FM 117

Introduction to Fashion Marketing

A customized text for this course, FM 117, Introduction to Fashion Marketing, was compiled by Gary Wolf, an FMM faculty member who is the instructor.

Taken from:
Consumer Behavior, Ninth Edition
by Leon G. Schiffman and Leslie Lazar Kanuk

Marketing: An Introduction, Ninth Edition
by Gary Armstrong and Philip Kotler

Fashion: From Concept to Consumer, Ninth Edition
by Gini Stephens Frings

Custom Publishing

New York   Boston   San Francisco
London   Toronto   Sydney   Tokyo   Singapore   Madrid
Mexico City   Munich   Paris   Cape Town   Hong Kong   Montreal

Cover Art: Illustration by Ellen Koch

Taken from:
Consumer Behavior, Ninth Edition
by Leon G. Schiffman and Leslie Lazar Kanuk
Copyright © 2007, 2004, 2000, 1997, 1991 by Pearson Education, Inc.
Published by Prentice Hall
Upper Saddle River, New Jersey 07458

Marketing: An Introduction, Ninth Edition
by Gary Armstrong and Philip Kotler
Copyright © 2009, 2007, 2005, 2003, 2000 by Pearson Education, Inc.
Published by Prentice Hall

Fashion: From Concept to Consumer, Ninth Edition
by Gini Stephens Frings
Copyright © 2008, 2006, 2002, 1999 by Pearson Education, Inc.
Published by Prentice Hall

This special edition published in cooperation with Pearson Custom Publishing.

All trademarks, service marks, registered trademarks, and registered service marks are the property of their respective owners and are used herein for identification purposes only.

Printed in the United States of America

10 9 8 7

2009160174

NM

Pearson
Custom Publishing
is a division of

www.pearsonhighered.com

ISBN 10: 0-558-34606-5
ISBN 13: 978-0-558-34606-5

Brief Contents

Chapters 4, 9, and 11–17 taken from *Consumer Behavior,* Ninth Edition, by Leon G. Schiffman and Leslie Lazar Kanuk

Chapters 1, 5–6, 8, 10, and 18–19 taken from *Marketing: An Introduction,* Ninth Edition, by Gary Armstrong and Philip Kotler

Chapters 2–3 and 7 taken from *Fashion: From Concept to Consumer,* Ninth Edition, by Gini Stephens Frings

chapter **1**
> **Define Marketing   1**

chapter **2**
> **Consumer Fashion Marketing   25**

chapter **3**
> **Retail Fashion Marketing   49**

chapter **4**
> **Marketing Research and Segmentation   63**

chapter **5**
> **Customer Relationships   111**

chapter **6**
> **Marketing Channels   131**

chapter **7**
> **Marketing Technology   151**

chapter **8**
> **Marketing Ethics and Social Responsibility   157**

chapter **9**
> **Diffusion   173**

chapter **10**
> **Product Life Cycle   209**

chapter **11**
> **Culture   229**

chapter **12**
> **Subcultures   251**

chapter **13**
> **Cross-Culture and Globalization   277**

chapter **14**
> **Consumer Motivation and Decision Making   295**

chapter **15**
> **Perception   339**

chapter **16**
> **Attitude   371**

chapter **17**
> **Learning   391**

chapter **18**
> **Business Buying Behavior   417**

chapter **19**
> **Price   429**

chapter 1

› **Define Marketing**

Understanding the marketplace and customer needs

As a first step, marketers need to understand customer needs and wants and the marketplace within which they operate. We now examine five core customer and marketplace concepts: (1) *needs, wants, and demands*; (2) *marketing offers (products, services, and experiences)*; (3) *value and satisfaction*; (4) *exchanges and relationships*; and (5) *markets.*

Customer needs, wants, and demands

The most basic concept underlying marketing is that of human needs. Human **needs** are states of felt deprivation. They include basic *physical* needs for food, clothing, warmth, and safety; *social* needs for belonging and affection; and *individual* needs for knowledge and self-expression. These needs were not created by marketers; they are a basic part of the human makeup.

Wants are the form human needs take as they are shaped by culture and individual personality. An American *needs* food but *wants* a Big Mac, french fries, and a soft drink. A person in Papua New Guinea *needs* food but *wants* taro, rice, yams, and pork. Wants are shaped by one's society and are described in terms of objects that will satisfy needs. When backed by buying power, wants become **demands**. Given their wants and resources, people demand products with benefits that add up to the most value and satisfaction.

Outstanding marketing companies go to great lengths to learn about and understand their customers' needs, wants, and demands. They conduct consumer research and analyze mountains of customer data. Their people at all levels—including top management—stay close to customers. For example, at Southwest Airlines, all senior executives handle bags, check in passengers, and serve as flight attendants once every quarter. Harley-Davidson's chairman regularly mounts his Harley and rides with customers to get feedback and ideas. And at Build-A-Bear Workshop, one of the country's fastest-growing retailers, founder and chief executive Maxine Clark regularly visits her stores around the world, meeting customers, chatting with employees, and just getting to know the young people who buy her products. "I'm on a lot of online buddy lists," she says.[6]

Market offerings—products, services, and experiences

Consumers' needs and wants are fulfilled through **market offerings**—some combination of products, services, information, or experiences offered to a market to satisfy a need or want. Market offerings are not limited to physical *products*. They also include *services*—activities or benefits offered for sale that are essentially intangible and do not result in the ownership of anything. Examples include banking, airline, hotel, tax preparation, and home repair services. More broadly, market offerings also include other entities, such as *persons, places, organizations, information,* and *ideas.* For example, beyond promoting its

Needs
States of felt deprivation.

Wants
The form human needs take as shaped by culture and individual personality.

Demands
Human wants that are backed by buying power.

Market offering
Some combination of products, services, information, or experiences offered to a market to satisfy a need or want.

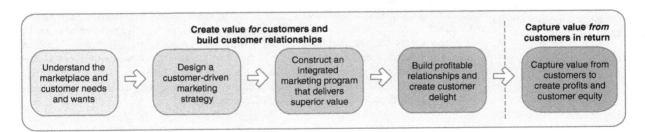

A Simple Model of the Marketing Process | **FIGURE 1.1**

Market offerings are not limited to physical products. For example, LaSalle Bank runs ads asking people to donate used or old winter clothing to the Salvation Army. In this case, the "marketing offer" is helping to keep those who are less fortunate warm.

banking services, LaSalle Bank runs ads asking people to donate used or old winter clothing to the Salvation Army. In this case, the "market offering" is helping to keep those who are less fortunate warm.

Many sellers make the mistake of paying more attention to the specific products they offer than to the benefits and experiences produced by these products. These sellers suffer from **marketing myopia**. They are so taken with their products that they focus only on existing wants and lose sight of underlying customer needs.[7] They forget that a product is only a tool to solve a consumer problem. A manufacturer of quarter-inch drill bits may think that the customer needs a drill bit. But what the customer *really* needs is a quarter-inch hole. These sellers will have trouble if a new product comes along that serves the customer's need better or less expensively. The customer will have the same *need* but will *want* the new product.

Smart marketers look beyond the attributes of the products and services they sell. By orchestrating several services and products, they create *brand experiences* for consumers. For example, Walt Disney World is an experience; so is a ride on a Harley-Davidson motorcycle or a visit to your local Starbucks. "We're not in the business of filling bellies," says Starbucks founder Howard Schultz, "we're in the business of filling souls."[8] Similarly, Hewlett-Packard recognizes that a personal computer is much more than just a collection of wires and electrical components. It's an intensely personal user experience: "There is hardly anything that you own that is *more* personal. Your personal computer is your backup brain. It's your life.... It's your astonishing strategy, staggering proposal, dazzling calculation. It's your autobiography, written in a thousand daily words."[9]

Marketing myopia
The mistake of paying more attention to the specific products a company offers than to the benefits and experiences produced by these products.

Customer value and satisfaction

Consumers usually face a broad array of products and services that might satisfy a given need. How do they choose among these many market offerings? Customers form expectations about the value and satisfaction that various market offerings will deliver and buy accordingly. Satisfied customers buy again and tell others about their good experiences. Dissatisfied customers often switch to competitors and disparage the product to others.

Marketers must be careful to set the right level of expectations. If they set expectations too low, they may satisfy those who buy but fail to attract enough buyers. If they raise expectations too high, buyers will be disappointed. Customer value and customer satisfaction are key building blocks for developing and managing customer relationships. We will revisit these core concepts later in the chapter.

Exchange
The act of obtaining a desired object from someone by offering something in return.

Exchanges and relationships

Marketing occurs when people decide to satisfy needs and wants through exchange relationships. **Exchange** is the act of obtaining a desired object from someone by offering something in return. In the broadest sense, the marketer tries to bring about a response to some market offering. The response may be more than simply buying or trading products and services. A political candidate, for instance, wants votes, a church wants membership, an orchestra wants an audience, and a social action group wants idea acceptance.

Marketing consists of actions taken to build and maintain desirable exchange *relationships* with target audiences involving a product, service, idea, or other object. Beyond simply attracting new customers and creating transactions, the goal is to retain customers and grow their business with the company. Marketers want to build strong relationships by consistently delivering superior customer value. We will expand on the important concept of managing customer relationships later in the chapter.

Markets

The concepts of exchange and relationships lead to the concept of a market. A **market** is the set of actual and potential buyers of a product. These buyers share a particular need or want that can be satisfied through exchange relationships.

Market
The set of all actual and potential buyers of a product or service.

Marketing means managing markets to bring about profitable customer relationships. However, creating these relationships takes work. Sellers must search for buyers, identify their needs, design good market offerings, set prices for them, promote them, and store and deliver them. Activities such as consumer research, product development, communication, distribution, pricing, and service are core marketing activities.

Although we normally think of marketing as being carried on by sellers, buyers also carry on marketing. Consumers do marketing when they search for the goods they need at prices they can afford. Company purchasing agents do marketing when they track down sellers and bargain for good terms.

Figure 1.2 shows the main elements in a modern marketing system. In the usual situation, marketing involves serving a market of final consumers in the face of competitors. The company and competitors research the market and interact with consumers to understand their needs and obtain their inputs. Then they assemble and send their respective market offerings and messages to consumers, either directly or through marketing intermediaries. All of the actors in the system are affected by major environmental forces (demographic, economic, physical, technological, political/legal, and social/cultural).

Each party in the system adds value for the next level. All of the arrows represent relationships that must be developed and managed. Thus, a company's success at building profitable relationships depends not only on its own actions but also on how

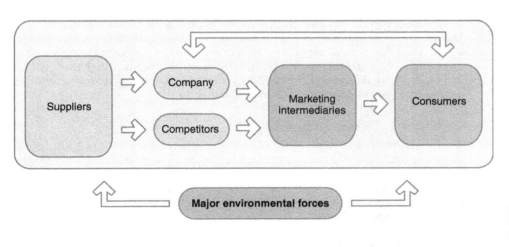

**Elements of a
Modern Marketing
System**

FIGURE 1.2

well the entire system serves the needs of final consumers. Wal-Mart cannot fulfill its promise of low prices unless its suppliers provide merchandise at low costs. And Ford cannot deliver high quality to car buyers unless its dealers provide outstanding sales and service.

Designing a customer-driven marketing strategy

Marketing management
The art and science of choosing target markets and building profitable relationships with them.

Once it fully understands consumers and the marketplace, marketing management can design a customer-driven marketing strategy. We define **marketing management** as the art and science of choosing target markets and building profitable relationships with them. The marketing manager's aim is to find, attract, keep, and grow target customers by creating, delivering, and communicating superior customer value.

To design a winning marketing strategy, the marketing manager must answer two important questions: *What customers will we serve (what's our target market)?* and *How can we serve these customers best (what's our value proposition)?* We will discuss these marketing strategy concepts briefly here.

Selecting customers to serve

The company must first decide *who* it will serve. It does this by dividing the market into segments of customers (*market segmentation*) and selecting which segments it will go after (*target marketing*). Some people think of marketing management as finding as many customers as possible and increasing demand. But marketing managers know that they cannot serve all customers in every way. By trying to serve all customers, they may not serve any customers well. Instead, the company wants to select only customers that it can serve well and profitably. For example, Nordstrom stores profitably target affluent professionals; Family Dollar stores profitably target families with more modest means.

Some marketers may even seek *fewer* customers and reduced demand. For example, Yosemite National Park is badly overcrowded in the summer and many power companies have trouble meeting demand during peak usage periods. In these and other cases of excess demand, companies may practice *demarketing* to reduce the number of customers or to shift their demand temporarily or permanently. For instance, many power companies now sponsor programs that help customers reduce their power usage through peak-load control devices, better energy use monitoring, and heating system tune-up incentives. Progress Energy even offers an Energy Manager on Loan program that provides school systems and other public customers with a cost-free on-site energy expert to help them find energy-savings opportunities.

Ultimately, marketing managers must decide which customers they want to target and on the level, timing, and nature of their demand. Simply put, marketing management is *customer management* and *demand management*.

Choosing a value proposition

The company must also decide how it will serve targeted customers—how it will *differentiate and position* itself in the marketplace. A company's *value proposition* is the set of benefits or values it promises to deliver to consumers to satisfy their needs. Keebler cookies are "baked by little elves in a hollow tree" but Nabisco's Oreos are "Milk's favorite cookie." With cell phones, Nokia is "Connecting People—anyone, anywhere," whereas with Apple's iPhone, "Touching is believing." And BMW promises "the ultimate driving machine," whereas Land Rover lets you "Go Beyond"—to "get a taste of adventure, whatever your tastes."

Such value propositions differentiate one brand from another. They answer the customer's question "Why should I buy your brand rather than a competitor's?" Companies must design strong value propositions that give them the greatest advantage in their target markets.

Marketing management orientations

Marketing management wants to design strategies that will build profitable relationships with target consumers. But what *philosophy* should guide these marketing strategies? What weight should be given to the interests of customers, the organization, and society? Very often, these interests conflict.

There are five alternative concepts under which organizations design and carry out their marketing strategies: the *production, product, selling, marketing,* and *societal marketing concepts*.

The Production Concept

The **production concept** holds that consumers will favor products that are available and highly affordable. Therefore, management should focus on improving production and distribution efficiency. This concept is one of the oldest orientations that guides sellers.

The production concept is still a useful philosophy in some situations. For example, computer maker Lenovo dominates the highly competitive, price-sensitive Chinese PC market through low labor costs, high production efficiency, and mass distribution. However, although useful in some situations, the production concept can lead to marketing myopia. Companies adopting this orientation run a major risk of focusing too narrowly on their own operations and losing sight of the real objective—satisfying customer needs and building customer relationships.

The Product Concept

The **product concept** holds that consumers will favor products that offer the most in quality, performance, and innovative features. Under this concept, marketing strategy focuses on making continuous product improvements.

Product quality and improvement are important parts of most marketing strategies. However, focusing *only* on the company's products can also lead to marketing myopia. For example, some manufacturers believe that if they can "build a better mousetrap, the world will beat a path to their door." But they are often rudely shocked. Buyers may well be looking for a better solution to a mouse problem but not necessarily for a better mousetrap. The better solution might be a chemical spray, an exterminating service, or something else that works even better than a mousetrap. Furthermore, a better mousetrap will not sell unless the manufacturer designs, packages, and prices it attractively; places it in convenient distribution channels; brings it to the attention of people who need it; and convinces buyers that it is a better product.

The Selling Concept

Many companies follow the **selling concept**, which holds that consumers will not buy enough of the firm's products unless it undertakes a large-scale selling and promotion effort. The concept is typically practiced with unsought goods—those that buyers do not normally think of buying, such as insurance or blood donations. These industries must be good at tracking down prospects and selling them on product benefits.

Such aggressive selling, however, carries high risks. It focuses on creating sales transactions rather than on building long-term, profitable customer relationships. The aim often is to sell what the company makes rather than making what the market wants. It assumes that customers who are coaxed into buying the product will like it. Or, if they don't like it, they will possibly forget their disappointment and buy it again later. These are usually poor assumptions.

The Marketing Concept

The **marketing concept** holds that achieving organizational goals depends on knowing the needs and wants of target markets and delivering the desired satisfactions better than competitors do. Under the marketing concept, customer focus and value are the *paths* to sales and profits. Instead of a product-centered "make and sell" philosophy, the marketing concept is a customer-centered "sense and respond" philosophy. It views marketing not as "hunting," but as "gardening." The job is not to find the right customers for your product but to find the right products for your customers.

Production concept
The idea that consumers will favor products that are available and highly affordable and that the organization should therefore focus on improving production and distribution efficiency.

Product concept
The idea that consumers will favor products that offer the most quality, performance, and features and that the organization should therefore devote its energy to making continuous product improvements.

Selling concept
The idea that consumers will not buy enough of the firm's products unless it undertakes a large-scale selling and promotion effort.

Marketing concept
The marketing management philosophy that holds that achieving organizational goals depends on knowing the needs and wants of target markets and delivering the desired satisfactions better than competitors do.

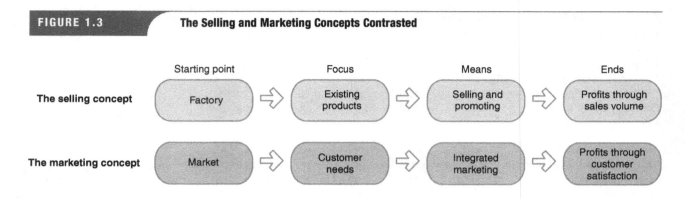

FIGURE 1.3	The Selling and Marketing Concepts Contrasted

Figure 1.3 contrasts the selling concept and the marketing concept. The selling concept takes an *inside-out* perspective. It starts with the factory, focuses on the company's existing products, and calls for heavy selling and promotion to obtain profitable sales. It focuses primarily on customer conquest—getting short-term sales with little concern about who buys or why.

In contrast, the marketing concept takes an *outside-in* perspective. As Herb Kelleher, Southwest Airlines' colorful CEO, puts it, "We don't have a marketing department; we have a customer department." The marketing concept starts with a well-defined market, focuses on customer needs, and integrates all the marketing activities that affect customers. In turn, it yields profits by creating lasting relationships with the right customers based on customer value and satisfaction.

Implementing the marketing concept often means more than simply responding to customers' stated desires and obvious needs. *Customer-driven* companies research current customers deeply to learn about their desires, gather new product and service ideas, and test proposed product improvements. Such customer-driven marketing usually works well when a clear need exists and when customers know what they want.

In many cases, however, customers *don't* know what they want or even what is possible. For example, even 20 years ago, how many consumers would have thought to ask for now-commonplace products such as cell phones, notebook computers, iPods, digital cameras, 24-hour online buying, and satellite navigation systems in their cars? Such situations call for *customer-driving* marketing—understanding customer needs even better than customers themselves do and creating products and services that meet existing and latent needs, now and in the future. As an executive at 3M puts it: "Our goal is to lead customers where they want to go before *they* know where they want to go."

The Societal Marketing Concept

Societal marketing concept
The idea that a company's marketing decisions should consider consumers' wants, the company's requirements, consumers' long-run interests, and society's long-run interests.

The **societal marketing concept** questions whether the pure marketing concept overlooks possible conflicts between consumer *short-run wants* and consumer *long-run welfare.* Is a firm that satisfies the immediate needs and wants of target markets always doing what's best for consumers in the long run? The societal marketing concept holds that marketing strategy should deliver value to customers in a way that maintains or improves both the consumer's *and the society's* well-being.

Consider the fast-food industry. You may view today's giant fast-food chains as offering tasty and convenient food at reasonable prices. Yet many consumer nutritionists and environmental groups have voiced strong concerns. They point to fast feeders such as Hardee's, who are promoting monster meals such as the Monster Thickburger—two 1/3-pound slabs of Angus beef, four strips of bacon, three slices of American cheese, and mayonnaise on a buttered bun, delivering 1,420 calories and 102 grams of fat. Such unhealthy fare, the critics claim, is leading consumers to eat too much of the wrong foods, contributing to a national obesity epidemic. What's more, the products are wrapped in convenient packaging but this leads to waste and pollution. Thus, in satisfying short-term consumer wants, the highly successful fast-food chains may be harming consumer health and causing environmental problems in the long run.[10]

FIGURE 1.4

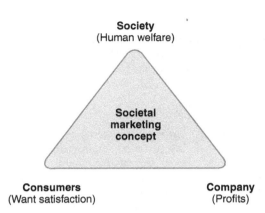

As Figure 1.4 shows, companies should balance three considerations in setting their marketing strategies: company profits, consumer wants, *and* society's interests. Johnson & Johnson does this well. Its concern for societal interests is summarized in a company document called "Our Credo," which stresses honesty, integrity, and putting people before profits. Under this credo, Johnson & Johnson would rather take a big loss than ship a bad batch of one of its products.

Consider the tragic tampering case in which eight people died in 1982 from swallowing cyanide-laced capsules of Tylenol, a Johnson & Johnson brand. Although Johnson & Johnson believed that the pills had been altered in only a few stores, not in the factory, it quickly recalled all of its product and launched an information campaign to instruct and reassure consumers. The recall cost the company $100 million in earnings. In the long run, however, the company's swift recall of Tylenol strengthened consumer confidence and loyalty, and today Tylenol remains one of the nation's leading brands of pain reliever.

Johnson & Johnson management has learned that doing what's right benefits both consumers and the company. Says former CEO Ralph Larsen, "The Credo should not be viewed as some kind of social welfare program . . . it's just plain good business. If we keep trying to do what's right, at the end of the day we believe the marketplace will reward us." Thus, over the years, Johnson & Johnson's dedication to consumers and community service has made it one of America's most-admired companies *and* one of the most profitable.[11]

Preparing an integrated marketing plan and program

The company's marketing strategy outlines which customers the company will serve and how it will create value for these customers. Next, the marketer develops an integrated marketing program that will actually deliver the intended value to target customers. The marketing program builds customer relationships by transforming the marketing strategy into action. It consists of the firm's *marketing mix,* the set of marketing tools the firm uses to implement its marketing strategy.

The major marketing mix tools are classified into four broad groups, called the *four Ps* of marketing: product, price, place, and promotion. To deliver on its value proposition, the firm must first create a need-satisfying market offering (product). It must decide how much it will charge for the offering (price) and how it will make the offering available to target consumers (place). Finally, it must communicate with target customers about the offering and persuade them of its merits (promotion). The firm must blend all of these marketing mix tools into a comprehensive *integrated marketing program* that communicates and delivers the intended value to chosen customers. We will explore marketing programs and the marketing mix in much more detail in later chapters.

Building customer relationships

The first three steps in the marketing process—understanding the marketplace and customer needs, designing a customer-driven marketing strategy, and constructing marketing programs—all lead up to the fourth and most important step: building profitable customer relationships.

Customer relationship management

Customer relationship management is perhaps the most important concept of modern marketing. Some marketers define customer relationship management narrowly as a customer data management activity (a practice called *CRM*). By this definition, it involves managing detailed information about individual customers and carefully managing customer "touch points" in order to maximize customer loyalty.

Most marketers, however, give the concept of customer relationship management a broader meaning. In this broader sense, **customer relationship management** is the overall process of building and maintaining profitable customer relationships by delivering superior customer value and satisfaction. It deals with all aspects of acquiring, keeping, and growing customers.

Customer relationship management
The overall process of building and maintaining profitable customer relationships by delivering superior customer value and satisfaction.

Relationship building blocks: customer value and satisfaction

The key to building lasting customer relationships is to create superior customer value and satisfaction. Satisfied customers are more likely to be loyal customers and to give the company a larger share of their business.

Customer Value Attracting and retaining customers can be a difficult task. Customers often face a bewildering array of products and services from which to choose. A customer buys from the firm that offers the highest **customer-perceived value**—the customer's evaluation of the difference between all the benefits and all the costs of a market offering relative to those of competing offers.

Customer-perceived value
The customer's evaluation of the difference between all the benefits and all the costs of a marketing offer relative to those of competing offers.

For example, consider the "premium denim" trend that has recently sent jeans prices skyrocketing. A pair of Paige Premium Denim jeans, for instance, starts at $169. A woman who buys a pair of Paige jeans gains a number of benefits. First, owner and designer Paige Adams-Gellar, a former model for premium denim brands, uses the knowledge she learned from the field to design jeans from the female perspective. Says Paige, "Most of us weren't blessed with perfect genes but we're bringing you the next best thing: perfect jeans." Her denim "will lift the derriere, lengthen your legs, and slenderize your hips and thighs—all with an uncompromising commitment to feminine detail and quality." In all, says Paige, her jeans are a real value—they will fit you better and last longer. When deciding whether to purchase a pair, customers will weigh these and other perceived values of owning Paige jeans against the money and psychic costs of acquiring them.

Customers often do not judge values and costs "accurately" or "objectively." They act on *perceived* value. For example, as compared to a pair of less expensive jeans that you'd pull off the shelf at Gap, do Paige jeans really provide superior quality and that perfect fit and look? If so, are they worth the much higher price? It's all a matter of personal value perceptions, but for many women the answer is yes. One woman notes that, for her, premium jeans always seem to fit just right, making the price irrelevant. "I work, so I have the money to buy them," she says. "I think they're worth it."[12]

Customer satisfaction
The extent to which a product's perceived performance matches a buyer's expectations.

Customer Satisfaction **Customer satisfaction** depends on the product's perceived performance relative to a buyer's expectations. If the product's performance falls short of expectations, the customer is dissatisfied. If performance matches expectations, the customer is satisfied. If performance exceeds expectations, the customer is highly satisfied or delighted.

Outstanding marketing companies go out of their way to keep important customers satisfied. Most studies show that higher levels of customer satisfaction lead to greater customer loyalty, which in turn results in better company performance. Smart companies aim to *delight* customers by promising only what they can deliver, then delivering *more* than they promise. Delighted customers not only make repeat purchases, they become "customer evangelists" who tell others about their good experiences with the product.[13]

For companies interested in delighting customers, exceptional value and service are more than a set of policies or actions—they are a companywide attitude, an important part of the overall company culture. For example, year after year, Lexus ranks at or near the top of the auto industry in terms of customer satisfaction. Its passion for satisfying customers is summed up in The Lexus Covenant, a founding philosophy in which the company pledges that "Lexus will treat each customer as we would a guest in our home." Lexus promises to create "the most satisfying automobile ownership experience" and "to always exceed expectations." Here's an example:[14]

> *A man bought his first new Lexus—a $45,000 piece of machinery. He could afford a Mercedes, a BMW, or a Cadillac, but he bought the Lexus. He took delivery of his new honey and started to drive it home, luxuriating in the smell of the leather interior and the glorious handling. On a whim, he turned on the radio. His favorite classical music station came on in splendid quadraphonic sound that ricocheted around the interior. He pushed the second button; it was his favorite news station. The third button brought his favorite talk station that kept him awake on long trips. The fourth button was set to his daughter's favorite rock station. In fact, every button was set to his specific tastes. The customer knew the car was smart, but was it psychic? No. The mechanic at Lexus had noted the radio settings on his trade-in and duplicated them on the new Lexus. The customer was delighted. This was his car now—through and through! No one told the mechanic to do it. It's just part of the Lexus philosophy: Delight a customer and continue to delight that customer, and you will have a customer for life. What the mechanic did cost Lexus nothing. Yet it solidified the relationship that could be worth high six figures to Lexus in customer lifetime value. Such relationship-building passions in dealerships around the country have made Lexus the nation's top-selling luxury vehicle.*

However, although the customer-centered firm seeks to deliver high customer satisfaction relative to competitors, it does not attempt to *maximize* customer satisfaction. A company can always increase customer satisfaction by lowering its price or increasing its services. But this may result in lower profits. Thus, the purpose of marketing is to generate customer value profitably. This requires a very delicate balance: The marketer must continue to generate more customer value and satisfaction but not "give away the house."

Customer relationship levels and tools

Companies can build customer relationships at many levels, depending on the nature of the target market. At one extreme, a company with many low-margin customers may seek to develop *basic relationships* with them. For example, Procter & Gamble does not phone or call on all of its Tide consumers to get to know them personally. Instead, P&G creates relationships through brand-building advertising, sales promotions, and its Tide Fabric-Care Network Web site (www.Tide.com). At the other extreme, in markets with few customers and high margins, sellers want to create *full partnerships* with key customers. For example, P&G customer teams work closely with Wal-Mart, Safeway, and other large retailers. In between these two extreme situations, other levels of customer relationships are appropriate.

Today, most leading companies are developing customer loyalty and retention programs. Beyond offering consistently high value and satisfaction, marketers can use specific marketing tools to develop stronger bonds with consumers. For example, many companies now offer *frequency marketing programs* that reward customers who buy frequently or in large amounts. Airlines offer frequent-flyer programs, hotels give room upgrades to their frequent guests, and supermarkets give patronage discounts to "very important customers." Some of these programs can be spectacular. To cater to its very best customers, Neiman Marcus created its InCircle Rewards program:

> *InCircle members, who must spend at least $5,000 a year using their Neiman Marcus credit cards to be eligible, earn points with each purchase—one point for each dollar charged. They then cash in points for anything from a New York lunch experience for two at one of the "Big Apple's hottest beaneries" (5,000 points) or a Sony home theater system (25,000 points) to a three-day personalized bullfighting course, including travel to a ranch in Northern Baja for some practical training (50,000 points). For 500,000 points, InCircle members can get a six-night Caribbean cruise, and for 1.5 million points, a Yamaha grand piano. Among the top prizes (for 5 million points!) are a J. Mendal custom-made sable coat valued at $200,000 and a private concert in the InCircler's home by jazz instrumentalist Chris Botti.[15]*

Other companies sponsor *club marketing programs* that offer members special benefits and create member communities. For example, Harley-Davidson sponsors the Harley Owners Group (H.O.G.), which gives Harley riders "an organized way to share their passion and show their pride." H.O.G membership benefits include two magazines (*Hog Tales* and *Enthusiast*), a *H.O.G. Touring Handbook,* a roadside assistance program, a specially designed insurance program, theft reward service, a travel center, and a "Fly & Ride" program enabling members to rent Harleys while on vacation. The worldwide club now numbers more than 1,500 local chapters and over 1 million members.[16]

To build customer relationships, companies can add structural ties as well as financial and social benefits. A business marketer might supply customers with special equipment or online linkages that help them manage their orders, payroll, or inventory. For example, McKesson Corporation, a leading pharmaceutical wholesaler, has set up a Supply Management Online system that helps retail pharmacy customers manage their inventories, order entry, and shelf space. The system also helps McKesson's medical-surgical supply and equipment customers optimize their supply purchasing and materials management operations.

The changing nature of customer relationships

Significant changes are occurring in the ways in which companies are relating to their customers. Yesterday's big companies focused on mass marketing to all customers at arm's length. Today's companies are building deeper, more direct, and more lasting relationships with more carefully selected customers. Here are some important trends in the way companies and customers are relating to one another.

Relating with more carefully selected customers

Few firms today still practice true mass marketing—selling in a standardized way to any customer who comes along. Today, most marketers realize that they don't want relationships with every customer. Instead, they now are targeting fewer, more profitable customers. Called *selective relationship management,* many companies now use customer profitability analysis to weed out losing customers and to target winning ones for pampering. Once they identify profitable customers, firms can create attractive offers and special handling to capture these customers and earn their loyalty.

But what should the company do with unprofitable customers? If it can't turn them into profitable ones, it may even want to "fire" customers that are too unreasonable or that cost more to serve than they are worth. For example, consumer electronics retailer Best Buy recently rolled out a new "Customer-Centricity" strategy that distinguishes between its best customers (called *angels*) and less profitable ones (called *demons*). The aim is to embrace the angels while ditching the demons.[17]

> *The angels include the 20 percent of Best Buy customers who produce the bulk of its profits. They snap up high-definition televisions, portable electronics, and newly released DVDs without waiting for markdowns or rebates. In contrast, the demons form an "underground of bargain-hungry shoppers intent on wringing every nickel of savings out of the big retailer. They load up on loss leaders . . . then flip the goods at a*

profit on eBay. They slap down rock-bottom price quotes from Web sites and demand that Best Buy make good on its lowest-price pledge."

To attract the angels, Best Buy's Customer-Centricity stores now stock more merchandise and offer better service to these good customers. For example, the stores set up digital photo centers and a "Geek Squad," which offers one-on-one in-store or at-home computer assistance to high-value buyers. Best Buy also set up a Reward Zone loyalty program, in which regular customers can earn points toward discounts on future purchases. To discourage the demons, Best Buy removed them from its marketing lists, reduced the promotions and other sales tactics that tended to attract them, and installed a 15 percent restocking fee.

However, Best Buy didn't stop there. Customer analysis revealed that its best customers fell into five groups: "Barrys," high-income men; "Jills," suburban moms; "Buzzes," male technology enthusiasts; "Rays," young family men on a budget; and small business owners. Each Customer-Centricity store now aligns its product and service mix to reflect the make-up of these customers in its market area. Best Buy then trains store clerks in the art of serving the angels and exorcising the demons. At stores targeting Barrys, for example, blue-shirted sales clerks steer promising candidates to the store's Magnolia Home Theater Center, a comfy store within a store that mimics the media rooms popular with home-theater fans. The centers feature premium home-theater systems and knowledgeable, no-pressure home-theater consultants. So far, Customer Centricity stores have "clobbered" the traditional Best Buy stores, with many posting sales gains more than triple those of stores with conventional formats. As one store manager puts it: "The biggest thing now is to build better relationships with [our best] customers."

Relating more deeply and interactively

Beyond choosing customers more selectively, companies are now relating with chosen customers in deeper, more meaningful ways. Rather than relying only on one-way, mass-media messages, today's marketers are incorporating new, more interactive approaches that help build targeted, two-way customer relationships.

The deeper nature of today's customer relationships results in part from the rapidly changing communications environment. New technologies have profoundly changed the ways in which people relate to one another. For example, thanks to explosive advances in Internet and computer technology, people can now interact in direct and surprisingly personal ways with large groups of others, whether nearby or scattered around the world. New tools for relating include everything from e-mail, blogs, Web sites, and video sharing to online communities and social networks such as MySpace, Facebook, YouTube, and Second Life.

This changing communications environment also affects how consumers relate to companies and products. Increasingly, marketers are using the new communications approaches in building closer customer relationships. The aim is to create deeper consumer involvement and a sense of community surrounding a brand—to make the brand a meaningful part of consumers' conversations and lives. "Becoming part of the conversation between consumers is infinitely more powerful than handing down information via traditional advertising," says one marketing expert. "It [makes] consumers . . . a part of the process, rather than being dumb recipients of the message from on high—and that is of huge potential value to brands."[18]

However, at the same time that the new communications tools create relationship-building opportunities for marketers, they also create challenges. They give consumers greater power and control. Today's consumers have more information about brands than ever before, and they have a wealth of platforms for airing and sharing their brand views with other consumers. And more than ever before, consumers can choose the brand conversations and exchanges in which they will participate. According to Mark Parker, chief executive of Nike, the new power of the consumer is "the most compelling change we've seen over the past four or five years. They are dictating what the dialogue is, how we're conducting it, and it's definitely a two-way conversation."[19]

Greater consumer control means that, in building customer relationships, companies can no longer rely on marketing by *intrusion*. They must practice marketing by *attraction*—creating market offerings and messages that involve consumers rather than interrupt them. Hence, most marketers now augment their mass-media marketing efforts with a rich mix of direct marketing approaches that promote brand-consumer interaction. For example, many are participating in the exploding world of *online social networks* or creating online communities of their own. Toyota, the world's fourth-largest advertiser, spends $2.8 billion a year on media advertising. But it also sells Scions at Second Life and maintains a Scion presence in MySpace, Gaia Online, and other cyber hangouts. And the company's Toyota.com/hybrids site creates a community in which more than 15,500 Prius, Camry, and Highlander hybrid "believers" meet to share videos and messages on their experiences with and reasons for buying hybrid vehicles.

Similarly, Nike spends close to $300 million a year on media advertising. But it also employs a host of other marketing activities designed to build brand community and deeper customer relationships.[20]

> *Twice a week, 30 or more people gather at the Nike store in Portland, Oregon, and go for an evening run. Afterward the members of the Niketown running club chat in the store over refreshments. Nike's staff keeps track of their performances and hails members who have logged more than 100 miles. The event is a classic example of up-close-and-personal relationship building with core customers. Nike augments such events with an online social network aimed at striking up meaningful long-term interactions with even more runners. Its Nike Plus running Web site lets customers with iPod-linked Nike shoes upload, track, and compare their performances. More than 200,000 runners are now using the Nike Plus site and more than half visit the site at least four times a week. The goal is to have 15 percent of the world's 100 million runners using the system.*
>
> *Another Nike social networking site—joga.com—targets the world's soccer fans. During the eight weeks surrounding the 2006 World Cup, the joga.com site was used by more than 1 million people to establish personalized World Cup pages. A related video of Ronaldinho, the Brazilian star, was downloaded 32 million times. According to Charlie Denson, president of the Nike brand, the huge success of such sites has persuaded the company to divide its Nike brand operations into six categories—running, basketball, soccer, men's fitness, women's fitness, and sports culture—with brand teams that will develop closer relationships with each specific consumer community.*

As a part of the new customer control and dialog, consumers themselves are now creating brand conversations and messages on their own. And increasingly, companies are even *inviting* consumers to play a more active role in shaping brand messages and ads. For example, Doritos and the NFL ran consumer-developed ads on last year's Super Bowl. Other companies, including marketing heavyweights such as Coca-Cola, McDonald's, and BMW, have snagged brand-related consumer videos from YouTube and other popular video-sharing sites and turned them into commercial messages. **Consumer-generated marketing**, whether invited by marketers or uninvited, has become a significant marketing force. In fact, last year, *Advertising Age* magazine awarded its coveted Ad Agency of the Year designation to—you guessed it—the consumer. "The explosion of video, blogs, Web sites, [and consumer-generated ads] confirmed what we knew all along," says the magazine. When it comes to creative messages, "the consumer is king."[21]

Consumer-generated marketing
Marketing messages, ads, and other brand exchanges created by consumers themselves—both invited and uninvited.

Partner relationship management

Partner relationship management
Working closely with partners in other company departments and outside the company to jointly bring greater value to customers.

When it comes to creating customer value and building strong customer relationships, today's marketers know that they can't go it alone. They must work closely with a variety of marketing partners. In addition to being good at *customer relationship management*, marketers must also be good at **partner relationship management**. Major changes are occurring in how marketers partner with others inside and outside the company to jointly bring more value to customers.

Partners inside the company

Traditionally, marketers have been charged with understanding customers and representing customer needs to different company departments. The old thinking was that marketing is done only by marketing, sales, and customer-support people. However, in today's more connected world, marketing no longer has sole ownership of customer interactions. Every functional area can interact with customers, especially electronically. The new thinking is that every employee must be customer focused. David Packard, late cofounder of Hewlett-Packard, wisely said, "Marketing is far too important to be left only to the marketing department."[22]

Today, rather than letting each department go its own way, firms are linking all departments in the cause of creating customer value. Rather than assigning only sales and marketing people to customers, they are forming cross-functional customer teams. For example, Procter & Gamble assigns "customer development teams" to each of its major retailer accounts. These teams—consisting of sales and marketing people, operations specialists, market and financial analysts, and others—coordinate the efforts of many P&G departments toward helping the retailer be more successful.

Marketing partners outside the firm

Changes are also occurring in how marketers connect with their suppliers, channel partners, and even competitors. Most companies today are networked companies, relying heavily on partnerships with other firms.

Marketing channels consist of distributors, retailers, and others who connect the company to its buyers. The *supply chain* describes a longer channel, stretching from raw materials to components to final products that are carried to final buyers. For example, the supply chain for personal computers consists of suppliers of computer chips and other components, the computer manufacturer, and the distributors, retailers, and others who sell the computers.

Through *supply chain management,* many companies today are strengthening their connections with partners all along the supply chain. They know that their fortunes rest not just on how well they perform. Success at building customer relationships also rests on how well their entire supply chain performs against competitors' supply chains. These companies don't just treat suppliers as vendors and distributors as customers. They treat both as partners in delivering customer value. On the one hand, for example, Lexus works closely with carefully selected suppliers to improve quality and operations efficiency. On the other hand, it works with its franchise dealers to provide top-grade sales and service support that will bring customers in the door and keep them coming back.

Capturing value from customers

The first four steps in the marketing process outlined in Figure 1.1 involve building customer relationships by creating and delivering superior customer value. The final step involves capturing value in return, in the form of current and future sales, market share, and profits. By creating superior customer value, the firm creates highly satisfied customers who stay loyal and buy more. This, in turn, means greater long-run returns for the firm. Here, we discuss the outcomes of creating customer value: customer loyalty and retention, share of market and share of customer, and customer equity.

Creating customer loyalty and retention

Good customer relationship management creates customer delight. In turn, delighted customers remain loyal and talk favorably to others about the company and its products. Studies show big differences in the loyalty of customers who are less satisfied, somewhat satisfied, and completely satisfied. Even a slight drop from complete satisfaction can create an enormous drop in loyalty. Thus, the aim of customer relationship management is to create not just customer satisfaction, but customer delight.[23]

Customer lifetime value
The value of the entire stream of purchases that the customer would make over a lifetime of patronage.

Companies are realizing that losing a customer means losing more than a single sale. It means losing the entire stream of purchases that the customer would make over a lifetime of patronage. For example, here is a dramatic illustration of **customer lifetime value**:

Stew Leonard, who operates a highly profitable four-store supermarket in Connecticut and New York, says that he sees $50,000 flying out of his store every time he sees a sulking customer. Why? Because his average customer spends about $100 a week, shops 50 weeks a year, and remains in the area for about 10 years. If this customer has an unhappy experience and switches to another supermarket, Stew Leonard's has lost $50,000 in revenue. The loss can be much greater if the disappointed customer shares the bad experience with other customers and causes them to defect. To keep customers coming back, Stew Leonard's has created what the New York Times *has dubbed the "Disneyland of Dairy Stores," complete with costumed characters, scheduled entertainment, a petting zoo, and animatronics throughout the store. From its humble beginnings as a small dairy store in 1969, Stew Leonard's has grown at an amazing pace. It's built 29 additions onto the original store, which now serves more than 300,000 customers each week. This legion of loyal shoppers is largely a result of the store's passionate approach to customer service. Rule #1 at Stew Leonard's—The customer is always right. Rule #2—If the customer is ever wrong, reread rule #1!*[24]

Stew Leonard is not alone in assessing customer lifetime value. Lexus estimates that a single satisfied and loyal customer is worth more than $600,000 in lifetime sales. The customer lifetime value of a Taco Bell customer exceeds $12,000.[25] Thus, working to retain and grow customers makes good economic sense. In fact, a company can lose money on a specific transaction but still benefit greatly from a long-term relationship.

This means that companies must aim high in building customer relationships. Customer delight creates an emotional relationship with a product or service, not just a rational preference. L.L.Bean, long known for its outstanding customer service and high customer loyalty, preaches the following "golden rule": Sell good merchandise, treat your customers like human beings, and they'll always come back for more." A customer relationships expert agrees: "If you want your customers to be more loyal, you must prove that you have their best interests at heart. Your concern for the customer's welfare must be so strong that it even occasionally trumps (gasp!) your own concern for immediate profits."[26]

Share of customer
The portion of the customer's purchasing that a company gets in its product categories.

Growing share of customer

Beyond simply retaining good customers to capture customer lifetime value, good customer relationship management can help marketers to increase their **share of customer**—the share they get of the customer's purchasing in their product categories. Thus, banks want to increase "share of wallet." Supermarkets and restaurants want to get more "share of stomach." Car companies want to increase "share of garage" and airlines want greater "share of travel."

To increase share of customer, firms can offer greater variety to current customers. Or they can train employees to cross-sell and up-sell in order to market more products and services to existing customers. For example, Amazon.com is highly skilled at leveraging relationships with its 50 million customers to

Customer lifetime value: To keep customers coming back, Stew Leonard's has created the "Disneyland of dairy stores." Rule #1—The customer is always right. Rule #2—If the customer is ever wrong, reread rule #1!

increase its share of each customer's purchases. Originally an online bookseller, Amazon.com now offers customers music, videos, gifts, toys, consumer electronics, office products, home improvement items, lawn and garden products, apparel and accessories, jewelry, and an online auction. In addition, based on each customer's purchase history, the company recommends related products that might be of interest. In this way, Amazon.com captures a greater share of each customer's spending budget.

Building customer equity

We can now see the importance of not just acquiring customers, but of keeping and growing them as well. One marketing consultant puts it this way: "The only value your company will ever create is the value that comes from customers—the ones you have now and the ones you will have in the future. Without customers, you don't have a business."[27] Customer relationship management takes a long-term view. Companies want not only to create profitable customers, but to "own" them for life, capture their customer lifetime value, and earn a greater share of their purchases.

What Is customer equity?

The ultimate aim of customer relationship management is to produce high *customer equity*.[28] **Customer equity** is the total combined customer lifetime values of all of the company's current and potential customers. Clearly, the more loyal the firm's profitable customers, the higher the firm's customer equity. Customer equity may be a better measure of a firm's performance than current sales or market share. Whereas sales and market share reflect the past, customer equity suggests the future. Consider Cadillac:

Customer equity
The total combined customer lifetime values of all of the company's customers.

> *In the 1970s and 1980s, Cadillac had some of the most loyal customers in the industry. To an entire generation of car buyers, the name "Cadillac" defined American luxury. Cadillac's share of the luxury car market reached a whopping 51 percent in 1976. Based on market share and sales, the brand's future looked rosy. However, measures of customer equity would have painted a bleaker picture. Cadillac customers were getting older (average age 60) and average customer lifetime value was falling. Many Cadillac buyers were on their last car. Thus, although Cadillac's market share was good, its customer equity was not. Compare this with BMW. Its more youthful and vigorous image didn't win BMW the early market share war. However, it did win BMW younger customers with higher customer lifetime values. The result: In the years that followed, BMW's market share and profits soared while Cadillac's fortunes eroded badly. Thus, market share is not the answer. We should care not just about current sales but also about future sales. Customer lifetime value and customer equity are the name of the game. Recognizing this, Cadillac is now making the Caddy cool again by targeting a younger generation of consumers with new high-performance models and its highly successful Break Through advertising campaign. Sales are up 35 percent over the past five years. More important, the future looks promising.[29]*

Building the right relationships with the right customers

Companies should manage customer equity carefully. They should view customers as assets that need to be managed and maximized. But not all customers, not even all loyal customers, are good investments. Surprisingly, some loyal customers can be unprofitable, and some disloyal customers can be profitable. Which customers should the company acquire and retain? "Up to a point, the choice is obvious: Keep the consistent big spenders and lose the erratic small spenders," says one expert. "But what about the erratic big spenders and the consistent small spenders? It's often unclear whether they should be acquired or retained, and at what cost."[30]

The company can classify customers according to their potential profitability and manage its relationships with them accordingly. Figure 1.5 classifies customers into one of four relationship groups, according to their profitability and projected loyalty.[31] Each group requires a different relationship management strategy. "Strangers" show low potential profitability and little projected loyalty. There is little fit between the

	Short-term customers	Long-term customers
High profitability	**Butterflies** Good fit between company's offerings and customer's needs; high profit potential	**True Friends** Good fit between company's offerings and customer's needs; highest profit potential
Low profitability	**Strangers** Little fit between company's offerings and customer's needs; lowest profit potential	**Barnacles** Limited fit between company's offerings and customer's needs; low profit potential

Potential profitability

Projected loyalty

company's offerings and their needs. The relationship management strategy for these customers is simple: Don't invest anything in them.

"Butterflies" are potentially profitable but not loyal. There is a good fit between the company's offerings and their needs. However, like real butterflies, we can enjoy them for only a short while and then they're gone. An example is stock market investors who trade shares often and in large amounts, but who enjoy hunting out the best deals without building a regular relationship with any single brokerage company. Efforts to convert butterflies into loyal customers are rarely successful. Instead, the company should enjoy the butterflies for the moment. It should use promotional blitzes to attract them, create satisfying and profitable transactions with them, and then cease investing in them until the next time around.

"True friends" are both profitable and loyal. There is a strong fit between their needs and the company's offerings. The firm wants to make continuous relationship investments to delight these customers and nurture, retain, and grow them. It wants to turn true friends into "true believers," who come back regularly and tell others about their good experiences with the company.

"Barnacles" are highly loyal but not very profitable. There is a limited fit between their needs and the company's offerings. An example is smaller bank customers who bank regularly but do not generate enough returns to cover the costs of maintaining their accounts. Like barnacles on the hull of a ship, they create drag. Barnacles are perhaps the most problematic customers. The company might be able to improve their profitability by selling them more, raising their fees, or reducing service to them. However, if they cannot be made profitable, they should be "fired."

The point here is an important one: Different types of customers require different relationship management strategies. The goal is to build the *right relationships* with the *right customers.*

Linking the Concepts

We've covered a lot of territory. Again, slow down for a moment and devdelop your own thoughts about marketing.

- In *your own words*, what *is* marketing and what does it seek to accomplish?
- How well does Lexus manage its relationships with customers? What customer relationship management strategy does it use? What relationship management strategy does Wal-Mart use?
- Think of a company for which you are a "true friend." What strategy does this company use to manage its relationship with you?

The changing marketing landscape

Every day, dramatic changes are occurring in the marketplace. Richard Love of Hewlett-Packard observes, "The pace of change is so rapid that the ability to change has now become a competitive advantage." Yogi Berra, the legendary New York Yankees catcher and manager, summed it up more simply when he said, "The future ain't what it used to be." As the marketplace changes, so must those who serve it.

In this section, we examine the major trends and forces that are changing the marketing landscape and challenging marketing strategy. We look at four major developments: the digital age, rapid globalization, the call for more ethics and social responsibility, and the growth of not-for-profit marketing.

The digital age

The recent technology boom has created a digital age. The explosive growth in computer, telecommunications, information, transportation, and other technologies has had a major impact on the ways companies bring value to their customers.

Now, more than ever before, we are all connected to each other and to things near and far in the world around us. Where it once took weeks or months to travel across the United States, we can now travel around the globe in only hours or days. Where it once took days or weeks to receive news about important world events, we now see them as they are occurring through live satellite broadcasts. Where it once took weeks to correspond with others in distant places, they are now only moments away by phone or the Internet.

The technology boom has provided exciting new ways to learn about and track customers, and to create products and services tailored to individual customer needs. Technology is also helping companies to distribute products more efficiently and effectively. And it's helping them to communicate with customers in large groups or one-to-one.

Through videoconferencing, marketing researchers at a company's headquarters in New York can look in on focus groups in Chicago or Paris without ever stepping onto a plane. With only a few clicks of a mouse button, a direct marketer can tap into online data services to learn anything from what car you drive to what you read to what flavor of ice cream you prefer. Or, using today's powerful computers, marketers can create their own detailed customer databases and use them to target individual customers with offers designed to meet their specific needs.

Technology has also brought a new wave of communication and advertising tools — ranging from cell phones, iPods, DVRs, Web sites, and interactive TV to video kiosks at airports and shopping malls. Marketers can use these tools to zero in on selected customers with carefully targeted messages. Through the Internet, customers can learn about, design, order, and pay for products and services, without ever leaving home. Then, through the marvels of express delivery, they can receive their purchases in less than 24 hours. From virtual reality displays that test new products to online virtual stores that sell them, the technology boom is affecting every aspect of marketing.

Perhaps the most dramatic new technology is the **Internet**. Today, the Internet links individuals and businesses of all types to each other and to information all around the world. It allows anytime, anywhere connections to information, entertainment, and communication. Companies are using the Internet to build closer relationships with customers and marketing partners. Beyond competing in traditional market*places,* they now have access to exciting new market*spaces.*

Internet
A vast public web of computer networks, which connects users of all types all around the world to each other and to an amazingly large information repository.

The Internet has now become a truly a global phenomenon. The number of Internet users worldwide now stands at almost 1.2 billion and will reach an estimated 1.8 billion by 2010.[32] This growing and diverse Internet population means that all kinds of people are now going to the Web for information and to buy products and services.

Internet usage surged in the 1990s with the development of the user-friendly World Wide Web. During the overheated Web frenzy of the late 1990s, dot-coms popped up everywhere, selling everything from books, toys, and CDs to furniture, home mortgages, and 100-pound bags of dog food via the Internet. The frenzy cooled during the "dot-com meltdown" of 2000, when many poorly conceived e-tailers and other Web start-ups went out of business. Today, a new version of the Internet has emerged—a "second coming" of the Web often referred to as *Web 2.0*. Web 2.0 involves a more reasoned and balanced approach to marketing online. It also offers a fast-growing set of new Web technologies for connecting with customers, such as Weblogs (blogs) and vlogs (video-based blogs), social networking sites, and video-sharing sites. The interactive, community-building nature of these new technologies makes them ideal for relating with consumers.[33]

Online marketing is now the fastest-growing form of marketing. These days, it's hard to find a company that doesn't use the Web in a significant way. In addition to the "click-only" dot-coms, most traditional "brick-and-mortar" companies have now become "click-and-mortar" companies. They have ventured online to attract new customers and build stronger relationships with existing ones. Today, some 65 percent of American online users now use the Internet to shop.[34] Business-to-business e-commerce is also booming. It seems that almost every business has set up shop on the Web.

Thus, the technology boom is providing exciting new opportunities for marketers. We will explore the impact of the new marketing technologies in Chapter 7.

Rapid globalization

As they are redefining their relationships with customers and partners, marketers are also taking a fresh look at the ways in which they relate with the broader world around them. In an increasingly smaller world, many marketers are now connected *globally* with their customers and marketing partners.

Today, almost every company, large or small, is touched in some way by global competition. A neighborhood florist buys its flowers from Mexican nurseries, and a large U.S. electronics manufacturer competes in its home markets with giant Korean rivals. A fledgling Internet retailer finds itself receiving orders from all over the world at the same time that an American consumer-goods producer introduces new products into emerging markets abroad.

American firms have been challenged at home by the skillful marketing of European and Asian multinationals. Companies such as Toyota, Nokia, Nestlé, Sony, and Samsung have often outperformed their U.S. competitors in American markets. Similarly, U.S. companies in a wide range of industries have developed truly global operations, making and selling their products worldwide. Quintessentially American McDonald's now serves 52 million customers daily in 31,600 restaurants worldwide— some 65 percent of its revenues come from outside the United States. Similarly, Nike markets in more than 160 countries, with non-U.S. sales accounting for 53 percent of its worldwide sales. Even MTV Networks has joined the elite of global brands—its 137 channels worldwide deliver localized versions of its pulse-thumping fare to teens in 419 million homes in 164 countries around the globe.[35]

Today, companies are not only trying to sell more of their locally produced goods in international markets, they also are buying more supplies and components abroad. For example, Isaac Mizrahi, one of America's top fashion designers, may choose cloth woven from Australian wool with designs printed in Italy. He will design a dress and e-mail the drawing to a Hong Kong agent, who will place the order with a Chinese factory. Finished dresses will be airfreighted to New York, where they will be redistributed to department and specialty stores around the country.

Thus, managers in countries around the world are increasingly taking a global, not just local, view of the company's industry, competitors, and opportunities. They are asking: What is global marketing? How does it differ from domestic marketing? How do global competitors and forces affect our business? To what extent should we "go global"? We will discuss the global marketplace in more detail in Chapter 13.

The call for more ethics and social responsibility

Marketers are reexamining their relationships with social values and responsibilities and with the very Earth that sustains us. As the worldwide consumerism and environmentalism movements mature, today's marketers are being called upon to take greater responsibility for the social and environmental impact of their actions. Corporate ethics and social responsibility have become hot topics for almost every business. And few companies can ignore the renewed and very demanding environmental movement.

The social-responsibility and environmental movements will place even stricter demands on companies in the future. Some companies resist these movements, budging only when forced by legislation or organized consumer outcries. More forward-looking companies, however, readily accept their responsibilities to the world around them. They view socially responsible actions as an opportunity to do well by doing good. They seek ways to profit by serving the best long-run interests of their customers and communities.

Some companies—such as Patagonia, Ben & Jerry's, Honest Tea, and others—are practicing "caring capitalism," setting themselves apart by being civic-minded and responsible. They are building social responsibility and action into their company value and mission statements. For example, when it comes to environmental responsibility, outdoor gear marketer Patagonia is "committed to the core." "Those of us who work here share a strong commitment to protecting undomesticated lands and waters," says the company's Web site. "We believe in using business to inspire solutions to the environmental crisis." Patagonia backs these words with actions. Each year it pledges at least 1 percent of its sales or 10 percent of its profits, whichever is greater, to the protection of the natural environment.[36] We will revisit the topic of marketing and social responsibility in greater detail in Chapter 8.

The growth of not-for-profit marketing

In the past, marketing has been most widely applied in the for-profit business sector. In recent years, however, marketing also has become a major part of the strategies of many not-for-profit organizations, such as colleges, hospitals, museums, zoos, symphony orchestras, and even churches. The nation's nonprofits face stiff competition for support and membership. Sound marketing can help them to attract membership and support. Consider the marketing efforts of the San Francisco Zoo:

The San Francisco Zoological Society aggressively markets the zoo's attractions to what might be its most important customer segment—children of all ages. It starts with a well-designed "product." The expanded Children's Zoo is specially designed to encourage parent-child interaction and discussions about living together with animals. The zoo provides close-up encounters with critters ranging from companion animals and livestock to the wildlife in our backyards and beyond. Children can groom livestock or collect eggs at the Family Farm, peer through microscopes in the Insect Zoo, crawl through a child-sized burrow at the Meerkats and Prairie Dogs exhibit, and lots more. To get the story out, attract visitors, and raise funds, the zoo sponsors innovative advertising, an informative Web site, and exciting family events. The most popular event is the annual ZooFest for Kids. "Bring your children, parents, grandparents, and friends to participate in the San Francisco Zoo's most popular annual family fundraiser—ZooFest for Kids!" the zoo invites. "Get your face painted, enjoy up-close encounters with animals, eat yummy treats, and much, much more." ZooFest planners market the event to local businesses, which supply food and entertainment. The event usually nets about $50,000, money that goes to support the

Not-for-profit marketing: The San Francisco Zoological Society aggressively markets the zoo's attractions to what might be its most important customer segment—children of all ages.

Zoo's conservation and education programs. "With music in the air and tables heaped high with food," notes one observer, "ZooFest for Kids [has] a magic about it befitting the beginning of summer"—magic created by good marketing.[37]

Similarly, private colleges, facing declining enrollments and rising costs, are using marketing to compete for students and funds. Many performing arts groups—even those with seasonal sellouts—face huge operating deficits that they must cover by more aggressive donor marketing. Finally, many long-standing not-for-profit organizations— the YMCA, the Salvation Army, the Girl Scouts—have lost members and are now modernizing their missions and "products" to attract more members and donors.[38]

Government agencies have also shown an increased interest in marketing. For example, the U.S. military has a marketing plan to attract recruits to its different services, and various government agencies are now designing *social marketing campaigns* to encourage energy conservation and concern for the environment or to discourage smoking, excessive drinking, and drug use. Even the once-stodgy U.S. Postal Service has developed innovative marketing to sell commemorative stamps, promote its priority mail services against those of its competitors, and lift its image. In all, the U.S. government is the nation's 29th-largest advertiser, with an annual advertising budget of more than $1.2 billion.[39]

So, what is marketing? Pulling it all together

At the start of this chapter, Figure 1.1 presented a simple model of the marketing process. Now that we've discussed all of the steps in the process, Figure 1.6 presents an expanded model that will help you pull it all together. What is marketing? Simply put, marketing is the process of building profitable customer relationships by creating value for customers and capturing value in return.

The first four steps of the marketing process focus on creating value for customers. The company first gains a full understanding of the marketplace by researching customer needs and managing marketing information. It then designs a customer-driven marketing strategy based on the answers to two simple questions. The first question is "What consumers will we serve?" (market segmentation and targeting). Good marketing companies know that they cannot serve all customers in every way. Instead, they need to focus their resources on the customers they can serve best and most profitably. The second marketing strategy question is "How can we best serve targeted customers?" (differentiation and positioning). Here, the marketer outlines a value proposition that spells out what values the company will deliver in order to win target customers.

With its marketing strategy decided, the company now constructs an integrated marketing program—consisting of a blend of the four marketing mix elements, or the four Ps—that transforms the marketing strategy into real value for customers. The company develops product offers and creates strong brand identities for them. It prices these offers to create real customer value and distributes the offers to make them available to target consumers. Finally, the company designs promotion programs that communicate the value proposition to target consumers and persuade them to act on the market offering.

Perhaps the most important step in the marketing process involves building value-laden, profitable relationships with target customers. Throughout the process, marketers practice customer relationship management to create customer satisfaction and delight. In creating customer value and relationships, however, the company cannot go

An Expanded Model of the Marketing Process   FIGURE 1.6

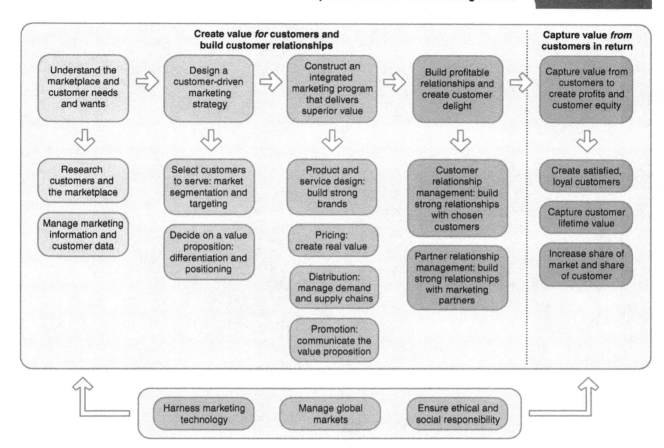

it alone. It must work closely with marketing partners both inside the company and throughout the marketing system. Thus, beyond practicing good customer relationship management, firms must also practice good partner relationship management.

The first four steps in the marketing process create value *for* customers. In the final step, the company reaps the rewards of its strong customer relationships by capturing value *from* customers. Delivering superior customer value creates highly satisfied customers who will buy more and will buy again. This helps the company to capture customer lifetime value and greater share of customer. The result is increased long-term customer equity for the firm.

Finally, in the face of today's changing marketing landscape, companies must take into account three additional factors. In building customer and partner relationships, they must harness marketing technology, take advantage of global opportunities, and ensure that they act in an ethical and socially responsible way.

chapter 2

Consumer Fashion Marketing

Fashion marketing is the entire process of researching, planning, promoting, and distributing the raw materials, apparel, and accessories that consumers want to buy. It involves everyone in the fashion industry and occurs throughout the entire channel of distribution. Marketing is the power behind the product development, production, distribution, retailing, and promotion of fibers, fabrics, leathers, furs, trimmings, apparel, and accessories.

Fashion marketing begins and ends with the consumer. This chapter first discusses the effect of consumer demand on marketing. It begins with a survey of consumer groups and demographic and psychographic trends, and explains how these help to define target markets. The chapter goes on to discuss economic, global, and technological influences on the fashion industry and ends with a discussion of the marketing chain.

Consumer demand

Consumers, people who buy and use merchandise, are the primary influence on marketing.

The history of the fashion industry in America is the story of a growing economy, based on manufacturing, that consumed more than it could produce. As competition increased, however, the consumer had more choice of products to the point of oversaturation. Consumers now have the income to influence fashion marketing by their buying decisions. In addition to better and cheaper products, consumers also demand constant availability, convenience, and a pleasant shopping experience. As a result, consumers' demands have shifted the industry from a production to a marketing orientation.

With this change in marketing philosophy, the industry now endeavors to find out what consumers will want to buy through research and then tries to develop the products to answer these needs. Fashion industry executives continually learn about consumer behavior to get clues as to what products consumers might need or want to buy in the future. They hire professional marketing firms to analyze lifestyles and buying behaviors. Professional analysts have developed sophisticated marketing research methods to determine consumer wants and needs. In turn, manufacturers and retailers have emphasized product development to answer these needs.

Fashion producers and retailers also spend large amounts of money on increased advertising and other marketing activities to *create* consumer demand. The ultimate achievement of advertising is to establish the identity of a particular brand name or store so solidly that consumers will seek it out, that it will become a "destination brand." Consumers are bombarded with million-dollar advertising campaigns. However, there is a limit to which marketing can win acceptance for a fashion. If the public is not ready for a product or is tired of it, no amount of advertising or publicity can gain or hold its acceptance.

Consumer groups

Fashion executives try to satisfy the wants and needs of particular consumer groups or market segments.

Consumers are not one homogeneous mass. Traditionally, society was divided by income classes. The wealthiest were the most fashionable, because only they could afford to buy expensive clothes. Those traditional class systems have broken down. Almost all clothing is mass-produced, and almost everyone can enjoy fashion on some price level.

The fashion industry has reached a consumer saturation point. In general, the U.S. population is spending less on apparel, along with food and entertainment, as they spend more on housing, health care, transportation, home furnishings and equipment, education, electronics, beauty, and fitness. Analysts believe that apparel purchases, as a percentage of spending, will continue to decline. In addition, busy schedules and multiple responsibilities limit the amount of time people have free to shop.

Demographic trends

Market research companies, manufacturers, and retailers try to understand consumer needs by studying information about society. Market researchers do sophisticated demographic and psychographic studies to classify the population into consumer groups or *market segments*, based on age, lifestyle, living area, educational and ethnic backgrounds, and so on. *Demographics* are statistical studies of measurable population characteristics such as birthrate, age distribution, and income. Demographic studies demonstrate that the American population is aging and diversifying.

The gray market

Americans born before 1945 are the most neglected by designers, retailers, and the media. In fact, the 60- to 75-year-old group is the second fastest growing age segment. People in this age group tend to feel 10 to 15 years younger than their actual age, but they have been marketed to as if they were 10 to 15 years older. Studies show that mature people have money to spend and enjoy new products as much as anyone and tend to dress up more often than younger people. Primarily, this age group prefers shopping for apparel and accessories by catalog, via the Internet, or at department stores. By 2010, one-third of the population will be over age 50, indicating that in the future marketers will need to cater to a more conservative value-, function-, comfort-, and quality-oriented customer.

Eileen Fisher ad showing three consumer groups of women. (Courtesy of Eileen Fisher, Inc.)

The postwar baby boom

Baby boomers, the age group caused by the increase in the birthrate between 1946 and 1964, are still the largest generation and the primary demographic spending group in the United States to influence the apparel market. These women shop a wide variety of retail venues from luxury specialty stores to discounters. Women 45 to 62 spend more on clothing per capita than any other age group.[1] Yet this group is also generally ignored by the fashion industry. Joan Kaner, former fashion director at Neiman Marcus, said, "The 45-and-up customer is not being represented, or even addressed, in most fashion advertising and editorial."[2]

Fashion advertisers have stereotypical ideas about the style sensibilities of people over 40 and are also afraid of alienating younger customers with multigenerational ads. However, a few advertisers are using older models, such as Sharon Stone for Badgley Mischka and Madonna for H&M. Baby boomers have distinct and firm ideas about what they want. They expect more service, comfort, and quality, but they want the same fashion as young people with appropriate length and fit.

The baby busters (generation X)

The generation born between 1965 and 1979 is referred to as the *baby busters*, because this age bracket is much smaller than the one preceding it. Now in their 30s and early 40s, they have become career- and family-oriented, and their spending patterns reflect these interests, with more spending on housing, home goods, transportation, and education.

The baby boomlet (generation Y)

Fashion marketing's most sought after consumer group is referred to as the *baby boomlet* or *generation Y* (also called the *millennial generation* or the *Net generation*), the children of the baby boomers, created by the rise in the birthrate that began in 1980. They are a racially diverse group with a global, sports, computer, and entertainment orientation that will affect their buying decisions in the future. Advertising, television shows, movies, Web sites, and magazines are created specifically for this market. This demographic group is fashion hungry and has a passion for buying clothes, but usually cannot afford to spend as much as baby boomers. The contemporary and young men's market is already strong as a result of people in this age group reaching their 20s, while teens spend heavily on junior fashions. Young people tend to prefer specialty apparel chains and small boutiques.

By 2010, the nation will be rather polarized, with the postwar boomers over 50 years of age and the millennial generation under 30. Some companies, such as the Gap and Eileen Fisher, are responding with multigenerational advertising campaigns.

Ethnic diversity

Another important demographic trend is the ethnic diversity of the U.S. population. The Immigration and Naturalization Service projects that legal immigration exceeds 700,000 per year. The Census Bureau has determined that the black, Hispanic, Asian, and Native American segments of the population will all grow much faster than the white majority. People of different cultural backgrounds look for different things in a fashion purchase. They have various cultural perceptions and partialities regarding styling, color, pattern, fabrics, fit, quality, and value. With a multicultural society, retailers and manufacturers try to cater to these various market segments.

Psychographic or lifestyle trends

People can share the same demographic characteristics and still be very different from each other. Whatever the age group, market researchers try to pinpoint delineations of lifestyles, called *psychographics*. These studies use psychological, sociological, and anthropological factors to further separate consumers based on the differences in their lifestyles. Manufacturers and retailers often turn to psychographics to further segment and analyze consumer groups and their fashion preferences.

Independent women

Today, more than 75 percent of the female population aged 20 to 60 are employed. More than 22 million women live alone or head single-women households. These circumstances have empowered women to make more purchasing decisions. For these women, who divide their days between the demands of home and career, time becomes a critical issue. Busy working women tend to shop less often and favor convenient, one-stop shopping, which has aided the growth of certain catalogs, Web sites, and superstores. However, like the majority of the population, they have more important claims on their paychecks than apparel and accessories.

Larger sizes

Another phenomenon influencing the fashion industry is the increasing number of people wearing larger sizes. As the population ages, people are getting heavier. Approximately 68 percent of all Americans are overweight. At Haggar, core sizes for its pants used to be sizes 32 to 40; now the core sizes go up to 44. As a result, retail stores are devoting more square footage to large-size apparel.

Other psychographic trends

The key to appealing to apparel shoppers is to merchandise according to consumer lifestyles—by relating to where shoppers work, as well as to their family demands, recreational activities, and cultural interests. Observers generally believe that the following are also important psychographic or lifestyle trends:

- **Community**—People are looking for a connection to the community; for the first time in more than 40 years, cities are gaining in population.
- **Renewed interest in family life**—People spend more money on the home and family activities than on fashion.
- **Cocooning**—Many people try to insulate themselves from the fears of terrorism, war, and crime by staying home as much as possible, shopping less, or shopping by catalog or on the Internet. At home they feel a sense of comfort and protection from an increasingly insecure and hostile world.
- **Work at home**—The number of people who work at home is expected to increase dramatically.
- **Increased at-home use of computers**—People are more likely to shop on the Internet.
- **Comfort**—People want relaxed and casual dressing at home and at work and activewear for exercise.
- **Value of time**—People are willing to trade money for free time, which makes shopping by catalog or the Internet appealing.
- **Stress**—Overwhelmed consumers have busy schedules and are overwhelmed with too much choice of merchandise; they prefer to limit shopping to a few favorite stores, catalogs, or Web sites.

Target marketing

Textile and apparel producers and retailers use demographic and psychographic information in an effort to understand the buying habits and preferences of each market segment. They also use direct customer contact in stores, informal interviews, surveys, consumer focus groups, and point-of-sale data analysis to define their *target market*, the group of consumers they want to reach. They try to be very specific to find even smaller potential *market niches* within larger markets. Ideally, appropriate consumer goods are then created for each of these groups of people to satisfy their wants and needs.

Database marketing (datamining)

Fashion merchants gather data about consumers to strengthen marketing strategies. Through their purchases, consumers unwittingly give manufacturers and retailers information about their shopping habits, size and color preferences, lifestyle, age, income, and address, which are recorded and stored in computers. Many retailers now issue their own store credit cards or cobranded cards (in partnership with a bank or a major credit card) to build more elaborate marketing databases.

This information is combined with answers to surveys and other sources, such as sweepstake entries, coupon request forms, and public records, and categorized into *databases*, consumer taste profiles for all consumer groups (see Market Research, Chapter 4). A retailer might evaluate credit card purchases by maternity customers, for example, and send these shoppers direct-mail advertising on baby goods nine months later.

Mapping   Merchants translate sales data and purchasing patterns into geographic maps, visual representations of their markets. Breaking out sales by customer zip codes vividly illustrates primary and secondary markets for each store location and helps management to understand traffic flow and sales potential.

Merchants use consumer profiles from databases to:

- Learn about their customers
- Find new customers
- Establish a target market
- Find or create new products to suit their target customers
- Help to find new ways to advertise to these markets
- Keep them focused on their customers

Manufacturers and retailers in touch with the needs of their target customers are the ones who succeed in an increasingly competitive marketplace. However, in spite of sophisticated research methods, fashion companies still have a problem understanding changing demographics and creating fashion products that their customers will want to buy.

The impact of economics on consumer demand

Consumer spending, the state of the economy, the international money market, and labor costs have an effect on fashion marketing.

Consumer spending

The amount of money that consumers spend on fashion and other goods depends on their income. Income, as it affects spending, is measured in three ways: personal income, disposable income, and discretionary income.

Personal income is the gross amount of income from all sources, such as wages and salaries, interest, and dividends.

Disposable income is personal income minus taxes. This amount determines a person's purchasing power.

Discretionary income is income left over after food, lodging, and other necessities have been paid for. This money is available to be spent or saved at will. The increase in discretionary income enjoyed by most people in our society means that more people are able to buy fashion. Young people spend the highest proportion of their income on clothes.

Purchasing power

Purchasing power is related to the economic situation. Although incomes in the Western world have risen in recent years, so have prices. Thus, income is meaningful only in relation to the amount of goods and services that it can buy, or its *purchasing power*. Credit, productivity, inflation, recession, and international currency values affect purchasing power.

Credit

The growth of consumer credit and the proliferation of credit cards have greatly extended consumer purchasing power. More and more retailers are offering their own credit cards to obtain consumer information for their databases. Now, there is too much easy credit available, which has resulted in a huge increase in personal bankruptcies, with losses to both retailers and banks.

Fashion companies, too, need credit to be able to operate through seasonal peaks and valleys and to finance their businesses through the long lead times required for buying supplies long before the finished product is paid for. The accumulation of too much

Rising domestic labor costs have caused U.S. and European manufacturers to seek cheaper labor in Asia, resulting in a huge increase in imports. *(Courtesy of Liz Claiborne)*

corporate debt is one of the factors that has led to many manufacturer and retailer bankruptcies and closings during the past 30 years.

Corporate ownership

Fashion manufacturers and retailers were traditionally privately owned companies. Now, most of these companies have grown into corporations or have been purchased by other corporations. There has been a steady barrage of mergers and acquisitions, resulting in giant "corporate groups" such as Liz Claiborne, Jones Apparel Group, and LVMH. In addition, many of these corporations sell stock to the public to gain broader access to funding. Their initial public offerings (IPOs) and the impressive performance of certain stocks have gained attention from the press. Bottom lines, instead of hemlines, often dominate the fashion news. These publicly held corporations now have an added responsibility to their shareholders. They are pressured to build sales and profits, increase cost efficiency, and sink millions into advertising to build their brand image.

Labor costs

As people receive higher salaries and live better, the cost of making products increases. Rising domestic labor costs have caused most manufacturers to search for cheaper sources of labor in Asia, Mexico, the Caribbean Basin, and elsewhere.

Inflation

In an inflationary period such as the United States experienced in the 1980s, people earn more money each year, but higher prices and higher taxes result in little or no real increase in purchasing power.

Recession

A recession, such as we experienced in 2002–2003, is a cycle beginning with a decrease in spending. Many companies are forced to cut back production, which results in unemployment and a drop in the gross national product (GNP). Unemployment furthers the cycle of reduced spending.

When the economic situation is unstable, the fashion picture is also unstable. Not only is money in short supply, but people seem to be confused about what they really want. In an economic upswing, colors are basically cheerful and happy, but they have a grayed palette when the economy is in trouble. Also, people are likely to buy conservatively or buy merchandise that they believe to be of lasting value in a recession, but they are more willing to pay for fashion in prosperous times.

Foreign exchange market

When the dollar is strong against other currencies, American consumers are able to buy foreign-made merchandise more cheaply. At the same time, American industry is hurt, because imported merchandise competes with domestic goods and exports become too expensive for other countries to buy.

On the other hand, when the dollar is weak (loses value relative to other currencies), foreign countries can buy American goods more cheaply. This situation encourages American fashion manufacturers to export and is good for business. In this case, however, imported goods are more expensive for Americans to buy.

The Euro   In 1999, the euro became the official common currency of 11 of the 15 members of the European Union (EU). The use of a single currency boosts European industries' ability to compete in world markets, especially against the dollar and yen, and makes trade easier by eliminating exchange rate fluctuations within Europe.

The impact of global trade on marketing

Fierce competition from imports and a saturated domestic market have led to a new global viewpoint in marketing on all levels of the industry.

A major trend in fashion marketing is globalization. World trade in apparel and accessories is growing despite high tariffs and drastic currency fluctuations. Many countries may be involved in the production of a single garment. For example, a garment could be designed in New York, made in China with fabric from Korea, and then distributed to retail stores all over the world. Retailers, too, are expanding globally. Stores as diverse as Christian Dior (French), H&M (Hennes & Mauritz, Swedish), Zara (Spanish), and the Gap (American) have opened stores worldwide.

Imports

Imports are goods that are brought in from a foreign country to sell here. The people or firms that import goods are usually manufacturers that produce apparel in another country, and wholesalers and retailers acting as *importers*. Retailers want to give their customers the best quality products at the lowest prices. Therefore, ever-increasing amounts of textiles, apparel, and accessories are being imported into the United States and the European Union (EU) because of the availability of cheaper labor in low-wage countries. U.S. and European manufacturers compete with labor rates of 69 cents per hour in parts of China and 60 cents or less in India.[3]

Imported Fashion merchandise

Traditionally, imports were fashion merchandise designed and produced by foreign designers and manufacturers and purchased by domestic retailers at international markets. The United States has long imported fashion from Paris, woolens from the British Isles, sweaters from Scandinavia, and leather goods from Italy. Currently, the European Economic Community, followed by the United States, is the largest importer and consumer of apparel in the world.

Knitwear by Gianfranco Ferré. The coveted "Made in Italy" label is disappearing as Italian manufacturers seek cheaper production in Eastern Europe and Asia. *(Courtesy of Gianfranco Ferré)*

Sourcing cheaper fabrics and production

Manufacturers *source* (search the world for) the best fabrics available at low cost to make into garments. U.S. textile and apparel imports increased from $10 billion in 1982 to $96 billion in 2006.[4] This corresponds to the enormous growth of the textile industries of China, Korea, Taiwan, and India. One reason for this is that U.S. manufacturers contracting production overseas tend to use fabrics from the region where production is done, thereby taking sales away from U.S. domestic textile producers. As a result, after the North American Free Trade Agreement (NAFTA) was passed in 1994, U.S. textile producers encouraged apparel production in Mexico and the Caribbean Basin, where U.S. textiles can be used, but this production is now limited to basics.

Today less than 10 percent of apparel sold in the United States is made here. Most manufacturers buy fabrics, patternmaking services, and production (cutting and sewing) from a contractor in a foreign country where labor is cheaper, especially China. The intense collaboration between the Chinese government and its textile and apparel sectors enables China to underprice its competitors. Government support takes the form of currency undervaluation, subsidized shipping costs, export tax rebates, and direct subsidization. Unless limited in some way, Chinese apparel exports will continue to grow, and China will eventually supply most of our apparel. The huge increase in imports in recent years has stimulated a great deal of controversy. The controversy revolves around two key points: the balance of trade and the loss of jobs at home.

Balance of trade

The *balance of trade* is the difference in value between a country's exports and its imports. Ideally, the two figures should be about equal. Lately, however, the United States has been importing much more than it exports, sending American dollars abroad to pay for these goods and creating a huge *trade deficit*. Many people believe that we should import fewer goods to balance trade. Others think that the consumer should be given the best merchandise at the best price, regardless of the balance of trade.

Labor versus free trade

There has been an enormous increase of imported fabric and apparel and accessory production. Labor unions have complained that overseas production has stolen thousands of domestic jobs in textile and apparel production. The American textile industry has lost more than 900,000 jobs, and thousands of plants have closed since 1980. The United States has lost its manufacturing base.

On the other hand, proponents of *free trade* (trade without restrictions), such as importers and retailers, believe that, in the long run, world trade should be based on specialization; each nation would contribute to the world market what it produces best at the most reasonable cost. In this way, consumers would obtain the most value for their money.

Import tariffs or duties

Duties or *tariffs* are customs charges imposed on imports in an attempt to protect domestic industry. Duties vary according to the type of garment, the fiber content, and whether the fabric is woven or knitted. However, the United States is considering eliminating them.

Harmonized Tariff Schedule The Harmonized Tariff Schedule (HTS) is an international system of product classification used since 1988 for international customs clearance and the collection of data on imports and exports. Formerly, every country had its own system of naming or numbering imports and exports. Now a system of six-digit codes allows participating countries to classify traded goods on a common basis.

World trade organization

The World Trade Organization (WTO), which governs worldwide trade, is located in Geneva. The organization has 149 member countries, which together account for over 90 percent of world merchandise trade. Its basic objectives are to achieve the expansion and progressive liberalization of world trade. Additional functions of the WTO are to set rules governing trade behavior, set environmental and labor standards, protect intellectual property, resolve disputes between members, and serve as a forum for trade negotiations. It was hoped that negotiations would help to alleviate poverty in poor countries with an increase of global commerce. However, the last meeting, called the Doha Round because it began in Doha, Qatar, in 2001, ended in deadlock in 2006.

The agreement on textiles and clothing

The Agreement on Textiles and Clothing (ATC) was negotiated under the auspices of the WTO. It provided for the 2005 quota removal from all apparel and textile imports for its 145 member countries.

A meeting of the World Trade Organization in Geneva, Switzerland. *(Photo by Tania Tang, courtesy of the WTO)*

Quota elimination

Many governments regulate imports by means of *quotas* that control the quantity of imported merchandise. Quotas are negotiated between two trading countries and are allocated for a 12-month period. Until now, a manufacturer or importer had to be sure that quotas were high enough to allow the merchandise in question to be produced in that country. Quotas involved a nightmare of complexities and middlemen. Governments allocated quotas to companies who paid for them. Countries were limited on what and how much they could export. However, in 2005, the international quota system was officially eliminated, except for countries that are not members of the World Trade Organization, although some special temporary limits on China still exist.

The end of the quota system on textiles and apparel will bring major economic changes to many parts of the world. It poses a great opportunity for China, but many other developing countries that rely on apparel exports for economic growth may lose their business to China. China's high unemployment and migration from rural areas to the cities will provide even more people willing to work for low wages. The National Textile Association (NTA) wants the U.S. government to impose safeguard measures, such as higher tariffs and duties, if China dominates world textile and apparel trade.

Fashion change and consumer acceptance

Career focus

Designers, merchandisers, and marketers at every level of the industry must be aware of fashion change, cycles, and consumer acceptance and how these concepts will affect product development and marketing. They also have to be aware of all the categories of apparel, particularly in their specialty area.

Consumers' wants and needs create a cycle of consumer demand, industry catering to that demand, and, finally, consumer acceptance with the purchase of merchandise in the retail market. The first part of this chapter discusses fashion acceptance and rejection, a cycle that creates fashion change. The middle of the chapter covers consumers' connection to fashion cycles, how cycles relate to fashion adoption, and what factors motivate consumers to buy fashion. Last, all the categories of women's wear, men's wear, and children's wear are described. To set the stage, the chapter begins with terms associated with fashion acceptance.

Fashion terms

All fashion executives use the following terms daily to discuss various aspects of fashion.

Fashion

Fashion is the style or styles most popular at a given time. The term implies four components: style, change, acceptance, and taste.

Style

Style is any particular characteristic or look in apparel or accessories. The term *style* can be interpreted three ways:

- Designers interpret fashion ideas into new styles and offer them to the public. The manufacturer assigns a *style number* to each new design in each collection, which is used to identify it throughout production, marketing, and retailing.

- Designs that have the same characteristics are referred to as a style, such as a blazer-style jacket, an empire-style dress, or an envelope-style handbag. A style may come and go in fashion, but that specific style always remains that style, whether it is in fashion or not. For example, the polo-shirt style will not always be in fashion, yet it will always have variations of the same styling and details, which make it a polo shirt.

- A person can have "style" by wearing fashionable clothes particularly suited to him or her, or a designer may become known for a certain "style" or look.

- A "stylist" is a fashion consultant who helps edit a designer's collection, selects flattering clothes for celebrities to wear, and/or puts fashion looks together with accessories for fashion photographers or a magazine.

Style #103 from the Andrew Gn fall women's collection.
(Courtesy of Andrew Gn, Paris)

Change

What makes fashion interesting is that it is always changing. Designer Karl Lagerfeld said, "What I like about fashion is change. Change means also that what we do today might be worthless tomorrow, but we have to accept that because we are in fashion. There's nothing safe forever in fashion . . . fashion is a train that waits for nobody. Get on it, or it's gone."[1] Vera Wang tells her assistants, "If you're afraid of change, you're in the wrong business."[2]

Many people criticize the fickleness of fashion, saying that fashion changes

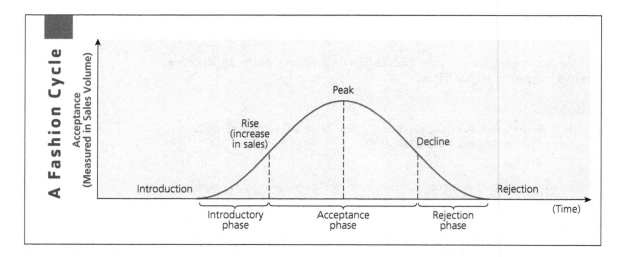

A Fashion Cycle

Acceptance (Measured in Sales Volume)

Peak

Rise (increase in sales)

Decline

Introduction

Rejection

(Time)

Introductory phase · Acceptance phase · Rejection phase

only to stimulate buying. And it is true that if fashion never changed, the public would not buy apparel and accessories so often. However, fashion is one way for consumers to visually express their relationship to current events and to life itself.

Fashion changes because

- It reflects changes in people's lifestyles and current events.
- People's needs change.
- People get bored with what they have.

As a result of modern communications, the public is quickly made aware of the existence of new styles. Thus, one of the greatest impacts on fashion is the acceleration of change. Consumers are aware of new styles before they reach the stores.

Because fashion is a product of change, a *sense of timing* (the ability to understand the speed of acceptance and change) is an important asset for anyone involved with product development or marketing in the fashion industry. Designers have to decide *when* their customers will be ready to accept a particular style. Italian designer Valentino remarked, "Timing is the key to a successful idea."[3]

Acceptance

Acceptance implies that consumers must buy and wear a style to make it a fashion. Karl Lagerfeld remarked, "There's no fashion if nobody buys it."[4] It is then up to the public to decide whether these styles will become fashion. Acceptance, that is, purchases by a large number of people, makes a style into fashion. The degree of acceptance also provides clues to fashion trends for coming seasons.

Taste

An individual's preference for one style or another is referred to as *taste*. "Good taste" in fashion implies sensitivity to what is beautiful and appropriate. People who have good taste also understand quality and simplicity. Good taste is developed by extensive exposure to beautiful design. People also develop individual tastes, often referred to as "personal style."

Fashion evolution

Generally, fashion change evolves gradually, giving consumers time to become accustomed to new looks.

Fashion cycles

Fashion acceptance is usually described as a fashion cycle. It is difficult to categorize or theorize about fashion without oversimplifying. Even so, the fashion cycle is usually depicted as a bell-shaped curve encompassing five stages: introduction, rise in popularity, peak of popularity, decline in popularity, and rejection. The cycle can reflect the acceptance of a single style from one designer or of a "trend" (general style direction), such as cropped pants.

Introduction of a style

Most new styles are introduced at a high price level. Designers who are respected for their talent may be given financial backing and allowed to design with very few limitations on creativity, quality of raw materials, or amount of fine workmanship. They create new apparel and accessory styles by changing elements such as line, shape, color, fabric, and details and their relationship to one another. Production costs are high and only a few people can afford the resulting garments. Production in small quantities gives a designer more freedom, flexibility, and room for creativity.

New styles are shown to retail buyers and the press at collection showings and market weeks. At this first stage of the cycle, fashion implies only style and newness. Some wealthy people are able to buy these clothes because they want to wear them to important events. Some new styles are loaned to movie and TV stars to wear so that they will be seen by many people.

Increase in popularity

When new styles are worn by celebrities on television or photographed in magazines, they attract the attention of the general public. Viewers and readers may wish to buy the new styles but perhaps cannot afford them.

Popular styles are copied or adapted by mainstream manufacturers to make them available to the general public. They use less expensive fabric and may modify the design to sell the style at lower prices. Some companies, such as ABS (Allen B. Schwartz), have built successful businesses imitating designer originals at lower prices. In self-defense, many couture and high-priced designers now have secondary, bridge, and/or diffusion lines, which sell at lower prices, so that they are able to sell adaptations of their original designs in greater quantities. Examples include Roberto Cavalli's "Just Cavalli" and Dolce & Gabbana's "D&G" collections.

Peak of popularity

When a fashion is at the height of popularity, it may be in such demand that more manufacturers copy it or produce adaptations of it at many price levels. Some designers are flattered by copying, and others are resentful. There is a very fine line between adaptations and "knockoffs"! However, volume production requires mass acceptance.

Decline in popularity

Eventually, so many copies are mass-produced that fashion-conscious people tire of the style and begin to look for something new. Consumers still wear garments in the style, but they are no longer willing to buy them at regular prices. Retail stores put declining styles on sale racks, hoping to make room for new merchandise. Many shoppers today wait to buy when merchandise goes on sale, causing price deflation.

Rejection of a style or obsolescence

In the last phase of the fashion cycle, some consumers have already turned to new looks, thus beginning a new cycle. The rejection or discarding of a style just because it is out of fashion is called *consumer obsolescence*. As early as 1600, Shakespeare wrote that "fashion wears out more apparel than the man."[5]

Length of cycles

Although all fashions follow the same cyclical pattern, there is no measurable timetable for a fashion cycle. Some fashions take a short time to peak in popularity, others take longer; some decline slowly, others swiftly. Some styles last a single selling season; others last several seasons. Certain fashions fade quickly; others never completely disappear.

Classics

Some styles never become completely obsolete, but instead remain more or less accepted for an extended period. A classic is characterized by simplicity of design, which keeps it from being easily dated. An example is the Chanel suit, which peaked in fashion in the late 1950s and enjoyed popularity again in the 1980s and 1990s. In the interim, the house of Chanel in Paris, as well as other manufacturers, have produced variations of these suits for a dedicated clientele at various price ranges. Other examples of classics include pea coats, blazers, cashmere sweaters, polo shirts, jeans, ballet flats, and loafers.

Fads

Short-lived fashions, or fads, such as pony prints or "charity" wristbands, can come and go in a single season. They lack the design strength to hold consumer attention for very long. Fads usually affect only a narrow consumer group, often begin in lower price ranges, are relatively simple and inexpensive to copy, and therefore flood the market in a very short time. Because of market saturation, the public tires of them quickly and they die out. Fads are more prevalent in the junior market.

Cycles within cycles

Design elements (such as color, texture, or silhouette) may change even though the style itself remains popular. Jeans became a fashion item in the late 1960s and remain classics. Therefore, their fashion cycle is very long. However, various details, silhouettes, and other features came and went during that time.

Recurring cycles

After a fashion dies, it may resurface. Designers often borrow ideas from the past. When a style reappears years later, it is reinterpreted for a new time; a silhouette or proportion may recur, but it is interpreted with a change in fabric and detail. Nothing is ever exactly the same—yet nothing is totally new. Designers are often inspired by nostalgic looks of the last century, but use different fabrics, colors, and details, which make the looks unique to today.

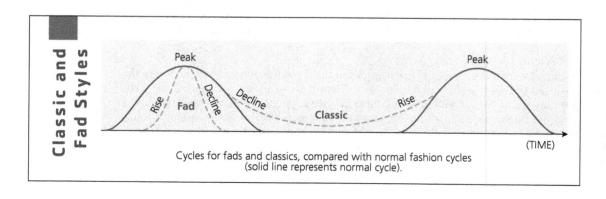

Cycles for fads and classics, compared with normal fashion cycles (solid line represents normal cycle).

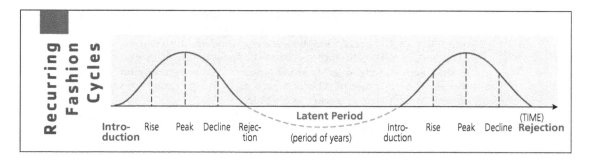

Consumer identification with fashion cycles

How customers relate to the phases of fashion cycles has to do with the consumer group to which they belong.

Consumer groups

Consumers can be identified with various stages of the fashion cycle. Fashion leaders buy and wear new styles at the beginning of their cycles; others tend to imitate: Manufacturers and retailers may also be identified as fashion leaders or followers, depending on which consumer groups they target.

Fashion leaders

The people who look for new fashion and wear it before it becomes generally acceptable are often referred to as fashion leaders. Fashion leaders are confident of their own taste or have a stylist to advise them. They dare to be different, and they attract the attention of others. Fashion leaders are a very small percentage of the public. They fall into two categories: fashion innovators and fashion role models.

Fashion Innovators   Some fashion leaders actually create fashion. They may be designers themselves or just want to express their own individual style. These fashion leaders constantly look for interesting new styles, colors, fabrics, and ways to accessorize their clothes. They try to find unique fashion in small boutiques or vintage clothing stores, or they design their own clothes. They are discerning shoppers who like to wear beautiful or unusual apparel. They may give impetus to a certain style by discovering and wearing it. They may be referred to as *avant garde* (French for "ahead of the pack") or fashion forward. Italian designer Donatella Versace explained, "Many people give us inspiration, the way they put their clothes together, and some have a style that goes beyond the clothes."[6]

Fashion Motivators or Role Models   A few fashion leaders have the beauty, status, and/or wealth to

Fashion leader Sarah Jessica Parker presents a CFDA Award to Narciso Rodriguez. *(Courtesy of the Council of Fashion Designers of America)*

become fashion role models. Designers lend new styles to celebrities, primarily film stars, to get publicity. They are seen at public events or on television and are photographed by the press. They become role models for everyone who identifies with them and, thereby, influence the way other people dress. For example, public interest in what actresses are wearing at the Academy Awards greatly influences the evening wear market. Because of their influence, fashion motivators are important to designers and to the fashion industry as a whole.

There are fashion leaders for every market segment. They can be any celebrity featured in the media, including royalty, politicians, TV and film stars, rock stars, and supermodels.

Fashion Victims   There are also those people with too much money to spend who become slaves to designer brands. Designer Jean-Paul Gaultier remarked, "Fashion victims are people who blindly and stupidly follow a brand without any discernment and without any analysis. As long as it's the latest rage, they buy it without thinking about adapting it to themselves."[7]

Fashion followers

Fashion needs followers, or it would not exist. Most men and women seek acceptance through conformity and like to emulate world, national, or community fashion leaders to feel confident. Fashion followers imitate others only after they are sure of fashion trends. Consumers become fashion followers for one or more of the following reasons:

- They lack the time, money, and interest to devote to fashion leadership. Dressing fashionably takes time and energy.
- They are busy with their jobs and families and think that fashion is unimportant.
- They need a period of exposure to new styles before accepting them.
- They are insecure about their tastes and, therefore, turn to what others have already approved as acceptable and appropriate.
- They want to fit in with their friends or peer group or to be accepted by them.
- They tend to imitate people whom they admire.

There are various degrees of fashion followers. Many busy people want to be judged by their intelligence and not on how they look or what they wear. This is true for many people with a life full of work, children, or other interests.

Because of fashion followers, most manufacturers are copyists or adapters. From a marketing point of view, fashion followers are very important. They make mass production possible, because volume production of fashion can only be profitable when similar merchandise is sold to many consumers.

Individuality

A recent styling trend of mixing unexpected garments, prints, colors, and textures together has given more fashion decision making to individuals. Mixing unrelated pieces takes skill and practice to make the mix look fashionable. Women who grew up on suits and coordinated outfits find this eclectic look very difficult to achieve. Even designers have problems with it; Miuccia Prada said, "It is not easy to do those combinations."[8] However, it does give consumers the opportunity to develop individuality.

Fashion leadership in manufacturing and retailing

Manufacturers and retailers respond to fashion leaders and followers in their product development and merchandising. They try to establish a particular merchandising identity with various consumer groups. Designer collections provide for the fashion leaders, whereas the majority of manufacturers provide merchandise for fashion followers.

Retailers, too, cater to fashion leaders or followers. Luxury brands featured at Bergdorf Goodman and Saks Fifth Avenue, for example, identify with and cater to fashion leaders, while Wal-Mart and Target are able to sell volume to the majority of followers. Stores like Macy's and the Gap fall in between.

Adoption of fashion

It is important to understand how new fashion ideas are disseminated, or spread, and how they are adapted to the tastes, lifestyles, and budgets of various consumers.

Basically, there are three variations of the fashion adoption process: traditional adoption, reverse adoption, and mass dissemination.

Traditional fashion adoption (trickle-down theory)

The trickle-down theory is based on the traditional process of copying and adapting trendsetting fashion from Paris, Milan, London, and New York designers. Sometimes it is even difficult to know where an idea began. Because couture or "signature" designer fashion is expensive, it is affordable to only a few people. As new styles are worn by publicized fashion leaders or shown in fashion publications, more consumers are exposed to these new looks. To appeal to this broader group of consumers, manufacturers produce less expensive adaptations of these fashions. These are copied again and again at lower prices until they have been seen often enough to become acceptable to the most conservative buyer. The cheapest versions are seen at discount houses soon after. Consumers then tire of the look, and its popularity fades. Fashion implies newness and freshness. Yet, as a fashion is copied, modified, and sold at lower and lower prices, it loses its newness, quality, and other essential design elements.

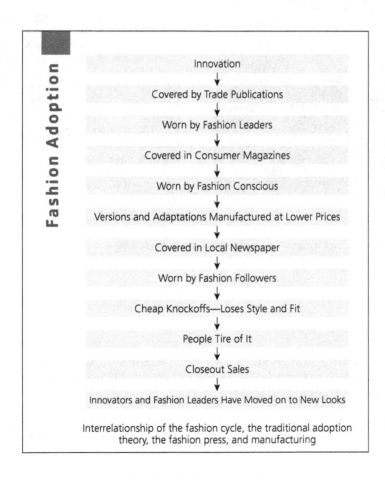

Fashion Adoption

Innovation
↓
Covered by Trade Publications
↓
Worn by Fashion Leaders
↓
Covered in Consumer Magazines
↓
Worn by Fashion Conscious
↓
Versions and Adaptations Manufactured at Lower Prices
↓
Covered in Local Newspaper
↓
Worn by Fashion Followers
↓
Cheap Knockoffs—Loses Style and Fit
↓
People Tire of It
↓
Closeout Sales
↓
Innovators and Fashion Leaders Have Moved on to New Looks

Interrelationship of the fashion cycle, the traditional adoption theory, the fashion press, and manufacturing

A dress from Prada, the much-copied Italian fashion company. *(Courtesy of Prada)*

Reverse adoption (trickle-up or bottom-up theory)

Since the 1960s, manufacturers and retailers have paid more attention to consumer preferences. Designers pay attention to what people are wearing. Dancewear and activewear, which began as functional needs of the consumer, also have influenced designer collections. Vintage fashion, purchased by young people in thrift shops, has influenced many recent collections. Designers now send out their own scouts or use shopping services to look for inspirational vintage styles.

Mass dissemination (trickle-across theory)

Modern communications bring fashion from around the world into our homes instantly. Consumers see the trends and want to look as fashionable as the celebrities. Manufacturers copy hot new styles almost immediately to meet the high demand; therefore, production speed is of the greatest importance. Mass dissemination is becoming the prevalent mode of fashion adoption. Oscar de la Renta commented that information is traveling a bit too fast—a denim coat from his collection had been copied and was selling at Bloomingdale's before his original version reached the stores.[9]

There is no longer one channel of fashion dissemination. Many separate markets have developed geared to various age ranges, lifestyles, tastes, and pocketbooks. What appeals to a junior customer would probably not appeal to a missy customer. Various designer and manufacturer labels appeal to various market segments at different price points. Increased diversity means that many different styles can be acceptable at the same time. There are many more options.

Motives for consumer buying

To help them make styling and merchandising decisions, designers, buyers, and other industry executives try to understand consumer motivation.

In the past, most people bought new clothes only when a need arose, for a very special occasion, or because their old clothes wore out. The average person simply could not afford to buy more than the basic necessities. In Western society today, discretionary income is larger, and people can buy new clothes frequently.

Therefore, buying motives have changed; people are able to buy clothes because they want or like them. Buying motives vary from consumer to consumer and from day to day. Motives are both rational and emotional:

To Fill an Emotional Need   New clothes help people to feel better psychologically. Being secure in the feeling that they are wearing appropriate fashion gives them confidence and self-assurance. A growing body of brain research shows that shopping activates the chemical dopamine. However, dopamine can cause impulse buying (buying without careful consideration), bad decisions, and compulsive shopping problems.

To Be Attractive   Consumers want clothes that are flattering, that make them look their best, or that show off their physical attributes.

To Be Fashionable   People may buy new clothing to make them feel that they are trendy or at least in the mainstream of fashion. They may discard clothing that is still wearable only because it is out of fashion.

To Impress Others   People may want to project a successful image or establish unique identities with fashion. They may want to exhibit their level of taste or income through clothing. Expensive brands have even served as status symbols.

To Be Accepted by Friends, Peer Groups, or Colleagues   Average Americans have conservative tastes; they do not want to differ from their peers. They may want to identify with a certain lifestyle. Buying patterns suggest that consumers like some direction or guidance as a framework for their choices.

To Fill Basic Lifestyle Needs   Based on their basic needs, individuals seek clothing for a particular event, climate or season, vacation, exercise or sport, job, or lifestyle.

Consumer buying patterns

Buying patterns change continually. To determine the acceptability of fashion, both designers and manufacturers find it helpful to consider these consumer shopping criteria.

- **Perceived value**—Consumers look for their idea of quality at reasonable prices; this is referred to as *perceived value*.
- **Item buying**—Consumers may buy only one item, such as a jacket, to update their wardrobes.
- **Multiple-use clothing**—Ideally, consumers look for comfortable, functional, multiple-use clothing.
- **Wear now**—People are buying closer to need, buying clothes they want to wear immediately.
- **Convenience**—With time and energy in increasingly short supply, consumers are looking for ways to make shopping easier. Consumers want to find what they need easily and quickly. In response to consumer needs, catalog and Internet shopping has increased.
- **Service**—Consumers are demanding personal service and in-stock assortments (clothing available in every size and color).

Fashion selection

Customers are attracted to a particular garment or accessory by its styling features. There are also practical considerations, including quality and price, that the consumer usually evaluates before making a purchase.

Styling Features

Styling features, which are the same as the elements of design, are considered here from the purchaser's point of view, rather than the creator's.

Ralph Rucci fitting one of his designs for a private client. *(Courtesy of Ralph Rucci, photo by Gini Stephens Frings)*

Color   People relate very personally to color, usually selecting or rejecting a fashion because the color does or does not appeal to them or is or is not flattering.

Texture   The surface interest in the fabric of a garment or accessory is called texture. Texture usually gives a clue as to fiber content.

Style   The elements that define a style include line, silhouette, and details. A consumer's selection is frequently influenced by his or her opinion of what is currently fashionable.

Practical Considerations

Price   Consumers want the best product at the best price. Price is probably the most important practical consideration for the average consumer. They must compare the total perceived worth of a style with the retail price and with their own budgets. As a result, discount retailers and inexpensive chains have taken market share away from middle market stores.

Fit   Sizing is not a guarantee of fit. The U.S. Department of Commerce has tried to set sizing standards, but it is difficult to set size ranges and grading rules to fit every figure. Each company tries its sample garments on models whose figures are typical of its target customers, which makes sizing vary from brand to brand. Fit Technologies has created a sizing system called Fit Logic, based on three body types. However, so far, Fit Logic and body scanning have not been widely adopted.

Comfort   Obviously, people need clothes to keep warm in cold weather or cool in warm weather. As the population ages and as travel increases, people also want clothes that are comfortable to move in, sit in, travel in, and so on. The increasing desire for comfortable clothes is one of the reasons for the popularity of spandex fiber (added to other fibers).

Appropriateness   It is important that consumers find suitable or acceptable fashions for specific occasions or to meet the needs of their lifestyles. Consumers consider their clothing needs for job and leisure-time activities, as well as what is appropriate for their figure type, personality, coloring, and age.

Brand or Designer Label   Brands are a manufacturer's means of product identification. Some consumers buy on the basis of a particular brand's reputation for styling or fit. Designer Giorgio Armani said, "A brand name is important as long as it is combined with a proper relationship of quality and price."[10]

Fiber or Fabric Performance and Care   The durability of a garment or accessory and the ease or difficulty of caring for it are often factors in garment selection. Many consumers prefer easy-care fabrics because they do not have the time for or the interest in ironing or the money to pay for dry cleaning. Consumer concern for easy-care prompted the textile industry to develop no-iron finishes and made wash-and-fold cotton garments popular. To protect the consumer, government regulations now require fiber content and care instruction labels to be sewn into apparel.

Quality and Durability   Consumer demand for quality has risen in recent years. The designer or bridge customer considers clothing an investment and may not mind spending more for the lasting qualities of fine detailing and workmanship. Some consumers may look for a particular brand or name on the basis of a reputation for quality.

chapter 3

Retail Fashion Marketing

Marketing

Marketing is the responsibility of everyone in retailing from management to sales associates.

In its broadest sense, marketing encompasses all of the activities needed to sell merchandise to consumers. *Marketing* involves communicating a retail fashion image and/or the availability of a product. It is also an attempt to attract the type of customer for whom the merchandise is intended. The primary challenges of marketing are to differentiate the store from competitors, attract new customers, get customers into the store, generate sales, and increase market share by inspiring new and current customers to buy more.

Retailers strive to differentiate themselves from their competitors; they try to show why a consumer should prefer their store, catalog, or Web site over another. Ideally, retailers should have several channels of distribution; store retailing should be balanced with online and catalog merchandising so that the customer has alternative ways to find merchandise. In retail stores, fashion marketing more specifically refers to the efforts to further those sales by means of advertising, publicity, special events, and visual merchandising.

This chapter deals with all aspects of retail fashion marketing, including market research, fashion leadership and image, visual merchandising, advertising, public relations, and special events. All these efforts tie into and complement each other. The methods used by retailers to market fashion vary considerably. Merchants must choose the approach best suited to their customers, the merchandise they carry, and the size of their business and budget.

Market research

Whether setting up a new store or reevaluating an existing one, retailers study the types of people who live in the community, their lifestyles, and, ultimately, their shopping wants and needs. Massimo Ferragamo explained, "You can't take the customer for granted and just hope they come floating into the store. We want to know who they are, their likes and their dislikes."[1] Retailers use telephone and online surveys, focus groups, feedback from sales associates, and point-of-sale (POS) data to study their customers.

Retailers analyze sales data on a store-by-store basis to uncover differences in customer buying habits. They issue their own credit cards to get even more precise information about their customers. All this information is entered into databases for use in store planning, merchandising, and marketing. Retailers develop *customer profile systems* that record the type, sizes, and frequency of merchandise purchased for each customer. They also use these databases to establish loyalty programs to reward good customers.

Retail target customers

Retail management decides which group of consumers it wants to reach and how it wants to reach them. The term *target market* describes the group of consumers the store wishes to attract. Customers comprising a specific target group are within a general age range, have similar lifestyles, and, therefore, have similar needs and tastes. No retail store can be all things to all people; it must select one or a few groups of people to serve.

While specialty stores may aim at one market segment, a department store tries to appeal to several categories of target customers. Separate departments, areas, or floors are created for each category. Once retail executives determine their target market(s), they tailor the store's image, merchandise focus, and marketing efforts toward these consumers.

Fashion leadership

Each store plays a role in fashion leadership according to the customer it wants to reach. Fashion leadership can be separated into three loosely defined categories:

- **Fashion-forward stores,** such as Bergdorf Goodman, Saks Fifth Avenue, Neiman Marcus, and Henri Bendel, seek leadership by carrying high-priced fashionable merchandise from around the world. These stores cater to the top 1 percent of the population, while Bloomingdale's and Nordstrom target the top 20 percent of the population. There are fewer of these stores because the percentage of customers who can afford their high prices is relatively small.
- **Mainstream retailers** identify with consumers who want fashion adaptations available to them at moderate and upper-moderate prices. Most of the department stores, such as Macy's and Dillard's, fall into this category, as do some specialty stores, such as Banana Republic and Gap.
- **Mass merchants** such as Wal-Mart and Target appeal to people who simply cannot or will not spend more money on their clothing. However, even at this price level, mass merchants find that they need a balance of fashionable and basic merchandise.

The retailer's Image

Saks Fifth Avenue is a fashion-forward, national multibrand specialty store. *(Photo by Gini Stephens Frings)*

Consumers are overwhelmed with so many choices, and it is often difficult for them to understand a store's message. It is important for a retailer to define its *image* clearly, the personality or character that it presents to the public. This image or uniqueness reflects

its degree of fashion leadership and its market niche and, therefore, appeals to its target customers. Ralph Lauren said, "Retailers have to have a point of view. It's the most important thing for retailers to have an identity, a sense of who they are."[2]

In keeping with that image, retailers strive for a store atmosphere that is both a complementary background for merchandise and an inviting, fun, and entertaining environment for the customer. The store's merchandising, advertising, interior decoration, and customer services develop, maintain, and reflect that image and try to generate excitement about the merchandise to create a desire to buy.

Planning and direction

The sales marketing director, fashion director, advertising and creative directors, visual merchandising director, merchandise managers, and buyers work together to plan and coordinate marketing strategies.

In small stores, a single person may direct all marketing activities with the help of outside consultants or agencies. In a large store, a marketing director may coordinate the joint efforts of advertising, special events, visual merchandising, public relations, and the fashion office. (Sometimes the fashion office is part of merchandising, and visual merchandising is part of store planning.) In large chains there may be a vice president to head each area.

A Bergdorf Goodman window featuring Celine fashions from Paris, with the visual merchandiser's usual sense of humor. *(Courtesy of Bergdorf Goodman, photo by Zehavi & Cordes)*

Buyers recommend plans for marketing activities in conjunction with their projected merchandise plans. The marketing director, fashion director, advertising and/or creative directors, visual merchandising director, merchandise managers, and buyers must agree on marketing strategies and how to reach their target market. At planning meetings, they discuss how to communicate fashion trends and important designer or brand promotions within the context of the store's image.

Stores schedule marketing activities for seasons and holidays throughout the retail calendar year as an integral part of the year's merchandising plan. Advertising and promotional events, such as holiday sales and customer appreciation weeks, are often scheduled up to a year ahead of time. In spite of all the scheduling, however, new promotions and other events can supersede all the best laid plans. For example, plans for scheduled activities could be cancelled in order to launch a new product and to react to new trends or the world situation. Marketing has to be flexible.

Visual merchandising

The corporate visual merchandising director, store planning director, architects, regional creative directors, and individual store visual managers and designers create a store's visual image.

Visual merchandising, or visual presentation, is one means to communicate a store's fashion, value, and quality message to prospective customers. The purpose of visual merchandising is to entice the customer into the store, enhance the stores' image, effectively present the merchandise the store has to offer, and show the customer how to wear that merchandise and accessorize it. With increased competition, retailers are trying to create more exciting and aggressive presentations. They use a variety of methods, such as humor, shock, elegance, and minimalism, to get attention or enhance store image. As visual presentation is an opportunity to create uniqueness, each retailer has its own approach.

A new Louis Vuitton store in Tokyo, Japan, is an example of modern "industrial" store design. *(Courtesy of Louis Vuitton, Paris)*

The visual merchandising team

Visual merchandising is a team effort involving management, including the fashion director and the marketing director; store planners; merchandise managers and buyers; the visual merchandising director, designers, and staff; the sign shop; and individual department managers and sales associates. The actual presentation set-up is done by staff designers.

Store planning

The building design plays an important part in establishing a store's image. Although building and renovations are managed by a separate *store planning division,* it is helpful to discuss them as a background to visual merchandising. A store's effectiveness and uniqueness lie in the retailer's ability to plan, create, and control the store's image in relation to the physical building. Store planning management must consider store image, location, architecture, and interior layout.

Store location

The location of a store is very important in relation to its potential customers. *Demographic research* is done to determine what location would best attract target customers. Computerized site-selection programs and marketing consultants provide data on area population forecasts, descriptions of households by income, median age of market-area residents, and information about the competition.

Store design

Store architects have to create an environment that is conducive to both retail operations and consumers' shopping needs. They consider the exterior design, major entrances, the relationship of the building to the mall or surrounding stores, interior layout, and space planning. Many stores are developing flexible interiors with movable panels instead of permanent walls. Interior aesthetics must enhance merchandise and be in keeping with the store image.

In addition, department relationships, aisle space, and traffic patterns are considered to make the departments and merchandise accessible and to help customers to find what they want easily. To comply with the Americans with Disabilities Act, aisles must be wide enough for easy wheelchair access. An environment is created to make the store easy for customers to shop.

Renovations

Many retailers are renovating existing stores, sometimes to reflect the characteristics of local communities and to increase market share. Many luxury retailers have been renovating to attract younger customers with a less intimidating and more accessible atmosphere, but in doing so, have lost their individuality and Old World charm. Renovation is a way to reposition a store, generate new traffic, and broaden the customer base without the expense of building a new store.

Interior Environment

The store's interior design and atmosphere should appeal to target customers. For example, to create a lavish environment, Neiman Marcus employs a full-time art curator to oversee its expansive art collection. Attracting the mature customer to a store or department with quality merchandise requires the creation of a warm, comfortable atmosphere. This may be achieved with wood paneling, comfortable seating, paintings, and furniture, such as those found in an elegant home. To appeal to overwhelmed baby boomers, merchandise might be presented in a simple, orderly environment with neatly folded merchandise, such as that found at the Gap. To attract teens, retailers employ graphics, humor, and music. Macy's, for example, launched teen shops with concrete floors, exposed steel tubing, rotating laser lights, media walls, and music videos to create a club atmosphere.

H&M uses both cutout figures and contemporary mannequins in the window of its Knightsbridge store in London. *(photo by Gini Stephens Frings)*

Seasonal visual merchandising

Visual merchandising managers, along with marketing and merchandising executives, make up a *seasonal calendar* indicating the dates on which specific merchandise is to be featured and the number and location of windows and interior displays that are to show the merchandise. Seasonal merchandising themes are planned up to a year in advance in conjunction with the seasons, other store promotions, and arrivals of new merchandise. In some cases, the theme may involve a tie-in with a vendor to introduce a new collection or brand. Planning a theme gives a focus to visual merchandising and a consistent look throughout the store.

An interior presentation at Fenwick, London. *(Courtesy of Fenwick, Ltd., photo by Gini Stephens Frings)*

The visual merchandising plan also includes a budget covering the cost of new mannequins or refurbishing existing ones, lighting, signage, props, special effects, posters and other background art, and the cost of paying staff needed to create and maintain the windows and interior displays.

Windows

The visual statements made in downtown store windows or at mall store entrances are the customers' first encounter with the store and must effectively and correctly convey the store's image and fashion focus and entice shoppers into the store. As marketing executive Virginia Meyer commented, "Store windows attract, compel, and persuade. . . . A good presentation can and should stop you, get your attention, and maybe even make you smile. In a very broad sense, visual presentation not only helps to sell the merchandise itself, but the store as well."[3] In addition, as Gilbert Vanderweide, a visual merchandising director, observed, "Windows tell you what's going on inside the store."[4]

A window is a total environment, a complete statement on its own. Windows are usually the most dramatic of the store's visual statements. They can be humorous or theatrical. To attract attention, windows may feature animation, posters, cutouts, video art, dramatic lighting, holograms, or other special effects. Some stores use look-through windows to make the windows part of the total store environment.

Window themes

Special event windows tie in to events and store promotions or convey the spirit of a holiday season. They create excitement and interest in visiting the store.

Fashion message windows feature a designer collection or the newest fashion trends and suggest ways to coordinate accessories. These windows are created to attract attention and coax customers to buy a new garment and/or accessory.

Interior presentations

Customers are further exposed to fashion and accessory purchase suggestions by interior presentations that may be located near the entrance to the store, at major focal points, at entrances to each floor, or in departments. In urban stores, the focus is on the main floor. However, stores in shopping malls, which may have few or no windows, must capitalize on the wide store entrance that gives the passing shopper a sweeping view of the selling area, giving entry area displays great impact.

Presentation areas positioned in front of each department or shop guide customers to that area. Different levels of interest are created on ledges, shelves, counters, platforms, or even hanging from the ceiling. Merchandise presentations may

take the form of groups of multiple mannequins or single items, shown on a form
or stand. Sportswear is usually shown in
groups, whereas eveningwear may be
shown individually.

Environments or *lifestyle presentations* feature appropriately dressed mannequins posed in lifelike situations. The
environment is enhanced with accessories, props, and furniture to complement the featured merchandise. Lifestyle
environments help customers to identify
with the apparel and accessories presented. Also, by showing total wardrobing
concepts, including accessories, they help
to educate and entice the customer.

Elements of visual merchandising
Enhancements

The elements used to show or enhance the
clothes on display include mannequins and
other forms, vitrines, fixtures, ladders, poles,
columns, platforms, tables or other furniture, boxes, paintings and other wall decoration, fabrics, banners, graphics (posters,
counter cards), lighting effects, accessories,
and other props. Most of all, visual merchandisers try to enhance merchandise with
other merchandise. Details are very important; every viewpoint has to be considered.

Technology

Retailers are using an increasing amount
of video technology to show merchandise.
Windows and departments may feature
video presentations of fashion shows to
add excitement and interest.

Mannequins

Mannequins change with fashion trends
and are made in the image of the current
ideal of beauty. For elegant fashion, perfectly coiffed, traditional lifelike man-
nequins are preferred. However, they are very expensive to buy and maintain. To save
money, many stores have replaced them with stylized mannequins.

Contemporary stylized
mannequins at Macy's,
designed by Mira
Kalman. (*Photo by Gini
Stephens Frings, courtesy
of Macy's*)

Visual merchandising in multi-unit stores
Standards manuals

The corporate office sets standards for consistent visual merchandising. Standards
manuals list exact specifications for all forms, fixtures, and props and their placement.
Quarterly addenda update the standards as new ideas are implemented. Visual merchandising designers set up the presentations, and then sales associates may be
trained to maintain these standards in each department.

A rich, warm, traditional environment created in Bergdorf Goodman's men's department. (*Courtesy of Bergdorf Goodman*)

Presentation packages

The corporate or central visual merchandising office may also create presentation packages for branch stores so that the entire group or chain will have the same look. Large presentation packages, including floor sets or *plan-o-grams* and digital photographs, are prepared at the flagship store and sent to other units to show them how to merchandise visually. Each retailer wants to have a total vision. This is easier to achieve in a private-label chain, such as Banana Republic or Ann Taylor, which has identical apparel and accessories in each store. It becomes more difficult to create a cohesive look for a multibrand retailer. They can set guidelines, but they have to be more flexible and allow customizing of packages for differences in various regions.

Telecommunications

Many stores are using teleconferencing to show actual visual presentations to other stores in their chain so that local visual artists will be able to replicate the presentations. They also use virtual computer mock-ups to share visual concepts with colleagues across the country via intranets.

Designer or brand in-store shops

In the case of in-store designer or brand boutiques, the vendor has visual merchandising requirements for presenting its line of merchandise. Apparel designers want to make a unique statement or create an atmosphere to complement their clothing. In some cases, the manufacturer supplies the fixtures and/or other enhancements so that they are the same in every store. It is often difficult to reconcile the individuality of these shops with the store's own identity. Some are de-emphasizing in-store shops or eliminating them altogether. Still other stores try to merge the look of the designer boutique with the store's image.

Departments

Large stores are divided into departments and designer or brand shops by fashion category or lifestyle. Traditionally, the main selling area is reserved for cosmetics, jewelry, and accessories. The rest of the store is divided into groups of departments and shops that relate to one another by category or price range. Department location is considered, and some shops are given prime location to attract attention. Destination departments, containing merchandise such as swimsuits, lingerie, or coats that customers seek because they are needed, can be in secondary locations. Retailers make an effort to drive foot traffic to the back merchandise walls of the store to prevent "dead zones."

Successful visual merchandising invites customers into a department. Visual merchandising must draw the customer to the department most suited to his or her lifestyle. There is no sign that says, "If you are age 38 to 50, live in the suburbs, and wear an average size 10, go to the Miss Macy department." Yet each department is merchandised with certain lifestyle statistics in mind. Visual environments, informational signing, and/or

Clothing fixtures at Gieves &
Hawkes, Savile Row, London.
(Courtesy of Gieves & Hawkes)

large lifestyle photographs on the walls help customers to find the department best
suited to their size and tastes.

Stock is arranged in an orderly, attractive manner to contribute to the visual effect
of the department and to help customers quickly find what they want. As popular
apparel or accessories are sold, the department manager and sales staff need to
rearrange the merchandise. Visual designers teach department staff members how to
layer clothes on hangers, how to display folded merchandise, and how to arrange merchandise by color groups.

Fixtures

In apparel departments, clothing is hung on fixtures that are arranged, usually in a
grid pattern, to give access and a clear view of the department from every angle.
Assortments may be displayed on *wall racks, rounders* (circular racks), *four-way* or
star fixtures (with four arms), *T-shaped stands* (with two arms), *I-beams* (straight
bars), or *collection fixtures* (with folded merchandise on shelves on one side and hanging clothes on the other). Assortment displays must permit customers to see an entire

range of colors or styles in each size. To avoid visual monotony, the fixtures are usually mixed. Although wall fixtures utilize space well and rounders show off a color story, they are not the most desirable means of display because the customer is confronted with nothing but sleeves. On frontal projection fixtures, such as the four-way or the T-stand, the garments face outward so that the customer can see the fronts. The first hanger on a sportswear T-stand is usually an H-shaped hanger showing a coordinated outfit so that the customer can see how the various pieces work together. Fixtures are becoming more sophisticated, and many stores are also creating their own unique custom fixtures to fit in better with overall store design.

Folding and stacking

Stores such as the Gap have made simple folding and stacking a popular and space-saving way to display merchandise. Store standards dictate placement of shelves or tables and how the merchandise should be folded and grouped. Many retailers have found that merchandise on tables is more accessible.

Accessories

Much more attention is being paid to visual merchandising of accessories. Traditionally located in the main selling area, some accessories are now available on apparel floors, too, so that customers can quickly accessorize their clothing purchases. Accessories can be shown in *vitrines* (glass cases), on shelves or tables, or on wall display racks. Stores must balance the salability of accessible, "open-sell" merchandise with the security and exclusivity of glass-case display.

E-commerce

The multimedia capabilities of the Internet allow advertisers to combine graphics, text, sound, and moving images on banner ads, sold on a cost-per-click or click-through basis. However, retailers have to differentiate their ads because millions of Web sites are competing for attention. Retailers continually evaluate design elements of their Web sites, searching for the best presentation to engage consumer response. They use A/B and multivariate testing (showing alternative designs) and analytical software to measure each design's success.

When a consumer makes a purchase from an e-commerce site, the retailer obtains the customer's e-mail address. The retailer can then use that address for advertising, delivering messages about special promotions and products, and inviting the consumer to trunk shows, parties, and designer appearances. E-mail allows the retailer to be much more specific and tailor the message to the consumer's demographics and buying history.

Fashion shows

Fashion shows are special events that communicate a fashion story. These are usually co-sponsored by a vendor. The selection and organization of the fashions and model bookings may be done by the fashion office, whereas invitations and other arrangements may be handled by the special events department. There are four possible ways to organize these presentations: as formal shows, department shows, designer trunk shows, or informal modeling.

Formal fashion shows take a great deal of advance planning involving booking models and fittings and arranging for a runway, scenery, lighting, microphones, music, seating, and assistants. Clothes are generally grouped according to styling, color, or other visual criteria. Models and music are selected to complement the clothes and set a mood. A designer-centered event can cost from $10,000 to $500,000. Because of their cost, these shows are usually reserved for charity events, and stores look for co-sponsors to share costs. For an Italian designer collection show, for example, costs could be split among the store, the designers, and the Italian Trade Commission.

Designer trunk shows are done in cooperation with a single vendor and are a popular way to sell expensive collections. Invitations are sent to the best customers according to customer profile databases. The designer or a representative travels from store to

A Randolph Duke fashion show at Neiman Marcus. *(Courtesy of Neiman Marcus, photo by Gini Stephens Frings)*

store with the collection, which is usually shown on models in the designer collections department. Customers get to see the entire collection unedited by a buyer and may order from the samples in their size. Some designers and retailers do 50 percent of their total business through trunk shows.

Department fashion shows, on a much smaller scale, are produced in-store to generate immediate sales. Usually, a platform is set up directly in the department that carries the clothes.

Informal fashion shows are the easiest to produce. A few models walk through the store showing the fashions they are wearing to customers who are shopping or having lunch in the store's restaurant. The models can take their time, and customers enjoy asking them questions. This is often done in conjunction with a trunk show.

Marketing evaluation

All the people involved in marketing—directors, managers, coordinators, artists, writers, designers, and buyers—evaluate the effectiveness of their efforts to plan for the future.

At the end of an event or advertising campaign, sales are analyzed and the campaign's effectiveness is evaluated. Advertising can be evaluated by sales volume, but it is very difficult to analyze sales results in relation to visual merchandising or special events. For example, unless a fashion show actually takes place in a department and people stay afterward to make purchases, how can the value of the event be measured? Some retailers are experimenting with electronic systems that track people window shopping and entering and exiting the store. Management usually evaluates the effectiveness of a campaign as a whole and makes recommendations for the next year.

chapter **4**

> **Marketing Research
and Segmentation**

The *marketing concept* states that, to be successful, a company must understand the needs of specific groups of consumers (i.e., target markets) and then satisfy these needs more effectively than the competition. The satisfaction of consumer needs is delivered in the form of the *marketing mix*, which consists of the so-called " 4 Ps": product, price, place, and promotion. Marketers who have a thorough under-standing of the consumer decision-making process are likely to design products, establish prices, select distribution outlets, and design promotional messages that will favorably influence consumer purchase decisions.

The field of consumer research developed as an extension of the field of market-ing research. Just as the findings of marketing research are used to improve manage-rial decision making, so too are the findings of consumer research. Studying consumer behavior, in all its ramifications, enables marketers to predict how consumers will react to promotional messages and to understand why they make the purchase deci-sions they do. Marketers realize that the more they know about their target con-sumers' decision-making process, the more likely they are to design marketing strate-gies and promotional messages that will favorably influence these consumers. Savvy marketers recognize that consumer research is a unique subset of marketing research, which merits the use of specialized research methods to collect customer data. *Consumer research* enables marketers to study and understand consumers' needs and wants, and how they make consumption decisions.

Consumer research paradigms

The early consumer researchers gave little thought to the impact of mood, emotion, or situation on consumer decisions. They believed that marketing was simply applied economics, and that consumers were rational decision makers who objec-tively evaluated the goods and services available to them and selected those that gave them the highest utility (satisfaction) at the lowest cost. Later on, researchers realized that consumers were not always consciously aware of why they made the decisions they did. Even when they were aware of their basic motivations, consumers were not always willing to reveal those reasons. In 1939, a Viennese psychoanalyst named Ernest Dichter began to use Freudian psychoanalytic techniques to uncover the hidden motivations of consumers. By the late 1950s, his research methodology (called **motivational research**), which was essentially qualitative in approach, was widely adopted by consumer researchers. As a result of Dichter's work and subsequent research designed to search deep within the con-sumer's psyche, consumer researchers today use two different types of research method-ology to study consumer behavior: **quantitative research** and **qualitative research**.

Quantitative research

Quantitative research is descriptive in nature and is used by researchers to understand the effects of various promotional inputs on the consumer, thus enabling marketers to "predict" consumer behavior. This research approach is known as **positivism**. The research methods used in quantitative research consist of experiments, survey techniques, and observation. The findings are descriptive, empirical, and, if collected randomly (i.e., using a probability sample), can be generalized to larger populations. Because the data col-lected are quantitative, they lend themselves to sophisticated statistical analysis.

Qualitative research

Qualitative research methods include depth interviews, focus groups, metaphor analy-sis, collage research, and projective techniques. These techniques are administered by highly trained interviewer–analysts who also analyze the findings; thus, the findings tend to be somewhat subjective. Because sample sizes are necessarily small, findings cannot be generalized to larger populations. They are primarily used to obtain new ideas for promotional campaigns and products that can be tested more thoroughly in larger, more comprehensive studies.

Qualitative methods are also used by consumer behavior researchers who are interested in the act of *consumption* rather than in the act of *buying* (i.e., decision making). They view consumer behavior as a subset of human behavior, and increased understanding as a key to reducing negative aspects of consumer behavior—the so-called "dark side" of consumer behavior—such as drug addiction, shoplifting, alcoholism, and compulsive buying. Research focused on understanding consumer *experiences* is called **interpretivism**. Table 4.1 compares the quantitative and qualitative research designs.

Combining qualitative and quantitative research findings

Marketers often use a combination of quantitative and qualitative research to help make strategic marketing decisions. For example, they use qualitative research findings to discover new ideas and to develop promotional strategy, and quantitative research findings to predict consumer reactions to various promotional inputs. Frequently, ideas stemming from qualitative research are tested empirically through quantitative studies. The predic-

TABLE 4.1	Comparisons Between Quantitative and Qualitative Research Designs	
	QUALITATIVE RESEARCH	**QUANTITATIVE RESEARCH**
Study Purpose	Studies designed to provide insights about new product ideas and positioning strategies. Ideas uncovered should be tested via quantitative studies. Often used in exploratory research to refine the objectives of quantitative studies.	Studies aimed at describing a target market—its characteristics and possible reactions of various segments to the elements of the marketing mix. Results are used for making strategic marketing decisions.
Types of Questions and Data Collection Methods	Open-ended, unstructured questions and further probing by the interviewer. Projective techniques include disguised questions where the respondents do not know the true purpose of the questions and are asked to freely respond to stimuli such as words or pictures. Depth interviews and focus groups are used.	Closed-ended questions with predefined possible responses and open-ended questions that have to be coded numerically. Most questionnaires include attitude scales and, generally, the questions are not disguised. Questionnaires are used in surveys conducted in person, by phone or mail, or online. Observation of respondents is also used. Experimentation is used to test cause-and-effect relationships.
Sampling Methods	Small, nonprobability samples; the findings are generally not representative of the universe under study.	Large, probability samples. Providing that the data collection instruments are valid and reliable, the results can be viewed as representative of the universe.
Data Analysis	Data collected are analyzed by the researchers who have collected it and who have expertise in the behavioral sciences. The analysis consists of looking for "key words" and establishing categories for the respondents' answers; it is subjective because it reflects the researchers' judgments.	The data is collected by a field force retained by the researcher, and then coded, tabulated, and entered into the database. The researcher analyzes the data by using objective, standardized statistical methods consisting mainly of comparisons of averages among the predefined variables and significance tests that estimate the extent to which the results represent the universe.

tions made possible by quantitative research and the understanding provided by qualitative research together produce a richer and more robust profile of consumer behavior than either research approach used alone. The combined findings enable marketers to design more meaningful and effective marketing strategies.

The consumer research process

The major steps in the consumer research process include (1) defining the objectives of the research, (2) collecting and evaluating secondary data, (3) designing a primary research study, (4) collecting primary data, (5) analyzing the data, and (6) preparing a report on the findings. Figure 4.1 depicts a model of the consumer research process.

Developing research objectives

The first and most difficult step in the consumer research process is to carefully define the objectives of the study. Is it to segment the market for plasma television sets? To find out consumer attitudes about and experiences with online shopping? To determine what percentage of households do their food shopping online? It is important for the marketing manager and the research manager (either in-house or retained for the specific study) to agree at the outset on the purposes and objectives of the study to ensure that the research design is appropriate. A carefully thought-out statement of objectives helps to define the type and level of information needed.

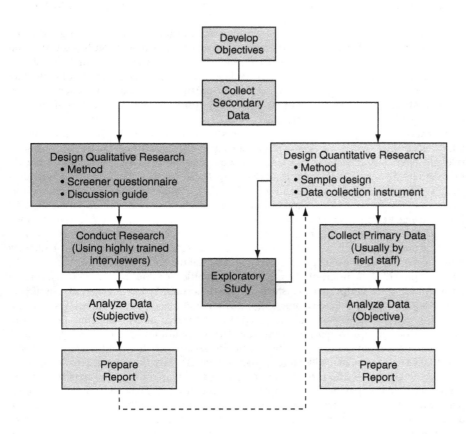

**The Consumer
Research Process**

FIGURE 4.1

For example, if the purpose of the study is to come up with new ideas for products or promotional campaigns, then a qualitative study is usually undertaken, in which respondents spend a significant amount of time face-to-face with a highly trained professional interviewer-analyst who also does the analysis. Because of the high costs of each interview, a fairly small sample of respondents is studied; thus, the findings are not projectable to the marketplace. If the purpose of the study is to find out how many people in the population (i.e., what percentage) use certain products and how frequently they use them, then a quantitative study that can be computer analyzed is undertaken. Sometimes, in designing a quantitative study, the researcher may not know what questions to ask. In such cases, before undertaking a full-scale study, the researcher is likely to conduct a small-scale *exploratory study* to identify the critical issues needed to develop narrow and more precise research objectives.

Collecting secondary data

A search for **secondary data** generally follows the statement of objectives. Secondary information is any data originally generated for some purpose other than the present research objectives. (Original data performed by individual researchers or organizations to meet specific objectives is called **primary data**.) Secondary data includes both **internal** and **external data**.

Internal secondary data consists of such information as data generated in-house for earlier studies as well as analysis of customer files, such as past customer transactions, letters from customers, sales-call reports, and data collected via warranty cards. Increasingly, companies use internal secondary data to compute **customer lifetime value profiles** for various customer segments. These profiles include customer acquisition costs (the resources needed to establish a relationship with the customer), the profits generated from individual sales to each customer, the costs of handling customers and their orders (some customers may place more complex and variable orders that cost more to handle), and the expected duration of the relationship.

External secondary data consists of any data collected by an outside organization. The major source of these data is the federal government, which publishes information collected by scores of government agencies about the economy, business, and virtually all demographics of the U.S. population. An excellent way to access selected parts of these data is FedStats (**www.fedstats.gov**). The U.S. Census Bureau (**www.census.gov**) collects data on the age, education, occupation, and income of U.S. residents by state and region and also provides projections on the future growth or decline of various demographic segments. Any firm operating globally may find key statistics about any country in the world in the CIA's electronic *The World Factbook* (**www.cia.gov/cia/publications/factbook**). Business-relevant secondary data from periodicals, newspapers, and books is readily accessible via two search engines—*ProQuest* and *Lexis-Nexis*. These engines access major newspapers such as *The Wall Street Journal* and *The New York Times*; business magazines such as *Business Week, Forbes, Fortune*, and *Harvard Business Review*; and journals focused specifically on marketing, such as *Advertising Age, Brandweek Magazine, Marketing News, Journal of Marketing, Journal of Marketing Research*, and *Journal of Consumer Research*.

Commercial data is available from marketing research companies that routinely monitor specific aspects of consumer behavior and sell the data to marketers. For example, *Claritas* provides demographic and lifestyle profiles of the consumers residing in each U.S. zip code (**http://www.clusterbigip1.claritas.com/MyBestSegments/Default.jsp? ID=0&SubID= &pageName=Home**). *Yankelovich* monitors consumers' lifestyles and consumption patterns, as well as more targeted studies focused on the consumer behavior of specific ethnic groups (**http://www.yankelovich.com/y-monitor.asp**). *Mediamark Research Inc.* conducts segmentation studies of consumers' leisure activities and buying styles, and also studies focused specifically on consumer innovators (**http://www.mediamark.com**).

Secondary data is also provided by companies that routinely monitor a particular consumption-related behavior. For example, one of the primary challenges marketers face is placing their advertisements in media that are most likely to reach their target customers. For decades, Nielsen Media Research has monitored the characteristics and size of audiences of TV programs. Nielsen did so through studying a presumably representative sample of U.S.

households who agreed to install computerized boxes with modems connected to each set in their homes; many of these households also used *people meters*, on which each family member watching a particular program "logged on" for the duration of their viewing. A company called *Arbitron* has provided similar data about the audiences of radio programs. Marketers use this data to decide where to place their promotional messages, and the managers of the TV and radio stations use this data to determine how much to charge the marketers. This figure is usually based on the size of the audience and is expressed as the *cpm*, or cost to reach 1000 people. Obviously, the larger the audience of a particular program, the more money is charged for the commercial time within it. Although marketers understand that, by using the Nielsen and Arbitron data, they are also reaching many consumers who are not within their target markets (and unfortunately paying for this "wasted" advertising), they have no other options since the Nielsen and Arbitron data are used universally.

Recognizing that new technologies provide opportunities for far more sophisticated monitoring techniques, Nielsen and Arbitron are now testing *portable people meters*. These meters are small devices that consumers clip to their belts or to other clothing and wear during their waking hours. This device monitors all the radio and TV programming a person is exposed to during the day. Eventually, the device will monitor the person's exposure to all media programming and advertising, such as Web streaming, supermarket Muzak, and, when GPS systems are integrated into the new meter, exposure to outdoor advertising. At night, the meter is plugged into a cradle that transmits this data for analysis. But perhaps the real future of researching consumers' exposure to media will not entail monitoring the behavior of several thousand consumers wearing portable meters, but monitoring the media exposure of almost all consumers via digital cable set-top boxes that are now present in many homes and are likely to be placed in the majority of American homes, as digital TV replaces analog broadcasts. Presently, digital cable boxes are primarily used to send signals to consumers' TVs in order to enable them to watch movies-on-demand. However, the digital boxes can easily record all the programs that consumers are tuned into, including, of course, channel surfing, attempts at avoiding commercial breaks, and recordings for later viewing, using devices such as TiVo or digital video recorders that cable companies increasingly offer to subscribers. So far, cable companies have been reluctant to use this data due to privacy concerns. However, some innovative companies are now developing methods that will transform data from digital cable boxes into information that can be used for precise targeting of consumers while still protecting privacy.[1] The portable people meters and the two-way digital cable boxes demonstrate the profound and dynamic changes that technology is bringing to consumer research. The numerous new technologies that are being developed will enable marketers to study consumers' media exposure much more precisely and collect data that will enable them to customize or *narrowcast* their promotional messages, and thus expend their advertising dollars more effectively.

For decades, marketers have purchased data from secondary data providers who collected data from **consumer panels**. The members of these panels were consumers who were paid for recording their purchases or media viewing habits in diaries that were then summarized and analyzed by the data providers. Today, online technologies enable companies to collect increasingly sophisticated data from respondents. For example, a manufacturer of customized snowboards had discovered that 10,000 snowboarding fans used its site to discuss their hobbies and buying habits, and also to rate different designs of snowboards. The snowboards marketer then started *selling* the data it collected from this online panel to other marketers interested in targeting the young, mostly male respondents who so enthusiastically revealed so much about themselves while discussing snowboards online. Similarly, GM is collecting data from 30,000 car buyers a month via an online site. One of the most important issues GM investigated was the point at which rising fuel prices significantly impact car buyers' priorities—data that can be used to alter production schedules as gas prices fluctuate and also in the design of future models.[2]

Obtaining secondary data before engaging in primary research offers several advantages. First, secondary data may provide a solution to the research problem and eliminate the need for primary research altogether. But even if this is not the case, secondary data, used in exploratory research, may help to clarify and redefine the objectives of the primary study and provide ideas for the methods to be used and the difficulties that are likely to occur during the full-scale study.

Although secondary information can be obtained more cheaply and quickly than primary data, it has some limitations. First, information may be categorized in units that are different from those that the researcher seeks (e.g., clustering consumers into the 15–20 and 21–25 age groups renders it useless to a researcher interested in consumers 17–24 years old). Some secondary data may not be accurate because of errors in gathering or analyzing the data for the original study or because the data had been collected in a biased fashion in order to support a particular point of view. Also, care must be taken not to use secondary data that may be outdated.

Designing primary research

The design of a research study is based on the purposes of the study. If descriptive information is needed, then a quantitative study is likely to be undertaken; if the purpose is to get new ideas (e.g., for positioning or repositioning a product), then a qualitative study is undertaken. Because the approach for each type of research differs in terms of method of data collection, sample design, and type of data collection instrument used, each research approach is discussed separately below.

Quantitative research designs

A quantitative research study consists of a research design, the data collection methods and instruments to be used, and the sample design. Three basic designs are used in quantitative research: observation, experimentation (in a laboratory or in the field, such as in a retail store), or survey (i.e., by questioning people).

Observational Research   **Observational research** is an important method of consumer research because marketers recognize that the best way to gain an in-depth understanding of the relationship between people and products is by watching them in the process of buying and/or using the products. Doing so enables observational researchers to comprehend what the product symbolizes to a consumer and provides greater insight into the bond between people and products that is the essence of brand loyalty. Many large corporations and advertising agencies use trained researchers/observers to watch, note, and sometimes videotape consumers in stores, malls, or their own homes. For example, in studying responses to a new mint-flavored Listerine, the Warner Lambert Company hired a research firm that paid 37 New York City families to let it install cameras in their bathrooms to videotape mouthwash usage. The study found that consumers who used Scope gave the product a swish and spit it out. On the other hand, users of the new Listerine kept the mouthwash in their mouths for much longer (one subject even held the mouthwash in his mouth as he left home and got into the car, and only spit it out after driving a couple of blocks).[3] Procter & Gamble (P&G) sent video crews to scores of households around the world, which enabled P&G executives in Cincinnati to watch a mother in Thailand feed her baby. They discovered that the mother was multitasking while feeding her baby and even glanced at her TV from time to time. Understanding such behavior can lead to the development of products and packages that will give P&G a strong competitive advantage in the marketplace.[4]

Mechanical observation uses a mechanical or electronic device to record customer behavior or response to a particular marketing stimulus. For example, when Duane Reade—a large chain of drugstores in New York City—considers a location for a new store, the company uses electronic beams or hand counters to count the numbers of passersby at different times and under different weather conditions.[5] Government planners use data collected from electronic EZ Pass devices in passenger cars to decide which roads should be expanded, and banks use security cameras to observe problems customers may have in using ATMs.

Increasingly, consumers use automated systems in their purchases because these instruments make purchases easier and often provide rewards for using them. For example, consumers who use supermarket frequency shopping cards often receive offers for promotional discounts tailored specifically for them at checkout counters. Moviegoers who order tickets online can pick them up at ATM-like devices at movie theaters and avoid waiting in line at the box office. As consumers use more and more highly convenient technologies, such as credit and ATM cards, EZ Passes, frequency cards, automated phone systems, and online shopping, there are more and more electronic records of their consumption patterns. As a consequence, observation of consumer behavior via electronic means has grown significantly and, as illustrated in the earlier discussion of portable people meters and two-way digital cable boxes, electronic observation of consumption behavior will become increasingly sophisticated.

Gambling casinos have been in the forefront of developing systems that track individual customer data collected during the various stages of a customer's visit, and cross-matching them with data collected on previous visits by that customer (including spending usage). They use this data to classify visitors into categories based on their "loyalty levels," and implement corresponding rewards that are delivered almost immediately. For example, normally about 50,000 people a day visit the Foxwood Casino in Connecticut. Most of them use magnetic cards called "frequent player cards." Sophisticated electronic network systems monitor the gaming patterns, eating habits, and room preferences of all visitors. When a player sits at a table, within seconds, the casino's manager can read the guest's history on the screen, including alcoholic beverages preferred and gaming habits. Because there are electronic tags in the chips issued to each player, when a player leaves the table, his or her record is updated instantly and made available at any contact point for that customer throughout the entire casino complex. Thus, the casino can instantly reward customers who are good for business by giving free meals and room upgrades and inviting them to gamble in designated VIP lounges. The customers love the frequency cards because they enable them to keep track of their spending, and the casinos benefit from each swipe of the card because it provides more information about customers. The casino has two identical computer systems and, if needed, can switch to a backup immediately and thus avoid the many thousands of dollars that may be lost during an even brief period of operating without computers.[6] Figure 4.2 depicts Foxwood's customer tracking system. More casinos are employing increasingly sophisticated software to create real-time and personal rewards to day-trippers who bet relatively small amounts of money—$50 to $100 per visit—but who visit the casinos frequently. Casinos have recognized that although these consumers wage little money per trip, they view gaming as their primary entertainment, and observing their behavior and immediately using the data to encourage them to spend more money is likely to increase profits greatly over time.[7]

Source: Courtesy of Kim S. Nash, "Casinos Hit Jackpot with Customer Data," *Computer World,* July 2, 2001, 17.

Foxwood's Casino Customer Tracking System FIGURE 4.2

An audit is another type of mechanical observation that entails monitoring the sales of products. A key component of Wal-Mart's competitive advantage is the retailing giant's use of technology in its product audits. At any given moment, the company knows what is selling, how fast, and how much of the product remains in its inventory. Maintaining small inventories and moving products quickly enables the company to lower its prices and attract more customers. Wal-Mart's record profits are derived from low per-item profits multiplied by selling billions of products quickly, and also moving products rapidly to where consumers are likely to buy them. For example, after observing that the sales of strawberry Pop-Tarts increased dramatically before a hurricane and that the top pre-seller before a hurricane was beer, the company quickly transports large quantities of these items to areas expected to be hit by an approaching storm.[8]

Marketers also use **physiological observation** devices that monitor respondents' patterns of information processing. For example, an electronic eye camera may be used to monitor the *eye movements* of subjects looking at a series of advertisements for various products, and electronic sensors placed on the subjects' heads can monitor the *brain activity* and attentiveness levels involved in viewing each ad. Neuroscientists monitoring cognitive functions in twelve different regions of the brain while consumers watched commercials for different products claimed that the data collected shows the respondents' levels of attention and the decoding and recall of the promotional messages.[9]

Experimentation   It is possible to test the relative sales appeal of many types of variables, such as package designs, prices, promotional offers, or copy themes through experiments designed to identify cause and effect. In such experiments (called *causal research*), only some variables are manipulated (the *independent variables*), while all other elements are kept constant. A **controlled experiment** of this type ensures that any difference in the outcome (the *dependent variable*) is due to different treatments of the variable under study and not to extraneous factors. For example, one study tested the effectiveness of using an attractive versus unattractive endorser in promoting two types of products: products that are used to enhance one's attractiveness (e.g., a men's cologne) and products that are not (e.g., a pen). The endorser used was a fictitious character named Phil Johnson who was described as a member of the U.S. Olympic water polo team. The photograph depicting the attractive endorser was a scanned image of an attractive athletic man, whereas the picture depicting the unattractive endorser was the same image graphically modified to reduce attractiveness. The subjects viewed each endorser-product combination for 15 seconds (simulating the viewing of an actual print ad) and then filled out a questionnaire that measured their attitudes and purchase intentions toward the products advertised. In this study, the combinations of the product (i.e., used/not used to enhance one's attractiveness) and the endorser's attractiveness (i.e., attractive/non-attractive endorser) were the *manipulated treatments* (i.e., the independent variables) and the combination of the attitudes and purchase intentions toward the product was the *dependent variable*. The study discovered that the attractive endorser was more effective in promoting both types of products.[10]

A major application of causal research is **test marketing**, in which, prior to launching a new product, elements such as package, price, and promotion are manipulated in a controlled setting in order to predict sales or gauge the possible responses to the product. Today some researchers employ *virtual reality methods*. For example, in a market test, respondents can view, on a computer screen, supermarket shelves that are stocked with many products, including different versions of the same product; they can "pick up" an item by touching the image, examine it by rotating the image with a track ball, and place it in a shopping cart if they decide to buy it. The researchers observe how long the respondents spend in looking at the product, the time spent in examining each side of the package, the products purchased, and the order of the purchases.

Surveys   If researchers wish to ask consumers about their purchase preferences and consumption experiences, they can do so in person, by mail, by telephone, or online. Each of these survey methods has certain advantages and certain disadvantages that the researcher must weigh when selecting the method of contact.

Personal interview surveys most often take place in the home or in retail shopping areas. The latter, referred to as *mall intercepts*, are used more frequently than home interviews because of the high incidence of not-at-home working women and the reluctance of many people today to allow a stranger into their home.

Telephone surveys are also used to collect consumer data; however, evenings and weekends are often the only times to reach telephone respondents, who tend to be less responsive—even hostile—to calls that interrupt dinner, television viewing, or general relaxation. The difficulties of reaching people with unlisted telephone numbers have been solved through random-digit dialing, and the costs of a widespread telephone survey are often minimized by using toll-free telephone lines. Other problems arise, however, from the increased use of answering machines and caller ID to screen calls. Some market research companies have tried to automate telephone surveys, but many respondents are even less willing to interact with an electronic voice than with a live interviewer.

Mail surveys are conducted by sending questionnaires directly to individuals at their homes. One of the major problems of mail questionnaires is a low response rate, but researchers have developed a number of techniques to increase returns, such as enclosing a stamped, self-addressed envelope, using a provocative questionnaire, and sending prenotification letters as well as follow-up letters. A number of commercial research firms that specialize in consumer surveys have set up panels of consumers who, for a token fee, agree to complete the research company's mail questionnaires on a regular basis. Sometimes panel members are also asked to keep diaries of their purchases.

Online surveys are sometimes conducted on the Internet. Respondents are directed to the marketer's (or researcher's) Web site by computer ads or home pages. Because the sample's respondents are self-selected, the results cannot be projected to the larger population. Most computer polls ask respondents to complete a profile consisting of demographic questions that enable the researchers to classify the responses to the substantive product or service questions.

Researchers who conduct computer polling believe that the anonymity of the Internet encourages respondents to be more forthright and honest than they would be if asked the same questions in person or by mail; others believe that the data collected may be suspect because some respondents may create new online personalities that do not reflect their own beliefs or behavior. Some survey organizations cite the inherent advantages of wide reach and affordability in online polling.

Quantitative research data collection instruments

Data collection instruments are developed as part of a study's total research design to systematize the collection of data and to ensure that all respondents are asked the same questions in the same order. Data collection instruments include questionnaires, personal inventories, and attitude scales. Data collection instruments are usually pretested and "debugged" to assure the validity and reliability of the research study. A study is said to have **validity** if it does, in fact, collect the appropriate data needed to answer the questions or objectives stated in the first (objectives) stage of the research process. A study is said to have **reliability** if the same questions, asked of a similar sample, produce the same findings. Often a sample is systematically divided in two, and each half is given the same questionnaire to complete. If the results from each half are similar, the questionnaire is said to have *split-half reliability*.

Questionnaires For quantitative research, the primary data collection instrument is the questionnaire, which can be sent through the mail to selected respondents for self-administration or can be administered by field interviewers in person or by telephone. In order to motivate respondents to take the time to respond to surveys, researchers have found that questionnaires must be interesting, objective, unambiguous, easy to complete, and generally not burdensome. To enhance the analysis and facilitate the classification of responses into meaningful categories, questionnaires include both substantive questions that are relevant to the purposes of the study and pertinent demographic questions.

The questionnaire itself can be *disguised* or *undisguised* as to its true purpose; a disguised questionnaire sometimes yields more truthful answers and avoids responses that

TABLE 4.2	Guidelines for Wording Questions

1. *Avoid leading questions.* For example, a question such as "Do you often shop at such cost-saving stores as Staples?" or "Weren't you satisfied with the service you received at Staples today?" introduce bias into the survey

2. *Avoid two questions in one.* For example, "In your view, did you save money and receive good service when you last visited Staples?" is really two questions combined and they should be stated separately.

3. *Questions must be clear.* For example, "Where do you usually shop for your home-office supplies?" is unclear because the term "usually" is vague.

4. *Use words that consumers routinely use.* For example, do not use the verb "to rectify"; use the verb "to correct."

5. *Respondents must be able to answer the question.* For example, it is unlikely that any respondent can accurately answer a question such as "how many newspaper or TV ads for Staples did you read or see during the past month?"

6. *Respondents must be willing to answer the question.* Questions about money, health issues, personal hygiene, or sexual preferences can embarrass respondents and cause them not to answer. Sometimes, asking the question in a less personal fashion might help generate more responses. For example, rather than asking older consumers whether they experience incontinence, the researcher should ask "millions of Americans experience some level of incontinence. Do you or anyone you know experience this difficulty?"

respondents may think are expected or sought. Questions can be *open-ended* (requiring answers in the respondent's own words) or *closed-ended* (the respondent merely checks the appropriate answer from a list of options). Open-ended questions yield more insightful information but are more difficult to code and to analyze; closed-ended questions are relatively simple to tabulate and analyze, but the answers are limited to the alternative responses provided (i.e., to the existing insights of the questionnaire designer). For example, a survey of U.S. merchant mariners in the late 1970s included both open-ended and closed-ended questions asking why the respondent first joined the merchant marine. The closed-ended question, which appeared toward the beginning of the 45-page questionnaire, resulted in a majority response that they were intrigued with the excitement and romance of the high seas. The open-ended question, which appeared toward the end of this very lengthy questionnaire, resulted in a preponderance of responses "to avoid the draft in World War II." This was an option the questionnaire designers never even contemplated.

Wording the questions represents the biggest challenge in constructing questionnaires; Table 4.2 includes guidelines for writing clear and effective questions. The sequence of questions is also important: The opening questions must be interesting enough to "draw" the respondent into participating, they must proceed in a logical order, and demographic (classification) questions should be placed at the end, where they are more likely to be answered. The format of the questionnaire and the wording and sequence of the questions affect the validity of the responses and, in the case of mail questionnaires, the number (rate) of responses received. Questionnaires usually offer respondents confidentiality or anonymity to dispel any reluctance about self-disclosure.

Attitude Scales   Researchers often present respondents with a list of products or product attributes for which they are asked to indicate their relative feelings or evaluations. The instruments most frequently used to capture this evaluative data are called **attitude scales**. The most frequently used attitude scales are Likert scales, semantic differential scales, behavior intention scales, and rank-order scales.

The *Likert scale* is the most popular form of attitude scale because it is easy for researchers to prepare and to interpret, and simple for consumers to answer. They check or write the number corresponding to their level of "agreement" or "disagreement" with each of a series of statements that describes the attitude object under investigation. The scale consists of an equal number of agreement/disagreement choices on either side of a neutral choice. A principal benefit of the Likert scale is that it gives the researcher the option of considering the responses to each statement separately or of combining the responses to produce an overall score.

The *semantic differential scale*, like the Likert scale, is relatively easy to construct and administer. The scale typically consists of a series of bipolar adjectives (such as good/bad, hot/cold, like/dislike, or expensive/inexpensive) anchored at the ends of an odd-numbered (e.g., five- or seven-point) continuum. Respondents are asked to evaluate a concept (or a product or company) on the basis of each attribute by checking the point on the continuum that best reflects their feelings or beliefs. Care must be taken to vary the location of positive and negative terms from the left side of the continuum to the right side to avoid consumer response bias. Sometimes an even-numbered scale is used to eliminate the option of a neutral answer. An important feature of the semantic differential scale is that it can be used to develop graphic consumer profiles of the concept under study. Semantic differential profiles are also used to compare consumer perceptions of competitive products and to indicate areas for product improvement when perceptions of the existing product are measured against perceptions of the "ideal" product.

The *behavior intention scale* measures the likelihood that consumers will act in a certain way in the future, such as buying the product again or recommending it to a friend. These scales are easy to construct, and consumers are asked to make subjective judgments regarding their future behavior.

With *rank-order scales*, subjects are asked to rank items such as products (or retail stores or Web sites) in order of preference in terms of some criterion, such as overall quality or value for the money. Rank-order scaling procedures provide important competitive information and enable marketers to identify needed areas of improvement in product design and product positioning.

Qualitative research designs and data collection methods

In selecting the appropriate research format for a qualitative study, the researcher has to take into consideration the purpose of the study and the types of data needed. Although the research methods used may differ in composition, they all have roots in psychoanalytic and clinical aspects of psychology, and they stress open-ended and free-response types of questions to stimulate respondents to reveal their innermost thoughts and beliefs.

The key data collection techniques for qualitative studies are depth interviews, focus groups, discussion guides, projective techniques, and metaphor analysis. These techniques are regularly used in the early stages of attitude research to pinpoint relevant product-related beliefs or attributes and to develop an initial picture of consumer attitudes (especially the beliefs and attributes they associate with particular products and services).

Depth Interviews   A **depth interview** is a lengthy (generally 30 minutes to an hour), nonstructured interview between a respondent and a highly trained interviewer, who minimizes his or her own participation in the discussion after establishing the general subject to be discussed. (However, as noted earlier, interpretative researchers often take a more active role in the discussion.) Respondents are encouraged to talk freely about their activities, attitudes, and interests in addition to the product category or brand under study. Transcripts, videotapes, or audiotape recordings of interviews are then carefully studied, together with reports of respondents' moods and any gestures or "body language" they may have used to convey attitudes or motives. Such studies provide marketers with valuable ideas about product design or redesign and provide insights for positioning or repositioning the product. Sometimes, as part of depth interviews, researchers show respondents photos, videos, and audiotapes of their own shopping behavior and ask them to explicitly comment on their consumption actions.

Focus Groups   A **focus group** consists of 8 to 10 respondents who meet with a moderator-analyst for a group discussion "focused" on a particular product or product category (or any other subject of research interest). Respondents are encouraged to discuss their interests, attitudes, reactions, motives, lifestyles, feelings about the product or product category, usage experience, and so forth.

Because a focus group takes about 2 hours to complete, a researcher can easily conduct two or three focus groups (with a total of 30 respondents) in one day, while it might take that same researcher five or six days to conduct 30 individual depth interviews. Analysis of responses in both depth interviews and focus groups requires a great deal of skill on the part of the researcher. Focus group sessions are invariably taped, and sometimes videotaped, to assist in the analysis. Interviews are usually held in specially designed conference rooms with one-way mirrors that enable marketers and advertising agency staff to observe the sessions without disrupting or inhibiting the responses.

Respondents are recruited on the basis of a carefully drawn consumer profile (called a **screener questionnaire**) based on specifications defined by marketing management, and usually are paid a fee for their participation. Sometimes users of the company's brands are clustered in one or more groups, and their responses are compared to those of nonusers interviewed in other groups.

Some marketers prefer focus groups to individual depth interviews because it takes less time overall to complete the study, and they feel that the freewheeling group discussions and group dynamics tend to yield a greater number of new ideas and insights than depth interviews. Other marketers prefer individual depth interviews because they feel that respondents are free of group pressure and thus are less likely to give socially acceptable (and not necessarily truthful) responses, are more likely to remain attentive during the entire interview, and—because of the greater personal attention received—are more likely to reveal private thoughts.

Projective Techniques   **Projective techniques** are designed to tap the underlying motives of individuals despite their unconscious rationalizations or efforts at conscious concealment. They consist of a variety of disguised "tests" that contain ambiguous stimuli, such as incomplete sentences, untitled pictures or cartoons, ink blots, word-association tests, and other-person characterizations. Projective techniques are sometimes administered as part of a focus group but more often are used during depth interviews. Because projective methods are closely associated with researching consumer needs and motivations they are more fully discussed later.

Metaphor Analysis   In the 1990s, a stream of consumer research emerged suggesting that most communication is nonverbal and that people do not think in words but in images. If consumers' thought processes consist of series of images, or pictures in their minds, then it is likely that many respondents cannot adequately convey their feelings and attitudes about the research subject (such as a product or brand) through the use of words alone. Therefore, it is important to enable consumers to represent their images in an alternate, nonverbal form—through the use, say, of sounds, music, drawings, or pictures. The use of one form of expression to describe or represent feelings about another is called a *metaphor*. A number of consumer theorists have come to believe that people use metaphors as the most basic method of thought and communication.

The **Zaltman Metaphor Elicitation Technique** (ZMET)—the first patented marketing research tool in the United States—relies on visual images to assess consumers' deep and subconscious thoughts about products, services, and marketing strategies. In one study about consumer perceptions of advertising, prescreened respondents were asked to bring into a depth interview pictures that illustrated their perceptions of the value of advertising. They were asked to bring pictures from magazines, newspapers, artwork, photos they took especially for the study or from existing collections, but not actual print advertisements. Each respondent participated in a two-hour videotaped interview (on average, each respondent brought in 13 images representing his or her impressions of the value of advertising). The interview used several methods that are part of the ZMET technique to elicit key metaphors and the interrelationships among them from the respondents. The interviews were then analyzed by qualified researchers according to the ZMET criteria. The findings revealed that the *ambivalent* respondents had both favorable (e.g., information and entertainment values) and unfavorable (e.g., misrepresentation of reality) impressions of advertising; *skeptics* had mostly negative, but some positive impressions of advertising; and *hostile* respondents viewed advertising as an all-negative force.[11]

Customer satisfaction measurement

Gauging the level of customer satisfaction and its determinants is critical for every company. Marketers can use such data to retain customers, sell more products and services, improve the quality and value of their offerings, and operate more effectively and efficiently. **Customer satisfaction measurement** includes quantitative and qualitative measures, as well as a variety of contact methods with customers.

Customer satisfaction surveys measure how satisfied the customers are with relevant attributes of the product or service, and the relative importance of these attributes (using an importance scale). Generally, these surveys use 5-point semantic differential scales ranging from "very dissatisfied" to "very satisfied." Research shows that customers who indicate they are "very satisfied" (typically a score of 5 on the satisfaction scale) are much more profitable and loyal than customers who indicate that they are "satisfied" (a score of 4). Therefore, companies that merely strive to have "satisfied" customers are making a crucial error.[12] Some marketers maintain that customers' satisfaction or dissatisfaction is a function of the difference between what they had *expected* to get from the product or service purchased and their perceptions of what they *received*. A group of researchers developed a scale that measures the performance of the service received against two expectation levels: *adequate* service and *desired* service, and also measures the customers' future intentions regarding purchasing the service.[13] This approach is more sophisticated than standard customer satisfaction surveys and more likely to yield results that can be used to develop corrective measures for products and services that fall short of customers' expectations.

Mystery shoppers are professional observers who pose as customers in order to interact with and provide unbiased evaluations of the company's service personnel in order to identify opportunities for improving productivity and efficiency. For example, one bank used mystery shoppers who, while dealing with a bank employee on another matter, dropped hints about buying a house or seeking to borrow college funds. Employees were scored on how quickly and effectively they provided information about the bank's pertinent products or services. A company that requires sales clerks to check youthful customers' IDs when they seek to buy video games with violent content may employ mystery shoppers to see whether their employees are actually doing so.

Analyzing customer complaints is crucial for improving products and customer service. Research indicates that only a few unsatisfied customers actually complain. Most unsatisfied customers say nothing but switch to competitors. A good **complaint analysis** system should encourage customers to (1) complain about an unsatisfactory product or service and (2) provide suggestions for improvements by completing forms asking specific questions beyond the routine "how was everything?" and (3) establish "listening posts" such as hotlines where specially designated employees either listen to customers' comments or actively solicit input from them (e.g., in a hotel lobby or on checkout lines). Since each complaint, by itself, provides little information, the company must have a system in which complaints are categorized and analyzed so that the results may be used to improve its operations.

Analyzing customer defections consists of finding out *why* customers leave the company. Customer loyalty rates are important because it is generally much cheaper to retain customers than to get new ones. Therefore, finding out why customers defect, and also *intervening* when customers' behaviors show that they may be considering leaving is crucial. For example, one bank that was losing about 20% of its customers every year discovered that segmenting defecting customers along demographic and family life-cycle characteristics was ineffective in reducing defection rates. The bank then compared 500 transaction records of loyal customers with 500 transaction records of defectors, using such dimensions as number of transactions, frequency of transactions, and fluctuations in average balances. The bank then identified transaction patterns that may indicate future defection and started targeting potential defectors and encouraging them to stay.[14]

Sampling and data collection

Since it is almost always impossible to obtain information from *every* member of the *population* or *universe* being studied, researchers use samples. A **sample** is a subset of the population that is used to estimate the characteristics of the entire population. Therefore, the sample must be *representative* of the universe under study. As the well-established Nielsen Media Research company recently found out, suspicions that a sample may not be representative of its universe endanger the credibility of all the data collected, and therefore must be addressed promptly. Although Nielsen's TV ratings have been used to estimate TV audiences and calculate advertising rates for many decades, its clients recently charged that the Nielsen sample was no longer representative of the U.S. population because it did not reflect accurately America's changing demographics and the large numbers of consumers who use devices such as TiVo to "time shift" and to avoid commercials during both live and recorded programs. In response to these criticisms, Nielsen has redesigned its sample to include significantly more ethnic groupings and to reflect the changes in TV viewing habits.[15]

An integral component of a research design is the sampling plan. Specifically, the sampling plan addresses three questions: whom to survey (the sampling unit), how many to survey (the sample size), and how to select them (the sampling procedure). Deciding whom to survey requires explicit definition of the *universe* or boundaries of the market from which data are sought so that an appropriate sample can be selected (such as working mothers). The size of the sample is dependent both on the size of the budget and on the degree of confidence that the marketer wants to place in the findings. The larger the sample, the more likely the responses will reflect the total universe under study. It is interesting to note, however, that a small sample can often provide highly reliable findings, depending on the sampling procedure adopted. (The exact number needed to achieve a specific level of confidence in the accuracy of the findings can be computed with a mathematical formula that is beyond the scope of this discussion.)

There are two types of samples: in a **probability sample**, respondents are selected in such a way that every member of the population studied has a known, non-zero chance of being selected. In a **nonprobability sample**, specific elements from the population under study have been predetermined in a nonrandom fashion on the basis of the researcher's judgment or decision to select a given number of respondents from a particular group. Table 4.3 summarizes the features of various types of probability and nonprobability designs.

As indicated earlier, qualitative studies usually require highly trained social scientists to collect data. A quantitative study generally uses a field staff that is either recruited and trained directly by the researcher or contracted from a company that specializes in conducting field interviews. In either case, it is often necessary to verify whether the interviews have, in fact, taken place. This is sometimes done by a postcard mailing to respondents asking them to verify that they participated in an interview on the date recorded on the questionnaire form. Completed questionnaires are reviewed on a regular basis as the research study progresses to ensure that the recorded responses are clear, complete, and legible.

Data analysis and reporting research findings

In qualitative research, the moderator or test administrator usually analyzes the responses received. In quantitative research, the researcher supervises the analysis: Open-ended responses are first coded and quantified (i.e., converted into numerical scores); then all of the responses are tabulated and analyzed using sophisticated analyti-

TABLE 4.3	Sampling
PROBABILITY SAMPLE	
Simple Random Sample	Every member of the population has a known and equal chance of being selected.
Systematic Random Sample	A member of the population is selected at random and then every "nth" person is selected.
Stratified Random Sample	The population is divided into mutually exclusive groups (such as age groups), and random samples are drawn from each group.
Cluster (area) Sample	The population is divided into mutually exclusive groups (such as blocks), and the researcher draws a sample of the groups to interview.
NONPROBABILITY SAMPLE	
Convenience Sample	The researcher selects the most accessible population members from whom to obtain information (e.g., students in a classroom).
Judgment Sample	The researcher uses his or her judgment to select population members who are good sources for accurate information (e.g., experts in the relevant field of study).
Quota Sample	The researcher interviews a prescribed number of people in each of several categories (e.g., 50 men and 50 women).

cal programs that correlate the data by selected variables and cluster the data by selected demographic characteristics.

In both qualitative and quantitative research, the research report includes a brief executive summary of the findings. Depending on the assignment from marketing management, the research report may or may not include recommendations for marketing action. The body of the report includes a full description of the methodology used and, for quantitative research, also includes tables and graphics to support the findings. A sample of the questionnaire is usually included in the appendix to enable management to evaluate the objectivity of the findings.

Conducting a research study

In designing a research study, researchers adapt the research processes described in the previous sections to the special needs of the study. For example, if a researcher is told that the purpose of the study is to develop a segmentation strategy for a new online dating service, he or she would first collect secondary data, such as population statistics (e.g., the number of men and women online in selected metropolitan areas within a certain age range, their marital status, and occupations). Then, together with the marketing manager, the researcher would specify the parameters (i.e., define the sampling unit) of the population to be studied (e.g., single, college-educated men and women between the ages of 18 and 45 who live or work within the Boston metropolitan area). A qualitative study (e.g., focus groups) might be undertaken first to gather information about the target population's attitudes and concerns about meeting people online, their special interests, and the specific services and precautions they would like an online dating service to provide. This phase of the research should result in tentative generalizations about the specific age group(s) to target and the services to offer.

The marketing manager then might instruct the researcher to conduct a quantitative study to confirm and attach "hard" numbers (percentages) to the findings that emerged from the focus groups. The first-phase study should have provided sufficient insights to develop a research design and to launch directly into a large-scale survey. If, however, there is still doubt about any element of the research design, such as question wording or format, they might decide first to do a small-scale exploratory study. Then, after refining the questionnaire and any other needed elements of the research design, they would launch a full-scale quantitative survey, using a probability sample that would allow them to project the findings to the total population of singles (as originally defined). The analysis should cluster prospective consumers of the online dating service into segments based on relevant sociocultural or lifestyle characteristics and on media habits, attitudes, perceptions, and geodemographic characteristics.

Ethics in consumer research

Consumer researchers must ensure that studies are objective and free of bias. Some studies are commissioned by organizations seeking to justify a particular position. For example, an organization opposed to the president of the United States may retain a research firm that will generate a national sample and ask respondents "do you believe that the president should be doing a better job in running the country?" Such a study may discover that, say, 65% of Americans believe that the president should be doing a better job. At the same time, another study using a national sample may ask respondents "do you approve or disapprove of the way the president is doing her job?" may also discover that 65% of Americans approve of the way the president is doing her job. The second study is more objective because the question was not stated in a biased fashion.

Researchers seeking to support a predetermined conclusion often do so by using biased samples and biased questions, manipulating statistical analyses, or ignoring relevant information. For example, a company offering a program for quitting smoking should not use only the successful graduates of its program in a study to be cited as evidence of the program's effectiveness.

Mistreating respondents is another ethical problem. Consumer researchers should avoid unnecessarily long interviews stemming from the logic that "as long as we are interviewing the person we may also try to find out . . ." Lengthy interviews where consumers are held on the phone for 30 minutes (and often lied to when they ask how much longer the call is going to take) or mall-intercept surveys where respondents are asked "can we have a few minutes of your time" and later subjected to a 40-minute questioning must be avoided. Such methods severely hurt the credibility of consumer research because they cause more and more people to refuse to participate in studies. Another unethical approach is sales pitches from telemarketers disguised as research studies.

At the start of all surveys, interviewers must clearly identify themselves and the company for which they are working, explain what the survey entails, and state the true expected duration of the interview. They should reassure respondents that there are no right or wrong answers to the questions. If the respondents are being paid, they should be so notified at the start of the interview. Perhaps most importantly, the privacy of respondents must be protected and guaranteed. Regrettably, although interviewers routinely promise research subjects the confidentiality of responses and anonymity (i.e., not identifying respondents by name in data analysis or reports), some unethical consumer researchers have sold data about consumers to marketers seeking persons with specific characteristics that will be targeted as prospective buyers.

SUMMARY

The field of consumer research developed as an extension of the field of marketing research to enable marketers to predict how consumers would react in the marketplace and to understand the reasons they made the purchase decisions they did. Consumer research undertaken from a managerial perspective to improve strategic marketing decisions is known as positivism. Positivist research is quantitative and empirical and tries to identify cause-and-effect relationships in buying situations. It is often supplemented with qualitative research.

Qualitative research is concerned with probing deep within the consumer's psyche to understand the motivations, feelings, and emotions that drive consumer behavior. Qualitative research findings cannot be projected to larger populations but are used primarily to provide new ideas and insights for the development of positioning strategies. Interpretivism, a qualitative research perspective, is generally more concerned with understanding the act of consuming rather than the act of buying (consumer decision making). Interpretivists view consumer behaviour as a subset of human behavior, and increased understanding as a key to eliminating some of the ills associated with destructive consumer behavior.

Each theoretical research perspective is based on its own specific assumptions and uses its own research techniques. Positivists typically use probability studies that can be generalized to larger populations. Interpretivists tend to view consumption experiences as unique situations that occur at specific moments in time; therefore, they cannot be generalized to larger populations. The two theoretical research orientations are highly complementary and, when used together, provide a deeper and more insightful understanding of consumer behavior than either approach used alone.

The consumer research process—whether quantitative or qualitative in approach—consists of six steps: defining objectives, collecting secondary data, developing a research design, collecting primary data, analyzing the data, and preparing a report of the findings. The research objectives should be formulated jointly by the marketer and the person or company that will conduct the actual research. Findings from secondary data and exploratory research are used to refine the research objectives. The collection of secondary data includes both internal and external sources. Quantitative research designs consist of observation, experimentation or surveys, and, for the most part, questionnaires (that often include attitude scales) are used to collect the data.

Qualitative designs and data collection methods include depth interviews, focus groups, projective techniques, and metaphor analysis. Customer satisfaction measurement is an integral part of consumer research. In large, quantitative studies, the researcher must make every effort to ensure that the research findings are reliable (that a replication of the study would provide the same results) and valid (that they answer the specific questions for which the study was originally undertaken). The selection and design of the sample is crucial since the type of sample used determines the degree to which the results of the study are representative of the population. Following the data collection, the results are analyzed and specific analytic techniques applied respectively to qualitative or quantitative data. Consumer researchers must also observe specific ethical guidelines to ensure the integrity of their studies and the privacy of respondents.

Market segmentation

Market segmentation and diversity are complementary concepts. Without a diverse marketplace composed of many different peoples with different backgrounds, countries of origin, interests, needs and wants, and perceptions, there would be little reason to segment markets. Diversity in the global marketplace makes market segmentation an attractive, viable, and potentially highly profitable strategy. The necessary conditions for successful segmentation of any market are a large enough population with sufficient money to spend (general affluence) and sufficient diversity to lend itself to partitioning the market into sizable segments on the basis of demographic, psychological, or other strategic variables. The presence of these conditions in the United States, Canada, Western Europe, Japan, Australia, and other industrialized nations makes these marketplaces extremely attractive to global marketers.

When marketers provide a range of product or service choices to meet diverse consumer interests, consumers are better satisfied, and their overall happiness, satisfaction, and quality of life are ultimately enhanced. Thus, market segmentation is a positive force for both consumers and marketers alike.

Market segmentation can be defined as the process of dividing a market into distinct subsets of consumers with common needs or characteristics and selecting one or more segments to target with a distinct marketing mix. Before the widespread acceptance of market segmentation, the prevailing way of doing business with consumers was through **mass marketing**—that is, offering the same product and marketing mix to all consumers. The essence of this strategy was summed up by the entrepreneur Henry Ford, who offered the Model T automobile to the public "in any color they wanted, as long as it was black."

If all consumers were alike—if they all had the same needs, wants, and desires, and the same background, education, and experience—mass (undifferentiated) marketing would be a logical strategy. Its primary advantage is that it costs less: Only one advertising campaign is needed, only one marketing strategy is developed, and usually only one standardized product is offered. Some companies, primarily those that deal in agricultural products or very basic manufactured goods, successfully follow a mass-marketing strategy. Other marketers, however, see major drawbacks in an undifferentiated marketing approach. When trying to sell the same product to every prospective customer with a single advertising campaign, the marketer must portray its product as a means for satisfying a common or generic need and, therefore, often ends up appealing to no one. A refrigerator may fulfill a widespread need to provide the home with a place to store perishable food that needs to be kept either cold or frozen (so that it does not spoil), but a standard-size refrigerator may be too big for a grandmother who lives alone and too small for a family of six. Without market differentiation, both the grandmother and the family of six would have to make do with the very same model, and, as we all know, "making do" is a far cry from being satisfied.

The strategy of segmentation allows producers to avoid head-on competition in the marketplace by differentiating their offerings, not only on the basis of price but also through styling, packaging, promotional appeal, method of distribution, and superior service. Marketers have found that the costs of consumer segmentation research, shorter production runs, and differentiated promotional campaigns are usually more than offset by increased sales. In most cases, consumers readily accept the passed-through cost increases for products that more closely satisfy their specific needs.

Market segmentation is just the first step in a three-phase marketing strategy. After segmenting the market into homogeneous clusters, the marketer then must select one or more segments to target. To accomplish this, the marketer must decide on a specific marketing mix—that is, a specific product, price, channel, and/or promotional appeal for each distinct segment. The third step is **positioning** the product so that it is perceived by the consumers in each target segment as satisfying their needs better than other competitive offerings.

Who uses market segmentation?

Because the strategy of market segmentation benefits both the consumer *and* the marketer, marketers of consumer goods are eager practitioners. For example, Chevrolet (**www.chevrolet.com**) targets its new Cobalt automobile with its sporty styling, minimal rear seat, and small trunk to young singles; it targets its Impala, a much larger vehicle, at the family car buyer needing a roomier vehicle. Another example is the market segmentation of marketers of wristwatches. To illustrate, Fossil (**www.fossil.com**), a manufacturer of popular priced fashion-conscious wristwatches, makes wristwatches to appeal to the demographics and functional-lifestyle need of consumers. More specifically, Fossil's watches (and those of many other wristwatch manufacturers) can be segmented in terms of four segments: (1) *gender of the wearer* (e.g., adult male versus adult female users), (2) *age of users* (e.g., first or starter watches, children's watches, or adult watches); (3) *function or lifestyle* (business dress, runners' watches, swimmers or divers watches, cell phone watches, etc.), and (4) *price* (e.g., watches costing less than $100, $100–$200, more than $200). Some limited edition and highly collectable wristwatches (e.g., some of those manufactured by firms like Carter, Rolex, and Patek Philippe) can cost $50,000 and up!

Hotels also segment their markets and target different chains to different market segments. For example, the Hilton Hotels family of brands (**www.hilton.com**) includes nine different hotel chains. A few examples of its lodging options and the prime target segments that Hilton is aiming at include *Embassy Suites Hotels* (for those desiring a two-room suite, cooked-to-order breakfast, and a nightly manager's reception), *Doubletree Hotels* (for those seeking contemporary, upscale accommodations), *Hampton Inns* (for price conscious travelers), *Homewood Suites* (for those seeking apartment-like accommodations for extended stays), and *Hilton Hotels* (stylish and sophisticated hotels for business and vacation travelers).

Industrial firms also segment their markets, as do not-for-profit organizations. For example, Peterbilt Motors Company (**www.peterbilt.com**) produces different models of trucks to meet the needs of long-haul truckers, construction projects, refuse collection companies, logging firms, and so on. The company's Web site offers a listing of its various vehicles by segment type. Charities such as the American Cancer Society (**www.cancer.org**) and UNICEF (**www.unicef.org**) frequently focus their fund-raising efforts on "heavy givers." Some performing arts centers segment their subscribers on the basis of *benefits sought* and have succeeded in increasing attendance through specialized promotional appeals.

How market segmentation operates

Segmentation studies are designed to discover the needs and wants of specific groups of consumers, so that specialized goods and services can be developed and promoted to satisfy each group's needs. Many new products have been developed to fill gaps in the marketplace revealed by segmentation research. For instance, Bayer Aspirin (**www.bayeraspirin.com**) has developed a variety of products that are designed to appeal directly to individuals with specific health issues (e.g., Bayer Rapid Headache Relief Formula, Bayer Back and Body Pain Formula, and Bayer Night Time Relief Formula).

In addition to filling product gaps, segmentation research is regularly used by marketers to identify the most appropriate media in which to place advertisements. Almost all media vehicles—from TV and radio stations to newspapers and magazines—use segmentation research to determine the characteristics of their audience and to publicize their findings in order to attract advertisers seeking a similar audience.

In some cases, if segments of customers are large enough and can attract enough advertising, the media will spin off separate programs or publications targeted to the specific segments. For example, *People* (**www.people.com**) has created a separate magazine for teenagers titled *Teen People* (**www.teenpeople.com**). In a somewhat similar fashion, *TIME* (**www.time.com**) targets different segments with special editions of its magazine. Not only does an advertiser have the choice of placing an ad in geographically based editions (e.g., international, U.S., regional, state, and spot market versions of each issue), but also some of the other editions offered by the magazine include a "Gold" edition for upscale mature adults, an "Inside Business" edition for top, middle, and technical management, and a "Women's" edition for affluent professional women. The magazine's Web site indicates that "there are more than 400 ways to buy advertising in *TIME.*" New magazines, TV stations, and radio stations are constantly being created to meet the unfulfilled needs of specific market segments.

Bases for segmentation

The first step in developing a segmentation strategy is to select the most appropriate base(s) on which to segment the market. Nine major categories of consumer characteristics provide the most popular bases for market segmentation. They include geographic factors, demographic factors, psychological factors, psychographic (lifestyle) characteristics, sociocultural variables, use-related characteristics, use-situation factors, benefits sought, and forms of **hybrid segmentation**—such as demographic-psychographic profiles, geodemographic factors, and values and lifestyles. Hybrid segmentation formats each use a combination of several segmentation bases to create rich and comprehensive profiles of particular consumer segments (e.g., a combination of a specific age range, income range, lifestyle, and profession). For example, the Bump Fighter Shaving System, manufactured by the American Safety Razor Company (**www.asrco.com**), is a replaceable-blade razor designed specifically for African American males. The product line has been expanded to now include shaving gel, skin conditioner, a disposable version of the razor, and a treatment mask (to be applied prior to sleeping). Table 4.4 lists the nine segmentation bases, divided into specific variables with examples of each. The following section discusses each of the nine segmentation bases. (Various psychological and sociocultural segmentation variables are examined in greater depth in later chapters.)

TABLE 4.4	Market Segmentation Categories and Selected Variables
SEGMENTATION BASE	**SELECTED SEGMENTATION VARIABLES**
GEOGRAPHIC SEGMENTATION	
Region	Southwest, Mountain states, Alaska, Hawaii
City size	Major metropolitan areas, small cities, towns
Density of area	Urban, suburban, exurban, rural
Climate	Temperate, hot, humid, rainy
DEMOGRAPHIC SEGMENTATION	
Age	Under 12, 12–17, 18–34, 35–49, 50–64, 65–74, 75–99, 100+
Sex	Male, female
Marital status	Single, married, divorced, living together, widowed
Income	Under $25,000, $25,000–$34,999, $35,000–$49,999, $50,000–$74,999, $75,000–$99,999, $100,000–$149,000, $150,000 and over
Education	Some high school, high school graduate, some college, college graduate, postgraduate
Occupation	Professional, blue-collar, white-collar, agricultural, military
PSYCHOLOGICAL SEGMENTATION	
Needs-motivation	Shelter, safety, security, affection, sense of self-worth
Personality	Extroverts, novelty seekers, aggressives, innovators
Perception	Low-risk, moderate-risk, high-risk
Learning-involvement	Low-involvement, high-involvement
Attitudes	Positive attitude, negative attitude
PSYCHOGRAPHIC	
(Lifestyle) Segmentation	Economy-minded, couch potatoes, outdoors enthusiasts, status seekers
SOCIOCULTURAL SEGMENTATION	
Cultures	American, Greek, Chinese, German, Mexican, French, Pakistani
Religion	Catholic, Protestant, Moslem, Jewish, other
Subcultures (race/ethnic)	African American, Caucasian, Asian, Hispanic
Social class	Lower, middle, upper
Family life cycle	Bachelors, young marrieds, full nesters, empty nesters
USE-RELATED SEGMENTATION	
Usage rate	Super heavy users, heavy users, medium users, light users, nonusers
Awareness status	Unaware, aware, interested, enthusiastic
Brand loyalty	None, some, strong
USE-SITUATION SEGMENTATION	
Time	Leisure, work, rush, morning, night
Objective	Personal, gift, snack, fun, achievement
Location	Home, work, friend's home, in-store
Person	Self, family members, friends, boss, peer

TABLE 4.4	Continued	
BENEFIT SEGMENTATION		
	Convenience, social acceptance, long lasting, economy, value-for-the-money	
HYBRID SEGMENTATION		
Demographic/psychographic	Combination of demographic and psychographic profiles of consumer segments profiles	
PRIZM NE (Geodemographics)	"Movers & Shakers," "New Empty Nests," "Boomtown Singles," "Bedrock America"	
SRI VALS™	Innovators, Thinkers, Believer, Achievers, Strivers, Experiencer, Makers, Survivors	

PRIZM NE is an example of a geodemographic profile. VALS™ is an example of a demographic/psychographic profile.

Geographic segmentation

In **geographic segmentation**, the market is divided by location. The theory behind this strategy is that people who live in the same area share some similar needs and wants and that these needs and wants differ from those of people living in other areas. To illustrate, certain supermarket and specialty related products sell better in one market, or a particular region, than in others. For example, whereas coffee-bean grinders are a "must have" in kitchens of people living in the Northwest, they are much less common anywhere else in the United States; and, similarly, Starbucks Coffee (**www.starbucks.com**) sells plenty of full-body coffees on the West Coast, but needed to introduce a line of Milder Dimensions® coffees to better satisfy its East Coast consumers (who tend to prefer a milder coffee than their West Coast counterparts).[1]

Some marketing scholars have argued that direct-mail merchandise catalogs, national toll-free telephone numbers, satellite television transmission, global communication networks, and especially the Internet have erased all regional boundaries and that geographic segmentation should be replaced by a single global marketing strategy. Clearly, any company that decides to put its catalog on the Internet makes it easy for individuals all over the world to browse and become customers. For example, vintage wristwatch dealers in New York, Boston, or Dallas (primarily selling 1940s–1970s high-end wristwatches to collectors) have posted their catalogs on the Web, advertise their Web addresses in *International Wristwatch* and other similar magazines, and gladly accept orders from both U.S. and overseas customers. For the consumers who shop on the Internet, it often makes little difference if online retailers are around the corner or halfway around the world—the only factor that differs is the shipping charge.

Other marketers have, for a number of years, been moving in the opposite direction and developing highly regionalized marketing strategies. For example, Campbell's Soup (**www.campbellsoup.com**) segments its domestic market into more than 20 regions, each with its own advertising and promotion budget. Within each region, Campbell's sales managers have the authority to develop specific advertising and promotional campaigns geared to local market needs and conditions, using local media ranging from newspapers to church bulletins. They work closely with local retailers on displays and promotions and report that their **micromarketing** strategies have won strong consumer support.

Marketers have observed divergent consumer purchasing patterns among urban, suburban, and rural areas. Throughout the United States, more furs and expensive jewelry are sold in cities than in small towns. Even within a large metropolitan area, different types of household furnishings and leisure products are sold in the central city than in the suburbs. Convertible sofas and small appliances are more likely to be bought by city apartment dwellers; suburban homeowners are better prospects for lawn mowers and barbecue grills. Probably the best example of successful segmentation based on geographic density is the giant Wal-Mart operation (**www.walmart.com**). Historically, Wal-Mart's basic marketing strategy was to locate discount stores in small towns (often in rural areas) that other major retail chain operations were ignoring at the time. Now that Wal-Mart has become the largest retailer in the world with 3,600 stores in the United States and 1,500 stores outside the United States, the firm has opened new stores in more populated locales, such as San Diego, California, and the Long Island, New York suburban towns of Westbury and East Meadow (both suburbs of New York City).

In summary, geographic segmentation is a useful strategy for many marketers. It is relatively easy to find geographically based differences for many products. In addition, geographic segments can be easily reached through the local media, including newspapers, TV and radio, and regional editions of magazines.

Demographic segmentation

Demography refers to the vital and measurable statistics of a population. **Demographic characteristics**, such as age, sex, marital status, income, occupation, and education, are most often used as the basis for market segmentation. Demographics help to *locate* a target market, whereas psychological and sociocultural characteristics help to *describe* how its members *think* and how they *feel*. Demographic information is often the most accessible and cost-effective way to identify a target market. Indeed, most secondary data, including census data, are expressed in demographic terms. Demographics are easier to measure than other segmentation variables; they are invariably included in psychographic and sociocultural studies because they add meaning to the findings.

Demographic variables reveal ongoing trends that signal business opportunities, such as shifts in age, gender, and income distribution. For example, demographic studies consistently show that the "mature-adult market" (the 50+ market) has a much greater proportion of disposable income than its younger counterparts. This factor alone makes consumers over age 50 a critical market segment for products and services that they buy for themselves, for their adult children, and for their grandchildren.

Age

Product needs and interests often vary with consumers' age. For instance, younger investors (those in their 30s to late 40s) as might be expected, tend to seek long-term gains when they invest, whereas those over 55 years of age tend to be more cautious and place more importance on the intermediate gain and current income of a potential investment. Because of such age-motivated differences, marketers have found age to be a particularly useful demographic variable for market segmentation.

The largest demographic segment in the U.S. population consists of baby boomers, the 78 million consumers born between 1946 and 1964. They spend over $1 trillion annually, and control 70 percent of the nation's wealth. While sometimes thought of as being "old" and "sickly," the reality is that 40 percent of all boomers believe that they are currently living the best years of their lives, and another 40 percent feel that the best years of their lives are still ahead of them. They are wealthy, optimistic, and have moved from a materialistic to a more experiential phase of their lives. Findings from a recent study, presented in Table 4.5 has segmented baby boomers into four subsegments—those "looking for balance," those "confident and living well," those "at ease," and those "overwhelmed."[2]

Many marketers have carved themselves a niche in the marketplace by concentrating on a specific age segment. For example, Heinz introduced EZ Squirt ketchup (which includes one version that is green in color) to better appeal to tweens,[3] and Aqua Velva, a 50-year-old brand of men's aftershave, is now targeting younger adult males with a new product, Ice Balm, which it advertises on both network and cable TV stations like Spike, ESPN, and the Speed Channel. Indeed, the men's grooming products category, which generates over $1 billion annually in sales, is experiencing a rapid expansion in terms of the number of new products being introduced each year. For instance, one firm, Sharps, positions itself as an outcast and tells users to "contemplate the goat" that appears on the product's package as part of the product usage instructions. It targets its

TABLE 4.5	Segmenting Baby Boomers			
SEGMENT NAME	**LOOKING FOR BALANCE**	**CONFIDENT AND LIVING WELL**	**AT EASE**	**OVERWHELMED**
Percent of Boomers	27%	23%	31%	19%
Characteristics	Very active and busy lifestyle. Money is important, but so is saving time.	Have highest incomes, are first to buy a new product or service. Technologically oriented, stylish, and trendy.	At peace with themselves and do not worry about the future. Lowest interest in luxury goods, and do not travel much. Most home-centric and family-oriented group.	Lowest income segment, worried about the future and financial security. Least active group— health is a big concern. Least social group. Do not use high-tech products.
Marketing Implications	Want great experiences— a market for travel-related businesses and food service businesses.	Travel is a favorite interest. Want luxury goods and services.	A good market for traditional household products and services. Like trusted brand names. Low interest in new products.	Opportunity for marketers of certain financial service and healthcare products/ services.

Source: Dick Chay, "New Segments of Boomers Reveal New Mktg. Implications," *Marketing News,* March 15, 2005, 24.

products to young men who do not fit into a Hugo Boss or Calvin Klein category, and who view themselves as risk takers and marginally countercultural.[4] Still further, while four years ago McDonald's (**www.mcdonalds.com**) spent 80 percent of its advertising budget on prime-time television, today it spends less than half its budget on prime-time TV and has increased its spending on Internet portals in an effort to reach young customers online. Similarly, Coke is spending more than $3 million on interactive media in an attempt to better connect with 12- to 24-year-old consumers.[5]

Age, especially chronological age, implies a number of underlying forces. In particular, demographers have drawn an important distinction between *age effects* (occurrences due to chronological age) and *cohort effects* (occurrences due to growing up during a specific time period). Examples of the *age effect* are the heightened interest in leisure travel that often occurs for people (single and married) during middle age (particularly in their late fifties or early sixties) and the interest in learning to play golf. Although people of all ages learn to play golf, it is particularly prevalent among people in their fifties. These two trends are examples of age effects because they especially seem to happen as people reach a particular age category.[6]

In contrast, the nature of *cohort effects* is captured by the idea that people hold onto the interests they grew up to appreciate. If 10 years from today it is determined that many rock-and-roll fans are over 55, it would not be because older people have suddenly altered their musical tastes but because the baby boomers who grew up with rock and roll have become older. As Bill Whitehead, CEO of the advertising agency Bates North America, noted: "When baby boomers are 70, they'll still eat pizza and still listen to the [Rolling] Stones."[7] It is important for marketers to be aware of the distinction between age effects and cohort effects: One stresses the impact of aging, whereas the second stresses the influence of the period when a person is born and the shared experiences with others of the same age. We must remember that cohort effects are ongoing and lifelong. To illustrate this point, Table 4.6 identifies and distinguishes among seven different American age cohort groupings.[8]

TABLE 4.6	**Four Selected American Cohorts**
Leading-edge baby boomer cohort (born from 1946–1954; came of age during the turmoil of the 1960s; aged 50–58 in 2004)	This group remembers the assassinations of John and Robert Kennedy and Martin Luther King, Jr. It was the loss of JFK that largely shaped this cohort's values. They became adults during the Vietnam War and watched as the first man walked on the moon. Leading-edge boomers were dichotomous: they championed causes (Greenpeace, civil rights, women's rights), yet were simultaneously hedonistic and self-indulgent (pot, 'free love,' sensuality).
Trailing-edge baby boomer cohort (born from 1955–1965; came of age during the first sustained economic downturn since the Depression; aged 39–49 in 2004)	This group witnessed the fall of Vietnam, Watergate Nixon's resignation. The oil embargo, the raging inflation rate, and the more than 30 percent decline in the S&P Index led these individuals, to be less optimistic about their financial future than the leading-edge boomers.
Generation X cohort (born from 1965–1976; came of age during a time of instability and uncertainty; aged 28–38 in 2004)	These are the latchkey children of divorce who have received the most negative publicity. This cohort has delayed marriage and children, and they do not take these commitments lightly. More than other groups, this cohort accepts cultural diversity and puts quality of personal life ahead of work life. They are 'free agents' not 'team players.' Despite a rocky start into adulthood, this group shows a spirit of entrepreneurship unmatched by any other cohort.
N Generation cohort (born from 1977–?; came of age during the 'Information Revolution'; aged 27 and under in 2004)	The youngest cohort is called the 'N Generation' or 'N-Gen' because the advent of the Internet is a defining event for them, and because they will be the 'engine' of growth over the next two decades. While still a work in progress, their core value structure seems to be quite different from that of Gen-X. They are more idealistic and social-cause oriented, without the cynical, 'What's in it for me?' free-agent mindset of many Gen-Xers.

Source: Charles D. Schewe and Geoffrey Meredith, "Segmenting Global Markets by Generational Cohorts: Determining Motivations by Age," *Journal of Consumer Behavior,* 4, October 2004, 54.

Sex

Like age, gender is quite frequently a distinguishing segmentation variable. Some products and services are quite naturely associated more or less with males or females. For instance, women have traditionally been the main users of such products as hair coloring and cosmetics, and men have been the main users of tools and shaving preparations. However, sex roles have blurred, and gender is no longer an accurate way to distinguish consumers in some product categories. For example, women are buying household repair tools, and men have become significant users of skin care and hair products. It is becoming increasingly common to see magazine ads and TV commercials that depict men and women in roles traditionally occupied by the opposite sex. For example, many ads reflect the expanded child-nurturing roles of young fathers in today's society.

Much of the change in sex roles has occurred because of the continued impact of dual-income households. One consequence for marketers is that women are not as readily accessible through traditional media as they once were. Because working women do not have much time to watch TV or listen to the radio, many advertisers now emphasize magazines in their media schedules, especially those specifically aimed at working women (e.g., *Working Mother*). Direct marketers also have been targeting time-pressured working women who use merchandise catalogs, convenient 800 numbers, and Internet sites as ways of shopping for personal clothing and accessories, as well as many household and family needs. Recent research has shown that men and women differ in terms of the way they look at their Internet usage. Specifically, men tend to "click on" a Web site because they are "information hungry," whereas women click because "they expect communications media to entertain and educate."[9] Interestingly, analysis undertaken by Wal-Mart has revealed that more women than men shop their Web site, and that their typical online customer is a working mom who uses the Internet to satisfy a

TABLE 4.7	Male and Female Segments of Internet Users	
	KEY USAGE SITUATION	**FAVORITE INTERNET MATERIALS**
FEMALE SEGMENTS		
Social Sally	Making friends	Chat and personal Web page
New Age Crusader	Fighting for causes	Books and government information
Cautious Mom	Nurturing children	Cooking and medical facts
Playful Pretender	Role-playing	Chat and games
Master Producer	Job productivity	White pages and government information
MALE SEGMENTS		
Bits and Bytes	Computers and hobbies	Investments, discovery, software
Practical Pete	Personal productivity	Investments, company listings
Viking Gamer	Competing and winning	Games, chat, software
Sensitive Sam	Helping family and friends	Investments, government information
World Citizen	Connecting with world	Discovery, software, investments

Source: Scott Smith and David Whitlark, "Men and Women Online: What Makes Them Click," *Marketing Research*, Summer 2001, 22.

portion of her shopping needs.[10] Still further, the research indicates that 92 percent of Wal-Mart's online shoppers visit a Wal-Mart store at least once a month, and these online customers have higher income and education levels than their only in-store shopper counterparts. Table 4.7 presents additional male and female differences when it comes to using the Internet and compares some key usage situations and favorite Internet materials for men versus women.

Furthermore, when it comes to being "hungry," research shows that young men are "more likely than average to go to a quick service restaurant for breakfast." Burger King, which controls only 10 percent of this breakfast market (compared to McDonald's 40 percent), has come to the conclusion that young men want tasty food, and are unconcerned about calories and fat content. Consequently, Burger King is now offering the *Enormous Omelet*, complete with 730 calories, 47 grams of fat, 415 mg of cholesterol, and 1,860 mg of sodium.[11] In contrast to both McDonalds and Burger King, Wendy's has tended to feature menu options like its *Fresh Fruit Bowl* that appeal to women.

Marital status
Traditionally, the family has been the focus of most marketing efforts, and for many products and services, the household continues to be the relevant consuming unit. Marketers are interested in the number and kinds of households that buy and/or own certain products. They also are interested in determining the demographic and media profiles of household decision makers (the persons involved in the actual selection of the product) to develop appropriate marketing strategies.

Marketers have discovered the benefits of targeting specific marital status groupings, such as singles, divorced individuals, single parents, and dual-income married couples. For instance, singles, especially one-person households with incomes greater than $50,000, comprise a market segment that tends to be above average in the usage of products not traditionally associated with supermarkets (e.g., cognac, books, loose tea) and below average in their consumption of traditional supermarket products (e.g., catsup, peanut butter, mayonnaise). Such insights can be particularly useful to a supermarket manager operating in a neighborhood of one-person households when deciding on the merchandise mix for the store. Some marketers target one-person households with single-serving foods (e.g., Bumble Bee tuna's 3 oz. easy-open cans, Pringles single serving-size cans, Orville Redenbacher's popcorn mini-bags, Campbell's Soup To Go!) and others with mini-appliances such as small microwave ovens and two-cup coffee makers.

Income, education, and occupation

Income has long been an important variable for distinguishing between market segments. Marketers commonly segment markets on the basis of income because they feel that it is a strong indicator of the ability (or inability) to pay for a product or a specific model of the product. For instance, consider *Panache*, the lifestyle magazine of the Fort Worth (TX) *Star-Telegram*. It struggled for six years at 16 pages per issue, and was basically going nowhere. But then, using the PRIZM geodemographic segmentation scheme from Claritas (which will be discussed later in this chapter), *Panache*'s distribution was changed so that it was only delivered to the homes of subscribers with $100,000+ annual incomes. Advertisers become enthusiastic about the magazine, and within a few months it grew to a 40 page per issue publication.[12]

Income is often combined with other demographic variables to more accurately define target markets. To illustrate, high income has been combined with age to identify the important *affluent elderly* segment. It also has been combined with both age and occupational status to produce the so-called *yuppie* segment, a sought-after subgroup of the baby boomer market.

Education, occupation, and income tend to be closely correlated in almost a cause-and-effect relationship. High-level occupations that produce high incomes usually require advanced educational training. Individuals with little education rarely qualify for high-level jobs. Insights on Internet usage preferences tend to support the close relationship among income, occupation, and education. Research reveals that consumers with lower incomes, lower education, as well as those with blue-collar occupations, tend to spend more time online at home than those with higher income, higher education, and white-collar occupations.[13] One possible reason for this difference is that those in blue-collar jobs often do not have access to the Internet during the course of the workday.

Psychological segmentation

Psychological characteristics refer to the inner or intrinsic qualities of the individual consumer. Consumer segmentation strategies are often based on specific psychological variables. For instance, consumers may be segmented in terms of their *motivations, personality, perceptions, learning,* and *attitudes.*

Psychographic segmentation

Marketing practitioners have heartily embraced psychographic research, which is closely aligned with psychological research, especially personality and attitude measurement. This form of applied consumer research (commonly referred to as lifestyle analysis) has proven to be a valuable marketing tool that helps identify promising consumer segments that are likely to be responsive to specific marketing messages.

The psychographic profile of a consumer segment can be thought of as a composite of consumers' measured **activities, interests, and opinions (AIOs)**. As an approach to constructing consumer psychographic profiles, AIO research seeks consumers' responses to a large number of statements that measure activities (how the consumer or family spends time, e.g., camping, volunteering at a local hospital, going to baseball games), interests (the consumer's or family's preferences and priorities, e.g., home, fashion, food), and opinions (how the consumer feels about a wide variety of events and political issues, social issues, the state of the economy, ecology). In their most common form, AIO-psychographic studies use a battery of statements (a **psychographic inventory**) designed to identify relevant aspects of a consumer's personality, buying

TABLE 4.8	A Hypothetical Psychographic Profile of the Techno-Road-Warrior

- *Goes on the Internet more than six times a week*
- *Sends and/or receives 15 or more e-mail messages a week*
- *Regularly visits Web sites to gather information and/or to comparison shop*
- *Often buys personal items via 800 numbers and/or over the Internet*
- *May trade stocks and/or make travel reservations over the Internet*
- *Earns $100,000 or more a year*
- *Belongs to several rewards programs (e.g., frequent flyer programs, hotel programs, rent-a-car programs)*

motives, interests, attitudes, beliefs, and values. Table 4.8 presents a likely psychographic profile of "techno-road-warriors," businesspeople who spend a high percentage of their workweek on the road, equipped with laptops, pagers, cellular telephones, and electronic organizers. The appeal of psychographic research lies in the frequently vivid and practical profiles of consumer segments that it can produce (which will be illustrated later in this chapter).

AIO research has even been employed to explore pet ownership as a segmentation base. One study has found that people who do ***not*** have pets are more conservative in nature, more brand loyal, and more likely to agree with statements such as "I am very good at managing money" and "It is important for me to look well dressed." Such findings can be used by marketers when developing promotional messages for their products and services.[14]

The results of psychographic segmentation efforts are frequently reflected in firms' marketing messages. For instance, Asics running shoes (see Figure 4.3) are targeted to individuals (in this case, women) who thrive on the challenge of running (**www.asics.com**). Psychographic segmentation is further discussed later in the chapter, where we consider hybrid segmentation strategies that combine psychographic and demographic variables to create rich descriptive profiles of consumer segments.

Sociocultural segmentation

Sociological (group) and *anthropological* (cultural) variables—that is, **sociocultural variables**—provide further bases for market segmentation. For example, consumer markets have been successfully subdivided into segments on the basis of stage in the family life cycle, social class, core cultural values, subcultural memberships, and cross-cultural affiliation.

Family life cycle

Family life-cycle segmentation is based on the premise that many families pass through similar phases in their formation, growth, and final dissolution. At each phase, the family unit needs different products and services. Young single people, for example, need basic furniture for their first apartment, whereas their parents, finally free of child rearing, often refurnish their homes with more elaborate pieces. Family life cycle is a composite variable based explicitly on *marital* and *family status* but implicitly reflects *relative age, income*, and *employment status.* Each of the stages in the traditional family life cycle (*bachelorhood, honeymooners, parenthood, postparenthood*, and *dissolution*) represents an important target segment to a variety of marketers. For example, the financial services industry frequently segments customers in terms of family life-cycle stages because families' financial needs tend to shift as they progress through the various stages of life.

Asics Targets a "Runner's" Lifestyle

Social class

Social class (or relative status in the community) can be used as a base for market segmentation and is usually measured by a weighted index of several demographic variables, such as education, occupation, and income. The concept of *social class* implies a hierarchy in which individuals in the same class generally have the same degree of status, whereas members of other classes have either higher or lower status. Studies have shown that consumers in different social classes vary in terms of values, product preferences, and buying habits. Many major banks and investment companies, for example, offer a variety of different levels of service to people of different social classes (e.g., private banking services to the upper classes). For example, some investment companies appeal to upper-class customers with offering them options that correspond to their wealthy status. In contrast, a financial program targeted to a lower social class might talk instead about savings accounts or certificates of deposit.

Culture and subculture

Some marketers have found it useful to segment their markets on the basis of cultural heritage because members of the same culture tend to share the same values, beliefs, and customs. Marketers who use cultural segmentation stress specific, widely held cultural values with which they hope consumers will identify (e.g., for American consumers, *youthfulness* and *fitness and health*). Cultural segmentation is particularly successful in international marketing, but it is important for the marketer to understand fully the target country's beliefs, values, and customs (the cross-cultural context).

Within the larger culture, distinct subgroups (subcultures) often are united by certain experiences, values, or beliefs that make effective market segments. These groupings could be based on a specific demographic characteristic (such as race, religion, ethnicity, or age) or lifestyle characteristic (teachers, joggers). In the United States, African Americans, Hispanic Americans, Asian Americans, and the elderly are important subcultural market segments. Research on subcultural differences, tends to reveal that consumers are more responsive to promotional messages that they perceive relate to their own ethnicity (e.g., African American consumers tend to respond favorably to marketers who recognize and respond positively to their specific interests and background).[15]

Culturally distinct segments can be prospects for the same product but often are targeted more efficiently with different promotional appeals. For example, a bicycle might be promoted as an efficient means of transportation in parts of Asia and as a health-and-fitness product in the United States. Moreover, a recent study that divided China's urban consumers into four segments ("working poor," "salary class," "little rich," and "yuppies") found that for all four groups, television was the most popular medium of entertainment and information. However, the working poor spend the most time listening to radio, while yuppies and the little rich spend the most time reading newspapers and magazines.[16]

Cross-cultural or global marketing segmentation

As the world has gotten smaller and smaller, a true global marketplace has developed. For example, as you read this you may be sitting on an IKEA chair or sofa (Sweden), drinking Earl Grey tea (England), wearing a Swatch watch (Switzerland), Nike sneakers (China), a Polo golf shirt (Mexico), and Dockers pants (Dominican Republic). Some global market segments, such as teenagers, appear to want the same types of products, regardless of which nation they call home—products that are trendy, entertaining, and image oriented. This global "sameness" allowed Reebok, for example, to launch its Instapump line of sneakers using the same global advertising campaign in approximately 140 countries.[17]

Use-related segmentation

An extremely popular and effective form of segmentation categorizes consumers in terms of product, service, or brand usage characteristics, such as level of usage, level of awareness, and degree of brand loyalty.

Rate of usage segmentation differentiates among heavy users, medium users, light users, and nonusers of a specific product, service, or brand. For example, research has consistently indicated that between 25 and 35 percent of beer drinkers account for more than 70 percent of all beer consumed. For this reason, most marketers prefer to target their advertising campaigns to heavy users rather than spend considerably more money trying to attract light users. This also explains the successful targeting of light beer to heavy drinkers on the basis that it is less filling (and, thus, can be consumed in greater quantities) than regular beer. Recent studies have found that heavy soup users were more socially active, creative, optimistic, witty, and less stubborn than light users and nonusers, and they were also less likely to read entertainment and sports magazines and more likely to read family and home magazines. Likewise, heavy users of travel agents in Singapore were more involved with and more enthusiastic about

TABLE 4.9	A Framework for Segmenting a Firm's Database of Customers	
SEGMENT NAME	**SEGMENT CHARACTERISTIC**	**COMPANY ACTION**
LoLows	Low current share, low-consumption customers	Starve
HiLows	High current share, low-consumption customers	Tickle
LowHighs	Low current share, high-consumption customers	Chase
HiHighs	High current share, high-consumption customers	Stroke

Source: Richard G. Barlow, "How to Court Various Target Markets," *Marketing News*, October 9, 2000, 22.

vacation travel, more innovative with regard to their selection of vacation travel products, more likely to travel for pleasure, and more widely exposed to travel information from the mass media.[18]

Marketers of a host of other products have also found that a relatively small group of heavy users accounts for a disproportionately large percentage of product usage; targeting these heavy users has become the basis of their marketing strategies. Other marketers take note of the gaps in market coverage for light and medium users and profitably target those segments. Table 4.9 presents an overview of a segmentation strategy especially suitable for marketers seeking to organize their database of customers into an action-oriented framework. The framework proposes a way to identify a firm's best customers by dividing the database into the following segments: (1) *LoLows* (low current share, low-consumption customers), (2) *HiLows* (high current share, low-consumption customers), (3) *LowHighs* (low current share, high-consumption customers), and (4) *HiHighs* (high current share, high-consumption customers). Moreover, the framework suggests the following specific strategies for each of the four segments: "starve" the *LoLows*, "tickle" the *HiLows*, "chase" the *LowHighs*, and "stroke" the *HiHighs*.[19]

In addition to segmenting customers in terms of rate of usage or other usage patterns, consumers can also be segmented in terms of their *awareness status*. In particular, the notion of consumer awareness of the product, interest level in the product, readiness to buy the product, or whether consumers need to be informed about the product are all aspects of awareness.

Sometimes *brand loyalty* is used as the basis for segmentation. Marketers often try to identify the characteristics of their brand-loyal consumers so that they can direct their promotional efforts to people with similar characteristics in the larger population. Other marketers target consumers who show no brand loyalty ("brand switchers") in the belief that such people represent greater market potential than consumers who are loyal to competing brands. Also, almost by definition, consumer innovators—often a prime target for new products—tend *not* to be brand loyal.

Increasingly, marketers stimulate and reward brand loyalty by offering special benefits to consistent or frequent customers. Such frequent usage or relationship programs often take the form of a membership club (e.g., Continental Airline's OnePass Platinum Elite Status, Hilton HHonors Diamond VIP Membership, Avis' Wizard Preferred Service Program). Relationship programs, such as The Hertz #1 Club®, tend to provide special accommodations and services, as well as free extras, to keep these frequent customers loyal and happy.

Usage-situation segmentation

Marketers recognize that the occasion or situation often determines what consumers will purchase or consume. For this reason, they sometimes focus on the **usage situation** as a segmentation variable.

The following three statements reveal the potential of situation segmentation: "Whenever our son Eric gets a raise or a promotion, we always take him out to dinner"; "When I'm away on business for a week or more, I try to stay at a Suites hotel"; "I always buy my wife candy on Valentine's Day." Under other circumstances, in other situations, and on other occasions, the same consumer might make other choices. Some situational factors that might influence a purchase or consumption choice includes whether it is a weekday or weekend (e.g., going to a movie); whether there is sufficient time (e.g., use of regular mail or express mail); whether it is a gift for a girlfriend, a parent, or a self-gift (a reward to one's self).

Many products are promoted for special usage occasions. The greeting card industry, for example, stresses special cards for a variety of occasions that seem to be increasing almost daily (Grandparents' Day, Secretaries' Day, etc.). The florist and candy industries promote their products for Valentine's Day and Mother's Day, the diamond industry promotes diamond rings as an engagement symbol, and the wristwatch industry promotes its products as graduation gifts.

A recent study found that individuals who purchase their magazines at newsstands are more active consumers and are more receptive to advertising than consumers who subscribe to the very same magazines. As the research noted, "this is the holy grail for advertisers."[20] Table 4.10 presents a comparison of newsstand magazine buyers versus magazine subscribers.

Situational factors as a base for segmentation have also been studied in relation to retailing. For example, in situations where the shopper has ample time, shopping atmosphere, stocking the right brands, and general familiarity with the retailer are important. Conversely, a shopper with less time wants to shop where a large selection of merchandise is immediately available, with no transaction hassles (i.e., for clothing, the ability to touch and try on merchandise).[21]

Benefit segmentation

Marketing and advertising executives constantly attempt to identify the one most important benefit of their product or service that will be most meaningful to consumers. Examples of benefits that are commonly used include *cleaner teeth* (Oral-B), *financial security* (Transamerica), *protection of data* (Norton Antivirus), *soft skin*

TABLE 4.10	**Newsstand Magazine Buyers versus Magazine Subscribers**

Consumers who buy magazines on the newsstand are:

- Two times as likely to enjoy reading ads in magazines
- 63 percent more likely to remember products advertised in magazines when they are shopping
- 48 percent more likely to shop frequently
- 50 percent more likely to buy things on the spur of the moment
- Twice as likely to spend more money on cosmetics than subscribers
- 58 percent more likely to buy leading cosmetic brands
- Nearly twice as likely to enjoy shopping for clothes
- 50 percent more likely to try new alcoholic drinks than subscribers
- 58 percent more likely to drink super-premium vodka
- Four times more likely to download music than subscribers
- More than twice as likely to purchase video games in the last 12 months
- Twice as likely to purchase designer jeans

Source: "New Study Reveals Newsstand Magazine Buyers to be More Active Consumers and More Receptive to Advertising," *Business Wire*, September 8, 2004, 1.

(Olay), *allergy relief* (Allegra), and *peace of mind* (Liberty Mutual Insurance Company).

In targeting Indian consumers in terms of benefits sought, research revealed that an important segment of Indian consumers of Dettol soap were hygiene-conscious and seeking protection from germs and contamination, rather than more common benefits of beauty, fragrance, freshness, or economy.[22] Still further, a segmentation study examining what drives consumer preferences for micro or craft beer, identified the following five strategic brand benefits: (1) functional (i.e., quality), (2) value for the money, (3) social benefit, (4) positive emotional benefits, and 5) negative emotional benefits.[23]

Changing lifestyles also play a major role in determining the product benefits that are important to consumers and provide marketers with opportunities for new products and services. For example, the microwave oven was the perfect solution to the needs of dual-income households, where neither the husband nor the wife has the time for lengthy meal preparation. Food marketers offer busy families the *benefit* of breakfast products that require only seconds to prepare.

Benefit segmentation can be used to position various brands within the same product category.[24] The classic case of successful benefit segmentation is the market for toothpaste, and a recent article suggested that if consumers are socially active, they want a toothpaste that can deliver white teeth and fresh breath; if they smoke, they want a toothpaste to fight stains; if disease prevention is their major focus, then they want a toothpaste that will fight germs; and if they have children, they want to lower their dental bills.[25]

Hybrid segmentation approaches

Marketers commonly segment markets by combining several segmentation variables rather than relying on a single segmentation base. This section examines three hybrid segmentation approaches that provide marketers with richer and more accurately defined consumer segments than can be derived from using a single segmentation variable. These include psychographic-demographic profiles, geodemographics, VALS, and Yankelovich's Mindbase Segmentation.

Psychographic, lifestyle, and demographic profiles

Psychographic (including lifestyles) and demographic profiles are highly complementary approaches that work best when used together. By combining the knowledge gained from including both demographic and psychographic factors, marketers are provided with powerful information about their target markets.

Demographic-psychographic profiling has been widely used in the development of advertising campaigns to answer three questions: "Whom should we target?" "What should we say?" "Where should we say it?" To help advertisers answer the third question, many advertising media vehicles sponsor demographic-lifestyle research on which they base very detailed *audience profiles*. Tables 4.11 and 4.12 present a portion of the demographic and psychographic-lifestyle profiles of *USA Today* (i.e., its newspaper, its Web site, and both) that is independently prepared by MMI (i.e., an audience research firm that prepares profiles of many magazine and newspaper readers). In the case of *USA Today*, such information is made available in the form of advertising information kits or alternatively is available on their Web sites (**www.usatoday.com**). *USA Today*, as well as many other newspapers and magazines, provide potential and current advertisers with such profiles to assist advertisers in making decisions as to where they are going to spend their advertising budgets. By offering media advertisers such carefully defined profiles of their audiences, mass media publishers and broadcasters make it possible for advertisers to select media whose audiences most closely resemble their target markets.

Finally, advertisers are increasingly designing ads that depict in words and/or pictures the essence of a particular target-market lifestyle or segment that they want to reach. In this spirit, Dream Catcher is seeking to inform its target audiences—about its cost effective destination club.

TABLE 4.11	Selected Demographic Profile of USA Today		
	USA TODAY	USATODAY.COM	USA TODAY NETWORK*
Total Readers	5,227,000	1,870,000	6,219,000
Gender			
Men	66%	70%	66%
Women	34%	30%	34%
Age			
Age 18–49	62%	73%	64%
Age 25–54	65%	78%	67%
Age 55+	27%	18%	25%
Average Age	45	43	45
Education			
Attended college or beyond	77%	83%	77%
College graduate or beyond	55%	65%	56%
Occupation			
Professional/Managerial	34%	52%	36%
Top/Middle Manager	33%	36%	32%
Employed	80%	85%	81%
Income			
HHI $50,000 or more	75%	79%	75%
HHI $60,000 or more	66%	68%	65%
HHI $75,000 or more	50%	56%	50%
HHI $100,000 or more	31%	30%	30%
Average HHI	$91,210	$90,861	$89,572
Median HHI	$74,715	$80,628	$74,838

* Unduplicated combined daily audience for USA TODAY and USATODAY.com.

Source: Fall 2004 MRI

Geodemographic segmentation

This type of hybrid segmentation scheme is based on the notion that people who live close to one another are likely to have similar financial means, tastes, preferences, lifestyles, and consumption habits (similar to the old adage, "Birds of a feather flock together"). This segmentation approach uses computers to generate geodemographic market clusters of like consumers. Specifically, computer software clusters the nation's 250,000+ neighborhoods into lifestyle groupings based on postal zip codes. Clusters are created based on consumer lifestyles, and a specific cluster includes zip codes that are composed of people with similar lifestyles widely scattered throughout the country. Marketers use the cluster data for direct-mail campaigns, to select retail sites and appropriate merchandise mixes, to locate banks and restaurants, and to design marketing strategies for specific market segments. For example, Eddie Bauer (**www.eddiebauer.com**) has employed Claritas demographics (**www.claritas.com**) to evaluate new retail store locations and is PRIZM coding current customers, and Duke Energy Corporation (**www.duke-energy.com**) has profiled its residential and small business customers with Claritas's databases as part of its customer retention program.[26] Table 4.13 presents four examples of geodemographic clusters.

TABLE 4.12	Selected Lifestyle Profile of USA Today		
		% COMP	**INDEX**
Tech Savvy Readers			
Use Internet more than once a day		32%	174
Internet access at home		79%	128
Online purchase for business or personal use in past 30 days		40%	182
Household owns a PC		84%	119
Own a digital camera		22%	130
Leisure Activities			
Attended movies in last 6 months		73%	120
Bought music CDs/tapes in last 12 months		46%	126
Attended live music performance in last 12 months		29%	123
Book reading		45%	120
Entertain friends or relatives at home in last 12 months		48%	123
Household subscribes to cable		69%	112
Sports Enthusiasts			
Golf—personally participated last 12 months		21%	185
Walking for exercise		30%	107
Engage in regular exercise program (2+ times a week)		50%	126
Personally participate in any sports in past 12 months		77%	120
Attend any sports events		48%	152
Watch any sports events on TV		79%	120
Financially Aware			
Tracked investments or traded securities online in past 30 days		26%	246
Banked via PC/Internet in last 12 months		26%	159
Own securities		30%	133
Own mutual funds		25%	143
Have retirement savings plan (401K, IRA, Keogh)		31%	139
Domestic and Foreign Travelers			
Any foreign travel in last 3 years		27%	118
Any domestic travel in past year		63%	117
Member of frequent flyer program		30%	173
Own a valid passport		31%	120

Source: Spring 2004 MRI

Over the past 25 years, as the firm that started the clustering phenomenon, Claritas has increased the number of segments in American society from the 40 segments used in the 1970s and 1980s to the 66 segments it uses today. The Claritas search engine will pick the top five lifestyle clusters for each zip code; you can find out about your zip code by visiting **www.yawyl.claritas.com**.

While cross-cultural or global marketing segmentation was discussed earlier in the chapter, it is of interest to note that Claritas recently extended its geodemographic segmentation tool, PRIZM, to the Canadian marketplace. Prism CE (CE = Canadian Edition) lists 66 different consumer "clusters," including 28 urban groups, 11 ethnic groups, and 15 francophone categories.[27]

TABLE 4.13	Four PRISM NE Geodemographic Segments

MOVERS & SHAKERS

- 1.59% of U.S. households
- Median household income: $95,372
- Predominant employment: Professional
- Social group: Elite suburbs
- Lifestage group: Midlife success
- Key education level: College grad+
- Adult age range: 35–64

CHARACTERISTICS: Movers & Shakers is home to America's up-and-coming business class: a wealthy suburban world of dual-income couples who are highly educated, typically between the ages of 35 and 54 and often with children. Given its high percentage of executives and white-collar professionals, there's a decided business bent to this segment: Movers & Shakers rank number-one for owning a small business and having a home office.

LIFESTYLE TRAITS:

- Go scuba diving/snorkeling
- Plan travel on the Internet
- Read *PC Magazine*
- Listen to adult contemporary radio
- Drive a Porsche

NEW EMPTY NESTS

- 1.05% of U.S. households
- Median household income: $65,832
- Predominant employment: Professional, white-collar
- Social group: The Affluentials
- Lifestage group: Conservative classics
- Key education level: College Grad+
- Adult age range: 65+

CHARACTERISTICS: With their grown-up children recently out of the house, New Empty Nests is composed of upscale older Americans who pursue active — and activist — lifestyles. Nearly three-quarters of residents are over 65 years old, but they show no interest in a rest-home retirement. This is the top-ranked segment for all-inclusive travel packages; the favorite destination is Italy.

LIFESTYLE TRAITS:

- Choose all-inclusive travel pkg.
- Belong to a fraternal order
- Read *Smithsonian*
- Watch *Meet the Press*
- Drive a Buick Park Avenue

BOOMTOWN SINGLES

- 1.22% of U.S. households
- Median household income: $37,407
- Predominant employment: White-collar, service
- Social group: City Centers
- Lifestage group: Young Achievers

(Continued)

TABLE 4.13	Continued

- Key education level: H.S./College
- Adult age range: Under 35

CHARACTERISTICS: Affordable housing, abundant entry-level jobs and a thriving singles scene—all have given rise to the Boomtown Singles segment in fast-growing satellite cities. Young, single and working-class, these residents pursue active lifestyles amid sprawling apartment complexes, bars, convenience stores, and laundromats.

LIFESTYLE TRAITS:

- Buy alternative music
- Play soccer
- Read *Muscle & Fitness*
- Watch MTV
- Drive a Daewoo

BEDROCK AMERICA

- 1.79% of U.S. households
- Median household income: $26,037
- Predominant employment: Service, BC, Farm
- Social group: Rustic living
- Lifestage group: Sustaining families
- Key education level: Elementary/H.S.
- Adult age range: Under 35

CHARACTERISTICS: Bedrock America consists of young, economically challenged families in small, isolated towns located throughout the nation's heartland. With modest educations, sprawling families, and blue-collar jobs, many of these residents struggle to make ends meet. One quarter live in mobile homes. One in three haven't finished high school. Rich in scenery, Bedrock America is a haven for fishing, hunting, hiking, and camping.

LIFESTYLE TRAITS:

- Go freshwater fishing
- Buy kids' bicycles
- Read baby magazines
- Watch *Days of Our Lives*
- Drive a Chevy S10 pickup

Source: Courtesy of Claritas Inc.

Geodemographic segmentation is most useful when an advertiser's or marketer's best prospects (in terms of consumer personalities, goals, and interests) can be isolated in terms of where they live. However, for products and services used by a broad cross section of the American public, other segmentation schemes may be more productive.

SRI consulting business intelligence's (SRIC–BI's) and VALS™ system

Drawing on Maslow's need hierarchy and the concept of social character, in the late 1970s researchers at SRI International (**www.sric-bi.com**) developed a generalized segmentation scheme of the American population known as the values and lifestyle (**VALS™**) system. This original system was designed to explain the dynamics of societal change, was based on social values, and was quickly adapted as a marketing tool.

In 1989 the VALS system was revised to focus more explicitly on explaining consumer purchasing behavior. The VALS typology classifies the American adult popu-

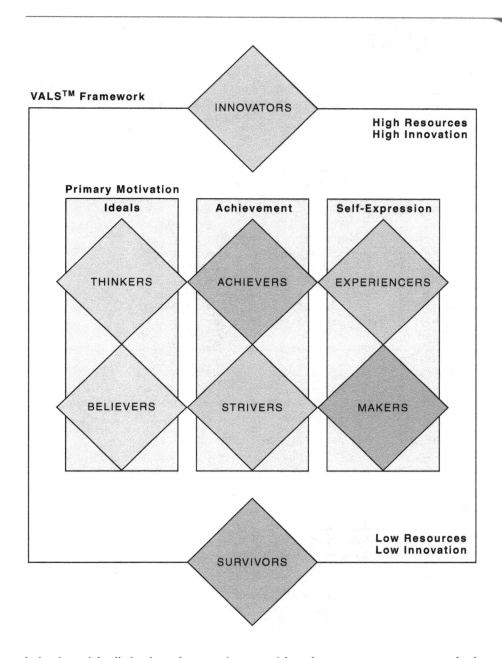

FIGURE 4.4

**Summary Diagram
of SRI VALS™
Segments**

Source: Reprinted with
permission of SRI Consulting
Business Intelligence.

lation into eight distinctive subgroups (segments) based on consumer responses to both
attitudinal and demographic questions. Figure 4.4 depicts the current VALS classification scheme. Examining the scheme, from left to right (Figure 4.4), the diagram identifies
three *primary motivations*: the *ideals motivated* (these consumer segments are guided by
knowledge and principles), the *achievement motivated* (these consumer segments are
looking for products and services that demonstrate success to their peers), and the *self-
expression motivated* (these consumer segments desire social or physical activity, variety,
and risk).[28] Furthermore, each of these three major self-motivations represents distinct
attitudes, lifestyles, and decision-making styles. Refocusing and examining Figure 4.4,
from top to bottom, the diagram reveals a kind of continuum in terms of resources and
innovation—that is, *high resources-high innovation* (on the top) to *low resources-low*
innovation (on the bottom). This range of resources/innovation (again, from most to
least) include the range of psychological, physical, demographic, and material means and

TABLE 4.14	A Brief Description of the Eight VALS™ New Edition Segments

INNOVATORS

Innovators are successful, sophisticated, take-charge people with high self-esteem. Because they have such abundant resources, they exhibit all three primary motivations in varying degrees. They are change leaders and are the most receptive to new ideas and technologies. Their purchases reflect cultivated tastes for upscale, niche products and services.

THINKERS*   Motivated by ideals; high resources

Thinkers are mature, satisfied, comfortable, and reflective. They tend to be well educated and actively seek out information in the decision-making process. They favor durability, functionality, and value in products.

BELIEVERS   Motivated by ideals; low resources

Believers are strongly traditional and respect rules and authority. Because they are fundamentally conservative, they are slow to change and technology averse. They choose familiar products and established brands.

ACHIEVERS   Motivated by achievement; high resources

Achievers have goal-oriented lifestyles that center on family and career. They avoid situations that encourage a high degree of stimulation or change. They prefer premium products that demonstrate success to their peers.

STRIVERS   Motivated by achievement; low resources

Strivers are trendy and fun loving. They have little discretionary income and tend to have narrow interests. They favor stylish products that emulate the purchases of people with greater material wealth.

EXPERIENCERS   Motivated by self-expression; high resources

Experiencers appreciate the unconventional. They are active and impulsive, seeking stimulation from the new, offbeat, and risky. They spend a comparatively high proportion of their income on fashion, socializing, and entertainment.

MAKERS   Motivated by self-expression; low resources

Makers value practicality and self-sufficiency. They choose hands-on constructive activities and spend leisure time with family and close friends. Because they prefer value to luxury, they buy basic products.

SURVIVORS

Survivors lead narrowly focused lives. Because they have the fewest resources, they do not exhibit a primary motivation and often feel powerless. They are primarily concerned about safety and security, so they tend to be brand loyal and buy discounted merchandise.

*VALS™ segments the U.S. English-speaking population age 18 or older into eight consumer groups. Their primary motivation and ability to express themselves in the marketplace distinguish the groups.

Source: Reprinted with permission of SRI Consulting Business Intelligence.

capacities consumers have to draw upon, including education, income, self-confidence, health, eagerness to buy, and energy level, as well as the consumer's propensity to try new products.

All eight VALS segments (defined in Table 4.14) contain between 10 and 17 percent of the U.S. adult population, with Believers, at 17 percent, being the largest VALS group. In terms of consumer characteristics, the eight VALS segments differ in some important

TABLE 4.15	Representative VALS™ Projects

COMMERCIALIZATION

- A European luxury automobile manufacturer used VALS to identify online, mobile applications that would appeal to affluent, early-adopter consumers within the next five years. VALS research identified early-adopter groups and explored their reactions to a variety of mobile services for use in automobiles. The VALS analysis enabled the company to prioritize applications for development and determine the best strategic alliances to pursue.
- A major telecommunications-product company used VALS to select an early-adopter target for a new telecommunications concept. VALS enabled the company to develop the product prototype and prioritize features and benefits, with a focus on the early-adopter target. The company used VALS to select the best name and logo, choose an overall positioning strategy, and set an initial price point.

POSITIONING

- A major stockbrokerage firm focused on providing excellent service to a select group of affluent consumers used VALS to redefine its image and develop a new corporate slogan. Within 18 months, advertising recall scores increased dramatically from 8% to 55%.
- A Minnesota medical center planned to offer a new line of service: cosmetic surgery. It used VALS to identify target consumers (those most interested and able to afford the service). By understanding the underlying motivations of the target, the center and its ad agency were able to develop a compelling selling proposition. The resulting advertising was so successful that just a few weeks into the campaign, the center exceeded its scheduling capabilities.

COMMUNICATIONS

- U.S. long-distance carrier used VALS to select its spokesperson in a major television campaign to increase its customer base. By understanding consumers who are heavy users of long-distance service, the company was able to select a spokesperson to whom the target could relate.
- An electric utility used VALS to increase participation in its energy-conservation program by developing a targeted direct mail campaign. Two distinctly different VALS segments were key targets. By developing unique strategies for each audience and identifying ZIP codes with high percentages of each target, the utility reported a 25% increase in participation.

Source: Reprinted with permission of SRI Consulting Business Intelligence.

ways. For instance, *Believers* tend to buy American-made products and are slow to alter their consumption-related habits, whereas *Innovators* are drawn to top-of-the-line and new products, especially innovative technologies. Therefore, it is not surprising that marketers of intelligent in-vehicle technologies (e.g., global positioning devices) must first target *Innovators*, because they are early adopters of new products.

In addition to the U.S. VALS system, there is a Japan VALS system and a U.K. VALS system. GeoVALS™ estimates the proportion of the eight U.S. VALS types by U.S. zip code and by black group.

To conclude our discussion of VALS, Table 4.15 presents a brief description of a number of different strategic applications of VALS.

Yankelovich mindbase® segmentation

Starting with their Monitor Survey of American Values and Attitudes, Yankelovich researchers have over the years created a number of different market segmentation methodologies that focus on household consumers (**see www.yankelovich.com**). A relatively recent effort has been the revision of the Yankelovich Mindbase,® which consists of eight consumer segments (see Table 4.16), and additional three smaller subsegments for each of the eight segments (for a total of 24 segments). A particularly attractive direct marketing feature of this segmentation framework is that it has been employed to categories the members of selected consumer databases (which contain the names and addresses of consumers who have been categories in terms of their Mindbase segmentation membership).

TABLE 4.16	**An Overview Profile of the Eight Yankelovich Mindbase® Segments**

SEGMENT 1—EXPRESSIVE CONSUMERS (11.1% OF THE U.S. POPULATION)

Personal Motto "Carpe Diem"

Profile:

Members of this segment see themselves as stylish, daring, and intense. They make an effort to live life to the fullest. They strive to reveal who they are to those they come in contact with—"It's who I am and I'm not afraid to express myself."

As shoppers they are open to the opinions of their friends; however, they personally look for brands that show their friends that they are "in the know." The interest in identifying "hot styles," and search magazines and online, and specialty stores and catalogs for what is new and in-style.

They are open to marketers who will entertain them, offer them "Stuff" that's new and that fits their personal definition of style.

Traits that sum them up:

-Bold

-Fun over work

-Active imagination

-Seek novelty

Their Demographics:

-Median age is 22

-Median income is $56,000

-Not married—68%

-Have children—37%

SEGMENT 2—DRIVEN CONSUMERS (14.9% OF THE U.S. POPULATION)

Personal Motto "Nothing ventured, nothing gained"

Profile:

Members of this segment are ambitious and working towards achieving their personal dreams and goals. They have an entrepreneurial spirit and seek to be the best in what they do at home and at work. They are well organized and self motivated to accomplish what they set out to do. They have a "life plan" and they are always working towards reaching it.

As consumers they especially like tools that help them achieve and accomplish. They like electronic gadgets because they are fun and because they are also useful.

They are open to marketers who will help them reach their dreams and goals.

Traits that sum them up:

-Looking for ways to excel

-Value education and personal growth

-See themselves as "workaholics"

-Wants to be seen as "unconventional"

TABLE 4.16	Continued

Their Demographics:

-Median age is 22

-Median income is $56,000

-Married—57%

-Have children—58%

SEGMENT 3—AT CAPACITY (12.0% OF THE U.S. POPULATION)

Personal Motto "Time is of the essence"

Profile:

This third segment consists of individuals who see their lives as busy and hectic and wish to simplify and take control of things. Besides reducing their obligations, a high priority is to invest in themselves and be more available to their families.

When shopping, online or in stores, convenience is especially important. They also demand excellent service, variety or choices, and even bargain.

Traits that sum them up:

-Seek control

-Crave to simplify and eliminate the nonessential

-Ambitious in their careers and desiring a more flexible work schedule

-Wish to be involved in their communities

Their Demographics:

-Median age is 32

-Median income is $50,000

-Married—67%

-Have children—75%

SEGMENT 4—ROCK STEADY CONSUMERS (11.3% OF THE U.S. POPULATION)

Personal Motto "Do the Right Thing"

Profile:

Members of this segment see themselves living a "contented life." They are content with themselves and their families. They see themselves as "dependable" and "generous" people, who are dedicated to enhancing their homes (by decorating and do-it-yourself projects).

As shoppers they do not like to be pressured nor do they pay much attention to "marketing tactics," rather they select retailers that give them a sense of providing quality products and good value.

Traits that sum them up:

-Happily married and spend their time at home

-Easygoing people

-They follow the rules

-They trust their instincts

Their Demographics:

-Median age is 45

-Median income is $67,000

-Married—80%

-Have children—85%

(Continued)

TABLE 4.16	Continued

SEGMENT 5—DOWN TO EARTH CONSUMERS (12.8% OF THE U.S. POPULATION)

Personal Motto "Easy on down the road"

Profile:

Members of this fifth segment seek to define their own path (their future) and want to maintain control over their own destiny. They are respectful of an individual having the right to have their own point of view. They are satisfied with their own lives and take every day as it comes. They are venturesome and interested in exploring other viewpoints, as well as new experiences.

In terms of consuming, members of this segment seek to "treat" themselves by buying "little things" (e.g., buying a piece of jewelry) or relaxing at home, possibly listening to music.

Traits that sum them up:

-Seek to "stretch" themselves

-Enjoy people with different viewpoints

-Don't do things just because they are "mainstream"

-Relax and take it easy on the weekends

Their Demographics:

-Median age is 44

-Median income is $55,000

-Married—64%

-Have children—76%

SEGMENT 6—SOPHISTICATED CONSUMERS (11.8% OF THE U.S. POPULATION)

Personal Motto "Sense and sensibility"

Profile:

This segment perceives themselves as being "intelligent," "confident," "sensitive," and as creative and expressive. Their work consumes most of their time and they define much of who they are through their work. Outside of work they seek to rejuvenate themselves by traveling, cooking, and spending time with their pets. For them new experiences tend to be more important than acquiring more "things."

They see themselves as being demanding consumers—they research what to buy and they expect the best in terms of quality, convenience, and service. They are also very vocal if a shopping experience falls short of what they were expecting.

Traits that sum them up:

-Value integrity

-Work to reduce personal stress

-Want to be a role model for others

-Are open-minded and seek new experiences

Their Demographics:

-Median age is 48

-Median income is $56,000

-Married—59%

-Have children—70%

TABLE 4.16	Continued

SEGMENT 7—MEASURE TWICE (11.9% OF THE U.S. POPULATION)

Personal Motto "An ounce of prevention"

Profile:

Segment 7 people are careful planners. They plan when it comes to their health, their financial well-being, and their future security. They remain open to new ideas as to ways to improve their lives, even to start a new career when they retire. They like to be up-to-date in terms of current events, and are active with regard to their hobbies and leisure-time pursuits.

They favor department stores and catalog shopping.

Traits that sum them up:

-On top of taking care of their health and financial security

-They have found a balanced life

-They are open to a new career when they retire

-They see themselves as "good citizens"

Their Demographics:

-Median age is 65

-Median income is $52,000

-Married—65%

-Have children—85%

SEGMENT 8—DEVOTED CONSUMERS (14.2% OF THE U.S. POPULATION)

Personal Motto "Home is where the heart is"

Profile:

The eighth and final segment is made up of individuals who see themselves as being "traditional" people. They are content with their lives, and do not feel that they are really missing anything. Their lives appear to be what they expected their lives to be. They are quite spiritual and have a great deal of faith in their religion. They hesitate to try something different, especially new technology; rather they are comfortable with what is familiar, especially their homes.

When shopping they favor familiar establishments with low prices.

Traits that sum them up:

-Share religious values with others

-Prefer things that are already proven trustworthy

-Feel closer to people with the same background

-Seen as feeling "complete"

Their Demographics:

-Median age is 67

-Median income is $32,000

-Married—60%

-Have children—85%

Source: "Yankelovich Mindbase® Segment Profiles, Introductory Information," PDF files supplied by Yankelovich, January 2005.

Criteria for effective targeting of market segments

The previous sections have described various bases on which consumers can be clustered into homogeneous market segments. The next challenge for the marketer is to select one or more segments to target with an appropriate marketing mix. To be an effective target, a market segment should be (1) identifiable, (2) sufficient (in terms of size), (3) stable or growing, and (4) accessible (reachable) in terms of both media and cost.

Identification

To divide the market into separate segments on the basis of a series of *common* or *shared* needs or characteristics that are relevant to the product or service, a marketer must be able to identify these relevant characteristics. Some segmentation variables, such as *geography* (location) or *demographics* (age, gender, occupation, race), are relatively easy to identify or are even observable. Others, such as *education, income,* or *marital status,* can be determined through questionnaires. However, other characteristics, such as *benefits sought* or *lifestyle,* are more difficult to identify. A knowledge of consumer behavior is especially useful to marketers who use such intangible consumer characteristics as the basis for market segmentation.

Sufficiency

For a market segment to be a worthwhile target, it must consist of a sufficient number of people to warrant tailoring a product or promotional campaign to its specific needs or interests. To estimate the size of each segment under consideration, marketers often use secondary demographic data, such as that provided by the United States Census Bureau (available at many libraries and online via the Internet), or they undertake a probability survey whose findings can be projected to the total market.

Stability

Most marketers prefer to target consumer segments that are relatively stable in terms of demographic and psychological factors and are likely to grow larger over time. They prefer to avoid "fickle" segments that are unpredictable in embracing fads. For example, teens are a sizable and easily identifiable market segment, eager to buy, able to spend, and easily reached. Yet, by the time a marketer produces merchandise for a popular teenage fad, interest in it may have waned.

Accessibility

A fourth requirement for effective targeting is accessibility, which means that marketers must be able to reach the market segments they want to target in an economical way. Despite the wide availability of special-interest magazines and cable TV programs, marketers are constantly looking for new media that will enable them to reach their target markets with minimum waste of circulation and competition. One way this can be accomplished is via the Internet. Upon the request of the consumer, a growing number of Web sites periodically send e-mail messages concerning a subject of special interest to the computer user. For example, a resident of Houston, Texas, who likes to take short vacation trips, might have Continental Airlines e-mail her the coming weekend's special airfare, hotel, and rent-a-car deals.

Implementing segmentation strategies

Firms that use market segmentation can pursue a *concentrated* marketing strategy or a *differentiated* marketing strategy. In certain instances, they might use a **countersegmentation** strategy.

Concentrated versus differentiated marketing

Once an organization has identified its most promising market segments, it must decide whether to target one segment or several segments. The premise behind market segmentation is that each targeted segment receives a specially designed marketing mix, that is, a specially tailored product, price, distribution network, and/or promotional campaign. Targeting several segments using individual marketing mixes is called **differentiated marketing**; targeting just one segment with a unique marketing mix is called **concentrated marketing**.

Differentiated marketing is a highly appropriate segmentation strategy for financially strong companies that are well established in a product category and competitive with other firms that also are strong in the category (e.g., soft drinks, automobiles, or detergents). However, if a company is small or new to the field, concentrated marketing is probably a better bet. A company can survive and prosper by filling a niche not occupied by stronger companies. For example, Viadent toothpaste has become a leader in the small but increasingly important submarket of the overall tooth care market that focuses on products that fight gingivitis and other gum diseases.

Countersegmentation

Sometimes companies find that they must reconsider the extent to which they are segmenting their markets. They might find that some segments have contracted over time to the point that they do not warrant an individually designed marketing program. In such cases, the company seeks to discover a more generic need or consumer characteristic that would apply to the members of two or more segments and recombine those segments into a larger single segment that could be targeted with an individually tailored product or promotional campaign. This is called a *countersegmentation* strategy. Some business schools with wide course offerings in each department were forced to adopt a countersegmentation strategy when they discovered that students simply did not have enough available credits to take a full spectrum of in-depth courses in their major area of study. As a result, some courses had to be canceled each semester because of inadequate registration. For some schools, a countersegmentation strategy effectively solved the problem (e.g., by combining *advertising, publicity, sales promotion*, and *personal selling* courses into a single course called Promotion).

chapter 5

> Customer Relationships

Companywide strategic planning: Defining marketing's role

Each company must find the game plan for long-run survival and growth that makes the most sense given its specific situation, opportunities, objectives, and resources. This is the focus of **strategic planning**—the process of developing and maintaining a strategic fit between the organization's goals and capabilities and its changing marketing opportunities.

Strategic planning sets the stage for the rest of the planning in the firm. Companies usually prepare annual plans, long-range plans, and strategic plans. The annual and long-range plans deal with the company's current businesses and how to keep them going. In contrast, the strategic plan involves adapting the firm to take advantage of opportunities in its constantly changing environment.

At the corporate level, the company starts the strategic planning process by defining its overall purpose and mission (see Figure 5.1). This mission then is turned into detailed supporting objectives that guide the whole company. Next, headquarters decides what portfolio of businesses and products is best for the company and how much support to give each one. In turn, each business and product develops detailed marketing and other departmental plans that support the companywide plan. Thus, marketing planning occurs at the business-unit, product, and market levels. It supports company strategic planning with more detailed plans for specific marketing opportunities.

Strategic planning
The process of developing and maintaining a strategic fit between the organization's goals and capabilities and its changing marketing opportunities.

Defining a market-oriented mission

An organization exists to accomplish something. At first, it has a clear purpose or mission, but over time its mission may become unclear as the organization grows, adds new products and markets, or faces new conditions in the environment. When management senses that the organization is drifting, it must renew its search for purpose. It is time to ask: What is our business? Who is the customer? What do consumers value? What *should* our business be? These simple-sounding questions are among the most difficult the company will ever have to answer. Successful companies continuously raise these questions and answer them carefully and completely.

Many organizations develop formal mission statements that answer these questions. A **mission statement** is a statement of the organization's purpose—what it wants to accomplish in the larger environment. A clear mission statement acts as an "invisible hand" that guides people in the organization. Studies have shown that firms with well-crafted mission statements have better organizational and financial performance.[2]

Some companies define their missions myopically in product or technology terms ("We make and sell furniture" or "We are a chemical-processing firm"). But mission statements should be *market oriented* and defined in terms of customer needs. Products and technologies eventually become outdated, but basic market needs may last forever.

A market-oriented mission statement defines the business in terms of satisfying basic customer needs. For example, Nike isn't just a shoe and apparel manufacturer—it wants "to bring inspiration and innovation to every athlete* in the world. (*If you have a

Mission statement
A statement of the organization's purpose—what it wants to accomplish in the larger environment.

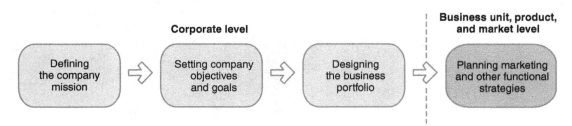

Corporate level			Business unit, product, and market level
Defining the company mission	Setting company objectives and goals	Designing the business portfolio	Planning marketing and other functional strategies

Steps in Strategic Planning **FIGURE 5.1**

body, you are an athlete.)" Likewise, eBay's mission isn't simply to hold online auctions and trading. Its mission is "to provide a global trading platform where practically anyone can trade practically anything—you can get *it* on eBay." It wants to be a unique Web community in which people can safely shop around, have fun, and get to know each other, for example, by chatting at the eBay Café. Table 5.1 provides several other examples of product-oriented versus market-oriented business definitions.[3]

Management should avoid making its mission too narrow or too broad. A pencil manufacturer that says it is in the communication equipment business is stating its mission too broadly. Missions should be *realistic*. Singapore Airlines would be deluding itself if it adopted the mission to become the world's largest airline. Missions should also be *specific*. Many mission statements are written for public relations purposes and lack specific, workable guidelines. Too often, they "are platitudes incorporating quality and customer satisfaction, often with an 'employees are our most important assets' kicker," say one analyst. "They're too long to remember, too vague to be meaningful, and too dull to inspire."[4] Such generic statements sound good but provide little real guidance or inspiration.

Missions should fit the *market environment*. The Girl Scouts of America would not recruit successfully in today's environment with its former mission: "to prepare young girls for motherhood and wifely duties." Today, its mission is to build girls of courage,

TABLE 5.1	Market-Oriented Business Definitions	
COMPANY	**PRODUCT-ORIENTED DEFINITION**	**MARKET-ORIENTED DEFINITION**
Amazon.com	We sell books, videos, CDs, toys, consumer electronics, and other products online.	We make the Internet buying experience fast, easy, and enjoyable—we're the place where you can discover anything you want to buy online.
America Online	We provide online services.	We create customer connectivity, anytime, anywhere.
Disney	We run theme parks.	We create fantasies— a place where America still works the way it's supposed to.
eBay	We hold online auctions.	We provide a global marketplace where practically anyone can trade practically anything—a Web community where people can shop around, have fun, and get to know each other.
Home Depot	We sell tools and home repair and improvement items.	We empower consumers to achieve the homes of their dreams.
Charles Schwab	We are a brokerage firm.	We are the guardian of our customers' financial dreams.
Revlon	We make cosmetics.	We sell lifestyle and self-expression; success and status; memories, hopes, and dreams.
Ritz-Carlton Hotels	We rent rooms.	We create the Ritz-Carlton experience—one that enlivens the senses, instills well-being, and fulfills even the unexpressed needs of our guests.
Wal-Mart	We run discount stores.	We deliver low prices every day and help people to save money so they can live better.

confidence, and character, who make the world a better place. The organization should also base its mission on its *distinctive competencies*. Finally, mission statements should be *motivating*. A company's mission should not be stated as making more sales or profits— profits are only a reward for undertaking a useful activity. A company's employees need to feel that their work is significant and that it contributes to people's lives. For example, Microsoft's aim is to help people to "realize their potential"—"your potential, our passion" says the company. Target's mission is to "Expect more. Pay less."

Setting company objectives and goals

The company needs to turn its mission into detailed supporting objectives for each level of management. Each manager should have objectives and be responsible for reaching them. For example, giant chemical company BASF makes and markets a diverse product mix includes everything from chemicals, plastics, and agricultural products to crude oil and natural gas. But BASF does more than just make chemicals. Its mission is to work with commercial customers in numerous industries to help them employ these chemicals to find innovative solutions and better products for their consumers.

This broad mission leads to a hierarchy of objectives, including business objectives and marketing objectives. BASF's overall objective is to build profitable customer relationships by developing better products. It does this by investing in research—nearly 10 percent of BASF's employees work in research and development. R&D is expensive and requires improved profits to plow back into research programs. So improving profits becomes another major BASF objective. Profits can be improved by increasing sales or reducing costs. Sales can be increased by improving the company's share of domestic and international markets. These goals then become the company's current marketing objectives.[5]

Marketing strategies and programs must be developed to support these marketing objectives. To increase its market share, BASF might increase its products' availability and promotion in existing markets. To enter new global markets, the company can create new local partnerships within targeted countries. For example, BASF's Agricultural Products division has begun targeting China's farmers with a line of insecticides. To bring the right crop protection solutions to these farmers, BASF has formed working relationships with several Chinese agricultural research organizations, such as Nanjing Agricultural University.[6]

These are BASF's broad marketing strategies. Each broad marketing strategy must then be defined in greater detail. For example, increasing the product's promotion may require more salespeople, advertising, and public relations efforts; if so, both requirements will need to be spelled out. In this way, the firm's mission is translated into a set of objectives for the current period.

Designing the business portfolio

Guided by the company's mission statement and objectives, management now must plan its **business portfolio**—the collection of businesses and products that make up the company. The best business portfolio is the one that best fits the company's strengths and weaknesses to opportunities in the environment. Business portfolio planning involves two steps. First, the company must analyze its *current* business portfolio and decide which businesses should receive more, less, or no investment. Second, it must shape the *future* portfolio by developing strategies for growth and downsizing.

Business portfolio
The collection of businesses and products that make up the company.

Analyzing the Current Business Portfolio

The major activity in strategic planning is business **portfolio analysis**, whereby management evaluates the products and businesses making up the company. The company will want to put strong resources into its more profitable businesses and phase down or drop its weaker ones.

Management's first step is to identify the key businesses making up the company. These can be called the strategic business units. A *strategic business unit* (SBU) is a unit of the company that has a separate mission and objectives and that can be planned

Portfolio analysis
The process by which management evaluates the products and businesses making up the company.

independently from other company businesses. An SBU can be a company division, a product line within a division, or sometimes a single product or brand.

The next step in business portfolio analysis calls for management to assess the attractiveness of its various SBUs and decide how much support each deserves. Most companies are well advised to "stick to their knitting" when designing their business portfolios. It's usually a good idea to focus on adding products and businesses that fit closely with the firm's core philosophy and competencies.

The purpose of strategic planning is to find ways in which the company can best use its strengths to take advantage of attractive opportunities in the environment. So most standard portfolio analysis methods evaluate SBUs on two important dimensions—the attractiveness of the SBU's market or industry and the strength of the SBU's position in that market or industry. The best-known portfolio-planning method was developed by the Boston Consulting Group, a leading management consulting firm.[7]

The Boston Consulting Group Approach   Using the Boston Consulting Group (BCG) approach, a company classifies all its SBUs according to the **growth-share matrix** shown in Figure 5.2. On the vertical axis, *market growth rate* provides a measure of market attractiveness. On the horizontal axis, *relative market share* serves as a measure of company strength in the market. The growth-share matrix defines four types of SBUs:

> *Stars.* Stars are high-growth, high-share businesses or products. They often need heavy investment to finance their rapid growth. Eventually their growth will slow down, and they will turn into cash cows.
>
> *Cash cows.* Cash cows are low-growth, high-share businesses or products. These established and successful SBUs need less investment to hold their market share. Thus, they produce a lot of cash that the company uses to pay its bills and to support other SBUs that need investment.
>
> *Question marks.* Question marks are low-share business units in high-growth markets. They require a lot of cash to hold their share, let alone increase it. Management must think hard about which question marks it should try to build into stars and which should be phased out.
>
> *Dogs.* Dogs are low-growth, low-share businesses and products. They may generate enough cash to maintain themselves but do not promise to be large sources of cash.

The 10 circles in the growth-share matrix represent a company's 10 current SBUs. The company has two stars, two cash cows, three question marks, and three dogs. The areas of the circles are proportional to the SBU's dollar sales. This company is in fair shape, although not in good shape. It wants to invest in the more promising question

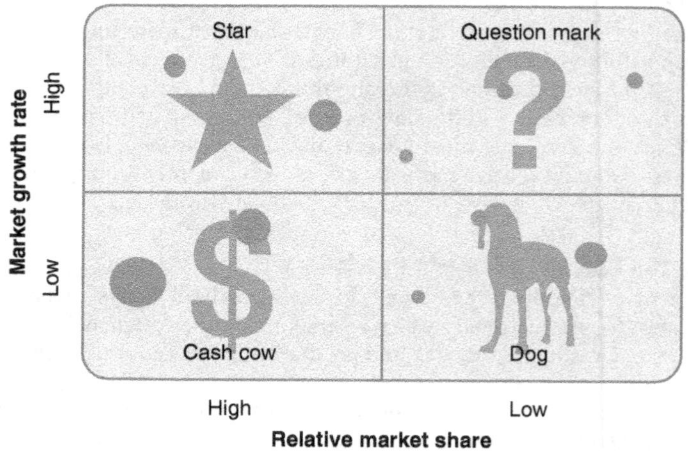

Growth-share matrix
A portfolio-planning method that evaluates a company's strategic business units in terms of their market growth rate and relative market share. SBUs are classified as stars, cash cows, question marks, or dogs.

The BCG Growth-Share Matrix

FIGURE 5.2

marks to make them stars and to maintain the stars so that they will become cash cows as their markets mature. Fortunately, it has two good-sized cash cows. Income from these cash cows will help finance the company's question marks, stars, and dogs. The company should take some decisive action concerning its dogs and its question marks. The picture would be worse if the company had no stars, if it had too many dogs, or if it had only one weak cash cow.

Once it has classified its SBUs, the company must determine what role each will play in the future. One of four strategies can be pursued for each SBU. The company can invest more in the business unit in order to *build* its share. Or it can invest just enough to *hold* the SBU's share at the current level. It can *harvest* the SBU, milking its short-term cash flow regardless of the long-term effect. Finally, the company can *divest* the SBU by selling it or phasing it out and using the resources elsewhere.

As time passes, SBUs change their positions in the growth-share matrix. Each SBU has a life cycle. Many SBUs start out as question marks and move into the star category if they succeed. They later become cash cows as market growth falls, then finally die off or turn into dogs toward the end of their life cycle. The company needs to add new products and units continuously so that some of them will become stars and, eventually, cash cows that will help finance other SBUs.

Problems with Matrix Approaches The BCG and other formal methods revolutionized strategic planning. However, such centralized approaches have limitations. They can be difficult, time consuming, and costly to implement. Management may find it difficult to define SBUs and measure market share and growth. In addition, these approaches focus on classifying *current* businesses but provide little advice for *future* planning.

Because of such problems, many companies have dropped formal matrix methods in favor of more customized approaches that are better suited to their specific situations. Moreover, unlike former strategic-planning efforts, which rested mostly in the hands of senior managers at company headquarters, today's strategic planning has been decentralized. Increasingly, companies are placing responsibility for strategic planning in the hands of cross-functional teams of divisional managers who are close to their markets.

For example, consider The Walt Disney Company. Most people think of Disney as theme parks and wholesome family entertainment. But in the mid-1980s, Disney set up a powerful, centralized strategic planning group to guide the company's direction and growth. Over the next two decades, the strategic planning group turned The Walt Disney Company into a huge but diverse collection of media and entertainment businesses. The sprawling Disney grew to include everything from theme resorts and film studios (Walt Disney Pictures, Touchstone Pictures, Hollywood Pictures, and others) to media networks (ABC plus Disney Channel, ESPN, A&E, History Channel, and a half dozen others) to consumer products and a cruise line. The newly transformed company proved hard to manage and performed unevenly. Recently, Disney's new chief executive disbanded the centralized strategic planning unit, decentralizing its functions to Disney division managers.

Developing strategies for growth and downsizing

Beyond evaluating current businesses, designing the business portfolio involves finding businesses and products the company should consider in the future. Companies need growth if they are to compete more effectively, satisfy their stakeholders, and attract top talent. "Growth is pure oxygen," states one executive. "It creates a vital, enthusiastic corporation where people see genuine opportunity." At the same time, a firm must be careful not to make growth itself an objective. The company's objective must be "profitable growth."

Marketing has the main responsibility for achieving profitable growth for the company. Marketing must identify, evaluate, and select market opportunities and lay down strategies for capturing them. One useful device for identifying growth opportunities is the **product/market expansion grid**, shown in Figure 5.3.[8]

First, Starbucks management might consider whether the company can achieve deeper **market penetration**—making more sales to current customers without changing

Product/market expansion grid
A portfolio-planning tool for identifying company growth opportunities through market penetration, market development, product development, or diversification.

Market penetration
A strategy for company growth by increasing sales of current products to current market segments without changing the product.

FIGURE 5.3

The Product/Market
Expansion Grid

	Existing products	New products
Existing markets	Market penetration	Product development
New markets	Market development	Diversification

its products. It might add new stores in current market areas to make it easier for more customers to visit. In fact, Starbucks is adding an average of 46 stores a week internationally, 52 weeks a year—its ultimate goal is 40,000 stores worldwide. Improvements in advertising, prices, service, menu selection, or store design might encourage customers to stop by more often, stay longer, or to buy more during each visit. For example, Starbucks has added drive-through windows to many of its stores. A Starbucks Card lets customers prepay for coffee and snacks or give the gift of Starbucks to family and friends. And to get customers to hang around longer, Starbucks offers wireless Internet access in most of its stores.

Market development

A strategy for company growth by identifying and developing new market segments for current company products.

Second, Starbucks management might consider possibilities for **market development**—identifying and developing new markets for its current products. For instance, managers could review new *demographic markets.* Perhaps new groups—such as seniors or ethnic groups—could be encouraged to visit Starbucks coffee shops for the first time or to buy more on each visit. Managers also could review new *geographical markets.* Starbucks is now expanding swiftly into new U.S. markets, especially smaller cities. And it's expanding rapidly in new global markets. In 1996, Starbucks had only 11 coffeehouses outside North America. It now has nearly 4,000, with plenty of room to grow. "We're just scratching the surface in China," says Starbucks' CEO. "We have [250] stores and the potential for more than 2,000 there."

Product development

A strategy for company growth by offering modified or new products to current market segments.

Third, management could consider **product development**—offering modified or new products to current markets. For example, Starbucks recently added fruit juice Frappuchino beverages to its menu to draw in more non-coffee drinkers and breakfast sandwiches to bolster its morning business. To capture consumers who brew their coffee at home, Starbucks has also pushed into America's supermarket aisles. It has a co-branding deal with Kraft, under which Starbucks roasts and packages its coffee and Kraft markets and distributes it. And the company is forging ahead into new consumer categories. For example, it has brought out a line of Starbucks coffee liqueurs.

Diversification

A strategy for company growth through starting up or acquiring businesses outside the company's current products and markets.

Fourth, Starbucks might consider **diversification**—starting up or buying businesses outside of its current products and markets. For example, Starbucks' 1999 purchase of Hear Music was so successful that it spurred the creation of a new Starbucks Entertainment division. Beginning with just selling and playing compilation CDs, Starbucks' Hear Music now has its own XM Satellite Radio station. It is also installing kiosks (called Media Bars) in select Starbucks stores that let customers download music and burn their own CDs while sipping their lattes. The newly formed Hear Music label has recently signed inaugural CDs by such legendary artists as Paul McCartney and Joni Mitchell.

In a more extreme diversification, Starbucks has partnered with Lion's Gate to coproduce movies and then market them in Starbucks coffeehouses. Starbucks supported the partnership's first film, *Akeelah and the Bee,* by sprinkling flashcards around the stores, stamping the movie's logo on its coffee cups, and placing spelling-bee-caliber words on the store chalkboards. Such new ventures have left some analysts asking whether Starbucks is diversifying too broadly, at the risk of diluting its market focus. They are asking, "What do movies have to do with Starbucks coffee and the Starbucks experience?"

Companies must not only develop strategies for *growing* their business portfolios but also strategies for **downsizing** them. There are many reasons that a firm might want to abandon products or markets. The market environment might change, making some of the company's products or markets less profitable. The firm may have grown too fast or entered areas where it lacks experience. This can occur when a firm enters too many foreign markets without the proper research or when a company introduces new products that do not offer superior customer value. Finally, some products or business units simply age and die.

When a firm finds brands or businesses that are unprofitable or that no longer fit its overall strategy, it must carefully prune, harvest, or divest them. Weak businesses usually require a disproportionate amount of management attention. Managers should focus on promising growth opportunities, not fritter away energy trying to salvage fading ones.

Downsizing
Reducing the business portfolio by eliminating products of business units that are not profitable or that no longer fit the company's overall strategy.

Planning marketing: Partnering to build customer relationships

The company's strategic plan establishes what kinds of businesses the company will operate in and its objectives for each. Then, within each business unit, more detailed planning takes place. The major functional departments in each unit—marketing, finance, accounting, purchasing, operations, information systems, human resources, and others—must work together to accomplish strategic objectives.

Marketing plays a key role in the company's strategic planning in several ways. First, marketing provides a guiding *philosophy*—the marketing concept—that suggests that company strategy should revolve around building profitable relationships with important consumer groups. Second, marketing provides *inputs* to strategic planners by helping to identify attractive market opportunities and by assessing the firm's potential to take advantage of them. Finally, within individual business units, marketing designs *strategies* for reaching the unit's objectives. Once the unit's objectives are set, marketing's task is to help carry them out profitably.

Customer value is the key ingredient in the marketer's formula for success. However, marketers alone cannot produce superior value for customers. Although marketing plays a leading role, it can be only a partner in attracting, keeping, and growing customers. In addition to *customer relationship management,* marketers must also practice *partner relationship management.* They must work closely with partners in other company departments to form an effective *value chain* that serves the customer. Moreover, they must partner effectively with other companies in the marketing system to form a competitively superior *value delivery network.* We now take a closer look at the concepts of a company value chain and value delivery network.

Partnering with other company departments

Each company department can be thought of as a link in the company's **value chain**.[9] That is, each department carries out value-creating activities to design, produce, market, deliver, and support the firm's products. The firm's success depends not only on how well each department performs its work but also on how well the various departments coordinate their activities.

For example, Wal-Mart's goal is to create customer value and satisfaction by providing shoppers with the products they want at the lowest possible prices. Marketers at Wal-Mart play an important role. They learn what customers need and stock the stores' shelves with the desired products at unbeatable low prices. They prepare advertising and merchandising programs and assist shoppers with customer service. Through these and other activities, Wal-Mart's marketers help deliver value to customers.

However, the marketing department needs help from the company's other departments. Wal-Mart's ability to offer the right products at low prices depends on the purchasing department's skill in developing the needed suppliers and buying from them at

Value chain
The series of departments that carry out value-creating activities to design, produce, market, deliver, and support a firm's products.

low cost. Wal-Mart's information technology department must provide fast and accurate information about which products are selling in each store. And its operations people must provide effective, low-cost merchandise handling.

A company's value chain is only as strong as its weakest link. Success depends on how well each department performs its work of adding customer value and on how well the activities of various departments are coordinated. At Wal-Mart, if purchasing can't obtain the lowest prices from suppliers, or if operations can't distribute merchandise at the lowest costs, then marketing can't deliver on its promise of lowest prices.

Ideally, then, a company's different functions should work in harmony to produce value for consumers. But, in practice, departmental relations are full of conflicts and misunderstandings. The marketing department takes the consumer's point of view. But when marketing tries to develop customer satisfaction, it can cause other departments to do a poorer job *in their terms*. Marketing department actions can increase purchasing costs, disrupt production schedules, increase inventories, and create budget headaches. Thus, the other departments may resist the marketing department's efforts.

Yet marketers must find ways to get all departments to "think consumer" and to develop a smoothly functioning value chain. Marketing managers need to work closely with managers of other functions to develop a system of functional plans under which the different departments can work together to accomplish the company's overall strategic objectives. The idea is to "maximize the customer experience across the organization and its various customer touch points," say a marketing consultant. Jack Welch, the highly regarded former GE CEO, told his employees: "Companies can't give job security. Only customers can!" He emphasized that all GE people, regardless of their department, have an impact on customer satisfaction and retention. His message: "If you are not thinking customer, you are not thinking."[10]

Marketing strategy and the marketing mix

The strategic plan defines the company's overall mission and objectives. Marketing's role and activities are shown in Figure 5.4, which summarizes the major activities involved in managing a customer-driven marketing strategy and the marketing mix.

Consumers stand in the center. The goal is to create value for customers and build profitable customer relationships. Next comes **marketing strategy**—the marketing logic by which the company hopes to create this customer value and achieve these profitable relationships. The company decides which customers it will serve (segmentation and targeting) and how (differentiation and positioning). It identifies the total market, then divides it into smaller segments, selects the most promising segments, and focuses on serving and satisfying customers in these segments.

Guided by marketing strategy, the company designs an integrated *marketing mix* made up of factors under its control—product, price, place, and promotion (the four Ps). To find the best marketing strategy and mix, the company engages in marketing analysis, planning, implementation, and control. Through these activities, the company watches and adapts to the actors and forces in the marketing environment. We will now look briefly at each activity. Then, in later chapters, we will discuss each one in more depth.

Customer-driven marketing strategy

To succeed in today's competitive marketplace, companies need to be customer centered. They must win customers from competitors, then keep and grow them by delivering greater value. But before it can satisfy consumers, a company must first understand their needs and wants. Thus, sound marketing requires a careful customer analysis.

Companies know that they cannot profitably serve all consumers in a given market—at least not all consumers in the same way. There are too many different kinds of consumers with too many different kinds of needs. And most companies are in a position to serve some segments better than others. Thus, each company must divide up the total market, choose the best segments, and design strategies for profitably serving chosen seg-

Marketing strategy
The marketing logic by which the business unit hopes to create customer value and achieve profitable customer relationships.

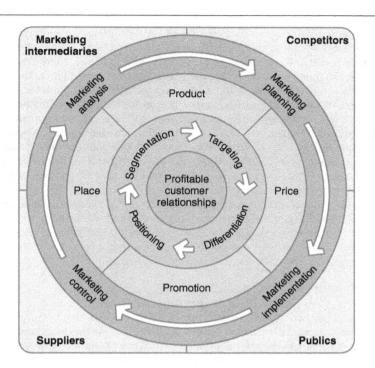

FIGURE 5.4

Managing Marketing Strategy and the Marketing Mix

ments. This process involves *market segmentation, market targeting, differentiation,* and *positioning*.

Market Segmentation

The market consists of many types of customers, products, and needs. The marketer must determine which segments offer the best opportunities. Consumers can be grouped and served in various ways based on geographic, demographic, psychographic, and behavioral factors. The process of dividing a market into distinct groups of buyers who have different needs, characteristics, or behavior who might require separate products or marketing programs is called **market segmentation**.

Every market has segments, but not all ways of segmenting a market are equally useful. For example, Tylenol would gain little by distinguishing between low-income and high-income pain reliever users if both respond the same way to marketing efforts. A **market segment** consists of consumers who respond in a similar way to a given set of marketing efforts. In the car market, for example, consumers who want the biggest, most comfortable car regardless of price make up one market segment. Consumers who care mainly about price and operating economy make up another segment. It would be difficult to make one car model that was the first choice of consumers in both segments. Companies are wise to focus their efforts on meeting the distinct needs of individual market segments.

Market Targeting

After a company has defined market segments, it can enter one or many of these segments. **Market targeting** involves evaluating each market segment's attractiveness and selecting one or more segments to enter. A company should target segments in which it can profitably generate the greatest customer value and sustain it over time.

A company with limited resources might decide to serve only one or a few special segments or "market niches." Such "nichers" specialize in serving customer segments that major competitors overlook or ignore. For example, Ferrari sells only 1,500 of its

Market segmentation
Dividing a market into distinct groups of buyers who have distinct needs, characteristics, or behavior and who might require separate products or marketing programs.

Market segment
A group of consumers who respond in a similar way to a given set of marketing efforts.

Market targeting
The process of evaluating each market segment's attractiveness and selecting one or more segments to enter.

very high-performance cars in the United States each year, but at very high prices—from an eye-opening $190,000 for its Ferrari F430 model to an absolutely astonishing $2 million for its FXX super sports car, which can be driven only on race tracks (it sold 10 in the United States last year). Most nichers aren't quite so exotic. White Wave, maker of Silk Soymilk, has found its niche as the nation's largest soymilk producer. And Veterinary Pet Insurance is tiny compared with the insurance industry giants, but it captures a profitable 60 percent share of all health insurance policies for our furry—or feathery—friends.

Alternatively, a company might choose to serve several related segments—perhaps those with different kinds of customers but with the same basic wants. Abercrombie & Fitch, for example, targets college students, teens, and kids with the same upscale, casual clothes and accessories in different outlets: the original Abercrombie & Fitch, Hollister, and Abercrombie. Or a large company might decide to offer a complete range of products to serve all market segments.

Most companies enter a new market by serving a single segment, and if this proves successful, they add segments. Large companies eventually seek full market coverage. They want to be the General Motors of their industry. GM says that it makes a car for every "person, purse, and personality." The leading company normally has different products designed to meet the special needs of each segment.

Market differentiation and positioning

After a company has decided which market segments to enter, it must decide how it will differentiate its market offering for each targeted segment and what positions it wants to occupy in those segments. A product's *position* is the place the product occupies, relative to competitors' products, in consumers' minds. Marketers want to develop unique market positions for their products. If a product is perceived to be exactly like others on the market, consumers would have no reason to buy it.

Positioning
Arranging for a product to occupy a clear, distinctive, and desirable place relative to competing products in the minds of target consumers.

Positioning is arranging for a product to occupy a clear, distinctive, and desirable place relative to competing products in the minds of target consumers. As one positioning expert puts it, positioning is "why a shopper will pay a little more for your brand."[13] Thus, marketers plan positions that distinguish their products from competing brands and give them the greatest advantage in their target markets.

Thus, Wal-Mart promises "save money, live better"; Target says "expect more, pay less." MasterCard gives you "priceless experiences"; and whether it's an everyday moment or the moment of a lifetime, "life takes Visa." And wireless provider Helio tells you "Don't call us a phone company. Don't call it a phone." Instead, Helio offers "advanced mobile services and exclusive, high-end, beautiful devices for consumers who have mobile at the center of their lives." Such deceptively simple statements form the backbone of a product's marketing strategy.

Differentiation
Actually differentiating the market offering to create superior customer value.

In positioning its product, the company first identifies possible customer value differences that provide competitive advantages upon which to build the position. The company can offer greater customer value either by charging lower prices than competitors do or by offering more benefits to justify higher prices. But if the company *promises* greater value, it must then *deliver* that greater value. Thus, effective positioning begins with **differentiation**— actually *differentiating* the company's market offering so that it gives consumers more value. Once the company has chosen a desired position, it must take strong steps to deliver and communicate that position to target consumers. The company's entire marketing program should support the chosen positioning strategy.

Developing an integrated marketing mix

Marketing mix
The set of controllable tactical marketing tools—product, price, place, and promotion—that the firm blends to produce the response it wants in the target market.

After deciding on its overall marketing strategy, the company is ready to begin planning the details of the marketing mix, one of the major concepts in modern marketing. The **marketing mix** is the set of controllable, tactical marketing tools that the firm blends to produce the response it wants in the target market. The marketing mix consists of everything the firm can do to influence the demand for its product. The many possibilities can be collected into four groups of variables known as the "four Ps": *product, price, place,* and *promotion.* Figure 5.5 shows the marketing tools under each P.

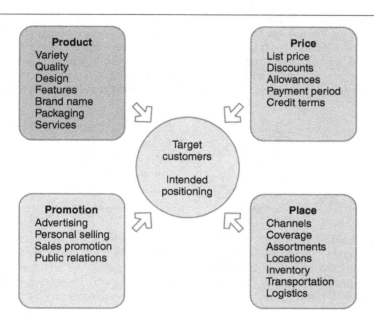

FIGURE 5.5

The Four *Ps* of the Marketing Mix

Product means the goods-and-services combination the company offers to the target market. Thus, a Ford Escape consists of nuts and bolts, spark plugs, pistons, headlights, and thousands of other parts. Ford offers several Escape models and dozens of optional features. The car comes fully serviced and with a comprehensive warranty that is as much a part of the product as the tailpipe.

Price is the amount of money customers must pay to obtain the product. Ford calculates suggested retail prices that its dealers might charge for each Escape. But Ford dealers rarely charge the full sticker price. Instead, they negotiate the price with each customer, offering discounts, trade-in allowances, and credit terms. These actions adjust prices for the current competitive situation and bring them into line with the buyer's perception of the car's value.

Place includes company activities that make the product available to target consumers. Ford partners with a large body of independently owned dealerships that sell the company's many different models. Ford selects its dealers carefully and supports them strongly. The dealers keep an inventory of Ford automobiles, demonstrate them to potential buyers, negotiate prices, close sales, and service the cars after the sale.

Promotion means activities that communicate the merits of the product and persuade target customers to buy it. Ford Motor Company spends more than $2.5 billion each year on U.S. advertising, more than $800 per vehicle, to tell consumers about the company and its many products.[14] Dealership salespeople assist potential buyers and persuade them that Ford is the best car for them. Ford and its dealers offer special promotions—sales, cash rebates, low financing rates—as added purchase incentives.

An effective marketing program blends all of the marketing mix elements into an integrated marketing program designed to achieve the company's marketing objectives by delivering value to consumers. The marketing mix constitutes the company's tactical tool kit for establishing strong positioning in target markets.

Some critics think that the four Ps may omit or underemphasize certain important activities. For example, they ask, "Where are services?" Just because they don't start with a *P* doesn't justify omitting them. The answer is that services, such as banking, airline, and retailing services, are products too. We might call them *service products*. "Where is packaging?" the critics might ask. Marketers would answer that they include packaging as just one of many product decisions. All said, as Figure 5.5 suggests, many marketing activities that might appear to be left out of the marketing mix are subsumed under one of the four Ps. The issue is not whether there should be 4, 6, or 10 Ps so much as what framework is most helpful in designing integrated marketing programs.

There is another concern, however, that is valid. It holds that the four Ps concept takes the seller's view of the market, not the buyer's view. From the buyer's viewpoint, in this age of customer value and relationships, the four Ps might be better described as the four Cs:[15]

4Ps	4Cs
Product	Customer solution
Price	Customer cost
Place	Convenience
Promotion	Communication

Thus, whereas marketers see themselves as selling products, customers see themselves as buying value or solutions to their problems. And customers are interested in more than just the price; they are interested in the total costs of obtaining, using, and disposing of a product. Customers want the product and service to be as conveniently available as possible. Finally, they want two-way communication. Marketers would do well to think through the four Cs first and then build the four Ps on that platform.

Managing the marketing effort

In addition to being good at the *marketing* in marketing management, companies also need to pay attention to the *management*. Managing the marketing process requires the four marketing management functions shown in Figure 5.6—*analysis, planning, implementation,* and *control*. The company first develops companywide strategic plans and then translates them into marketing and other plans for each division, product, and brand. Through implementation, the company turns the plans into actions. Control consists of measuring and evaluating the results of marketing activities and taking corrective action where needed. Finally, marketing analysis provides information and evaluations needed for all of the other marketing activities.

Marketing Analysis, Planning, Implementation, and Control

FIGURE 5.6

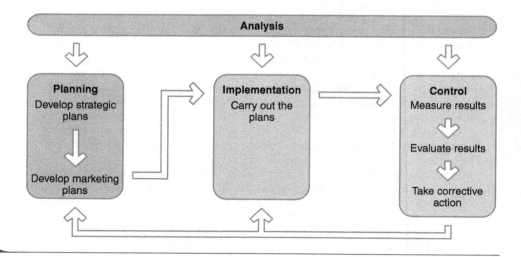

FIGURE 5.7

SWOT Analysis

	Strengths Internal capabilities that may help a company reach its objectives	Weaknesses Internal limitations that may interfere with a company's ability to achieve its objectives
Internal		
External	Opportunities External factors that the company may be able to exploit to its advantage	Threats Current and emerging external factors that may challenge the company's performance
	Positive	Negative

Marketing analysis

Managing the marketing function begins with a complete analysis of the company's situation. The marketer should conduct a **SWOT analysis**, by which it evaluates the company's overall strengths (S), weaknesses (W), opportunities (O), and threats (T) (see Figure 5.7). Strengths include internal capabilities, resources, and positive situational factors that may help the company to serve its customers and achieve its objectives. Weaknesses include internal limitations and negative situational factors that may interfere with the company's performance. Opportunities are favorable factors or trends in the external environment that the company may be able to exploit to its advantage. And threats are unfavorable external factors or trends that may present challenges to performance.

The company should analyze its markets and marketing environment to find attractive opportunities and identify environmental threats. It should analyze company strengths and weaknesses as well as current and possible marketing actions to determine which opportunities it can best pursue. The goal is to match the company's strengths to attractive opportunities in the environment, while eliminating or overcoming the weaknesses and minimizing the threats. Marketing analysis provides inputs to each of the other marketing management functions.

Marketing planning

Through strategic planning, the company decides what it wants to do with each business unit. Marketing planning involves deciding on marketing strategies that will help the company attain its overall strategic objectives. A detailed marketing plan is needed for each business, product, or brand. What does a marketing plan look like? Our discussion focuses on product or brand marketing plans.

Table 5.2 outlines the major sections of a typical product or brand marketing plan. The plan begins with an executive summary, which quickly overviews major assessments, goals, and recommendations. The main section of the plan presents a detailed SWOT analysis of the current marketing situation as well as potential threats and opportunities. The plan next states major objectives for the brand and outlines the specifics of a marketing strategy for achieving them.

A *marketing strategy* consists of specific strategies for target markets, positioning, the marketing mix, and marketing expenditure levels. It outlines how the company intends to create value for target customers in order to capture value in return. In this section, the planner explains how each strategy responds to the threats, opportunities, and critical issues spelled out earlier in the plan. Additional sections of the marketing plan lay out an action program for implementing the marketing strategy along with the details of a supporting *marketing budget*. The last section outlines the controls that will be used to monitor progress, measure return on marketing investment, and take corrective action.

SWOT analysis
An overall evaluation of the company's strengths (S), weaknesses (W), opportunities (O), and threats (T).

TABLE 5.2	Contents of a Marketing Plan
SECTION	**PURPOSE**
Executive summary	Presents a brief summary of the main goals and recommendations of the plan for management review, helping top management to find the plan's major points quickly. A table of contents should follow the executive summary.
Current marketing situation	Describes the target market and company's position in it, including information about the market, product performance, competition, and distribution. This section includes: ■ A *market description,* which defines the market and major segments then reviews customer needs and factors in the marketing environment that may affect customer purchasing. ■ A *product review,* which shows sales, prices, and gross margins of the major products in the product line. ■ A review of *competition,* which identifies major competitors and assesses their market positions and strategies for product quality, pricing, distribution, and promotion. ■ A review of *distribution,* which evaluates recent sales trends and other developments in major distribution channels.
Threats and opportunities analysis	Assesses major threats and opportunities that the product might face, helping management to anticipate important positive or negative developments that might have an impact on the firm and its strategies.
Objectives and issues	States the marketing objectives that the company would like to attain during the plan's term and discusses key issues that will affect their attainment. For example, if the goal is to achieve a 15 percent market share, this section looks at how this goal might be achieved.
Marketing strategy	Outlines the broad marketing logic by which the business unit hopes to create customer value and relationships and the specifics of target markets, positioning, and marketing expenditure levels. How will the company create value for customers in order to capture value from customers in return? This section also outlines specific strategies for each marketing mix element and explains how each responds to the threats, opportunities, and critical issues spelled out earlier in the plan.
Action programs	Spells out how marketing strategies will be turned into specific action programs that answer the following questions: *What* will be done? *When* will it be done? *Who* will do it? *How* much will it cost?
Budgets	Details a supporting marketing budget that is essentially a projected profit-and-loss statement. It shows expected revenues (forecasted number of units sold and the average net price) and expected costs (of production, distribution, and marketing). The difference is the projected profit. Once approved by higher management, the budget becomes the basis for materials buying, production scheduling, personnel planning, and marketing operations.
Controls	Outlines the control that will be used to monitor progress and allow higher management to review implementation results and spot products that are not meeting their goals. It includes measures of return on marketing investment.

Marketing implementation

Planning good strategies is only a start toward successful marketing. A brilliant marketing strategy counts for little if the company fails to implement it properly. **Marketing implementation** is the process that turns marketing *plans* into marketing *actions* in order to accomplish strategic marketing objectives. Whereas marketing planning addresses the *what* and *why* of marketing activities, implementation addresses the *who, where, when,* and *how.*

Many managers think that "doing things right" (implementation) is as important as, or even more important than, "doing the right things" (strategy). The fact is that both are critical to success, and companies can gain competitive advantages through effective implementation. One firm can have essentially the same strategy as another, yet win in the marketplace through faster or better execution. Still, implementation is difficult—it is often easier to think up good marketing strategies than it is to carry them out.

In an increasingly connected world, people at all levels of the marketing system must work together to implement marketing strategies and plans. At Black & Decker, for example, marketing implementation for the company's power tools, outdoor equipment, and other products requires day-to-day decisions and actions by thousands of people both inside and outside the organization. Marketing managers make decisions about target segments, branding, packaging, pricing, promoting, and distributing. They talk with engineering about product design, with manufacturing about production and inventory levels, and with finance about funding and cash flows. They also connect with outside people, such as advertising agencies to plan ad campaigns and the news media to obtain publicity support. The sales force urges Home Depot, Lowe's, Wal-Mart, and other retailers to advertise Black & Decker products, provide ample shelf space, and use company displays.

Successful marketing implementation depends on how well the company blends its people, organizational structure, decision and reward systems, and company culture into a cohesive action program that supports its strategies. At all levels, the company must be staffed by people who have the needed skills, motivation, and personal characteristics. The company's formal organization structure plays an important role in implementing marketing strategy; so do its decision and reward systems. For example, if a company's compensation system rewards managers for short-run profit results, they will have little incentive to work toward long-run market-building objectives.

Finally, to be successfully implemented, the firm's marketing strategies must fit with its company culture, the system of values and beliefs shared by people in the organization. Studies show that the most successful companies have almost cultlike cultures built around strong, market-oriented missions. At companies such as Dell, Nordstrom, Toyota, P&G, and Four Seasons Hotels, employees share a strong vision and know in their hearts what's right for their company and its customers.

Marketing implementation
The process that turns marketing strategies and plans into marketing actions in order to accomplish strategic marketing objectives.

Marketing department organization

The company must design a marketing organization that can carry out marketing strategies and plans. If the company is very small, one person might do all of the research, selling, advertising, customer service, and other marketing work. As the company expands, a marketing department emerges to plan and carry out marketing activities. In large companies, this department contains many specialists. Thus, General Electric and Microsoft have product and market managers, sales managers and salespeople, market researchers, advertising experts, and many other specialists. To head up such large marketing organizations, many companies have now created a *chief marketing officer* (or CMO) position.

Modern marketing departments can be arranged in several ways. The most common form of marketing organization is the *functional organization.* Under this organization, different marketing activities are headed by a functional specialist—a sales manager, advertising manager, marketing research manager, customer-service manager, or new-product manager. A company that sells across the country or internationally often uses a *geographic organization.* Its sales and marketing people are assigned to specific countries, regions, and districts. Geographic organization allows salespeople to settle into a territory, get to know their customers, and work with a minimum of travel time and cost.

Companies with many very different products or brands often create a *product management organization*. Using this approach, a product manager develops and implements a complete strategy and marketing program for a specific product or brand. Product management first appeared at Procter & Gamble in 1929. A new company soap, Camay, was not doing well, and a young P&G executive was assigned to give his exclusive attention to developing and promoting this product. He was successful, and the company soon added other product managers.[16] Since then, many firms, especially consumer-products companies, have set up product management organizations.

For companies that sell one product line to many different types of markets and customers that have different needs and preferences, a *market* or *customer management organization* might be best. A market management organization is similar to the product management organization. Market managers are responsible for developing marketing strategies and plans for their specific markets or customers. This system's main advantage is that the company is organized around the needs of specific customer segments.

Large companies that produce many different products flowing into many different geographic and customer markets usually employ some *combination* of the functional, geographic, product, and market organization forms. This ensures that each function, product, and market receives its share of management attention. However, it can also add costly layers of management and reduce organizational flexibility. Still, the benefits of organizational specialization usually outweigh the drawbacks.

Marketing organization has become an increasingly important issue in recent years. Many companies are finding that today's marketing environment calls for less focus on products, brands, and territories and more focus on customers and customer relationships. More and more companies are shifting their brand management focus toward *customer management*—moving away from managing just product or brand profitability and toward managing customer profitability and customer equity. And many companies now organize their marketing operations around major customers. They think of themselves not as managing portfolios of brands but as managing portfolios of customers. For example, companies such as Procter & Gamble and Black & Decker have large teams, or even whole divisions, set up to serve large customers such as Wal-Mart, Target, Safeway, or Home Depot.

Marketing control

Marketing control
The process of measuring and evaluating the results of marketing strategies and plans and taking corrective action to ensure that objectives are achieved.

Because many surprises occur during the implementation of marketing plans, the marketing department must practice constant marketing control. **Marketing control** involves evaluating the results of marketing strategies and plans and taking corrective action to ensure that objectives are attained. Marketing control involves four steps. Management first sets specific marketing goals. It then measures its performance in the marketplace and evaluates the causes of any differences between expected and actual performance. Finally, management takes corrective action to close the gaps between its goals and its performance. This may require changing the action programs or even changing the goals.

Operating control involves checking ongoing performance against the annual plan and taking corrective action when necessary. Its purpose is to ensure that the company achieves the sales, profits, and other goals set out in its annual plan. It also involves determining the profitability of different products, territories, markets, and channels.

Strategic control involves looking at whether the company's basic strategies are well matched to its opportunities. Marketing strategies and programs can quickly become outdated, and each company should periodically reassess its overall approach to the marketplace. A major tool for such strategic control is a **marketing audit**. The marketing audit is a comprehensive, systematic, independent, and periodic examination of a company's environment, objectives, strategies, and activities to determine problem areas and opportunities. The audit provides good input for a plan of action to improve the company's marketing performance.[17]

Marketing audit
A comprehensive, systematic, independent, and periodic examination of a company's environment, objectives, strategies, and activities to determine problem areas and opportunities and to recommend a plan of action to improve the company's marketing performance.

The marketing audit covers *all* major marketing areas of a business, not just a few trouble spots. It assesses the marketing environment, marketing strategy, marketing organization, marketing systems, marketing mix, and marketing productivity and profitability. The audit is normally conducted by an objective and experienced outside party. The findings may come as a surprise—and sometimes as a shock—to management. Management then decides which actions make sense and how and when to implement them.

Measuring and managing return on marketing investment

Marketing managers must ensure that their marketing dollars are being well spent. In the past, many marketers spent freely on big, expensive marketing programs, often without thinking carefully about the financial returns on their spending. They believed that marketing produces intangible outcomes, which do not lend themselves readily to measures of productivity or return. But all that is changing:

> For years, corporate marketers have walked into budget meetings like neighborhood junkies. They couldn't always justify how well they spent past handouts or what difference it all made. They just wanted more money—for flashy TV ads, for big-ticket events, for, you know, getting out the message and building up the brand. But those heady days of blind budget increases are fast being replaced with a new mantra: measurement and accountability. Armed with reams of data, increasingly sophisticated tools, and growing evidence that the old tricks simply don't work, there's hardly a marketing executive today who isn't demanding a more scientific approach to help defend marketing strategies in front of the chief financial officer. Marketers want to know the actual return on investment (ROI) of each dollar. They want to know it often, not just annually.... Companies in every segment of American business have become obsessed with honing the science of measuring marketing performance. "Marketers have been pretty unaccountable for many years," notes one expert. "Now they are under big pressure to estimate their impact."[18]

In response, marketers are developing better measures of *return on marketing investment*. **Return on marketing investment** (or *marketing ROI*) is the net return from a marketing investment divided by the costs of the marketing investment. It measures the profits generated by investments in marketing activities.

It's true that marketing returns can be difficult to measure. In measuring financial ROI, both the *R* and the *I* are uniformly measured in dollars. But there is as yet no consistent definition of marketing ROI. "It's tough to measure, more so than for other business expenses," says one analyst. "You can imagine buying a piece of equipment . . . and then measuring the productivity gains that result from the purchase," he says. "But in marketing, benefits like advertising impact aren't easily put into dollar returns. It takes a leap of faith to come up with a number."[19] A recent survey of top marketing executives found that although 58 percent of the companies surveyed have formal accountability programs, only 28 percent are satisfied with their ability to use marketing ROI measures to take action.[20]

A company can assess return on marketing in terms of standard marketing performance measures, such as brand awareness, sales, or market share. Campbell Soup uses sales and share data to evaluate specific advertising campaigns. For example, analysis revealed that its recent Soup at Hand advertising campaign, which depicted real-life scenarios of consumers using the portable soup, nearly doubled both the product's trial rate and repeat use rate after the first year. The Soup at Hand campaign received a Gold Effie, an advertising industry award based on marketing effectiveness.[21]

Many companies are assembling such measures into *marketing dashboards*—meaningful sets of marketing performance measures in a single display used to monitor strategic marketing performance. Just as automobile dashboards present drivers with details on how their cars are performing, the marketing dashboard gives marketers the detailed measures they need to assess and adjust their marketing strategies.[22]

Return on marketing investment (or *marketing ROI*)
The net return from a marketing investment divided by the costs of the marketing investment.

FIGURE 5.8

Return on Marketing

Source: Adapted from Roland T. Rust, Katherine N. Lemon, and Valerie A. Zeithamal, "Return on Marketing: Using Consumer Equity to Focus Marketing Strategy," *Journal of Marketing,* January 2004, p. 112.

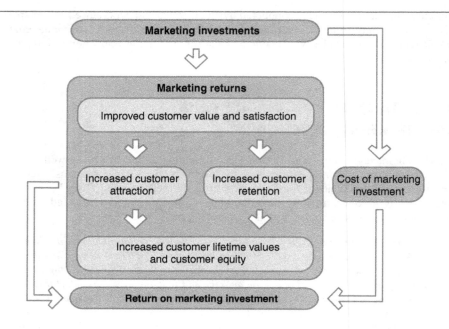

Increasingly, however, beyond standard performance measures, marketers are using customer-centered measures of marketing impact, such as customer acquisition, customer retention, and customer lifetime value. Figure 5.8 views marketing expenditures as investments that produce returns in the form of more profitable customer relationships.[23] Marketing investments result in improved customer value and satisfaction, which in turn increases customer attraction and retention. This increases individual customer lifetime values and the firm's overall customer equity. Increased customer equity, in relation to the cost of the marketing investments, determines return on marketing investment.

Regardless of how it's defined or measured, the return on marketing investment concept is here to stay. "Marketing ROI is at the heart of every business," says an AT&T marketing executive. "[We've added another P to the marketing mix]—for *profit and loss* or *performance.* We absolutely have to . . . quantify the impact of marketing on the business. You can't improve what you can't measure."[24]

chapter **6**

› **Marketing Channels**

Most firms cannot bring value to customers by themselves. Instead, they must work closely with other firms in a larger value delivery network.

Supply chains and the value delivery network

Producing a product or service and making it available to buyers requires building relationships not just with customers, but also with key suppliers and resellers in the company's *supply chain*. This supply chain consists of "upstream" and "downstream" partners. Upstream from the company is the set of firms that supply the raw materials, components, parts, information, finances, and expertise needed to create a product or service. Marketers, however, have traditionally focused on the "downstream" side of the supply chain—on the *marketing channels* (or *distribution channels*) that look forward toward the customer. Downstream marketing channel partners, such as wholesalers and retailers, form a vital connection between the firm and its customers.

Both upstream and downstream partners may also be part of other firms' supply chains. But it is the unique design of each company's supply chain that enables it to deliver superior value to customers. An individual firm's success depends not only on how well *it* performs, but also on how well its entire supply chain and marketing channel competes with competitors' channels.

The term *supply chain* may be too limited—it takes a *make-and-sell* view of the business. It suggests that raw materials, productive inputs, and factory capacity should serve as the starting point for market planning. A better term would be *demand chain* because it suggests a *sense-and-respond* view of the market. Under this view, planning starts with the needs of target customers, to which the company responds by organizing a chain of resources and activities with the goal of creating customer value.

Even a demand chain view of a business may be too limited, because it takes a step-by-step, linear view of purchase-production-consumption activities. With the advent of the Internet and other technologies, however, companies are forming more numerous and complex relationships with other firms. For example, Ford manages numerous supply chains. It also sponsors or transacts on many B2B Web sites and online purchasing exchanges as needs arise. Like Ford, most large companies today are engaged in building and managing a continuously evolving *value delivery network*.

A **value delivery network** is made up of the company, suppliers, distributors, and ultimately customers who "partner" with each other to improve the performance of the entire system. For example, Nike subsidiary Converse does more than just make and market sneakers. It manages an entire network of materials and equipment suppliers, company shoe designers and manufacturing people, and thousands of online and off-line resellers who must work effectively together to bring superior value to Converse customers. It even involves customers themselves in the value creation process by inviting them to design their own Chucks online or to submit their own "Made by You" Converse video shorts to conversegallery.com.

This chapter focuses on marketing channels—on the downstream side of the value delivery network. However, it is important to remember that this is only part of the full value network. In creating customer value, companies need upstream supplier partners just as they need downstream channel partners. Increasingly, marketers are participating in and influencing their company's upstream activities as well as its downstream activities. More than marketing channel managers, they are becoming full value network managers.

The chapter examines four major questions concerning marketing channels: What is the nature of marketing channels and why are they important? How do channel firms interact and organize to do the work of the channel? What problems do companies face in designing and managing their channels? What role do physical distribution and supply chain management play in attracting and satisfying customers?

Value delivery network
The network made up of the company, suppliers, distributors, and ultimately customers who "partner" with each other to improve the performance of the entire system in delivering customer value.

The nature and importance of marketing channels

Marketing channel (distribution channel)
A set of interdependent organizations that help make a product or service available for use or consumption by the consumer or business user.

Few producers sell their goods directly to the final users. Instead, most use intermediaries to bring their products to market. They try to forge a **marketing channel** (or **distribution channel**)—a set of interdependent organizations that help make a product or service available for use or consumption by the consumer or business user.

A company's channel decisions directly affect every other marketing decision. Pricing depends on whether the company works with national discount chains, uses high-quality specialty stores, or sells directly to consumers via the Web. The firm's sales force and communications decisions depend on how much persuasion, training, motivation, and support its channel partners need. Whether a company develops or acquires certain new products may depend on how well those products fit the capabilities of its channel members.

Companies often pay too little attention to their distribution channels, sometimes with damaging results. In contrast, many companies have used imaginative distribution systems to *gain* a competitive advantage. FedEx's creative and imposing distribution system made it a leader in express delivery. Dell revolutionized its industry by selling personal computers directly to consumers rather than through retail stores. Amazon.com pioneered the sales of books and a wide range of other goods via the Internet. And Calyx & Corolla led the way in selling fresh flowers and plants direct to consumers by phone and from its Web site, cutting a week or more off the time it takes flowers to reach consumers through conventional retail channels.

Distribution channel decisions often involve long-term commitments to other firms. For example, companies such as Ford, Hewlett-Packard, or McDonald's can easily change their advertising, pricing, or promotion programs. They can scrap old products and introduce new ones as market tastes demand. But when they set up distribution channels through contracts with franchisees, independent dealers, or large retailers, they cannot readily replace these channels with company-owned stores or Web sites if conditions change. Therefore, management must design its channels carefully, with an eye on tomorrow's likely selling environment as well as today's.

How channel members add value

Why do producers give some of the selling job to channel partners? After all, doing so means giving up some control over how and to whom they sell their products. Producers use intermediaries because they create greater efficiency in making goods available to target markets. Through their contacts, experience, specialization, and scale of operation, intermediaries usually offer the firm more than it can achieve on its own.

Figure 6.1 shows how using intermediaries can provide economies. Figure 6.1A shows three manufacturers, each using direct marketing to reach three customers. This system requires nine different contacts. Figure 6.1B shows the three manufacturers working through one distributor, which contacts the three customers. This system requires only six contacts. In this way, intermediaries reduce the amount of work that must be done by both producers and consumers.

From the economic system's point of view, the role of marketing intermediaries is to transform the assortments of products made by producers into the assortments wanted by consumers. Producers make narrow assortments of products in large quantities, but consumers want broad assortments of products in small quantities. Marketing channel members buy large quantities from many producers and break them down into the smaller quantities and broader assortments wanted by consumers.

For example, Unilever makes millions of bars of Lever 2000 hand soap each day, but you want to buy only a few bars at a time. So big food, drug, and discount retailers, such as Kroger, Walgreens, and Wal-Mart, buy Lever 2000 by the truckload and stock it on their store's shelves. In turn, you can buy a single bar of Lever 2000, along with a shopping cart full of small quantities of toothpaste, shampoo, and other related products as

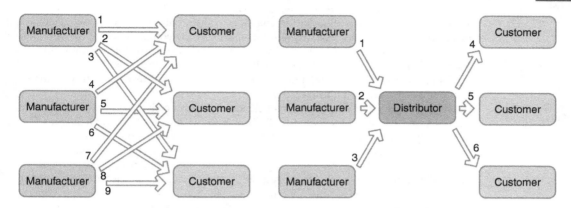

How a Distributor Reduces the Number of Channel Transactions FIGURE 6.1

A. Number of contacts without a distributor
M x C = 3 x 3 = 9

B. Number of contacts with a distributor
M + C = 3 + 3 = 6

you need them. Thus, intermediaries play an important role in matching supply and demand.

In making products and services available to consumers, channel members add value by bridging the major time, place, and possession gaps that separate goods and services from those who would use them. Members of the marketing channel perform many key functions. Some help to complete transactions:

- *Information:*Gathering and distributing marketing research and intelligence information about actors and forces in the marketing environment needed for planning and aiding exchange
- *Promotion:*Developing and spreading persuasive communications about an offer
- *Contact:*Finding and communicating with prospective buyers
- *Matching:*Shaping and fitting the offer to the buyer's needs, including activities such as manufacturing, grading, assembling, and packaging
- *Negotiation:*Reaching an agreement on price and other terms of the offer so that ownership or possession can be transferred

Others help to fulfill the completed transactions:

- *Physical distribution:*Transporting and storing goods
- *Financing:*Acquiring and using funds to cover the costs of the channel work
- *Risk taking:*Assuming the risks of carrying out the channel work

The question is not *whether* these functions need to be performed—they must be—but rather *who* will perform them. To the extent that the manufacturer performs these functions, its costs go up and its prices must be higher. When some of these functions are shifted to intermediaries, the producer's costs and prices may be lower, but the intermediaries must charge more to cover the costs of their work. In dividing the work of the channel, the various functions should be assigned to the channel members who can add the most value for the cost.

Number of channel levels

Companies can design their distribution channels to make products and services available to customers in different ways. Each layer of marketing intermediaries that performs some work in bringing the product and its ownership closer to the final buyer is a

Channel level
A layer of intermediaries that performs some work in bringing the product and its ownership closer to the final buyer.

Direct marketing channel
A marketing channel that has no intermediary levels.

Indirect marketing channel
A channel containing one or more intermediary levels.

channel level. Because the producer and the final consumer both perform some work, they are part of every channel.

The *number of intermediary levels* indicates the *length* of a channel. Figure 6.2A shows several consumer distribution channels of different lengths. Channel 1, called a **direct marketing channel**, has no intermediary levels; the company sells directly to consumers. For example, Mary Kay and Amway sell their products door-to-door, through home and office sales parties, and on the Web; GEICO sells direct via the telephone and the Internet. The remaining channels in Figure 6.2A are **indirect marketing channels**, containing one or more intermediaries.

Figure 6.2B shows some common business distribution channels. The business marketer can use its own sales force to sell directly to business customers. Or it can sell to various types of intermediaries, who in turn sell to these customers. Consumer and business marketing channels with even more levels can sometimes be found, but less often. From the producer's point of view, a greater number of levels means less control and greater channel complexity. Moreover, all of the institutions in the channel are connected by several types of *flows*. These include the *physical flow* of products, the *flow of ownership,* the *payment flow,* the *information flow,* and the *promotion flow.* These flows can make even channels with only one or a few levels very complex.

Channel behavior and organization

Distribution channels are more than simple collections of firms tied together by various flows. They are complex behavioral systems in which people and companies interact to accomplish individual, company, and channel goals. Some channel systems consist only of informal interactions among loosely organized firms. Others consist of formal interactions guided by strong organizational structures. Moreover, channel systems do not stand still—new types of intermediaries emerge and whole new channel systems evolve. Here we look at channel behavior and at how members organize to do the work of the channel.

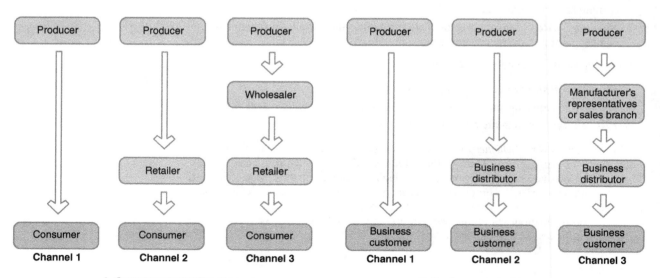

A. Customer marketing channels

B. Business marketing channels

FIGURE 6.2 **Consumer and Business Marketing Channels**

Channel behavior

A marketing channel consists of firms that have partnered for their common good. Each channel member depends on the others. For example, a Ford dealer depends on Ford to design cars that meet consumer needs. In turn, Ford depends on the dealer to attract consumers, persuade them to buy Ford cars, and service cars after the sale. Each Ford dealer also depends on other dealers to provide good sales and service that will uphold the brand's reputation. In fact, the success of individual Ford dealers depends on how well the entire Ford marketing channel competes with the channels of other auto manufacturers.

Each channel member plays a specialized role in the channel. For example, Samsung's role is to produce consumer electronics products that consumers will like and to create demand through national advertising. Best Buy's role is to display these Samsung products in convenient locations, to answer buyers' questions, and to complete sales. The channel will be most effective when each member assumes the tasks it can do best.

Ideally, because the success of individual channel members depends on overall channel success, all channel firms should work together smoothly. They should understand and accept their roles, coordinate their activities, and cooperate to attain overall channel goals. However, individual channel members rarely take such a broad view. Cooperating to achieve overall channel goals sometimes means giving up individual company goals. Although channel members depend on one another, they often act alone in their own short-run best interests. They often disagree on who should do what and for what rewards. Such disagreements over goals, roles, and rewards generate **channel conflict**.

Horizontal conflict occurs among firms at the same level of the channel. For instance, some Ford dealers in Chicago might complain the other dealers in the city steal sales from them by pricing too low or by advertising outside their assigned territories. Or Holiday Inn franchisees might complain about other Holiday Inn operators overcharging guests or giving poor service, hurting the overall Holiday Inn image.

Vertical conflict, conflicts between different levels of the same channel, is even more common. For example, Goodyear created hard feelings and conflict with its premier independent-dealer channel when it began selling through mass-merchant retailers. Similarly, Revlon came into serious conflict with its department store channels when it cozied up to mass merchants:[2]

> *A few years back, Revlon made a big commitment to mass-market retailers such as Wal-Mart, Target, and CVS, all but snubbing better department stores in the process. That strategy worked well initially. However, the mass merchants are sophisticated and demanding, and they quickly abandon brands that aren't working. That happened recently with Revlon's important new Vital Radiance cosmetics line, which targeted aging boomers. When Revlon failed to deliver on the promised marketing support for Vital Radiance—it spent only $700,000 during the three-month launch versus P&G's $9 million during the same period for its Cover Girl Advanced Radiance cosmetics—the mass-merchant channels backed away from the brand. For example, only 647 of CVS's 5,300 stores carried the new line. Meanwhile, the department stores, which Revlon had chosen to ignore with Vital Radiance, were lukewarm in their reaction to Revlon's attempted launch of a new prestige fragrance, Flair. Federated Department Stores, which operates Macy's and Bloomingdale's, refused to carry Revlon's new fragrance altogether. Says one retailing expert, "The prestige channel [didn't] trust Revlon not to run back to the discount channel if sales for Flair [didn't] fly." In the end, Revlon withdrew Vital Radiance, and Flair never made it to market. Thanks to bungled marketing channel relationships, Revlon lost more than $100 million in one year.*

Some conflict in the channel takes the form of healthy competition. Such competition can be good for the channel—without it, the channel could become passive and noninnovative. But severe or prolonged conflict, as in the case of Goodyear and Revlon, can disrupt

Channel conflict
Disagreement among marketing channel members on goals and roles—who should do what and for what rewards.

Conventional distribution channel
A channel consisting of one or more independent producers, wholesalers, and retailers, each a separate business seeking to maximize its own profits even at the expense of profits for the system as a whole.

Vertical marketing system (VMS)
A distribution channel structure in which producers, wholesalers, and retailers act as a unified system. One channel member owns the others, has contracts with them, or has so much power that they all cooperate.

Corporate VMS
A vertical marketing system that combines successive stages of production and distribution under single ownership—channel leadership is established through common ownership.

Corporate VMS: Effective vertical integration makes Zara faster, more flexible, and more efficient than competitors. It can take a new line from design to production to worldwide distribution in its own stores in less than a month (versus an industry average of nine months).

channel effectiveness and cause lasting harm to channel relationships. Companies should manage channel conflict to keep it from getting out of hand.

Vertical marketing systems

For the channel as a whole to perform well, each channel member's role must be specified and channel conflict must be managed. The channel will perform better if it includes a firm, agency, or mechanism that provides leadership and has the power to assign roles and manage conflict.

Historically, *conventional distribution channels* have lacked such leadership and power, often resulting in damaging conflict and poor performance. One of the biggest channel developments over the years has been the emergence of *vertical marketing systems* that provide channel leadership.

A **conventional distribution channel** consists of one or more independent producers, wholesalers, and retailers. Each is a separate business seeking to maximize its own profits, perhaps even at the expense of the system as a whole. No channel member has much control over the other members, and no formal means exists for assigning roles and resolving channel conflict.

In contrast, a **vertical marketing system (VMS)** consists of producers, wholesalers, and retailers acting as a unified system. One channel member owns the others, has contracts with them, or wields so much power that they must all cooperate. The VMS can be dominated by the producer, wholesaler, or retailer.

We look now at three major types of VMSs: *corporate, contractual,* and *administered.* Each uses a different means for setting up leadership and power in the channel.

Corporate VMS

A **corporate VMS** integrates successive stages of production and distribution under single ownership. Coordination and conflict management are attained through regular organizational channels. For example, grocery giant Kroger owns and operates 42 factories that crank out more than 8,000 private label items found on its store shelves. Similarly, to help supply products for its 1,760 grocery stores, Safeway owns and operates nine milk plants, eight bakery plants, four ice cream plants, four soft drink bottling plants, and four fruit and vegetable processing plants. And little-known Italian eyewear maker Luxottica produces many famous eyewear brands—including its own Ray-Ban brand and licensed brands such as Polo Ralph Lauren, Dolce & Gabbana, Prada, Versace, and Bvlgari. It then sells these brands through two of the world's largest optical chains, LensCrafters and Sunglass Hut, which it also owns.[3]

Controlling the entire distribution chain has turned Spanish clothing chain Zara into the world's fastest-growing fashion retailer.

The secret to Zara's success is its control over almost every aspect of the supply chain, from design and production to its own worldwide distribution network. Zara makes 40 percent of its own fabrics and produces more than half of its own clothes, rather than relying on a hodgepodge of slow-moving suppliers. New designs feed into Zara manufacturing centers, which ship finished products directly to 1,021 Zara stores in 64 countries, saving time, eliminating the need for warehouses, and keeping inventories low. Effective vertical integration makes Zara faster, more flexible, and more efficient than international competitors such as Gap, Benetton, and H&M. And Zara's low costs let it offer mid-market chic at down-market prices.

> *Last summer, Zara managed to latch onto one of the season's hottest trends in just four weeks (versus an industry average of nine months). The process started when trend-spotters spread the word back to headquarters: White eyelet—cotton with tiny holes in it—was set to become white-hot. A quick telephone survey of Zara store managers confirmed that the fabric could be a winner, so in-house designers got down to work. They zapped patterns electronically to Zara's factory across the street, and the fabric was cut. Local subcontractors stitched white-eyelet V-neck belted dresses—think Jackie Kennedy, circa 1960—and finished them in less than a week. The $129 dresses were inspected, tagged, and transported through a tunnel under the street to a distribution center. From there, they were quickly dispatched to Zara stores from New York to Tokyo—where they were flying off the racks just two days later. In all, the company's stylish but affordable offerings have attracted a cult following. Zara store sales grew 19 percent last year to more than $7 billion.[4]*

Contractual VMS

A **contractual VMS** consists of independent firms at different levels of production and distribution who join together through contracts to obtain more economies or sales impact than each could achieve alone. Channel members coordinate their activities and manage conflict through contractual agreements.

The **franchise organization** is the most common type of contractual relationship—a channel member called a *franchisor* links several stages in the production-distribution process. In the United States alone, some 1,500 franchise businesses and 750,000 franchise outlets account for more than $1.5 trillion in annual sales. Industry analysts estimate that a new franchise outlet opens somewhere in the United States every eight minutes and that about one out of every 12 retail business outlets is a franchised business.[5] Almost every kind of business has been franchised—from motels and fast-food restaurants to dental centers and dating services, from wedding consultants and maid services to fitness centers and funeral homes.

There are three types of franchises. The first type is the *manufacturer-sponsored retailer franchise system*—for example, Ford and its network of independent franchised dealers. The second type is the *manufacturer-sponsored wholesaler franchise system*—Coca-Cola licenses bottlers (wholesalers) in various markets who buy Coca-Cola syrup concentrate and then bottle and sell the finished product to retailers in local markets. The third type is the *service-firm-sponsored retailer franchise system*—examples are found in the auto-rental business (Hertz, Avis), the fast-food service business (McDonald's, Burger King), and the motel business (Holiday Inn, Ramada Inn).

The fact that most consumers cannot tell the difference between contractual and corporate VMSs shows how successfully the contractual organizations compete with corporate chains.

Administered VMS

In an **administered VMS**, leadership is assumed not through common ownership or contractual ties but through the size and power of one or a few dominant channel members. Manufacturers of a top brand can obtain strong trade cooperation and support from resellers. For example, General Electric, Procter & Gamble and Kraft can command unusual cooperation from resellers regarding displays, shelf space, promotions, and price policies. Large retailers such as Wal-Mart, Home Depot, and Barnes & Noble can exert strong influence on the manufacturers that supply the products they sell.

Horizontal marketing systems

Another channel development is the **horizontal marketing system**, in which two or more companies at one level join together to follow a new marketing opportunity. By working together, companies can combine their financial, production, or marketing resources to accomplish more than any one company could alone.

Companies might join forces with competitors or noncompetitors. They might work with each other on a temporary or permanent basis, or they may create a separate company. For example, McDonald's now places "express" versions of its restaurants in

Contractual VMS
A vertical marketing system in which independent firms at different levels of production and distribution join together through contracts to obtain more economies or sales impact than they could achieve alone.

Franchise organization
A contractual vertical marketing system in which a channel member, called a franchiser, links several stages in the production-distribution process.

Administered VMS
A vertical marketing system that coordinates successive stages of production and distribution, not through common ownership or contractual ties, but through the size and power of one of the parties.

Horizontal marketing system
A channel arrangement in which two or more companies at one level join together to follow a new marketing opportunity.

Wal-Mart stores. McDonald's benefits from Wal-Mart's heavy store traffic, and Wal-Mart keeps hungry shoppers from needing to go elsewhere to eat.

Such channel arrangements also work well globally. For example, McDonald's recently joined forces with Sinopec, China's largest gasoline retailer, to place drive-through restaurants at Sinopec's more than 31,000 gas stations. The move greatly speeds McDonald's expansion into China while at the same time pulling hungry motorists into Sinopec gas stations.[6] As another example, Coca-Cola and Nestlé formed a joint distribution venture, Beverage Partners Worldwide, to market ready-to-drink coffees, teas, and flavored milks in more than 40 countries worldwide. Coke provides worldwide experience in marketing and distributing beverages, and Nestlé contributes two established brand names—Nescafé and Nestea.[7]

Multichannel distribution systems

Multichannel distribution system
A distribution system in which a single firm sets up two or more marketing channels to reach one or more customer segments.

In the past, many companies used a single channel to sell to a single market or market segment. Today, with the proliferation of customer segments and channel possibilities, more and more companies have adopted **multichannel distribution systems**—often called *hybrid marketing channels*. Such multichannel marketing occurs when a single firm sets up two or more marketing channels to reach one or more customer segments. The use of multichannel systems has increased greatly in recent years.

Figure 6.3 shows a multichannel marketing system. In the figure, the producer sells directly to consumer segment 1 using direct-mail catalogs, telemarketing, and the Internet and reaches consumer segment 2 through retailers. It sells indirectly to business segment 1 through distributors and dealers and to business segment 2 through its own sales force.

These days, almost every large company and many small ones distribute through multiple channels. For example, John Deere sells its familiar green and yellow lawn and garden tractors, mowers, and outdoor power products to consumers and commercial users through several channels, including John Deere retailers, Lowe's home improvement stores, and online. It sells and services its tractors, combines, planters, and other agricultural equipment through its premium John Deere dealer network. And it sells large construction and forestry equipment through selected large, full-service dealers and their sales forces.

Apparel and accessories marketer Coldwater Creek started as an out-of-home mail-order business in Sand Point, Idaho. The founder began by selling 18 items and

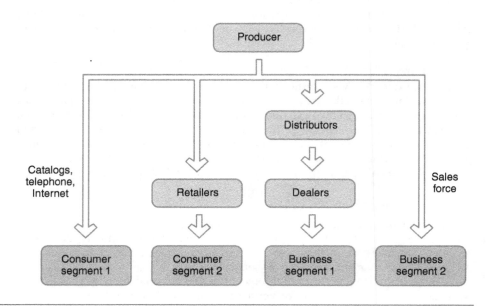

Multichannel Distribution System

FIGURE 6.3

shipping orders by peddling them to the local post office in his backpack. As the company grew, it added new marketing channels to reach new consumers. It now sells through four different catalogs, a direct-response Web site (www.coldwatercreek.com), and more than 250 Coldwater Creek retail outlets, all serviced by a state-of-the-art distribution and customer-service center in West Virginia.[8]

Multichannel distribution systems offer many advantages to companies facing large and complex markets. With each new channel, the company expands its sales and market coverage and gains opportunities to tailor its products and services to the specific needs of diverse customer segments. But such multichannel systems are harder to control, and they generate conflict as more channels compete for customers and sales. For example, when John Deere began selling selected consumer products through Lowe's home improvement stores, many of its dealers felt betrayed and complained loudly. To avoid such conflicts in its Internet marketing channels, the company routes all of its Web site sales to John Deere dealers.

Changing channel organization

Changes in technology and the explosive growth of direct and online marketing are having a profound impact on the nature and design of marketing channels. One major trend is toward **disintermediation**—a big term with a clear message and important consequences. Disintermediation occurs when product or service producers cut out intermediaries and go directly to final buyers, or when radically new types of channel intermediaries displace traditional ones.

Thus, in many industries, traditional intermediaries are dropping by the wayside. For example, companies such as Dell and Southwest Airlines sell directly to final buyers, cutting retailers and sales agents from their marketing channels altogether. In other cases, new forms of resellers are displacing traditional intermediaries. For example, online marketing is growing rapidly, taking business from traditional brick-and-mortar retailers. Consumers can buy electronics from sonystyle.com; clothes and accessories from bluefly.com; and books, videos, toys, jewelry, sports, consumer electronics, home and garden items, and almost anything else from Amazon.com; all without ever stepping into a traditional retail store. Online music download services such as iTunes and Musicmatch are threatening the very existence of traditional music-store retailers. In fact, once-dominant music retailer Tower Records recently declared bankruptcy and closed its doors for good.

Disintermediation presents both opportunities and problems for producers and resellers. Channel innovators who find new ways to add value in the channel can sweep

Disintermediation
The cutting out of marketing channel intermediaries by product or service producers, or the displacement of traditional resellers by radical new types of intermediaries.

Disintermediation: Online music download services are threatening to make traditional CD sellers obsolete. For example, once dominant Tower Records recently closed its doors for good. Courtesy of Michael Nagle/The New York Times

aside traditional resellers and reap the rewards. In turn, traditional intermediaries must continue to innovate in order to avoid being swept aside. For example, when Netflix pioneered online video rentals, it sent traditional brick-and-mortar video-rental stores such as Blockbuster reeling. To meet the threat, Blockbuster developed its own online DVD-rental service. Now, both Netflix and Blockbuster face disintermediation threats from an even hotter channel—digital video distribution.

Similarly, to remain competitive, product and service producers must develop new channel opportunities, such as Internet and other direct channels. However, developing these new channels often brings them into direct competition with their established channels, resulting in conflict.

To ease this problem, companies often look for ways to make going direct a plus for the entire channel. For example, Black & Decker knows that many customers would prefer to buy its power tools and outdoor power equipment online. But selling directly through its Web site would create conflicts with important and powerful retail partners, such as Home Depot, Lowe's, Target, Wal-Mart, and Amazon.com. So, although Black & Decker's Web site provides detailed information about the company's products, you can't buy a Black & Decker cordless drill, laser level, leaf blower, or anything else there. Instead, the Black & Decker site refers you to resellers' Web sites and stores. Thus, Black & Decker's direct marketing helps both the company and its channel partners.

Channel design decisions

We now look at several channel decisions manufacturers face. In designing marketing channels, manufacturers struggle between what is ideal and what is practical. A new firm with limited capital usually starts by selling in a limited market area. Deciding on the best channels might not be a problem: The problem might simply be how to convince one or a few good intermediaries to handle the line.

If successful, the new firm can branch out to new markets through the existing intermediaries. In smaller markets, the firm might sell directly to retailers; in larger markets, it might sell through distributors. In one part of the country, it might grant exclusive franchises; in another, it might sell through all available outlets. Then, it might add a Web store that sells directly to hard-to-reach customers. In this way, channel systems often evolve to meet market opportunities and conditions.

For maximum effectiveness, however, channel analysis and decision making should **Marketing channel design** be more purposeful. **Marketing channel design** calls for analyzing consumer needs, setting channel objectives, identifying major channel alternatives, and evaluating them.

Marketing channel design
Designing effective marketing channels by analyzing consumer needs, setting channel objectives, identifying major channel alternatives, and evaluating them.

Analyzing consumer needs

As noted previously, marketing channels are part of the overall *customer-value delivery network*. Each channel member and level adds value for the customer. Thus, designing the marketing channel starts with finding out what target consumers want from the channel. Do consumers want to buy from nearby locations or are they willing to travel to more distant centralized locations? Would they rather buy in person, by phone, through the mail, or online? Do they value breadth of assortment or do they prefer specialization? Do consumers want many add-on services (delivery, credit, repairs, installation), or will they obtain these elsewhere? The faster the delivery, the greater the assortment provided, and the more add-on services supplied, the greater the channel's service level.

Providing the fastest delivery, greatest assortment, and most services may not be possible or practical. The company and its channel members may not have the resources or skills needed to provide all the desired services. Also, providing higher levels of service results in higher costs for the channel and higher prices for consumers. The company must balance consumer needs not only against the feasibility and costs of meeting these needs but also against customer price preferences. The success of discount retailing shows that consumers will often accept lower service levels in exchange for lower prices.

Setting channel objectives

Companies should state their marketing channel objectives in terms of targeted levels of customer service. Usually, a company can identify several segments wanting different levels of service. The company should decide which segments to serve and the best channels to use in each case. In each segment, the company wants to minimize the total channel cost of meeting customer-service requirements.

The company's channel objectives are also influenced by the nature of the company, its products, its marketing intermediaries, its competitors, and the environment. For example, the company's size and financial situation determine which marketing functions it can handle itself and which it must give to intermediaries. Companies selling perishable products may require more direct marketing to avoid delays and too much handling.

In some cases, a company may want to compete in or near the same outlets that carry competitors' products. In other cases, producers may avoid the channels used by competitors. Mary Kay Cosmetics, for example, sells direct to consumers through its corps of more than one million independent beauty consultants in 34 markets worldwide rather than going head-to-head with other cosmetics makers for scarce positions in retail stores. Amazon.com has become the Wal-Mart of the Internet by selling exclusively via the Internet rather than through stores. And GEICO markets auto and homeowner's insurance directly to consumers via the telephone and Web rather than through agents.

Finally, environmental factors such as economic conditions and legal constraints may affect channel objectives and design. For example, in a depressed economy, producers want to distribute their goods in the most economical way, using shorter channels and dropping unneeded services that add to the final price of the goods.

Identifying major alternatives

When the company has defined its channel objectives, it should next identify its major channel alternatives in terms of *types* of intermediaries, the *number* of intermediaries, and the *responsibilities* of each channel member.

Types of Intermediaries

A firm should identify the types of channel members available to carry out its channel work. For example, suppose a manufacturer of test equipment has developed an audio device that detects poor mechanical connections in machines with moving parts. Company executives think this product would have a market in all industries in which electric, combustion, or steam engines are made or used. The company's current sales force is small, and the problem is how best to reach these different industries. The following channel alternatives might emerge:

> *Company sales force:* Expand the company's direct sales force. Assign outside salespeople to territories and have them contact all prospects in the area, or develop separate company sales forces for different industries. Or, add an inside telesales operation in which telephone salespeople handle small or mid-size companies.
>
> *Manufacturer's agents:* Hire manufacturer's agents—independent firms whose sales forces handle related products from many companies—in different regions or industries to sell the new test equipment.
>
> *Industrial distributors:* Find distributors in the different regions or industries who will buy and carry the new line. Give them exclusive distribution, good margins, product training, and promotional support.

Number of marketing intermediaries

Companies must also determine the number of channel members to use at each level. Three strategies are available: intensive distribution, exclusive distribution, and selective distribution. Producers of convenience products and common raw materials typically seek **intensive distribution**—a strategy in which they stock their products in as many outlets as possible. These products must be available where and when consumers want them. For

Intensive distribution
Stocking the product in as many outlets as possible.

Exclusive distribution
Giving a limited number of dealers the exclusive right to distribute the company's products in their territories.

Selective distribution
The use of more than one, but fewer than all, of the intermediaries who are willing to carry the company's products.

example, toothpaste, candy, and other similar items are sold in millions of outlets to provide maximum brand exposure and consumer convenience. Kraft, Coca-Cola, Kimberly-Clark, and other consumer-goods companies distribute their products in this way.

By contrast, some producers purposely limit the number of intermediaries handling their products. The extreme form of this practice is **exclusive distribution**, in which the producer gives only a limited number of dealers the exclusive right to distribute its products in their territories. Exclusive distribution is often found in the distribution of luxury automobiles and prestige women's clothing. For example, Bentley dealers are few and far between—even large cities may have only one dealer. By granting exclusive distribution, Bentley gains stronger distributor selling support and more control over dealer prices, promotion, credit, and services. Exclusive distribution also enhances the car's image and allows for higher markups.

Between intensive and exclusive distribution lies **selective distribution**—the use of more than one, but fewer than all, of the intermediaries who are willing to carry a company's products. Most television, furniture, and home appliance brands are distributed in this manner. For example, Whirlpool and General Electric sell their major appliances through dealer networks and selected large retailers. By using selective distribution, they can develop good working relationships with selected channel members and expect a better-than-average selling effort. Selective distribution gives producers good market coverage with more control and less cost than does intensive distribution.

Responsibilities of Channel Members

The producer and intermediaries need to agree on the terms and responsibilities of each channel member. They should agree on price policies, conditions of sale, territorial rights, and specific services to be performed by each party. The producer should establish a list price and a fair set of discounts for intermediaries. It must define each channel member's territory, and it should be careful about where it places new resellers.

Mutual services and duties need to be spelled out carefully, especially in franchise and exclusive distribution channels. For example, McDonald's provides franchisees with promotional support, a record-keeping system, training at Hamburger University, and general management assistance. In turn, franchisees must meet company standards for physical facilities and food quality, cooperate with new promotion programs, provide requested information, and buy specified food products.

Evaluating the major alternatives

Suppose a company has identified several channel alternatives and wants to select the one that will best satisfy its long-run objectives. Each alternative should be evaluated against economic, control, and adaptive criteria.

Using *economic criteria,* a company compares the likely sales, costs, and profitability of different channel alternatives. What will be the investment required by each channel alternative, and what returns will result? The company must also consider *control issues.* Using intermediaries usually means giving them some control over the marketing of the product, and some intermediaries take more control than others. Other things being equal, the company prefers to keep as much control as possible. Finally, the company must apply *adaptive criteria.* Channels often involve long-term commitments, yet the company wants to keep the channel flexible so that it can adapt to environmental changes. Thus, to be considered, a channel involving long-term commitments should be greatly superior on economic and control grounds.

Designing international distribution channels

International marketers face many additional complexities in designing their channels. Each country has its own unique distribution system that has evolved over time and changes very slowly. These channel systems can vary widely from country to country. Thus, global marketers must usually adapt their channel strategies to the existing structures within each country.

In some markets, the distribution system is complex and hard to penetrate, consisting of many layers and large numbers of intermediaries. At the other extreme, distribution systems in developing countries may be scattered, inefficient, or altogether lacking. For example, China and India are huge markets, each with populations well over one billion people. However, because of inadequate distribution systems, most companies can profitably access only a small portion of the population located in each country's most affluent cities. "China is a very decentralized market," notes a China trade expert. "[It's] made up of two dozen distinct markets sprawling across 2,000 cities. Each has its own culture. . . . It's like operating in an asteroid belt." China's distribution system is so fragmented that logistics costs amount to 15 percent of the nation's GDP, far higher than in most other countries. After 10 years of effort, even Wal-Mart executives admit that they have been unable to assemble an efficient supply chain in China.[9]

Sometimes customs or government regulation can greatly restrict how a company distributes products in global markets. For example, it wasn't an inefficient distribution structure that caused problems for Avon in China—it was restrictive government regulations. Fearing the growth of multilevel marketing schemes, the Chinese government banned door-to-door selling altogether in 1998, forcing Avon to abandon its traditional direct marketing approach and sell through retail shops. The Chinese government recently gave Avon and other direct sellers permission to sell door-to-door again, but that permission is tangled in a web of restrictions. Fortunately for Avon, its earlier focus on store sales is helping it weather the restrictions better than most other direct sellers.[10]

International marketers face a wide range of channel alternatives. Designing efficient and effective channel systems between and within various country markets poses a difficult challenge.

Channel management decisions

Once the company has reviewed its channel alternatives and decided on the best channel design, it must implement and manage the chosen channel. **Marketing channel management** calls for selecting, managing, and motivating individual channel members and evaluating their performance over time.

Marketing channel management
Selecting, managing, and motivating individual channel members and evaluating their performance over time.

Selecting channel members

Producers vary in their ability to attract qualified marketing intermediaries. Some producers have no trouble signing up channel members. For example, when Toyota first introduced its Lexus line in the United States, it had no trouble attracting new dealers. In fact, it had to turn down many would-be resellers.

At the other extreme are producers who have to work hard to line up enough qualified intermediaries. When Polaroid started, for example, it could not get photography stores to carry its new cameras, and it had to go to mass-merchandising outlets. Similarly, when the U.S. Time Company first tried to sell its inexpensive Timex watches through regular jewelry stores, most jewelry stores refused to carry them. The company then managed to get its watches into mass-merchandise outlets. This turned out to be a wise decision because of the rapid growth of mass merchandising.

When selecting intermediaries, the company should determine what characteristics distinguish the better ones. It will want to evaluate each channel member's years in business, other lines carried, growth and profit record, cooperativeness, and reputation. If the intermediaries are sales agents, the company will want to evaluate the number and character of other lines carried and the size and quality of the sales force. If the intermediary is a retail store that wants exclusive or selective distribution, the company will want to evaluate the store's customers, location, and future growth potential.

Managing and motivating channel members

Once selected, channel members must be continuously managed and motivated to do their best. The company must sell not only *through* the intermediaries but *to* and *with* them. Most companies see their intermediaries as first-line customers and partners. They practice strong *partner relationship management (PRM)* to forge long-term partnerships with channel members. This creates a marketing system that meets the needs of both the company *and* its marketing partners.

In managing its channels, a company must convince distributors that they can succeed better by working together as a part of a cohesive value delivery system. Thus, Procter & Gamble works closely with Wal-Mart to create superior value for final consumers. The two jointly plan merchandising goals and strategies, inventory levels, and advertising and promotion programs. Similarly, Samsung's Information Technology Division works closely with value-added resellers through the industry-leading Samsung Power Partner Program (P3).

> *The Samsung P3 program creates close partnerships with important value-added resellers (VARs)—channel firms that assemble IT solutions for their own customers using products from Samsung and other manufacturers. Through the Power Partner Program, Samsung provides extensive presale, selling, and postsale tools and support to some 17,255 registered North America VAR partners at one of three levels—silver, gold, or platinum. For example, platinum-level partners—those selling $500,000 or more of Samsung IT products per year—receive access to a searchable online product and pricing database and downloadable marketing materials. They can tap into partner-only Samsung training programs, special seminars, and conferences. A dedicated Samsung P3 team helps partners to find good sales prospects and initiate sales. Then, a dedicated Samsung field sales rep works with each partner to close deals, and inside sales reps provide the partner with information and technical support. Platinum partners even participate in Samsung's Reseller Council. Finally, the P3 program rewards high-performing reseller-partners with rebates, discount promotions, bonuses, and sales awards. In all, the Power Partner Program turns important resellers into strong, motivated marketing partners by helping them to be more effective and profitable at selling Samsung.[11]*

Many companies are now installing integrated high-tech partner relationship management systems to coordinate their whole-channel marketing efforts. Just as they use customer relationship management (CRM) software systems to help manage relationships with important customers, companies can now use PRM and supply chain management (SCM) software to help recruit, train, organize, manage, motivate, and evaluate relationships with channel partners.

Evaluating channel members

The producer must regularly check channel member performance against standards such as sales quotas, average inventory levels, customer delivery time, treatment of damaged and lost goods, cooperation in company promotion and training programs, and services to the customer. The company should recognize and reward intermediaries who are performing well and adding good value for consumers. Those who are performing poorly should be assisted or, as a last resort, replaced. A company may periodically "requalify" its intermediaries and prune the weaker ones.

Finally, manufacturers need to be sensitive to their dealers. Those who treat their dealers poorly risk not only losing dealer support but also causing some legal problems. The next section describes various rights and duties pertaining to manufacturers and their channel members.

Marketing logistics and supply chain management

In today's global marketplace, selling a product is sometimes easier than getting it to customers. Companies must decide on the best way to store, handle, and move their products and services so that they are available to customers in the right assortments, at the right time, and in the right place. Physical distribution and logistics effectiveness have a major impact on both customer satisfaction and company costs. Here we consider the nature and importance of logistics management in the supply chain, goals of the logistics system, major logistics functions, and the need for integrated supply chain management.

Nature and importance of marketing logistics

To some managers, marketing logistics means only trucks and warehouses. But modern logistics is much more than this. **Marketing logistics**—also called **physical distribution**—involves planning, implementing, and controlling the physical flow of goods, services, and related information from points of origin to points of consumption to meet customer requirements at a profit. In short, it involves getting the right product to the right customer in the right place at the right time.

In the past, physical distribution planners typically started with products at the plant and then tried to find low-cost solutions to get them to customers. However, today's marketers prefer customer-centered logistics thinking, which starts with the marketplace and works backward to the factory, or even to sources of supply. Marketing logistics involves not only *outbound distribution* (moving products from the factory to resellers and ultimately to customers) but also *inbound distribution* (moving products and materials from suppliers to the factory) and *reverse distribution* (moving broken, unwanted, or excess products returned by consumers or resellers). That is, it involves entire **supply chain management**—managing upstream and downstream value-added flows of materials, final goods, and related information among suppliers, the company, resellers, and final consumers, as shown in Figure 6.4.

The logistics manager's task is to coordinate activities of suppliers, purchasing agents, marketers, channel members, and customers. These activities include forecasting, information systems, purchasing, production planning, order processing, inventory, warehousing, and transportation planning.

Companies today are placing greater emphasis on logistics for several reasons. First, companies can gain a powerful competitive advantage by using improved logistics to give customers better service or lower prices. Second, improved logistics can yield tremendous cost savings to both the company and its customers. As much as 20 percent of an average product's price is accounted for by shipping and transport alone. This far exceeds the cost of advertising and many other marketing costs. American companies spend almost $1.2 trillion each year—about 9.6 percent of gross domestic product—to wrap, bundle, load, unload, sort, reload, and transport goods. That's more than the national GDPs of all but 12 countries worldwide. What's more, these costs have risen more than 50 percent over the past decade. By itself, Ford has more than 500 million tons of finished vehicles, production parts, and aftermarket parts in transit at any given time, running up an annual logistics bill of around $4 billion.[13] Shaving off even a small fraction of these costs can mean substantial savings.

Third, the explosion in product variety has created a need for improved logistics management. For example, in 1911 the typical A&P grocery store carried only 270 items. The store manager could keep track of this inventory on about 10 pages of notebook paper stuffed in a shirt pocket. Today, the average A&P carries a bewildering stock of

Marketing logistics (physical distribution)
Planning, implementing, and controlling the physical flow of materials, final goods, and related information from points of origin to points of consumption to meet customer requirements at a profit.

Supply chain management
Managing upstream and downstream value-added flows of materials, final goods, and related information among suppliers, the company, resellers, and final consumers.

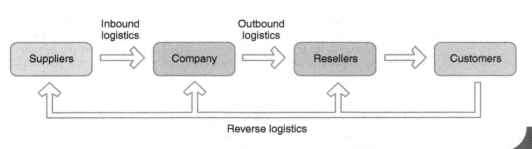

Supply Chain Management

FIGURE 6.4

more than 25,000 items. A Wal-Mart Supercenter store carries more than 100,000 products, 30,000 of which are grocery products.[14] Ordering, shipping, stocking, and controlling such a variety of products presents a sizable logistics challenge.

Finally, improvements in information technology have created opportunities for major gains in distribution efficiency. Today's companies are using sophisticated supply chain management software, Web-based logistics systems, point-of-sale scanners, uniform product codes, satellite tracking, and electronic transfer of order and payment data. Such technology lets them quickly and efficiently manage the flow of goods, information, and finances through the supply chain.

Goals of the logistics system

Some companies state their logistics objective as providing maximum customer service at the least cost. Unfortunately, no logistics system can *both* maximize customer service *and* minimize distribution costs. Maximum customer service implies rapid delivery, large inventories, flexible assortments, liberal return policies, and other services—all of which raise distribution costs. In contrast, minimum distribution costs imply slower delivery, smaller inventories, and larger shipping lots—which represent a lower level of overall customer service.

The goal of marketing logistics should be to provide a *targeted* level of customer service at the least cost. A company must first research the importance of various distribution services to customers and then set desired service levels for each segment. The objective is to maximize *profits,* not sales. Therefore, the company must weigh the benefits of providing higher levels of service against the costs. Some companies offer less service than their competitors and charge a lower price. Other companies offer more service and charge higher prices to cover higher costs.

Major logistics functions

Given a set of logistics objectives, the company is ready to design a logistics system that will minimize the cost of attaining these objectives. The major logistics functions include *warehousing, inventory management, transportation,* and *logistics information management.*

Warehousing

Production and consumption cycles rarely match. So most companies must store their goods while they wait to be sold. For example, Snapper, Toro, and other lawn mower manufacturers run their factories all year long and store up products for the heavy spring and summer buying seasons. The storage function overcomes differences in needed quantities and timing, ensuring that products are available when customers are ready to buy them.

A company must decide on *how many* and *what types* of warehouses it needs and *where* they will be located. The company might use either *storage warehouses* or *distribution centers.* Storage warehouses store goods for moderate to long periods. **Distribution centers** are designed to move goods rather than just store them. They are large and highly automated warehouses designed to receive goods from various plants and suppliers, take orders, fill them efficiently, and deliver goods to customers as quickly as possible.

Like almost everything else these days, warehousing has seen dramatic changes in technology in recent years. Older, multistoried warehouses with outdated materials-handling methods are steadily being replaced by newer, single-storied *automated warehouses* with advanced, computer-controlled materials-handling systems requiring few employees. Computers and scanners read orders and direct lift trucks, electric hoists, or robots to gather goods, move them to loading docks, and issue invoices.

For example, Wal-Mart operates a network of 129 huge U.S. distribution centers and another 57 around the globe. A single center, which might serve the daily needs of 120 Wal-Mart stores, typically contains some 1 million square feet of space (about 20 football fields) under a single roof. At a typical center, laser scanners

Distribution center
A large, highly automated warehouse designed to receive goods from various plants and suppliers, take orders, fill them efficiently, and deliver goods to customers as quickly as possible.

route as many as 190,000 cases of goods per day along 11 miles of conveyer belts, and the center's 1,000 workers load or unload some 500 trucks daily. Wal-Mart's Monroe, Georgia, distribution center contains a 127,000-square-foot freezer (that's about 1/2 a football field) that can hold 10,000 pallets—room enough for 58 million Popsicles.[15]

Inventory management

Inventory management also affects customer satisfaction. Here, managers must maintain the delicate balance between carrying too little inventory and carrying too much. With too little stock, the firm risks not having products when customers want to buy. To remedy this, the firm may need costly emergency shipments or production. Carrying too much inventory results in higher-than-necessary inventory-carrying costs and stock obsolescence. Thus, in managing inventory, firms must balance the costs of carrying larger inventories against resulting sales and profits.

Many companies have greatly reduced their inventories and related costs through *just-in-time* logistics systems. With such systems, producers and retailers carry only small inventories of parts or merchandise, often only enough for a few days of operations. For example, Dell, a master just-in-time producer, carries as little as three days of inventory, whereas competitors and their retail channels might carry 40 days or even 60.[16] New stock arrives exactly when needed, rather than being stored in inventory until being used. Just-in-time systems require accurate forecasting along with fast, frequent, and flexible delivery so that new supplies will be available when needed. However, these systems result in substantial savings in inventory-carrying and handling costs.

Marketers are always looking for new ways to make inventory management more efficient. In the not-too-distant future, handling inventory might even become fully automated. For example, in Chapter 3, we discussed RFID or "smart tag" technology, by which small transmitter chips are embedded in or placed on products and packaging on everything from flowers and razors to tires. "Smart" products could make the entire supply chain—which accounts for nearly 75 percent of a product's cost—intelligent and automated.

Companies using RFID would know, at any time, exactly where a product is located physically within the supply chain. "Smart shelves" would not only tell them when it's time to reorder, but would also place the order automatically with their suppliers. Such exciting new information technology applications will revolutionize distribution as we know it. Many large and resourceful marketing companies, such as Wal-Mart, Procter & Gamble, Kraft, IBM, Hewlett-Packard, and Best Buy, are investing heavily to make the full use of RFID technology a reality.[17]

Integrated logistics management

Today, more and more companies are adopting the concept of **integrated logistics management**. This concept recognizes that providing better customer service and trimming distribution costs require *teamwork,* both inside the company and among all the marketing channel organizations. Inside, the company's various departments must work closely together to maximize the company's own logistics performance. Outside, the company must integrate its logistics system with those of its suppliers and customers to maximize the performance of the entire distribution system.

Integrated logistics management
The logistics concept that emphasizes teamwork, both inside the company and among all the marketing channel organizations, to maximize the performance of the entire distribution system.

Cross-functional teamwork inside the company

Most companies assign responsibility for various logistics activities to many different departments—marketing, sales, finance, operations, purchasing. Too often, each function tries to optimize its own logistics performance without regard for the activities of the other functions. However, transportation, inventory, warehousing, and order-processing activities interact, often in an inverse way. Lower inventory levels reduce inventory-carrying costs. But they may also reduce customer service and increase costs from stock-outs, back orders, special production runs, and costly fast-freight shipments. Because distribution activities involve strong trade-offs, decisions by different functions must be coordinated to achieve better overall logistics performance.

The goal of integrated supply chain management is to harmonize all of the company's logistics decisions. Close working relationships among departments can be achieved in several ways. Some companies have created permanent logistics committees, made up of managers responsible for different physical distribution activities. Companies can also create supply chain manager positions that link the logistics activities of functional areas. For example, Procter & Gamble has created supply managers, who manage all of the supply chain activities for each of its product categories. Many companies have a vice president of logistics with cross-functional authority.

Finally, companies can employ sophisticated, systemwide supply chain management software, now available from a wide range of software enterprises large and small, from SAP and Oracle to Infor and Logility. The worldwide market for supply chain management software topped an estimated $6 billion last year.[20] The important thing is that the company must coordinate its logistics and marketing activities to create high market satisfaction at a reasonable cost.

Building logistics partnerships

Companies must do more than improve their own logistics. They must also work with other channel partners to improve whole-channel distribution. The members of a marketing channel are linked closely in creating customer value and building customer relationships. One company's distribution system is another company's supply system. The success of each channel member depends on the performance of the entire supply chain. For example, IKEA can create its stylish but affordable furniture and deliver the "IKEA lifestyle" only if its entire supply chain—consisting of thousands of merchandise designers and suppliers, transport companies, warehouses, and service providers—operates at maximum efficiency and customer-focused effectiveness.

Smart companies coordinate their logistics strategies and forge strong partnerships with suppliers and customers to improve customer service and reduce channel costs. Many companies have created *cross-functional, cross-company teams.* For example, Procter & Gamble has a team of more than 200 people working in Bentonville, Arkansas, home of Wal-Mart.[21] The P&Gers work jointly with their counterparts at Wal-Mart to find ways to squeeze costs out of their distribution system. Working together benefits not only P&G and Wal-Mart but also their shared final consumers.

Other companies partner through *shared projects.* For example, many large retailers conduct joint in-store programs with suppliers. Home Depot allows key suppliers to use its stores as a testing ground for new merchandising programs. The suppliers spend time at Home Depot stores watching how their product sells and how customers relate to it. They then create programs specially tailored to Home Depot and its customers. Clearly, both the supplier and the customer benefit from such partnerships. The point is that all supply chain members must work together in the cause of bringing value to final consumers.

chapter 7

› **Marketing Technology**

The impact of technology on marketing

Changes in technology, for communications, information gathering, textile development, and apparel production, have a great effect on the marketing of fashion.

Communications

The development of modern communications has had a huge impact on the fashion industry. Communications that formerly took days or weeks happen instantly. A variety of communication systems provide fashion business executives and consumers alike with up-to-the-minute fashion information. Accurate, timely, and useful communications are critical to the success of fashion companies.

Business communications

Fashion industry executives use the latest technology to make communications easier. They have to assess the viability of the myriad of new communication options.

- **Computers**—Fashion industry executives are able to communicate with their offices from anywhere in the world on their laptop computers via satellite.
- **Intranet**—Industry executives may use electronic mail (E-mail) on a closed Intranet networksystem to share information internally, both among departments and with branch offices and stores. These private systems allow people to share information without worrying about data security.
- **Internet**—Executives also use E-mail via the Internet to communicate worldwide with their associates. Manufacturers can communicate with their suppliers and production facilities worldwide and exchange digital design and pattern images.
- **Video**—Videoconferencing provides communications and visuals on products, trends, floor presentations, selling techniques, and electronic staff meetings, acting as a *virtual boardroom*. Videoconferencing is used between manufacturers and factories, manufacturers and retailers, management and sales representatives, and among chain stores of a retail organization. It is especially helpful when travel is impossible due to terrorists or war.
- **Fax**—A facsimile (fax) machine can send a fashion sketch or list of specifications around the world in seconds.

Communication with consumers

The Internet, fax machines, and television bring fashion from around the world into our homes instantly.

- **Television**—Television is a vehicle for home shopping, infomercials, and direct-response commercials.
- **Telephone**—The 800 number revolutionized telephone ordering. Now, fiber-optic cables carry digital signals to facilitate interactive shopping.
- **Web sites**—Many manufacturers and retailers have created Web sites to advertise their brands and to give information to consumers. Even small companies can afford to advertise globally.
- **E-commerce**—The Internet opens up global markets. Forecasters predict strong growth for fashion sales on the Internet as more consumers go online and more retailers develop "shops" in cyberspace.

On camera at QVC Cable Shopping Network. *(Photo by Gini Stephens Frings)*

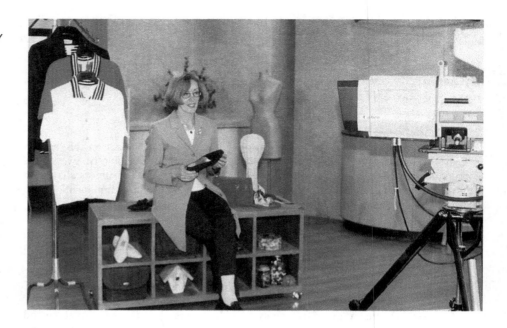

Information technology

Manufacturers and retailers also use computer technology to collect information, or *data*, to help them to make accurate marketing decisions.

- **Databases**—As discussed earlier in the chapter, retailers use information gathered from their customers to help them to determine target markets and customer preferences and to develop marketing activities and directional selling relevant to that market.

- **Research**—Manufacturers and retailers use the Internet to do research to help them to make important merchandising decisions. The Internet can provide fashion industry members with global information on suppliers, fashion services, directories, and libraries.

Information systems

Each manufacturer and retailer works with computer experts to develop software programs and systems based on its company's needs. These systems bring order out of chaos by keeping track of and controlling planning, production, inventory, sales, and distribution, and they allow companies to collaborate with factories and supply-chain partners around the world.

- In product development, designers and merchandisers rely on consumer statistics and sales data to track trends. Customer relation management (CRM) systems keep track of customer preferences and purchasing patterns.

- Product data management (PDM) and product lifecycle management (PLM) systems coordinate each step of the design process from initial concept through production, including keeping track of resources for fabrics and trims, specifications, work-in-progress, and inventory.

- In production, goods are given *universal product codes* (UPC) that identify style, color, size, price, and fabrication.

- Radio frequency identification (RFID) tags, embedded in fabric with a computer chip, keep track of inventory so that everyone knows what is on order, in work, or in inventory at all times.

Electronic data interchange

In an attempt to reduce waiting time in ordering and distribution, textile producers, apparel manufacturers, and retailers use *electronic data interchange (EDI)*, the exchange of business data between two parties by means of computers. Inventory information is fed through the EDI pipeline from textile producers to manufacturers and retailers.

Automatic Replenishment   Agreements between suppliers and retailers allow the manufacturer to ship goods to stores automatically when inventory levels are low. Coded information immediately informs the retail buyer to replenish stock, the apparel manufacturer in turn to issue new cuts, and the fabric producer to send more fabric to the apparel manufacturer.

Value Chain Initiative (VCI)   Standardized codes and linkage systems have been developed throughout the industry. A consortium of approximately 90 leading software, hardware, transportation, and logistics companies has developed a set of international standards for sharing information among retailers, manufacturers, and suppliers. VCI covers nearly all aspects of the supply chain, including distribution management, electronic data interchange, import and export transportation, inventory control, and warehouse management.

Textile and apparel production technology

Modern technology makes fashion production more efficient. Computer-aided yarn spinning, fabric design, weaving, knitting, dyeing, and finishing allow our domestic textile industry to compete with imports.

Technological research has made it possible to develop nanotechnology, which controls the structure of matter at the molecular level, to create fibers with multifunctional properties as well as finishes that change fabric characteristics. Color-technology software has been developed to speed collaboration on color choices and matching

Using a digitizer to record pattern shapes into a patternmaking computer system. *(Courtesy of Gerber Technology)*

between designers and fabric producers. Manufacturers are even experimenting with conductive fibers to build electronics into clothing.

The development of modern production machinery, such as power sewing machines and cutting tools, has streamlined the process of manufacturing. Modern cutting techniques include the use of computers, water jets, and laser beams. Computer technology has revolutionized manufacturing with computer-aided design (CAD), patternmaking, grading, cutting, unit and modular production systems, pressing, and distribution systems. Today's power machines can run faster than a car engine, sewing more than 5000 stitches per minute. Specialized machines make seamless activewear. Engineers are linking all phases of production from design to delivery.

The marketing chain

The marketing chain is the flow of product development, production, and distribution from concept to consumer.

The traditional chain of marketing—textiles to apparel manufacturers to retailers to consumers—is no longer clearly divided. The old relationships between suppliers and retailers are disappearing.

Traditional marketing chain

This textbook follows the sequential order of the traditional marketing chain. Formerly, each level of the industry was clearly separated. The textile industry developed and produced fibers, yarns, and fabrics and sold them to their customers, the apparel and accessory manufacturers. The manufacturers designed and produced the apparel and accessories and sold them to the retailers. The retailers sold it all to consumers. All levels did their own marketing activities, such as advertising, sometimes in cooperation with each other. Today, the old divisions have broken down.

Traditional Marketing Chain

Fibers
Product Development
Production
Sales & Distribution

Yarns
Product Development
Production
Sales & Distribution

Fabrics
Product Development
Weaving & Knitting
Sales & Distribution

Apparel & Accessories
Product Development
Production
Sales & Distribution

Retailers
Merchandising
Sales

Consumers

Vertical integration

Many companies are combining fabric production and apparel manufacturing, or manufacturing and retailing, a strategy called *vertical integration*. A completely vertical company produces fabrics, manufactures clothing, and sells the finished apparel in its own stores. Cutting out distribution costs (from manufacturer to retailer) increases profits and keeps prices down for the consumer. Vertical companies also like having total control of the supply, production, and marketing chain.

Full Package manufacturing

With today's focus on global production, most American and European manufacturers and retailers design their own fashion, but buy "full garment packages" from contractors in Asia and elsewhere. They source (find the best production available at the cheapest price) contract production to suppliers who can handle everything from buying piece goods to booking space on ships.

Manufacturer–retailer alliances

Fierce competition has forced manufacturers and retailers to work together to achieve quick and cost-effective *seamless distribution*. They form informal partnerships or alliances to integrate the marketing chain. Retailers discuss their needs with their manufacturer-partner; they work on product development together and plan production and shipping timetables together. For this arrangement to work, manufacturers and retailers must have complete trust in each other and open communications. In addition, many retailers have become manufacturers themselves.

chapter **8**

> ## Marketing Ethics and Social Responsibility

Social criticisms of marketing

Marketing receives much criticism. Some of this criticism is justified; much is not. Social critics claim that certain marketing practices hurt individual consumers, society as a whole, and other business firms.

Marketing's impact on individual consumers

Consumers have many concerns about how well the American marketing system serves their interests. Surveys usually show that consumers hold mixed or even slightly unfavorable attitudes toward marketing practices. Consumer advocates, government agencies, and other critics have accused marketing of harming consumers through high prices, deceptive practices, high-pressure selling, shoddy or unsafe products, planned obsolescence, and poor service to disadvantaged consumers.

High prices

Many critics charge that the American marketing system causes prices to be higher than they would be under more "sensible" systems. They point to three factors—*high costs of distribution, high advertising and promotion costs,* and *excessive markups.*

High Costs of Distribution   A long-standing charge is that greedy channel intermediaries mark up prices beyond the value of their services. Critics charge that there are too many intermediaries, that intermediaries are inefficient, or that they provide unnecessary or duplicate services. As a result, distribution costs too much, and consumers pay for these excessive costs in the form of higher prices.

How do resellers answer these charges? They argue that intermediaries do work that would otherwise have to be done by manufacturers or consumers. Markups reflect services that consumers themselves want—more convenience, larger stores and assortments, more service, longer store hours, return privileges, and others. In fact, they argue, retail competition is so intense that margins are actually quite low. For example, after taxes, supermarket chains are typically left with barely 1 percent profit on their sales. If some resellers try to charge too much relative to the value they add, other resellers will step in with lower prices. Low-price stores such as Wal-Mart, Costco, and other discounters pressure their competitors to operate efficiently and keep their prices down.

High Advertising and Promotion Costs   Modern marketing is also accused of pushing up prices to finance heavy advertising and sales promotion. For example, a few dozen tablets of a heavily promoted brand of pain reliever sell for the same price as 100 tablets of less-promoted brands. Differentiated products—cosmetics, detergents, toiletries—include promotion and packaging costs that can amount to 40 percent or more of the manufacturer's price to the retailer. Critics charge that much of the packaging and promotion adds only psychological value to the product rather than functional value.

Marketers respond that advertising does add to product costs. But it also adds value by informing potential buyers of the availability and merits of a brand. Brand name products may cost more but branding gives buyers assurances of consistent quality. Moreover, consumers can usually buy functional versions of products at lower prices. However, they *want* and are willing to pay more for products that also provide psychological benefits—that make them feel wealthy, attractive, or special. Also, heavy advertising and promotion may be necessary for a firm to match competitors' efforts—the business would lose "share of mind" if it did not match competitive spending. At the same time, companies are cost conscious about promotion and try to spend their money wisely.

Excessive Markups   Critics also charge that some companies mark up goods excessively. They point to the drug industry, where a pill costing five cents to make may cost the consumer $2 to buy. They point to the pricing tactics of funeral homes that prey on the confused emotions of bereaved relatives and to the high charges for auto repair and other services.

Marketers respond that most businesses try to deal fairly with consumers because they want to build customer relationships and repeat business. Most consumer abuses are unintentional. When shady marketers do take advantage of consumers, they should be reported to Better Business Bureaus and to state and federal agencies. Marketers also respond that consumers often don't understand the reasons for high markups. For example, pharmaceutical markups must cover the costs of purchasing, promoting, and distributing existing medicines plus the high research and development costs of formulating and testing new medicines. As pharmaceuticals company GlaxoSmithKline states in its ads, "Today's medicines finance tomorrow's miracles."

Deceptive practices

Marketers are sometimes accused of deceptive practices that lead consumers to believe they will get more value than they actually do. Deceptive practices fall into three groups: pricing, promotion, and packaging. *Deceptive pricing* includes practices such as falsely advertising "factory" or "wholesale" prices or a large price reduction from a phony high retail list price. *Deceptive promotion* includes practices such as misrepresenting the product's features or performance or luring the customers to the store for a bargain that is out of stock. *Deceptive packaging* includes exaggerating package contents through subtle design, using misleading labeling, or describing size in misleading terms.

To be sure, questionable marketing practices do occur. Consider the advertising of airline ticket prices:[2]

> When is $49 not $49? When it's the advertised price for an airline ticket. In newspaper ads and radio commercials, we are lured with the promise of $49 round-trip tickets to Bermuda. But by the time you add in all the extras, that bargain ticket will cost nearly $200. What ever happened to truth in advertising? Technically, the advertising is legal. But the average airline consumer needs a magnifying glass to get an idea of the actual ticket cost. For the Bermuda ticket, radio commercials warn that the discount price comes with conditions and fees, but you must read the fine print across the bottom of a newspaper ad to discover the true cost. "Prepaid government taxes and fees of up to $86.00, September 11 Security Fees of up to $10.00, and Passenger Facility Charges up to $18.00 per person . . . are not included in listed prices," we're told. "Listed prices include fuel-related and all other increases as of 7/1, but may increase additionally due to unanticipated expenses beyond our control." Add them up, and that ticket costs $163, not counting whatever fuel surcharge may have been imposed over the past nine months. Not quite the $49 in the big print at the top of the ad.

Deceptive practices have led to legislation and other consumer protection actions. For example, in 1938, Congress reacted to such blatant deceptions as Fleischmann's Yeast's claim to straighten crooked teeth by enacting the Wheeler-Lea Act giving the Federal Trade Commission (FTC) power to regulate "unfair or deceptive acts or practices." The FTC has published several guidelines listing deceptive practices. Despite new regulations, some critics argue that deceptive claims are still the norm.

The toughest problem is defining what is "deceptive." For instance, an advertiser's claim that its powerful laundry detergent "makes your washing machine 10 feet tall," showing a surprised homemaker watching her appliance burst through her laundry room ceiling, isn't intended to be taken literally. Instead, the advertiser might claim, it is "puffery"—innocent exaggeration for effect. One noted marketing thinker, Theodore Levitt, once claimed that advertising puffery and alluring imagery are bound to occur—and that they may even be desirable: "There is hardly a company that would not go down in ruin if it refused to provide fluff, because nobody will buy pure functionality.... Worse, it denies . . . people's honest needs and values. Without distortion, embellishment, and elaboration, life would be drab, dull, anguished, and at its existential worst."[3]

However, others claim that puffery and alluring imagery can harm consumers in subtle ways. Think about the popular and long-running MasterCard Priceless commercials that paint pictures of consumers fulfilling their priceless dreams despite the costs. Similarly, Visa invites consumers to "Enjoy life's opportunities." Both suggest that your credit card can make it happen. But critics charge that such imagery by credit card companies encourages a spend-now-pay-later attitude that causes many consumers to *over*use their cards. The critics point to statistics showing that sixty percent of Americans are carrying a balance on their credit cards and that one in every four American families is maxed out on at least one credit card. One in every seven Americans today is dealing with a debt collector because they can't make their payments.[4]

Marketers argue that most companies avoid deceptive practices because such practices harm their business in the long run. Profitable customer relationships are built upon a foundation of value and trust. If consumers do not get what they expect, they will switch to more reliable products. In addition, consumers usually protect themselves from deception. Most consumers recognize a marketer's selling intent and are careful when they buy, sometimes to the point of not believing completely true product claims.

High-pressure selling

Salespeople are sometimes accused of high-pressure selling that persuades people to buy goods they had no thought of buying. It is often said that insurance, real estate, and used cars are *sold,* not *bought*. Salespeople are trained to deliver smooth, canned talks to entice purchase. They sell hard because sales contests promise big prizes to those who sell the most.

But in most cases, marketers have little to gain from high-pressure selling. Such tactics may work in one-time selling situations for short-term gain. However, most selling involves building long-term relationships with valued customers. High-pressure or deceptive selling can do serious damage to such relationships. For example, imagine a Procter & Gamble account manager trying to pressure a Wal-Mart buyer, or an IBM salesperson trying to browbeat a General Electric information technology manager. It simply wouldn't work.

Shoddy, harmful, or unsafe products

Another criticism concerns poor product quality or function. One complaint is that, too often, products are not made well and services are not performed well. A second complaint is that many products deliver little benefit, or that they might even be harmful. For example, many critics have pointed out the dangers of today's fat-laden fast food. In fact, McDonald's recently faced a class-action lawsuit charging that its fare has contributed to the nationwide obesity epidemic.

Who's to blame for the nation's obesity problem? And what should responsible food companies do about it? As with most social responsibility issues, there are no easy answers. McDonald's has worked to improve its fare and make its menu and its customers healthier. However, other fast feeders seem to be going the other way. Hardee's, for example, serves up a 1,410-calorie Monster Thickburger, and Burger King promotes its Enormous Omelet breakfast sandwich, packing an unapologetic 47 grams of fat. Are these companies being socially irresponsible? Or are they simply serving customers choices they want?

A third complaint concerns product safety. Product safety has been a problem for several reasons, including company indifference, increased product complexity, and poor quality control. For years, Consumers Union—the nonprofit testing and information organization that publishes the *Consumer Reports* magazine and Web site—has reported various hazards in tested products: electrical dangers in appliances, carbon monoxide poisoning from room heaters, injury risks from lawn mowers, and faulty automobile design, among many others. The organization's testing and other activities have helped consumers make better buying decisions and encouraged businesses to eliminate product flaws.

However, most manufacturers *want* to produce quality goods. The way a company deals with product quality and safety problems can damage or help its reputation. Companies selling poor-quality or unsafe products risk damaging conflicts with consumer groups and regulators. Unsafe products can result in product liability suits and large awards for damages. More fundamentally, consumers who are unhappy with a firm's products may avoid future purchases and talk other consumers into doing the same. Thus, quality missteps can have severe consequences. Today's marketers know that good quality results in customer value and satisfaction, which in turn creates profitable customer relationships.

Planned obsolescence

Critics also have charged that some companies practice planned obsolescence, causing their products to become obsolete before they actually should need replacement. Some producers are accused of using materials and components that will break, wear, rust, or rot sooner than they should. One writer put it this way: "The marvels of modern technology include the development of a soda can which, when discarded, will last forever—and a . . . car, which, when properly cared for, will rust out in two or three years."[6]

Others are charged with continually changing consumer concepts of acceptable styles to encourage more and earlier buying. An obvious example is constantly changing clothing fashions. Still others are accused of introducing planned streams of new products that make older models obsolete. Critics claim that this occurs in the consumer electronics and computer industries. For example, consider this writer's tale about an aging cell phone:

> Today, most people, myself included, are all agog at the wondrous outpouring of new technology, from cell phones to iPods, iPhones, laptops, BlackBerries, and on and on. Even though I am a techno-incompetent and like to think I shun these new devices, I actually have a drawer filled with the detritus of yesterday's hottest product, now reduced to the status of fossils. I have video cameras that use tapes no longer available, laptops with programs incompatible with anything on today's market, portable CD players I no longer use, and more. But what really upsets me is how quickly some still-useful gadgets become obsolete, at least in the eyes of their makers.
>
> I recently embarked on an epic search for a cord to plug into my wife's cell phone to recharge it. We were traveling and the poor phone kept bleating that it was running low and the battery needed recharging. So, we began a search—from big-box technology superstores to smaller suppliers and the cell phone companies themselves—all to no avail. Finally, a salesperson told my wife, "That's an old model, so we don't stock the charger any longer." "But I only bought it last year," she sputtered. "Yeah, like I said, that's an old model," he replied without a hint of irony or sympathy. So, in the world of insanely rapid obsolescence, each successive model is incompatible with the previous one it replaces. The proliferation and sheer waste of this type of practice is mind-boggling.[7]

Marketers respond that consumers *like* style changes; they get tired of the old goods and want a new look in fashion. Or they *want* the latest high-tech innovations, even if older models still work. No one has to buy the new product, and if too few people like it, it will simply fail. Finally, most companies do not design their products to break down earlier, because they do not want to lose customers to other brands. Instead, they seek constant improvement to ensure that products will consistently meet or exceed customer expectations. Much of the so-called planned obsolescence is the working of the competitive and technological forces in a free society—forces that lead to ever-improving goods and services.

Poor service to disadvantaged consumers

Finally, the American marketing system has been accused of serving disadvantaged consumers poorly. For example, critics claim that the urban poor often must shop in smaller stores that carry inferior goods and charge higher prices. The presence of large national chain stores in low-income neighborhoods would help to keep prices down. However, the critics accuse major chain retailers of "redlining," drawing a red line around disadvantaged neighborhoods and avoiding placing stores there.[8]

Similar redlining charges have been leveled at the insurance, consumer lending, banking, and health care industries. Home and auto insurers have been accused of assigning higher premiums to people with poor credit ratings. The insurers claim that individuals with bad credit tend to make more insurance claims, and that this justifies charging them higher premiums. However, critics and consumer advocates have accused the insurers of a new form of redlining. Says one writer, "This is a new excuse for denying coverage to the poor, elderly, and minorities."[9]

More recently, consumer advocates have charged that income tax preparers such as H&R Block and Jackson Hewitt are taking advantage of the working poor by offering them "rapid refunds" after preparing their taxes. Customers receive these rapid refunds when their taxes are prepared, rather than waiting two weeks to a month for the IRS to send the refund. The big problem is that the refunds are not free. In fact, they're "refund anticipation loans" (RALs) with fees starting around $130, which represents an APR (annual percentage rate) of 245 percent of the average working poor person's refund. In one year alone, more than 10.6 million low-income families requested rapid refunds, and tax preparers made more than $1.4 billion in profits on them. Consumer advocates are pressuring state legislatures to pass laws requiring loan materials to be written in a language that the average consumer can understand. And the state of California recently filed a lawsuit against H&R Block for deceptive practices associated with RALs.[10]

Clearly, better marketing systems must be built to service disadvantaged consumers. In fact, many marketers profitably target such consumers with legitimate goods and services that create real value. In cases where marketers do not step in to fill the void, the government likely will. For example, the FTC has taken action against sellers who advertise false values, wrongfully deny services, or charge disadvantaged customers too much.

Marketing's impact on society as a whole

The American marketing system has been accused of adding to several "evils" in American society at large. Advertising has been a special target—so much so that the American Association of Advertising Agencies once launched a campaign to defend advertising against what it felt to be common but untrue criticisms.

False wants and too much materialism

Critics have charged that the marketing system urges too much interest in material possessions. People are judged by what they *own* rather than by who they *are*. This drive for wealth and possessions hit new highs in the 1980s and 1990s, when phrases such as "greed is good" and "shop till you drop" seemed to characterize the times.

In the current decade, many social scientists have noted a reaction against the opulence and waste of the previous decades and a return to more basic values and social commitment. However, our infatuation with material things continues.

> *If you made a graph of American life since the end of World War II, every line concerning money and the things that money can buy would soar upward, a statistical monument to materialism. Inflation-adjusted income per American has almost tripled. The size of the typical new house has more than doubled. A two-car garage was once a goal; now we're nearly a three-car nation. Designer everything, personal electronics, and other items that didn't even exist a half-century ago are now affordable. Although our time spent shopping has dropped in recent years to just three hours a week, American households currently spend on average $1.22 for every $1 earned. Some consumers will let nothing stand between them and their acquisitions. Recently, in a Florida Wal-Mart, post-Thanksgiving shoppers rushing to buy DVD players (on sale for $29) knocked down a woman, trampled her, and left her unconscious.*[11]

The critics do not view this interest in material things as a natural state of mind but rather as a matter of false wants created by marketing. Businesses hire Madison Avenue to stimulate people's desires for goods, and Madison Avenue uses the mass media to create materialistic models of the good life. People work harder to earn the necessary money. Their purchases increase the output of American industry, and industry in turn uses Madison Avenue to stimulate more desire for the industrial output.

Thus, marketing is seen as creating false wants that benefit industry more than they benefit consumers. Some critics even take their concerns to the streets.

> *For almost a decade Bill Talen, also known as Reverend Billy, has taken to the streets, exhorting people to resist temptation—the temptation to shop. With the zeal of a street-corner preacher and the schmaltz of a street-corner Santa, Reverend Billy will tell anyone willing to listen that people are walking willingly into the hellfires of consumption. Reverend Billy, leader of the Church of Stop Shopping believes that shoppers have almost no resistance to the media messages that encourage them, around the clock, to want things and buy them. He sees a population lost in consumption, the meaning of individual existence vanished in a fog of wanting, buying, and owning too many things, ultimately leading to a "Shopocalypse." Sporting a televangelist's pompadour, a priest's collar, and a white megaphone, Reverend Billy is often accompanied by his gospel choir when he strides into stores he considers objectionable or shows up at protests like the annual post-Thanksgiving Buy Nothing Parade in front of Macy's in Manhattan. When the choir, which is made up of volunteers, erupts in song, it is hard to ignore: "Stop shopping! Stop shopping! We will never shop again!"[12]*

These criticisms overstate the power of business to create needs, however. People have strong defenses against advertising and other marketing tools. Marketers are most effective when they appeal to existing wants rather than when they attempt to create new ones. Furthermore, people seek information when making important purchases and often do not rely on single sources. Even minor purchases that may be affected by advertising messages lead to repeat purchases only if the product delivers the promised customer value. Finally, the high failure rate of new products shows that companies are not able to control demand.

On a deeper level, our wants and values are influenced not only by marketers but also by family, peer groups, religion, cultural background, and education. If Americans are highly materialistic, these values arose out of basic socialization processes that go much deeper than business and mass media could produce alone.

Too few social goods

Business has been accused of overselling private goods at the expense of public goods. As private goods increase, they require more public services that are usually not forthcoming. For example, an increase in automobile ownership (private good) requires more highways, traffic control, parking spaces, and police services (public goods). The overselling of private goods results in "social costs." For cars, some of the social costs include traffic congestion, gasoline shortages, and air pollution. For example, in 85 of the most congested U.S. urban areas, drivers sat through 3.7 billion hours of traffic delays in one year. In the process, they wasted 2.3 billion gallons of fuel and emitted millions of tons of greenhouse gases.[13]

A way must be found to restore a balance between private and public goods. One option is to make producers bear the full social costs of their operations. The government could require automobile manufacturers to build cars with more efficient engines and better pollution-control systems. Automakers would then raise their prices to cover extra costs. If buyers found the price of some cars too high, however, the producers of these cars would disappear. Demand would then move to those producers that could support the sum of the private and social costs.

A second option is to make consumers pay the social costs. For example, many cities around the world are starting to charge "congestion tolls" in an effort to reduce traffic congestion. To unclog its streets, the city of London now levies a congestion charge of $16.50 per day per car to drive in an eight-square-mile area downtown. The charge has not only reduced traffic congestion by 30 percent and increased mass transit use by 16 percent, it also raises money to shore up London's public transportation system.

Based on London's success, cities such as San Diego and Denver have turned some of their HOV (high-occupancy vehicle) lanes into HOT (high-occupancy toll) lanes for drivers carrying too few passengers. Regular drivers can use the HOV lanes, but they must pay tolls ranging from $0.50 off-peak to $8.50 during rush hour. The U.S. government has recently proposed a bill that would create rush-hour fees in congested urban areas across the country. If the costs of driving rise high enough, the government hopes, consumers will travel at nonpeak times or find alternative transportation modes, ultimately helping to curb America's oil addiction.[14]

Cultural pollution

Critics charge the marketing system with creating *cultural pollution*. Our senses are being constantly assaulted by marketing and advertising. Commercials interrupt serious programs; pages of ads obscure magazines; billboards mar beautiful scenery; spam fills our e-mailboxes. These interruptions continually pollute people's minds with messages of materialism, sex, power, or status. A recent study found that 63 percent of Americans feel constantly bombarded with too many marketing messages, and some critics call for sweeping changes.[15]

Marketers answer the charges of "commercial noise" with these arguments: First, they hope that their ads reach primarily the target audience. But because of mass-communication channels, some ads are bound to reach people who have no interest in the product and are therefore bored or annoyed. People who buy magazines addressed to their interests—such as *Vogue* or *Fortune*—rarely complain about the ads because the magazines advertise products of interest.

Second, ads make much of television and radio free to users and keep down the costs of magazines and newspapers. Many people think commercials are a small price to pay for these benefits. Finally, today's consumers have alternatives. For example, they can zip or zap TV commercials on recorded programs or avoid them altogether on many paid cable or satellite channels. Thus, to hold consumer attention, advertisers are making their ads more entertaining and informative.

Marketing's impact on other businesses

Critics also charge that a company's marketing practices can harm other companies and reduce competition. Three problems are involved: acquisitions of competitors, marketing practices that create barriers to entry, and unfair competitive marketing practices.

Critics claim that firms are harmed and competition reduced when companies expand by acquiring competitors rather than by developing their own new products. The large number of acquisitions and the rapid pace of industry consolidation over the past several decades have caused concern that vigorous young competitors will be absorbed and that competition will be reduced. In virtually every major industry—retailing, entertainment, financial services, utilities, transportation, automobiles, telecommunications, health care—the number of major competitors is shrinking.

Acquisition is a complex subject. Acquisitions can sometimes be good for society. The acquiring company may gain economies of scale that lead to lower costs and lower prices. A well-managed company may take over a poorly managed company and improve its efficiency. An industry that was not very competitive might become more competitive after the acquisition. But acquisitions can also be harmful and, therefore, are closely regulated by the government.

Critics have also charged that marketing practices bar new companies from entering an industry. Large marketing companies can use patents and heavy promotion spending or tie up suppliers or dealers to keep out or drive out competitors. Those concerned with antitrust regulation recognize that some barriers are the natural result of the economic advantages of doing business on a large scale. Other barriers could be challenged by existing and new laws. For example, some critics have proposed a progressive tax on advertising spending to reduce the role of selling costs as a major barrier to entry.

Finally, some firms have in fact used unfair competitive marketing practices with the intention of hurting or destroying other firms. They may set their prices below costs, threaten to cut off business with suppliers, or discourage the buying of a competitor's products. Various laws work to prevent such predatory competition. It is difficult, however, to prove that the intent or action was really predatory.

In recent years, Wal-Mart has been accused of using predatory pricing in selected market areas to drive smaller, mom-and-pop retailers out of business. Wal-Mart has become a lightning rod for protests by citizens in dozens of towns who worry that the megaretailer's unfair practices will choke out local businesses. However, whereas critics charge that Wal-Mart's actions are predatory, others assert that its actions are just the healthy competition of a more efficient company against less efficient ones.

For instance, when Wal-Mart recently began a program to sell generic drugs at $4 a prescription, local pharmacists complained of predatory pricing. They charged that at those low prices, Wal-Mart must be selling under cost to drive them out of business. But Wal-Mart claimed that, given its substantial buying power and efficient operations, it could make a profit at those prices. The $4 pricing program was not aimed at putting competitors out of business. Rather, it was simply a good competitive move that served customers better and brought more of them in the door.[16]

Citizen and public actions to regulate marketing

Because some people view business as the cause of many economic and social ills, grass-roots movements have arisen from time to time to keep business in line. The two major movements have been *consumerism* and *environmentalism*.

Consumerism

American business firms have been the target of organized consumer movements on three occasions. The first consumer movement took place in the early 1900s. It was fueled by rising prices, Upton Sinclair's writings on conditions in the meat industry, and scandals in the drug industry. The second consumer movement, in the mid-1930s, was sparked by an upturn in consumer prices during the Great Depression and another drug scandal.

The third movement began in the 1960s. Consumers had become better educated, products had become more complex and potentially hazardous, and people were unhappy with American institutions. Ralph Nader appeared on the scene to force many issues, and other well-known writers accused big business of wasteful and unethical practices. President John F. Kennedy declared that consumers had the right to safety and to be informed, to choose, and to be heard. Congress investigated certain industries and proposed consumer-protection legislation. Since then, many consumer groups have been organized and several consumer laws have been passed. The consumer movement has spread internationally and has become very strong in Europe.

But what is the consumer movement? **Consumerism** is an organized movement of citizens and government agencies to improve the rights and power of buyers in relation to sellers. Traditional *sellers' rights* include:

Consumerism
An organized movement of citizens and government agencies to improve the rights and power of buyers in relation to sellers.

- The right to introduce any product in any size and style, provided it is not hazardous to personal health or safety; or, if it is, to include proper warnings and controls
- The right to charge any price for the product, provided no discrimination exists among similar kinds of buyers
- The right to spend any amount to promote the product, provided it is not defined as unfair competition
- The right to use any product message, provided it is not misleading or dishonest in content or execution
- The right to use any buying incentive programs, provided they are not unfair or misleading

Traditional *buyers' rights* include:

- The right not to buy a product that is offered for sale
- The right to expect the product to be safe
- The right to expect the product to perform as claimed

Comparing these rights, many believe that the balance of power lies on the seller's side. True, the buyer can refuse to buy. But critics feel that the buyer has too little information, education, and protection to make wise decisions when facing sophisticated sellers. Consumer advocates call for the following additional consumer rights:

- The right to be well informed about important aspects of the product
- The right to be protected against questionable products and marketing practices
- The right to influence products and marketing practices in ways that will improve the "quality of life"

Each proposed right has led to more specific proposals by consumerists. The right to be informed includes the right to know the true interest on a loan (truth in lending), the true cost per unit of a brand (unit pricing), the ingredients in a product (ingredient labeling), the nutritional value of foods (nutritional labeling), product freshness (open dating), and the true benefits of a product (truth in advertising). Proposals related to consumer protection include strengthening consumer rights in cases of business fraud, requiring greater product safety, ensuring information privacy, and giving more power to government agencies. Proposals relating to quality of life include controlling the ingredients that go into certain products and packaging, reducing the level of advertising "noise," and putting consumer representatives on company boards to protect consumer interests.

Consumers have not only the *right* but also the *responsibility* to protect themselves instead of leaving this function to someone else. Consumers who believe they got a bad deal have several remedies available, including contacting the company or the media; contacting federal, state, or local agencies; and going to small-claims courts.

Environmentalism

Whereas consumerists consider whether the marketing system is efficiently serving consumer wants, environmentalists are concerned with marketing's effects on the environment and with the environmental costs of serving consumer needs and wants. **Environmentalism** is an organized movement of concerned citizens, businesses, and government agencies to protect and improve people's living environment.

Environmentalists are not against marketing and consumption; they simply want people and organizations to operate with more care for the environment. The marketing system's goal, they assert, should not be to maximize consumption, consumer choice, or consumer satisfaction, but rather to maximize life quality. And "life quality" means not only the quantity and quality of consumer goods and services, but also the quality of the environment. Environmentalists want environmental costs included in both producer and consumer decision making.

The first wave of modern environmentalism in the United States was driven by environmental groups and concerned consumers in the 1960s and 1970s. They were concerned with damage to the ecosystem caused by strip-mining, forest depletion, acid rain, loss of the atmosphere's ozone layer, toxic wastes, and litter. They also were concerned with the loss of recreational areas and with the increase in health problems caused by bad air, polluted water, and chemically treated food.

The second environmentalism wave was driven by government, which passed laws and regulations during the 1970s and 1980s governing industrial practices impacting the environment. This wave hit some industries hard. Steel companies and utilities had to invest billions of dollars in pollution control equipment and costlier fuels. The auto industry had to introduce expensive emission controls in cars. The packaging industry had to find ways to reduce litter. These industries and others have often resented and resisted environmental regulations, especially when they have been imposed too rapidly to allow companies to make proper adjustments. Many of these companies claim they have had to absorb large costs that have made them less competitive.

The first two environmentalism waves have now merged into a third and stronger wave in which companies are accepting more responsibility for doing no harm to the environment. They are shifting from protest to prevention, and from regulation to

Environmentalism
An organized movement of concerned citizens and government agencies to protect and improve people's living environment.

Environmental sustainability
A management approach that involves developing strategies that both sustain the environment and produce profits for the company.

responsibility. More and more companies are adopting policies of **environmental sustainability**. Simply put, environmental sustainability is about generating profits while helping to save the planet. Sustainability is a crucial but difficult societal goal.

Some companies have responded to consumer environmental concerns by doing only what is required to avert new regulations or to keep environmentalists quiet. Enlightened companies, however, are taking action not because someone is forcing them to, or to reap short-run profits, but because it is the right thing to do—for both the company and for the planet's environmental future.

Figure 8.1 shows a grid that companies can use to gauge their progress toward environmental sustainability. In includes both internal and external "greening" activities that will pay off for the firm and environment in the short run and "beyond greening" activities that will pay off in the longer term. At the most basic level, a company can practice *pollution prevention*. This involves more than pollution control—cleaning up waste after it has been created. Pollution prevention means eliminating or minimizing waste before it is created. Companies emphasizing prevention have responded with internal "green marketing" programs—designing and developing ecologically safer products, recyclable and biodegradable packaging, better pollution controls, and more energy-efficient operations.

For example, Sony has reduced the amount of heavy metals—such as lead, mercury, and cadmium—in its electronic products. Nike produces PVC-free shoes, recycles old sneakers, and educates young people about conservation, reuse, and recycling. And UPS is now developing a "green fleet" of alternative-fuel vehicles to replace its old fleet of boxy brown, smoke-belching diesel delivery trucks. It recently deployed 50 new next-generation hybrid electric delivery vehicles to join the roughly 20,000 low-emission and alternative-fuel trucks already in use. The hybrid vehicles produce 45 percent better fuel economy and a dramatic decrease in vehicle emissions.[17]

At the next level, companies can practice *product stewardship*—minimizing not just pollution from production and product design but all environmental impacts throughout the full product life cycle, and all the while reducing costs. Many companies are adopting *design for environment (DFE)* and *cradle-to-cradle* practices. This involves thinking ahead to design products that are easier to recover, reuse, or recycle and developing programs to reclaim products at the end of their lives. DFE not only helps to sustain the environment, it can be highly profitable for the company.

An example is Xerox Corporation's Equipment Remanufacture and Parts Reuse Program, which converts end-of-life office equipment into new products and parts. Equipment returned to Xerox can be remanufactured reusing 70 to 90 percent by weight of old machine components, while still meeting performance standards for equipment made with all new parts. The program creates benefits for both the environment and for the company. So far, it has diverted nearly two billion pounds of waste from landfills. And it reduces the amount of raw material and energy needed to produce new parts. Energy savings from parts reuse total an estimated 320,000 megawatt hours annually—enough energy to light more than 250,000 U.S. homes for the year.[18]

The Environmental Sustainability Portfolio

Source: Stuart L. Hart, "Innovation, Creative Destruction, and Sustainability," *Research Technology Management,* September–October 2005, pp. 21–27.

	Today: Greening	Tomorrow: Beyond Greening
Internal	**Pollution prevention** Eliminating or reducing waste before it is created	**New clean technology** Developing new sets of environmental skills and capabilities
External	**Product stewardship** Minimizing environmental impact throughout the entire product lifecycle	**Sustainability vision** Creating a strategic framework for future sustainability

FIGURE 8.1

Today's "greening" activities focus on improving what companies already do to protect the environment. The "beyond greening" activities identified in Figure 8.1 look to the future. First, internally, companies can plan for *new clean technology*. Many organizations that have made good sustainability headway are still limited by existing technologies. To create fully sustainable strategies, they will need to develop innovative new technologies. Wal-Mart is doing this. It recently opened two experimental superstores designed to test dozens of environmentally friendly and energy-efficient technologies:[19]

> *A 143-foot-tall wind turbine stands outside a Wal-Mart Supercenter in Aurora, Colorado. Incongruous as it might seem, it is clearly a sign that something about this particular store is different. On the outside, the store's facade features row upon row of windows to allow in as much natural light as possible. The landscaping uses native, drought-tolerant plants well adapted to the hot, dry Colorado summers, cutting down on watering, mowing, and the amount of fertilizer and other chemicals needed. Inside the store, an efficient high-output linear fluorescent lighting system saves enough electricity annually from this store alone to supply the needs of 52 single-family homes. The store's heating system burns recovered cooking oil from the deli's fryers. The oil is collected, mixed with waste engine oil from the store's Tire and Lube Express, and burned in the waste-oil boiler. All organic waste, including produce, meats, and paper, is placed in an organic waste compactor, which is then hauled off to a company that turns it into mulch for the garden.*
>
> *These and dozens more technological touches make the supercenter a laboratory for efficient and Earth-friendly retail operations. In the long run, Wal-Mart's environmental goals are to use 100 percent renewable energy, to create zero waste, and to sell products that sustain its resources and environment. Moreover, Wal-Mart is eagerly spreading the word by encouraging visitors—even from competing companies. "We had Target in here not too long ago, and other retail chains and independents have also taken a tour of the store," notes the store manager. "This is not something we're keeping to ourselves. We want everyone to know about it."*

Finally, companies can develop a *sustainability vision,* which serves as a guide to the future. It shows how the company's products and services, processes, and policies must evolve and what new technologies must be developed to get there. This vision of sustainability provides a framework for pollution control, product stewardship, and new environmental technology for the company and others to follow.

Most companies today focus on the upper-left quadrant of the grid in Figure 8.1, investing most heavily in pollution prevention. Some forward-looking companies practice product stewardship and are developing new environmental technologies. Few companies have well-defined sustainability visions. However, emphasizing only one or a few quadrants in the environmental sustainability grid can be shortsighted. Investing only in the left half of the grid puts a company in a good position today but leaves it vulnerable in the future. In contrast, a heavy emphasis on the right half suggests that a company has good environmental vision but lacks the skills needed to implement it. Thus, companies should work at developing all four dimensions of environmental sustainability.

Environmentalism creates some special challenges for global marketers. As international trade barriers come down and global markets expand, environmental issues are having an ever-greater impact on international trade. Countries in North America, Western Europe, and other developed regions are developing strict environmental standards. In the United States, for example, more than two dozen major pieces of environmental legislation have been enacted since 1970, and recent events suggest that more regulation is on the way. A side accord to the North American Free Trade Agreement (NAFTA) set up the Commission for Environmental Cooperation resolving environmental matters. The European Union has passed "end-of-life" regulations affecting automobiles and consumer electronics products. And the EU's Eco-Management and Audit Scheme provides guidelines for environmental self-regulation.[21]

However, environmental policies still vary widely from country to country. Countries such as Denmark, Germany, Japan, and the United States have fully developed environmental policies and high public expectations. But major countries such as China, India, Brazil, and Russia are in only the early stages of developing such policies. Moreover, environmental factors that motivate consumers in one country may have no impact on consumers in another. For example, PVC soft-drink bottles cannot be used in Switzerland or Germany. However, they are preferred in France, which has an extensive recycling process for them. Thus, international companies have found it difficult to develop standard environmental practices that work around the world. Instead, they are creating general policies and then translating these policies into tailored programs that meet local regulations and expectations.

Public actions to regulate marketing

Citizen concerns about marketing practices will usually lead to public attention and legislative proposals. New bills will be debated—many will be defeated, others will be modified, and a few will become workable laws.

There are many laws that will affect marketing. The task is to translate these laws into the language that marketing executives understand as they make decisions about competitive relations, products, price, promotion, and channels of distribution.

Business actions toward socially responsible marketing

At first, many companies opposed consumerism and environmentalism. They thought the criticisms were either unfair or unimportant. But by now, most companies have grown to embrace the new consumer rights, at least in principle. They might oppose certain pieces of legislation as inappropriate ways to solve specific consumer problems, but they recognize the consumer's right to information and protection. Many of these companies have responded positively to consumerism and environmentalism as a way to create greater customer value and to strengthen customer relationships.

Enlightened marketing

Enlightened marketing
A marketing philosophy holding that a company's marketing should support the best long-run performance of the marketing system.

The philosophy of **enlightened marketing** holds that a company's marketing should support the best long-run performance of the marketing system. Enlightened marketing consists of five principles: *consumer-oriented marketing, customer-value marketing, innovative marketing, sense-of-mission marketing,* and *societal marketing.*

Consumer-oriented marketing

Consumer-oriented marketing
The philosophy of enlightened marketing that holds that the company should view and organize its marketing activities from the consumer's point of view.

Consumer-oriented marketing means that the company should view and organize its marketing activities from the consumer's point of view. It should work hard to sense, serve, and satisfy the needs of a defined group of customers. All of the good marketing companies that we've discussed in this text have had this in common: an all-consuming passion for delivering superior value to carefully chosen customers. Only by seeing the world through its customers' eyes can the company build lasting and profitable customer relationships.

Customer-value marketing

Customer-value marketing
A principle of enlightened marketing that holds that a company should put most of its resources into customer value-building marketing investments.

According to the principle of **customer-value marketing**, the company should put most of its resources into customer-value-building marketing investments. Many things marketers do—one-shot sales promotions, cosmetic packaging changes, direct-response advertising—may raise sales in the short run but add less *value* than would actual improvements in the product's quality, features, or convenience. Enlightened marketing calls for building long-run consumer loyalty and relationships by continually improving the value consumers receive from the firm's market offering. By creating value *for* consumers, the company can capture value *from* consumers in return.

Innovative marketing

The principle of **innovative marketing** requires that the company continuously seek real product and marketing improvements. The company that overlooks new and better ways to do things will eventually lose customers to another company that has found a better way. An excellent example of an innovative marketer is Samsung Electronics:

A dozen years ago, Samsung was a copycat consumer electronics brand you bought off a shipping pallet at Costco if you couldn't afford a Sony. But today, the brand holds a high-end, cutting-edge aura. In 1996, Samsung Electronics made an inspired decision. It turned its back on cheap knock-offs and set out to overtake rival Sony. The company hired a crop of fresh, young designers, who unleashed a torrent of new products—not humdrum, me-too products, but sleek, bold, and beautiful products targeted to high-end users. Samsung called them "lifestyle works of art"—from brightly colored cell phones and elegantly thin DVD players to flat-panel TV monitors that hung on walls like paintings. Every new product had to pass the "Wow!" test: If it didn't get a "Wow!" reaction during market testing, it went straight back to the design studio.

Samsung also changed its distribution to match its new caché. It initially abandoned low-end distributors such as Wal-Mart and Kmart, instead building strong relationships with specialty retailers such as Best Buy and Circuit City. Interbrand calculates Samsung's brand value at more than $16 billion, highest in the consumer electronics business and 38 percent higher than Sony's. Samsung is the world leader in CDMA cell phones and is battling for the number-two spot in total handsets sold. It's also number-one worldwide in color TVs, flash memory, and LCD panels. "Samsung's performance continues to astound brand watchers," says one analyst. The company has become a model for others that "want to shift from being a cheap supplier to a global brand." Says a Samsung designer, "We're not el cheapo anymore."[22]

Innovative marketing
A principle of enlightened marketing that requires that a company seek real product and marketing improvements.

Sense-of-mission marketing

Sense-of-mission marketing means that the company should define its mission in broad *social* terms rather than narrow *product* terms. When a company defines a social mission, employees feel better about their work and have a clearer sense of direction. Brands linked with broader missions can serve the best long-run interests of both the brand and consumers. For example, Dove wants to do more than just sell its beauty care products. It's on a mission to discover "real beauty" and to help women be happy just the way they are.

Sense-of-mission marketing
A principle of enlightened marketing that holds that a company should define its mission in broad social terms rather than narrow product terms.

Societal marketing

Following the principle of **societal marketing**, an enlightened company makes marketing decisions by considering consumers' wants and interests, the company's requirements, and society's long-run interests. The company is aware that neglecting consumer and societal long-run interests is a disservice to consumers and society. Alert companies view societal problems as opportunities.

A societally oriented marketer wants to design products that are not only pleasing but also beneficial. The difference is shown in Figure 8.2. Products can be classified

Societal marketing
A principle of enlightened marketing that holds that a company should make marketing decisions by considering consumers' wants, the company's requirements, consumers' long-run interests, and society's long-run interests.

IMMEDIATE SATISFACTION

		Low	High
LONG-RUN CONSUMER BENEFIT	**High**	Salutary products	Desirable products
	Low	Deficient products	Pleasing products

Societal Classification of Products

FIGURE 8.2

Deficient products

Products that have neither immediate appeal nor long-run benefits.

Pleasing products

Products that give high immediate satisfaction but may hurt consumers in the long run.

Salutary products

Products that have low appeal but may benefit consumers in the long run.

Desirable products

Products that give both high immediate satisfaction and high long-run benefits.

according to their degree of immediate consumer satisfaction and long-run consumer benefit. **Deficient products**, such as bad-tasting and ineffective medicine, have neither immediate appeal nor long-run benefits. **Pleasing products** give high immediate satisfaction but may hurt consumers in the long run. Examples include cigarettes and junk food. **Salutary products** have low appeal but may benefit consumers in the long run; for instance, bicycle helmets or some insurance products. **Desirable products** give both high immediate satisfaction and high long-run benefits, such as a tasty *and* nutritious breakfast food.

As with environmentalism, the issue of ethics presents special challenges for international marketers. Business standards and practices vary a great deal from one country to the next. For example, whereas bribes and kickbacks are illegal for U.S. firms, they are standard business practice in many South American countries. One recent study found that companies from some nations were much more likely to use bribes when seeking contracts in emerging-market nations. The most flagrant bribe-paying firms were from India, Russia, and China. Other countries where corruption is common include Iraq, Myanmar, and Haiti. The least corrupt were companies from Iceland, Finland, New Zealand, and Denmark.[27]

The question arises as to whether a company must lower its ethical standards to compete effectively in countries with lower standards. The answer: No. Companies should make a commitment to a common set of shared standards worldwide. For example, John Hancock Mutual Life Insurance Company operates successfully in Southeast Asia, an area that by Western standards has widespread questionable business and government practices. Despite warnings from locals that Hancock would need to bend its rules to succeed, the company set out strict guidelines. "We told our people that we had the same ethical standards, same procedures, and same policies in these countries that we have in the United States, and we do," says Hancock Chairman Stephen Brown. "We just felt that things like payoffs were wrong—and if we had to do business that way, we'd rather not do business." Hancock employees feel good about the consistent levels of ethics. "There may be countries where you have to do that kind of thing," says Brown. "We haven't found that country yet, and if we do, we won't do business there."[28]

Many industrial and professional associations have suggested codes of ethics, and many companies are now adopting their own codes. For example, the American Marketing Association, an international association of marketing managers and scholars, developed a code of ethics. Companies are also developing programs to teach managers about important ethics issues and help them find the proper responses. They hold ethics workshops and seminars and set up ethics committees. Furthermore, most major U.S. companies have appointed high-level ethics officers to champion ethics issues and to help resolve ethics problems and concerns facing employees.

Desirable products: Haworth's Zody office chair is not only attractive and functional but also environmentally responsible.

chapter 9

> **Diffusion**

What is opinion leadership?

The power and importance of personal influence are captured in the following comment by an ad agency executive: "Perhaps the most important thing for marketers to understand about word-of-mouth is its huge potential economic impact."[1] This decade-old comment is more true today than ever before!

Opinion leadership (or word-of-mouth communications) is the process by which one person (the opinion leader) informally influences the actions or attitudes of others, who may be opinion seekers or opinion recipients. The key characteristic of the influence is that it is interpersonal and informal and takes place between two or more people, *none of whom represents a commercial selling source that would gain directly from the sale of something.* Word-of-mouth implies personal, or face-to-face, communication, although it may also take place in a telephone conversation or within the context of e-mail or a chat group on the Internet. This communication process is likely, at times, to also be reinforced by nonverbal observations of the appearance and behavior of others.

One of the parties in a word-of-mouth encounter usually offers advice or information about a product or service, such as which of several brands is best or how a particular product may be used. This person, the **opinion leader**, may become an **opinion receiver** when another product or service is brought up as part of the overall discussion.

Individuals who actively seek information and advice about products sometimes are called **opinion seekers**. For purposes of simplicity, the terms *opinion receiver* and *opinion recipient* will be used interchangeably in the following discussion to identify both those who actively seek product information from others and those who receive unsolicited information. Simple examples of opinion leadership at work include the following:

1. *A family decides that they need a new gas barbeque for their backyard, and they ask a few of their neighbors which brand they should purchase.*

2. *A person shows his cousin photographs of his recent vacation in Costa Rica, and the cousin suggests that using a different film might produce better pictures of the rain forest.*

3. *During a coffee break, a coworker talks about the new TV series she saw last night and recommends seeing it.*

Most studies of opinion leadership are concerned with the measurement of the behavioral impact that opinion leaders have on the consumption habits of others. Available research, for example, suggests that "influentials" or opinion leaders are almost four times more likely than others to be asked about political and government issues, as well as how to handle teens; three times more likely to be asked about computers or investments; and twice as likely to be asked about health issues and restaurants.[2] There is also research to suggest that when an information seeker feels that he or she knows little about a particular product or service, a "strong-tie source" will be sought (such as a friend or family member), but when the consumer has some prior knowledge of the subject area, then a "weak-tie source" is acceptable (acquaintances or strangers).[3]

Word-of-mouth in today's *always in contact* world

Over the past decade, with the proliferation of cell phone usage and e-mail (and the invention of combination devices like BlackBerry and Web-capable cell phones), many people find themselves, by choice, to be "always" available to friends, family, and business associates. Although Americans have been somewhat slower than consumers in other countries to embrace the notion of receiving e-mail via their cellular telephones, this may be due, in part, to the great number of PCs in use in the United States. Table 9.1 shows, whereas almost 68 percent of Americans are Internet users, the second-place nation in terms of the number of Internet users, China, has only 7.3 percent of its citizens on the Web. In contrast, there are presently about 310 million cellular telephone users in China, which adds up to about 25 percent of its population.[4]

TABLE 9.1	Top 15 Countries in Terms of the Number of Internet Users in 2005	
COUNTRY	NUMBER OF INTERNET USERS (IN MILLIONS)	INTERNET PENETRATION
United States	200.9	67.8
China	94.0	7.3
Japan	67.7	52.8
Germany	46.3	56.0
India	39.2	3.6
United Kingdom	35.2	58.7
South Korea	31.6	63.3
Italy	28.6	48.8
France	24.8	41.2
Russia	22.3	15.5
Canada	20.5	63.8
Brazil	17.9	9.9
Indonesia	15.3	7.0
Spain	14.6	1.4
Australia	13.6	66.4

Source: **http://www.internetworldstats.com/top20.htm**, accessed May 27, 2005.

Along with the explosion of Web-capable cellular telephones is the creation of the "thumb generation," which is known in Japan as *oya yubi sedai*. Young people in Japan learn to send e-mail messages from the cell phones by using their thumbs, and some Japanese TV stations have even held thumbing speed contests. This is just a natural extension of the thumb usage learned from using handheld computer games.[5]

Just how important is word-of-mouth?

A recent study in the United Kingdom asked consumers which information sources would make them "more comfortable" with a company. The answer at the top of the list was "friend's recommendation" (the response of 71 percent of respondents), whereas "past experience" was the response of 63 percent of respondents. Only 15 percent of the consumers mentioned "advertising."[6] Additionally, it has been reported that over 40 percent of U.S. consumers will actively seek the advice of family and friends when in the market for a doctor, lawyer, or automobile mechanic, and the importance of word-of-mouth is even greater with respect to the diffusion of new products.[7]

Dynamics of the opinion leadership process

The opinion leadership process is a very dynamic and powerful consumer force. As informal communication sources, opinion leaders are remarkably effective at influencing consumers in their product-related decisions. Some of the reasons for the effectiveness of opinion leaders are discussed next.

Credibility

Opinion leaders are highly credible sources of information because they usually are perceived as objective concerning the product or service information or advice they dispense.

Their intentions are perceived as being in the best interests of the opinion recipients because they receive no compensation for the advice and apparently have no "ax to grind." Because opinion leaders often base their product comments on firsthand experience, their advice reduces for opinion receivers the perceived risk or anxiety inherent in buying new products. The average person is exposed to anywhere from 200 to 1,000 sales communications a day, but he or she is thousands of times more likely to act on the basis of a friend's or colleague's recommendation. Whereas the advertiser has a vested interest in the message being advertised, the opinion leader offers advice that does not have a commercial motive.

Positive and negative product information

Information provided by marketers is invariably favorable to the product and/or brand. Thus, the very fact that opinion leaders provide both favorable and unfavorable information adds to their credibility. An example of an unfavorable or negative product comment is, "The problem with those inexpensive kitchen knives is that they soon go from being sharp to being dull." Compared with positive or even neutral comments, negative comments are relatively uncommon. For this reason, consumers are especially likely to note such information and to avoid products or brands that receive negative evaluations. Over the years, motion pictures have failed due to negative "buzz" about the film, and negative word-of-mouth about new food products have retarded sales or caused the early death of a product. Consumers, it turns out, are generally much more likely to share a negative experience than a positive one.

Information and advice

Opinion leaders are the source of both information and advice. They may simply talk about their *experience* with a product, relate what they know about a product, or, more aggressively, *advise* others to buy or to avoid a specific product. The kinds of product or service information that opinion leaders are likely to transmit during a conversation include the following:

1. Which of several brands is best: *"In my opinion, when you consider picture quality versus price, Sony offers the best value in small digital cameras."*
2. How to best use a specific product: *"I find that my walls look best when I paint with a roller rather than a pad."*
3. Where to shop: *"When Brooks Brothers has a sale, the values are terrific."*
4. Who provides the best service: *"Over the past few years, I've had my car serviced and repaired at Tom's Garage, and I think its service can't be beat."*

Many of the messages being sent and received these days deal with movies, restaurants, shopping, computer games, and other areas of interest to young adults—word-of-mouth communication in the form of telephone or e-mail. Figure 9.1 presents the results of a survey estimating the percentage of Americans that acted on a referral from an opinion leader for selected important product and service categories during the past year.

Opinion leadership is category specific

Opinion leadership tends to be *category specific;* that is, opinion leaders often "specialize" in certain product categories about which they offer information and advice. When other product categories are discussed, however, they are just as likely to reverse their roles and become opinion receivers. A person who is considered particularly knowledgeable about home electronics may be an opinion leader in terms of this subject, yet when it comes to purchasing a new washing machine, the same person may seek advice from someone else—perhaps even from someone who has sought his advice on home electronics.

Opinion leadership is a two-way street

As the preceding example suggests, consumers who are opinion leaders in one product-related situation may become opinion receivers in another situation, even for the same product. Consider the following example. Rob, a new father contemplating the purchase

Word-of-Mouth in Action

Source: Business Week (based on an online survey of 1,000 adults, February 2002, Goodmind LLC), May 6, 2002, 10.

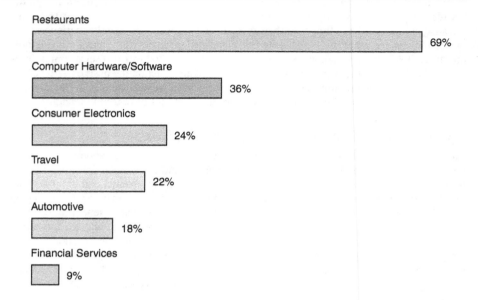

Restaurants — 69%

Computer Hardware/Software — 36%

Consumer Electronics — 24%

Travel — 22%

Automotive — 18%

Financial Services — 9%

of a baby car seat, may seek information and advice from other people to reduce his indecision about which brand to select. Once the car seat has been bought, however, he may experience postpurchase dissonance and have a compelling need to talk favorably about the purchase to other people to confirm the correctness of his own choice. In the first instance, he is an opinion receiver (seeker); in the second, he assumes the role of opinion leader.

An opinion leader may also be influenced by an opinion receiver as the result of a product-related conversation. For example, a person may tell a friend about a favorite hotel getaway in Lake Como, Italy, and, in response to comments from the opinion receiver, come to realize that the hotel is too small, too isolated, and offers vacationers fewer amenities than other hotels.

The motivation behind opinion leadership

To understand the phenomenon of opinion leadership, it is useful to examine the motivation of those who provide and those who receive product-related information.

The needs of opinion leaders

What motivates a person to talk about a product or service? Motivation theory suggests that people may provide information or advice to others to satisfy some basic need of their own. However, opinion leaders may be unaware of their own underlying motives. As suggested earlier, opinion leaders may simply be trying to reduce their own postpurchase dissonance by confirming their own buying decisions. For instance, if Bradley subscribes to a satellite TV service and then is uncertain that he made the right choice, he may try to reassure himself by "talking up" the service's advantages to others. In this way, he relieves his own psychological discomfort. Furthermore, when he can influence a friend or neighbor to also get satellite TV, he confirms his own good judgment in selecting the service first. Thus, the opinion leader's true motivation may really be self-confirmation or self-involvement. Furthermore, the information or advice that an opinion leader dispenses may provide all types of tangential personal benefits: It may confer attention, imply some type of status, grant superiority, demonstrate awareness and expertise, and give the feeling of possessing inside information and the satisfaction of "converting" less adventurous souls.

In addition to *self*-involvement, the opinion leader may also be motivated by *product* involvement, *social* involvement, and *message* involvement. Opinion leaders who are motivated by product involvement may find themselves so pleased or so disappointed with a product that they simply must tell others about it. Those who are motivated by social involvement need to share product-related experiences. In this type of situation, opinion leaders use their product-related conversations as expressions of friendship, neighborliness, and love.

The needs of opinion receivers

Opinion receivers satisfy a variety of needs by engaging in product-related conversations. First, they obtain new-product or new-usage information. Second, they reduce their perceived risk by receiving firsthand knowledge from a user about a specific product or brand. Third, they reduce the search time entailed in the identification of a needed product or service. Moreover, opinion receivers can be certain of receiving the approval of the opinion leader if they follow that person's product endorsement or advice and purchase the product. For all of these reasons, people often look to friends, neighbors, and other acquaintances for product information. Indeed, research examining the importance of four specific information sources on a hypothetical $100 purchase of consumer services revealed that *advice from others* was more important than the combined impact of sales representatives, advertising and promotion, and other sources.[8] Table 9.2 compares the motivations of opinion receivers with those of opinion leaders.

Purchase pals

Researchers have also examined the influence of "purchase pals" as information sources who actually accompany consumers on shopping trips. Although purchase pals were used only 9 percent of the time for grocery items, they were used 25 percent of the time for purchases of electronic equipment (e.g., computers, VCRs, TV sets).[9] Interestingly,

TABLE 9.2	A Comparison of the Motivations of Opinion Leaders and Opinion Receivers

OPINION LEADERS	OPINION RECEIVERS
Self-Improvement Motivations	
• *Reduce postpurchase uncertainty or dissonance*	• *Reduce the risk of making a purchase commitment*
• *Gain attention or status*	• *Reduce search time (e.g., avoid the necessity of shopping around)*
• *Assert superiority and expertise*	
• *Feel like an adventurer*	
• *Experience the power of "converting" others*	
Product-Involvement Motivations	
• *Express satisfaction or dissatisfaction with a product or service*	• *Learn how to use or consume a product*
	• *Learn what products are new in the marketplace*
Social-Involvement Motivations	
• *Express neighborliness and friendship by discussing products or services that may be useful to others*	• *Buy products that have the approval of others, thereby ensuring acceptance*
Message-Involvement Motivations	
• *Express one's reaction to a stimulating advertisement by telling others about it*	

male purchase pals are more likely to be used as sources of product category expertise, product information, and retail store and price information. Female purchase pals are more often used for moral support and to increase confidence in the buyer's decisions. Similarly, it seems that when a weak tie exists between the purchase pal and the shopper (e.g., neighbor, classmate, or work colleague), the purchase pal's main contribution tends to be functional—the source's specific product experiences and general marketplace knowledge are being relied on. In contrast, when strong ties exist (such as mother, son, husband, or wife), what is relied on is the purchase pal's familiarity and understanding of the buyer's individual characteristics and needs (or tastes and preferences).

Surrogate buyers versus opinion leaders

Although the traditional model of new product adoption shows opinion leaders influencing the purchase of many new products and services, there are instances in which surrogate buyers replace opinion leaders in this role. For example, working women are increasingly turning to wardrobe consultants for help in purchasing business attire, most new drugs start out requiring a doctor's prescription, and many service providers make decisions for their clients (e.g., your service station decides which brand of disk brake pads to install on your car). Consequently, in an increasing number of decision situations, it is a surrogate buyer who primarily influences the purchase. Table 9.3 presents the key differences between opinion leaders and surrogate buyers.

TABLE 9.3	Key Differences Between Opinion Leaders and Surrogate Buyers
OPINION LEADER	**SURROGATE BUYER**
1. Informal relationship with end users	1. Formal relationship; occupation-related status
2. Information exchange occurs in the context of a casual interaction	2. Information exchange in the form formal instructions/advice
3. Homophilous (to a certain extent) to end users	3. Heterophilous to end users (that in fact is the source of power)
4. Does not get paid for advice	4. Usually hired, therefore gets paid
5. Usually socially more active than end users	5. Not necessarily socially more active than end users
6. Accountability limited regarding the outcome of advice	6. High level of accountability
7. As accountability limited, rigor in search and screening of alternatives low	7. Search and screening of alternatives more rigorous
8. Likely to have (although not always) used the product personally	8. May not have used the product for personal consumption
9. More than one can be consulted before making a final decision	9. Second opinion taken on rare occasions
10. Same person can be an opinion leader for a variety of related product categories	10. Usually specializes for a specific product/service category

Source: Praveen Aggarwal and Taihoon Cha, "Surrogate Buyers and the New Product Adoption Process: A Conceptualization and Managerial Framework," *Journal of Consumer Marketing* 14, no. 5 (1997): 394. Reprinted by permission.

Measurement of opinion leadership

Consumer researchers are interested in identifying and measuring the impact of the opinion leadership process on consumption behavior. In measuring opinion leadership, the researcher has a choice of four basic measurement techniques: (1) the *self-designating method,* (2) the *sociometric method,* (3) the *key informant method,* and (4) the *objective method.*

In the *self-designating method*, respondents are asked to evaluate the extent to which they have provided others with information about a product category or specific brand or have otherwise influenced the purchase decisions of others. There are two types of self-designating question formats that can be used to determine a consumer's opinion leadership activity. The first consists of a single question, whereas the second consists of a series of questions. The use of multiple questions enables the researcher to determine a respondent's opinion leadership more reliably because the statements are interrelated. The self-designating technique is used more often than other methods for measuring opinion leadership because consumer researchers find it easy to include in market research questionnaires. Because this method relies on the respondent's self-evaluation, however, it may be open to bias should respondents perceive "opinion leadership" (even though the term is not used) to be a desirable characteristic and, thus, overestimate their own roles as opinion leaders.

The *sociometric method* measures the person-to-person informal communication of consumers concerning products or product categories. In this method, respondents are asked to identify (a) the specific individuals (if any) to whom they provided advice or information about the product or brand under study and (b) the specific individuals (if any) who provided them with advice or information about the product or brand under study. In the first instance, if respondents identify one or more individuals to whom they have provided some form of product information, they are tentatively classified as opinion leaders. In the second instance, respondents are asked to identify the individuals (if any) who provided them with information about a product under investigation. Individuals designated by the primary respondent are tentatively classified as opinion leaders. In both cases, the researcher attempts to validate the determination by asking the individuals named whether they did, in fact, either provide or receive the relevant product information.

Opinion leadership can also be measured through the use of a *key informant*, a person who is keenly aware of or knowledgeable about the nature of social communications among members of a specific group. The key informant is asked to identify those individuals in the group who are most likely to be opinion leaders. However, the key informant does not have to be a member of the group under study. For example, a professor may serve as the key informant for a college class, identifying those students who are most likely to be opinion leaders with regard to a particular issue. This research method is relatively inexpensive because it requires that only one individual or at most several individuals be intensively interviewed, whereas the self-designating and sociometric methods require that a consumer sample or entire community be interviewed. However, the key informant method is generally not used by marketers because of the difficulties inherent in identifying an individual who can objectively identify opinion leaders in a relevant consumer group.

Finally, the *objective method* of determining opinion leadership is much like a "controlled experiment"—it involves placing new products or new-product information with selected individuals and then tracing the resulting "web" of interpersonal communication concerning the relevant product(s). In a practical sense, a new restaurant in a downtown business district might apply this approach to speed up the creation of a core customer base by sending out invitations to young, influential business executives to dine with their friends at a reduced introductory price any time during the first month of the restaurant's operations. If the restaurant's food and drink are judged to be superior, the restaurant is likely to enjoy the benefits of enhanced positive word-of-mouth generated by the systematic encouragement of the young clientele to "try it out" and who "talk it up" to their friends after experiencing the new restaurant.

Table 9.4 presents an overview of each of the four methods of measuring opinion leadership, together with advantages and limitations.

| TABLE 9.4 | Methods of Measuring Opinion Leadership: Advantages and Limitations | | | |

OPINION LEADERSHIP MEASUREMENT METHOD	DESCRIPTION OF METHOD	SAMPLE QUESTIONS ASKED	ADVANTAGES	LIMITATIONS
Self-Designating Method	Each respondent is asked a series of questions to determine the degree to which he or she perceives himself or herself to be an opinion leader.	"Do you influence other people in their selection of products?"	Measures the individual's own perceptions of his or her opinion leadership.	Depends on the objectivity with which respondents can identify and report their personal influence.
Sociometric Method	Members of a social system are asked to identify to whom they give advice and to whom they go for advice and information about a product category.	"Whom do you ask?" "Who asks you for information about that product category?"	Sociometric questions have the greatest degree of validity and are easy to administer.	It is very costly and analysis often is very complex. Requires a large number of respondents. Not suitable for sample design where only a portion of the social system is interviewed.
Key Informant Method	Carefully selected key informants in a social system are asked to designate opinion leaders.	"Who are the most influential people in the group?"	Relatively inexpensive and less time consuming than the sociometric method.	Informants who are not thoroughly familiar with the social system are likely to provide invalid information.
Objective Method	Artificially places individuals in a position to act as opinion leaders and measures results of their efforts.	"Have you tried the product?"	Measures individual's ability to influence others under controlled circumstances.	Requires the establishment of an experimental design and the tracking of the resulting impact on the participants.

Source: Adapted with the permission of The Free Press, a division of Simon & Schuster, from *Diffusion of Innovations*. Fourth Edition by Everett M. Rogers. Copyright © 1995 by Everett M. Rogers. Copyright © 1962, 1971, 1983 by the Free Press.

A profile of the opinion leader

Just who are opinion leaders? Can they be recognized by any distinctive characteristics? Can they be reached through specific media? Marketers have long sought answers to these questions, for if they are able to identify the relevant opinion leaders for their products, they can design marketing messages that encourage them to communicate with and influence the consumption behavior of others. For this reason, consumer researchers have attempted to develop a realistic profile of the opinion leader. This has not been easy to do. As was pointed out earlier, opinion leadership tends to be category specific; that is, an individual who is an opinion *leader* in one product category may be an opinion *receiver* in another product category. Thus, the generalized profile of opinion leaders is likely to be influenced by the context of specific product categories.

Although it is difficult to construct a generalized profile of the opinion leader without considering a particular category of interest (or a specific product or service category), Table 9.5 does present a summary of the generalized characteristics that

TABLE 9.5	Profile of Opinion Leaders

GENERALIZED ATTRIBUTES ACROSS PRODUCT CATEGORIES	CATEGORY-SPECIFIC ATTRIBUTES
Innovativeness	Interest
Willingness to talk	Knowledge
Self-confidence	Special-interest media exposure
Gregariousness	Same age
Cognitive differentiation	Same social status
	Social exposure outside group

appear to hold true regardless of product category. The evidence indicates that opinion leaders across all product categories generally exhibit a variety of defining characteristics. First, they reveal a keen sense of knowledge and interest in the particular product or service area, and they are likely to be consumer innovators. They also demonstrate a greater willingness to talk about the product, service, or topic; they are more self-confident; and they are more outgoing and gregarious ("more sociable"). Furthermore, within the context of a specific subject area, opinion leaders receive more information via nonpersonal sources and are considered to have expertise in their area of influence. They also usually belong to the same socioeconomic and age groups as their opinion receivers.

When it comes to their mass-media exposure or habits, opinion leaders are likely to read special-interest publications devoted to the specific topic or product category in which they "specialize."[10] For example, an automobile opinion leader might read publications such as *Car and Driver, Motor Trend*, and *Automobile*. These special-interest magazines serve not only to inform automotive-oriented consumers about new cars, tires, audio systems, and accessories that may be of personal interest, but also provide them with the specialized knowledge that enables them to make recommendations to relatives, friends, and neighbors. Thus, the opinion leader tends to have greater exposure to media specifically relevant to his or her area of interest than the nonleader. Summing up it for us, a recent study found that opinion leaders "gain influence through their informational advantages relative to others in the same environment."[11]

Frequency and overlap of opinion leadership

Opinion leadership is not a rare phenomenon. Often more than one-third of the people studied in a consumer research project are classified as opinion leaders with respect to some self-selected product category. The frequency of consumer opinion leadership suggests that people are sufficiently interested in at least one product or product category to talk about it and give advice concerning it to others.

This leads to the interesting question: Do opinion leaders in one product category tend to be opinion leaders in other product categories? The answer to this question comes from an area of research aptly referred to as *opinion leadership overlap*. Accordingly, opinion leadership tends to overlap across certain combinations of interest areas. Overlap is likely to be highest among product categories that involve similar interests (such as televisions and VCRs, high-fashion clothing and cosmetics, household cleansers and detergents, expensive wristwatches and writing instruments, hunting gear, and fishing tackle). Thus, opinion leaders in one product area often are opinion leaders in related areas in which they are also interested.

Market mavens

Research suggests the existence of a special category of consumer influencer, the **market maven**. These consumers possess a wide range of information about many different types of products, retail outlets, and other dimensions of markets. They both initiate discussions with other consumers and respond to requests for market information. Market mavens like to shop, and they also like to share their shopping expertise with others. However, although they appear to fit the profile of opinion leaders in that they have high levels of brand awareness and tend to try more brands, unlike opinion leaders their influence extends beyond the realm of high-involvement products. For example, market mavens may help diffuse information on such low-involvement products as razor blades and laundry detergent.[12] Furthermore, market mavens appear to be motivated by a sense of obligation to share information, a desire to help others, and the feeling of pleasure that comes with telling others about products.[13]

While both innovators and market mavens spend more time shopping than other consumers, innovators tend to be price insensitive. Market mavens are not primarily concerned with price, but are nevertheless more value conscious than other shoppers and are heavy users of coupons.[14] Table 9.6 compares consumer innovators to market mavens, including breadth of knowledge and reaction to promotions. The table, for example, reveals that while the opinion leader's knowledge extends only to a specific product category, market mavens possess a wide range of market information. Table 9.7

TABLE 9.6	Consumer Innovativeness and Market Mavenism Compared	
CONSTRUCT OF INTEREST	**INNOVATIVENESS**	**MARKET MAVENISM**
Information and Knowledge	Knowledgeable about specific product categories	Wide variety of market information; information seekers
Opinion Leadership	Act as opinion leaders for new products	Act as opinion leaders for many aspects of the marketplace
Search Behavior	Exposed to a variety of information sources	Exposed to a variety of information sources
Involvement	Involved in the marketplace; especially new products	Involved in many aspects of the marketplace
Promotion	Interested in information heavy or centrally processed communications	Heavy users of coupons, shopping lists, grocery budgets, and ads
Brand Awareness	Aware of new brands in specific product fields	Aware of new brands in many fields
Assertiveness	No reason to expect an assertive style of shopping and buying.	More assertive than other consumers
Value conscious	More interested in newness than price; not bargain conscious	More value conscious than other consumers; seek bargain prices
Fashion Consciousness	Fashion innovators are fashion conscious	Market Mavens are not fashion conscious

Source: Ronald E. Goldsmith, Leisa R. Flynn, and Elizabeth B. Goldsmith, "Innovation Consumers and Market Mavens," *Journal of Marketing Theory and Practice* 11 (Fall 2003): 56.

TABLE 9.7	Market Maven Scale (Six-point Agree/Disagree Response Format)

1. I like introducing new brands and products to my friends.
2. I like helping people by providing them with information about many kinds of products.
3. People ask me for information about products, places to shop, or sales.
4. If someone asked where to get the best buy on several products, I could tell him or her where to shop.
5. My friends think of me as a good source of information when it comes to new products or sales.
6. Think about a person who has information about a variety of products and likes to share this information with others. This person knows about new products, sales, stores, and so on, but does not necessarily feel he or she is an expert on one particular product. How well would you say that this description fits you?

Source: Ronald E. Goldsmith, Leisa R. Flynn, and Elizabeth B. Goldsmith, "Innovation Consumers and Market Mavens," *Journal of Marketing Theory and Practice* 11 (Fall 2003): 58.

presents a Market Maven Scale that uses a 7-point Agree/Disagree response format to identify market mavens.

It would be wrong to discuss market mavens without specifically citing the role played by teenagers. Seventy percent of teens use the Internet regularly, and they know how to search for and find information both for themselves and as information requests from others. Research has found that in families where both parents and teenagers are heavy Internet users, both the teens and their parents recognize the teens' expertise and value the child's contribution to family decision-making.[15]

Just as the examination of the relationship between being an opinion leader and being an innovator led to the recognition of the existence of the market maven, research on the market maven has uncovered yet another category of consumers, the *social hub*. These are individuals who direct social traffic—they have relationships with many people, they frequently bring these people together, and they do so for personal pleasure (rather than for some tangible reward). It is possible that social hubs may prove to be an excellent way to predict the number of people that are told about a consumption experience.[16]

The situational environment of opinion leadership

Product-related discussions between two people do not take place in a vacuum. Two people are not likely to meet and spontaneously break into a discussion in which product-related information is sought or offered. Rather, product discussions generally occur within relevant situational contexts, such as when a specific product or a similar product is used or served or as an outgrowth of a more general discussion that touches on the product category. For example, while drinking coffee, one person might tell the other person about a preferred brand of coffee.

Moreover, it is not surprising that opinion leaders and opinion receivers often are friends, neighbors, or work associates, for existing friendships provide numerous opportunities for conversation concerning product-related topics. Close physical proximity is likely to increase the occurrences of product-related conversations. A local health club or community center, for example, or even the local supermarket, provides opportunities for neighbors to meet and engage in informal communications about products or services. In a similar fashion, the rapid growth in the use of the Internet is also creating a type of close "electronic proximity" or "communities"—one in which people of like minds, attitudes, concerns, backgrounds, and experiences are coming together in "chat sessions" to explore their common interests. Within this context, the Internet is a fertile environment for word-of-mouth communications of the kind that consumer marketers are interested in impacting.

The interpersonal flow of communication

A classic study of voting behavior concluded that ideas often flow from mass media (e.g., newspapers, magazines radio, TV) to opinion leaders and from them to the general public.[17] This so-called **two-step flow of communication theory** portrays opinion leaders as direct receivers of information from impersonal mass-media sources, who in turn, transmit (and interpret) this information to the masses. This theory views the opinion leader as an intermediary between the impersonal mass media and the majority of society. Figure 9.2 presents a model of the two-step flow of communication theory. Information is depicted as flowing in a single direction (or one way) from the mass media to opinion leaders (Step 1) and then from the opinion leaders (who interpret, legitimize, and transmit the information) to friends, neighbors, and acquaintances, who constitute the "masses" (Step 2).

Multistep flow of communication theory

A more comprehensive model of the interpersonal flow of communication depicts the transmission of information from the media as a multistep flow. The revised model takes into account the fact that information and influence often are two-way processes in which opinion leaders both influence and are influenced by opinion receivers. Figure 9.3 presents a model of the **multistep flow of communication theory**. Steps 1a and 1b depict the flow of information from the mass media simultaneously to opinion leaders, opinion receivers/seekers, and information receivers (who neither influence nor are influenced by others). Step 2 shows the transmission of information and influence from opinion leaders to opinion receivers/seekers. Step 3 reflects the transfer of information and influence from opinion receivers to opinion leaders.

Advertising designed to stimulate/simulate word-of-mouth

In a world before the Internet, Weblogs, and viral or buzz marketing, firms' advertising and promotional programs largely relied on *stimulating or persuading consumers* to "tell your friends how much you like our product." This is one way in which marketers encourage consumer discussions of their products or services. For instance, Daffy's, an off-price retailer operating in several northeastern states (**www.daffys.com**), used an outdoor poster (at bus shelters and subway stations) to boldly state that "Friends don't let friends pay retail." Here the implication is that you should share your knowledge and experience with others. The objective of a promotional strategy of stimulation is to run advertisements or a direct-marketing program that is sufficiently interesting and informative to provoke consumers into discussing the benefits of the product with others.

Two-Step Flow of Communication Theory

FIGURE 9.2

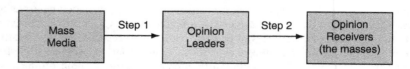

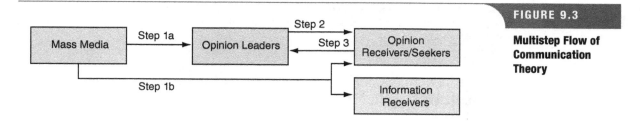

FIGURE 9.3

Multistep Flow of Communication Theory

In a classic study, a group of socially influential high school students (class presidents and sports captains) were asked to become members of a panel that would rate newly released musical recordings. As part of their responsibilities, panel participants were encouraged to discuss their record choices with friends. Preliminary examination suggested that these influentials would not qualify as opinion leaders for musical recordings because of their relatively meager ownership of the product category.[18] However, some of the records the group evaluated made the Top 10 charts in the cities in which the members of the group lived; these same recordings did not make the Top 10 charts in any other city. This study suggests that product-specific opinion leaders can be created by taking socially involved or influential people and deliberately increasing their enthusiasm for a product category.

A more recent research effort explored the notion of increasing enthusiasm for a product category. Over a 12-week period of time, half the participants were assigned to look at corporate Web sites (i.e., marketer-generated information sources), and half were asked to look at online discussions (e.g., chat rooms, forums). Consumers who got their information from online discussions reported greater interest in the product category. It is felt that chat rooms and other forums provide consumers with personal experiences and may offer greater credibility, trustworthiness, relevance, and empathy than marketer-generated Internet Web sites.[19]

Another related form of advertising message (much less common than ads designed to stimulate word-of-mouth) are ads designed to *simulate word-of-mouth* was from time-to-time used by a small number of marketing firms to supplement their regular advertising image or brand advertising. Ads designed to *simulate word-of-mouth* portrayed people in the act of informal communication.

Word-of-mouth may be uncontrollable

Although most marketing managers believe that word-of-mouth communication is extremely effective, one problem that they sometimes overlook is the fact that informal communication is difficult to control. Negative comments, frequently in the form of rumors that are untrue, can sweep through the marketplace to the detriment of a product.

Some common rumor themes that have plagued marketers in recent years and unfavorably influenced sales include the following: (1) The product was produced under unsanitary conditions, (2) the product contained an unwholesome or culturally unacceptable ingredient, (3) the product functioned as an undesirable depressant or stimulant, (4) the product included a cancer-causing element or agent, and (5) the firm was owned or influenced by an unfriendly or misguided foreign country, governmental agency, or religious cult.

A particularly challenging form of "negative" word-of-mouth can be generated today over the Internet, when a dissatisfied consumer decides to post his or her story on a bulletin board for all to see. Consider, for example, the Apple iPod. When two brothers in New York City found that a failed battery could not be easily or inexpensively replaced (Apple was charging $200 to replace the battery), they went online (**www.ipodsdirtysecret.com**). Consumers critical of Starbucks can vent their anger at **www.ihatestarbucks.com**, and people who dislike Microsoft can always log onto

www.watchingmicrosoft.com. As one advertising industry executive has commented, "One determined detractor can do as much damage as 100,000 positive mentions can do good."[20]

Marketers seek to take control of the opinion leadership process

Marketers have long been aware of the power that opinion leadership exerts on consumers' preferences and actual purchase behavior. For this reason marketers are increasingly designing products with characteristics or design factors that make them easy to talk about and whip up interest about. They are also looking at ways to more directly intervene and take control of the word-of-mouth process. This effort to control the flow of word-of-mouth about a product is not new. However, what is new is the degree of interest and available technologies that makes it easier to accomplish (e.g., consumers' buddy lists).

Marketers are now moving beyond primarily employing advertising to stimulate or simulate word-of-mouth, to an environment where they are seeking to manage (i.e., to create and control) word-of-mouth. In this section we will consider marketers' efforts to create products with greater word-of-mouth potential, and to harness the power of mouth by either hiring paid actors to go out and create product buzz; or securing the involvement of largely unpaid consumer volunteers, who act as buzz agents to drum up awareness, interest, and intention to purchase the clients' new products. As part of this discussion we will consider viral marketing and Weblogs.

Creating products with built-in buzz potential

New-product designers take advantage of the effectiveness of word-of-mouth communication by deliberately designing products to have word-of-mouth potential. A new product should give customers something to talk about ("buzz potential"). Examples of products and services that have had such word-of-mouth appeal include iPods, cell phones with digital cameras, and a host of other sought after technologies and luxury brands. Such high-demand products have attained market share advantages because consumers are willing to "sell" them to each other by means of word-of-mouth. Motion pictures also appear to be one form of entertainment in which word-of-mouth operates with some degree of regularity and a large degree of impact. It is very common to be involved directly or overhear people discussing which movies they liked and which movies they advise others to skip. Proof of the power of word-of-mouth are those cases in which critics hate a movie and the viewing public like it and tell their friends.

For instances in which informal word-of-mouth does not spontaneously emerge from the uniqueness of the product or its marketing strategy, some marketers have deliberately attempted to stimulate or to simulate opinion leadership.

Strategy designed to simulate buzz

The nature and scope of the Internet has inspired marketers to expand opportunities to take control of the process of word-of-mouth. For instance, they are increasingly hiring buzz marketing agencies that maintain large armies of largely volunteer consumer buzz agents who seem to greatly enjoy telling other consumers (often friends and family, and people on their buddy list) about a product that they have been exposed to and feel that they would like to talk about. An example of such a consulting agency is Bzzagent (see **www.bzzagent.com**). They assist their clients in creating word-of-mouth or buzz marketing campaigns. For instance, for chicken sausage producers and a publisher of mass-appeal books, Bzzagent agent assisted these clients to use their largely voluntary bzzagents to talk about these products and to dramatically enhance their market success.[21]

Similarly, P&G has created a company known as Tremor (see the Web site at **www.tremor.com**) that specializes in the teen market and the market of their mothers. In contrast to Bzzagent, which does not screen their agents to ascertain that they would be good at stimulating interest, Tremor actually provides a series of screening tests and only selects those who meet their standards in terms of being likely to be an effective word-of-mouth communicator.

Some marketers prefer to hire actors to go out and simulate for a product. For instance, a campaign for Hennessy Cognac used paid actors to visit Manhattan bars and nightclubs and order Cognac martinis made with Hennessy. Although they were instructed to act as if they were ordering a new fad drink, in reality they were attempting to create a new fad drink.[22] The objective of a promotional strategy of stimulation is to run advertisements or a direct-marketing program that is sufficiently interesting and informative to provoke consumers into discussing the benefits of the product with others.

There has also been a tremendous growth in product placements over the past few years. For instance, reality shows like *The Apprentice* and *Survivor* have shown just how valuable product placements can be, and the amount spent on product placements reached a record $4.25 billion in 2005, a 23 percent increase over the prior year.[23]

Viral marketing

Also known as "buzz marketing," "wildfire marketing," "avalanche marketing," or any one of a dozen other names, *viral marketing* "describes any strategy that encourages individuals to pass on a marketing message to others, creating the potential for exponential growth in the message's exposure and influence."[24] Viral marketing is the marriage of e-mail and word-of-mouth. It is also named "viral" because it allows a message to spread like a virus. Consider HotMail, the first free Web e-mail service. By giving away free e-mail addresses and services, and by attaching a tag to the bottom of every message that reads "Get your private, free e-mail at **http://www.hotmail.com**," every time a HotMail user sent an e-mail, there was a good chance that the receiver of the e-mail would consider signing up for a free HotMail account. And with the expectation of more than 150 million Instant Messenger (IM) users, companies like ActiveBuddy create custom software applications to connect IM users to information that they want, while "mimicking, in a crude way, the banter of a fellow IM user at the other end of the data link."[25] Table 9.8 presents the demographic characteristics of adult Instant Messenger users.

Consider some other recent examples of viral marketing in action. M80 Interactive Marketing (a viral marketing firm) has its employees surf the Web to locate enthusiastic music fans who can be used to generate "buzz" about Britney Spears, one of the firm's clients. These fans may be asked, for example, to swamp MTV's request line demanding the star's latest hit. Beanie Babies, the VW Beetle, the movie *The Blair Witch Project,* and ICQ (an Internet chat service) were also able to generate word-of-mouth hype that resulted in explosive consumer demand. Volkswagen even sold 2,000 Reflex Yellow and Vapor Blue Beetles online, and *only* online. Vespa, the Italian motor scooter manufacturer, has its in-house agency hire models to hang out on scooters outside trendy nightclubs and cafes in Los Angeles.[26] Procter & Gamble is using viral marketing in a big way. The company has developed kiosks for shopping malls that present and sell new P&G products—all in the hope that shoppers will tell their friends what they have seen. And if shoppers purchase a product at the kiosk, they are invited to join an "Innovator's Club" that offers discounts, a Web site, and puts the shopper into the P&G database for future new product introductions.[27]

There appears to be two principal types of "buzz." *Uncodified buzz* occurs when an innovator encounters a new product, movie, etc., that he or she likes and passes on the information. While the level of trust and credibility that a consumer gives such communication, because it comes from a friend, is very high, this type of buzz is not something that is controllable by the firm, and could be either positive or negative. In contrast, *codified buzz* is something that is "incubated, fostered, and underwritten by the firm," and may take the form of trial versions, testimonials, observable usage, endorsements, gift certificates, hosted chat rooms, and so on. The firm should understand that the observ-

TABLE 9.8	A Profile of Adult Instant Messaging (IM) Users

Who uses instant messaging

The IM population is dominated by young adults and suburbanites. High percentages of minorities and those living in households with modest incomes also trade instant messages. The percentages in the right column do not at times add up to 100 because of rounding

	The percent of internet users in each group who are IM users (e.g. 42% of online men are IM users)	The proportion of the IM population each group makes up (e.g. 50% of all IM-ers are men)
Men	42%	50%
Women	42	50
Race/ethnicity		
Whites	41%	73%
Blacks	44	8
Hispanics	52	9
Other	40	10
Age		
Gen Y (ages 18–27)	62%	31%
Gen X (ages 28–39)	37	28
Trailing Boomers (ages 40–49)	33	20
Leading Boomers (ages 50–58)	29	12
Matures (ages 59–68)	25	7
After Work (age 69+)	29	3
Household income		
Less than $30,000	53%	31%
$30,000–$50,000	42	24
$50,000–$75,000	36	19
$75,000+	39	27
Educational attainment		
Did not graduate from HS	49%	8%
High school grad	44	31
Some college	48	32
College degree+	34	29
Community type		
Urban	45%	30%
Suburban	42	49
Rural	40	21
Type of internet connection at home		
Broadband	46%	41%
Dialup	39	59

Source: Eulynn Shiu and Amada Lenhart, "How Americans Use Instant Messaging," *Pew Internet & American Life Project*, September 1, 2004, accessed at **www.Pewinternet.org**.

ability and the trialability of the viral marketing program for the new product (these two concepts will be fully discussed later in this chapter) are critical elements. For example, a money-back guarantee makes trialability a win-win undertaking for the consumers because it reduces the risk perceived with regard to making a purchase.[28]

One way in which the "buzz" can spread quickly is through the forwarding of e-mails. It is estimated that 90 percent of Internet users use e-mail, and about 50 percent of them use it daily. The term *Viral Maven* has been coined to refer to an individual who receives and sends pass-along e-mail frequently, as opposed to *Infrequent Senders*. One Viral Maven, for example, forwarded an e-mail about the band Nsync to 500 of her friends because it contained video messages from band members that were not available anywhere else.[29] Recently, Nescafé Café con Leche (Nestle Argentina) recruited 50 of the drink's target consumers who were "big" e-mail forwarders and asked them to forward a spot for the product to at least 15 people each. In the month after the product's introduction, the spot and link were forwarded 100,000 times, and 15 to 20 percent of visitors to the site answered a four-question survey.[30]

To learn more about viral and buzz marketing check out the Web site of the Viral and Buzz Marketing Association, a group of marketing practitioners who desire to advance the art and science of word-of-mouth and to benefit and protect interests of consumers (**www.vbma.net**).

Weblogs as word-of-mouth

One of the newest mediums for disseminating word-of-mouth is the blog (short for Weblog), with over five million of these Web journals appearing on the Internet over the past few years. Recently, *Fortune Magazine* named the blog the number one tech trend, and estimated that 23,000 new Weblogs are created daily—both by consumers and by companies. Consider the power and impact of blogs on a company's products. Specifically, when a person posted information on a group discussion site that U-shaped Kryptonite bicycle locks could be picked with a Bic ballpoint pen, within a few days a number of blogs had videos demonstrating how this could be done. Four days after the original posting, Kryptonite issued a statement promising that their new line of bicycle locks would be tougher. But bloggers kept up the pressure, and shortly thereafter *The New York Times* and The Associated Press published articles about the problem. Over a ten-day period about 1.8 million people read postings about Kryptonite, and the company announced that it would offer free exchange for any affected lock. And anyone can create a blog. For example, you can just go to Google's Blogger.com or Spaces.MSN.com and create an account. If you're interested if anyone is reading your blog, you can register with a service like Feedburner to see how many hits you're getting.[31]

Diffusion of innovations

The second part of this chapter examines a major issue in marketing and consumer behavior—the acceptance of new products and services. The framework for exploring consumer acceptance of new products is drawn from the area of research known as the **diffusion of innovations**. Consumer researchers who specialize in the diffusion of innovations are primarily interested in understanding two closely related processes: the **diffusion process** and the **adoption process**. In the broadest sense, diffusion is a macro process concerned with the spread of a new product (an innovation) from its source to the consuming public. In contrast, adoption is a micro process that focuses on the stages through which an individual consumer passes when deciding to accept or reject a new product. In addition to an examination of these two interrelated processes, we present a profile of **consumer innovators**, those who are the first to purchase a new product. The ability of marketers to identify and reach this important group of consumers plays a major role in the success or failure of new-product introductions.

And why are new-product introductions so important? Consider General Motors' OnStar system, which is in widespread use today. When it was first introduced, it was a dealer-installed option that required consumers to obtain their own cellular accounts. When dealers informed GM that this procedure was overly cumbersome and was limiting sales, General Motors made a deal with a cellular telephone company, which allowed OnStar to be packaged as a factory-installed fully functioning communications device. GM was also told by consumers that they did not need the detailed diagnostic engine reports that the system was providing—they only needed to know the difference between a problem that required immediate emergency attention and one that could wait for a routine service appointment.[32] These changes to the original GM version of OnStar undoubtedly increased its popularity with GM vehicle purchasers.

The diffusion process

The diffusion process is concerned with how innovations spread, that is, how they are assimilated within a market. More precisely, diffusion is the process by which the acceptance of an innovation (a new product, new service, new idea, or new practice) is spread by communication (mass media, salespeople, or informal conversations) to members of a social system (a target market) over a period of time. This definition includes the four basic elements of the diffusion process: (1) the innovation, (2) the channels of communication, (3) the social system, and (4) time.

The innovation

No universally accepted definition of the terms product **innovation** or *new product* exists. Instead, various approaches have been taken to define a new product or a new service; these can be classified as *firm-, product-, market-,* and *consumer-oriented definitions of innovations.*

Firm-oriented definitions

A *firm-oriented* approach treats the newness of a product from the perspective of the company producing or marketing it. When the product is "new" to the company, it is considered new. This definition ignores whether or not the product is actually new to the marketplace (i.e., to competitors or consumers). Consistent with this view, copies or modifications of a competitor's product would qualify as new. Although this definition has considerable merit when the objective is to examine the impact that a "new" product has on the firm, it is not very useful when the goal is to understand consumer acceptance of a new product.

Product-oriented definitions

In contrast to firm-oriented definitions, a *product-oriented* approach focuses on the features inherent in the product itself and on the effects these features are likely to have on consumers' established usage patterns. One product-oriented framework considers the extent to which a new product is likely to disrupt established behavior patterns. It defines the following three types of product innovations:[33]

1. *A **continuous innovation** has the least disruptive influence on established patterns. It involves the introduction of a modified product rather than a totally new product. Examples include the redesigned BMW 3-Series, the latest version of Microsoft Windows, reduced-fat Vienna Finger cookies, Hershey dark chocolate Kisses, American Express Travel Checque Card, and Band-Aid Tough Strips.*

2. *A **dynamically continuous innovation** is somewhat more disruptive than a continuous innovation but still does not alter established behavior patterns. It may involve the creation of a new product or the modification of an existing product. Examples*

FIGURE 9.4

The Telephone Has Led to Related Innovations

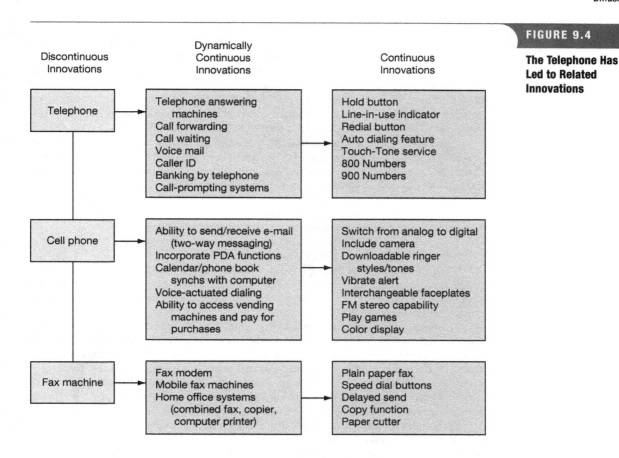

Discontinuous Innovations	Dynamically Continuous Innovations	Continuous Innovations
Telephone	Telephone answering machines Call forwarding Call waiting Voice mail Caller ID Banking by telephone Call-prompting systems	Hold button Line-in-use indicator Redial button Auto dialing feature Touch-Tone service 800 Numbers 900 Numbers
Cell phone	Ability to send/receive e-mail (two-way messaging) Incorporate PDA functions Calendar/phone book synchs with computer Voice-actuated dialing Ability to access vending machines and pay for purchases	Switch from analog to digital Include camera Downloadable ringer styles/tones Vibrate alert Interchangeable faceplates FM stereo capability Play games Color display
Fax machine	Fax modem Mobile fax machines Home office systems (combined fax, copier, computer printer)	Plain paper fax Speed dial buttons Delayed send Copy function Paper cutter

include digital cameras, digital video recorders, MP3 players, tablet PCs, USB flash drives, and disposable diapers.

3. *A **discontinuous innovation** requires consumers to adopt new behavior patterns. Examples include airplanes, radios, TVs, automobiles, fax machines, PCs, videocassette recorders, medical self-test kits, and the Internet.*

Figure 9.4 shows how the telephone, a discontinuous innovation of major magnitude, has produced a variety of both dynamically continuous and continuous innovations and has even stimulated the development of other discontinuous innovations.

Market-oriented definitions

A *market-oriented* approach judges the newness of a product in terms of how much exposure consumers have to the new product. Two market-oriented definitions of product innovation have been used extensively in consumer studies:

1. *A product is considered new if it has been purchased by a relatively small (fixed) percentage of the potential market.*

2. *A product is considered new if it has been on the market for a relatively short (specified) period of time.*

Both of these market-oriented definitions are basically subjective because they leave the researcher with the task of establishing the degree of sales penetration within the market that qualifies the product as an "innovation" (such as the first 5 percent of the potential market to use the new product) or how long the product can be on the market and still be considered "new" (i.e., the first three months that the product is available).

Consumer-oriented definitions

Although each of the three approaches described have been useful to consumer researchers in their study of the diffusion of innovations, some researchers have favored a *consumer-oriented* approach in defining an innovation.[34] In this context, a "new" product is any product that a potential consumer judges to be new. In other words, newness is based on the consumer's perception of the product rather than on physical features or market realities. Although the consumer-oriented approach has been endorsed by some advertising and marketing practitioners, it has received little systematic research attention.

Additionally, it should be pointed out that although this portion of the chapter deals primarily with what might be described as "purchase" innovativeness (or time of adoption), a second type of innovativeness, "use innovativeness," has been the subject of some thought and research. A consumer is being *use innovative* when he or she uses a previously adopted product in a novel or unusual way. In one study that dealt with the adoption of VCRs and PCs, early adopters showed significantly higher use innovativeness than those who adopted somewhat later along the cycle of acceptance of the innovation.[35]

Product characteristics that influence diffusion

All products that are new do not have equal potential for consumer acceptance. Some products seem to catch on almost overnight (cordless telephones), whereas others take a very long time to gain acceptance or never seem to achieve widespread consumer acceptance (trash compactors).

The uncertainties of product marketing would be reduced if marketers could anticipate how consumers will react to their products. For example, if a marketer knew that a product contained inherent features that were likely to inhibit its acceptance, the marketer could develop a promotional strategy that would compensate for these features or decide not to market the product at all. Pickups trucks are now being designed for the female driver, and manufacturers are careful to design door handles that do not break nails. Ford even offers adjustable gas and brake pedals.[36]

Although there are no precise formulas by which marketers can evaluate a new product's likely acceptance, diffusion researchers have identified five product characteristics that seem to influence consumer acceptance of new products: (1) relative advantage, (2) compatibility, (3) complexity, (4) trialability, and (5) observability.[37] Based on available research, it has been estimated that these five product characteristics account for much of the dynamic nature of the rate or speed of adoption.[38]

Relative Advantage   The degree to which potential customers perceive a new product as superior to existing substitutes is its *relative advantage*. For example, although many people carry beepers so that their business offices or families can contact them, a cellular telephone enables users to be in nearly instant communication with the world and allows users to both receive and place calls. The fax machine is another example of an innovation that offers users a significant relative advantage in terms of their ability to communicate. A document can be transmitted in as little as 15 to 18 seconds at perhaps one-tenth the cost of an overnight express service, which will not deliver the document until the following day.

Compatibility   The degree to which potential consumers feel a new product is consistent with their present needs, values, and practices is a measure of its *compatibility*. For instance, an advantage of 3M's Scotch™ Pop-up Tape Strips is that they are easier to use than roll-tape for certain tasks (such as wrapping gifts), yet they represent no new learning for the user. Similarly, in the realm of shaving products, it is not too difficult to imagine that a few years ago when Gillette introduced the MACH3 razor, some men made the transition from inexpensive disposable razors and other men shifted from competitive nondisposable razors (including Gillette's own Sensor razors). This new product is fully compatible with the established wet-shaving rituals of many men. However, it is difficult to imagine male shavers shifting to a new depilatory cream designed to remove facial hair. Although potentially simpler to use, a cream would be basically *incompatible* with most men's current values regarding daily shaving practices.

Complexity   *Complexity*, the degree to which a new product is difficult to understand or use, affects product acceptance. Clearly, the easier it is to understand and use a product, the more likely it is to be accepted. For example, the acceptance of such convenience foods as frozen french fries, instant puddings, and microwave dinners is generally due to their ease of preparation and use. Interestingly, although VCRs can be found in most American homes, millions of adults still need help from their children in programming the machine to record a particular television program. The introduction, awhile ago, of VCR Plus+ and TV have helped a little to reduce the ongoing challenge to easily use a VCR to record a TV program.

The issue of complexity is especially important when attempting to gain market acceptance for high-tech consumer products. Four predominant types of "technological fear" act as barriers to new product acceptance: (1) fear of technical complexity, (2) fear of rapid obsolescence, (3) fear of social rejection, and (4) fear of physical harm. Of the four, *technological complexity* was the most widespread concern of consumer innovators.[39]

Trialability   *Trialability* refers to the degree to which a new product is capable of being tried on a limited basis. The greater the opportunity to try a new product, the easier it is for consumers to evaluate it and ultimately adopt it. In general, frequently purchased household products tend to have qualities that make trial relatively easy, such as the ability to purchase a small or "trial" size. Because a computer program cannot be packaged in a smaller size, many computer software companies offer free working models of their latest software to encourage computer users to try the program and subsequently buy the program.

Aware of the importance of trial, marketers of new supermarket products commonly use substantial cents-off coupons or free samples to provide consumers with direct product experience. On the other hand, durable items, such as refrigerators or ovens, are difficult to try without making a major commitment. This may explain why publications such as *Consumer Reports* are so widely consulted for their ratings of infrequently purchased durable goods.

Observability   *Observability* (or communicability) is the ease with which a product's benefits or attributes can be observed, imagined, or described to potential consumers. Products that have a high degree of social visibility, such as fashion items, are more easily diffused than products that are used in private, such as a new type of deodorant. Similarly, a tangible product is promoted more easily than an intangible product (such as a service).

It is also important to recognize that a particular innovation may diffuse differently throughout different cultures. For example, although shelf-stable milk (milk that does not require refrigeration) has been successfully sold for years in Europe, Americans thus far have resisted the aseptic milk package. Table 9.9 summarizes the product characteristics that influence diffusion.

Resistance to innovation

What makes some new products almost instant successes, while others must struggle to achieve consumer acceptance? To help answer such a question, marketers look at the product characteristics of an innovation. Such characteristics offer clues to help determine the extent of consumer resistance, which increases when perceived relative advantage, perceived compatibility, trialability, and communicability are low, and perceived complexity is high. The term *innovation overload* is used to describe the situation in which the increase in information and options available to the consumer is so great that it seriously impairs decision making. As a result, the consumer finds it difficult to make comparisons among the available choices. In a world in which consumers often find themselves with too little time and too much stress, increased complexity of products wastes time and may reduce or eliminate acceptance of the product.

The channels of communication

How quickly an innovation spreads through a market depends to a great extent on communications between the marketer and consumers, as well as communication among

TABLE 9.9	Product Characteristics That Influence Diffusion	
CHARACTERISTICS	**DEFINITION**	**EXAMPLES**
Relative Advantage	The degree to which potential customers perceive a new product as superior to existing substitutes	HDTV over standard TV, MP3 player over a traditional CD player
Compatibility	The degree to which potential consumers feel a new product is consistent with their present needs, values, and practices	Gillette MACH3 Turbo over disposable razors, digital alarm clocks over analog alarm clocks
Complexity	The degree to which a new product is difficult to understand or use	Products low in complexity include hot and cold cereals, disposable razors, and soap
Trialability	The degree to which a new product is capable of being tried on a limited basis	Trial-size jars and bottles of new products, free trials of software, free samples, cents-off coupons
Observability	The degree to which a product's benefits or attributes can be observed, imagined, or described to potential customers	Clothing, such as Ralph Lauren jeans, sneakers, laptops, messenger bags

consumers (word-of-mouth communication). Of central concern is the uncovering of the relative influence of impersonal sources (advertising and editorial matter) and interpersonal sources (salespeople and informal opinion leaders). Over the past decade or so, we have also seen the rapid increase of the Internet as a major consumer-related source of information. The Internet is particularly interesting since it can on the one hand be seen as an interpersonal source of information (e.g., with its Internet ads, e-commerce Web sites that function like a direct-mail category, and the introduction and growth of Webpods). In contrast, the Internet can concurrently be seen as a highly personal and interpersonal source of information. In this second context, the Internet consumers have an incredible number of company- and noncompany-sponsored forums and discussion groups to chat away with people who have expertise and experience that is vital to making an informed decision.

Still further, in recent years, a variety of new channels of communication have been developed to inform consumers of innovative products and services. Consider the growth of interactive marketing messages, in which the consumer becomes an important part of the communication rather than just a "passive" message recipient. For example, for the past several years, an increasing number of companies, such as the Ford Motor Company, General Motors, and other major automobile manufactures, have used CD-ROMs to promote their products.

As of this writing, perhaps the newest and rapidly growing medium for word-of-mouth is the podcast, which some consumers are seeking out as alternatives to TV, radio, and print. It has been estimated that there are now thousands of podcasts available on the Internet, which the consumer can download as an audio file (e.g., computer, MP3 player). For example, the *Harvard Business Review* is available in audio format as a podcast.[40]

The social system

The diffusion of a new product usually takes place in a social setting frequently referred to as a *social system*. In the context of consumer behavior, the terms *market segment* and target market may be more relevant than the term *social system* used in diffusion research. A social system is a physical, social, or cultural environment to which people belong and within which they function. For example, for a new hybrid- seed corn, the social system might consist of all farmers in a number of local communities. For a new drug, the social system might consist of all physicians within a specific medical specialty (e.g., all neurologists). For a new special diet product, the social system might include all residents of a geriatric community. As these examples indicate, the social system serves as the *boundary* within which the diffusion of a new product is examined.

The orientation of a social system, with its own special values or norms, is likely to influence the acceptance or rejection of new products. When a social system is modern in orientation, the acceptance of innovations is likely to be high. In contrast, when a social system is traditional in orientation, innovations that are perceived as radical or as infringements on established customs are likely to be avoided. According to one authority, the following characteristics typify a *modern social system:* [41]

- *A positive attitude toward change*
- *An advanced technology and skilled labor force*
- *A general respect for education and science*
- *An emphasis on rational and ordered social relationships rather than on emotional ones*
- *An outreach perspective, in which members of the system frequently interact with outsiders, thus facilitating the entrance of new ideas into the social system*
- *A system in which members can readily see themselves in quite different roles*

Furthermore, a social system (either modern or traditional) may be national in scope and may influence members of an entire society or may exist at the local level and influence only those who live in a specific community. The key point to remember is that a social system's orientation is the climate in which marketers must operate to gain acceptance for their new products. For example, in recent years, the United States has experienced a decline in the demand for beef, from just under 80 pounds per person in 1970 to a little over 60 pounds per person in the first few years of this century.[42] The growing interest in health and fitness throughout the nation has created a climate in which beef is considered too high in fat and in caloric content. At the same time, the consumption of chicken and fish has increased because these foods satisfy the prevailing nutritional values of a great number of consumers.

Time

Time is the backbone of the diffusion process. It pervades the study of diffusion in three distinct but interrelated ways: (1) the *amount of purchase time,* (2) the identification of *adopter categories,* and (3) the *rate of adoption.*

Purchase time

Purchase time refers to the amount of time that elapses between consumers' initial awareness of a new product or service and the point at which they purchase or reject it. Table 9.10 illustrates the scope of purchase time by tracking a hypothetical professor's purchase of a new PC for his home.

Table 9.10 illustrates not only the length and complexity of consumer decision making but also how different information sources become important at successive steps in the process. Purchase time is an important concept because the average time a consumer takes to adopt a new product is sometimes a useful predictor of the overall length of time it will take for the new product to achieve widespread adoption. For example, when the individual purchase time is short, a marketer can expect that the overall rate of diffusion will be faster than when the individual purchase time is long.

TABLE 9.10	Time Line for Selecting a Computer

WEEK	PRECIPITATING SITUATIONS/FACTORS
0	Richard is a college professor, who, in addition to teaching, is also a marketing researcher. He uses his home computer to create PowerPoint presentations for use in class, to tabulate and analyze marketing research survey data, to create marketing research reports, to search the Internet for information, and to communicate (via e-mail) with both students, clients, and friends. His current computer is almost 5 years old, and at times can be a bit slow, especially compared to the new, state-of-the-art computer that was recently installed in his college office.
	DECISION PROCESS BEGINS
1–2	Richard visits a number of computer stores and talks to salespeople about the pros and cons of various computer brands and models. He also visits several dozen Web sites where he reads both the specifications of different computers and a number of computer model reviews.
3–7	The transmission in the family's 5-year-old SUV breaks and has to be replaced. Because of the expense involved, Richard puts the notion of buying a new computer on "hold" for a while.
	INTEREST IS RETRIGGERED
8	As July is drawing to a close and with the start of the new fall semester only a month away, Richard again starts thinking about buying a new computer, in order to have it set up in his home, with his software installed, before the beginning of the new semester.
	CONSUMER ACQUIRES A MENTOR (OPINION LEADER)
9	Richard asks one of his colleagues at the college, a fellow teacher who knows a great deal about computers, to serve as his mentor (opinion leader) with respect to PCs, and he agrees.
	FEATURES AND BRAND OPTIONS ARE REVIEWED
10–11	With the advice of the mentor, Richard narrows down his choice to one Sony Vaio model, one Hewlett Packard model, and one Dell model. While he knows that he wants a 19-inch LCD display, he is unsure about how much memory he really needs, and whether a DVD burner is really necessary.
12–13	Richard revisits several computer stores to look at the Sony and HP models of interest, and spends time on the Dell Web site reading about the numerous ways that this brand of PC can be configured.
14	After his mentor tells him to check the **www.gotapex.com** Web site daily, he discovers one morning that the site is offering a Dell coupon worth $400. So the Dell PC that he was considering, which was going to cost $1,200, now will cost only $800.
	ORDERING THE COMPUTER
	Richard calls his mentor and tells him about the coupon, and his mentor replies "It's a great deal—take it!" So Richard accesses the Dell Web site, orders the computer (which includes free shipping), and five days later, via UPS delivery, the computer arrives at his front door. He unpacks it, follows the color-coded directions for setting it up, and turns it on. Everything works perfectly, and he spends the next day installing his software, his files, and his broadband Internet connection. By the time the new semester begins, Richard has a computer that is up-and-running and is several times faster than his old one.

Adopter categories

The concept of **adopter categories** involves a classification scheme that indicates where a consumer stands in relation to other consumers in terms of time (or when the consumer adopts a new product). Five adopter categories are frequently cited in the diffusion literature: *innovators, early adopters, early majority, late majority,* and *laggards.* Table 9.11 describes each of these adopter categories and estimates their relative proportions within the total population that eventually adopts the new product. It should also be mentioned that the person first to buy an innovation is often an individual who serves as a bridge to other networks, an opinion broker between groups, rather than within groups.[43]

TABLE 9.11	Adopter Categories	
ADOPTER CATEGORY	**DESCRIPTION**	**RELATIVE PERCENTAGE WITHIN THE POPULATION THAT EVENTUALLY ADOPTS**
Innovators	*Venturesome*—very eager to try new ideas; acceptable if risk is daring; more cosmopolite social relationships; communicate with other innovators	2.5%
Early Adopters	*Respect*—more integrated into the local social system; the persons to check with before adopting a new idea; category contains greatest number of opinion leaders; are role models	13.5
Early Majority	*Deliberate*—adopt new ideas just prior to the average time; seldom hold leadership positions; deliberate for some time before adopting	34.0
Late Majority	*Skeptical*—adopt new ideas just after the average time; adopting may be both an economic necessity and a reaction to peer pressures; innovations approached cautiously	34.0
Laggards	*Traditional*—the last people to adopt an innovation; most "localite" in outlook; oriented to the past; suspicious of the new	16.0
		100.0%

Source: Adapted/Reprinted with the permission of The Free Press, a division of Simon & Schuster, from *Diffusion of Innovations,* 3rd edition, by Everett M. Rogers. Copyright © 1995 by Everett M. Rogers. Copyright © 1962, 1971, 1983 by The Free Press.

As Figure 9.5 indicates, the adopter categories are generally depicted as taking on the characteristics of a normal distribution (a bell-shaped curve) that describes the total population that ultimately adopts a product. Some argue that the bell curve is an erroneous depiction because it may lead to the inaccurate conclusion that 100 percent of the members of the social system under study (the target market) eventually will accept the product innovation. This assumption is not in keeping with marketers' experiences, because very few, if any, products fit the precise needs of all potential consumers. For example, all renters/purchasers of movies who have in the past rented video cassettes could theoretically be expected to use (or try) DVDs. In fact, it is unrealistic for the movie rental/sales industry to expect all prerecorded movie renters/purchasers to switch to DVD. For this reason, it is appropriate to add an additional category, that of *non-adopters.* The "nonadopter" category is in accord with marketplace reality—that *not* all potential consumers adopt a particular product or service innovation. For example, 28 percent of U.S. adults do not own a cell phone.[44]

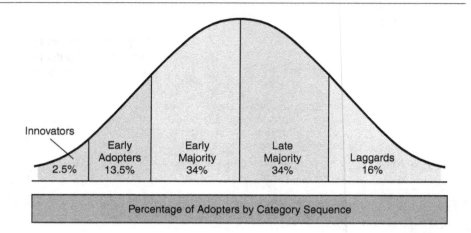

FIGURE 9.5

The Sequence and Proportion of Adopter Categories Among the Population That Eventually Adopts

Source: Adapted/Reprinted with the permission of The Free Press, a division of Simon & Schuster, from *Diffusion of Innovations*, 3rd edition, by Everett M. Rogers. Copyright © 1995 by Everett M. Rogers. Copyright © 1962, 1971, 1983 by The Free Press.

Innovators

| Innovators 2.5% | Early Adopters 13.5% | Early Majority 34% | Late Majority 34% | Laggards 16% |

Percentage of Adopters by Category Sequence

Instead of the classic five-category adopter scheme, many consumer researchers have used other classification schemes, most of which consist of two or three categories that compare *innovators* or *early triers* with *later triers* or nontriers. As we will see, this focus on the innovator or early trier has produced several important generalizations that have practical significance for marketers planning the introduction of new products.

Rate of adoption

The rate of adoption is concerned with how long it takes a new product or service to be adopted by members of a social system, that is, how quickly it takes a new product to be accepted by those who will ultimately adopt it. The general view is that the rate of adoption for new products is getting faster or shorter. Fashion adoption is a form of diffusion, one in which the rate of adoption is important. Cyclical fashion trends or "fads" are extremely "fast," whereas "fashion classics" may have extremely slow or "long" cycles.

In general, the diffusion of products worldwide is becoming a more rapid phenomenon. For example, it took black-and-white TVs about 12 years longer to reach the same level of penetration in Europe and Japan as in the United States. For color TVs, the lag time dropped to about five years for Japan and several more years for Europe. In contrast, for VCRs there was only a three- or four-year spread, with the United States (with its emphasis on cable TV) lagging behind Europe and Japan. Finally, for compact disk players, penetration levels in all three countries were about even after only three years.[45] Table 9.12 presents the time required for a sample of electronic products to penetrate 10 percent of the mass market in the United Kingdom.

The objective in marketing new products is usually to gain wide acceptance of the product as quickly as possible. Marketers desire a rapid rate of product adoption to penetrate the market and quickly establish market leadership (obtain the largest share of the market) before competition takes hold. A *penetration policy* is usually accompanied by a relatively low introductory price designed to discourage competition from entering the market. Rapid product adoption also demonstrates to marketing intermediaries (wholesalers and retailers) that the product is worthy of their full and continued support.

Under certain circumstances, marketers might prefer to avoid a rapid rate of adoption for a new product. For example, marketers who wish to use a pricing strategy that will enable them to recoup their development costs quickly might follow a *skimming policy:* They first make the product available at a very high price to consumers who are willing to pay top dollar and then gradually lower the price in a stepwise fashion to attract additional market segments at each price reduction plateau. For example, when 17-inch computer

TABLE 9.12	Time Required for Electronic Products to Penetrate 10 Percent of the Mass Market in the United Kingdom
PRODUCT	**NUMBER OF YEARS**
Pager	41
Telephone	38
Cable television	25
Fax machine	22
VCR	9
Cellular phone	9
Personal computer	7
CD-ROM*	6
Wireless data service*	6
Screen-phone*	6
Interactive television*	3

*Predicted.
Source: Eric Chi-Chung Shiu and John A. Dawson, "Cross-National Consumer Segmentation of Internet Shopping for Britain and Taiwan," *The Service Industries Journal (London),* 22, January 2002, 163. Reprinted by permission.

monitors (not flat-screen LCD panels) were first introduced, they sold for more than $700. Today they can be purchased for $100 or less.

In addition to how long it takes from introduction to the point of adoption (or when the purchase actually occurs), it is useful to track the extent of adoption (the diffusion rate). For instance, a particular corporation might not upgrade its employees' computer systems to the Windows XP environment until after many other companies in the area have already begun to do so. However, once it decides to upgrade, it might install Windows XP software in a relatively short period of time on all of its employees' PCs. Thus, although the company was relatively "late" with respect to *time* of adoption, its *extent* of adoption was very high.

Although sales graphs depicting the adoption categories (again, see Figure 9.5) are typically thought of as having a normal distribution in which sales continue to increase prior to reaching a peak (at the top of the curve), some research evidence indicates that a third to a half of such sales curves, at least in the consumer electronics industry, involve an initial peak, a trough, and then another sales increase. Such a "saddle" in the sales curve has been attributed to the early market adopters and the main market adopters being two separate markets.[46]

The adoption process

The second major process in the diffusion of innovations is *adoption*. The focus of this process is the stages through which an individual consumer passes while arriving at a decision to try or not to try, or to continue using or to discontinue using a new product. (The *adoption process* should not be confused with *adopter categories*.)

Stages in the adoption process

It is often assumed that the consumer moves through five stages in arriving at a decision to purchase or reject a new product: (1) awareness, (2) interest, (3) evaluation, (4) trial, and (5) adoption (or rejection). The assumption underlying the adoption process is that

TABLE 9.13	**The Stages in the Adoption Process**	
NAME OF STAGE	**WHAT HAPPENS DURING THIS STAGE**	**EXAMPLE**
Awareness	Consumer is first exposed to the product innovation.	Eric sees an ad for a 23-inch thin LCD HDTV in a magazine he is reading.
Interest	Consumer is interested in the product and searches for additional information.	Eric reads about the HDTV set on the manufacturer's Web site and then goes to an electronics store near his apartment and has a salesperson show him the unit.
Evaluation	Consumer decides whether or not to believe that this product or service will satisfy the need—a kind of "mental trial."	After talking to a knowledgeable friend, Eric decides that this TV will fit nicely on top of the chest in his bedroom. He also calls his cable company and finds out that he can exchange his "standard" TV cable box for an HDTV cable box at no cost and no additional monthly fee.
Trial	Consumer uses the product on a limited basis.	Since an HDTV set cannot be "tried" like a small tube of toothpaste, Eric buys the TV at his local electronics store on his way home from work. The store offers a 14-day (from the date of purchase) full refund policy.
Adoption (Rejection)	If trial is favorable, consumer decides to use the product on a full rather than a limited basis—if unfavorable, the consumer decides to reject it.	Eric loves his new HDTV set and expects many years of service from it.

consumers engage in extensive information search, whereas consumer involvement theory suggests that for some products, a limited information search is more likely (for low-involvement products). The five **stages in the adoption process** are described in Table 9.13.

Although the traditional adoption process model is insightful in its simplicity, it does not adequately reflect the full complexity of the consumer adoption process. For one, it does not adequately acknowledge that there is quite often a need or problem-recognition stage that consumers face before acquiring an awareness of potential options or solutions (a need recognition preceding the awareness stage). Moreover, the adoption process does not adequately provide for the possibility of evaluation and rejection of a new product or service after each stage, especially after trial (i.e., a consumer may reject the product after trial or never use the product on a continuous basis). Finally, it does not explicitly include post-adoption or postpurchase evaluation, which can lead to a strengthened commitment or to a decision to discontinue use. Figure 9.6 presents an enhanced representation of the adoption process model, one that includes the additional dimensions or actions described here.

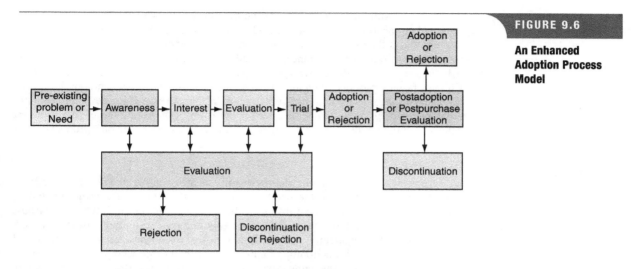

FIGURE 9.6

An Enhanced Adoption Process Model

The adoption of some products and services may have minimal consequences, whereas the adoption of other innovations may lead to major behavioral and lifestyle changes. Examples of innovations with such major impact on society include the automobile, the telephone, the electric refrigerator, the television, the airplane, the personal computer, and the Internet.

The adoption process and information sources

The adoption process provides a framework for determining which types of information sources consumers find most important at specific decision stages. For example, early purchasers of USB storage devices or keys (often used to back up or store computer files) might first become aware of the products via mass-media sources (e.g., *PC Magazine* or Internet sites like **www.news.com**). Then these early or innovative consumers' final pretrial information might be an outcome of informal discussions with personal sources (e.g., other innovators at a technology forum or chat room). The key point is that impersonal mass-media sources tend to be most valuable for creating initial product awareness; as the purchase decision progresses, however, the relative importance of these sources declines while the relative importance of interpersonal sources (friends, salespeople, and others) increases.

A profile of the consumer innovator

Who is the consumer innovator? What characteristics set the innovator apart from later adopters and from those who never purchase? How can the marketer reach and influence the innovator? These are key questions for the marketing practitioner about to introduce a new product or service.

Defining the consumer innovator

Consumer innovators can be defined as the relatively small group of consumers who are the earliest purchasers of a new product. The problem with this definition, however, concerns the concept of *earliest,* which is, after all, a relative term. Sociologists have treated this issue by sometimes defining innovators as the first 2.5 percent of the social system to adopt an innovation. In many marketing diffusion studies, however, the definition of the consumer innovator has been derived from the status of the new product under investigation. For example, if researchers define a new product as an innovation for the first three months of its availability, then they define the consumers who purchase it during this period as "innovators." Other researchers have defined innovators in terms of their *innovativeness*, that is, their purchase of some minimum number of new products from a selected group of new products. For instance, in the adoption of new fashion items, innovators can be defined as those consumers who purchase more than one fashion product from a group of 10 new fashion products. Noninnovators would be defined as those who purchase none or only one of the new fashion products. In other instances, researchers have defined innovators as those falling within an arbitrary proportion of the total market (e.g., the first 10 percent of the population in a specified geographic area to buy the new product).

Interest in the product category

Not surprisingly, consumer innovators are much more interested than either later adopters or nonadopters in the product categories that they are among the first to purchase. If what is known from diffusion theory holds true in the future, the earliest purchasers of small electric automobiles are likely to have substantially greater interest in automobiles (they will enjoy looking at automotive magazines and will be interested in the performance and functioning of automobiles) than those who purchased conventional small cars during the same period or those who purchased small electric cars during a later period. Also, early adopters of products containing a nonfat synthetic cooking oil (i.e., olestra) were found to have a high interest in such a product because of health and diet concerns.

Consumer innovators are more likely than noninnovators to seek information concerning their specific interests from a variety of informal and mass-media sources. They are more likely to give greater deliberation to the purchase of new products or services in their areas of interest than noninnovators.

The innovator is an opinion leader

When discussing the characteristics of the opinion leader earlier in this chapter, we indicated a strong tendency for consumer opinion leaders to be innovators. In the present context, an impressive amount of research on the diffusion of innovations has found that consumer innovators provide other consumers with information and advice about new products and that those who receive such advice frequently follow it. Thus, in the role of opinion leader, the consumer innovator often influences the acceptance or rejection of new products.

When innovators are enthusiastic about a new product and encourage others to try it, the product is likely to receive broader and quicker acceptance. When consumer innovators are dissatisfied with a new product and discourage others from trying it, its acceptance will be severely limited, and it may die a quick death. For products that do not generate much excitement (either positive or negative), consumer innovators may not be sufficiently motivated to provide advice. In such cases, the marketer must rely almost entirely on mass media and personal selling to influence future purchasers; the absence of informal influence is also likely to result in a somewhat slower rate of acceptance (or rejection) of the new product. Because motivated consumer innovators can influence the rate of acceptance or rejection of a new product, they influence its eventual success or failure.

Personality traits

Earlier, we examined the personality traits that distinguish the consumer innovator from the noninnovator. In this section, we will briefly highlight what researchers have learned about the personality of the consumer innovator.

First, consumer innovators generally are *less dogmatic* than noninnovators. They tend to approach new or unfamiliar products with considerable openness and little anxiety. In contrast, noninnovators seem to find new products threatening to the point where they prefer to delay purchase until the product's success has been clearly established.

Consistent with their open-mindedness, it appears that innovative behavior is an expression of an individual's *need for uniqueness*.[47] Some researchers have found that a tension exists in decision making between two opposing objectives—conformity and distinction. The need for uniqueness allows an individual to distinguish himself by purchasing a rare item, which is a socially acceptable behavior. Consequently, those new products, both branded and unbranded, that represent a greater change in a person's consumption habits were viewed as superior when it came to satisfying the need for uniqueness. Therefore, to gain more rapid acceptance of a new product, marketers might consider appealing to a consumer's need for uniqueness.

Still further, consumer innovators also differ from noninnovators in terms of *social character*. Consumer innovators are *inner-directed;* that is, they rely on their own values or standards when making a decision about a new product. In contrast, noninnovators are *other-directed,* relying on others for guidance on how to respond to a new product rather than trusting their own personal values or standards. Thus, the initial purchasers of a new line of automobiles might be inner-directed, whereas the later purchasers of the same automobile might be other-directed. This suggests that as acceptance of a product progresses from early to later adopters, a gradual shift occurs in the personality type of adopters from inner-directedness to other-directedness.

There also appears to be a link between *optimum stimulation level* and consumer innovativeness. Specifically, individuals who seek a lifestyle rich with novel, complex, and unusual experiences (high optimum stimulation levels) are more willing to risk trying new products, to be innovative, to seek purchase-related information, and to accept new retail facilities.

Researchers have isolated a link between *variety seeking* and purchase behavior that provides insights into consumer innovators. Variety-seeking consumers tend to be brand switchers and purchasers of innovative products and services. They also possess the following innovator-related personality traits: They are open-minded (or low in dogmatism), extroverts, liberal, low in authoritarianism, able to deal with complex or ambiguous stimuli, and creative.[48]

To sum up, consumer innovators seem to be more receptive to the unfamiliar and the unique; they are more willing to rely on their own values or standards than on the judgment of others. They also are willing to run the risk of a poor product choice to increase their exposure to new products that will be satisfying. For the marketer, the personality traits that distinguish innovators from noninnovators suggest the need for separate promotional campaigns for innovators and for later adopters.

Perceived risk and venturesomeness

Perceived risk is another measure of a consumer's likelihood to try new brands or products. Perceived risk is the degree of uncertainty or fear about the consequences of a purchase that a consumer feels when considering the purchase of a new product. For example, consumers experience uncertainty when they are concerned that a new product will not work properly or as well as other alternatives. Research on perceived risk and the trial of new products overwhelmingly indicates that consumer innovators are low-risk perceivers; that is, they experience little fear of trying new products or services. Consumers who perceive little or no risk in the purchase of a new product are much more likely to make innovative purchases than consumers who perceive a great deal of risk. In other words, high-risk perception limits innovativeness.

Venturesomeness is a broad-based measure of a consumer's willingness to accept the risk of purchasing new products. Measures of venturesomeness have been used to evaluate a person's general values or attitudes toward trying new products. A typical measurement scale might include such items as:

- *I prefer to (try a shampoo when it first comes out) (wait and learn how good it is before trying it).*
- *When I am shopping and see a brand of coffee I know about but have never tried, I am (very anxious or willing to try it), (hesitant about trying it), (very unwilling to try it).*
- *I like to be among the first people to buy and use new products that are on the market (measured on a five-point "agreement" scale).*

Research that has examined venturesomeness has generally found that consumers who indicate a willingness to try new products tend to be consumer innovators (as measured by their actual purchase of new products). On the other hand, consumers who express a reluctance to try new products are, in fact, less likely to purchase new products. Therefore, venturesomeness seems to be an effective barometer of actual innovative behavior.

Purchase and consumption characteristics

Consumer innovators possess purchase and usage traits that set them apart from noninnovators. For example, consumer innovators are *less* brand loyal; that is, they are more apt to switch brands. This is not surprising, for brand loyalty would seriously impede a consumer's willingness to try new products.

Consumer innovators are more likely to be *deal prone* (to take advantage of special promotional offers such as free samples and cents-off coupons). They are also likely to be *heavy users* of the product category in which they innovate. Specifically, they purchase larger quantities and consume more of the product than noninnovators. Finally, for products like VCRs, PCs, microwave ovens, 35-mm cameras, and food processors, usage variety is likely to be a relevant dimension of new-product diffusion. An understanding of how consumers might be "usage innovators"—that is, finding or "inventing" new uses for an innovation—might create entirely new market opportunities for marketers' products. Still further, a recent study of Indian consumers' attitudes toward the purchase of new food products found that "intention to buy" was an accurate predictor of behavior for highly innovative consumers, but failed to predict purchase behavior for less innovative Indian consumers.[49] This suggests that more innovative consumers are more likely to act on their reported intentions to purchase than less innovative consumers with the same intention of purchase.

To sum up, a positive relationship exists between innovative behavior and heavy usage. Consumer innovators are not only an important market segment from the standpoint of being the first to use a new product, but they also represent a substantial market in terms of product volume. However, their propensity to switch brands or to use products in different or unique ways and their positive response to promotional deals also suggest that innovators will continue to use a specific brand only as long as they do not perceive that a new and potentially better alternative is available.

Media habits

Comparisons of the media habits of innovators and noninnovators across such widely diverse areas of consumption as fashion clothing and new automotive services suggest that innovators have somewhat greater total exposure to magazines than noninnovators, particularly to special-interest magazines devoted to the product category in which they innovate. For example, fashion innovators are more likely to read magazines such as *Gentlemen's Quarterly* and *Vogue* than noninnovators; financial services innovators have greater exposure to such special-interest magazines as *Money* and *Financial World*.

Consumer innovators are also less likely to watch television than noninnovators. This view is consistently supported by research that over the past decade or so has compared the magazine and TV exposure levels of consumer innovators. The evidence indicates that consumer innovators have higher-than-average magazine exposure and lower-than-average TV exposure. It will be interesting, though, to observe over the next few years what the impact of the convergence of computers and television will be. Studies concerning the relationship between innovative behavior and exposure to other mass media, such as radio and newspapers, have been too few, and the results have been too varied to draw any useful conclusions.

Social characteristics

Consumer innovators are more socially accepted and socially involved than noninnovators. For example, innovators are more socially integrated into the community, better accepted by others, and more socially involved; that is, they belong to more social groups and organizations than noninnovators. This greater social acceptance and involvement of consumer innovators may help explain why they function as effective opinion leaders.

Demographic characteristics

It is reasonable to assume that the age of the consumer innovator is related to the specific product category in which he or she innovates; however, research suggests that consumer innovators tend to be younger than either late adopters or noninnovators. This is no doubt because many of the products selected for research attention (such as fashion, convenience grocery products, or new automobiles) are particularly attractive to younger consumers.

Consumer innovators have more formal education, have higher personal or family incomes, and are more likely to have higher occupational status (to be professionals or hold managerial positions) than late adopters or noninnovators. In other words, innovators tend to be more upscale than other consumer segments and can, therefore, better afford to make a mistake should the innovative new product or service being purchased prove to be unacceptable.

Table 9.14 summarizes the major differences between consumer innovators and late adopters or noninnovators. The table includes the major distinctions examined in our current presentation of the *consumer innovator profile*.

TABLE 9.14	Comparative Profiles of the Consumer Innovator and the Noninnovator or Late Adopter	
CHARACTERISTIC	INNOVATOR	NONINNOVATOR (OR LATE ADOPTER)
Product Interest	More	Less
Opinion Leadership	More	Less
Personality		
Dogmatism	Open-minded	Closed-minded
Need for uniqueness	Higher	Lower
Social character	Inner-directed	Other-directed
Optimum stimulation level	Higher	Lower
Variety seeking	Higher	Lower
Perceived risk	Less	More
Venturesomeness	More	Less
Purchase and Consumption Traits		
Brand loyalty	Less	More
Deal proneness	More	Less
Usage	More	Less
Media Habits		
Total magazine exposure	More	Less
Special-interest magazines	More	Less
Television	Less	More
Social Characteristics		
Social integration	More	Less
Social striving (e.g., social, physical, and occupational mobility)	More	Less
Group memberships	More	Less
Demographic Characteristics		
Age	Younger	Older
Income	Higher	Lower
Education	More	Less
Occupational status	Higher	Lower

Are there generalized consumer innovators?

Do consumer innovators in one product category tend to be consumer innovators in other product categories? The answer to this strategically important question is a guarded "no." The overlap of innovativeness across product categories, like opinion leadership, seems to be limited to product categories that are closely related to the same basic interest area. Consumers who are innovators of one new food product or one new appliance are more likely to be innovators of other new products in the same general product category. In other words, although no single or generalized consumer-innovativeness trait seems to operate *across* broadly different product categories, evidence suggests that consumers who innovate *within* a specific product category will innovate again within the same product category. For example, up to the point of "innovator burnout" (i.e., "what I have is good enough"), a person who was an innovator in buying an early 2 megapixel digital camera in the 1990s was most likely again to be an innovator in buying a 3 megapixel digital camera, a 5 megapixel digital camera, and a 7 megapixel digital camera, and is likely again to be an innovator when it comes to the next generation of digital cameras. For the marketer, such a pattern suggests that it is generally a good marketing strategy to target a new product to consumers who were the first to try other products in the same basic product category.

Technology and innovators

In the realm of high-tech innovations, there is evidence suggesting that there is a generalized "high-tech" innovator—known as a "change leader."[50] Such individuals tend to embrace and popularize many of the innovations that are ultimately accepted by the mainstream population, such as computers, cellular telephones, and fax machines. They tend to have a wide range of personal and professional contacts representing different occupational and social groups; most often these contacts tend to be "weak ties" or acquaintances. Change leaders also appear to fall into one of two distinct groups: a *younger group* that can be characterized as being stimulation seeking, sociable, and having high levels of fashion awareness or a *middle-aged group* that is highly self-confident and has very high information-seeking needs.

Similar to change leaders, "technophiles" are individuals who purchase technologically advanced products soon after their market debut. Such individuals tend to be technically curious people. Also, another group responding to technology are adults who are categorized as "techthusiasts"—people who are most likely to purchase or subscribe to emerging products and services that are technologically oriented. These consumers are typically younger, better educated, and more affluent.[51]

Advancing our understanding of the relationship between technology and consumer innovation has been explored within the context of the technology acceptance model (TAM). Within the domain of work perceived usefulness or utilitarian aspect of a technology has been revealed to be most important; however, within consumer context of consumers' response to a new handheld Internet device, the most powerful determinant of attitudes toward usage was the "fun" of using the device—a hedonic aspect. The implication for marketers is clear—a consumer may purchase a new bit of technology more for the fun they can have with the device than for the ability it gives them to accomplish particular functions.[52]

Research conducted with over 500 adult Internet users found that purchasing online was positive related to technology-related innovativeness. Still further, the gathering of store or product information online was positively related to the number of years online and the weekly number of hours spent online.[53] Still further, when exploring the adoption of mobile gaming (games delivered via cell phone), a market that is expected to grow worldwide from $950 million in 2001 to $17.5 billion in 2006, researchers discovered important additions to the traditional list of product characteristics that influence the rate of adoption (e.g., relative advantage, complexity). What they perceived as risk were navigation (maneuvering ergonomics associated with the mobile device), critical mass (the more people that have adopted the innovation, the more attractive it is to others), and payment options (because of the expense of the mobile device, trialability is not an option). Perceived risk was found to play the most important role in the adoption process, followed by complexity and compatibility.[54]

chapter 10

> ## Product Life Cycle

Companies that excel at developing and managing new products reap big rewards. Every product seems to go through a life cycle—it is born, goes through several phases, and eventually dies as newer products come along that create greater value for customers. This product life cycle presents two major challenges: First, because all products eventually decline, a firm must be good at developing new products to replace aging ones (the challenge of *new-product development*). Second, the firm must be good at adapting its marketing strategies in the face of changing tastes, technologies, and competition as products pass through life-cycle stages (the challenge of *product life-cycle strategies*). We first look at the problem of finding and developing new products and then at the problem of managing them successfully over their life cycles.

New-product development strategy

A firm can obtain new products in two ways. One is through *acquisition*—by buying a whole company, a patent, or a license to produce someone else's product. The other is through the firm's own **new-product development** efforts. By *new products* we mean original products, product improvements, product modifications, and new brands that the firm develops through its own research-and-development efforts. In this chapter, we concentrate on new-product development.

New-product development
The development of original products, product improvements, product modifications, and new brands through the firm's own product development efforts.

New products are important—to both customers and the marketers who serve them. "Both consumers and companies love new products," declares a new-product consultant, "consumers because they solve problems and bring variety to their lives, and companies because they are a key source of growth."[2]

Yet, innovation can be very expensive and very risky. For example, Texas Instruments lost $660 million before withdrawing from the home computer business. Webvan burned through a staggering $1.2 billion trying to create a new online grocery business before shuttering its cyberdoors for a lack of customers. And despite a huge investment and fevered speculation that it could be even bigger than the Internet, Segway sold an underwhelming 23,500 of its human transporters in the more than five years following its launch, a tiny fraction of projected sales. Segway has yet to do more than gain small footholds in niche markets, such as urban touring and police departments.[3]

New products face tough odds. Other costly product failures from sophisticated companies include New Coke (Coca-Cola Company), Eagle Snacks (Anheuser-Busch), Zap Mail electronic mail (FedEx), Premier "smokeless" cigarettes (R.J. Reynolds), Arch Deluxe sandwiches (McDonald's), and Breakfast Mates cereal-and-milk combos (Kellogg). Studies indicate that up to 90 percent of all new consumer products fail. For example, of the 30,000 new food, beverage, and beauty products launched each year, an estimated 70 to 90 percent fail within just 12 months.[4]

Why do so many new products fail? There are several reasons. Although an idea may be good, the company may overestimate market size. The actual product may be poorly designed. Or it might be incorrectly positioned, launched at the wrong time, priced too high, or poorly advertised. A high-level executive might push a favorite idea despite poor marketing research findings. Sometimes the costs of product development are higher than expected, and sometimes competitors fight back harder than expected. However, the reasons behind some new-product failures seem pretty obvious. Try the following on for size:[5]

Strolling the aisles at NewProductWorks Showcase and Learning Center collection is like finding yourself in some nightmare version of a supermarket. Many of the 86,553 products on display were abject flops. Behind each of them are squandered dollars and hopes and the classic question, "What were they thinking?" Some products failed because they simply failed to bring value to customers—for example, Look of Buttermilk shampoo, Cucumber antiperspirant spray, or Premier smokeless cigarettes. Smokeless cigarettes? What were they thinking? Other companies failed because they attached trusted brand names to something totally out of character. Can you imagine swallowing Ben-Gay aspirin? Or how about Gerber Singles food for adults (perhaps the tasty pureed sweet-and-sour pork or chicken Madeira)? Other misbegotten attempts to stretch a good name include Cracker Jack cereal, Exxon fruit punch, Smucker's premium ketchup, Fruit of the Loom laundry detergent, and Harley-Davidson cake-decorating kits. Really, what were they thinking?

The new-product development process

So companies face a problem—they must develop new products, but the odds weigh heavily against success. In all, to create successful new products, a company must understand its consumers, markets, and competitors and develop products that deliver superior value to customers. It must carry out strong new-product planning and set up a systematic, customer-driven *new-product development process* for finding and growing new products. Figure 10.1 shows the eight major steps in this process.

Idea generation

Idea generation
The systematic search for new-product ideas.

New-product development starts with **idea generation**—the systematic search for new-product ideas. A company typically generates hundreds of ideas, even thousands, in order to find a few good ones. For example, IBM recently held an "Innovation Jam"—a kind of online suggestion box—in which it invited IBM and customer employees worldwide to submit ideas for new products and services. The mammoth brainstorming session generated some 37,000 ideas from 104 countries. Since the jam fest, however, IBM has whittled down this surge of ideas to only 10 products, businesses, and services that it plans to develop.[6]

Major sources of new-product ideas include internal sources and external sources such as customers, competitors, distributors and suppliers, and others.

Internal idea sources

Using *internal sources,* the company can find new ideas through formal research and development. Or it can pick the brains of employees—from executives to scientists, engineers, and manufacturing staff to salespeople—as IBM did with its Innovation Jam. Everyone in the company can contribute good new-product ideas. "Most companies operate under the assumption that big ideas come from a few big brains: the inspired founder, the eccentric inventor, the visionary boss," says one analyst. But in today's fast-moving and competitive environment, "it's time to invent a less top-down approach to innovation, to make it everybody's business to come up with great ideas."[7]

Some companies have developed successful "intrapreneurial" programs that encourage employees to think up and develop new-product ideas. For example, Samsung built a special Value Innovation Program (VIP) Center in Suwon, South Korea, to encourage and support internal new-product innovation. The VIP Center is the ultimate round-the-clock idea factory in which company researchers, engineers, and designers commingle to come up with new-product ideas and processes. The center features workrooms, dorm rooms, training rooms, a kitchen, and a basement filled with games, a gym, and sauna. Recent ideas sprouting from the VIP Center include a 102-inch plasma HDTV and a

Major Stages in New-Product Development

FIGURE 10.1

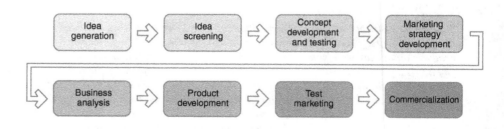

process to reduce material costs on a multifunction printer by 30 percent. The center has helped Samsung, once known as the maker of cheap knock-off products, become one of the world's most innovative and profitable consumer electronics companies.[8]

External idea sources

Companies can also obtain good new-product ideas from any of a number of external sources. For example, *distributors and suppliers* can contribute ideas. Distributors are close to the market and can pass along information about consumer problems and new-product possibilities. Suppliers can tell the company about new concepts, techniques, and materials that can be used to develop new products. *Competitors* are another important source. Companies watch competitors' ads to get clues about their new products. They buy competing new products, take them apart to see how they work, analyze their sales, and decide whether they should bring out a new product of their own. Other idea sources include trade magazines, shows, and seminars; government agencies; advertising agencies; marketing research firms; university and commercial laboratories; and inventors.

Some companies seek the help of outside new-product consultancies and design firms, such as ZIBA, Frog Design, or IDEO, for new-product ideas and designs. For example, when Procter & Gamble needed innovative ideas for reinventing its Pringles snack chip line, it turned to IDEO. After interviewing kids and moms about snacking, lunching, and eating habits, IDEO landed on the idea that the uniform chips could have entertainment value. It came up with Pringles Prints, printable chips with individual images, trivia questions, and jokes printed on every chip. Now, more than just a snack, the highly successful Pringles Prints create an interactive customer experience. P&G has even developed co-branding efforts with partners such as Hasbro and Trivial Pursuit to broaden the product's appeal.[9]

Perhaps the most important source of new-product ideas is *customers* themselves. The company can analyze customer questions and complaints to find new products that better solve consumer problems. For example, Staples developed its Easy Rebate program in response to concerns expressed by small-business customers that lost rebates were one of their biggest frustrations.[10]

Company engineers or salespeople can meet with and work alongside customers to get suggestions and ideas. LEGO did just that when it invited 250 LEGO train-set enthusiasts to visit its New York office to assess new designs. "We pooh-poohed them all," says one LEGO fan, an Intel engineer from Portland. But the group gave LEGO lots of new ideas, and the company put them to good use. The result was the "Santa Fe Super Chief" set. Thanks to "word-of-mouse" endorsements from the 250 enthusiasts, LEGO sold out the first 10,000 units in less than two weeks with no additional marketing.[11]

Other companies actively solicit ideas from customers and turn customers into cocreators. For example, Dell set up a Web site forum called IdeaStorm that asks consumers for insights on how to improve its product offering. Users post suggestions, the community votes, and the most popular ideas rise to the top. Only two months after launch, the site had received some 3,850 ideas and 236,000 votes. Michael Dell sees such customer-driven innovation as a key to reenergizing Dell. "We need to think differently about the market and engage our customers in almost everything we do," says Dell.

Finally, customers often create new products and uses on their own, and companies can benefit by putting them on the market. For example, for years customers were spreading the word that Avon Skin-So-Soft bath oil and moisturizer was also a terrific bug repellent. Whereas some consumers were content simply to bathe in water scented with the fragrant oil, others carried it in their backpacks to mosquito-infested campsites or kept a bottle on the decks of their beach houses. Avon turned the idea into a complete line of Skin-So-Soft Bug Guard products, including Bug Guard Mosquito Repellent Moisturizing Towelettes and Bug Guard Plus, a combination moisturizer, insect repellent, and sunscreen.[12]

Although customer input on new products yields many benefits, companies must be careful not to rely *too* heavily on what customers say. For some products, especially highly technical ones, customers may not know what they need. "Merely giving people what they want isn't always enough," says one innovation management consultant.

"People want to be surprised; they want something that's better than they imagined, something that stretches them in what they like."[13]

Idea screening

The purpose of idea generation is to create a large number of ideas. The purpose of the succeeding stages is to *reduce* that number. The first idea-reducing stage is **idea screening**, which helps spot good ideas and drop poor ones as soon as possible. Product development costs rise greatly in later stages, so the company wants to go ahead only with the product ideas that will turn into profitable products.

Many companies require their executives to write up new-product ideas in a standard format that can be reviewed by a new-product committee. The write-up describes the product or service, the proposed customer value proposition, the target market, and the competition. It makes some rough estimates of market size, product price, development time and costs, manufacturing costs, and rate of return. The committee then evaluates the idea against a set of general criteria.

For example, at Kao Corporation, the large Japanese consumer-products company, the new-product committee asks questions such as these: Is the product truly useful to consumers and society? Is it good for our particular company? Does it mesh well with the company's objectives and strategies? Do we have the people, skills, and resources to make it succeed? Does it deliver more value to customers than do competing products? Is it easy to advertise and distribute? Many companies have well-designed systems for rating and screening new-product ideas.

Concept development and testing

An attractive idea must be developed into a **product concept**. It is important to distinguish between a product idea, a product concept, and a product image. A *product idea* is an idea for a possible product that the company can see itself offering to the market. A *product concept* is a detailed version of the idea stated in meaningful consumer terms. A *product image* is the way consumers perceive an actual or potential product.

Concept development

Suppose that a car manufacturer has developed a practical battery-powered all-electric car. Its initial prototype is a sleek, sporty convertible that sells for about $100,000.[14] However, later this decade, it plans to introduce more-affordable, mass-market models that will compete with today's hybrid-powered cars. This 100 percent electric car will accelerate from 0 to 60 in four seconds, travel more than 250 miles on a single charge, recharge from a normal 120-volt electrical outlet, and cost about one cent per mile to power.

Looking ahead, the marketer's task is to develop this new product into alternative product concepts, find out how attractive each concept is to customers, and choose the best one. It might create the following product concepts for the electric car:

> *Concept 1:* An affordably priced midsize car designed as a second family car to be used around town for running errands and visiting friends
>
> *Concept 2:* A midpriced sporty compact appealing to young singles and couples
>
> *Concept 3:* A "green" car appealing to environmentally conscious people who want practical, low-polluting transportation
>
> *Concept 4:* A high-end midsize utility vehicle appealing to those who love the space SUVs provide but lament the poor gas mileage

Concept testing

Concept testing calls for testing new-product concepts with groups of target consumers. The concepts may be presented to consumers symbolically or physically. Here, in words, is concept 3:

> *An efficient, fun-to-drive, battery-powered compact car that seats four. This 100 percent electric wonder provides practical and reliable transportation with no pollution.*

TABLE 10.1	Questions for Battery-Powered Electric Car Concept Test

1. Do you understand the concept of a battery-powered electric car?
2. Do you believe the claims about the car's performance?
3. What are the major benefits of the battery-powered electric car compared with a conventional car?
4. What are its advantages compared with a gas-electric hybrid car?
5. What improvements in the car's features would you suggest?
6. For what uses would you prefer a battery-powered electric car to a conventional car?
7. What would be a reasonable price to charge for the car?
8. Who would be involved in your decision to buy such a car? Who would drive it?
9. Would you buy such a car (definitely, probably, probably not, definitely not)?

It goes more than 250 miles on a single charge and costs pennies per mile to operate. It's a sensible, responsible alternative to today's pollution-producing gas-guzzlers. It's priced, fully equipped, at $25,000.

Many firms routinely test new-product concepts with consumers before attempting to turn them into actual new products. For some concept tests, a word or picture description might be sufficient. However, a more concrete and physical presentation of the concept will increase the reliability of the concept test. After being exposed to the concept, consumers then may be asked to react to it by answering questions such as those in Table 10.1.

The answers to such questions will help the company decide which concept has the strongest appeal. For example, the last question asks about the consumer's intention to buy. Suppose 10 percent of consumers say they "definitely" would buy, and another 5 percent say "probably." The company could project these figures to the full population in this target group to estimate sales volume. Even then, the estimate is uncertain because people do not always carry out their stated intentions.

Marketing strategy development

Suppose the car maker finds that concept 3 for the fuel-cell-powered electric car tests best. The next step is **marketing strategy development**, designing an initial marketing strategy for introducing this car to the market.

The *marketing strategy statement* consists of three parts. The first part describes the target market; the planned value proposition; and the sales, market share, and profit goals for the first few years. Thus:

Marketing strategy development
Designing an initial marketing strategy for a new product based on the product concept.

The target market is younger, well-educated, moderate- to high-income individuals, couples, or small families seeking practical, environmentally responsible transportation. The car will be positioned as more fun to drive and less polluting than today's internal combustion engine or hybrid cars. The company will aim to sell 100,000 cars in the first year, at a loss of not more than $15 million. In the second year, the company will aim for sales of 120,000 cars and a profit of $25 million.

The second part of the marketing strategy statement outlines the product's planned price, distribution, and marketing budget for the first year:

The battery-powered electric car will be offered in three colors—red, white, and blue—and will have a full set of accessories as standard features. It will sell at a retail price of $25,000—with 15 percent off the list price to dealers. Dealers who sell more than 10 cars per month will get an additional discount of 5 percent on each car sold that month. A marketing budget of $50 million will be split 50-50 between a national *media campaign and local event marketing. Advertising and a Web site will emphasize the car's fun spirit and low emissions. During the first year, $100,000 will be spent on marketing research to find out who is buying the car and their satisfaction levels.*

The third part of the marketing strategy statement describes the planned long-run sales, profit goals, and marketing mix strategy:

We intend to capture a 3 percent long-run share of the total auto market and realize an after-tax return on investment of 15 percent. To achieve this, product quality will start high and be improved over time. Price will be raised in the second and third years if competition permits. The total marketing budget will be raised each year by about 10 percent. Marketing research will be reduced to $60,000 per year after the first year.

Business analysis

Business analysis
A review of the sales, costs, and profit projections for a new product to find out whether these factors satisfy the company's objectives.

Once management has decided on its product concept and marketing strategy, it can evaluate the business attractiveness of the proposal. **Business analysis** involves a review of the sales, costs, and profit projections for a new product to find out whether they satisfy the company's objectives. If they do, the product can move to the product development stage.

To estimate sales, the company might look at the sales history of similar products and conduct market surveys. It can then estimate minimum and maximum sales to assess the range of risk. After preparing the sales forecast, management can estimate the expected costs and profits for the product, including marketing, R&D, operations, accounting, and finance costs. The company then uses the sales and costs figures to analyze the new product's financial attractiveness.

Product development

Product development
Developing the product concept into a physical product in order to ensure that the product idea can be turned into a workable market offering.

So far, for many new-product concepts, the product may have existed only as a word description, a drawing, or perhaps a crude mock-up. If the product concept passes the business test, it moves into **product development**. Here, R&D or engineering develops the product concept into a physical product. The product development step, however, now calls for a large jump in investment. It will show whether the product idea can be turned into a workable product.

The R&D department will develop and test one or more physical versions of the product concept. R&D hopes to design a prototype that will satisfy and excite consumers and that can be produced quickly and at budgeted costs. Developing a successful prototype can take days, weeks, months, or even years depending on the product and prototype methods.

Often, products undergo rigorous tests to make sure that they perform safely and effectively, or that consumers will find value in them. Companies can do their own product testing or outsource testing to other firms that specialize in testing. Here are some examples of such product tests:[15]

Thunk. Thunk. Thunk. Behind a locked door in the basement of Louis Vuitton's elegant Paris headquarters, a mechanical arm hoists a brown-and-tan handbag a half-meter off the floor—then drops it. The bag, loaded with an 8-pound weight, will be lifted and dropped, over and over again, for four days. This is Vuitton's test laboratory, a high-tech torture chamber for its fabled luxury goods. Another piece of lab equipment bombards handbags with ultraviolet rays to test resistance to fading. Still another tests zippers by tugging them open and shutting them 5,000 times. There's even a mechanized mannequin hand, with a Vuitton charm bracelet around its wrist, being shaken vigorously to make sure none of the charms fall off.

At Gillette, almost everyone gets involved in new-product testing. Every working day at Gillette, 200 volunteers from various departments come to work unshaven, troop to the second floor of the company's gritty South Boston plant, and enter small booths with a sink and mirror. There they take instructions from technicians on the other side of a small window as to which razor, shaving cream, or aftershave to use. The volunteers evaluate razors for sharpness of blade, smoothness of glide, and ease of handling. In a nearby shower room, women perform the same ritual on their legs, underarms, and what the company delicately refers to as the "bikini area." "We bleed so you'll get a good shave at home," says one Gillette employee.

A new product must have the required functional features and also convey the intended psychological characteristics. The battery-powered electric car, for example, should strike consumers as being well built, comfortable, and safe. Management must learn what makes consumers decide that a car is well built. To some consumers, this means that the car has "solid-sounding" doors. To others, it means that the car is able to withstand heavy impact in crash tests. Consumer tests are conducted in which consumers test-drive the car and rate its attributes.

Test marketing

If the product passes concept and product tests, the next step is **test marketing**, the stage at which the product and marketing program are introduced into realistic market settings. Test marketing gives the marketer experience with marketing the product before going to the great expense of full introduction. It lets the company test the product and its entire marketing program—targeting and positioning strategy, advertising, distribution, pricing, branding and packaging, and budget levels.

The amount of test marketing needed varies with each new product. Test marketing costs can be high, and it takes time that may allow competitors to gain advantages. When the costs of developing and introducing the product are low, or when management is already confident about the new product, the company may do little or no test marketing. In fact, test marketing by consumer-goods firms has been declining in recent years. Companies often do not test-market simple line extensions or copies of successful competitor products.

However, when introducing a new product requires a big investment, or when management is not sure of the product or marketing program, a company may do a lot of test marketing. For instance, McDonald's tested its Redbox subsidiary's automated DVD rental kiosks in its own restaurants and in supermarkets for more than two years in six major U.S. markets. Using the kiosks, consumers can rent DVDs for $1 a day using their credit cards. Based on the success of these test markets—in Denver tests alone, the Redbox kiosks quickly commanded more than a 10 percent share of all DVD rentals— McDonald's is rolling out kiosks in all of its restaurants and in a slew of supermarkets across the country.[16]

Although test-marketing costs can be high, they are often small when compared with the costs of making a major mistake. Still, test marketing doesn't guarantee success. For example, Procter & Gamble tested its Fit produce rinse product heavily for five years and Olay cosmetics for three years. Although market tests suggested the products would be successful, P&G pulled the plug on both shortly after their introductions.[17]

Many marketers are now using new technologies to reduce the costs of test marketing and to speed up the process. For example, Frito-Lay worked with research firm Decision Insight to create an online virtual convenience store in which to test new products and marketing ideas.[18]

Decision Insight's SimuShop online shopping environment lets Frito-Lay's marketers test shopper reactions to different extensions, shelf placements, pricing, and packaging of its Lay's, Doritos, Cheetos, and Fritos brands in a variety of store setups without investing huge amounts of time and money on actual in-store research in different locations. Recruited shoppers visit the online store, browse realistic virtual shelves featuring Frito-Lay's and competing products, click on individual products to view them in more detail, and select products to put in their carts. When the shopping is done, selected customers are questioned in one-on-one, on-screen interviews about why they chose the products they did. Watching the entire decision process unfold gives Frito-Lay marketers reams of information about what would happen in the real world. With

Test marketing
The stage of new-product development in which the product and marketing program are tested in realistic market settings.

200-some bags of Frito-Lay products sitting on a typical store shelf, the company doesn't have the luxury of test marketing in actual market settings. "For us, that can only really be done virtually," says a Frito-Lay marketer. The SimuShop tests produce a 90 percent or better correlation to real shopper behavior when compared with later real-world data.

Commercialization

Test marketing gives management the information needed to make a final decision about whether to launch the new product. If the company goes ahead with **commercialization**—introducing the new product into the market—it will face high costs. The company may need to build or rent a manufacturing facility. And, in the case of a major new consumer packaged good, it may spend hundreds of millions of dollars for advertising, sales promotion, and other marketing efforts in the first year. For example, when Unilever introduced its Sunsilk hair care line, it spent $200 million in the United States alone, including $30 million for nontraditional media such as MySpace ads and profiles, mall displays that used audio to catch passersby, 3-D ads in tavern bathrooms, and cinema ads.[19]

The company launching a new product must first decide on introduction *timing*. If the car maker's new battery-powered electric car will eat into the sales of the company's other cars, its introduction may be delayed. If the car can be improved further, or if the economy is down, the company may wait until the following year to launch it. However, if competitors are ready to introduce their own battery-powered models, the company may push to introduce its car sooner.

Next, the company must decide *where* to launch the new product—in a single location, a region, the national market, or the international market. Few companies have the confidence, capital, and capacity to launch new products into full national or international distribution. They will develop a planned *market rollout* over time. In particular, small companies may enter attractive cities or regions one at a time. Larger companies, however, may quickly introduce new models into several regions or into the full national market. For example, Procter & Gamble launched the Gillette Fusion six-blade razor with a full national $300 million blitz. The launch began with 2006 Super Bowl ads costing more than $6 million. Within the first week of launch, P&G had blanketed U.S. stores with some 180,000 Fusion displays. After three months, Fusion brand awareness exceeded 60 percent, and the new brand contributed to a 44 percent rise in overall U.S. sales of nondisposable razors.[20]

Companies with international distribution systems may introduce new products through swift global rollouts. Microsoft recently did this with its Windows Vista operating system. Microsoft used a mammoth $500 million promotional blitz to launch Vista simultaneously in more than 30 markets worldwide. The campaign targeted 6.6 billion global impressions in just its first two months. "There won't be a PC sold anywhere in the world that doesn't have Vista within the next six months," said an industry analyst at the start of the campaign.[21]

Managing new-product development

The new-product development process shown in Figure 10.1 highlights the important activities needed to find, develop, and introduce new products. However, new-product development involves more than just going through a set of steps. Companies must take a holistic approach to managing this process. Successful new-product development requires a customer-centered, team-based, and systematic effort.

Customer-centered new-product development

Above all else, new-product development must be customer centered. When looking for and developing new products, companies often rely too heavily on technical research in their R&D labs. But like everything else in marketing, successful new-product develop-

Commercialization
Introducing a new product into the market.

ment begins with a thorough understanding of what consumers need and value. **Customer-centered new-product development** focuses on finding new ways to solve customer problems and create more customer-satisfying experiences.

One recent study found that the most successful new products are ones that are differentiated, solve major customer problems, and offer a compelling customer value proposition.[22] Thus, for products ranging from bathroom cleaners to jet engines, today's innovative companies are getting out of the research lab and mingling with customers in the search for new customer value. Consider these examples:[23]

> People at all levels of Procter & Gamble, from brand managers to the CEO, look for fresh ideas by tagging along with and talking to customers as they shop for and use the company's products. When one P&G team tackled the problem of "reinventing bathroom cleaning," it started by "listening with its eyes." The group spent many hours watching consumers clean their bathrooms. They focused on "extreme users," ranging from a professional house cleaner who scrubbed grout with his fingernail to four single guys whose idea of cleaning the bathroom was pushing a filthy towel around the floor with a big stick. If they could make both users happy, they figured they had a home run. One big idea—a cleaning tool on a removable stick that could both reach shower walls and get into crannies—got the green light quickly. Consumers loved the prototype, patched together with repurposed plastic, foam, and duct tape. Some refused to return it. The idea became P&G's highly successful Mr. Clean Magic Reach bathroom cleaning tool.
>
> General Electric wants to infuse customer-centered new-product development thinking into all of its diverse divisions. So executives from the GE Money division—which offers credit cards, loans, and other consumer finance solutions—recently took a tour of San Francisco. During the tour, they watched how people use money—where they get it, how they spend it, even how they carry it. Similarly, to unleash creativity in 15 top executives from GE's jet-engine business, the company took them out to talk with airplane pilots and mechanics. "We even went to meet Larry Flynt's private jet team," says a manager who arranged the trip. "It's a way to . . . increase their empathy and strengthen their ability to make innovation decisions."

Thus, customer-centered new-product development begins and ends with solving customer problems. As one expert asks: "What is innovation after all, if not products and services that offer fresh thinking in a way that meets the needs of customers?"[24] Says another expert, "Getting consumer insights at the beginning of the process, using those insights consistently and respectfully throughout the process, and communicating them in a compelling form when you go to market is critical to a product's success in the market these days."[25]

Team-based new-product development

Good new-product development also requires a total-company, cross-functional effort. Some companies organize their new-product development process into the orderly sequence of steps shown in Figure 10.1, starting with idea generation and ending with commercialization. Under this *sequential product development* approach, one company department works individually to complete its stage of the process before passing the new product along to the next department and stage. This orderly, step-by-step process can help bring control to complex and risky projects. But it also can be dangerously slow. In fast-changing, highly competitive markets, such slow-but-sure product development can result in product failures, lost sales and profits, and crumbling market positions.

In order to get their new products to market more quickly, many companies use a **team-based new-product development** approach. Under this approach, company departments work closely together in cross-functional teams, overlapping the steps in the product development process to save time and increase effectiveness. Instead of passing the new product from department to department, the company assembles a team of people from various departments that stays with the new product from start to

Customer-centered new-product development
New-product development that focuses on finding new ways to solve customer problems and create more customer-satisfying experiences.

Team-based new-product development
An approach to developing new products in which various company departments work closely together, overlapping the steps in the product development process to save time and increase effectiveness.

finish. Such teams usually include people from the marketing, finance, design, manufacturing, and legal departments, and even supplier and customer companies. In the sequential process, a bottleneck at one phase can seriously slow the entire project. In the team-based approach, if one area hits snags, it works to resolve them while the team moves on.

The team-based approach does have some limitations. For example, it sometimes creates more organizational tension and confusion than the more orderly sequential approach. However, in rapidly changing industries facing increasingly shorter product life cycles, the rewards of fast and flexible product development far exceed the risks. Companies that combine a customer-centered approach with team-based new-product development gain a big competitive edge by getting the right new products to market faster.

Systematic new-product development

Finally, the new-product development process should be holistic and systematic rather than compartmentalized and haphazard. Otherwise, few new ideas will surface, and many good ideas will sputter and die. To avoid these problems, a company can install an *innovation management system* to collect, review, evaluate, and manage new-product ideas.

The company can appoint a respected senior person to be the company's innovation manager. It can set up Web-based idea management software and encourage all company stakeholders—employees, suppliers, distributors, dealers—to become involved in finding and developing new products. It can assign a cross-functional innovation management committee to evaluate proposed new-product ideas and help bring good ideas to market. It can create recognition programs to reward those who contribute the best ideas.[26]

The innovation management system approach yields two favorable outcomes. First, it helps create an innovation-oriented company culture. It shows that top management supports, encourages, and rewards innovation. Second, it will yield a larger number of new-product ideas, among which will be found some especially good ones. The good new ideas will be more systematically developed, producing more new-product successes. No longer will good ideas wither for the lack of a sounding board or a senior product advocate.

Thus, new-product success requires more than simply thinking up a few good ideas, turning them into products, and finding customers for them. It requires a holistic approach for finding new ways to create valued customer experiences, from generating and screening new-product ideas to creating and rolling out want-satisfying products to customers.

More than this, successful new-product development requires a whole-company commitment. At companies known for their new-product prowess—such as Apple, Google, 3M, Procter & Gamble, and General Electric—the entire culture encourages, supports, and rewards innovation. Consider GE, which has topped *Fortune's* list of most admired companies 7 of the past 10 years, largely because of its innovative culture. GE's companywide emphasis on innovation is summed up in its well-known advertising tagline: "Imagination at Work."[27]

> At GE, innovation is a key to future growth. But GE's vision of an imagination-driven company can't be realized unless everyone in the company is looking for innovation. So three years ago, GE launched a companywide movement called "Imagination Breakthroughs" that challenged every GE business unit to identify at least five breakthrough big ideas that were capable of generating $50 million to $100 million of new revenue within three to seven years. Under the program, the chief marketing officers in each GE business have become innovation project leaders, responsible for finding new ideas, filtering them, and matching them to customer needs. Marketing executives throughout the company now receive regular creativity training. For example, each year, 60 of GE's most senior marketers experience a three and one-half week "odyssey of creativity." (Remember those customer-interaction

Linking the Concepts

Take a break. Think about new products and how companies find and develop them.

- Suppose that you're on a panel to nominate the "best new products of the year." What products would you nominate and why? See what you can learn about the new-product development process for one of these products.
- Applying the new-product development process you've just studied, develop an idea for an innovative new snack-food product and sketch out a brief plan for bringing it to market. Loosen up and have some fun with this.

field trips by GE executives described in a previous example?) GE's broad-based support for innovation is producing results. Imagination Breakthroughs has already yielded more than 100 projects that are on track to meet their $50 million targets. Says GE CEO Jeffrey Immelt, "for GE, imagination is more than a slogan or a tagline. It is a reason for being."

Product life-cycle strategies

After launching the new product, management wants the product to enjoy a long and happy life. Although it does not expect the product to sell forever, the company wants to earn a decent profit to cover all the effort and risk that went into launching it. Management is aware that each product will have a life cycle, although its exact shape and length is not known in advance.

Figure 10.2 shows a typical **product life cycle (PLC)**, the course that a product's sales and profits take over its lifetime. The product life cycle has five distinct stages:

1. *Product development* begins when the company finds and develops a new-product idea. During product development, sales are zero and the company's investment costs mount.
2. *Introduction* is a period of slow sales growth as the product is introduced in the market. Profits are nonexistent in this stage because of the heavy expenses of product introduction.
3. *Growth* is a period of rapid market acceptance and increasing profits.

Product life cycle
The course of a product's sales and profits over its lifetime.

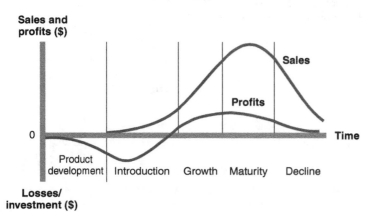

Sales and Profits Over the Product's Life from Inception to Decline

FIGURE 10.2

4. *Maturity* is a period of slowdown in sales growth because the product has achieved acceptance by most potential buyers. Profits level off or decline because of increased marketing outlays to defend the product against competition.

5. *Decline* is the period when sales fall off and profits drop.

Not all products follow this product life cycle. Some products are introduced and die quickly; others stay in the mature stage for a long, long time. Some enter the decline stage and are then cycled back into the growth stage through strong promotion or repositioning. It seems that a well-managed brand could live forever. Such venerable brands as Coca-Cola, Gillette, Budweiser, American Express, Wells-Fargo, Kikkoman, and TABASCO®, for instance, are still going strong after more than 100 years.

The PLC concept can describe a *product class* (gasoline-powered automobiles), a *product form* (SUVs), or a *brand* (the Ford Escape). The PLC concept applies differently in each case. Product classes have the longest life cycles—the sales of many product classes stay in the mature stage for a long time. Product forms, in contrast, tend to have the standard PLC shape. Product forms such as "dial telephones" and "cassette tapes" passed through a regular history of introduction, rapid growth, maturity, and decline.

A specific brand's life cycle can change quickly because of changing competitive attacks and responses. For example, although laundry soaps (product class) and powdered detergents (product form) have enjoyed fairly long life cycles, the life cycles of specific brands have tended to be much shorter. Today's leading brands of powdered laundry soap are Tide and Cheer; the leading brands 75 years ago were Fels-Naptha, Octagon, and Kirkman.

The PLC concept also can be applied to what are known as styles, fashions, and fads. Their special life cycles are shown in Figure 10.3. A **style** is a basic and distinctive mode of expression. For example, styles appear in homes (colonial, ranch, transitional), clothing (formal, casual), and art (realist, surrealist, abstract). Once a style is invented, it may last for generations, passing in and out of vogue. A style has a cycle showing several periods of renewed interest. A **fashion** is a currently accepted or popular style in a given field. For example, the more formal "business attire" look of corporate dress of the 1980s and 1990s gave way to the "business casual" look of today. Fashions tend to grow slowly, remain popular for a while, and then decline slowly.

Fads are temporary periods of unusually high sales driven by consumer enthusiasm and immediate product or brand popularity.[28] A fad may be part of an otherwise normal lifecycle, as in the case of recent surges in the sales of poker chips and accessories and scrapbooking supplies. Or the fad may comprise a brand's or product's entire lifecycle. "Pet rocks" are a classic example. Upon hearing his friends complain about how expensive it was to care for their dogs, advertising copywriter Gary Dahl joked about his pet rock. He soon wrote a spoof of a dog-training manual for it, titled "The Care and Training of Your Pet Rock." Soon Dahl was selling some 1.5 million ordinary beach pebbles at $4 a pop. Yet the fad, which broke one October, had sunk like a stone by the next February. Dahl's advice to those who want to succeed with a fad: "Enjoy it while it lasts." Other examples of such fads include the Rubik's Cube and low-carb diets.[29]

Style
A basic and distinctive mode of expression.

Fashion
A currently accepted or popular style in a given field.

Fad
A temporary period of unusually high sales driven by consumer enthusiasm and immediate product or brand popularity.

Styles, Fashions, and Fads

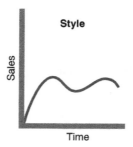
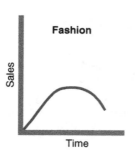
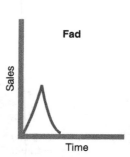

FIGURE 10.3

The PLC concept can be applied by marketers as a useful framework for describing how products and markets work. And when used carefully, the PLC concept can help in developing good marketing strategies for different stages of the product life cycle. But using the PLC concept for forecasting product performance or for developing marketing strategies presents some practical problems. For example, managers may have trouble identifying which stage of the PLC the product is in or pinpointing when the product moves into the next stage. They may also find it hard to determine the factors that affect the product's movement through the stages.

In practice, it is difficult to forecast the sales level at each PLC stage, the length of each stage, and the shape of the PLC curve. Using the PLC concept to develop marketing strategy also can be difficult because strategy is both a cause and a result of the product's life cycle. The product's current PLC position suggests the best marketing strategies, and the resulting marketing strategies affect product performance in later life-cycle stages.

Moreover, marketers should not blindly push products through the traditional stages of the product life cycle. "As marketers instinctively embrace the old life-cycle paradigm, they needlessly consign their products to following the curve into maturity and decline," notes one marketing professor. Instead, marketers often defy the "rules" of the life cycle and position their products in unexpected ways. By doing this, "companies can rescue products foundering in the maturity phase of their life cycles and return them to the growth phase. And they can catapult new products forward into the growth phase, leapfrogging obstacles that could slow consumers' acceptance."[30]

We looked at the product development stage of the product life cycle in the first part of the chapter. We now look at strategies for each of the other life-cycle stages.

Introduction stage

The **introduction stage** starts when the new product is first launched. Introduction takes time, and sales growth is apt to be slow. Well-known products such as instant coffee and frozen foods lingered for many years before they entered a stage of rapid growth.

In this stage, as compared to other stages, profits are negative or low because of the low sales and high distribution and promotion expenses. Much money is needed to attract distributors and build their inventories. Promotion spending is relatively high to inform consumers of the new product and get them to try it. Because the market is not generally ready for product refinements at this stage, the company and its few competitors produce basic versions of the product. These firms focus their selling on those buyers who are the most ready to buy.

A company, especially the *market pioneer,* must choose a launch strategy that is consistent with the intended product positioning. It should realize that the initial strategy is just the first step in a grander marketing plan for the product's entire life cycle. If the pioneer chooses its launch strategy to make a "killing," it may be sacrificing long-run revenue for the sake of short-run gain. As the pioneer moves through later stages of the life cycle, it must continuously formulate new pricing, promotion, and other marketing strategies. It has the best chance of building and retaining market leadership if it plays its cards correctly from the start.

Growth stage

If the new product satisfies the market, it will enter a **growth stage**, in which sales will start climbing quickly. The early adopters will continue to buy, and later buyers will start following their lead, especially if they hear favorable word of mouth. Attracted by the opportunities for profit, new competitors will enter the market. They will introduce new product features, and the market will expand. The increase in competitors leads to an increase in the number of distribution outlets, and sales jump just to build reseller inventories. Prices remain where they are or fall only slightly. Companies keep their promotion spending at the same or a slightly higher level. Educating the market remains a goal, but now the company must also meet the competition.

Profits increase during the growth stage, as promotion costs are spread over a large volume and as unit manufacturing costs fall. The firm uses several strategies to sustain

Introduction stage
The product life-cycle stage in which the new product is first distributed and made available for purchase.

Growth stage
The product life-cycle stage in which a product's sales start climbing quickly.

rapid market growth as long as possible. It improves product quality and adds new product features and models. It enters new market segments and new distribution channels. It shifts some advertising from building product awareness to building product conviction and purchase, and it lowers prices at the right time to attract more buyers.

In the growth stage, the firm faces a trade-off between high market share and high current profit. By spending a lot of money on product improvement, promotion, and distribution, the company can capture a dominant position. In doing so, however, it gives up maximum current profit, which it hopes to make up in the next stage.

Maturity stage

Maturity stage
The product life-cycle stage in which sales growth slows or levels off.

At some point, a product's sales growth will slow down, and the product will enter a **maturity stage**. This maturity stage normally lasts longer than the previous stages, and it poses strong challenges to marketing management. Most products are in the maturity stage of the life cycle, and therefore most of marketing management deals with the mature product.

The slowdown in sales growth results in many producers with many products to sell. In turn, this overcapacity leads to greater competition. Competitors begin marking down prices, increasing their advertising and sales promotions, and upping their product development budgets to find better versions of the product. These steps lead to a drop in profit. Some of the weaker competitors start dropping out, and the industry eventually contains only well-established competitors.

Although many products in the mature stage appear to remain unchanged for long periods, most successful ones are actually evolving to meet changing consumer needs. Product managers should do more than simply ride along with or defend their mature products—a good offense is the best defense. They should consider modifying the market, product, and marketing mix.

In *modifying the market,* the company tries to increase the consumption of the current product. It may look for new users and new market segments, as when John Deere targeted the retiring baby-boomer market with the Gator, a vehicle traditionally used on a farm. For this new market, Deere has repositioned the Gator, promising that it can "take you from a do-it-yourselfer to a do-it-a-lot-easier." As one ad for the Gator XUV puts it, "When your plans include landscaping, gardening, or transporting people and materials on your property, the XUV provides a smooth, comfortable ride with heavy-duty performance."

The manager may also look for ways to increase usage among present customers. For example, Glad Products Company helps customers to find new uses for its Press'n Seal wrap, the plastic wrap that creates a Tupperware-like seal. As more and more customers contacted the company about alternative uses for the product, Glad set up a special "1000s of Uses. What's Yours?" Web site (www.1000uses.com) at which customers could swap usage tips. "We found out our heavy users use it for a lot more than just covering food," says a Glad brand manager. "And they all became heavy users when they had an 'aha' moment with Press'n Seal." Suggested uses for Press'n Seal range from protecting a computer keyboard from dirt and spills and keeping garden seeds fresh to use by soccer moms sitting on damp benches while watching their tykes play. "We just roll out the Glad Press'n Seal over the long benches," says the mom who shared the tip, "and everyone's bottom stays nice and dry."[31]

The company might also try *modifying the product*—changing characteristics such as quality, features, style, or packaging to attract new users and to inspire more usage. It can improve the product's styling and attractiveness. It might improve the product's quality and performance—its durability, reliability, speed, taste. Thus, makers of consumer food and household products introduce new flavors, colors, scents, ingredients, or packages to enhance performance and revitalize consumer buying. For example, P&G regularly adds new versions and features to its Tide line, such as Tide with a Touch of Downey, 2X concentrated liquids, Tide Simple Pleasures scents, and the Tide to Go instant stain removal pen.

Finally, the company can try *modifying the marketing mix*—improving sales by changing one or more of the marketing mix elements. The company can offer new or improved services to buyers. It can cut prices to attract new users and competitors' cus-

Linking the Concepts

Pause for a moment and think about some products that have been around for a long time.

- Ask a grandparent or someone else who shaved back then to compare a 1950s or 1960s Gillette razor to the most current model. Is Gillette's latest razor really a new product or just a "retread" of the previous version? What do you conclude about product life cycles?
- Crayola Crayons have been a household staple for more than 100 years. But the brand remains vital. Sixty-five percent of all American children aged two to eight pick up a crayon at least once a day and color for an average of 28 minutes. Nearly 80 percent of the time, they pick up a Crayola crayon. How has the Binney & Smith division of Hallmark protected the Crayola brand from old age and decline (check out www.crayola.com and www.binney-smith.com)?

tomers. It can launch a better advertising campaign or use aggressive sales promotions—trade deals, cents-off, premiums, and contests. In addition to pricing and promotion, the company can also move into new marketing channels to help serve new users.

Decline stage

The sales of most product forms and brands eventually dip. The decline may be slow, as in the case of oatmeal cereal, or rapid, as in the cases of cassette and VHS tapes. Sales may plunge to zero, or they may drop to a low level where they continue for many years. This is the **decline stage**.

> **Decline stage**
> The product life-cycle stage in which a product's sales decline.

Sales decline for many reasons, including technological advances, shifts in consumer tastes, and increased competition. As sales and profits decline, some firms withdraw from the market. Those remaining may prune their product offerings. They may drop smaller market segments and marginal trade channels, or they may cut the promotion budget and reduce their prices further.

Carrying a weak product can be very costly to a firm, and not just in profit terms. There are many hidden costs. A weak product may take up too much of management's time. It often requires frequent price and inventory adjustments. It requires advertising and sales-force attention that might be better used to make "healthy" products more profitable. A product's failing reputation can cause customer concerns about the company and its other products. The biggest cost may well lie in the future. Keeping weak products delays the search for replacements, creates a lopsided product mix, hurts current profits, and weakens the company's foothold on the future.

For these reasons, companies need to pay more attention to their aging products. The firm's first task is to identify those products in the decline stage by regularly reviewing sales, market shares, costs, and profit trends. Then, management must decide whether to maintain, harvest, or drop each of these declining products.

Management may decide to *maintain* its brand without change in the hope that competitors will leave the industry. For example, Procter & Gamble made good profits by remaining in the declining liquid soap business as others withdrew. Or management may decide to reposition or reinvigorate the brand in hopes of moving it back into the growth stage of the product life cycle. P&G has done this with several brands, including Mr. Clean and Old Spice.

Management may decide to *harvest* the product, which means reducing various costs (plant and equipment, maintenance, R&D, advertising, sales force) and hoping that sales hold up. If successful, harvesting will increase the company's profits in the short run. Or management may decide to *drop* the product from the line. It can sell it to another firm or simply liquidate it at salvage value. In recent years, Procter & Gamble

TABLE 10.2	Summary of Product Life-Cycle Characteristics, Objectives, and Strategies			
CHARACTERISTICS	**INTRODUCTION**	**GROWTH**	**MATURITY**	**DECLINE**
Sales	Low sales	Rapidly rising sales	Peak sales	Declining sales
Costs	High cost per customer	Average cost per customer	Low cost per customer	Low cost per customer
Profits	Negative	Rising profits	High profits	Declining profits
Customers	Innovators	Early adopters	Middle majority	Laggards
Competitors	Few	Growing number	Stable number beginning to decline	Declining number
MARKETING OBJECTIVES				
	Create product awareness and trial	Maximize market share	Maximize profit while defending market share	Reduce expenditure and milk the brand
STRATEGIES				
Product	Offer a basic product	Offer product extensions, service, warranty	Diversify brand and models	Phase out weak items
Price	Use cost-plus	Price to penetrate market	Price to match or beat competitors	Cut price
Distribution	Build selective distribution	Build intensive distribution	Build more intensive distribution	Go selective: phase out unprofitable outlets
Advertising	Build product awareness among early adopters and dealers	Build awareness and interest in the mass market	Stress brand differences and benefits	Reduce to level needed to retain hard-core loyals
Sales Promotion	Use heavy sales promotion to entice trial	Reduce to take advantage of heavy consumer demand	Increase to encourage brand switching	Reduce to minimal level

Source: Philip Kotler and Kevin Lane Keller, *Marketing Management,* 12th ed. (Upper Saddle River, N.J.: Prentice Hall, 2006), p. 332.

has sold off a number of lesser or declining brands such as Crisco oil, Comet cleanser, Duncan Hines cake mixes, and Jif peanut butter. If the company plans to find a buyer, it will not want to run down the product through harvesting.

Table 10.2 summarizes the key characteristics of each stage of the product life cycle. The table also lists the marketing objectives and strategies for each stage.[32]

Additional product and service considerations

Here, we'll wrap up our discussion of products and services with two additional considerations: social responsibility in product decisions and issues of international product and service marketing.

Product decisions and social responsibility

Product decisions have attracted much public attention. Marketers should carefully consider public policy issues and regulations regarding acquiring or dropping products, patent protection, product quality and safety, and product warranties.

Regarding new products, the government may prevent companies from adding products through acquisitions if the effect threatens to lessen competition. Companies dropping products must be aware that they have legal obligations, written or implied, to their suppliers, dealers, and customers who have a stake in the dropped product. Companies must also obey U.S. patent laws when developing new products. A company cannot make its product illegally similar to another company's established product.

Manufacturers must comply with specific laws regarding product quality and safety. The Federal Food, Drug, and Cosmetic Act protects consumers from unsafe and adulterated food, drugs, and cosmetics. Various acts provide for the inspection of sanitary conditions in the meat- and poultry-processing industries. Safety legislation has been passed to regulate fabrics, chemical substances, automobiles, toys, and drugs and poisons. The Consumer Product Safety Act of 1972 established a Consumer Product Safety Commission, which has the authority to ban or seize potentially harmful products and set severe penalties for violation of the law.

If consumers have been injured by a product that has a defective design, they can sue manufacturers or dealers. Product liability suits are now occurring in federal courts at the rate of almost 24,000 per year. Although manufacturers are found at fault in only 6 percent of all product liability cases, when they are found guilty, the median jury award is $1.5 million and individual awards can run into the tens or even hundreds of millions of dollars. For example, a jury recently ordered Merck to pay $253 million to the widow of a man who died from a heart attack after using the painkiller Vioxx for his arthritis. Although the judge later reduced the award to a "mere" $26.1 million, this was only the first of more than 4,000 Vioxx product liability suits.[33]

This phenomenon has resulted in huge increases in product liability insurance premiums, causing big problems in some industries. Some companies pass these higher rates along to consumers by raising prices. Others are forced to discontinue high-risk product lines. Some companies are now appointing "product stewards," whose job is to protect consumers from harm and the company from liability by proactively ferreting out potential product problems.

Many manufacturers offer written product warranties to convince customers of their products' quality. To protect consumers, Congress passed the Magnuson-Moss Warranty Act in 1975. The act requires that full warranties meet certain minimum standards, including repair "within a reasonable time and without charge" or a replacement or full refund if the product does not work "after a reasonable number of attempts" at repair. Otherwise, the company must make it clear that it is offering only a limited warranty. The law has led several manufacturers to switch from full to limited warranties and others to drop warranties altogether.

International product and service marketing

International product and service marketers face special challenges. First, they must figure out what products and services to introduce and in which countries. Then, they must decide how much to standardize or adapt their products and services for world markets.

On the one hand, companies would like to standardize their offerings. Standardization helps a company to develop a consistent worldwide image. It also lowers the product design, manufacturing, and marketing costs of offering a large variety of products. On the other hand, markets and consumers around the world differ widely. Companies must usually respond to these differences by adapting their product offerings. For example, Cadbury sells kiwi-filled Cadbury Kiwi Royale in New Zealand. Frito-Lay sells Nori Seaweed Lay's potato chips for Thailand and A la Turca corn chips with poppy seeds and a dried tomato flavor for Turkey.[34] And P&G adapts the flavors of its Crest toothpaste to satisfy the palettes of local consumers.

> *In America, P&G sells Crest toothpaste in flavors designed for Western palettes—everything from its regular soft mint flavor to vanilla mint, citrus clean mint, lemon ice, and cinnamon. But it has to rethink these flavors for the Chinese market, even within the Chinese market. China's rural populations like simplistic natural tastes, such as fruit or herbs. Drawing upon cultural beliefs about good health, P&G*

devised an herbal formulation. The company also created a salt version, as the Chinese consider salt a teeth-whitening agent. More affluent city dwellers, however, have palettes similar to those of U.S. consumers, preferring more complex flavors like mint. For them, P&G made a tea-flavored Crest, based on the Chinese belief that tea treats halitosis.

Packaging also presents new challenges for international marketers. Packaging issues can be subtle. For example, names, labels, and colors may not translate easily from one country to another. A firm using yellow flowers in its logo might fare well in the United States but meet with disaster in Mexico, where a yellow flower symbolizes death or disrespect. Similarly, although Nature's Gift might be an appealing name for gourmet mushrooms in America, it would be deadly in Germany, where *gift* means poison. Packaging may also need to be tailored to meet the physical characteristics of consumers in various parts of the world. For instance, soft drinks are sold in smaller cans in Japan to fit the smaller Japanese hand better. Thus, although product and package standardization can produce benefits, companies must usually adapt their offerings to the unique needs of specific international markets.

Service marketers also face special challenges when going global. Some service industries have a long history of international operations. For example, the commercial banking industry was one of the first to grow internationally. Banks had to provide global services in order to meet the foreign exchange and credit needs of their home country clients wanting to sell overseas. In recent years, many banks have become truly global. Germany's Deutsche Bank, for example, serves more than 13 million customers through 1,717 branches in 73 countries. For its clients around the world who wish to grow globally, Deutsche Bank can raise money not only in Frankfurt but also in Zurich, London, Paris, Tokyo, and Moscow.[35]

Professional and business services industries such as accounting, management consulting, and advertising have also globalized. The international growth of these firms followed the globalization of the client companies they serve. For example, as more clients employ worldwide marketing and advertising strategies, advertising agencies have responded by globalizing their own operations. McCann Worldgroup, a large U.S.-based advertising and marketing services agency, operates in more than 130 countries. It serves international clients such as Coca-Cola, General Motors, ExxonMobile, Microsoft, MasterCard, Johnson & Johnson, and Unilever in markets ranging from the United States and Canada to Korea and Kazakhstan. Moreover, McCann Worldgroup is one company in the Interpublic Group of Companies, an immense, worldwide network of advertising and marketing services companies.[36]

Retailers are among the latest service businesses to go global. As their home markets become saturated, American retailers such as Wal-Mart, Office Depot, and Saks Fifth Avenue are expanding into faster-growing markets abroad. For example, since 1995, Wal-Mart has entered 15 countries; its international division's sales grew more than 11 percent last year, skyrocketing to more than $62.7 billion. Foreign retailers are making similar moves. Asian shoppers can now buy American products in French-owned Carrefour stores. Carrefour, the world's second-largest retailer behind Wal-Mart, now operates in more than 12,000 stores in more than 30 countries. It is the leading retailer in Europe, Brazil, and Argentina and the largest foreign retailer in China.[37]

The trend toward growth of global service companies will continue, especially in banking, airlines, telecommunications, and professional services. Today service firms are no longer simply following their manufacturing customers. Instead, they are taking the lead in international expansion.

chapter **11**

› **Culture**

The study of culture is a challenging undertaking because its primary focus is on the broadest component of social behavior—*an entire society*. In contrast to the psychologist, who is principally concerned with the study of individual behavior, or the sociologist, who is concerned with the study of groups, the anthropologist is primarily interested in identifying the very fabric of society itself.

This chapter explores the basic concepts of culture, with particular emphasis on the role that culture plays in influencing consumer behavior. We will first consider the specific dimensions of culture that make it a powerful force in regulating human behavior. After reviewing several measurement approaches that researchers use to understand the impact of culture on consumption behavior, we will show how a variety of core American cultural values influence consumer behavior.

This chapter is concerned with the general aspects of culture; the following two chapters focus on subculture and on cross-culture and show how marketers can use such knowledge to shape and modify their marketing strategies.

What is culture?

Given the broad and pervasive nature of **culture**, its study generally requires a detailed examination of the character of the total society, including such factors as language, knowledge, laws, religions, food customs, music, art, technology, work patterns, products, and other artifacts that give a society its distinctive flavor. In a sense, culture is a society's personality. For this reason, it is not easy to define its boundaries.

Because our objective is to understand the influence of culture on consumer behavior, we define culture as the *sum total of learned beliefs, values, and customs that serve to direct the consumer behavior of members of a particular society.*

The *belief* and *value* components of our definition refer to the accumulated feelings and priorities that individuals have about "things" and possessions. More precisely, *beliefs* consist of the very large number of mental or verbal statements (i.e., "I believe . . . ") that reflect a person's particular knowledge and assessment of something (another person, a store, a product, a brand). *Values* also are beliefs. Values differ from other beliefs, however, because they meet the following criteria: (1) They are relatively few in number; (2) they serve as a guide for culturally appropriate behavior; (3) they are enduring or difficult to change; (4) they are not tied to specific objects or situations; and (5) they are widely accepted by the members of a society.

Therefore, in a broad sense, both values and beliefs are mental images that affect a wide range of specific attitudes that, in turn, influence the way a person is likely to respond in a specific situation. For example, the criteria a person uses to evaluate alternative brands in a product category (such as Samsung versus Panasonic HDTV sets), or his or her eventual preference for one of these brands over the other, are influenced by both a person's general values (perceptions as to what constitutes quality and the meaning of country of origin) and specific beliefs (particular perceptions about the quality of South Korean-made versus Japanese-made televisions).

In contrast to beliefs and values, customs are *overt modes of behavior that constitute culturally approved or acceptable ways of behaving in specific situations.* Customs consist of everyday or routine behavior. For example, a consumer's routine behavior, such as adding a diet sweetener to coffee, putting ketchup on scrambled eggs, putting mustard on frankfurters, and having a pasta dish *before* rather than *with* the main course of a meal, are customs. Thus, whereas beliefs and values are guides for behavior, customs are *usual and acceptable ways of behaving.*

By our definition, it is easy to see how an understanding of various cultures of a society helps marketers predict consumer acceptance of their products.

The invisible hand of culture

The impact of culture is so natural and automatic that its influence on behavior is usually taken for granted. For instance, when consumer researchers ask people why they do certain things, they frequently answer, "Because it's the right thing to do." This seemingly superficial response partially reflects the ingrained influence of culture on our behavior. Often it is only when we are exposed to people with different cultural values or customs (as when visiting a different region or a different country) that we become aware of how culture has molded our own behavior. Thus, a true appreciation of the influence that culture has on our daily life requires some knowledge of at least one other society with different cultural characteristics. For example, to understand that brushing our teeth twice a day with flavored toothpaste is a cultural phenomenon requires some awareness that members of another society either do not brush their teeth at all or do so in a distinctly different manner than our own society.

Perhaps the following statement expresses it best:

> Consumers both view themselves in the context of their culture and react to their environment based upon the cultural framework that they bring to that experience. Each individual perceives the world through his own cultural lens.[1]

Culture can exist and sometimes reveal itself at different perceived or subjective levels.[2] For those of us interested in consumer behavior, we would be most concerned with three "levels" of subjective culture that are especially relevant to the exploration of consumer behavior and formation of marketing strategy. The first-level can be thought of as the *supranational level;* it reflects the underlying dimensions of culture that impact multiple cultures or different societies (i.e., cross-national or cross-cultural boundaries). For instance, it might reflect regional character (e.g., people living in several nations in a particular region of Europe), or racial and religious similarities or differences, or shared or different languages. The second level is concerned with *national level* factors, such as shared core values, customs, personalities, and predispositional factors that tend to capture the essence of the "national character" of the citizens of a particular country (mostly the content of this chapter). Finally, *group level* factors are concerned with various subdivisions of a country or society. They might include subcultures' difference, and membership and reference group differences. Figure 11.1 presents a model depicting the role that subjective culture (on the left side of the model) plays in determining our beliefs, practices, and values, which in turn impact our social norms, attitudes, behavioral intentions, and, ultimately, our behavior.

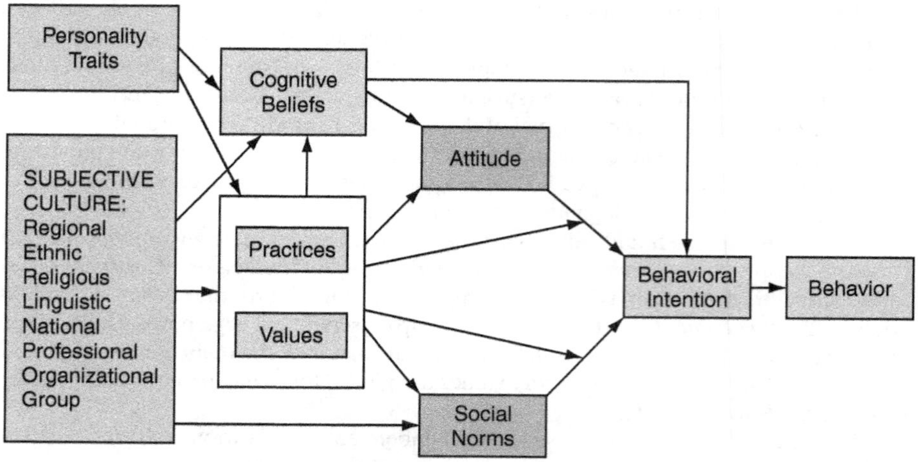

A Theoretical Model of Culture's Influence on Behavior

Source: Elena Karahanna, J. Roberto Evaristo, and Mark Strite, "Levels of Culture and Individual Behavior: An Integrative Perspective," *Journal of Global Information Management* 13 (April–June 2005): 8.

FIGURE 11.1

Culture satisfies needs

Culture exists to satisfy the needs of the people within a society. It offers order, direction, and guidance in all phases of human problem solving by providing "tried-and-true" methods of satisfying physiological, personal, and social needs. For example, culture provides standards and "rules" about when to eat ("not between meals"); where to eat ("in a busy restaurant, because the food is likely to be good"); what is appropriate to eat for breakfast (eggs and toast), lunch (a sandwich), dinner ("something hot and good and healthy"), and snacks ("something with quick energy, but not too many calories"); and what to serve to guests at a dinner party ("a formal sit-down meal"), at a picnic (barbecued "franks and hamburgers"), or at a wedding (champagne). Culture is also associated with what a society's members consider to be a necessity and what they view as a luxury. For instance, 55 percent of American adults consider a microwave to be a necessity, and 36 percent consider a remote control for a TV or VCR to be a necessity.[3]

Similarly, culture also provides insights as to suitable dress for specific occasions (such as what to wear around the house, what to wear to school, to work, to church, at a fast-food restaurant, or to a movie theater). Dress codes have shifted dramatically; people are dressing more casually most of the time. Today, only a few big-city restaurants and clubs have business dress requirements. With the relaxed dress code in the corporate work environment, fewer men are wearing dress shirts, ties, and business suits, and fewer women are wearing dresses, suits, and panty hose. In their place casual slacks, sports shirts and blouses, jeans, and the emerging category of "dress casual" have been increasing in sales.

Soft-drink companies would prefer that consumers received their morning "jolt" of caffeine from one of their products rather than from coffee. Because most Americans do not consider soda a suitable breakfast beverage, the real challenge for soft-drink companies is to overcome culture, not competition. Indeed, coffee has been challenged on all fronts by juices, milk, teas (hot and iced), a host of different types of soft drinks, and now even caffeinated waters. Not resting on their "cultural advantage" as a breakfast drink and the namesake of the "coffee break," coffee marketers have been fighting back by targeting gourmet and specialty coffees (e.g., espresso, cappuccino, and café mocha) to young adults (those 18 to 24 years of age). These efforts have been paying off as young adults (an important segment of the soft-drink market) have been responding positively to gourmet coffees.

Cultural beliefs, values, and customs continue to be followed as long as they yield satisfaction. When a specific standard no longer satisfies the members of a society, however, it is modified or replaced, so that the resulting standard is more in line with current needs and desires. For instance, it was once considered a sign of a fine hotel that it provided down or goose feather pillows in rooms. Today, with so many guests allergic to such materials, synthetic polyfill pillows are becoming more the rule. Thus, culture gradually but continually evolves to meet the needs of society.

Culture is learned

Unlike innate biological characteristics (e.g., sex, skin, hair color, or intelligence), culture is learned. At an early age, we begin to acquire from our social environment a set of beliefs, values, and customs that make up our culture. For children, the learning of these acceptable cultural values and customs is reinforced by the process of playing with their toys. As children play, they act out and rehearse important cultural lessons and situations. This cultural learning prepares them for later real-life circumstances.

How culture is learned

Anthropologists have identified three distinct forms of cultural learning: *formal learning,* in which adults and older siblings teach a young family member "how to behave"; *informal learning,* in which a child learns primarily by imitating the behavior of selected others, such as family, friends, or TV heroes; and *technical learning*, in which teachers instruct the child in an educational environment about what should be done, how it should be done, and why it should be done. Although a firm's advertising can influence all three types of cultural learning, it is likely that many product advertisements enhance informal cultural learning by providing the audience with a model of behavior to imitate. This is especially true for visible or conspicuous products that are evaluated in public settings (such as designer clothing, cell phones, or status golf clubs), where peer influence is likely to play an important role. Additionally, "not only are cultural values cited in advertising copy, they also are often coded in the visual imagery, colors, movements, music, and other nonverbal elements of an advertisement."[4]

The repetition of advertising messages creates and reinforces cultural beliefs and values. For example, many advertisers continually stress the same selected benefits of their products or services. Ads for wireless phone service often stress the clarity of their connection, or the nationwide coverage of their service, or the free long distance calling, as well as the flexibility of their pricing plans. It is difficult to say whether wireless phone subscribers *inherently* desire these benefits from their wireless service providers or whether, after several years of cumulative exposure to advertising appeals stressing these benefits, they have been taught by marketers to desire them. In a sense, although specific product advertising may reinforce the benefits that consumers want from the product (as determined by consumer behavior research), such advertising also "teaches" future generations of consumers to expect the same benefits from the product category.

Figure 11.2 shows that cultural meaning moves from the culturally constituted world to consumer goods and from there to the individual consumer by means of various *consumption-related vehicles* (e.g., advertising or observing or imitating others' behavior). Imagine the ever-popular T-shirt and how it can furnish cultural meaning and identity for wearers. T-shirts can function as *trophies* (as proof of participation in sports or travel) or as self-proclaimed labels of *belonging to a cultural category* ("World Series Attendee"). T-shirts can also be used as a means of *self-expression,* which may provide wearers with the additional benefit of serving as a "topic" initiating social dialogue with others. Still further, although we might expect that a New York T-shirt would be worn by a person who has been to New York (or has received it as a gift from someone else who has visited New York), this is not necessarily so. In such a world of "virtual identities," consumers can now just buy a New York T-shirt at a local retailer and create the impression that they have been there.

Enculturation and acculturation

When discussing the acquisition of culture, anthropologists often distinguish between the learning of one's own, or native, culture and the learning of some "new" (other) culture. The learning of one's own culture is known as **enculturation**. The learning of a new or foreign culture is known as **acculturation**. Acculturation is an important concept for marketers who plan to sell their products in foreign or multinational markets. In such cases, marketers must study the specific culture(s) of their potential target markets to determine whether their products will be acceptable to its members and, if so, how they can best communicate the characteristics of their products to persuade the target market to buy.

Language and symbols

To acquire a common culture, the members of a society must be able to communicate with each other through a common language. Without a common language, shared meaning could not exist and true communication would not take place.

To communicate effectively with their audiences, marketers must use appropriate **symbols** to convey desired product images or characteristics. These symbols can be verbal or nonverbal. Verbal symbols may include a television announcement or an advertisement in a

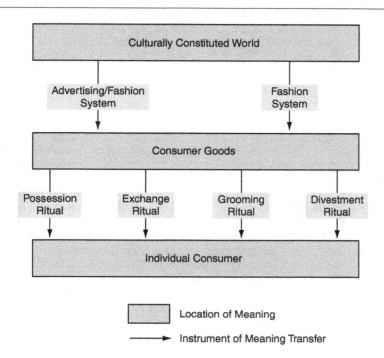

FIGURE 11.2

The Movement of Cultural Meaning

Source: Grant McCracken, "Culture and Consumption: A Theoretical Account of the Structure and Movement of the Cultural Meaning of Consumer Goods," *Journal of Consumer Research*, 13 (June 1986): 72. Reprinted by permission of The University of Chicago Press as publishers.

magazine. Nonverbal communication includes the use of such symbols as figures, colors, shapes, and even textures to lend additional meaning to print or broadcast advertisements, to trademarks, and to packaging or product designs.

Basically, the symbolic nature of human language sets it apart from all other animal communication. A symbol is anything that stands for something else. Any word is a symbol. The word *razor* calls forth a specific image related to an individual's own knowledge and experience (possibly either a shaving-related image or a Motorola cell phone-related image). The word *tsunami* calls forth the notion of waves and water and also has the power to stir us emotionally, arousing feelings of danger and the need for protection and safety. Similarly, the word *mercedes* has symbolic meaning: To some it suggests a fine luxury automobile; to others it implies wealth and status; to still others it reminds them of a woman named Mercedes.

Because the human mind can process symbols, it is possible, for example, for a person to "experience" cognitively a visualization for a product, like the advertisement for a skin moisturizing gel, which contrasts two scenes—one of a parched desert without the gel and one of a rich green landscape with the gel. Such a comparison presents the idea that a skin-moisturizing gel will transform a person's dry skin to a comfortable moist state. The capacity to learn symbolically is primarily a human phenomenon; most other animals learn by direct experience. Clearly, the ability of humans to understand symbolically how a product, service, or idea can satisfy their needs makes it easier for marketers to sell the features and benefits of their offerings. Through a shared language and culture, individuals already know what the image means; thus, an association can be made without actively thinking about it.

A symbol may have several, even contradictory, meanings, so the advertiser must ascertain exactly what the symbol is communicating to its intended audience. For example, the advertiser who uses a trademark depicting an old craftsman to symbolize careful workmanship may instead be communicating an image of outmoded methods and lack of style. The marketer who uses slang in an advertisement to attract a teenage audience must do so with great care; slang that is misused or outdated will symbolically date the marketer's firm and product.

Price and channels of distribution also are significant symbols of the marketer and the marketer's product. For example, price often implies quality to potential buyers. For certain products (such as clothing), the type of store in which the product is sold also is an important symbol of quality. In fact, all the elements of the marketing mix—the product, its promotion, price, and the stores at which it is available—are symbols that communicate ranges of quality to potential buyers.

Ritual

In addition to language and symbols, culture includes various ritualized experiences and behaviors that until recently have been largely neglected by consumer researchers. A **ritual** is a type of symbolic activity consisting of a series of steps (multiple behaviors) occurring in a fixed sequence and repeated over time.[5]

In practice, rituals extend over the human life cycle from birth to death, including a host of intermediate events (such as confirmation, graduations, and marriage). These rituals can be very public, elaborate, religious, or civil ceremonies, or they can be as mundane as an individual's grooming behavior or flossing. Ritualized behavior is typically rather formal and often is scripted behavior (as a religious service requiring a prayer book or the code of proper conduct in a court of law). It is also likely to occur repeatedly over time (such as singing the national anthem before a basketball game).

Most important from the standpoint of marketers is the fact that rituals tend to be replete with ritual artifacts (products) that are associated with or somehow enhance the performance of the ritual. For instance, turkey, stuffing, and other various food items are linked to the ritual of a Thanksgiving Day, New Year's Day, or other holiday celebrations; other rituals (such as a graduation, a wedding or wedding anniversary, a Tuesday night card game, or a Saturday morning visit to the hair salon) have their own specific artifacts associated with them. For special occasions, such as wedding anniversaries, some types of artifacts are perceived as more appropriate as gifts than others, for example, jewelry rather than everyday household items (Table 11.1).

TABLE 11.1 Selected Rituals and Associated Artifacts

SELECTED RITUALS	TYPICAL ARTIFACTS
Wedding	White gown (something old, something new, something borrowed, something blue)
Birth of child	U.S. savings bond, silver baby spoon
Birthday	Card, present, cake with candles
50th wedding anniversary	Catered party, card and gift, display of photos of the couple's life together
Graduation	Pen, U.S. savings bond, card, wristwatch
Valentine's Day	Candy, card, flowers
New Year's Eve	Champagne, party, fancy dress
Thanksgiving	Prepare a turkey meal for family and friends
Going to the gym	Towel, exercise clothes, water, portable tape player
Sunday football	Beer, potato chips, pretzels
Super Bowl party	Same as Sunday football (just more)
Starting a new job	Get a haircut, buy some new clothing
Getting a job promotion	Taken out to lunch by coworkers, receive token gift
Retirement	Company party, watch, plaque
Death	Send a card, give to charity in the name of the deceased

In addition to a ritual, which is the way that something is traditionally done, there is also *ritualistic behavior,* which can be defined as any behavior that is made into a ritual. For example, a tennis player may bounce the ball a few times or swing the arm holding the tennis racket in a big arc once or twice before every serve. Table 11.2 describes a young woman's ritualistic behavior with respect to facial beauty care.

Culture is shared

To be considered a cultural characteristic, a particular belief, value, or practice must be shared by a significant portion of the society. Thus, culture frequently is viewed as group *customs* that link together the members of a society. Of course, common language is the critical cultural component that makes it possible for people to share values, experiences, and customs.

Various social institutions within a society transmit the elements of culture and make the sharing of culture a reality. Chief among such institutions is the *family,* which serves as the primary agent for enculturation—the passing along of basic cultural beliefs, values, and customs to society's newest members. A vital part of the enculturation role of the family is the consumer socialization of the young. This includes teaching such basic consumer-related values and skills as the meaning of money; the relationship between price and quality; the establishment of product tastes, preferences, and habits; and appropriate methods of response to various promotional messages.

In addition to the family, two other institutions traditionally share much of the responsibility for the transfer of selected aspects of culture: *educational institutions* and *houses of worship.* Educational institutions specifically are charged with imparting basic learning skills, history, patriotism, citizenship, and the technical training needed to prepare people for significant roles within society. Religious institutions provide and perpetuate religious consciousness, spiritual guidance, and moral training. Although the young receive much of their consumer training within the family setting, the educational and religious systems reinforce this training by teaching economic and ethical concepts.

A fourth, frequently overlooked, social institution that plays a major role in the transfer of culture throughout society is the mass media. Given the extensive exposure of the American population to both print and broadcast media, as well as the easily ingested, entertaining format in which the contents of such media usually are presented, it is not surprising that the mass media are powerful vehicles for imparting a wide range of cultural values.

TABLE 11.2	**Facial Beauty Ritual of a Young TV Advertising Sales Representative**

1. I pull my hair back with a headband.
2. I take all my makeup off with L'Oréal eye makeup remover.
3. Next, I use a Q-tip with some moisturizer around my eyes to make sure all eye makeup is removed.
4. I wash my face with Noxzema facial wash.
5. I apply Clinique Dramatically Different Lotion to my face, neck, and throat.
6. If I have a blemish, I apply Clearasil Treatment to the area to dry it out.
7. Twice weekly (or as necessary) I use Aapri Facial Scrub to remove dry and dead skin.
8. Once a week I apply Clinique Clarifying Lotion 2 with a cotton ball to my face and throat to remove deep-down dirt and oils.
9. Once every three months I get a professional salon facial to deep-clean my pores.

We are exposed daily to advertising, an important component of the media. Advertising not only underwrites, or makes economically feasible, the editorial or programming contents of the media, but it also transmits much about our culture. Without advertising, it would be almost impossible to disseminate information about products, ideas, and causes.

Consumers receive important cultural information from advertising. For example, it has been hypothesized that one of the roles of advertising in sophisticated magazines such as *Vogue* (**www.vogue.com**), *Bon Appetit* (**www. epicurious.com/bonappetit**), and *Architectural Digest* (**www.architecturaldigest.com**) is to instruct readers how to dress, how to decorate their homes, and what foods and wines to serve guests, or in other words, what types of behavior are most appropriate to their particular social class. Thus, although the scope of advertising is often considered to be limited to influencing the demand for specific products or services, in a cultural context, advertising has the expanded mission of reinforcing established cultural values and aiding in the dissemination of new tastes, habits, and customs. In planning their advertising, marketers should recognize that advertising is an important agent for social change in our society.

Culture is dynamic

To fulfill its need-gratifying role, culture continually must evolve if it is to function in the best interests of a society. For this reason, the marketer must carefully monitor the sociocultural environment in order to market an existing product more effectively or to develop promising new products.

This is not an easy task because many factors are likely to produce cultural changes within a given society (new technology, population shifts, resource shortages, wars, changing values, and customs borrowed from other cultures). For example, major ongoing cultural changes in American society reflect the expanded career options open to women. Today, most women work outside the home, frequently in careers that once were considered exclusively male oriented. These career women are increasingly not waiting for marriage or a man to buy them luxury items—such as fur coats, expensive wristwatches, and diamond rings. More and more such women are saying, "I earn a good living, why wait? I will buy it for myself."

The changing nature of culture means that marketers have to consistently reconsider *why* consumers are now doing what they do, *who* the purchasers and the users of their products are (males only, females only, or both), *when* they do their shopping, *how* and *where* they can be reached by the media, and *what* new product and service needs are emerging. Marketers who monitor cultural changes also often find new opportunities to increase corporate profitability. For example, marketers of such products and services as life insurance, financial and investment advice, casual clothing, toy electric trains, and cigars are among those who have attempted to take advantage of shifts in what is feminine and how to communicate with female consumers. As yet another example, "design has (re)emerged as a major force in American consumers' lives." Since today even basic consumer goods deliver on their promises of performance, design has become a way for a company to differentiate its products.[6] If all MP3 players, for example, sound great, then why not purchase the one that looks the "coolest," which is probably the iPod. One writer has recently described the period we are now living in "as the age of aesthetics," wherein the way things look, feel, and smell have come to matter—not just among the upper-middle classes but among all consumers.[7]

A recently longitudinal study of how women have been depicted in *Fortune* magazine serves as yet another example of how culture is dynamic. The study employed content analysis (discussed later in this chapter) as its methodology, and concluded that the changes in advertising tended to reflect the changing role of women during the decade starting in 1990.[8] In particular, the research reveals a fourfold increase in the number of women as the "figure" (i.e., presented in the foreground of the print advertisement) compared to men. Women were also substantially more likely to be portrayed as being a "professional."

Insights about cultural change are also secured from lists that trend observers create as to "what's hot" and "what's not." Such lists often reflect the dynamic nature of a particular society or culture.

The measurement of culture

A wide range of measurement techniques are used in the study of culture. For example, the projective tests used by psychologists to study motivation and personality and the attitude measurement techniques used by social psychologists and sociologists are relatively popular tools in the study of culture.

In addition, *content analysis, consumer fieldwork,* and *value measurement instruments* are three research approaches that are frequently used to examine culture and to spot cultural trends. There are also several commercial services that track emerging values and social trends for businesses and governmental agencies.

Content analysis

Conclusions about a society, or specific aspects of a society, or a comparison of two or more societies sometimes can be drawn from examining the content of particular messages. **Content analysis**, as the name implies, focuses on the content of verbal, written, and pictorial communications (such as the copy and art composition of an ad).

Content analysis can be used as a relatively objective means of determining what social and cultural changes have occurred in a specific society or as a way of contrasting aspects of two different societies. A content analysis of more than 250 ads appearing in eight issues of *Seventeen* magazine, four Japanese issues, and four American issues, found that teenage girls are portrayed differently. The research concluded that these "differences correspond to each country's central concepts of self and society." Whereas American teen girls are often associated with images of "independence and determination," Japanese teen girls are most often portrayed with a "happy, playful, childlike girlish image."[9] In another content analysis study—this one comparing American and Chinese television commercials targeted to children—the research revealed that 82 percent of the Chinese ads aimed at children were for food products, whereas 56 percent of the ads directed at American children were for toys.[10]

Content analysis is useful to both marketers and public policymakers interested in comparing the advertising claims of competitors within a specific industry, as well as for evaluating the nature of advertising claims targeted to specific audiences (e.g., women, the elderly, or children).

Consumer fieldwork

When examining a specific society, anthropologists frequently immerse themselves in the environment under study through **consumer fieldwork**. As trained researchers, they are likely to select a small sample of people from a particular society and carefully observe their behavior. Based on their observations, researchers draw conclusions about the values, beliefs, and customs of the society under investigation. For example, if researchers were interested in how men select neckties, they might position trained observers in department and clothing stores and note how neckties are selected (solid versus patterned, striped versus paisley, and so on). The researchers also may be interested in the degree of search that accompanies the choice, that is, how often consumers tend to take a necktie off the display, examine it, compare it to other neckties in the store, and place it back again before selecting the necktie that they finally purchase.

The distinct characteristics of **field observation** are that (1) it takes place within a natural environment; (2) it is performed sometimes without the subject's awareness; and (3) it focuses on observation of behavior. Because the emphasis is on a natural environment and observable behavior, field observation concerned with consumer behavior often focuses on in-store shopping behavior and, less frequently, on in-home preparation and consumption.

In some cases, instead of just observing behavior, researchers become **participant-observers** (i.e., they become active members of the environment that they are studying). For example, if researchers were interested in examining how consumers select computer software, they might take a sales position in a computer superstore to observe directly and even to interact with customers in the transaction process.

Today, there are consumer research firms that specialize in studying consumer rituals and values. These firms often videotape subjects at work, at home, in their cars, and in public places. For instance, researchers might ask a teenager why he's buying a certain backpack, and you might not get a useful response. Rather, watching a teenager as he shops for that backpack, and you might "learn a few things." This type of research, used by Nissan in the 1990s when it was designing its line of Infinity automobiles, discovered that the Japanese notion of luxury was very different than the American version— whereas the Japanese crave simplicity, Americans crave visible opulence.[11]

Both field observation and participant-observer research require highly skilled researchers who can separate their own preferences and emotions from what they actually observe in their professional roles. Both techniques provide valuable insight that might not easily be obtained through survey research that simply asks consumers questions about their behavior.

In addition to fieldwork methods, depth interviews and focus-group sessions are also often used by marketers to get a "first look" at an emerging social or cultural change. In the relatively informal atmosphere of focus group discussions, consumers are apt to reveal attitudes or behavior that may signal a shift in values that, in turn, may affect the long-run market acceptance of a product or service. For instance, focus group studies can be used to identify marketing programs that reinforce established customer loyalty and goodwill (or relationship marketing). A common thread running throughout these studies showed that established customers, especially for services (such as investment and banking services), want to have their loyalty acknowledged in the form of *personalized services*. These observations have led various service and product companies to refine or establish loyalty programs that are more personalized in the way that they treat their established customers (e.g., by recognizing the individuality of such core customers). This is just one of numerous examples showing how focus groups and depth interviews are used to spot social trends.

Value measurement survey instruments

Anthropologists have traditionally observed the behavior of members of a specific society and inferred from such behavior the dominant or underlying values of the society. In recent years, however, there has been a gradual shift to measuring values directly by means of survey (questionnaire) research. Researchers use data collection instruments called *value instruments* to ask people how they feel about such basic personal and social concepts as freedom, comfort, national security, and peace.

A variety of popular value instruments have been used in consumer behavior studies, including the **Rokeach Value Survey**, the *List of Values (LOV),* and the *Values and Lifestyles—VALS.* The widely used Rokeach Value Survey is a self-administered value inventory that is divided into two parts, each part measuring different but complementary types of personal values (see Table 11.3). The first part consists of 18 *terminal value* items, which are designed to measure the relative importance of end states of existence (or personal goals). The second part consists of 18 *instrumental value* items, which measure basic approaches an individual might take to reach end-state values. Thus, the first half of the measurement instrument deals with ends, and the second half considers means.

Using the Rokeach Value Survey, adult Brazilians were categorized into six distinctive value segments.[12] For example, Segment A (representing 13 percent of the sample) was most concerned with "world peace," followed by "inner harmony" and "true friendship." Members of this segment were found to be especially involved in domestic-oriented activities (such as gardening, reading, and going out with the family to visit relatives). Because of their less materialistic and nonhedonistic orientation, this segment also may be the least prone to experiment with new products. In contrast, Segment B (representing 9 percent of the sample) was most concerned with self-centered values such as self-respect, a comfortable life, pleasure, an exciting life, a sense of accomplishment, and social recognition. They were least concerned with values related to the family, such as friendship, love, and equality. These self-centered, achievement-oriented pleasure seekers were expected to prefer provocative clothes in the latest fashion, to enjoy an active lifestyle, and be more likely to try new products.

The LOV scale is a related measurement instrument that is also designed to be used in surveying consumers' personal values. The LOV scale asks consumers to identify their

---

| TABLE 11.3 | The Rokeach Value Survey Instrument |

TERMINAL VALUES	INSTRUMENTAL VALUES
A Comfortable Life (a prosperous life)	Ambitious (hardworking, aspiring)
An Exciting Life (a stimulating, active life)	Broad-Minded (open-minded)
A World at Peace (free of war and conflict)	Capable (competent, effective)
Equality (brotherhood, equal opportunity for all)	Cheerful (lighthearted, joyful)
Freedom (independence and free choice)	Clean (neat, tidy)
Happiness (contentedness)	Courageous (standing up for your beliefs)
National Security (protection from attack)	Forgiving (willing to pardon others)
Pleasure (an enjoyable life)	Helpful (working for the welfare of others)
Salvation (saved, eternal life)	Honest (sincere, truthful)
Social Recognition (respect and admiration)	Imaginative (daring, creative)
True Friendship (close companionship)	Independent (self-reliant, self-sufficient)
Wisdom (a mature understanding of life)	Intellectual (intelligent, reflective)
A World of Beauty (beauty of nature and the arts)	Logical (consistent, rational)
Family Security (taking care of loved ones)	Loving (affectionate, tender)
Mature Love (sexual and spiritual intimacy)	Obedient (dutiful, respectful)
Self-Respect (self-esteem)	Polite (courteous, well-mannered)
A Sense of Accomplishment (lasting contribution)	Responsible (dependable, reliable)
Inner Harmony (freedom from inner conflict)	Self-Controlled (restrained, self-disciplined)

two most important values from a nine-value list (such as "warm relationships with others," "a sense of belonging," or "a sense of accomplishment") that is based on the terminal values of the Rokeach Value Survey.[13]

American core values

What is the American culture? In this section, we identify a number of **core values** that both affect and reflect the character of American society. This is a difficult undertaking for several reasons. First, the United States is a diverse country, consisting of a good number of **subcultures** (religious, ethnic, regional, racial, and economic groups), each of which interprets and responds to society's basic beliefs and values in its own specific way. Second, America is a dynamic society that has undergone an almost constant change in response to the development of new technology. This element of rapid change makes it especially difficult to monitor changes in cultural values. Finally, the existence of contradictory values in American society is somewhat confusing. For instance, Americans traditionally embrace freedom of choice and individualism, yet simultaneously they show great tendencies to conform (in dress, in furnishings, and in fads) to the rest of society. In the context of consumer behavior, Americans like to have a wide choice of products and prefer those that uniquely express what they envison to be their personal lifestyles. Yet, there is often a considerable amount of implicit pressure to conform to the values of family members, friends, and other socially important groups. It is difficult to reconcile these seemingly inconsistent values; their existence, however, demonstrates that America is a complex society with numerous paradoxes.

When selecting the specific core values to be examined, we were guided by three criteria:

1. The value must be pervasive. *A significant portion of the American people must accept the value and use it as a guide for their attitudes and actions.*

2. The value must be enduring. *The specific value must have influenced the actions of the American people over an extended period of time (as distinguished from a short-run trend).*

3. The value must be consumer related. *The specific value must provide insights that help us to understand the consumption actions of the American people.*

Meeting these criteria are a number of basic values that expert observers of the American scene consider the "building blocks" of that rather elusive concept called the "American character."

Achievement and success

In a broad cultural context, achievement is a major American value, with historical roots that can be traced to the traditional religious belief in the Protestant work ethic, which considers hard work to be wholesome, spiritually rewarding, and an appropriate end in itself. Indeed, substantial research evidence shows that the achievement orientation is closely associated with the technical development and general economic growth of American society.[14]

Individuals who consider a "sense of accomplishment" an important personal value tend to be achievers who strive hard for success. Although historically associated with men, especially male business executives, today *achievement* is very important for women, who are increasingly enrolled in undergraduate and graduate business programs and are more commonly seeking top-level business careers.

A recent study that examined the interplay between the Internet and personal values found that those individuals scoring high in "sense of accomplishment" were more likely to use the Internet for learning or gathering information, making reservations or researching travel, work/business, buying goods or services, looking up stock quotes, and participating in online auctions by buying or selling products. Conversely, Internet activities not associated with a high "sense of accomplishment" included surfing the Web, communication with others in chat rooms, and gathering product or retail store information.[15]

Success is a closely related American cultural theme. However, achievement and success do differ. Specifically, achievement is its own direct reward (it is implicitly satisfying to the individual achiever), whereas success implies an extrinsic reward (such as luxury possessions, financial compensation, or status improvement). Moreover, it is the widespread embracing of achievement and success that has led to the great success and progress of the United States.[16] A recent study examining what influences college students' choice of major found that the most important influence for incoming freshmen was interest in the subject. However, while for female students the next most influential factor was aptitude in the subject, for male students it was "the major's potential for career advancement, and job opportunities and the level of compensation in the field."[17]

Both achievement and success influence consumption. They often serve as social and moral justification for the acquisition of goods and services. For example, "You owe it to yourself," "You worked for it," and "You deserve it" are popular achievement themes used by advertisers to coax consumers into purchasing their products. Regardless of gender, achievement-oriented people often enjoy conspicuous consumption because it allows them to display symbols of their personal achievement. When it comes to personal development and preparation for future careers, the themes of achievement and success are also especially appropriate.

Activity

Americans attach an extraordinary amount of importance to being *active* or *involved*. Keeping busy is widely accepted as a healthy and even necessary part of the American lifestyle. The hectic nature of American life is attested to by foreign visitors, who frequently comment that they cannot understand why Americans are always "on the run" and seemingly unable to relax. It is easy to identify ads in the mass media for products and services that are designed to assist consumers in dealing with their hectic or "overfull" lives.

The premium placed on activity has had both positive and negative effects on the popularity of various products. For example, a principal reason for the enormous growth of fast-food chains, such as McDonald's and Kentucky Fried Chicken, is that so many people want quick, prepared meals when they are away from the house. Americans rarely eat a full breakfast because they usually are too rushed in the morning to prepare and consume a traditional morning meal.

Research suggests that "being busy," in and of itself, is not enough and not necessarily healthy. For example, some researchers have reported that although it is important for elderly people to "keep busy," it is important that the activities they engage in be fulfilling. Similarly, it is being questioned whether keeping young children busy all the time is healthy for them—it's been suggested that kids need time to relax![18]

Efficiency and practicality

With a basic philosophy of down-to-earth pragmatism, Americans pride themselves on being efficient and practical. When it comes to *efficiency,* they admire anything that saves time and effort. In terms of *practicality,* they generally are receptive to any new product that makes tasks easier and can help solve problems. For example, today it is possible for manufacturers of many product categories to offer the public a wide range of interchangeable components. Thus, a consumer can design his or her own customized wall unit from such standard components as compatible metals and woods, legs, door facings, and style panels at a cost not much higher than a completely standardized unit. The capacity of manufacturers to create mass-produced components offers consumers the practical option of a customized product at a reasonable price. If you are unfamiliar with such furniture, just browse through an IKEA catalog or the "virtual catalog" on the IKEA Web site (**www.ikea.com**). As another example, if you go to the Dell Computer Web site (**www.dell.com**) you can observe the myriad of ways in which almost any model of a Dell computer can be customized by the purchaser (e.g., memory upgrades, video card upgrades, hard drive size upgrades, software upgrades, etc.).

Another illustration of Americans' attentiveness to efficiency and practicality is the extreme importance attached to *time*. Americans seem to be convinced that "time waits for no one," which is reflected in their habitual attention to being prompt. Another sign of America's preoccupation with time is the belief that time is in increasingly short supply. Americans place a great deal of importance on getting there first, on the value of time itself, on the notion that time is money, on the importance of not wasting time, and on identifying "more" time. In our attempt to get more and more out of each day, one author has concluded that we may become trapped in a vicious circle in which we feel as if we are getting less and less out of each day.[19]

The frequency with which Americans look at their watches and the importance attached to having an accurate timepiece tend to support the American value of *punctuality*.

Progress

Progress is another watchword of American society. Americans respond favorably to the promise of progress. Receptivity to progress appears to be closely linked to the other core values already examined (*achievement, success, efficiency,* and *practicality*) and to the central belief that people can always improve themselves, that tomorrow should be better than today. In a consumption-oriented society, such as that of the United States, progress often means the acceptance of change, new products, or services designed to fulfill previously undersatisfied or unsatisfied needs. A new type of counselor, the "life coach" or "personal coach," works with individuals in order to help them improve themselves and seek "fulfillment and balance in careers, family, health, and hobbies." The coach tracks the client's progress and tries to keep the client heading in the direction of his or her fulfillment. Ideally, the coach makes the client excited about prospects for the future.

In the name of progress, Americans appear to be receptive to product claims that stress "new," "improved," "longer-lasting," "speedier," "quicker," "smoother and closer," and "increased strength."

Material comfort

For most Americans (even young children), *material comfort* signifies the attainment of "the good life," a life that may include a new car, a dishwasher, an air conditioner, a hot tub, and an almost infinite variety of other convenience-oriented and pleasure-providing goods and services. It appears that consumers' idea of material comfort is largely a *relative* view; that is, consumers tend to define their own satisfaction with the amount of material goods they have in terms of a comparison of what they have to what others have. If a comparison suggests that they have more than others do, then they are more likely to be satisfied.[20] On the other hand, as many popular songs point out, the ownership of material goods does not always lead to happiness. For instance, many people, especially affluent people, might be willing to trade money for more free time to spend with family and friends.

Vivre (**www.vivre.com**) offers a mail-order and online catalog aimed at "connecting luxury brands with affluent shoppers that is dedicated to providing material comfort for its customers." Consider how the company responds to the question "What is Vivre?" (taken from its Web site):

> *One might consider Vivre to be a revival of the classic "first floor" of a department store, which traditionally displayed only the best of the best to a discriminating clientele. Likewise, Vivre presents only that which is deemed to be relevant, inspiring and exquisitely crafted. With a modern sensibility, the resulting treasure trove is delivered to doorsteps in the form of a glossy catalog . . . and to desktops via a full-service e-commerce website. Therein shoppers will find the best of the world at their fingertips.*
>
> *By presenting each season's collection in a lifestyle context, we create an emotional connection with our customers, who rely upon us to offer an edited collection of the very best of each season. By interspersing our selections with editorial and advice, we create an inspirational shopping experience — one where Vivre is considered to be a trusted advisor to "A Beautiful Life."*[21]

Material comfort has often been associated with "bigger quantities of things" or "more of something." Recently, however, there has been a noticeable shift away from such a "more is better" viewpoint to a "better is better" vision—one that stresses better quality and better design. Americans today increasingly want *better,* and *better looking,* products. Such a state of affairs has been referred to as "the design economy"—that is, an economy that is based on the interaction of four elements: sustained prosperity, ongoing technology, a culture open to change, and marketing expertise.[22] Consider, for example, how the famous designer, Michael Graves, has helped Target (mass-merchandise retailer) accomplish its goal of being a standout provider of finely designed products at mass-market prices.

Individualism

Americans value "being themselves." Self-reliance, self-interest, self-confidence, self-esteem, and self-fulfillment are all exceedingly popular expressions of *individualism.* Striving for individualism seems to be linked to the rejection of dependency; that is, it is better to rely on oneself than on others. American "rugged individualism" is a form of individualism. It is based on the notion of self-reliance with competition (i.e., we try to meet our needs through personal effort, and in a way that outperforms our peers). Still further, solo performance, to the rugged individualist, is more important than teamwork—tasks should be accomplished alone, and victory should be earned alone.[23] Table 11.4 presents an interesting elaboration of the concept of "rugged individualism." Please examine it.

In terms of consumer behavior, an appeal to individualism frequently takes the form of reinforcing the consumer's sense of identity with products or services that both

TABLE 11.4	An Elaboration of the Cultural Dynamics of the "Rugged Individual"	
LABEL	**DEFINITION**	**IMAGERY**
Competition against self/Competition against others	Sees both self-weakness and others' strengths as foes to overcome.	Transforming self from a weakling to a warrior.
Manual labor/Purchased labor	The choice to make or buy competitive equipment.	Becoming completely self-sufficient.
Solo performance/Team work	Accomplishing goals by self or as a team.	The solo performer as the ideal.
Technology and machines/Aesthetics and fashion	Exaltation to utility, denigration of beauty.	Aesthetics as a seductive siren.
Instrumentalism/Anthropomorphism	The extended self as alive, nonself as target or tool.	Dog as partner, deer as prey.
Nature/Culture	Culture as inadequate for testing manhood; nature as both refuge and providing ground.	The wilderness as heaven and hell.
Individual freedom/Rule of law	Any form of government is restrictive of personal freedom and therefore undesirable.	The warrior as the quintessence of selfhood, the embodiment of freedom, and the exemplar of natural law.

Source: Elizabeth C. Hirschman, "Men, Dogs, Guns, and Cars: The Semiotics of Rugged Individualism," *Journal of Advertising* 32 (Spring 2003): 11.

reflect and emphasize that identity. For example, advertisements for high-style clothing and cosmetics usually promise that their products will enhance the consumer's exclusive or distinctive character and set him or her apart from others.

Freedom

Freedom is another very strong American value, with historical roots in such democratic ideals as freedom of speech, freedom of the press, and freedom of worship. As an outgrowth of these beliefs in freedom, Americans have a strong preference for *freedom of choice,* the opportunity to choose from a wide range of alternatives. This preference is reflected in the large number of competitive brands and product variations that can be found on the shelves of the modern supermarket or department store. For many products, consumers can select from a wide variety of sizes, colors, flavors, features, styles, and even special ingredients. It also explains why many companies offer consumers many choices .

However, there are decision-making situations when consumers are faced with too many choices. In such cases they may feel overwhelmed by the sheer number of choices and respond by running away from the stressful situation. Research with English consumers found that many of the respondents reported feeling bewildered and irritated by the fact that they were being offered "too much choice."[24]

External conformity

Although Americans deeply embrace freedom of choice and individualism, they nevertheless accept the reality of conformity. *External conformity* is a necessary process by which the individual adapts to society.

In the realm of consumer behavior, conformity (or uniformity) takes the form of standardized goods and services. Standardized products have been made possible by mass production. The availability of a wide choice of standardized products places the consumer in the unique position of being *individualistic* (by selecting specific products that close friends do not have) or of *conforming* (by purchasing a similar or identical product). In this context, individualism and conformity exist side by side as choices for the consumer.

An interesting example of the "Ping-Pong" relationship between seeking individualism and accepting conformity is the widespread acceptance of more casual dressing in the workplace. For instance, male and female executives are conforming less to workplace dress codes (i.e., there are more "total" dress options open to business executives). For instance, some male executives are wearing casual slacks and sport shirts to work; others are wearing blazers and slacks rather than business suits. Greater personal confidence and an emphasis on comfort appear to be the reasons that many executives are wearing less traditional business attire. Nevertheless, in some companies the appearance of male executives in blue blazers and gray slacks does seem like a "business uniform" (which is a kind of conformity). Consumer research examining the types of clothing that men and women wear to the office suggests that the majority of American workers are wearing some type of casual clothing to work.[25] For men, it is commonly "everyday casual" (jeans, shorts, T-shirts, etc.); for women it is "casual" (casual pants with or without a jacket, sweaters, separates, and pantsuits). Moreover, more than 50 percent of workers surveyed feel that it increases their productivity to wear casual clothing to work.

Humanitarianism

Americans are often generous when it comes to giving to those in need. They support with a passion many humane and charitable causes, and they sympathize with the underdog who must overcome adversity to get ahead. They also tend to be charitable and willing to come to the aid of people who are less fortunate than they are. To make the study of charitable giving more fruitful, consumer researchers have validated two scales that deal with *attitudes toward helping others* (AHO) and *attitudes toward charitable organizations* (ACO).[26]

Within the context of making charitable decisions, the Web site of the Planned Giving Design Center (**www.pgdc.net**) assists charities in their efforts to establish and cultivate relationships with professionals who advise clients in a position to make charitable contributions (e.g., lawyers, financial planners, trust officers).[27] Other Web sites are designed to provide individual givers with assistance in donating to specific charities (e.g., **www.charityguide.org**, **www.guidestar.org**, and **www.charitynavigator.org**).

Beyond charitable giving, other social issues have an impact on both what consumers buy and where they invest. For example, some investors prefer mutual funds that screen companies for such social concerns as military contracts, pollution problems, and equal opportunity employment. Investments in socially conscious mutual funds are now quite commonplace. Many companies try to appeal to consumers by emphasizing their concern for environmental or social issues.

Youthfulness

Americans tend to place an almost sacred value on *youthfulness*. This emphasis is a reflection of America's rapid technological development. In an atmosphere where "new" is constantly stressed, "old" is often equated with being outdated. This is in contrast to traditional European, African, and Asian societies, in which the elderly are revered for having the wisdom of experience that comes with age.

Youthfulness should not be confused with youth, which describes an age grouping. Americans are preoccupied with *looking* and *acting* young, regardless of their chronological age. For Americans, youthfulness is a state of mind and a state of being, sometimes expressed as being "young at heart," "young in spirit," or "young in appearance."

A great deal of advertising is directed to creating a sense of urgency about retaining one's youth and fearing aging.[28] Hand-cream ads talk about "young hands"; skin-treatment ads state "I dreaded turning 30¼"; fragrance and makeup ads stress looking "sexy and young" or "denying your age"; detergent ads ask the reader, "Can you match their hands with their ages?" These advertising themes, which promise the consumer the benefits of youthfulness, reflect the high premium Americans place on appearing and acting young.

Fitness and health

Americans' preoccupation with *fitness* and *health* has emerged as a core value. This value has manifested itself in a number of ways, including tennis, racquetball, and jogging, and the continued increases in sales of vitamins. Added to these trends is an enhanced consciousness on the part of Americans that "You are what you eat." It has been suggested that the fitness boom of the 1980s was a result of a perceived lack of social control in America—people just felt anxious, insecure, and had self-doubts. A person feeling a lack of external self-control turns inward—if you can't control the world, you can control and change your own body through exercise.[29]

Fitness and health have increasingly become lifestyle choices for many consumers. Therefore, it is not surprising to find an almost constant stream of new products and services designed to assist health-focused consumers to achieve a healthier lifestyle. This trend has stimulated Reebok to open a series of exercise–retail complexes that seek to build a cultural connection with consumers that goes beyond the normal marketing approach. Traditional food manufacturers have begun modifying their ingredients to cater to the health conscious consumer. Frozen dinners have become more nutritious in recent years, and manufacturers of traditional "junk food" are trying to make it more healthful. "Light" or "fat-free" versions of snack chips or pretzels, along with "low-sodium," "no-cholesterol," "no-preservative" snack products, are an attempt to provide consumers with tasty and healthy options. There are even Web sites for the fitness-minded consumer (see **www.fitnessonline.com**) offering workout tips, nutritional information, and fitness-related products and services. And the *Wall Street Journal* has reported that 100 million Americans sought health information over the Internet in the year 2000—up 30 million from the prior year.

Although there is no denying the "fitness and healthy living" trend in American society, there is evidence that consumers find it difficult "to be good" in terms of their personal health. For instance, people miss their desserts. Research suggests that more than 75 percent of American consumers think about dessert between one and eight times a day. The main activities that seem to put people in the mood for desserts are exercise, working, entertainment, eating, and studying.[30] Also, many Americans are unwilling to compromise on flavor for health benefits, with the result being a kind of reverse trend toward full-flavored, rich foods. This countertrend reveals the diversity of preferences that exist side by side within the marketplace.[31] It points out that low-fat, low-cholesterol, and low-carb food products are not for everyone. Moreover, it suggests that there is an important market segment whose members seek to indulge their taste buds and their waistlines. Indeed, the World Health Organization has released a report stating that obesity is an increasing problem in both developed and developing countries.[32]

Core values are not only an american phenomenon

The cultural values just examined are not all uniquely or originally American. Some may have originally been borrowed, particularly from European society, as people emigrated to the United States. Some values that originated in America are now part of the fabric of other societies. For example, there is evidence that the good life may be nearly a universal notion and that global brands are used as an external sign of attaining the good life.[33]

In addition, not all Americans necessarily accept each of these values. However, as a whole, these values do account for much of the American character. Table 11.5 summarizes a number of American core values and indicates their relevance to consumer behavior.

Toward a shopping culture

It appears that the role that shopping plays in the American life has been elevated to the point that the American culture has become a *shopping culture* (which is a parallel perspective to the commonly held view that America's culture is a *consumer culture*). One authority has even noted that shopping has remade our culture and now defines the way we understand the world around us—"shopping is what we do to create value in our lives."[34] Making this possible is the reality that great shopping experiences are no longer just for the rich, as consumers from all walks of life can enjoy the low prices found in discount stores. Still further, shopping "has become an increasingly acceptable and popular pastime even for younger, single guys." Specifically, men between 25 and 49 years of age now account for over half of all male buying power, and this market is expected to grow to $6.7 trillion by 2009, an increase of almost 25 percent. A recent study found that one in four men under age 40 claim to shop frequently, compared to less than 20 percent of men in their 40s and 50s.[35]

Much of this "shop 'til you drop" mentality has propelled shopping to the "all American" pastime, an obsession that is driving an increasing number of Americans to be in credit card debt. It appears that consumers' credit card usage is more and more defining the meaning of a *consumption lifestyle,* one that unfortunately fosters consumers' attainment through their consumption of unfulfilling possessions and burdensome debt.[36]

TABLE 11.5	Summary of American Core Values	
VALUE	**GENERAL FEATURES**	**RELEVANCE TO CONSUMER BEHAVIOR**
Achievement and Success Activity	Hard work is good; success flows from hard work. Keeping busy is healthy and natural.	Acts as a justification for acquisition of goods ("You deserve it"). Stimulates interest in products that are time-savers and enhance leisure time.
Efficiency and Practicality	Admiration of things that solve problems (e.g., saves time and effort). People can improve themselves; tomorrow should be better than today.	Stimulates purchase of products that function well and save time. Stimulates desire for new products that fulfill unsatisfied needs; ready acceptance of products that claim to be "new and improved."
Material Comfort	"The good life."	Fosters acceptance of convenience and luxury products that make life more comfortable and enjoyable.
Individualism	Being oneself (e.g., self-reliance, self-interest, self-esteem).	Stimulates acceptance of customized or unique products that enable a person to "express his or her own personality."
Freedom	Freedom of choice.	Fosters interest in wide product lines and differentiated products.
External Conformity	Uniformity of observable behavior; desire for acceptance.	Stimulates interest in products that are used or owned by others in the same social group.
Humanitarianism	Caring for others, particularly the underdog.	Stimulates patronage of firms that compete with market leaders.
Youthfulness	A state of mind that stresses being "young at heart" and having a youthful appearance.	Stimulates acceptance of products that provide the illusion of maintaining or fostering youthfulness.
Fitness and Health	Caring about one's body, including the desire to be physically fit and healthy.	Stimulates acceptance of food products, activities, and equipment perceived to maintain or increase physical fitness.

chapter 12

› **Subcultures**

Culture has a potent influence on all consumer behavior. Individuals are brought up to follow the beliefs, values, and customs of their society and to avoid behavior that is judged unacceptable or considered taboo. In addition to segmenting in terms of cultural factors, marketers also segment overall societies into smaller subgroups (subcultures) that consist of people who are similar in terms of their ethnic origin, their customs, and the ways they behave. These subcultures provide important marketing opportunities for astute marketing strategists.

Our discussion of subcultures, therefore, has a narrower focus than the discussion of culture. Instead of examining the dominant beliefs, values, and customs that exist within an entire society, this chapter explores the marketing opportunities created by the existence of certain beliefs, values, and customs shared by members of specific subcultural groups within a society.

These subcultural divisions are based on a variety of sociocultural and demographic variables, such as nationality, religion, geographic locality, race, age, and sex.

What is subculture?

The members of a specific **subculture** possess beliefs, values, and customs that set them apart from other members of the same society. In addition, they adhere to most of the dominant cultural beliefs, values, and behavioral patterns of the larger society. We define subculture, then, as *a distinct cultural group that exists as an identifiable segment within a larger, more complex society.*

Thus, the cultural profile of a society or nation is a composite of two distinct elements: (1) the unique beliefs, values, and customs subscribed to by members of specific subcultures; and (2) the central or core cultural themes that are shared by most of the population, regardless of specific subcultural memberships. Figure 12.1 presents a simple model of the relationship between two subcultural groups (Hispanic Americans and African Americans) and the larger or "more general" culture. As the figure depicts, each subculture has its own unique traits, yet both groups share the dominant traits of the overall American culture.

Let us look at it in another way: Each American is, in large part, a product of the "American way of life." Each American, however, is at the same time a member of various subcultures. For example, a 10-year-old girl may simultaneously be African American, Baptist, a preteen, and a Texan. We would expect that membership in each

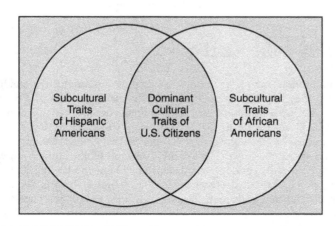

Relationship Between Culture and Subculture

FIGURE 12.1

TABLE 12.1	Examples of Major Subcultural Categories
CATEGORIES	**EXAMPLES**
Nationality (i.e., birthplace of ancestors)	Greek, Italian, Russian
Religion	Catholic, Hindu, Mormon
Geographic region	Eastern, Southern Southwestern
Race	African American, Asian, Caucasian
Age	Teenager, Xers, elderly
Gender	Female, male
Occupation	Bus driver, cook, scientist
Social class	Lower, middle, upper

different subculture would provide its own set of specific beliefs, values, attitudes, and customs. Table 12.1 lists typical subcultural categories and corresponding examples of specific subcultural groups. This list is by no means exhaustive: Electricians, Democrats, Cub Scouts, and millionaires—in fact, any group that shares common beliefs and customs—may be classified as a subculture.

Subcultural analysis enables the marketing manager to focus on sizable and natural market segments. When carrying out such analyses, the marketer must determine whether the beliefs, values, and customs shared by members of a specific subgroup make them desirable candidates for special marketing attention. Subcultures, therefore, are relevant units of analysis for market research. And these subcultures are dynamic— for example, the different ethnic groups that comprise the U.S. population have been changing and will continue to change in size and economic power in the coming years. More specifically, the white (non-Hispanic) population of the United States, which made up 71 percent of Americans in the year 2000 (date of the last U.S. Census), is projected to represent about 53 percent of the U.S. population by the year 2050.[1] Frequently a "window on the future," the State of California has estimated that the state's multicultural or combined minority population is now the state's majority population.

A recent study of ethnic media usage in California also found that over 80 percent of Asian American, African American, and Hispanic American respondents claimed to get information from ethnic television, radio, and publications. Furthermore, 68 percent preferred ethnic-language TV stations over English channels for news, and 40 percent reported paying greater attention to ethnic language ads than English-language ads.[2]

The following sections examine a number of important subcultural categories: nationality, religion, geographic location, race, age, and sex.

Nationality subcultures

For many people, **nationality** is an important subcultural reference that guides what they value and what they buy. This is especially true for the population of a country like the United States that has a history of attracting people from all over the globe. Supporting this pattern are the results of the 2000 U.S. Census, which found that about one in ten Americans is foreign born.[3] It has also been reported that Queens County (one of the five boroughs that make up the City of New York) is the most multicultural county in America, and that 46 percent of its residents were born outside of the United States.[4] For these Americans, as well as Americans born in the United States, there is frequently a strong sense of identification and pride in the language and customs of their ancestors.

TABLE 12.2	Hispanics Become the Largest Minority Group in the United States			
	POPULATION, IN MILLIONS			PERCENTAGE OF THE
	JULY 2001*	APRIL 2000	PERCENTAGE CHANGE	POPULATION, JULY 2001
Total population	284.8	281.4	1.2%	100.0%
Hispanic (of any race)	37.0	35.3	4.7	13.0
One race	280.7	277.5	1.2	98.6
White	230.3	228.1	1.0	80.9
Non-Hispanic white	196.2	195.6	0.3	68.9
Black or African American	36.2	35.7	1.5	12.7
American Indian or Alaska Native	2.7	2.7	2.3	1.0
Asian	11.0	10.6	3.7	3.9
Native Hawaiian/ Pacific Islander	0.5	0.5	3.0	0.2
Two or more races	4.1	3.9	4.6	1.4
				*Estimated

Source: "Largest Minority Group: Hispanics," *The New York Times*, January 22, 2003, A17.

When it comes to consumer behavior, this ancestral pride is manifested most strongly in the consumption of ethnic foods, in travel to the "homeland," and in the purchase of numerous cultural artifacts (ethnic clothing, art, music, foreign-language newspapers). Interest in these goods and services has expanded rapidly as younger Americans attempt to better understand and more closely associate with their ethnic roots. To illustrate the importance of ethnic origin as a subcultural market segment, the next section examines the **Hispanic American subculture**.

Hispanic subcultures

The 2000 U.S. Census found that the number of Hispanic Americans (of all races) had grown by 58 percent during the decade of the 1990s (compared to an overall U.S. population growth of 13.2 percent). And, according to the Census Bureau, in July of 2002 Hispanics replaced African Americans as the largest minority group in the United States (see Table 12.2). Hispanics are currently 14 percent of the U.S. population, and their number is estimated to reach 24 percent of the population by the year 2050, giving the United States a Hispanic population of over 100 million.[5] These Hispanic Americans had an estimated purchasing power in 2004 of $687 billion, which is expected to climb to $992 billion by 2009.[6] In contrast to other American population segments, Hispanic Americans are younger—in 2005 almost 38 percent of Hispanics are 19 years old or younger, whereas only 28 percent of the U.S. population is 19 or younger. The median age for Hispanics is 26 years of age, whereas the median age for the rest of America is 35 years of age.[7] Hispanic Americans also tend to be members of larger families (average Hispanic household size is 3.5 people compared to an average U.S. household size of 2.6 people).[8] They are also more likely to live in an extended family household consisting of several generations of family members. Not only are Hispanic households more likely than black or non-Hispanic American white families to contain children, but also Hispanics spend more time caring for their children.[9]

As of this writing, 88 percent of all Hispanics under the age of 18 living in the United States were born here. And by 2020, only 34 percent of Hispanics living here will be foreign-born first generation, 36 percent will be U.S. born second-generation children of immigrants, and 30 percent will be third-generation children of U.S. born Hispanics.[10] In terms of acculturation, only 20 percent of the Hispanic/Latino market has recently migrated to the United States and speak only Spanish. Of the remaining 80 percent, 20 percent speak only English and 60 percent speak both Spanish and English.

Of the more than 41 million Hispanics currently living in the United States, the most recent Census found that 77 percent live in the seven states that have a Hispanic population of one million or more (California, Texas, New York, Florida, Illinois, Arizona, and New Jersey). Still further, while Hispanics represented 42 percent of New Mexico's total population, the highest percentage of any state, some counties in North Carolina, Georgia, Iowa, Arkansas, Minnesota, and Nebraska are between 6 and 25 percent Hispanic.[11] Table 12.3 presents the 25 largest U.S. Hispanic markets, the Hispanic population of each, and the Hispanic percentage of the total residents of that market.

TABLE 12.3	Top 25 U.S. Hispanic Markets		
RANK	**MARKET**	**HISPANIC POPULATION**	**HISPANIC % OF TOTAL**
1	Los Angeles	7,811,100	44.5
2	New York	4,316,400	20.5
3	Chicago	1,838,000	19.0
4	Miami	1,836,800	43.1
5	Houston	1,822,600	33.4
6	Dallas-Fort Worth	1,509,700	23.5
7	San Francisco	1,491,800	21.3
8	San Antonio	1,293,700	60.3
9	Phoenix	1,208,000	27.2
10	McAllen, Texas	1,142,000	94.8
11	San Diego	927,600	31.2
12	Fresno-Visalia, Calif.	893,000	50.7
13	Sacramento, Calif.	892,400	24.1
14	El Paso, Texas	782,500	87.7
15	Albuquerque, N.M.	740,700	41.6
16	Denver	740,600	19.7
17	Washington	545,200	9.0
18	Philadelphia	534,300	6.9
19	Austin, Texas	471,700	29.0
20	Las Vegas	438,800	26.0
21	Atlanta	433,600	7.5
22	Orlando	432,200	13.2
23	Boston	417,700	6.6
24	Tampa, Fla.	415,400	10.4
25	Tucson-Nogales, Ariz.	385,900	35.4

Source: "Hispanic Fact Pack, 2004 Edition," *A Supplement to Advertising Age*, 40.

This subcultural group can be considered as a single market, based on a common language and culture, or as separate subcultural markets that correspond to different Hispanic countries of origin. There are 12 Hispanic subgroups identified in the United States. The three largest Hispanic subcultural groups consist of Mexican Americans (about 58.5 percent of total Hispanic Americans), Puerto Ricans (approximately 9.6 percent of the total), and Cubans (about 3.5 percent of the total). These subcultures are heavily concentrated geographically, with more than 70 percent of their members residing in California, Texas, New York, and Florida; Los Angeles alone is home to one-fifth of the Hispanic population of the United States. Also, whereas more than 60 percent of all Mexican Americans (the largest Hispanic group) were born in the United States, 72 percent of Cuban Americans were born in Cuba.[12]

Understanding Hispanic consumer behavior

Available evidence indicates that Hispanic and Anglo consumers differ in terms of a variety of important buyer behavior variables. For instance, Hispanic consumers have a strong preference for well-established brands and traditionally prefer to shop at smaller stores. In the New York metropolitan area, for example, Hispanic consumers spend a substantial portion of their food budgets in *bodegas* (relatively small food specialty stores), despite the fact that supermarket prices generally are lower. Table 12.4 presents these and other distinctive characteristics of the overall Hispanic market.

Although mindful of their tradition, Hispanic Americans, like other major subcultural groups, are a dynamic and evolving portion of the overall society. For this reason, a growing number of Hispanic consumers are shifting their food shopping to nonethnic, large, American-style supermarkets. They appear to be engaged in a process of acculturation; that is, they are gradually adopting the consumption patterns of the majority of U.S. consumers. Similarly, when it comes to clothes shopping, Hispanic youths are more fashion conscious and are more likely to seek out and be loyal to well-known brands and to generally like the act of shopping more than their non-Hispanic counterparts.[13] While about half of Hispanic Americans have a computer at home (as compared to about three-quarters of the U.S. population), and only about 35 percent have Internet access at home (as compared to about 65 percent of the U.S. population), the number of Hispanic households with computers with Internet access has been increasing annually.[14] Perhaps one of the reasons why Mattel has introduced a Spanish-language "Barbie" site targeted to young girls (**www.barbielatina.com**) is because of the increasing number of Hispanic households with personal computers and Internet connections.[15]

TABLE 12.4	Traditional Characteristics of the Hispanic American Market

Prefer well-known or familiar brands
Buy brands perceived to be more prestigious
Are fashion conscious
Historically prefer to shop at smaller personal stores
Buy brands advertised by their ethnic-group stores
Tend not to be impulse buyers (i.e., are deliberate)
Increasingly clipping and using cents-off coupons
Likely to buy what their parents bought
Prefer fresh to frozen or prepared items
Tend to be negative about marketing practices and government intervention in business

Defining and segmenting the Hispanic market

Marketers who are targeting the diversity within the Hispanic subcultures are concerned with finding the best ways to define and segment this overall subculture. In terms of definition, Table 12.5 presents six variables marketers have used to determine who is Hispanic. Of these measures, the combination of *self-identification* and *degree of identification* are particularly appealing, because they permit consumers to define or label themselves. Research shows that those who strongly identify with being Hispanic (*Strong Hispanic Identifiers*) are more frequent users of Spanish-language media, are more brand loyal, are more likely to buy prestige brands, are more likely to seek the advice of another and to more often be influenced by friends or family, and are more likely to buy brands advertised to Hispanics than Weak Hispanic Identifiers.[16] This pattern suggests that the degree of Hispanic identification is a useful segmentation variable.

Some marketers feel that it is worthwhile to target each Hispanic American market separately. Other marketers, especially larger marketers, have been targeting the Hispanic market as a single market, using Spanish-language mass media. For instance, to cater to the Hispanic market, Toyota launched an interactive soccer game on its Spanish-language Web site (**www.toyota.com/español**), which asked the player to defend their Corolla.[17] Johnson & Johnson has outfitted a 53 foot trailer as a six-room home (including life-size cutouts of family members) and has sent it on a cross-country tour, making stops at 100 Wal-Marts and 20 Hispanic fiestas. Individuals visiting the trailer learn about 15 different J&J brands and will receive free product samples.[18] While the Spanish language is often regarded as the bridge that links the various Hispanic subcultures, nevertheless, there is considerable variation among Hispanics regarding their language preferences (such as Spanish only, Spanish preferred, English only, or English preferred). This language categorization provides still another basis for segmenting the Hispanic American market. Available research indicates that Hispanic Americans spend the most time with mass media in the first language that they learn to speak. So those whose first language is Spanish tend to prefer TV, radio, magazines, and newspapers in Spanish,

TABLE 12.5	Ways in Which "Hispanic" Has Been Defined
NAME OF INDICATOR	**NATURE/SCOPE AND COMMENTARY**
Spanish surname	Not a definitive; since a non-Hispanic person might have a Spanish surname, or a Hispanic person might have a non-Spanish surname.
Country of origin	The birthplace of persons born in the United States of Hispanic parents (e.g., of Puerto Rican parentage) would not reveal their Hispanic background.
Country of family ancestry	Includes those individuals who may not be Hispanic despite coming from a particular Spanish-Latin country (e.g., people of German parentage who may be brought up in a Latin country).
Spanish spoken at home	A significant minority of Hispanic households may speak English at home, yet consider themselves to be culturally Hispanic.
Self-identification	It is reasonable that if an adequate number of self-report choices are offered, a person might identify himself or herself as "Hispanic."
Degree of identification	This measure captures the "degree" of personal identification as "Hispanic" and augments the self-identification measure.

whereas those Hispanic Americans who first learn English prefer their media exposure to be in English.[19] For instance, supporting this point of view, the number of Spanish-language stations is growing; Discovery Communications launched two new networks—Discovery Kids en Espanol and Discovery Viajar y Vivir (Travel and Living).[20] With respect to the medium of radio, Clear Channel Radio recently flipped a general market to a Spanish-language format radio station in Atlanta and went from a 1.6 to an 11.3 share among listeners 18 to 34 years old.[21] Table 12.6 presents the language preferences of Hispanic Americans, 18 years of age and older, with respect to language usage. Note that in all categories, a smaller than average percentage of 18- to 24-year-olds prefer "only Spanish."

Recently, Cohorts, Inc., a Denver company that provides information to database marketers, developed a segmentation scheme for the Hispanic market that contains 19 lifestyle segments. These segments ranged from "Affluent Grandparents" (successful, dual-income couples) to "Latinos with Roommates" (less-educated single Latinos with roommates).

Religious subcultures

The United States reportedly has more than 200 different organized **religious subcultures**. Of this number, Protestant denominations, Roman Catholicism, and Judaism are the principal organized religious faiths. The members of all these religious groups at times are likely to make purchase decisions that are influenced by their religious identity. Commonly, consumer behavior is directly affected by religion in terms of products that are *symbolically* and *ritualistically* associated with the celebration of various religious holidays. For example, Christmas has become the major gift-purchasing season of the year.

Consider born-again Christians, the fastest-growing religious affiliation in America. Members of this group are generally defined as individuals "who follow literal interpretations of the Bible and acknowledge being born again through religious conversion." These consumers make up about 72 million of the 235 million Christians in the United States. Religion is part of their daily activity, and their interests and opinions are often tied to their religion. From a marketer's perspective, born-again Christians tend to be fiercely loyal to a brand that supports their causes and viewpoint.[22]

Religious requirements or practices sometimes take on an expanded meaning beyond their original purpose. For instance, dietary laws for an observant Jewish family represent an obligation, so there are toothpastes and artificial sweeteners that are kosher for Passover. The *U* and *K* marks on food packaging are symbols that the food meets Jewish dietary laws. For nonobservant Jews and an increasing number of non-Jews, however, these marks often signify that the food is pure and wholesome—a kind of "Jewish *Good Housekeeping* Seal of Approval." In response to the broader meaning given to kosher-certified products, a number of national brands, such as Coors beer and Pepperidge Farm cookies, have secured kosher certification for their products. Indeed, most Kosher food is consumed by non-Jews.[23] A kosher Manhattan steak house, the Prime Grill, claims that about half of its clientele are non-Jews, and that its success is based on the fact that it has a fine dining menu (without "Jewish types of food") that "just happens to be kosher."[24] Packaging and print ads for food items that are kosher often display a *K* or a *U* inside a circle and sometimes the word *parve*. This word tells the shopper that the product is kosher and that it can be eaten with either meat or dairy products (but not both). Targeting specific religious groups with specially designed marketing programs can be really profitable. For instance, the Shaklee Corporation, a multilevel marketer of the Shaklee Performance drink mix, recruits salespeople from a variety of different religious groups (e.g., Hasidic Jews, Amish, and Mennonites) to sell its products to members of their communities.[25] It is likely that such shared religious identity and membership aid a salesperson in his or her effort to communicate with and persuade potential customers.

| TABLE 12.6 | Selected Dimensions of Language Usage by U.S. Hispanic Adults | | | | | | |

	ALL HISPANIC ADULTS	% BY AGE GROUP					
		18–24	25–34	35–44	45–54	55–64	65+
SPEAK AT HOME:							
Only English	12.3	10.1	13.2	12.1	13.9	13.5	10.8
Mostly Eng., some Span.	20.9	22.9	19.6	19.1	25.8	15.6	23.7
Eng. & Span. equally	15.8	19.4	8.2	16.3	16.1	32.8	15.6
Mostly Span., some Eng.	29.8	35.2	31.3	31.2	26.7	20.3	22.5
Only Spanish	20.4	12.4	27.2	20.4	17.2	16.2	24.2
SPEAK OUTSIDE THE HOME:							
Only English	16.7	23.3	13.3	16.1	17.2	17.0	13.6
Mostly Eng., some Span.	32.0	33.5	29.5	34.4	37.5	27.0	27.4
Eng. & Span. equally	8.3	12.1	2.3	7.7	9.1	17.8	11.3
Mostly Span., some Eng.	24.9	19.1	35.0	23.0	20.8	21.0	17.5
Only Spanish	14.0	8.1	16.1	15.8	14.0	12.0	17.4
PREFER SPEAKING IN:							
Only English	17.2	24.8	17.0	13.6	16.3	17.4	11.5
Mostly Eng., some Span.	27.4	31.9	20.3	31.3	21.7	40.5	27.6
Mostly Span., some Eng.	24.5	23.9	26.8	23.2	32.3	13.9	19.2
Only Spanish	25.4	14.6	32.2	27.0	24.1	22.0	27.0
PREFER READING IN:							
Only English	33.2	38.0	28.2	28.2	36.5	49.0	31.5
Mostly Eng., some Span.	21.8	25.3	17.6	25.0	23.2	17.1	22.8
Mostly Span., some Eng.	16.7	14.5	22.9	17.7	12.6	10.3	10.3
Only Spanish	24.4	18.5	29.3	25.6	23.4	21.3	21.2
PREFER WATCHING TV IN:							
Only English	25.9	30.3	22.1	24.7	22.5	38.5	25.7
Mostly Eng., some Span.	29.9	32.3	26.9	25.7	42.0	29.5	26.8
Mostly Span., some Eng.	25.8	23.3	29.2	31.6	21.4	14.4	22.5
Only Spanish	13.8	7.7	19.0	13.6	10.6	14.6	14.5
PREFER LISTENING RADIO IN:							
Only English	23.4	31.3	20.9	23.5	19.0	24.2	20.6
Mostly Eng., some Span.	21.0	24.0	17.3	22.1	23.4	24.7	16.9
Mostly Span., some Eng.	25.6	24.8	28.0	22.7	31.0	19.4	24.4
Only Spanish	25.0	15.2	30.2	26.8	22.8	25.9	27.2

Source: "Hispanic Fact Pack, 2004 Edition," *Advertising Age,* 42 (Data from Simmons Market Research Bureau's Fall 2005 Full-Year National Consumer Study).

Geographic and regional subcultures

The United States is a large country, one that enjoys a wide range of climatic and geographic conditions. Given the country's size and physical diversity, it is only natural that many Americans have a sense of **regional** identification and use this identification as a way of describing others (such as "he is a true Southerner"). These labels often assist us in developing a mental picture and supporting *stereotype* of the person in question.

Anyone who has traveled across the United States has probably noted many regional differences in consumption behavior, especially when it comes to food and drink. For example, a *mug* of black coffee typifies the West, while a *cup* of coffee with milk and sugar is preferred in the East. There also are geographic differences in the consumption of a staple food such as bread. Specifically, in the South and Midwest, soft white bread is preferred, whereas on the East and West coasts, firmer breads (rye, whole wheat, and French and Italian breads) are favored. Regional differences also include brand preferences. Why do you suppose Skippy is the best-selling brand of peanut butter on both the East and West coasts, while Peter Pan sells best in the South and Jif sells best in the Midwest?[26]

Consumer research studies document regional differences in consumption patterns. For instance, Table 12.7 illustrates that differences in product purchase, ownership, or usage levels occur between major metropolitan areas. This distribution helps redefine local markets in terms of specific urban lifestyles. Still further, Table 12.8 reveals that San Francisco leads the nation's 10 largest markets when it comes to ordering anything from

TABLE 12.7	Product Purchase/Usage by Leading Metropolitan Market	
PRODUCT PURCHASE/USAGE	**HIGHEST PURCHASE/USAGE**	**LOWEST PURCHASE/USAGE**
Body power	New York	San Francisco
Energy drinks	San Francisco	Philadelphia
Artificial sweetener	Los Angeles	Dallas-Forth Worth
Total beer/ale	Chicago	Philadelphia
Ground coffee	Boston	Los Angeles
Gasoline	Dallas-Fort Worth	New York
Jams and jellies	Cleveland	San Francisco
Hair growth products	New York	Boston
Attend an auto show	Detroit	Washington, DC
Grated cheese	Philadelphia	Los Angeles
Attend a movie once a month	Boston	Dallas-Fort Worth
Own a mountain bike	San Francisco	New York
Boxed chocolates	Chicago	Dallas-Fort Worth
Personally have a valid passport	San Francisco	Cleveland
Vegetarian frozen burger	Boston	Dallas-Fort Worth

Source: Doublebase Mediamark Research, Inc. 2005 Doublebase Report. All rights reserved. Reprinted by permission.

TABLE 12.8	Ranking of Leading Metropolitan Markets in Terms of Ordering Anything from Amazon.com During the Past 12 Months

MARKET	U.S. AVERAGE = 100
San Francisco	203
Washington, DC	168
Boston	152
New York	138
Philadelphia	114
Chicago	114
Los Angeles	92
Dallas-Fort Worth	83
Detroit	82
Cleveland	69

Source: Doublebase Mediamark Research, Inc. 2005 Doublebase Report. All rights reserved. Reprinted by permission.

Amazon.com during a past 12 month period. An examination of this table and the other evidence presented here supports marketers who argue that it is important to take geographic consumption patterns into account when planning marketing and promotional efforts.

In general, large metropolitan areas, with a substantial number of affluent middle-age households, dominate many, but not all, consumer-spending categories. Two examples are the San Jose, California, metro area, which leads in apparel purchasing, and Nassau-Suffolk counties in New York, which lead in purchasing of insurance and pension programs.[27]

Racial subcultures

The major **racial subcultures** in the United States are Caucasian, African American, Asian American, and American Indian. Although differences in lifestyles and consumer-spending patterns exist among these groups, the vast majority of racially oriented consumer research has focused on consumer differences between African Americans and Caucasians. More recently, particular research attention has been given to Asian American consumers.

The African American consumer

The U.S. Census Bureau estimates the African American population of the United States to be more than 39 million people, or more than 13 percent of the U.S. population.[28] While the overall U.S. population grew 13 percent between 1990 and 2000, the African American population in the U.S. grew by 21 percent.[29] As such, **African American consumers** currently constitute the second largest minority in the United States. With a purchasing power currently estimated to be $723 billion, and expected to grow to $965 billion by 2010, more than half of African American consumers are less than 35 years of age.[30] However, this important subcultural grouping is frequently portrayed as a single, undifferentiated African American market, consisting of consumers who have a uniform set of consumer needs. In reality they are a diverse group, consisting of numerous subgroups, each with distinctive backgrounds, needs, interests, and opinions. For example, in addition to the African Americans who have been in the United States for many generations, there are Caribbean Americans, from such islands as Jamaica and Haiti, who have recently immigrated to the United States.[31] Therefore, just as the white majority has been divided into a variety of market segments, each with its own distinctive needs and tastes, so, too, can the African American market be segmented.

Consumer behavior characteristics of African American consumers

Although there are many similarities between African Americans and the rest of America in terms of consumer behavior, there are also some meaningful differences in terms of product preferences and brand purchase patterns. African American consumers tend to prefer popular or leading brands, are brand loyal, and are unlikely to purchase private-label and generic products. One study, for example, found that almost two-thirds of African Americans are willing to pay more to get "the best," even if the brand or product is not widely recognized (only 51 percent of whites were reported to feel this way), and African Americans have been reported to buy high fashions and name brands "as signals of their success."[32] Still further, African American consumers tend to make more trips during the course of a week to the grocery store (2.2 trips versus 1.8 trips for the average shopper), and they also spend more per week ($94 versus $85 for the average shopper) than other consumers.[33]

African Americans account for over 30 percent of spending in the $4 billion hair care market, and they spend more on telephone services than any other consumer segment. Still further, they spend an average of $1,427 annually on clothing for themselves, which is $458 more than all U.S. consumers.[34] Similarly, African American teens spend more on clothing and fine jewelry than all U.S. teens.

Some meaningful differences exist among Anglo-White, African American, and Hispanic American consumers in the purchase, ownership, and use of a diverse group of products. For marketers, these findings confirm the wisdom of targeting racial market segments.

Reaching the African American audience

A question of central importance to marketers is how to best reach *African American consumers*. Traditionally, marketers have subscribed to one of two distinct marketing strategies. Some have followed the policy of running all their advertising in general mass media in the belief that African Americans have the same media habits as whites; others have followed the policy of running additional advertising in selected media directed exclusively to African Americans.

Both strategies may be appropriate in specific situations and for specific product categories. For products of very broad appeal (as aspirin or toothpaste), it is possible that the mass media (primarily television) may effectively reach all relevant consumers, including African American and white. For other products (such as personal grooming products or food products), marketers may find that mass media do not communicate effectively with the African American market. Because the media habits of African American consumers differ from those of the general population, media specifically targeted to African Americans are likely to be more effective. The notion that African Americans have cultural values subtly different from the U.S. population as a whole is supported by a Yankelovich survey in which a majority of African Americans believe that most advertising is designed for white people.[35] Furthermore, a recent study of ethnic identification found that African American adolescents with a stronger sense of black ethnic identity tend to identify more closely with black models or characters appearing in ads than do African American adolescents with weaker ethnic identification.[36] Research studies have also concluded that the socializing effects of the media may be greater for African Americans than for Caucasians. For example, while 7.5 hours a day is the average daily TV viewing for all TV households in America, African American households average 10 hours of TV per day, and both children and adolescents often use television as a source of guidance (e.g., African American adolescents use TV to learn about occupations and to learn dating behavior).[37] Other research reveals that African American adults tend to place a great deal of trust in African American centric media (i.e., black magazines, black TV news, black-owned local newspapers, and black radio news) as a source of information about companies and their products.[38] Approximately $400 million of the $1.7 billion spent annually on ads targeted to African Americans is spent on magazine advertising, which includes such publications as *Black Enterprise, Ebony, Essence, Jet, The Source*, and *Vibe*.[39] Many marketers supplement their general advertising with advertisements in magazines, newspapers, and other media directed specifically to African Americans. For example, Pepsi has a promotion that they run in February, which is Black History Month. In conjunction with a Web site featuring black history and art, students are asked to "write your own history." Ten $10,000 college scholarships are awarded as first prize. New fragrances are being offered to the African American woman—"Goddess" from Coty with Kimora Lee Simmons as spokesperson and P. Diddy's "Carol's Daughter" from Estée Lauder, also backed by celebrities like Jada Pinkett Smith. And entrepreneurs Russell Simmons and Keven Liles have started a company called Def Jam Mobile. The company will deliver ring tones, news alerts, and other content to subscribers (the ring tone market is expected to reach $1 billion by 2007). And let's not forget that Hallmark Cards has a division called "Mahogany," which creates and sells cards targeted to the African American audience.[40]

Major advertisers targeting the African American market have increasingly used the specialized services of African American advertising agencies. These specialized agencies generally provide marketers wanting to target African Americans with the distinctive advantage of access to a staff of African American marketing professionals who thoroughly know the values and customs of this market and its specific subsegments.

Asian American consumers

The **Asian American** population is approximately 14 million in size and is the fastest-growing American minority (on a percentage basis). While Asians and Pacific Islanders made up 3.9 percent of the U.S. population in 2000, this group is expected to account for 8.9 percent of America's population in 2050.[41] According to the 2000 Census, six different ethnicities make up about 88 percent of the Asian American population: Chinese (2.4 million), Filipinos (1.9 million), Indian (1.7 million), Vietnamese (1.12 million), Korean (1.1 million), and Japanese (797,000).[42] Asian Americans are today the most diverse ethnic group in the United States, and includes the influences of 15 different cultures and a wide range of languages.[43]

Asian Americans are largely family oriented, highly industrious, and strongly driven to achieve a middle-class lifestyle. They are an attractive market for increasing numbers of marketers. Indeed, in 2001, 40 percent of all Asian and Pacific Islander families had incomes of at least $75,000, compared with 35 percent of non-Hispanic white families, and an average household income for this group, at $55,026, is 28 percent more than the U.S. average. With respect to occupations, a higher proportion of Asians and Pacific Islanders (than non-Hispanic whites) were concentrated in managerial and professional jobs. Still further, educational attainment is an important goal for this segment of the population. For the Asian and Pacific Islander population age 25 and older, 51 percent of the men (compared to 32 percent for non-Hispanic white men) and 44 percent of the women (compared to 27 percent for non-Hispanic white women) have earned a Bachelor's Degree or more.[44]

Where are the Asian Americans?

Asian Americans are largely urban people concentrated in neighborhoods situated in and around a small number of large American cities (95 percent live in metropolitan areas). Nearly half of all Asian Americans live in Los Angeles, San Francisco, and New York, and at present, more than 10 percent of California's population is Asian American. The stereotype that most Chinese live in "Chinatown" is incorrect. Most Chinese, as well as most other Asian Americans, do not live in downtown urban areas; they live in the suburbs.[45] Figure 12.2 presents a comparison of region of residence for Asian and Pacific Islanders versus non-Hispanic whites. It is of interest to note that while close to 20 percent of non-Hispanic whites live in the West, slightly more than half of Asians and Pacific Islanders do.

FIGURE 12.2

(Percent distribution of population)

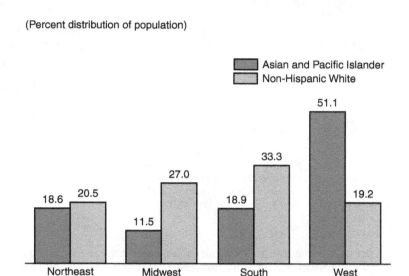

Region of Residence for Selected Subcultural Groups

Source: U.S. Census Bureau, Annual Demographic Supplement to the March 2002 Current Population Survey, as contained in "The Asian and Pacific Islander Population of the United States: March 2002," *U.S. Census Bureau,* accessed at www.census.gov/ prod/2003pubs/ p20-540.pdf, 2.

Understanding the Asian American consumer

U.S. Census Bureau data reveal that more Asian Americans, on a per capita basis, own their own businesses than non–Asian American minorities. Those who do not own their own businesses are largely in professional, technical, or managerial occupations. Additionally, many Asian Americans are young and live a good part of their lives in multi-income households. Asian Americans also tend to be more computer literate than the general population. English-speaking Asian Americans are more likely than other Americans to get their news and information online. Asian Americans who go online also tend to be young. Still further, Asian American households are more likely than Hispanic and African American households to have Internet access.[46] Two general-interest Internet sites, **www.Click2Asia.com** and **www.AsianAvenue.com**, have helped create cyberspace communities for Asian Americans.[47] Still further, Asian Americans are much more likely to purchase online than other segments of the U.S. population.

Asian Americans as consumers

During the decade of the 1990s, the buying power of Asian Americans increased about 125 percent, to over $250 billion, and is expected to reach about $530 billion by 2009.[48] As consumers, Asian Americans value quality (associated quality with well-known upscale brands). This population segment tends to be loyal customers, frequently more male oriented when it comes to consumption decisions, and attracted to retailers that make it known that they welcome Asian American patronage.

It is important to remember that Asian Americans are really drawn from diverse cultural backgrounds. Therefore, although Asian Americans have many similarities, marketers should avoid treating Asian Americans as a single market because they are far from being so homogeneous. For example, Vietnamese Americans are more likely to follow the traditional model, wherein the man makes the decision for large purchases; however, Chinese American husbands and wives are more likely to share in the decision-making process.[49] Vietnamese Americans also frown on credit, because in their culture owing money is viewed negatively. In contrast, Korean Americans and Chinese Americans, many of whom have been in the United States for years, accept credit as the American way.[50] A recent article, though, does mention several Asian American youth trends, including the belief among females that the way to stay slim is through self-discipline, and not through fad diets, the desire to be the first to own high-tech gadgets, the addition of Canton Pop artists to MP3 playlists, and a more open-minded attitude toward interracial coupling.[51]

TABLE 12.9	Language Preference of Specific Asian American Groups	
ASIAN AMERICAN GROUP	**% WHO PREFER NATIVE LANGUAGE**	**% SPEAKING NATIVE LANGUAGE AT HOME**
Vietnamese	93	71
Chinese	83	66
Korean	81	66
Filipino	66	56
Asian Indian	55	59
Japanese	42	29

Source: www.ewowfacts.com/pdfs/chapters/61.pdf (page 609); and *Orienting the U.S. Food and Beverage Market: Strategies Targeting Asian Americans to 2010* (Alexandria, VA: Promar International), June 2000, 87.

The use of Asian American models in advertising is effective in reaching this market segment. Research reveals that responses to an ad for stereo speakers featuring an Asian model were significantly more positive than responses to the same ad using a Caucasian model.[52] Additionally, the percentage of Asian Americans who prefer advertisements that are not in the English language varies among different Asian American groups. For instance, according to Table 12.9, 93 percent of Vietnamese consumers prefer ad messages in the Vietnamese language, whereas only 42 percent of Japanese Americans prefer ad messages in Japanese. Aware of the increased importance of the Asian American market, Proctor & Gamble Company has named its first Asian American advertising agency, and Wal-Mart has just begun running TV commercials in Mandarin, Cantonese, and Vietnamese, as well as Filipino print ads.[53]

Age subcultures

It's not difficult to understand why each major age subgrouping of the population might be thought of as a separate subculture. After all, don't you listen to different music than your parents and grandparents, dress differently, read different magazines, and enjoy different TV shows? Clearly, important shifts occur in an individual's demand for specific types of products and services as he or she goes from being a dependent child to a retired senior citizen. In this chapter, we will limit our examination of **age subcultures** to four age groups, moving from youngest to oldest: **Generation Y**, **Generation X**, **baby boomers**, and **seniors**. These four age segments have been singled out because their distinctive lifestyles qualify them for consideration as subcultural groups.

The generation Y market

This age cohort (a cohort is a group of individuals born over a relatively short and continuous period of time) includes the approximately 71 million Americans born between the years 1977 and 1994 (i.e., the children of baby boomers). Members of Generation Y (also known as "echo boomers" and the "millennium generation") can be divided into three subsegments: Gen Y adults (age 19–28), Gen Y teens (age 13–18), and Gen Y kids, or "tweens" (age 8–12).[54] Keep in mind that while "tweens" are too young to have been born between 1977 and 1994, they nevertheless are still considered to be part of the Gen Y market.

TABLE 12.10	Selected Profile of the "Tween" Market

- Consists of 8- to 14-year-olds
- Spend and influence $1.18 trillion in purchases worldwide
- They know brand images better than an advertising expert
- Tweens in the U.S., U.K., and Australia average seeing 20,000 to 40,000 commercials a year
- Tweens affect their parents' brand choices
  - They may influence up to 80 percent of family brand choices
  - They may have a substantial influence on the final decision in over 60 percent of choices
- They no longer expect to be informed by traditional media (e.g., TV, radio)
- The concept of individual brand loyalty may no longer exist—it is a group decision (i.e., the tween and his/her peers)
- Up to 25 percent of all tweens communicate every week with tweens in other countries
- Almost half of all tweens consider the use of grammatically correct language to be outdated, and prefer TweenSpeak, which combines words, icons, illustrations, and phrases
- Globally, 24 percent of tweens use the Internet as their primary communication tool
- 21 percent of tweens claim that the Internet is the easiest way to find new friends

Source: Adapted from Martin Lindstrom, "Branding Is No Longer Child's Play!," *Journal of Consumer Marketing* 21, no. 3 (2004): 175–182.

Appealing to generation Y

The teen segment of Generation Y directly spend over $150 billion annually and furthermore influence the purchases of their parents for a substantial amount of other goods and services. They have grown up in a media-saturated environment and tend to be aware of "marketing hype." For example, they would tend to immediately understand that when a shopping center locates popular teen stores at opposite ends of the mall they are being encouraged "to walk the mall."

This age cohort has shifted some of its TV viewing time to the Internet and, when compared with their parents, they are less likely to read newspapers and often do not trust the stores that their parents shop in.[55] Smart retailers have found it profitable to develop Web sites specifically targeted to the interests of the Gen Y consumer. For example, Limited Too (**www.limitedtoo.com**), Rave Girl (**www.goravegirl.com**), and Abercrombie & Fitch (**www.abercrombiekids.com**) have all developed sites targeted to the tween market, despite the fact that a person is supposed to be at least 18 years old to place an order. Still further, about half of all 9- to 17-year-olds are asked by their parents to go online to research products or services.

Tweens

In the United States, the 29 million members of the "tween" market (generally considered to consist of 8- to 14-year-olds) spend an average of $1,294 each, for a total of $38 billion. And their parents will spend almost $126 billion more on them. Still further, in households that include a tween, food purchases account for almost 50 percent of total household spending.[56] Table 12.10 provides some additional information about the tween market. Teenagers also visit shopping malls more frequently than any other age group, spending an average of $46.80 per mall visit.[57]

Gen Y adults are the largest users of cell phone text messaging. A recent study found that 63 percent of Gen Y adults use text messaging, compared with only 31 percent of Gen Xers, 18 percent of cell phone users in their 40s, and 13 percent of those 50-year-olds. In today's cell phone market, 76 percent of 15- to 19-year-olds and 90 percent of consumers in their early 20s regularly use their cell phones for text messaging, ringtones, and games.[58]

Twixters

Spanning the Gen Y and Gen X markets is a group of 21- to 29-year-olds who continue to live with their parents. Many of them are out of college and have decent jobs and incomes—but they are not moving out to get married, nor are they leaving their parents' home. Over half of Twixters graduated college more than $10,000 in debt (some taking 6 years to do so). They tend to have trust in their parents and in established institutions, and often do not marry before they reach their 30th birthday. While these individuals cannot afford to purchase "anything that could be considered an asset," they do purchase gadgets and clothes.[59]

The generation X market

This age grouping—often referred to as *Xers, busters,* or *slackers*—consists of the almost 50 million individuals born between about 1965 and 1979 (different experts quote different starting and ending years). As consumers, these 25- to 40-year-olds represented $1.4 trillion in spending power in 2004.[60] They do not like labels, are cynical, and do not want to be singled out and marketed to.

Also, unlike their parents, who are frequently baby boomers, they are in no rush to marry, start a family, or work excessive hours to earn high salaries. For Generation X consumers, job satisfaction is typically more important than salary. It has been said, for example, that "Baby Boomers live to work, Gen Xers work to live!" Xers reject the values of older coworkers who may neglect their families while striving to secure higher salaries and career advancement, and many have observed their parents getting laid off after many years of loyalty to an employer. They, therefore, are not particularly interested in long-term employment with a single company but instead prefer to work for a company that can offer some worklife flexibility and can bring some fun aspects into the environment. Gen Xers understand the necessity of money but do not view salary as a sufficient reason for staying with a company—the quality of the work itself and the relationships built on the job are much more important. For Generation X, it is more important to enjoy life and to have a lifestyle that provides freedom and flexibility.

Some additional facts about Generation X are:

- 62 percent are married
- 29.7 million are parents
- 51 percent of children under 18 living at home are in households headed by an Xer
- 31 percent of Gen Xers have earned a college degree
- 81 percent of Xers are employed full-time or part-time
- 37 percent of Gen Xers' mothers worked outside the home when they (as kids) were growing up[61]

Appealing to generation X

Members of Generation X often pride themselves on their sophistication. Although they are not necessarily materialistic, they do purchase good brand names (such as Sony) but not necessarily designer labels. They want to be recognized by marketers as a group in their own right and not as mini–baby boomers. Therefore, advertisements targeted to this audience must focus on their style in music, fashions, and language. One key for marketers appears to be sincerity. Xers are not against advertising but only opposed to insincerity.

Baby boomer media does not work with Generation X members. For example, while 65 percent of 50- to 64-year-olds, and 55 percent of 30- to 49-year-olds read a newspaper regularly, only 39 percent of adults under 30 (the younger Xers) regularly read a newspaper.[62] Xers are the MTV generation, and whereas the three major U.S. TV networks attract an average of only 18 percent of the 18- to 29-year-old group, the Fox network claims that 38 percent of its viewers are in this age group. Still further, Xers use the Internet more than any other age cohort. For example, 60 percent of Xers have tried online banking, while only 38 percent of Generation Y has tried online banking.[63]

Hotel chains are also making changes in their offerings in order to better attract the Gen X traveler, the fastest-growing group of hotel patrons. Marriott, for example, is remodeling rooms to include flat-panel LCD TVs, high-speed Internet access, ergonomic desk chairs, and high thread-count sheets.[64] Additionally, Gen Xers are generally dissatisfied with most current shopping malls—they want to do more than just shop. Xers want to be able to eat a proper sitdown meal at the mall, rather than something quick at the food court. They also want to be able to get a cup of coffee while doing work on their laptop, and perhaps also see a movie.[65]

The baby boomer market

Marketers have found baby boomers a particularly desirable target audience because (1) they are the single largest distinctive age category alive today; (2) they frequently make important consumer purchase decisions; and (3) they contain small subsegments of trendsetting consumers (sometimes known as yuppies, or young upwardly mobile professionals) who have influence on the consumer tastes of other age segments of society.

Who are the baby boomers?

The term *baby boomers* refers to the age segment of the population that was born between 1946 and 1964. Thus, baby boomers are in the broad age category that extends from about 40 to 60. These 78 million or so baby boomers represent more than 40 percent of the adult population. The magnitude of this statistic alone would make them a much sought-after market segment. However, they also are valued because they comprise about 50 percent of all those in professional and managerial occupations and more than one-half of those with at least a college degree.

Although each year more baby boomers turn 50 years of age, they do not necessarily like the idea. Increases in health club memberships and a boom in the sales of vitamin and health supplements are evidence that these consumers are trying hard to look and feel "young"—they do not want to age gracefully but will fight and kick and pay whatever is necessary to look young. In advertisements they want to be portrayed as they see themselves—lively and attractive.[66] Most important to marketers, who understand them, they have money and they want to spend it on what they feel advances the quality of their lives.

Consumer characteristics of baby boomers

Baby boomers tend to be motivated consumers. They enjoy buying for themselves, for their homes or apartments, and for others—they are consumption oriented. As baby boomers age, the nature of the products and services they most need or desire changes. For example, because of the aging of this market segment, sales of "relaxed fit" jeans, and "lineless" bifocal glasses are up substantially, as is the sales of walking shoes. Men's and women's pants with elastic waistbands are also enjoying strong sales. Moreover, bank marketers and other financial institutions are also paying more attention to assisting boomers who are starting to think about retirement. Even St. Joseph's Aspirin has switched its target from babies to boomers, and Disney has ads to entice baby boomers to vacation at their theme parks without their kids.

Yuppies are by far the most sought-after subgroup of baby boomers. Although constituting only 5 percent of the population, they generally are well off financially, well educated, and in enviable professional or managerial careers. They often are associated with status brand names, such as BMWs or Volvo station wagons, Rolex watches, cable TV, and Cuisinart food processors. The Gap, for example, is opening a new chain of stores called Forth & Towne, aimed at women age 35 and older. These women were GAP shoppers for many years, but today they primarily shop department stores, because the specialty stores generally target younger audiences.[67]

Today, though, as many yuppies are maturing, they are shifting their attention away from expensive status-type possessions to travel, physical fitness, planning for second careers, or some other form of new life directions. Indeed, there has been a move away from wanting possessions, to wanting experiences—"boomers today are more interested in doing things than having things."[68]

Recent articles dealing with the baby boom generation have noted that some members of this group are planning to keep working, either full-time or part-time beyond age 65 (which, for the oldest boomers, is just a few years away). While some need to do this for the money, most just want to stay active, and/or are even planning, upon retirement, to start new careers. The majority of this group will not need to work in order to support themselves—by 2020, when the youngest baby boomers turn 55, this age cohort will own $20 trillion in assets.[69]

To sum up, Gen Yers, Gen Xers, and baby boomers differ in their purchasing behavior, attitudes toward brands, and behavior toward ads. Table 12.11 captures some of the differences among these three age cohorts.

Older consumers

America is aging. A portion of the baby boomers are about to turn 60, and there are plenty of preboomers—those 60 to 65 years old. According to the U.S. Census Bureau (in 2004), there were more than 36 million people in this country who are 65 years of age or older (12 percent of the population). Projecting ahead to the year 2050, it is anticipated that there will be more than 86 million Americans (21 percent of the total population) who will be 65 years of age or older.[70] Still further, from the start to the end of the twentieth century, life expectancy in the United States rose from about 47 years to 77 years,

TABLE 12.11	Comparison of Selected Age Cohorts Across Marketing-Related Issues		
THEMES	**GENERATION Y**	**GENERATION X**	**BOOMERS**
Purchasing behavior	Savvy, pragmatic	Materialistic	Narcissistic
Coming of age technology	Computer in every home	Microwave in every home	TV in every home
Price–quality attitude	Value oriented: weighing price–quality relationships	Price oriented: concerned about the cost of individual items	Conspicuous consumption: buying for indulgence
Attitude toward brands	Brand embracing	Against branding	Brand loyal
Behavior toward ads	Rebel against hype	Rebel against hype	Respond to image-building type

Source: Stephanie M. Noble and Charles H. Noble, "Getting to Know Y: The Consumption Behaviors of a New Cohort," *AMA Winter Educators' Conference* 11 (Chicago: American Marketing Association, 2000), *Marketing Theory,* Conference Proceedings, 294.

and whereas a 65-year-old in 1900 could expect, on average, to live about 12 more years, a 65-year-old in 2000 can expect about 18 more years of life.[71]

It should also be kept in mind that "later adulthood" (i.e., those who are 50 years of age or older) is the longest adult life stage for most consumers (i.e., often 29 or more years in duration). This is in contrast to "early adulthood" (i.e., those who are 18 to 34 years of age), a stage lasting 16 years, and "middle adulthood" (i.e., those who are 35 to 49 years of age), a stage lasting 14 years. Remember that people over age 50 comprise about one-third of the adult U.S. market.

Although some people think of older consumers as consisting of people without substantial financial resources, in generally poor health, and with plenty of free time on their hands, the fact is that more than 30 percent of men and more than 20 percent of women aged 65 to 69 are employed, as are 19 percent of men and 12 percent of women aged 70 to 74. Additionally, millions of seniors are involved in the daily care of a grandchild, and many do volunteer work. The annual discretionary income of this group amounts to 50 percent of the discretionary income of the United States, and these older consumers are major purchasers of luxury products such as cars, alcohol, vacations, and financial products. Americans over 65 now control about 70 percent of the nation's wealth.

Defining "older" in older consumer

Driving the growth of the elderly population are three factors: the declining birthrate, the aging of the huge baby boomer segment, and improved medical diagnoses and treatment. In the United States, "old age" is officially assumed to begin with a person's 65th birthday (or when the individual qualifies for full Social Security and Medicare). However, people over age 60 tend to view themselves as being 15 years younger than their chronological age.

It is generally accepted that people's perceptions of their ages are more important in determining behavior than their chronological ages (or the number of years lived). In fact, people may at the same time have a number of different perceived or **cognitive ages**. Specifically, elderly consumers perceive themselves to be younger than their chronological ages on four perceived age dimensions: *feel age* (how old they feel); *look age* (how old they look); *do age* (how involved they are in activities favored by members of a specific age group); and *interest age* (how similar their interests are to those of members of a specific age group).[72] The results support other research that indicates that elderly consumers are more likely to consider themselves younger (to have a younger cognitive age) than their chronological age.

For marketers, these findings underscore the importance of looking beyond chronological age to perceived or cognitive age when appealing to mature consumers and to the possibility that cognitive age might be used to segment the mature market. The "New-Age Elderly," when compared to the "Traditional Elderly," are more adventurous, more likely to perceive themselves to be better off financially, and more receptive to marketing information.[73]

Segmenting the elderly market

The elderly are by no means a homogeneous subcultural group. There are those who, as a matter of choice, do not have color TVs or Touch-Tone telephone service, whereas others have the latest desktop computers and spend their time surfing the Internet (cyberseniors will be discussed later in this section).

One consumer gerontologist has suggested that the elderly are more diverse in interests, opinions, and actions than other segments of the adult population.[74] Although this view runs counter to the popular myth that the elderly are uniform in terms of attitudes and lifestyles, both gerontologists and market researchers have repeatedly demonstrated that age is not necessarily a major factor in determining how older consumers respond to marketing activities.

With an increased appreciation that the elderly constitute a diverse age segment, more attention is now being given to identifying ways to segment the elderly into meaningful groupings. One relatively simple segmentation scheme partitions the elderly into three chronological age categories: the *young-old* (65 to 74 years of age); the *old* (those 75 to 84); and the *old-old* (those 85 years of age and older). This market segmentation approach provides useful consumer-relevant insights.

The elderly can also be segmented in terms of motivations and *quality-of-life orientation*. Table 12.12 presents a side-by-side comparison of new-age elderly consumers and the more traditional older consumers. The increased presence of the new-age elderly suggests that marketers need to respond to the value orientations of older consumers whose lifestyles remain relatively ageless. Clearly, the new-age elderly are individuals who feel, think, and do according to a cognitive age that is younger than their chronological age. All this suggests the declining importance of chronological age, and increasing importance of perceived or cognitive age as an indicator of the "aging experience" and age-related quality of life.

TABLE 12.12   Comparison of New-Age and Traditional Elderly

NEW-AGE ELDERLY	TRADITIONAL/STEREOTYPICAL ELDERLY
• Perceive themselves to be different in outlook from other people their age	• Perceive all older people to be about the same in outlook
• Age is seen as a state of mind	• See age as more of a physical state
• See themselves as younger than their chronological age	• See themselves at or near their chronological age
• Feel younger, think younger, and "do" younger	• Tend to feel, think, and do things that they feel match their chronological age
• Have a genuinely youthful outlook	• Feel that one should act one's age
• Feel there is a considerable adventure to living	• Feel life should be dependable and routine
• Feel more in control of their own lives	• Normal sense of being in control of their own lives
• Have greater self-confidence when it comes to making consumer decisions	• Normal range of self-confidence when it comes to making consumer decisions
• Less concerned that they will make a mistake when buying something	• Some concern that they will make a mistake when buying something
• Especially knowledgeable and alert consumers	• Low-to-average consumer capabilities
• Selectively innovative	• Not innovative
• Seek new experiences and personal challenges	• Seek stability and a secure routine
• Less interested in accumulating possessions	• Normal range of interest in accumulating possessions
• Higher measured life satisfaction	• Lower measured life satisfaction
• Less likely to want to live their lives over differently	• Have some regrets as to how they lived their lives
• Perceive themselves to be healthier	• Perceive themselves to be of normal health for their age
• Feel financially more secure	• Somewhat concerned about financial security

Source: Reprinted by permission from "The Value Orientation of New-Age Elderly: The Coming of an Ageless Market" by Leon G. Schiffman and Elaine Sherman in *Journal of Business Research* 22 (April 1991): 187–194. Copyright 1991 by Elsevier Science Publishing Co., Inc.

Cyberseniors

Although some people might think of older Americans as individuals who still use rotary phones and are generally resistant to change, this stereotype is far from the truth. Few older consumers are fearful of new technology, and there are more Internet users over the age of 50 than under the age of 20. Research studies have found that those over 55 are more likely than the average adult to use the Internet to purchase books, stocks, and computer equipment—92 percent of surfing seniors have shopped online and 78 percent have purchased online.[75] In fact, older Internet users are the fastest-growing demographic group with respect to the U.S. Internet market, and it has been forecast that 48 percent of all seniors will be online by the end of 2005. Additionally, a recent study found that 46 percent of cyberseniors use the Internet more than 10 hours weekly.[76]

What's the attraction for seniors to go online? Certainly, the Internet is a great way to communicate with friends and family members living in other states, including grand-children in college. But the Web is also a place to find information (e.g., stock prices, health and medication-related information), entertainment, and a sense of community. There also appears to be a relationship between the amount of time an older adult spends on the Internet and his or her level of out-of-home mobility (using the Internet may serve as a substitute for going out of the house). Having a computer and modem "empowers" older consumers—it allows them to regain some of the control that was lost due to the physical and/or social deterioration in their lives. For example, a consumer can pay bills, shop, and e-mail friends. This may be part of the reason why the American Association of Retired Persons (AARP) claims that 2 million of its members are computer users.[77]

Marketing to the older consumer

Older consumers are open to be marketed to, but only for the "right" kinds of products and services and using the "right" advertising presentation. For example, older models tend to be underrepresented in advertisements or are often shown as being infirm or feeble. Part of the problem, according to some writers on the subject, is that the advertising professionals who create the ads are often in their 20s and 30s and have little under-standing or empathy for older consumers. Seniors often want to be identified not for what they did in the past but by what they would like to accomplish in the future. Retirement or moving to a sunbelt community is viewed as the opening of a new chapter in life and not a quiet withdrawal from life. In the same vein, the increase in the number of older adults taking vacation cruises and joining health clubs signifies a strong commit-ment to remaining "functionally young."

For some products and services, seniors do exhibit different shopping habits than younger consumers. For example, when shopping for a car, older consumers consider fewer brands, fewer models, and fewer dealers. They also are more likely to choose a long-established brand of automobile.[78] Older shoppers tend to be more store-loyal than younger age groups, especially with respect to supermarkets. Still further, the importance of factors like store location (e.g., distance from home) are often a function of the health status of the senior.[79]

Sex as a subculture

Because **sex roles** have an important cultural component, it is quite fitting to examine **gender** as a subcultural category.

Sex roles and consumer behavior

All societies tend to assign certain traits and roles to males and others to females. In American society, for instance, aggressiveness and competitiveness often were consid-ered traditional *masculine traits*; neatness, tactfulness, gentleness, and talkativeness were considered traditional *feminine traits*. In terms of role differences, women have historically been cast as homemakers with responsibility for child care and men as the providers or breadwinners. Because such traits and roles are no longer relevant for many individuals, marketers are increasingly appealing to consumers' broader vision of gender-related role options. However, many studies are still suggesting that even with the large number of middle-class women in the workplace, men are not doing more in terms of housework (e.g., cleaning, cooking, laundry).[80]

A recent study also found that men and women exhibit different reactions to identical print advertisements. Women show superior affect and purchase intention toward ads that are verbal, harmonious, complex, and category-oriented. In contrast, men exhibit superior affect and purchase intention toward ads that are comparative, simple, and attribute-oriented. Consequently, it may be best, where feasible, to advertise differently to men and women.[81]

Consumer products and sex roles

Within every society, it is quite common to find products that are either exclusively or strongly associated with the members of one sex. In the United States, for example, shaving equipment, cigars, pants, ties, and work clothing were historically male products; bracelets, hair spray, hair dryers, and sweet-smelling colognes generally were considered feminine products. For most of these products, the **sex role** link has either diminished or disappeared; for others, the prohibition still lingers. Specifically, although women have historically been the major market for vitamins, men are increasingly being targeted for vitamins exclusively formulated for men. Furthermore, in the past few years men have exhibited more of an interest in personal health and wellness, closing the gap with women with regard to these areas of personal concern.[82]

The appeal of the Internet seems to differ somewhat for men and women. For instance, women go online to seek out reference materials, online books, medical information, cooking ideas, government information, and chat sites. In contrast, men tend to focus on exploring, discovery, identifying free software, and investments. This seems to provide further support for the notion that men are "hunters," whereas women are "nurturers."[83] Still further, although men and women are equally likely to browse commercial sites, women are less likely to purchase online (32% for men versus 19% for women). Evidence suggests that the lower incidence of women purchasing online is due to their heightened concerns about online security and privacy.[84]

Women as depicted in media and advertising

Many women feel that the media and advertising create an expectation of beauty that most women can never achieve. Consequently, they want the definition of "beauty" to change. Dove has an advertising campaign that is challenging the traditional sense of beauty and has been well received by women. "Real" women are portrayed in the company's ads—with gray hair, winkles, and flawed skin—i.e., real people! Importantly, the campaign lets women know that beauty comes in many sizes, shapes, and ages.[85] Supporting Dove's realistic approach, a recent study found that 65 percent of women 35 to 40 years of age felt that most advertisements aimed at them were patronizing, and 50 percent also found the ads to be "old-fashioned."[86]

The working woman

Marketers are keenly interested in the **working woman**, especially the married working woman. They recognize that married women who work outside of the home are a large and growing market segment, one whose needs differ from those of women who do not work outside the home (frequently self-labeled "stay-at-home moms"). It is the size of the working woman market that makes it so attractive. Approximately 60 percent of

American women 16 years of age and older are in the labor force, which represents a market of over 65 million individuals. Whereas more than half of all women with children under the age of 1 are working (55 percent), almost 78 percent of women with children ages 6 to 17 are employed.[87]

Because 40 percent of all business travelers today are women, hotels have begun to realize that it pays to provide the services women want, such as healthy foods, gyms, and spas and wellness centers. Female business travelers are also concerned about hotel security and frequently use room service because they do not want to go to the hotel bar or restaurant. The Hilton in Paris, for example, discreetly hands key cards to female patrons, offers valet parking, and allows women to receive guests in an executive lounge located on the hotel's business floor.[88]

Segmenting the working woman market

To provide a richer framework for segmentation, marketers have developed categories that differentiate the motivations of working and nonworking women. For instance, a number of studies have divided the female population into four segments: *stay-at-home* housewives; *plan-to-work* housewives; *just-a-job* working women; and *career-oriented* working women.[89] The distinction between "just-a-job" and "career-oriented" working women is particularly meaningful. "Just-a-job" working women seem to be motivated to work primarily by a sense that the family requires the additional income, whereas "career-oriented" working women, who tend to be in a managerial or professional position, are driven more by a need to achieve and succeed in their chosen careers. Today, though, with more and more female college graduates in the workforce, the percentage of career-oriented working women is on the rise. As evidence of this fact, 25 percent of all working women bring home a paycheck that is larger than their husband's (10 years ago it was only 17 percent).[90]

Working women spend less time shopping than nonworking women. They accomplish this "time economy" by shopping less often and by being brand and store loyal. Not surprisingly, working women also are likely to shop during evening hours and on weekends, as well as to buy through direct-mail catalogs.

Businesses that advertise to women should also be aware that magazines are now delivering a larger women's audience than television shows. Whereas early 1980s' TV shows had higher ratings than popular magazines, today the top 25 women's magazines have larger audiences than the top 25 television shows targeted to females.[91]

Every year, more and more products and retailers target to women. Recent examples include Beringer's introduction of White Lie Early Season Chardonnay ("This wine speaks to us in our language") and Godiva Chocolate's notion that their product is something that a woman deserves to buy for herself (rather than as a gift for someone else). Best Buy, and other similar electronics stores, are trying harder than ever to make women feel comfortable shopping in their outlets, since women spend $55 billion annually on consumer electronics. A recent study by the Consumer Electronics Association found that 46 percent of women claim that they have the most influence in their households with respect to consumer electronics purchases.[92]

Subcultural interaction

All consumers are simultaneously members of more than one subcultural segment (e.g., a consumer may be a young, Hispanic, Catholic homemaker living in the Midwest). The reality of **subcultural interaction** suggest that marketers should strive to understand how multiple *subcultural* memberships *interact* to influence target consumers' relevant consumption behavior. Promotional strategy should not be limited to target a single subcultural membership.

SUMMARY

Subcultural analysis enables marketers to segment their markets to meet the specific needs, motivations, perceptions, and attitudes shared by members of a specific subcultural group. A subculture is a distinct cultural group that exists as an identifiable segment within a larger, more complex society. Its members possess beliefs, values, and customs that set them apart from other members of the same society; at the same time, they hold to the dominant beliefs of the overall society. Major subcultural categories in this country include nationality, religion, geographic location, race, age, and sex. Each of these can be broken down into smaller segments that can be reached through special copy appeals and selective media choices. In some cases (such as the elderly consumer), product characteristics can be tailored to the specialized needs of the market segment. Because all consumers simultaneously are members of several subcultural groups, the marketer must determine for the product category how specific subcultural memberships interact to influence the consumer's purchase decisions.

chapter 13

Cross-Culture and Globalization

In our examination of psychological, social, and cultural factors, we have consistently pointed out how various segments of the American consuming public differ. If so much diversity exists among segments of a single society, then even more diversity is likely to exist among the members of two or more societies. To succeed, international marketers must understand the nature and extent of differences between the consumers of different societies—"cross-cultural" differences—so that they can develop effective targeted marketing strategies to use in each foreign market of interest.

In this chapter, we broaden our scope of analysis and consider the marketing implications of cultural differences and similarities that exist between the people of two or more nations. We also compare the views that pin a global marketing perspective—one that stresses the *similarities* of consumers worldwide—against a localized marketing strategy that stresses the *diversity* of consumers in different nations and their specific cultural orientations. Our own view is that marketers must be aware of and sensitive to cross-cultural similarities and differences that can provide expanded sales and profit opportunities. Multinational marketers must be ready to tailor their marketing mixes to the specific customs of each nation that they want to target.

The imperative to be multinational

Today, almost all major corporations are actively marketing their products beyond their original homeland borders. In fact, the issue is generally not *whether* to market a brand in other countries but rather *how* to do it (as the same product with the same "global" advertising campaign, or "tailored" products and localized ads for each country). Because of this emphasis on operating as a multinational entity, the vocabulary of marketing now includes terms such as *glocal*, which refers to companies that are both "global" and "local"; that is, they include in their marketing efforts a blend of standardized and local elements in order to secure the benefits of each strategy.

This challenge has been given special meaning by the efforts of the **European Union** (EU) to form a single market. Although the movement of goods and services among its 25 members (with the potential of becoming 27 members in 2007) has been eased, it is unclear whether this diverse market will really be transformed into a single market of almost 460 million homogeneous "Euroconsumers" with the same or very similar wants and needs.[1] Many people hope that the recent introduction of the euro as a common EU currency will help shape Europe into a huge, powerful, unified market. Furthermore, the rapid acceptance of capitalism by many Eastern European countries also presents a major opportunity and challenge to marketers. Firms such as Coca-Cola, General Motors, Nabisco, P&G, and R.J. Reynolds have been investing extensive sums on product development and marketing to satisfy the needs of Eastern European consumer markets.

The **North American Free Trade Agreement** (NAFTA), which currently consists of the United States, Canada, and Mexico, provides free-market access to more than 430 million consumers. Since its inception, for example, the markets in Canada and Mexico for packaged software from U.S. firms has grown to three times its pre-NAFTA market size.[2] The emerging Association of Southeast Asian Nations (ASEAN), consisting of Indonesia, Singapore, Thailand, the Philippines, Malaysia, Brunei, and Vietnam, is another important economic alliance that offers marketers new global markets. The members of this group have formed the ASEAN Free Trade Area (AFTA) to promote regional trade.

Many firms are developing strategies to take advantage of these and other emerging economic opportunities. A substantial number of firms are now jockeying for market share in foreign markets. For instance, Starbucks has opened a store within the

TABLE 13.1	The World's Most Valuable Brands	
RANK	**BRAND**	**2004 BRAND VALUE ($BILLIONS)**
1	Coca-Cola	67.4
2	Microsoft	61.4
3	IBM	53.8
4	GE	44.1
5	Intel	33.5
6	Disney	27.1
7	McDonald's	25.0
8	Nokia	24.0
9	Toyota	22.7
10	Marlboro	22.1

Note: Only includes brands that obtain at least one-third of their earnings outside of their home country.

Source: Diane Brady, Robert D. Hof, Andy Reinhardt, Moon Ihlwan, Stanley Holmes, and Kerry Capell, "The Top 100 Brands," *Business Week*, August 2, 2004, 68.

Forbidden City in Beijing, China, and MTV Networks has formed a partnership with @JapanMedia to establish a new 24-hour Japanese language music TV channel.[3]

Firms are selling their products worldwide for a variety of reasons. First, with the buildup of "multinational fever" and the general attractiveness of multinational markets, products or services originating in one country are increasingly being sought out by consumers in other parts of the world. Second, many firms have learned that overseas markets represent the single most important opportunity for their future growth when their home markets reach maturity. This realization is propelling them to expand their horizons and seek consumers scattered all over the world. Moreover, consumers all over the world are increasingly eager to try "foreign" products that are popular in different and far-off places. Consider the following story:

> There was this Englishman who worked in the London office of a multinational cor-
> poration based in the United States. He drove home one evening in his Japanese car.
> His wife, who worked in a firm which imported German kitchen equipment, was
> already home. Her small Italian car was often quicker through the traffic. After a meal
> which included New Zealand lamb, California carrots, Mexican honey, French cheese
> and Spanish wine, they settled down to watch a program on their television set, which
> has been made in Finland. The program was a retrospective celebration of the war to
> recapture the Falkland Islands. As they watched it they felt warmly patriotic, and very
> proud to be British.[4]

According to *Business Week*, Coca-Cola is the most valuable brand in the world, with a brand value of about $65 billion. Table 13.1 presents a list of the world's 10 most valuable brands.

Acquiring exposure to other cultures

As more and more consumers come in contact with the material goods and lifestyles of people living in other parts of the world, they have the opportunity to adopt these different products and practices. How consumers in one culture secure exposure to the goods of other people living in other cultures is an important part of consumer behavior. It impacts the well-being of consumers worldwide and of marketers trying to gain acceptance for their products in countries that are often quite different from their home country. After all, by the time you read this, there may be five models of automobiles available for you to purchase that were made in China, thanks to a deal between Chery Automobiles of China and Malcom Bricklin, chairman of Visionary Vehicles.[5]

Consider Mexico, America's neighbor to the South. While the Mexican culture shares many similarities with those of Central and South American nations, consumers in Mexico differ when it comes to attitude — they have an affinity for American values. Mexican consumers use brands to display status, making conspicuous consumption a part of life, even for the poor. For example, a working class household might keep a large American refrigerator in the living room, instead of the kitchen, because it is viewed as a sign of financial success. Still further, the largest market for Martell cognac outside of France is Mexico, because the product allows the affluent to display their success and wealth.[6]

A portion of consumers' exposure to different cultures tends to come about through consumers' own initiatives — their travel, their living and working in foreign countries, or even their immigration to a different country. Additionally, consumers obtain a "taste" of different cultures from contact with foreign movies, theater, art and artifacts, and most certainly, from exposure to unfamiliar and different products. This second major category of cultural exposure is often fostered by marketers seeking to expand their markets by bringing new products, services, practices, ideas, and experiences to potential consumers residing in a different country and possessing a different cultural view. Within this context, international marketing provides a form of "culture transfer."

Country-of-origin effects

When consumers are making purchase decisions, they may take into consideration the countries of origin (COO) of their choices. Researchers have shown that consumers use their knowledge of where products are made in the evaluation of their purchase options.[7] Such a country-of-origin effect seems to come about because consumers are often aware that a particular firm or brand name is associated with a particular country. For example, a Volkswagen's "Fahrvergnügen" campaign touted German engineering, and Land-Rover's advertising conveys a sophisticated British image. In contrast, Jaguar does not tend to play on its British heritage when marketing its cars in the United States. And then there's Chevrolet, the General Motors division responsible for over half of GM's vehicle sales. Over the years, Chevrolet has used slogans such as "See the U.S.A. in your Chevrolet," and it is currently using the theme "An American Revolution" to introduce 10 new cars and trucks.[8]

In general, many consumers associate France with wine, fashion clothing, and perfume and other beauty products; Italy with pasta, designer clothing, furniture, shoes, and sports cars; Japan with cameras and consumer electronics; and Germany with cars, tools, and machinery. Moreover, consumers tend to have an established *attitude* or even a preference when it comes to a particular product being made in a particular country. This attitude might be positive, negative, or neutral, depending on perceptions or experience. For instance, a consumer in one country might positively value a particular product made in another country (e.g., affluent American consumers may feel that an English Thomas Pink dress shirt or a Bosch dishwasher from Germany are worthwhile investments). In contrast, another consumer might be negatively influenced when he learns that a television set he is considering is made in a country that he does not associate with fine electronics (e.g., a TV made in Costa Rica). Such country-of-origin effects influence how consumers rate quality and which brands they will ultimately select. Recent research suggests, though, that when consumer motivation is high and when a specific model of a product is being evaluated (as opposed to a range of products manufactured in a particular country), then consumers are *less* likely to base judgments on country-of-origin information.[9] However, when consumers are less familiar with foreign products, COO becomes an important extrinsic cue.[10]

Refining the country-of-origin concept, a study that contrasted U.S. and Mexican consumers decomposed country-of-origin into three separate entities: country of design (COD), country of assembly (COA), and country of parts (COP). Of the three, country

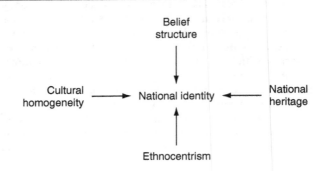

FIGURE 13.1

Dimensions of National Identity

of parts (COP) had the strongest influence on product evaluations.[11] The study also found that COD was a more important cue in the United States than in Mexico, and that younger Mexicans exhibited a stronger COO effect than older Mexicans.

Beyond perceptions of a product's attributes based on its country of manufacture, research evidence exists that suggests that some consumers may refrain from purchasing products from particular countries due to animosity. A study of this issue found that *high-animosity consumers* in the People's Republic of China owned fewer Japanese products than *low-animosity consumers* (during World War II, Japan occupied parts of China). Although some Chinese consumers might consider Sony to be a high-end, high-quality brand (or perceptions of the product itself might be very positive), they might nevertheless refuse to bring a product manufactured in Japan into the home. Similarly, some Jewish consumers avoid purchasing German-made products due to the Holocaust, and some New Zealand and Australian consumers boycott French products due to France's nuclear tests in the South Pacific.[12]

What is national identity?

One way to explain why a consumer prefers buying products made in one country and does not wish to buy products made in another, or why consumers in different countries exhibit different behaviors, is the existence of a "national identity." As presented in Figure 13.1, national identity consists of four dimensions (for each dimension a sample item from a scale to measure it is included, the entire measure is composed of 17 items): *belief structure* (e.g., "A true American would never reject their religious belief"), *cultural homogeneity* (e.g., "People frequently engage in activities that identify them as American"), *national heritage* (e.g., "Important people from the country's past are admired by people today"), and *consumer ethnocentrism* (e.g., "Only those products that are unavailable in the USA should be imported"). Using the national identity scale, research has studied consumers in South Korea, Taiwan, Thailand, and Singapore.[13] The research, for example, revealed that Thailand had the strongest national identity and Singapore the weakest. Generally, countries with a weak sense of national identity, coupled with low ethnocentric tendencies, are suitable for use as places to launch new products, because foreign firms are not viewed as threats.

Cross-cultural consumer analysis

To determine whether and how to enter a foreign market, marketers need to conduct some form of **cross-cultural consumer analysis**. Within the scope of this discussion, cross-cultural consumer analysis is defined as the effort to determine to what extent the consumers of two or more nations are similar or different. Such analyses can provide marketers with an understanding of the psychological, social, and cultural characteristics of the foreign consumers they wish to target, so that they can design effective marketing strategies for the specific national markets involved.

TABLE 13.2	A Comparison of Chinese and American Cultures

CHINESE CULTURAL TRAITS	AMERICAN CULTURAL TRAITS
• Centered on a set of relationships defined by Confucian doctrine	• Centered on the individual
• Submissive to authority	• Greater emphasis on self-reliance
• Ancestor worship	• Resents class-based distinctions
• Passive acceptance of fate by seeking harmony with nature	• Active mastery in the person–nature relationship
• Emphasizes inner experiences of meaning and feeling	• Concerned with external experiences and the world of things
• A closed worldview, prizing stability and harmony	• An open view of the world, emphasizing change and movement
• Culture rests on kinship ties and tradition with a historical orientation	• Places primary faith in rationalism and is oriented toward the future
• Places weight on vertical interpersonal relationships	• Places weight on horizontal dimensions of interpersonal relationship
• Values a person's duties to family, clan, and state	• Values the individual personality

Source: Adapted from Carolyn A. Lin, "Cultural Values Reflected in Chinese and American Television Advertising," *Journal of Advertising* 30, no. 4 (Winter 2001): 83–94.

In a broader context, cross-cultural consumer analysis might also include a comparison of subcultural groups within a single country (such as English and French Canadians, Cuban Americans and Mexican Americans in the United States, or Protestants and Catholics in Northern Ireland). For our purposes, however, we will limit our discussion of cross-cultural consumer analysis to comparisons of consumers of *different* countries.

Similarities and differences among people

A major objective of cross-cultural consumer analysis is to determine how consumers in two or more societies are similar and how they are different. For instance, Table 13.2 presents at least a partial depiction of the differences between Chinese and American cultural traits. Such an understanding of the similarities and differences that exist between nations is critical to the multinational marketer who must devise appropriate strategies to reach consumers in specific foreign markets. The greater the similarity between nations, the more feasible it is to use relatively similar marketing strategies in each nation. On the other hand, if the cultural beliefs, values, and customs of specific target countries are found to differ widely, then a highly *individualized* marketing strategy is indicated for each country. To illustrate, in addition to IKEA furniture company's generic global Web site that uses English, the firm also offers 14 localized Web sites (in selected languages) and 30 minisites (in more languages) that only provide contact information. And whereas the IKEA Italian Web site shows a group of people frolicking on their IKEA furniture (nudity is acceptable and commonplace in Italian advertising), the Saudi Arabian Web site uses extremely conservative photographs (**www.ikea.com**).[14] As another example, while 88 percent of adults in both France and Germany drink mineral water, French consumption is strongly associated with concern over the quality of tap water, while German consumption is closely linked to vegetarians.[15]

A firm's success in marketing a product or service in a number of foreign countries is likely to be influenced by how similar the beliefs, values, and customs are that govern the use of the product in the various countries. For example, the worldwide TV commercials of major international airlines (American Airlines, Continental Airlines, Air France, Lufthansa, Swissair, United Airlines, and British Airways) tend to depict the luxury and pampering offered to their business-class and first-class international travelers. The reason for their general cross-cultural appeal is that these commercials speak to the same types of individuals worldwide—upscale international business travelers—who share much in common. In contrast, knowing that "typical" American advertising would not work in China, Nike hired Chinese-speaking art directors and copywriters to develop specific commercials that would appeal to the Chinese consumer within the boundaries of the Chinese culture. The resulting advertising campaign appealed to national pride in China.[16] Yet another example of cultural differences necessitating a change in marketing would be the efforts of Western banks to attract Muslim customers. The shari'ah (the sacred law of Islam based on what is written in the Koran) forbids Muslims from charging interest, and prohibits such Western-type financial transactions such as speculation, selling short, and conventional debt financing. Consequently, Western banks in the United Kingdom that want to appeal to that country's two million Muslim residents must develop a new range of products for this group of target consumers.[17]

Further supporting the importance of cultural differences or orientation, consider that Southeast Asia is frequently the largest market for prestige and luxury brands from the West, and that luxury brand companies such as Louis Vuitton, Rolex, Gucci, and Prada are looking to markets such as Hanoi and Guangzhou when they are thinking of expanding their market reach. Indeed, in fine-tuning their marketing, these luxury-brand marketers need to be especially responsive to cultural differences that compel luxury purchases in the Asian and Western markets. To this end, research suggests that while Western consumers tend to "use" a prestige item to enhance their sense of individualism or serve as a source of personal pleasure, for Southeast Asian consumers the same prestige item might serve to further bond the individual with others and to provide visible evidence of the person's value to others.[18] Still further, within the scope of a visible luxury product, a woman in Hong Kong might carry a Fendi handbag (a visible and conspicuous item), but is not likely to be receptive to luxury lingerie because it is not an item that "shows" in public.[19]

The growing global middle class

The growing middle class in developing countries is a phenomenon that is very attractive to global marketers who are often eager to identify new customers for their products. The news media has given considerable coverage to the idea that the rapidly expanding middle class in countries of Asia, South America, and Eastern Europe is based on the reality that, although per capita income may be low, there is nevertheless considerable buying power in a country such as China, where $1,500 of income is largely discretionary income. This means that a Chinese family with $1,500 is middle class and is a target customer for TVs, VCRs, and computers. Indeed, this same general pattern of the growing middle class has also been observed in many parts of South America, Asia, and Eastern Europe.[20] In many parts of the world, an income equivalent to $5,000 is considered the point at which a person becomes "middle class," and it has been estimated that somewhat more than one billion people in the world's developing countries meet this income standard.[21] It is important to note though, that consumers in less-developed nations often cannot afford to pay as much for a product as consumers in the more advanced economies do. As an example, Nestlé has introduced low-price ice cream in China—the product sells for 12 cents.[22] Table 13.3 lists the size of the emerging middle class in 12 different countries. The results reveal that more than 90 percent of the population of South Korea can be considered middle class, whereas less than 5 percent of the populations of Nigeria and Pakistan can be similarly categorized.

The rather rapid expansion of middle-class consumers, over the past 50 years, have attracted the attention of many well-established marketing powerhouses, who were already finding their home markets to be rather mature and reaching what was felt to be

TABLE 13.3	Size of the Emerging Middle Class in Selected Countries	
	PERCENT OF THE POPULATION	**NUMBER OF PEOPLE (MILLIONS)**
Brazil	35	57.9
China	23	290.4
India	9	91.4
Indonesia	10	21.0
Korea, Republic of	93	44.0
Malaysia	46	10.7
Mexico	46	45.1
Nigeria	<5	<6.3
Pakistan	<5	<6.9
Peru	27	6.9
Philippines	25	18.9
Russian Federation	45	65.5

Source: Benjamin Senauer and Linda Goetz, "The Growing Middle Class in Developing Countries and the Market for High-Value Food Products," *Prepared for the Workshop on Global Markets for High-Value Food, Economic Research Service, USDA*, Washington D.C., February 14, 2003, 13, accessed at **www.farmfoundation.org/documents/ben-sanauerpaper2−10−3-13-03_000.pdf**

a saturation point in terms of sales opportunities. While in 1960 two-thirds of the world's middle class lived in industrialized nations, by the year 2000, some 83 percent of middle-class citizens were living in developing countries. These changes strongly suggest that more people are now living longer, healthier, and better lives—literacy rates in developing countries have risen dramatically in the past 50 years, and today two-thirds, rather than only one-third of the people living in these nations are literate.[23] Table 13.4 captures the global progress over the past 50 years and projects it to year 2050. Note how in 1950 the caloric intake in emerging markets was only 55 percent of industrial countries, while today it is more than 80 percent.

Although a growing middle class provides a market opportunity for products like Big Macs and fries, it should always be remembered that the same product may have different meanings in different countries. For example, whereas a U.S. consumer wants his or her "fast food" to be fast, a Korean consumer is more likely to view a meal as a social or family-related experience. Consequently, convenient store hours may be valued more by a Korean consumer than shorter service time.[24] In China, despite a traditional emphasis on "fresh" (just picked or killed) food, the emerging middle class, with rising incomes and rising demands on their time, are often willing to spend money to save time, in the form of alternatives to home-cooked meals.[25]

Regulations in different countries may preclude the use of some of the marketing practices that a firm employs in the United States. For example, German advertising rules do not allow an ad to compare one brand to another, nor do they permit Lands' End to offer a "lifetime guarantee." And whereas consumers in the United States like to buy with charge cards, the French prefer an invoice and the Germans prefer COD.[26]

Many transnational corporations (a company that had direct foreign investments and owns or controls activities in more than one nation) think in terms of regions as markets, or even the entire world as their market. For example, Nestlé, a giant Swiss firm, generates only 2 percent of its sales in Switzerland, and bases only 4 percent of its workers there. Whenever possible, transnational firms try to avoid having products identified with a particular country, rather they seek to make their product feel "local and natural" to their target customers. Of course, there are exceptions to such strategy. In particular, we might speculate that people throughout the world might generally be expected to

TABLE 13.4	Measured Global Progress 1950–2050		
	1950	**2000**	**2050**
Global Output, Per Capita ($)	586	6,666	15,155
Global Financial Market Capitalization, Per Capita ($)	158	13,333	75,000
Percent of Global GDP			
Emerging Markets	5	50	55
Industrial Countries	95	75	45
Life Expectancy (years)			
Emerging Markets	41	64	76
Industrial Countries	65	77	82
Daily Caloric Intake			
Emerging Markets	1,200	2,600	3,000
Industrial Countries	2,200	3,100	3,200
Infant Mortality (per 1000)			
Emerging Markets	140	65	10
Industrial Countries	30	8	4
Literacy Rate (per 100)			
Emerging Markets	33	64	90
Industrial Countries	95	98	99

Sources: Bloomberg, World Bank, United Nations, and author's estimates. Output and financial market capitalization figures are inflation-adjusted. Peter Marber, "Globalization and Its Contents," *World Policy Journal* (Winter 2004/05): 30.

prefer a precision Swiss wristwatch, to a wristwatch that is made in their own country. Also fashion clothing items, made in France or Italy, are also likely to be perceived to be more desirable than locally made clothing.

The bottom line, though, is that more consumer goods are sold each year because of the growth of the world's middle-class population, and a marketer would do well to focus more on the emerging middle class in other nations than on people who cannot afford to buy its products in its home market. As a recent article concluded, "Coke is the global soft drink, Macs the global fast-food, and CNN the global television. These are the commodities of a new global middle-class."[27]

The global teenage market

As part of growth of the world middle class, there has been a parallel growth in an affluent global teenage and young adult markets. To be expected, these youthful markets have attracted the attention of marketers. Within reason, these teenagers (and their somewhat older brothers and sisters—"the young adult segment") appear to have quite similar interests, desires, and consumption behavior no matter where they live. Therefore, in response to this perspective, consumer researchers have explored the makeup, composition, and behavior of this segment(s). One particular study considered the fashion consciousness of teenagers in the United States, Japan, and China.[28] The research revealed that American and Japanese teens were highly similar, differing only in that the Japanese teens were more likely to choose style over comfort (most likely because of the importance, in the Japanese Confucian society, of meeting the expectations of group members). In contrast, Chinese teens were less fashion conscious than both the American and Japanese teens, which supports the idea that differ-

TABLE 13.5	Fashion Consciousness Scale Results for Chinese, Japanese, and U.S. Teenagers			
ITEM	CHINA (μ)	JAPAN (μ)	USA (μ)	GRAND (μ)
1. I usually have one or more outfits that are of the very latest style	3.06	4.23	4.53	4.17
2. When I must choose between the two, I usually dress for style, not comfort	2.49	4.26	3.57	3.57
3. An important part of my life and activities involves dressing stylishly	2.24	3.72	3.34	3.26
4. Fashionable, attractive styling is very important to me	2.60	3.96	3.77	3.62

Source: R. Stephen Parker, Charles M. Hermans, and Allen D. Schaefer, "Fashion Consciousness of Chinese, Japanese and American Teenagers," *Journal of Fashion Marketing and Management* 8, no. 2 (2004): 181.

ences exist between highly developed and less high-developed nations with respect to teen fashion consciousness. Table 13.5 presents the four-item scale employed in the study to measure fashion consciousness; each item was measured using a 7-point Likert-type scale (1="strongly disagree" and 7="strongly agree") with the mean score for each question shown.

Acculturation is a needed marketing viewpoint

Too many marketers contemplating international expansion make the strategic error of believing that if its product is liked by local or domestic consumers, then everyone will like it. This biased viewpoint increases the likelihood of marketing failures abroad. It reflects a lack of appreciation of the unique psychological, social, cultural, and environmental characteristics of distinctly different cultures. To overcome such a narrow and culturally myopic view, marketers must also go through an *acculturation process*. They must learn everything that is relevant about the usage or potential usage of their products and product categories in the foreign countries in which they plan to operate. Take the Chinese culture, for example. For Western marketers to succeed in China, it is important for them to take into consideration *guo qing* (pronounced "gwor ching"), which means "to consider the special situation or character of China."[29] An example of *guo qing* for Western marketers is the Chinese policy of limiting families to one child. An appreciation of this policy means that foreign businesses will understand that Chinese families are open to particularly high-quality baby products for their single child (or "the little emperor").[30] One result of this one-child policy is that in the large cities in China, children are given more than $3 billion a year by their parents to spend as they wish and influence approximately 68 percent of their parents' spending. These Chinese children are also less culture bound than their parents and are, therefore, more open to Western ideas and products.[31]

In a sense, cross-cultural **acculturation** is a dual process for marketers. First, marketers must thoroughly orient themselves to the values, beliefs, and customs of the new society to appropriately position and market their products (being sensitive to and consistent with traditional or prevailing attitudes and values). Second, to gain acceptance for a culturally new product in a foreign society, they must develop a strategy that encourages members of that society to modify or even break with their own traditions (to change their attitudes and possibly alter their behavior). To illustrate the point, a social marketing effort designed to encourage consumers in developing nations to secure polio vaccinations for their children would require a two-step acculturation process. First, the marketer must obtain an in-depth picture of a society's present attitudes and customs with regard to preventive medicine and related concepts. Then the marketer must devise promotional strategies that will convince the members of a target market to have their children vaccinated, even if doing so requires a change in current attitudes.

Distinctive characteristics of cross-cultural analysis

It is often difficult for a company planning to do business in foreign countries to undertake **cross-cultural consumer research**. For instance, it is difficult in the Islamic countries of the Middle East to conduct Western-style market research. In Saudi Arabia, for instance, it is illegal to stop people on the streets, and focus groups are impractical because most gatherings of four or more people (with the exception of family and religious gatherings) are outlawed.[32] American firms desiring to do business in Russia have found a limited amount of information regarding consumer and market statistics. Similarly, marketing research information on China is generally inadequate, and surveys that ask personal questions arouse suspicion. So marketers have tried other ways to elicit the data they need. For example, Grey Advertising has given cameras to Chinese children so they can take pictures of what they like and do not like, rather than ask them to explain it to a stranger. Moreover, AC Nielsen conducts focus groups in pubs and children's playrooms rather than in conference rooms; and Leo Burnett has sent researchers to China to simply "hang out" with consumers.[33]

Applying research techniques

Although the same basic research techniques used to study domestic consumers are useful in studying consumers in foreign lands, in cross-cultural analysis an additional burden exists because language and word usage often differ from nation to nation. Another issue in international marketing research concerns scales of measurement. In the United States, a 5- or 7-point scale may be adequate, but in other countries a 10- or even 20-point scale may be needed. Still further, research facilities, such as telephone interviewing services, may or may not be available in particular countries or areas of the world.

To avoid such research measurement problems, consumer researchers must familiarize themselves with the availability of research services in the countries they are evaluating as potential markets and must learn how to design marketing research studies that will yield useful data. Researchers must also keep in mind that cultural differences may make "standard" research methodologies inappropriate. Table 13.6 identifies basic issues that multinational marketers must consider when planning cross-cultural consumer research.

Alternative multinational strategies: global versus local

Some marketers have argued that world markets are becoming more and more similar and that standardized marketing strategies are, therefore, becoming more feasible. For example, Exxon Mobil has launched a $150 million marketing campaign to promote its brands (Exxon, Esso, Mobil, and General), and the firm wants all the ads to carry the same look and feel, regardless of which one of the 100 countries in the world the ad will appear.[34] In contrast, other marketers feel that differences between consumers of various nations are far too great to permit a standardized marketing strategy. In a practical sense, a basic challenge for many executives contemplating multinational marketing is to decide whether to use *shared needs and values* as a segmentation strategy (i.e., to appeal to consumers in different countries in terms of their "common" needs, values, and goals) or to use *national borders* as a segmentation strategy (i.e., to use relatively different, "local," or specific marketing strategies for members of distinctive cultures or countries).

TABLE 13.6	Basic Research Issues in Cross-Cultural Analysis
FACTORS	**EXAMPLES**
Differences in language and meaning	Words or concepts (e.g., "personal checking account") may not mean the same in two different countries.
Differences in market segmentation opportunities	The income, social class, age, and sex of target customers may differ dramatically between two different countries.
Differences in consumption patterns	Two countries may differ substantially in the level of consumption or use of products or services (e.g., mail catalogs).
Differences in the perceived benefits of products and services	Two nations may use or consume the same product (e.g., yogurt) in very different ways.
Differences in the criteria for evaluating products and services	The benefits sought from a service (e.g., bank cards) may differ from country to country.
Differences in economic and social conditions and family structure	The "style" of family decision making may vary significantly from country to country.
Differences in marketing research and conditions	The types and quality of retail outlets and direct-mail lists may vary greatly among countries.
Differences in marketing research possibilities	The availability of professional consumer researchers may vary considerably from country to country.

Favoring a world brand

An increasing number of firms have created **world brand** products that are manufactured, packaged, and positioned in exactly the same way regardless of the country in which they are sold. It is quite natural for a "world class" upscale brand of wristwatches such as Patek Philippe to create a global or uniform advertising campaign to reach its sophisticated worldwide target market. Although the advertising copy is in specific target languages, one might speculate that many of Patek Philippe's affluent target customers do read and write English. Nevertheless, to maximize their "comfort zone," it is appropriate to speak to them in their native languages.

Marketers of products with a wide or almost mass-market appeal have also embraced a world branding strategy. For instance, multinational companies, such as General Motors, Gillette, Estée Lauder, Unilever, and Fiat, have each moved from a local strategy of nation-by-nation advertising to a global advertising strategy.

Still other marketers selectively use a world branding strategy. For example, you might think that Procter & Gamble (P&G), which markets hundreds of brands worldwide, is a company with an abundance of world brands. Recently, though, it was revealed that of its 16 largest brands, only three are truly global brands—Always/Whisper, Pringles, and Pantene. Some of P&G's other brands, such as Pampers, Tide/Ariel, Safeguard, and Oil of Olay, are just starting to establish common positioning in the world market.[35]

Are global brands different?

According to a 12 nation consumer research project, global brands are viewed differently than local brands, and consumers, worldwide, associate global brands with three characteristics: *quality signal*, *global myth*, and *social responsibility*. First, consumers believe that the more people who purchase a brand, the higher the brand's quality (which often results in a global brand being able to command a premium price). Still further, consumers worldwide believe that global brands develop new products and breakthrough technologies at a faster pace than local brands. The second characteristic, global myth, refers to the fact that consumers view global brands as a kind of "cultural ideals," and their purchase and use makes the consumer feel like a citizen of the world, and gives them an identity (i.e., "*Local brands show what we are; global brands show what we want to be*"). Finally, global companies are held to a higher level of corporate social responsibility than local brands, and are expected to respond to social problems associated with what they sell. For the 12 nations studied in this research, the importance of these three dimensions was consistent, and accounted for 64 percent of the variation in the overall brand preferences (quality signal accounts for 44 percent of the explanation, global myth accounts for 12 percent of the explanation, and social responsibility accounts for 8 percent of the explanation).[36]

Additionally, while there was not much variation across the 12 nations studied, there were intracountry differences, which resulted in the conclusion that there were four major segments in each country with respect to how its citizens view global brands. *Global Citizens* (55 percent of the total respondents) use a company's global success as an indication of product quality and innovativeness, and are also concerned that the firm acts in a socially responsible manner. *Global Dreamers* (23 percent of the total respondents) view global brands as quality products, and are not particularly concerned about the social responsible issue. *Antiglobals* (13 percent of the total respondents) feel that global brands are higher quality than local brands, but they dislike brands that preach U.S. values and do not trust global companies to act responsibly. Generally, they try to avoid purchasing global brands. Lastly, *Global Agnostics* (8%) evaluate global brands in the same way they evaluate local brands.[37]

Multinational reactions to brand extensions

Just because a brand may be global in character does not mean that consumers around the world will necessarily respond similarly to a brand extension. A recent study examined reactions to brand extensions among Western culture (U.S.) and Eastern culture (India) consumers, hypothesizing that the Eastern holistic way of thinking (which focuses on the relationships between objects), rather than the Western analytic style of thinking (which focuses on the attributes or parts of objects and on category-based induction) would affect the manner in which consumers judge the "fit" of a brand extension. Indeed, the research results confirmed this hypothesis—low-fit extensions (McDonald's chocolate bar and Coke popcorn) received more positive evaluations from the Eastern culture subjects, while moderate-fit extensions (Kodak greeting cards and Mercedes Benz watches) garnered equal responses from both cultural groups. For the Eastern culture participants, liking Coke products, and the fact that Coke and popcorn were complementary products, in that they can be consumed together, was enough to make the brand extension acceptable. The American subjects, in contrast, saw little product class similarity between Coke and popcorn.[38]

Adaptive global marketing

In contrast to the marketing communication strategy that stresses a common message, some firms embrace a strategy that adapts their advertising messages to the specific values of particular cultures. McDonald's is an example of a firm that tries to localize its advertising and other marketing communications to consumers in each of the cross-cultural markets in which it operates, making it a "glocal" company. For example, the Ronald McDonald that we all know has been renamed Donald McDonald in Japan, because the Japanese language does not contain the "R" sound. Additionally, the McDonald's menu in Japan has been localized to include corn soup and green tea milkshakes.[39] And in Sweden McDonald's developed a new package using woodcut illustrations and a softer design to appeal to the interest the consumers of that nation have in food value and the outdoors.[40]

Like McDonald's, Levi's and Reebok also tend to follow multilocal strategies that calculate cultural differences in creating brand images for their products. For instance, Levi's tends to position its jeans to American consumers, stressing a social-group image, whereas it uses a much more individualistic, sexual image when communicating with European consumers.[41] Still further, Yahoo!, one of the most successful Web sites on the Internet, modifies both its content and communications for each of its 23 country-specific Web sites. Moreover, in a number of Coke's 140-plus markets, what we know as Diet Coke is called Coca-Cola Light, because the word *diet* has an undesirable connotation or no relevance.[42] Similarly, Coke's best-selling beverage in Japan is not Coke Classic—it's Georgia Coffee—packaged in a can and available in more than 10 versions (e.g., black, black with sugar, with milk and sugar, and so on). Other marketers, too, feel that the world brand concept may be going too far. Specifically, when it comes to the marketing of Tiger Woods, one of the premier golfers of our time. In the United States, he is seen as an example of African American success, in Asia he is a sports star with Asian heritage, and in Europe he is seen as a great young athlete who regularly beats older golfers.[43]

When it comes to the design of e-commerce Web sites, a five-nation research study suggests that consumers react best when content is adapted to their local needs. While in the past some companies felt that local adaptation involved no more than simply translating Web pages into the local language, it is now felt that special attention must also be paid to a number of other factors, including local time and date formats, units of measurement, addresses and telephone numbers, layout and orientation of Web pages, icons, symbols, color, and aesthetics.[44] Still further, one study of American and German Internet users reveals that German users were more likely to withhold or alter personal information on the Internet than American users. Analysis suggests that the German personality has a large private space and a small public space, which translates into a great sense of personal privacy; whereas the opposite is true of the American personality.[45]

Combining global and local marketing strategies

Some firms follow a mixed or combination strategy. For instance, Unilever, Playtex, and Black & Decker have augmented their global strategies with local executions. In taking such an adaptive approach, global advertisers with a knowledge of cross-cultural differences can tailor their supplemental messages more effectively to suit individual local markets. For example, a study has indicated that while U.S. consumers focus more on the product-related claims made in advertisements, Taiwanese consumers focus more on the appropriateness of the ad, such as its aesthetic qualities.[46] There is also some evidence to suggest that Spanish ads may contain a larger proportion of affiliation appeals than U.S. ads do because of Spain's cultural inclination toward femininity in its societal norms (U.S. societal norms tend to reflect masculinity).[47] Because concepts and words often do not easily translate and many regions of the country have their own language, advertisements in China are likely to be more effective if they rely heavily on symbols rather than text.[48] A recent study dealing with visual standardization in print ads concluded that "the standardized approach to global advertising may be able to convey a degree of uniformity in meaning when relying on visually explicit messages. . . . This suggests that there is an ability to create a general consensus of meaning across various cultures by using strong visual images whose fundamental message is highly apparent."[49] It is also important to note that consumers in different countries of the world have vastly different amounts of exposure to advertisements. For instance, the daily amount of advertising aimed at Japanese consumers, at almost $6 a day, is 14 times the amount aimed at the average Laotian consumer over the course of an entire year.[50]

A recent study of foreign advertisers in China found that 11 percent employed a standardized (or global) strategy, 12 percent used a localized strategy, and the remaining 77 percent favored a combination strategy. Of the seven advertising components that were studied, localizing language to blend with the local culture was considered to be the most important, followed by the need to localize product attributes, models, colors of ads, humor, scenic background, and music.[51] Additionally, it has been reported that many of the Western companies that have not been successful in China have acted as if what had worked well in other parts of the world would also prove successful in China. This is a too common mistake.

Perhaps the latest creative hotbed for advertising is Thailand, a nation that generally requires a different advertising focus than most other countries. While over 90 percent of the population is literate, Thais tend not to read as a leisure activity. Consequently, advertisements are designed to visually catch the attention of consumers, and are typically original, humorous, and often slapstick. An example is an ad in which Coke is paired with kung fu, which is not how Coke would be advertised in other markets.[52]

Frameworks for assessing multinational strategies

Multinational marketers face the challenge of creating marketing and advertising programs capable of communicating effectively with a diversity of target markets. To assist in this imposing task, various frameworks have been developed to determine the degree to which marketing and advertising efforts should be either globalized or localized, or mixed or combined.

To enable international marketers to assess the positions their products enjoy in specific foreign markets, Table 13.7 presents a five-stage continuum that ranges from mere awareness of a foreign brand in a local market area to complete global identification of the brand; that is, the brand is accepted "as is" in almost every market, and consumers do not think about its country of origin—"it belongs."

Table 13.8 presents a framework that focuses on four marketing strategies available to a firm contemplating doing business on a global basis. A firm might decide either to standardize or localize its product and either standardize or localize its communications program (thus forming a two-by-two matrix). The four possibilities that this decision framework considers range from a company incorporating a **global strategy** (or standardizing both product and communications program) to developing a completely **local strategy** (or customizing both the product and communications program) for each unique market. In the middle there are two *mixed strategies*. All four cells may represent growth opportunities for the firm. To determine which cell represents the firm's best strategy, the marketer must conduct cross-cultural consumer analysis to obtain consumer reactions to alternative product and promotional executions. To illustrate the strategic importance of product uniformity, Frito-Lay, the U.S. snack-food giant, has been standardizing quality and reducing the many local brand names of potato chip companies that it owns throughout the world. This effort is moving the company along a common global visual appearance that features the Lay's logo as a global brand. Its efforts are driven by research that reveals that potato chips are a snack food that has widespread appeal throughout much of the world.[53]

Another orientation for assessing whether to use a global versus local marketing strategy concentrates on a high-tech to high-touch continuum. **Product standardization** appears to be most successful for high-involvement products that approach either end of the high-tech/high-touch continuum. In other words, products that are at either extreme are more suitable for positioning as global brands. In contrast, low-involvement products in the midrange of the high-tech/high-touch continuum are more suitably marketed as local brands, using market-by-market executions.[54] To illustrate, on a worldwide basis, consumers interested in high-involvement, high-tech products share a common language (such as "bytes" and "microprocessors"), whereas advertisements for high-involvement, high-touch products tend to use more emotional appeals and to emphasize visual images. In either case, according to this perspective (high-involvement products that are either high-tech or high-touch), such products are candidates for global promotional communications.

Some researchers have written that globalization (or standardization) and localization should be viewed as two ends of a continuum and that often the key to success is to "be global but act local." It is also generally an error to assume that demographic segments in other nations would want to be or act like Americans. When looking for success in a foreign

TABLE 13.7	A Product Recognition Continuum for Multinational Marketing
FACTORS	**EXAMPLES**
Stage One	Local consumers have heard or read of a brand marketed elsewhere but cannot get it at home; a brand is "alien" and unavailable but may be desirable [e.g., Rover (English autos), Havana cigars (made in Cuba), or medicine not approved by the FDA but sold in Europe].
Stage Two	Local consumers view a brand made elsewhere as "foreign," made in a particular country but locally available (e.g., Saab autos, French wine). The fact that the brand is foreign makes a difference in the consumer's mind, sometimes favorable, sometimes not.
Stage Three	Local consumers accord imported brand "national status"; that is, its national origin is known but does not affect their choice (e.g., Molson beer in the United States, Ford autos in southern Europe).
Stage Four	Brand owned by a foreign company is made (wholly or partly) domestically and has come to be perceived by locals as a local brand; its foreign origins may be remembered but the brand has been "adopted" ("naturalized"). Examples are Sony in the United States, Coca-Cola in Europe and Japan.
Stage Five	Brand has lost national identity and consumers everywhere see it as "borderless" or global; not only can people not identify where it comes from but they never ask this question. Examples include the Associated Press and CNN news services, Nescafé, Bayer aspirin.

Source: Adapted from George V. Priovolos, "How to Turn National European Brands into Pan-European Brands." Working paper. Hagan School of Business, Iona College, New Rochelle, NY.

TABLE 13.8	A Framework for Alternative Global Marketing Strategies	
PRODUCT STRATEGY	**COMMUNICATION STRATEGY**	
	Standardized Communications	**Localized Communications**
Standardized Product	**Global Strategy:** Uniform Product/ Uniform Message	**Mixed Strategy:** Uniform Product/ Customized Message
Localized Product	**Mixed Strategy:** Customized Product/ Uniform Message	**Local Strategy:** Customized Product/ Customized Message

market, it has been suggested that a company should remember the following 3 P's—place, people, and product. Table 13.9 presents the specific elements of these 3 P's and cites the appropriate marketing strategy when using a standardization approach and when using a localization approach.[55]

TABLE 13.9	Degree of Fit Between Marketing Strategies and the 3 P's		
		MARKETING STRATEGIES	
THE 3 P'S	**SPECIFIC ELEMENTS**	**STANDARDIZATION**	**LOCALIZATION**
Place	Economy	Prosperous	Struggling
	Partners	Few	Plentiful
	Competition	Low	Intense
People	Tastes	Little preference	High preference
	Sophistication	High	Low
	Segments	Few	Many
	Classification	Industrial/consumer durables	Consumer nondurables
Products	Technology	High	Low
	Culture bound	Low	High
	Reputation	Sterling	Poor or unknown
	Product perception	High	Low

Source: Sangeeta Ramarapu, John E. Timmerman, and Narender Ramarapu, "Choosing Between Globalization and Localization as a Strategic Thrust for Your International Marketing Effort," *Journal of Marketing Theory and Practice* 7, no. 2 (Spring 1999): 101. Reprinted by permission.

When marketing high-tech products abroad, it is important to note that many industrialized nations lag behind the United States in computer usage. For example, although more than 90 percent of U.S. white-collar workers use a PC, only 55 percent of Western European white-collar workers do so. Often the goal in many European firms is to rise to a high enough position in the company so you do not have to use a PC (i.e., not using a PC as a status symbol).[56] Moreover, approximately 68 percent of all existing Web pages are in English, 6 percent are in Japanese, 6 percent are in German, and 4 percent are in Chinese (these are the top four languages on the Internet).[57]

Perhaps because of the dominance of English-language pages on the Internet, specific non–English-speaking European nations appear to be out to distinguish themselves and their cultures by designing Web sites that in some way or other reflect their countries and specific cultures. So German Web sites might employ bright colors and a geometrical layout to give it a "German feel"; a French Web site might have a black background; a Dutch Web site might offer video downloads; and a Scandinavian Web site might provide a variety of images of nature.[58] Indeed, a recent study of global American brands examined how these brands standardize their Web sites in Europe (U.K., France, Germany, and Spain). The study found that while manufacturers' Web sites did have a minimal level of uniformity with respect to color, logo, and layout, the textual information and visual images were dissimilar from one market to the next. Still further, as with traditional advertising media, standardization for durable goods was higher than for nondurables.[59] In yet another study, researchers examined the domestic and Chinese Web sites of U.S.-based multinational companies. Findings show that the Internet is not a culturally neutral medium, but is full of cultural markers that allow country-specific Web sites to possess a feel and a look that is unique to the local culture. For example, while Web sites intended for the U.S. consumer often contained patriotic phrases and references to September 11th, Chinese Web sites were loaded with Chinese cultural symbols (e.g., the Great Wall of China, Chinese festivals). The managerial implication of the research is that consumers relate best to Web sites that have a local feel because it reduces the anxiety associated with the Internet (it is a relatively new medium) and makes navigation easier.[60]

chapter **14**

> **Consumer Motivation and Decision Making**

Consumer motivation

Human needs—consumer needs—are the basis of all modern marketing. Needs are the essence of the marketing concept. The key to a company's survival, profitability, and growth in a highly competitive marketplace is its ability to identify and satisfy unfulfilled consumer needs better and sooner than the competition.

Marketers do not create needs, though in some instances they may make consumers more keenly aware of unfelt needs. Successful marketers define their markets in terms of the needs they presume to satisfy, not in terms of the products they sell. This is a market-oriented, rather than a production-oriented, approach to marketing. A marketing orientation focuses on the needs of the buyer; a production orientation focuses on the needs of the seller. The marketing concept implies that the manufacturer will make only what it knows people will buy; a production orientation implies that the manufacturer will try to sell whatever it decides to make.

The philosophy and marketing strategy of Charles Revson, the builder of the Revlon cosmetics empire, depict an insightful understanding of consumer needs. Charles Revson started by manufacturing nail polish, but he defined nail polish as a fashion accessory and not merely a nail covering. His strategy was designed to induce women to use different shades of nail polish to match different outfits, moods, and occasions. This approach vastly broadened the market for the product, because it persuaded women to buy and use many different colors of nail polish in the same season rather than wait to finish one bottle before buying another one. And Revson ensured that women would buy more and more bottles of nail polish by introducing new nail color fashions every season. Emulating GM's strategy of planned obsolescence (i.e., introducing new automobile models every year), Revlon would introduce new nail colors every fall and spring and, through heavy and effective advertising, would persuade women that buying the new colors would satisfy their needs to appear fashionable and attractive.[1]

Similar to GM's segmentation strategy, Revson developed separate cosmetic lines targeting different consumer segments, such as the popularly priced *Revlon* (which Revson equated with the positioning of the Pontiac), *Natural Wonder* (targeting the youth market), and *Marcella Borghese* (positioned as the high-class line with international "flavor"). Most importantly, Revson understood that he was not selling women the physical product (e.g., nail lacquer to cover their nails) but the fantasy that the nail polish would attract attention and bestow class and glamour on the user. Thus, Revson did not sell deep red polish; he sold *Fire and Ice*. He did not sell dark red polish; he sold *Berry Bon Bon*. Charles Revson summed up his philosophy by saying "In the factory, we make cosmetics; in the store, we sell hope." And selling hope, rather than the physical product known as cosmetics, allowed Revson to charge much more for his products. Rather than compete with other manufacturers on the basis of price, Revson competed on the basis of perceived quality and greater satisfaction of women's needs for fantasy and attention.[2]

Savvy companies define their missions in terms of the consumer needs they satisfy rather than the products they produce and sell. Because consumers' basic needs do not change but the products that satisfy them do, a corporate focus on developing products that will satisfy consumers' needs ensures that the company stays in the forefront of the search for new and effective solutions. By doing so, such companies are likely to survive and grow despite strong competition or adverse economic conditions. On the other hand, companies that define themselves in terms of the products they make may suffer or even go out of business when their products are replaced by competitive offerings that better satisfy the same need. Table 14.1 includes examples of companies that define themselves as need-oriented rather than product-oriented.

This chapter discusses basic needs that operate in most people to motivate behavior. It explores the influence that such needs have on consumption behavior. Later chapters explain why and how these basic human needs, or motives, are expressed in so many diverse ways.

TABLE 14.1	Companies Can Define Themselves as Product-Oriented versus Need-Oriented	
	PRODUCT-ORIENTED	**NEED-ORIENTED**
Pfizer	We make pharmaceuticals.	"We dedicate ourselves to humanity's quest for longer, healthier, happier lives through innovation in pharmaceutical, consumer, and animal health products." (**www.pfizer.com**)
Logitech	We make cameras and PC tracking devices.	"Logitech designs, manufactures and markets personal peripherals that enable people to effectively work, play, and communicate in the digital world. The company's products combine essential core technologies, continuing innovation, award-winning industrial design and excellent price performance." (**www.logitech.com**)
Ritz-Carlton	We rent rooms and provide facilities for meetings and events.	The company's credo stresses the genuine care and comfort of the guests, the finest personal service and facilities, a warm yet refined ambience, and an experience that fulfills even the unexpressed needs and wishes of the guests. (**www.ritzcarlton.com**)

Motivation as a psychological force

Motivation is the *driving force within individuals that impels them to action.* This driving force is produced by a state of tension, which exists as the result of an unfulfilled need. Individuals strive both consciously and subconsciously to reduce this tension through behavior that they anticipate will fulfill their needs and thus relieve them of the stress they feel. The specific goals they select and the patterns of action they undertake to achieve their goals are the results of individual thinking and learning. Figure 14.1 presents a model of the motivational process. It portrays motivation as a state of need-induced tension that "drives" the individual to engage in behavior that he or she believes will satisfy the need and thus reduce the tension. Whether gratification is actually achieved depends on the course of action pursued. The specific goals that consumers wish to achieve and the courses of action they take to attain these goals are selected on the basis of their thinking processes (cognition) and previous learning (e.g., experience). Therefore, marketers must view motivation as the force that induces consumption and, through consumption experiences, the process of consumer learning.

Needs

Every individual has needs: some are innate, others are acquired. **Innate needs** are physiological (i.e., *biogenic*); they include the needs for food, water, air, clothing, shelter, and sex. Because they are needed to sustain biological life, the biogenic needs are considered **primary needs** or motives.

Acquired needs are needs that we learn in response to our culture or environment. These may include needs for self-esteem, prestige, affection, power, and learning. Because acquired needs are generally psychological (i.e., *psychogenic*), they are considered **secondary needs** or motives. They result from the individual's subjective psychological state

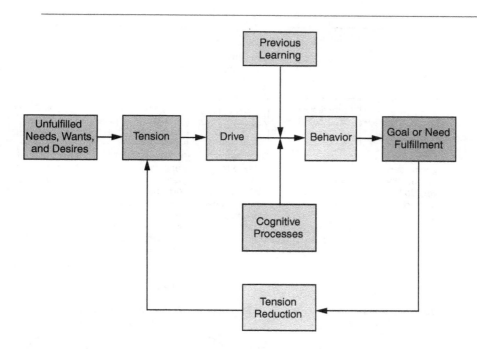

FIGURE 14.1

**Model of the
Motivation Process**

Source: From Jeffrey F. Dugree et al., "Observations: Translating Values into Product Wants," *Journal of Advertising Research,* 36, 6 (November 1996). Reprinted by permission of the *Journal of the American Marketing Association.*

and from relationships with others. For example, all individuals need shelter from the elements; thus, finding a place to live fulfills an important primary need for a newly transferred executive. However, the kind of home she rents or buys may be the result of secondary needs. She may seek a place in which she and her husband can entertain large groups of people (and fulfill social needs); she may want to live in an exclusive community to impress her friends and family (and fulfill ego needs). The place where an individual ultimately chooses to live thus may serve to fulfill both primary and secondary needs.

Goals

Goals are the sought-after results of motivated behavior. As Figure 14.1 indicated, all behavior is goal oriented. Our discussion of motivation in this chapter is in part concerned with **generic goals**, that is, the general classes or categories of goals that consumers see as a means to fulfill their needs. If a student tells his parents that he wants to become a medical doctor, he has stated a generic goal. If he says he wants to get an M.D. degree from UCLA, he has expressed a **product-specific goal**. Marketers are particularly concerned with product-specific goals, that is, the specifically branded products and services that consumers select for goal fulfillment.

Individuals set goals on the basis of their personal values, and they select means (or behaviors) that they believe will help them achieve their desired goals. Figures 14.2 A, B, and C depict a framework of the goal structure behind losing weight and maintaining weight loss and the results of a study based on this model. Figure 14.2A depicts an overall framework for pursuing consumption-related goals. Figure 14.2B depicts the interrelationship among the needs driving the goal of losing weight (e.g., increased self-confidence, looking and feeling better, and living longer) and the behaviors required to achieve the goal (i.e., exercising and/or dieting). Figure 14.2C depicts the complex nature of goal setting based on subjects' responses to questions regarding their reasons for selecting weight loss as a goal, providing justification for each reason, and explaining each justification.[3] The three diagrams together depict the complexity of goal setting and the difficulties in understanding this process through a set theoretical model. Figure 14.3

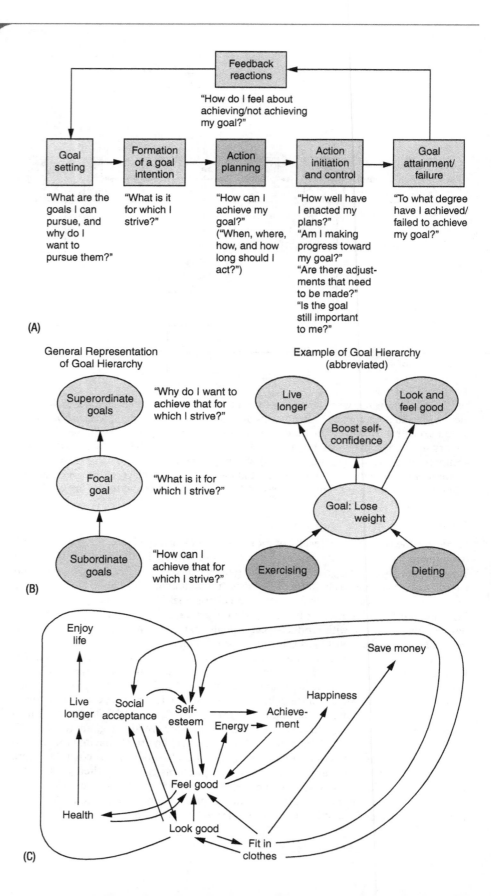

FIGURE 14.2

The Needs and Goals Behind Losing or Maintaining Body Weight

Source: From "Goal Setting and Goal Pursuit in the Regulation of Body Weight," by Richard Bagozzi and Elizabeth Edwards originally published in *Psychology and Health, 13,* 1998. Reprinted by permission of Taylor & Francis Ltd., www.tandf.co.uk/journals.

depicts an ad that portrays subscribing to a health magazine as a means to achieve several physical appearance-related goals.

The selection of goals

For any given need, there are many different and appropriate goals. The goals selected by individuals depend on their personal experiences, physical capacity, prevailing cultural norms and values, and the goal's accessibility in the physical and social environment. For example, a young woman may wish to get a deep, even tan and may envision spending time in the sun as a way to achieve her goal. However, if her dermatologist advises her to avoid direct exposure to the sun, she may settle for a self-tanning cosmetic product instead. The goal object has to be both socially acceptable and physically accessible. If cosmetic companies did not offer effective alternatives to tanning in the sun, our young woman would have to either ignore the advice of her dermatologist or select a substitute goal, such as untanned (but undamaged) youthful-looking skin.

An individual's personal characteristics and own perception of self also influence the specific goals selected. Research on personal goal orientation distinguished two types of people: (1) persons with *promotion focus* are interested in their growth and development, have more hopes and aspirations and favor the presence of positive outcomes; (2) persons with a *prevention focus* are interested in safety and security, are more concerned with duties and obligations and favor the absence of negative outcomes. One study found that, in forming consumption-related goals, consumers with a prevention focus favored the status quo and inaction over action.[4] Another study distinguished between two types of goals: (1) **ideals**, which represent hopes, wishes, and aspirations; and (2) **oughts**, which represent duties, obligations, and responsibilities. The study showed that people concerned with *ideals* relied more on feelings and affects in evaluating advertisements, while people more concerned with *oughts* relied more heavily on the substantive and factual contents of ads.[5] In yet another study, some consumers were led to believe that they obtained a discount in the purchase price of a PC because of their good negotiating skills and were encouraged to feel proud, while others were led to believe that they received the discount because the computer was on sale and were not encouraged to feel proud. In addition, the goals that the consumers were encouraged to believe they had obtained were stated as either gains (i.e., promotion goals) or the avoidance of losses (i.e., prevention goals). The study showed that people who felt proud of their negotiating skills and also believed that they avoided losses were less likely to repurchase the product than persons who felt proud and also believed that they had achieved gains. For the people who did not feel proud, the type of goals they believed they had accomplished had no impact on intentions to repurchase the product.[6]

Goals are also related to negative forms of consumption behavior. One study found that personal goals that focus on extrinsic benefits (such as financial success, social status, and being attractive to others) are associated with higher degrees of compulsive buying than goals that stress intrinsic benefits (such as self-acceptance, affiliation, and connection with community).[7] These studies illustrate the complexity of the ways consumers conceptualize goals and the impact of set or achieved goals on consumption behavior.

Interdependence of needs and goals

Needs and goals are interdependent; neither exists without the other. However, people are often not as aware of their needs as they are of their goals. For example, a teenager may not consciously be aware of his social needs but may join a number of chat groups online to meet new friends. A person may not consciously be aware of a power need but may choose to run for public office when an elective position becomes available. A college student may not consciously recognize her need for achievement but may strive to attain a straight A grade point average.

Individuals are usually somewhat more aware of their *physiological* needs than they are of their *psychological* needs. Most people know when they are hungry, thirsty, or cold, and they take appropriate steps to satisfy these needs. The same people may not consciously be aware of their needs for acceptance, self-esteem, or status. They may, however, subconsciously engage in behavior that satisfies their psychological (acquired) needs.

Positive and negative motivation

Motivation can be **positive** or **negative** in direction. We may feel a driving force *toward* some object or condition or a driving force *away* from some object or condition. For example, a person may be impelled toward a restaurant to fulfill a hunger need, and away from motorcycle transportation to fulfill a safety need.

Some psychologists refer to positive drives as needs, wants, or desires and to negative drives as fears or aversions. However, although positive and negative motivational forces seem to differ dramatically in terms of physical (and sometimes emotional) activity, they are basically similar in that both serve to initiate and sustain human behavior. For this reason, researchers often refer to both kinds of drives or motives as *needs, wants*, and *desires*. Some theorists distinguish *wants* from *needs* by defining wants as product-specific needs. Others differentiate between desires, on the one hand, and needs and wants on the other. Thus, there is no uniformly accepted distinction among the terms needs, wants, and desires.

Needs, wants, or desires may lead to goals that can be positive or negative. A positive goal is one toward which behavior is directed; thus, it is often referred to as an **approach object**. A negative goal is one from which behavior is directed away and is referred to as an **avoidance object**. Because both approach and avoidance goals are the results of motivated behavior, most researchers refer to both simply as *goals*. Consider this example: A middle-aged woman with a positive goal of fitness may join a health club to work out regularly. Her husband, who views getting fat as a negative goal, joins a health club to guide his exercise. In the former case, the wife's actions are designed to achieve the *positive* goal of health and fitness; in the latter case, her husband's actions are designed to avoid a *negative* goal—a flabby physique.

Rational versus emotional motives

Some consumer behaviorists distinguish between so-called **rational motives** and **emotional motives**. They use the term *rationality* in the traditional economic sense, which assumes that consumers behave rationally by carefully considering all alternatives and choosing those that give them the greatest utility. In a marketing context, the term *rationality* implies that consumers select goals based on totally objective criteria, such as size, weight, price, or miles per gallon. Emotional motives imply the selection of goals according to personal or subjective criteria (e.g., pride, fear, affection, or status).

The assumption underlying this distinction is that subjective or emotional criteria do not maximize utility or satisfaction. However, it is reasonable to assume that consumers always attempt to select alternatives that, in their view, serve to best satisfy their needs. Obviously, the assessment of satisfaction is a very personal process, based on the individual's own need structure, as well as on past behavioral and social (or learned) experiences. What may appear irrational to an outside observer may be perfectly rational in the context of the consumer's own psychological field. For example, a person who pursues extensive facial cosmetic surgery in order to appear younger uses significant economic resources (e.g., hefty surgical fees, time lost in recovery, inconvenience, and the risk that something may go wrong) to achieve her goal. To that person, undergoing the surgery, and expending the considerable financial and physical costs required, are perfectly rational decisions to achieve her goal. However, to many other persons within the same culture who are less concerned with aging, and to persons from other cultures that are not so preoccupied with personal appearance, these decisions appear completely irrational.

The dynamics of motivation

Motivation is a highly dynamic construct that is constantly changing in reaction to life experiences. Needs and goals change and grow in response to an individual's physical condition, environment, interactions with others, and experiences. As individuals attain their goals, they develop new ones. If they do not attain their goals, they continue to strive for old goals or they develop substitute goals. Some of the reasons why need-driven human activity never ceases include the following: (1) Many needs are never fully satisfied; they continually impel actions designed to attain or maintain satisfaction. (2) As needs become satisfied, new and higher-order needs emerge that cause tension and induce activity. (3) People who achieve their goals set new and higher goals for themselves.

Needs are never fully satisfied

Most human needs are never fully or permanently satisfied. For example, at fairly regular intervals throughout each day individuals experience hunger needs that must be satisfied. Most people regularly seek companionship and approval from others to satisfy their social needs. Even more complex psychological needs are rarely fully satisfied. For example, a person may partially satisfy a need for power by working as administrative assistant to a local politician, but this vicarious taste of power may not sufficiently satisfy her need; thus, she may strive to work for a state legislator or even to run for political office herself. In this instance, temporary goal achievement does not adequately satisfy the need for power, and the individual strives ever harder to more fully satisfy that need.

New needs emerge as old needs are satisfied

Some motivational theorists believe that a hierarchy of needs exists and that new, higher-order needs emerge as lower-order needs are fulfilled.[8] For example, a man whose basic physiological needs (e.g., food, housing, etc.) are fairly well satisfied may turn his efforts to achieving acceptance among his neighbors by joining their political clubs and supporting their candidates. Once he is confident that he has achieved acceptance, he then may seek recognition by giving lavish parties or building a larger house. Marketers must be attuned to changing needs.

Success and failure influence goals

A number of researchers have explored the nature of the goals that individuals set for themselves. Broadly speaking, they have concluded that individuals who successfully achieve their goals usually set new and higher goals for themselves; that is, they raise their **levels of aspiration**. This may be due to the fact that their success in reaching lower goals makes them more confident of their ability to reach higher goals. Conversely, those who do not reach their goals sometimes lower their levels of aspiration.[9] Thus, goal selection is often a function of success and failure. For example, a college senior who is not accepted into medical school may try instead to become a dentist or a podiatrist.

The nature and persistence of an individual's behavior are often influenced by expectations of success or failure in reaching certain goals. Those expectations, in turn, are often based on past experience. A person who takes good snapshots with an inexpensive camera may be motivated to buy a more sophisticated camera in the belief that it will enable him to take even better photographs, and eventually he may upgrade his camera by several hundred dollars. On the other hand, a person who has not been able to take good photographs is just as likely to keep the same camera or even to lose all interest in photography.

These effects of success and failure on goal selection have strategy implications for marketers. Goals should be reasonably attainable. Advertisements should not promise more than the product will deliver. Products and services are often evaluated by the size and direction of the gap between consumer expectations and objective performance. Thus, even a good product will not be repurchased if it fails to live up to unrealistic expectations created by ads that "overpromise." Similarly, a consumer is likely to regard a mediocre product with greater satisfaction than it warrants if its performance exceeds her expectations.

Substitute goals

When an individual cannot attain a specific goal or type of goal that he or she anticipates will satisfy certain needs, behavior may be directed to a **substitute goal**. Although the substitute goal may not be as satisfactory as the primary goal, it may be sufficient to dispel uncomfortable tension. Continued deprivation of a primary goal may result in the substitute goal assuming primary-goal status. For example, a woman who has stopped drinking whole milk because she is dieting may actually begin to prefer skim milk. A man who cannot afford a BMW may convince himself that a new sporty Chrysler Sebring has an image he clearly prefers.

Frustration

Failure to achieve a goal often results in feelings of frustration. At one time or another, everyone has experienced the frustration that comes from the inability to attain a goal. The barrier that prevents attainment of a goal may be personal to the individual (e.g., limited physical or financial resources) or an obstacle in the physical or social environment (e.g., a storm that causes the postponement of a long-awaited vacation). Regardless of the cause, individuals react differently to frustrating situations. Some people manage to cope by finding their way around the obstacle or, if that fails, by selecting a substitute goal. Others are less adaptive and may regard their inability to achieve a goal as a personal failure. Such people are likely to adopt a defense mechanism to protect their egos from feelings of inadequacy. The creation of a new type of children's board game represents a creative response to the concept of frustration. Unlike most board games, where a child who has lost may be frustrated and subject to the ridicule of other children, the new game is centered on skill-building activities and provides every child with a chance to shine. While the game is built on a "nobody loses" concept, the designers have carefully built in an element of competition because a complete lack of competition may make a game seem boring.[10]

Defense mechanisms

People who cannot cope with frustration often mentally redefine their frustrating situations in order to protect their self-images and self-esteem. For example, a young woman may yearn for a European vacation she cannot afford. The coping individual may select a less expensive vacation trip to Disneyland or to a national park. The person who cannot cope may react with anger toward her boss for not paying her enough money to afford the vacation she prefers, or she may persuade herself that Europe is unseasonably warm this year. These last two possibilities are examples, respectively, of *aggression* and *rationalization*, **defense mechanisms** that people sometimes adopt to protect their egos from feelings of failure when they do not attain their goals. Other defense mechanisms include *regression, withdrawal, projection, daydreaming, identification*, and *repression*. These defense mechanisms are described in Table 14.2. This listing of defense mechanisms is far from exhaustive, because individuals tend to develop their own ways of redefining frustrating situations to protect their self-esteem from the anxieties that result from experiencing failure. Marketers often consider this fact in their selection of advertising appeals and construct advertisements that portray a person resolving a particular frustration through the use of the advertised product.

TABLE 14.2	Defense Mechanisms
DEFENSE MECHANISM	**DESCRIPTION AND ILLUSTRATIONS**
Aggression	In response to frustration, individuals may resort to aggressive behavior in attempting to protect their self-esteem. The tennis pro who slams his tennis racket to the ground when disappointed with his game or the baseball player who physically intimidates an empire for his call are examples of such conduct. So are consumer boycotts of companies or stores.
Rationalization	People sometimes resolve frustration by inventing plausible reasons for being unable to attain their goals (e.g., not having enough time to practice) or deciding that the goal is not really worth pursuing (e.g., how important is it to achieve a high bowling score?).
Regression	An individual may react to a frustrating situation with childish or immature behavior. A shopper attending a bargain sale, for example, may fight over merchandise and even rip a garment that another shopper will not relinquish rather than allow the other person to have it.
Withdrawal	Frustration may be resolved by simply withdrawing from the situation. For instance, a person who has difficulty achieving officer status in an organization may decide he can use his time more constructively in other activities and simply quit that organization.
Projection	An individual may redefine a frustrating situation by projecting blame for his or her own failures and inabilities on other objects or persons. Thus, the golfer who misses a stroke may blame his golf clubs or his caddy.
Daydreaming	Daydreaming, or fantasizing, enables the individual to attain imaginary gratification of unfulfilled needs. A person who is shy and lonely, for example, may daydream about a romantic love affair.
Identification	People resolve feelings of frustration by subconsciously identifying with other persons or situations that they consider relevant. For example, slice-of-life commercials often portray a stereotypical situation in which an individual experiences a frustration and then overcomes the problem by using the advertised product. If the viewer can identify with the frustrating situation, he or she may very likely adopt the proposed solution and buy the product advertised.
Repression	Another way that individuals avoid the tension arising from frustration is by repressing the unsatisfied need. Thus, individuals may "force" the need out of their conscious awareness. Sometimes repressed needs manifest themselves indirectly. The wife who is unable to bear children may teach school or work in a library; her husband may do volunteer work in a boys' club. The manifestation of repressed needs in a socially acceptable form is called *sublimation*, another type of defense mechanism.

Multiplicity of needs and variation of goals

A consumer's behavior often fulfills more than one need. In fact, it is likely that specific goals are selected because they fulfill several needs. We buy clothing for protection and for a certain degree of modesty; in addition, our clothing fulfills a wide range of personal and social needs, such as acceptance or ego needs.

One cannot accurately infer motives from behavior. People with different needs may seek fulfillment through selection of the same goal; people with the same needs may seek fulfillment through different goals. Consider the following examples. Five people who are active in a neighborhood association may each belong for a different reason. The first may be genuinely concerned with protecting the interests of the neighborhood's residents; the second may be concerned about the possibility of increased crime in the area; the third may seek social contacts from organizational meetings; the fourth may enjoy the power of directing a large group; and the fifth may enjoy the status provided by membership in an attention-getting organization.

Similarly, five people may be driven by the same need (e.g., an ego need) to seek fulfillment in different ways. The first may seek advancement and recognition through a professional career; the second may become active in a political organization; the third may run in regional marathons; the fourth may take professional dance lessons; and the fifth may seek attention by monopolizing classroom discussions.

Realizing that many people have a need to make new friends as well as have a place to live, new apartment buildings in New York City now include such facilities as private parks, entertainment rooms, card rooms, exercise rooms, billiard rooms adjacent to laundry rooms, and other types of common areas that convey a sense of community and facilitate meetings with neighbors.[11]

Arousal of motives

Most of an individual's specific needs are dormant much of the time. The arousal of any particular set of needs at a specific moment in time may be caused by internal stimuli found in the individual's physiological condition, by emotional or cognitive processes, or by stimuli in the outside environment.

Physiological arousal

Bodily needs at any one specific moment in time are based on the individual's physiological condition at that moment. A drop in blood sugar level or stomach contractions will trigger awareness of a hunger need. Secretion of sex hormones will awaken the sex need. A decrease in body temperature will induce shivering, which makes the individual aware of the need for warmth. Most of these physiological cues are involuntary; however, they arouse related needs that cause uncomfortable tensions until they are satisfied. For example, a person who is cold may turn up the heat in his bedroom and also make a mental note to buy a warm cardigan sweater to wear around the house.

Emotional arousal

Sometimes daydreaming results in the arousal or stimulation of latent needs. People who are bored or who are frustrated in trying to achieve their goals often engage in daydreaming (autistic thinking), in which they imagine themselves in all sorts of desirable situations. These thoughts tend to arouse dormant needs, which may produce uncomfortable tensions that drive them into goal-oriented behavior. A young woman who daydreams of a torrid romance may spend her free time in Internet single chat rooms; a young man who dreams of being a famous novelist may enroll in a writing workshop.

Cognitive arousal

Sometimes random thoughts can lead to a cognitive awareness of needs. An advertisement that provides reminders of home might trigger instant yearning to speak with one's parents. This is the basis for many long-distance telephone company campaigns that stress the low cost of international long-distance rates.

Environmental (or situational) arousal

The set of needs an individual experiences at a particular time are often activated by specific cues in the environment. Without these cues, the needs might remain dormant. For example, the 6 o'clock news, the sight or smell of bakery goods, fast-food commercials on television, the end of the school day—all of these may arouse the "need" for food. In such cases, modification of the environment may be necessary to reduce the arousal of hunger.

A most potent form of situational cue is the goal object itself. A woman may experience an overwhelming desire to visit Australia when she is drawn to the scene depicted in a magazine; a man may suddenly experience a "need" for a new car when passing a dealer's display window. Sometimes an advertisement or other environmental cue produces a psychological imbalance in the viewer's mind. For example, a young college student who constantly uses his cell phone may see a new, slick-looking cell phone model with more features displayed in a store window. The exposure may make him unhappy with his old cell phone and cause him to experience tension that will be reduced only when he buys himself the new cell phone model.

When people live in a complex and highly varied environment, they experience many opportunities for need arousal. Conversely, when their environment is poor or deprived, fewer needs are activated. This explains why television has had such a mixed effect on the lives of people in underdeveloped countries. It exposes them to various lifestyles and expensive products that they would not otherwise see, and it awakens wants and desires that they have little opportunity or even hope of satisfying. Thus, while television enriches many lives, it also serves to frustrate people with little money or education or hope, and may result in the adoption of such aggressive defense mechanisms as robbery, boycotts, or even revolts.

There are two opposing philosophies concerned with the arousal of human motives. The **behaviorist school** considers motivation to be a mechanical process; behavior is seen as the response to a stimulus, and elements of conscious thought are ignored. An extreme example of the *stimulus–response* theory of motivation is the impulse buyer who reacts largely to external stimuli in the buying situation. According to this theory, the consumer's cognitive control is limited; he or she does not act but reacts to stimuli in the marketplace (e.g., an ice cream truck on the corner). The **cognitive school** believes that all behavior is directed at goal achievement. Needs and past experiences are reasoned, categorized, and transformed into attitudes and beliefs that act as predispositions focused on helping the individual satisfy needs, and they determine the actions that he or she takes to achieve this satisfaction.

Types and systems of needs

For many years, psychologists and others interested in human behavior have attempted to develop exhaustive lists of human needs. Most lists of human needs tend to be diverse in content as well as in length. Although there is little disagreement about specific physiological needs, there is considerable disagreement about specific psychological (i.e., psychogenic) needs.

In 1938, the psychologist Henry Murray prepared a detailed list of 28 psychogenic needs. This research was probably the first systematic approach to the understanding of nonbiological human needs. Murray believed that everyone has the same basic set of needs but that individuals differ in their priority ranking of these needs. Murray's basic needs include many motives that are assumed to play an important role in consumer behavior, such as acquisition, achievement, recognition, and exhibition (see Table 14.3).

Hierarchy of needs

Dr. Abraham Maslow, a clinical psychologist, formulated a widely accepted theory of human motivation based on the notion of a universal hierarchy of human needs.[12]

TABLE 14.3	Murray's List of Psychogenic Needs

NEEDS ASSOCIATED WITH INANIMATE OBJECTS

Acquisition
Conservancy
Order
Retention
Construction

NEEDS THAT REFLECT AMBITION, POWER, ACCOMPLISHMENT, AND PRESTIGE

Superiority
Achievement
Recognition
Exhibition
Inviolacy (inviolate attitude)
Infavoidance (to avoid shame, failure, humiliation, ridicule)
Defendance (defensive attitude)
Counteraction (counteractive attitude)

NEEDS CONCERNED WITH HUMAN POWER

Dominance
Deferrence
Similance (suggestible attitude)
Autonomy
Contrariance (to act differently from others)

SADOMASOCHISTIC NEEDS

Aggression
Abasement

NEEDS CONCERNED WITH AFFECTION BETWEEN PEOPLE

Affiliation
Rejection
Nurturance (to nourish, aid, or protect the helpless)
Succorance (to seek aid, protection, or sympathy)
Play

NEEDS CONCERNED WITH SOCIAL INTERCOURSE (THE NEEDS TO ASK AND TELL)

Cognizance (inquiring attitude)
Exposition (expositive attitude)

Source: Adapted from Henry A. Murray, "Types of Human Needs," in David C. McClelland, *Studies in Motivation* (New York: Appleton-Century-Crofts, 1955), 63–66. Reprinted by permission of Irvington Publishers, Inc.

Maslow's theory identifies five basic levels of human needs, which rank in order of importance from lower-level (biogenic) needs to higher-level (psychogenic) needs. The theory postulates that individuals seek to satisfy lower-level needs before higher-level needs emerge. The lowest level of chronically unsatisfied need that an individual experiences serves to motivate his or her behavior. When that need is "fairly well" satisfied, a new (and higher) need emerges that the individual is motivated to fulfill. When this need is satisfied, a new (and still higher) need emerges, and so on. Of course, if a lower-level

FIGURE 14.3

Maslow's Hierarchy of Needs

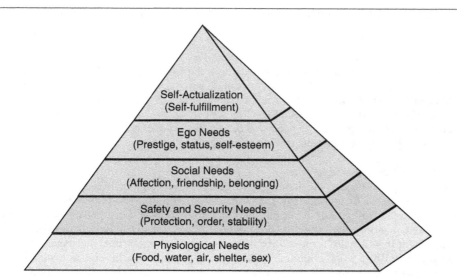

need experiences some renewed deprivation (e.g., thirst), it may temporarily become dominant again.

Figure 14.3 presents a diagram of **Maslow's hierarchy of needs**. For clarity, each level is depicted as mutually exclusive. According to the theory, however, there is some overlap between each level, as no need is ever completely satisfied. For this reason, although all levels of need below the level that is currently dominant continue to motivate behavior to some extent, the prime motivator—the major driving force within the individual— is the lowest level of need that remains largely unsatisfied.

Physiological needs

In the hierarchy-of-needs theory, physiological needs are the first and most basic level of human needs. These needs, which are required to sustain biological life, include food, water, air, shelter, clothing, sex—all the biogenic needs, in fact, that were listed as primary needs earlier.

According to Maslow, physiological needs are dominant when they are chronically unsatisfied: "For the man who is extremely and dangerously hungry, no other interest exists but food. He dreams food, he remembers food, he thinks about food, he emotes only about food, he perceives only food, and he wants only food."[13] For many people in this country, the biogenic needs tend to be satisfied, and higher-level needs are dominant. Unfortunately, however, the lives of the many homeless people in major cities and in physically devastated areas are focused almost entirely on satisfying their biogenic needs, such as the needs for food, clothing, and shelter.

Safety needs

After the first level of need is satisfied, safety and security needs become the driving force behind an individual's behavior. These needs are concerned not only with physical safety but also include order, stability, routine, familiarity, and control over one's life and environment. Health and the availability of health care are important safety concerns. Savings accounts, insurance policies, education, and vocational training are all means by which individuals satisfy the need for security.

Social needs

The third level of Maslow's hierarchy includes such needs as love, affection, belonging, and acceptance. People seek warm and satisfying human relationships with other people and are motivated by love for their families. Because of the importance of social motives in our society, advertisers of many product categories emphasize this appeal in their advertisements.

Egoistic needs

When social needs are more or less satisfied, the fourth level of Maslow's hierarchy becomes operative. This level is concerned with egoistic needs. These needs can take either an inward or an outward orientation, or both. Inwardly directed ego needs reflect an individual's need for self-acceptance, self-esteem, success, independence, and personal satisfaction with a job well done. Outwardly directed ego needs include the needs for prestige, reputation, status, and recognition from others.

Need for self-actualization

According to Maslow, most people do not satisfy their ego needs sufficiently to ever move to the fifth level—the need for self-actualization (self-fulfillment). This need refers to an individual's desire to fulfill his or her potential—to become everything he or she is capable of becoming. In Maslow's words, "What a man can be, he must be."[14] This need is expressed in different ways by different people. A young man may desire to be an Olympic star and work single-mindedly for years to become the best in his sport. An artist may need to express herself on canvas; a research scientist may strive to find a new drug that eradicates cancer. Maslow noted that the self-actualization need is not necessarily a creative urge but that it is likely to take that form in people with some capacity for creativity. Some of our largest corporations encourage their highly paid employees to look beyond their paychecks to find gratification and self-fulfillment in the workplace—to view their jobs as the way to become "all they can be."

An evaluation of the need hierarchy and marketing applications

Maslow's hierarchy-of-needs theory postulates a five-level hierarchy of prepotent human needs. Higher-order needs become the driving force behind human behavior as lower-level needs are satisfied. The theory says, in effect, that dissatisfaction, not satisfaction, motivates behavior.

The need hierarchy has received wide acceptance in many social disciplines because it appears to reflect the assumed or inferred motivations of many people in our society. The five levels of need are sufficiently generic to encompass most lists of individual needs. The major problem with the theory is that it cannot be tested empirically; there is no way to measure precisely how satisfied one level of need must be before the next higher need becomes operative. The need hierarchy also appears to be very closely bound to our contemporary American culture (i.e., it appears to be both culture- and time-bound).

Despite these limitations, the hierarchy offers a highly useful framework for marketers trying to develop appropriate advertising appeals for their products. It is adaptable in two ways: First, it enables marketers to focus their advertising appeals on a need level that is likely to be shared by a large segment of the target audience; second, it facilitates product positioning or repositioning.

Segmentation and promotional applications

Maslow's need hierarchy is readily adaptable to market segmentation and the development of advertising appeals because there are consumer goods designed to satisfy each of the need levels and because most needs are shared by large segments of consumers. For example, individuals buy health foods, medicines, and low-fat products to satisfy physiological needs. They buy insurance, preventive medical services, and home security systems to satisfy safety and security needs. Almost all personal care and grooming products (e.g., cosmetics, mouthwash, shaving cream), as well as most clothes, are bought to satisfy social needs. High-tech products such as elaborate sound systems and luxury products (e.g., furs, big cars, or expensive furniture) are often bought to fulfill ego and esteem needs. Postgraduate college education, hobby-related products, exotic and physically challenging adventure trips are sold as ways of achieving self-fulfillment.

The need hierarchy is often used as the basis for market segmentation, with specific advertising appeals directed to one or more need-segment levels. For example, an ad for a very expensive sports car may use a self-actualization appeal such as "you deserve the very best."

Advertisers may use the need hierarchy for **positioning** products—that is, deciding how the product should be perceived by prospective consumers. The key to positioning is to find a niche—an unsatisfied need—that is not occupied by a competing product or brand. The need hierarchy is a very versatile tool for developing positioning strategies because different appeals for the same product can be based on different needs included in this framework. For example, many ads for soft drinks stress social appeal by showing a group of young people enjoying themselves and the advertised product; others stress refreshment (a physiological need); still others may focus on low caloric content (thus indirectly appealing to the ego need).

A trio of needs

Some psychologists believe in the existence of a trio of basic needs: the needs for power, for affiliation, and for achievement. These needs can each be subsumed within Maslow's need hierarchy; considered individually, however, each has a unique relevance to consumer motivation.

Power

The power need relates to an individual's desire to control his or her environment. It includes the need to control other persons and various objects. This need appears to be closely related to the ego need, in that many individuals experience increased self-esteem when they exercise power over objects or people.

Affiliation

Affiliation is a well-known and well-researched social motive that has far-reaching influence on consumer behavior. The affiliation need suggests that behavior is strongly influenced by the desire for friendship, for acceptance, for belonging. People with high affiliation needs tend to be socially dependent on others. They often select goods they feel will meet with the approval of friends. Teenagers who hang out at malls or techies who congregate at computer shows often do so more for the satisfaction of being with others than for making a purchase. An appeal to the affiliation needs of young adults is shown in Figure 14.4. The affiliation need is very similar to Maslow's social need.

Achievement

A considerable number of research studies have focused on the achievement need.[15] Individuals with a strong need for achievement often regard personal accomplishment as an end in itself. The achievement need is closely related to both the egoistic need and the self-actualization need. People with a high need for achievement tend to be more self-confident, enjoy taking calculated risks, actively research their environments, and value feedback. Monetary rewards provide an important type of feedback as to how they are doing. People with high achievement needs prefer situations in which they can take personal responsibility for finding solutions. High achievement is a useful promotional strategy for many products and services targeted to educated and affluent consumers.

In summary, individuals with specific psychological needs tend to be receptive to advertising appeals directed at those needs. They also tend to be receptive to certain kinds of products. Thus, a knowledge of motivational theory provides marketers with key bases for segmenting markets and developing promotional strategies.

Source: Photograph by James Mollison. Courtesy of United Colors of Benetton.

Appeal to the Affiliation Need

UNITED COLORS
OF BENETTON.

Consumer decision making and beyond

This section draws together many of the psychological, social, and cultural concepts developed throughout the book into an overview framework for understanding how consumers make decisions. It takes a broad perspective and examines **consumer decision making** in the context of all types of *consumption choices,* ranging from the consumption of new products to the use of old and established products. It also considers consumers' decisions not as the end point but rather as the beginning point of a **consumption process**.

What is a decision?

Every day, each of us makes numerous decisions concerning every aspect of our daily lives. However, we generally make these decisions without stopping to think about how we make them and what is involved in the particular decision-making process itself. In the most general terms, a decision is the selection of an option from two or more alternative choices. In other words, for a person to make a decision, a choice of alternatives must be available. When a person has a choice between making a purchase and not making a purchase, a choice between brand X and brand Y, or a choice of spending time doing A or B, that person is in a position to make a decision. On the other hand, if the consumer has no alternatives from which to choose and is literally *forced* to make a particular purchase or take a particular action (e.g., use a prescribed medication), then this single "no-choice" instance does not constitute a decision; such a no-choice decision is commonly referred to as a "Hobson's choice."

In actuality, no-choice purchase or consumption situations are fairly rare. You may recall from our discussion of core American cultural values that for consumers, *freedom* is often expressed in terms of a wide range of product choices. Thus, if there is almost always a choice, then there is almost always an opportunity for consumers to make decisions. Moreover, experimental research reveals that providing consumers with a choice when there was originally none can be a very good business strategy, one that can substantially increase sales.[1] For instance, when a direct-mail electrical appliance catalog displayed two coffeemakers instead of just one (the original coffeemaker at $149 and a "new" only slightly larger one at $229), the addition of the second *comparison* coffeemaker seemed to stimulate consumer evaluation that significantly increased the sales of the original coffeemaker.

Table 14.4 summarizes various types of consumption and purchase-related decisions. Although not exhaustive, this list does serve to demonstrate that the scope of consumer decision making is far broader than the mere selection of one brand from a number of brands.

Levels of consumer decision making

Not all consumer decision-making situations receive (or require) the same degree of information research. If all purchase decisions required extensive effort, then consumer decision making would be an exhausting process that left little time for anything else. On the other hand, if all purchases were routine, then they would tend to be monotonous and would provide little pleasure or novelty. On a continuum of effort ranging from very high to very low, we can distinguish three specific levels of consumer decision making: **extensive problem solving**, **limited problem solving**, and **routinized response behavior**.

Extensive problem solving

When consumers have no established criteria for evaluating a product category or specific brands in that category or have not narrowed the number of brands they will

TABLE 14.4	Types of Purchase or Consumption Decisions	
DECISION CATEGORY	**ALTERNATIVE A**	**ALTERNATIVE B**
Basic Purchase or Consumption Decision Brand Purchase or Consumption Decision	To purchase or consume a product (or service)	Not to purchase or consume a product (or service)
	To purchase or consume a specific brand	To purchase or consume another brand
	To purchase or consume one's usual brand	To purchase or consume another established brand (possibly with special features)
	To purchase or consume a basic model	To purchase or consume a luxury or status model
	To purchase or consume a new brand	To purchase or consume one's usual brand or some other established brand
	To purchase or consume a standard quantity	To purchase or consume more or less than a standard quantity
	To purchase or consume an on-sale brand	To purchase or consume a nonsale brand
	To purchase or consume a national brand	To purchase or consume a store brand
Channel Purchase Decisions	To purchase from a specific type of store (e.g., a department store)	To purchase from some other type of store (e.g., a discount store)
	To purchase from one's usual store	To purchase from some other store
	To purchase in-home (by phone or catalog or Internet)	To purchase in-store merchandise
	To purchase from a local store	To purchase from a store requiring some travel (outshopping)
Payment Purchase Decisions	To pay for the purchase with cash	To pay for the purchase with a credit card
	To pay the bill in full when it arrives	To pay for the purchase in installments

consider to a small, manageable subset, their decision-making efforts can be classified as *extensive problem solving*. At this level, the consumer needs a great deal of information to establish a set of criteria on which to judge specific brands and a correspondingly large amount of information concerning each of the brands to be considered.

Limited problem solving

At this level of problem solving, consumers already have established the basic criteria for evaluating the product category and the various brands in the category. However, they have not fully established preferences concerning a select group of brands. Their search for additional information is more like "fine-tuning"; they must gather additional brand information to discriminate among the various brands.

Routinized response behavior

At this level, consumers have experience with the product category and a well-established set of criteria with which to evaluate the brands they are considering. In some situations, they may search for a small amount of additional information; in others, they simply review what they already know.

Just how extensive a consumer's problem-solving task is depends on how well established his or her criteria for selection are, how much information he or she has about each brand being considered, and how narrow the set of brands is from which the choice will be made. Clearly, extensive problem solving implies that the consumer must seek more information to make a choice, whereas routinized response behavior implies little need for additional information.

All decisions in our lives cannot be complex and require extensive research and consideration—we just cannot exert the level of effort required. Some decisions have to be "easy ones."

Models of consumers: Four views of consumer decision making

Before presenting an overview model of how consumers make decisions, we will consider several schools of thought that depict consumer decision making in distinctly different ways. The term *models of consumers* refers to a general view or perspective as to how (and why) individuals behave as they do. Specifically, we will examine models of consumers in terms of the following four views: (1) an *economic view*, (2) a *passive view*, (3) a *cognitive view*, and (4) an *emotional view*.

An economic view

In the field of theoretical economics, which portrays a world of perfect competition, the consumer has often been characterized as making rational decisions. This model, called the *economic man* theory, has been criticized by consumer researchers for a number of reasons. To behave rationally in the economic sense, a consumer would have to (1) be aware of all available product alternatives, (2) be capable of correctly ranking each alternative in terms of its benefits and disadvantages, and (3) be able to identify the one best alternative. Realistically, however, consumers rarely have all of the information or sufficiently accurate information or even an adequate degree of involvement or motivation to make the so-called "perfect" decision.

It has been argued that the classical economic model of an all-rational consumer is unrealistic for the following reasons: (a) People are limited by their existing skills, habits, and reflexes; (b) people are limited by their existing values and goals; and (c) people are limited by the extent of their knowledge.[2] Consumers operate in an imperfect world in which they do not maximize their decisions in terms of economic considerations, such as price–quantity relationships, marginal utility, or indifference curves. Indeed, the consumer generally is unwilling to engage in extensive decision-making activities and will settle, instead, for a "satisfactory" decision, one that is "good enough."[3] For this reason, the economic model is often rejected as too idealistic and simplistic. As an example, recent research has found that consumers' primary motivation for price haggling, which was long thought to be the desire to obtain a better price (i.e., better dollar value for the purchase), may instead be related to the need for achievement, affiliation, and dominance.[4]

A passive view

Quite opposite to the rational economic view of consumers is the *passive* view that depicts the consumer as basically submissive to the self-serving interests and promotional efforts of marketers. In the passive view, consumers are perceived as impulsive and irrational purchasers, ready to yield to the aims and into the arms of marketers. At least to some degree, the passive model of the consumer was subscribed to by the hard-driving supersalespeople of old, who were trained to regard the consumer as an object to be manipulated.

The principal limitation of the passive model is that it fails to recognize that the consumer plays an equal, if not dominant, role in many buying situations—sometimes by seeking information about product alternatives and selecting the product that appears to offer the greatest satisfaction and at other times by impulsively selecting a product that satisfies the mood or emotion of the moment. All that we have studied about motivation, selective perception, learning, attitudes, communication, and opinion leadership serves to support the proposition that consumers are rarely objects of manipulation. Therefore, this simple and single-minded view should also be rejected as unrealistic.

A cognitive view

The third model portrays the consumer as a *thinking problem solver*. Within this framework, consumers frequently are pictured as either receptive to or actively searching for products and services that fulfill their needs and enrich their lives. The cognitive model focuses on the processes by which consumers seek and evaluate information about selected brands and retail outlets.

Within the context of the cognitive model, consumers are viewed as information processors. Information processing leads to the formation of preferences and, ultimately, to purchase intentions. The cognitive view also recognizes that the consumer is unlikely to even attempt to obtain all available information about every choice. Instead, consumers are likely to cease their information-seeking efforts when they perceive that they have sufficient information about some of the alternatives to make a "satisfactory" decision. As this information-processing viewpoint suggests, consumers often develop shortcut decision rules (called **heuristics**) to facilitate the decision-making process. They also use decision rules to cope with exposure to too much information (i.e., **information overload**).

The cognitive, or problem-solving, view describes a consumer who falls somewhere between the extremes of the economic and passive views, who does not (or cannot) have total knowledge about available product alternatives and, therefore, cannot make *perfect* decisions, but who nonetheless actively seeks information and attempts to make *satisfactory* decisions.

Consistent with the problem-solving view is the notion that a great deal of consumer behavior is goal directed. For example, a consumer might purchase a computer in order to manage finances or look for a laundry detergent that will be gentle on fabrics. Goal setting is especially important when it comes to the adoption of new products because the greater the degree of "newness," the more difficult it would be for the consumer to evaluate the product and relate it to his or her need (because of a lack of experience with the product). Figure 14.5 diagrams goal setting and goal pursuit in consumer behavior.

An emotional view

Although long aware of the *emotional* or *impulsive* model of consumer decision making, marketers frequently prefer to think of consumers in terms of either economic or passive models. In reality, however, each of us is likely to associate deep feelings or emotions, such as joy, fear, love, hope, sexuality, fantasy, and even a little "magic," with certain purchases or possessions. These feelings or emotions are likely to be highly involving. For instance, a person who misplaces a favorite fountain pen might go to great lengths to look for it, despite the fact that he or she has six others at hand.

Possessions also may serve to preserve a sense of the past and act as familiar transitional objects when one is confronted with an uncertain future. For example, members of the armed forces invariably carry photographs of "the girl (or guy) back home," their families, and their lives in earlier times. These memorabilia frequently serve as hopeful reminders that normal activities will someday resume.

If we were to reflect on the nature of our recent purchases, we might be surprised to realize just how impulsive some of them were. Rather than carefully searching, deliberating, and evaluating alternatives before buying, we are just as likely to have made many of these purchases on impulse, on a whim, or because we were emotionally driven.

When a consumer makes what is basically an emotional purchase decision, less emphasis is placed on the search for prepurchase information. Instead, more emphasis is placed on current mood and feelings ("Go for it!"). This is not to say that emotional deci-

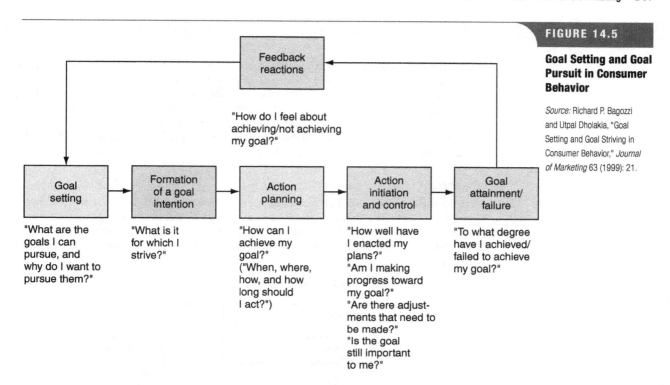

FIGURE 14.5

Goal Setting and Goal Pursuit in Consumer Behavior

Source: Richard P. Bagozzi and Utpal Dholakia, "Goal Setting and Goal Striving in Consumer Behavior," *Journal of Marketing* 63 (1999): 21.

sions are not rational. Buying products that afford emotional satisfaction is a perfectly rational consumer decision. Some emotional decisions are expressions that "you deserve it" or "treat yourself." For instance, many consumers buy designer-label clothing, not because they look any better in it, but because status labels make them feel better. This is a rational decision. Of course, if a man with a wife and three children purchases a two-seater Porsche 911 Carrera (**www.porsche.com**) for himself, the neighbors might wonder about his level of rationality (although some might think it was deviously high). No such question would arise if the same man selected a box of Godiva chocolate (**www.godiva.com**), instead of a Whitman Sampler (**www.whitmans.com**), although in both instances, each might be an impulsive, emotional purchase decision.

Consumers' **moods** are also important to decision making. Mood can be defined as a "feeling state" or state of mind.[5] Unlike an emotion, which is a response to a particular environment, a mood is more typically an unfocused, preexisting state—already present at the time a consumer "experiences" an advertisement, a retail environment, a brand, or a product. Compared to emotions, moods are generally lower in intensity and longer last-ing and are not as directly coupled with action tendencies and explicit actions as emotions.

Mood appears to be important to consumer decision making, because it impacts on *when* consumers shop, *where* they shop, and *whether* they shop alone or with others. It also is likely to influence *how* the consumer responds to actual shopping environ-ments (i.e., at point of purchase). Some retailers attempt to create a mood for shoppers, even though shoppers enter the store with a preexisting mood. Research suggests that a store's image or atmosphere can affect shoppers' moods; in turn, shoppers' moods can influence how long they stay in the store, as well as other behavior that retailers wish to encourage.[6]

In general, individuals in a positive mood recall more information about a product than those in a negative mood. As the results of one study suggest, however, inducing a positive mood at the point-of-purchase decision (as through background music, point-of-purchase displays, etc.) is unlikely to have a meaningful impact on specific brand choice unless a previously stored brand evaluation already exists.[7]

A model of consumer decision making

This section presents an overview model of consumer decision making that reflects the *cognitive* (or *problem-solving*) consumer and, to some degree, the *emotional consumer.* The model is designed to tie together many of the ideas on consumer decision making and consumption behavior discussed throughout the book. It does not presume to provide an exhaustive picture of the complexities of consumer decision making. Rather, it is designed to synthesize and coordinate relevant concepts into a significant whole. The model, presented in Figure 14.6, has three major components: input, process, and output.

Input

The *input* component of our consumer decision-making model draws on external influences that serve as sources of information about a particular product and influence a consumer's product-related values, attitudes, and behavior. Chief among these input factors are the *marketing mix activities* of organizations that attempt to communicate the benefits

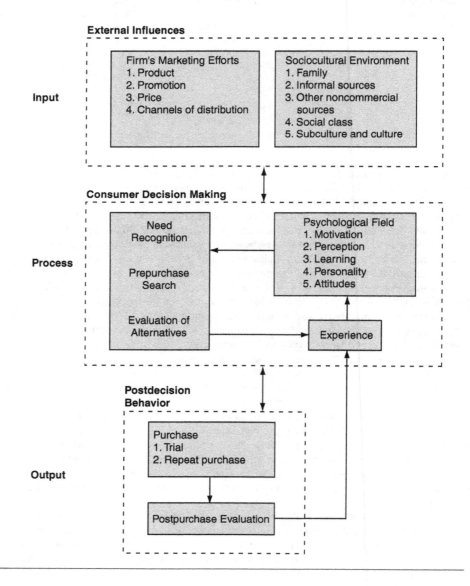

A Simple Model of Consumer Decision Making

FIGURE 14.6

of their products and services to potential consumers and the nonmarketing *sociocultural influences*, which, when internalized, affect the consumer's purchase decisions.

Marketing inputs

The firm's marketing activities are a direct attempt to reach, inform, and persuade consumers to buy and use its products. These inputs to the consumer's decision-making process take the form of specific marketing mix strategies that consist of the product itself (including its package, size, and guarantees); mass-media advertising, direct marketing, personal selling, and other promotional efforts; pricing policy; and the selection of distribution channels to move the product from the manufacturer to the consumer.

Ultimately, the impact of a firm's marketing efforts in large measure is governed by the consumer's perception of these efforts. Thus, marketers do well to remain diligently alert to consumer perceptions by sponsoring consumer research, rather than to rely on the *intended* impact of their marketing messages.

Sociocultural inputs

The second type of input, the *sociocultural environment*, also exerts a major influence on the consumer. Sociocultural inputs consist of a wide range of noncommercial influences. For example, the comments of a friend, an editorial in the newspaper, usage by a family member, an article in *Consumer Reports*, or the views of experienced consumers participating in a special-interest discussion group on the Internet are all noncommercial sources of information. The influences of social class, culture, and subculture, although less tangible, are important input factors that are internalized and affect how consumers evaluate and ultimately adopt (or reject) products. The unwritten codes of conduct communicated by culture subtly indicate which consumption behavior should be considered "right" or "wrong" at a particular point in time. For example, Japanese mothers maintain much more control over their children's consumption than American mothers, because in the United States children are socialized to be individualistic (*to stand out*), whereas in Japan children are socialized to be integrated with others (*to stand in*).

The cumulative impact of each firm's marketing efforts; the influence of family, friends, and neighbors; and society's existing code of behavior are all inputs that are likely to affect what consumers purchase and how they use what they buy. Because these influences may be directed to the individual or actively sought by the individual, a two-headed arrow is used to link the *input* and *process* segments of the model (Figure 14.6).

Process

The *process* component of the model is concerned with how consumers make decisions. To understand this process, we must consider the influence of psychological concepts. The *psychological field* represents the internal influences (motivation, perception, learning, personality, and attitudes) that affect consumers' decision-making processes (what they need or want, their awareness of various product choices, their information-gathering activities, and their evaluation of alternatives). As pictured in the *process* component of the overview decision model (Figure 14.6), the act of making a consumer decision consists of three stages: (1) **need recognition**, (2) **prepurchase search**, and (3) **evaluation of alternatives**.

Need recognition

The *recognition of a need* is likely to occur when a consumer is faced with a "problem." For example, consider the case of Eric, a 25-year-old college graduate working for an equity research firm in New York. He is totally computer literate, having had computers in the classroom since elementary school, and, like others his age, knows a great deal about other high-tech gadgets, such as MP3 players, HDTV, and cell phones. In fact, he recently purchased a thin 23-inch LCD HDTV for his bedroom, and exchanged his digital cable box, with a digital video recorder, for its HDTV equivalent. Eric frequently visits Web sites to find out about new state-of-the-art digital and electronic equipment, knows which Web sites offer reviews and comparisons of high-tech gear, and knows a number of Web sites where highly specialized e-tailers are offering state-of-the-art equipment. In the messenger bag, which he carries almost everywhere, is his Dell MP3 player (with hard drive), a USB flash drive, and, sometimes, his personal laptop computer. Interestingly, while in college he scheduled his life using his PDA, he no longer bothers to carry it around.

Eric often gets together with his friends for birthday parties, holiday parties, or just plain "let's meet at a restaurant for the evening," and he also likes to travel during his three weeks of annual vacation time. He has been taking photos for the past six or seven years with a small, 35mm zoom lens film camera that was a gift from his parents. Since he is part of the "digital age," he would like to replace his film camera with an even smaller digital camera that, for the sake of convenience, can fit easily into his pants or jacket pocket.

Among consumers, there seem to be two different need or problem recognition styles. Some consumers are *actual state* types, who perceive that they have a problem when a product fails to perform satisfactorily (as a cordless telephone that develops constant static). In contrast, other consumers are *desired state* types, for whom the desire for something new may trigger the decision process.[8] Since Eric's current camera can do the job, he appears to be a desired state consumer.

Prepurchase search

Prepurchase search begins when a consumer perceives a need that might be satisfied by the purchase and consumption of a product. The recollection of past experiences (drawn from storage in long-term memory) might provide the consumer with adequate information to make the present choice. On the other hand, when the consumer has had no prior experience, he or she may have to engage in an extensive search of the outside environment for useful information on which to base a choice.

The consumer usually searches his or her memory (the *psychological field* depicted in the model) before seeking external sources of information regarding a given consumption-related need. Past experience is considered an internal source of information. The greater the relevant past experience, the less external information the consumer is likely to need to reach a decision. Many consumer decisions are based on a combination of past experience (internal sources) and marketing and noncommercial information (external sources). The degree of perceived risk can also influence this stage of the decision process. In high-risk situations, consumers are likely to engage in complex and extensive information search and evaluation; in low-risk situations, they are likely to use very simple or limited search and evaluation tactics.

The act of shopping is an important form of external information. According to a recent consumer study, there is a big difference between men and women in terms of their response to shopping. Whereas most men do not like to shop, most women claim to like the experience of shopping; and although the majority of women found shopping to be relaxing and enjoyable, the majority of men did not feel that way.[9]

An examination of the external search effort associated with the purchase of different product categories (TVs, VCRs, or personal computers) found that, as the amount of total search effort increased, consumer attitudes toward shopping became more positive, and more time was made available for shopping. Not surprisingly, the external search effort was greatest for consumers who had the least amount of product category knowledge.[10] It follows that the less consumers know about a product category and the more important the purchase is to them, the more time they will make available and the more extensive their prepurchase search activity is likely to be. Conversely, research studies have indicated that consumers high in subjective knowledge (a self-assessment of how much they know about the product category) rely more on their own evaluations than on dealer recommendations.

It is also important to point out that the Internet has had a great impact on prepurchase search. Rather than visiting a store to find out about a product or calling the manufacturer and asking for a brochure, manufacturers' Web sites can provide consumers with much of the information they need about the products and services they are considering. For example, many automobile Web sites provide product specifications, sticker prices and dealer cost information, reviews, and even comparisons with competing vehicles. Audi's Web site (**www.audiusa.com**), for example, lets you "build" your own car, and see how it would look, for example, in different colors. Some auto company Web sites will even list a particular auto dealer's new and used car inventory. And then there are Web sites such as The Fox Company (**www.thefoxcompany.net**) that allow women to customize any number of cosmetic and beauty care products, and My Tailor (**www.mytailor.com**) that lets men design their own clothing, such as dress shirts.

With respect to surfing the Internet for information, consider one consumer's comments drawn from a recent research study: "I like to use the Web because it's so easy to find information, and it's really easy to use. The information is at my finger-tips and I don't have to search books in libraries."[11] However, a Roper Starch Survey found that an average user searching the Internet gets frustrated in about 12 minutes, on average, and new research findings suggest that although the Internet may reduce physical effort, "the cognitive challenge of interacting with computers and online information limits consumer information search in the Web-based marketspace."[12]

How much information a consumer will gather also depends on various situational factors. Getting back to Eric, while he works long hours in Manhattan, he is willing to spend time researching his desired purchase. He starts by sitting at his office desk with his office computer connected to the firm's network broadband connection. He visits the Web sites of digital camera manufacturers such as Nikon (**www.nikonusa.com**), Canon (**www.canonusa.com**), Sony (**www.sony.com**), Pentax (**www.pentaximaging.com**), and Hewlett Packard (**www.hp.com**), as well as e-tailer Web sites like Amazon (**www.amazon.com**) and Newegg (**www.newegg.com**), to see which brands and models of digital cameras are small and lightweight. Still further, he visits the Web sites of two major New York City camera stores—B&H (**www.bhphotovideo.com**) and Adorama (**www.adorama.com**). He finds several small lightweight digital cameras that seem like possibilities.

Eric also talks to some of his friends and coworkers who are even more into digital cameras than he is. One suggests that he try to find product reviews of any camera that he considers to be a possibility on such Web sites as as CNET (**www.cnet.com**), Digital Photograph Review (**www.dpreview.com**), Digital Camera Resource (**www.dcresource.com**), and Steve's Digicams (**www.steves-digicams.com**).

As Table 14.5 indicates, a number of factors are likely to increase consumers' prepurchase search. For some products and services, the consumer may have ongoing experience on which to draw (such as a skier purchasing a "better" pair of skis), or the purchase may essentially be discretionary in nature (rather than a necessity), so there is no rush to make a decision. In the case of Eric, our equity researcher, while there is no particular need to rush into the purchase of the digital camera, he would like to have it in a month, when he is planning to take a week's vacation.

Let's consider several of the prepurchase search alternatives open to a digital camera buyer. At the most fundamental level, search alternatives can be classified as either personal or impersonal. *Personal* search alternatives include more than a consumer's past experience with the product or service. They also include asking for information and advice from friends, relatives, coworkers, and sales representatives. For instance, Eric spoke with a few friends and coworkers and asked them what they know about digital cameras. Eric also investigated whether photography magazines, such as *Popular Photography*, or computer magazines, such as *Computer Shopper*, might have rated the various brands or models of digital cameras. Table 14.6 presents some of the sources of information that Eric might use as part of his prepurchase search. Any or all of these sources might be used as part of a consumer's search process.

Evaluation of alternatives

When evaluating potential alternatives, consumers tend to use two types of information: (1) a "list" of brands (or models) from which they plan to make their selection (the evoked set) and (2) the criteria they will use to evaluate each brand (or model). Making a selection from a *sample* of all possible brands (or models) is a human characteristic that helps simplify the decision-making process.

TABLE 14.5	Factors That Are Likely to Increase Prepurchase Search

Product Factors

Long interpurchase time (a long-lasting or infrequently used product)

Frequent changes in product styling

Frequent price changes

Volume purchasing (large number of units)

High price

Many alternative brands

Much variation in features

Situational Factors

EXPERIENCE

First-time purchase

No past experience because the product is new

Unsatisfactory past experience within the product category

SOCIAL ACCEPTABILITY

The purchase is for a gift

The product is socially visible

VALUE-RELATED CONSIDERATIONS

Purchase is discretionary rather than necessary

All alternatives have both desirable and undesirable consequences

Family members disagree on product requirements or evaluation of alternatives

Product usage deviates from important reference groups

The purchase involves ecological considerations

Many sources of conflicting information

Product Factors

DEMOGRAPHIC CHARACTERISTICS OF CONSUMER

Well educated

High income

White-collar occupation

Under 35 years of age

PERSONALITY

Low dogmatic

Low-risk perceiver (broad categorizer)

Other personal factors such as high product involvement and enjoyment of shopping and search

Evoked Set   Within the context of consumer decision making, the **evoked set** refers to the specific brands (or models) a consumer considers in making a purchase within a particular product category. (The evoked set is also called the *consideration set*.) A consumer's evoked set is distinguished from his or her **inept set**, which consists of brands (or models) the consumer excludes from purchase consideration because they are felt to be unacceptable (or they are seen as "inferior"), and from the **inert set**, which consists of brands (or models) the consumer is indifferent toward because they are perceived as not having any particular advantages. Regardless of the total number of brands (or models)

TABLE 14.6	Alternative Prepurchase Information Sources for an Ultralight Laptop

PERSONAL	IMPERSONAL
Friends	Newspaper articles
Neighbors	Magazine articles
Relatives	*Consumer Reports*
Coworkers	Direct-mail brochures
Computer salespeople	Information from product advertisements
	Internal Web sites

in a product category, a consumer's evoked set tends to be quite small on average, often consisting of only three to five brands (or models).

The evoked set consists of the small number of brands the consumer is familiar with, remembers, and finds acceptable. Figure 14.7 depicts the evoked set as a subset of all available brands in a product category. As the figure indicates, it is essential that a product be part of a consumer's evoked set if it is to be considered at all. The five terminal positions in the model that do not end in purchase would appear to have perceptual problems. For example, (1) brands (or models) may be *unknown* because of the consumer's selective exposure to advertising media and selective perception of advertising stimuli; (2) brands (or models) may be *unacceptable* because of poor qualities or attributes or inappropriate positioning in either advertising or product characteristics; (3) brands (or models) may be perceived as not having any special benefits and are regarded *indifferently* by the consumer; (4) brands (or models) may be *overlooked* because they have not been clearly positioned or sharply targeted at the consumer market segment under study; and (5) brands (or models) may not be selected because they are perceived by consumers as *unable to satisfy* perceived needs as fully as the brand that is chosen.

In each of these instances, the implication for marketers is that promotional techniques should be designed to impart a more favorable, perhaps more relevant, product

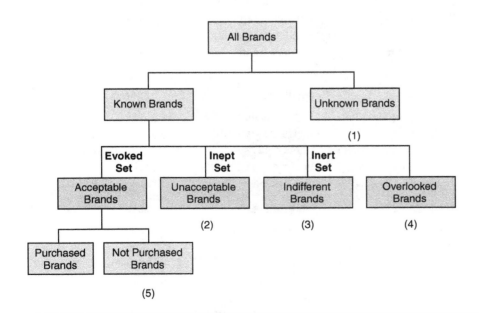

The Evoked Set as a Subset of All Brands in a Product Class

FIGURE 14.7

image to the target consumer. This may also require a change in product features or attributes (more or better features). An alternative strategy is to invite consumers in a particular target segment to consider a specific offering and possibly put it in their evoked set.

Research also suggests that the use of white space and choice of typeface in advertisements may influence the consumer's image of the product. For example, quality, prestige, trust, attitude toward the brand, and purchase intention have been shown to be positively conveyed by white space, and typefaces that were perceived as being attractive, warm, and liked when they were simple, more natural, and include a typefont with serifs.[13]

It has also been suggested that consumers may not, all at once, reduce down the number of possible choices into their evoked set, but instead may make several decisions within a single decision process. These screening decisions, or decision waves, are used to eliminate unsuitable alternatives before gathering information or comparing options, and help reduce decision complexity to a more manageable level.[14]

Criteria Used for Evaluating Brands The criteria consumers use to evaluate the alternative products that constitute their evoked sets usually are expressed in terms of important product attributes. Examples of product attributes that consumers have used as criteria in evaluating nine product categories are listed in Table 14.7.

When a company knows that consumers will be evaluating alternatives, it sometimes advertises in a way that recommends the criteria that consumers should use in assessing product or service options.

We have probably all had the experience of comparing or evaluating different brands or models of a product and finding the one that just feels, looks, and/or performs "right." Interestingly, research shows that when consumers discuss such "right products," there is little or no mention of price; brand names are not often uppermost in consumers'

TABLE 14.7   **Possible Product Attributes Used as Purchase Criteria for Nine Product Categories**

PERSONAL COMPUTERS	CD PLAYERS	WRISTWATCHES
Processing speed	Mega bass	Watchband
Price	Electronic shock protection	Alarm feature
Type of display	Length of play on batteries	Price
Hard-disk size	Random play feature	Water resistant
Amount of memory	Water resistant	Quartz movement
Laptop or desktop		Size of dial

VCRS	COLOR TVS	FROZEN DINNERS
Ease of programming	Picture quality	Taste
Number of heads	Length of warranty	Type of main course
Number of tape speeds	Cable ready	Type of side dishes
Slow-motion feature	Price	Price
Automatic tracking	Size of screen	Preparation requirements

35MM CAMERAS	FOUNTAIN PENS	COLOR INKJET PRINTERS
Autofocus	Balance	Output speed
Built-in flash	Price	Number of ink colors
Automatic film loading	Gold nib	Resolution (DPI)
Lens type	Smoothness	Length of warranty
Size and weight	Ink reserve	USB capability

minds; items often reflect personality characteristics or childhood experiences; and it is often "love at first sight." In one study, the products claimed to "just feel right" included Big Bertha golf clubs, old leather briefcases, Post-it notes, and the Honda Accord.[15] And, a product's country of origin can also play a role in how a consumer evaluates a brand.

Research has explored the role of brand credibility (which consists of trustworthiness and expertise) on brand choice, and has found that brand credibility improves the chances that a brand will be included in the consideration set. Three factors that impact a brand's credibility are: the perceived quality of the brand, the perceived risk associated with the brand, and the information costs saved with that brand (due to the time and effort saved by not having to shop around).[16] Still further, the study indicates that trustworthiness is more important than expertise when it comes to making a choice.

Let's return for a moment to Eric and his search for a small, lightweight digital camera. As part of his search process, he has acquired information about a number of relevant issues (or attributes) that could influence his final choice. For example, Eric has learned that the overall size of a digital camera is very much a function of the features that it contains, such as whether or not the camera has a viewfinder, how powerful its flash is, whether it offers manual control of functions such as shutter speed and aperture, and the size of its camera back LCD screen. Still further, Eric realizes that the higher the megapixel count of the pictures the camera takes, the higher the camera's price is going to be (i.e., a 5 megapixel digital camera can typically take photos that can be enlarged to 8×10 inches and still be sharp, while a 3 megapixel camera's photos may not appear sharp when enlarged bigger than 5×7 inches). He reasoned that for the types of photos that he takes (he gets 4×6-inch prints and on rare occasions makes a 5×7-inch enlargement), 5 megapixels is plenty.

As part of his search process, Eric has also acquired information about other relevant issues (or attributes) that could influence his final choice (see Table 14.8). For example, he has learned that some digital camera zoom lenses have less of a zoom range than others, and that all LCD screens are not equally sharp because some have only half or two-thirds the number of pixels of others (the greater the number of pixels, the sharper the image on the camera-back LCD screen).

TABLE 14.8	Comparison of Selected Characteristics of Digital Cameras		
FEATURE	**NIKON**	**CANON**	**PENTAX**
Megapixels	5.1	5.0	5.0
Weight (oz.)	4.2	4.6	3.7
Dimensions	3.5×2.3×0.8	3.4×2×0.8	3.3×2×0.8
Lens focal length (35mm equivalent)	35–105	35–105	36–107
Viewfinder	No	Yes	Yes
LCD screen size	2.5 inches	2 inches	1.8 inches
LCD resolution	110,000 pixels	118,000 pixels	85,000 pixels
Media	SD card	SD card	SD card
Manual control	Program auto	Program & exposure compensation	Program & exposure compensation
Battery/Charger	Proprietary battery, camera charges on proprietary cradle	Proprietary battery, small plug-in charger	Proprietary battery, camera charges on proprietary cradle
Price	$340	$345	$330

Source: Information from B&H catalog (Summer 2005) and manufacturers' Web sites.

On the basis of his information search, Eric realizes that he is going to have to make a decision regarding what he really wants from this new digital camera. Does he want just a digital version of his current 35mm point-and-shoot camera, or is he willing to sacrifice some features for a camera that is substantially smaller and lighter? He comes to realize that he always has his current camera set to "auto" when he takes pictures, and that the only features he really wants, in addition to small size, is autofocus (which all the digital cameras he's investigated have) and a zoom lens. Thus, Eric realizes that he is willing to give up some functionality (such as manual control of shutter speed) in exchange for reduced size and weight.

Consumer Decision Rules Consumer decision rules, often referred to as *heuristics, decision strategies*, and *information-processing strategies*, are procedures used by consumers to facilitate brand (or other consumption-related) choices. These rules reduce the burden of making complex decisions by providing guidelines or routines that make the process less taxing.

Consumer decision rules have been broadly classified into two major categories: **compensatory** and **noncompensatory decision rules**. In following a compensatory decision rule, a consumer evaluates brand or model options in terms of each relevant attribute and computes a weighted or summated score for each brand. The computed score reflects the brand's relative merit as a potential purchase choice. The assumption is that the consumer will select the brand that scores highest among the alternatives evaluated. Referring to Table 14.9, it is clear that when using a compensatory decision rule, the Canon digital camera scores highest.

A unique feature of a compensatory decision rule is that it allows a positive evaluation of a brand on one attribute to balance out a negative evaluation on some other attribute. For example, a positive assessment of the energy savings made possible by a particular brand or type of lightbulb may offset an unacceptable assessment in terms of the bulb's diminished light output.

In contrast, noncompensatory decision rules do not allow consumers to balance positive evaluations of a brand on one attribute against a negative evaluation on some other attribute. For instance, in the case of an energy-saving lightbulb, the product's negative (unacceptable) rating on its light output would not be offset by a positive evaluation of its energy savings. Instead, this particular lightbulb would be disqualified from further consideration. If Eric's choice of a digital camera was based on the desire to have a built-in viewfinder, rather than just an LCD screen on the camera's back

TABLE 14.9	Hypothetical Ratings for Digital Cameras		
FEATURE	**NIKON**	**CANON**	**PENTAX**
MegaPixels	9	9	9
Weight	7	6	8
Dimensions	6	8	8
Lens focal length	9	9	9
Viewfinder	4	8	8
LCD screen size	9	8	6
LCD resolution	8	9	5
Media	9	9	9
Manual Control	5	9	9
Battery/Charger	5	9	5
Price	8	8	8
Total	79	92	84

(refer again to Table 14.8), a noncompensatory decision rule would have eliminated the Nikon.

Three noncompensatory rules are considered briefly here: the *conjunctive* rule, the *disjunctive* rule, and the *lexicographic* rule.

In following a **conjunctive decision rule**, the consumer establishes a separate, minimally acceptable level as a cutoff point for each attribute. If any particular brand or model falls below the cutoff point on any one attribute, the option is eliminated from further consideration. Because the conjunctive rule can result in several acceptable alternatives, it becomes necessary in such cases for the consumer to apply an additional decision rule to arrive at a final selection, for example, to accept the first satisfactory brand. The conjunctive rule is particularly useful in quickly reducing the number of alternatives to be considered. The consumer can then apply another more refined decision rule to arrive at a final choice.

The **disjunctive rule** is the "mirror image" of the conjunctive rule. In applying this decision rule, the consumer establishes a separate, minimally acceptable cutoff level for each attribute (which may be higher than the one normally established for a conjunctive rule). In this case, if an option meets or exceeds the cutoff established for any one attribute, it is accepted. Here again, a number of brands (or models) might exceed the cutoff point, producing a situation in which another decision rule is required. When this occurs, the consumer may accept the first satisfactory alternative as the final choice or apply another decision rule that is perhaps more suitable.

In following a **lexicographic decision rule**, the consumer first ranks the attributes in terms of perceived relevance or importance. The consumer then compares the various alternatives in terms of the single attribute that is considered most important. If one option scores sufficiently high on this top-ranked attribute (regardless of the score on any of the other attributes), it is selected and the process ends. When there are two or more surviving alternatives, the process is repeated with the second highest-ranked attribute (and so on), until reaching the point that one of the options is selected because it exceeds the others on a particular attribute.

With the lexicographic rule, the highest-ranked attribute (the one applied first) may reveal something about the individual's basic consumer (or shopping) orientation. For instance, a "buy the best" rule might indicate that the consumer is *quality oriented*; a "buy the most prestigious brand" rule might indicate that the consumer is *status oriented*; a "buy the least expensive" rule might reveal that the consumer is *economy minded*.

A variety of decision rules appear quite commonplace. According to a consumer survey, 9 out of 10 shoppers who go to the store for frequently purchased items possess a specific shopping strategy for saving money. The consumer segment and the specific shopping rules that these segments employ are:[17]

1. *Practical loyalists—those who look for ways to save on the brands and products they would buy anyway.*
2. *Bottom-line price shoppers—those who buy the lowest-priced item with little or no regard for brand.*
3. *Opportunistic switchers—those who use coupons or sales to decide among brands and products that fall within their evoked set.*
4. *Deal hunters—those who look for the best bargain and are not brand loyal.*

We have considered only the most basic of an almost infinite number of consumer decision rules. Most of the decision rules described here can be combined to form new variations, such as conjunctive-compensatory, conjunctive-disjunctive, and disjunctive-conjunctive rules. It is likely that for many purchase decisions, consumers maintain in long-term memory overall evaluations of the brands in their evoked sets. This would make assessment by individual attributes unnecessary. Instead, the consumer would simply select the brand with the highest perceived overall rating. This type of synthesized decision rule is known as the **affect referral decision rule** and may represent the simplest of all rules.

TABLE 14.10	Hypothetical Use of Popular Decision Rules in Making a Decision to Purchase a Digital Camera
DECISION RULE	**MENTAL STATEMENT**
Compensatory rule	"I selected the digital camera that came out best when I balanced the good ratings against the bad ratings."
Conjunctive rule	"I selected the digital camera that had no bad features."
Disjunctive rule	"I picked the digital camera that excelled in at least one attribute."
Lexicographic rule	"I looked at the feature that was most important to me and chose the camera that ranked highest on that attribute."
Affect referral rule	"I bought the brand with the highest overall rating."

Table 14.10 summarizes the essence of many of the decision rules considered in this chapter in terms of the kind of mental statements that Eric might make in selecting a digital camera.

How Do Functionally Illiterate Consumers Decide? The National Adult Literacy Survey found that a bit more than 20 percent of American consumers did not possess the rudimentary skills in language and arithmetic needed for the typical retail environment, and that perhaps as much as half of all U.S. consumers lack the skills needed to master specific aspects of shopping, such as sales agreements and credit applications. Furthermore, despite the fact that functionally illiterate consumers have only 40 percent as much purchasing power as their literate counterparts, they may spend as much as $380 billion annually.[18]

Research has found that functionally illiterate consumers do make decisions differently, in terms of cognitive predilections, decision rules and trade-offs, and coping behaviors (see Figure 14.8). For example, they use concrete reasoning and noncompensatory decision rules, meaning that they base the purchase decision on a single piece of information, without regard to other product attributes (e.g., "I just look at the tag and see what's cheapest. I don't look by their sizes"). Such consumers, if confronted with two boxes of a product at the same price, would tend to purchase the one in the physically

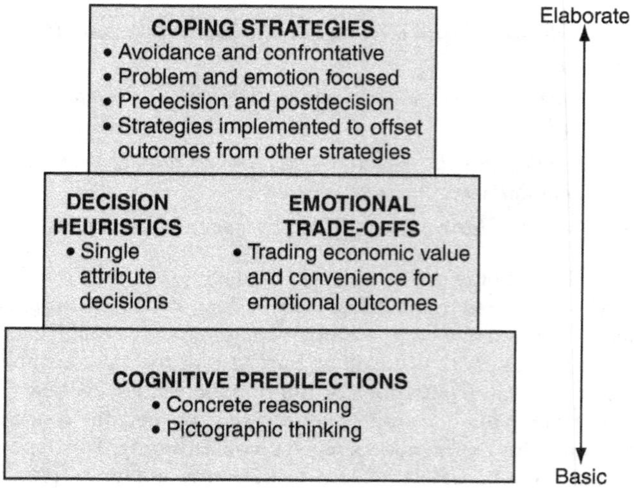

The Decision Process for Functionally Illiterate Consumers

Source: Madhubalan Viswanathan, José Antonio Rosa, and James Edwin Harris, "Decision Making and Coping of Functionally Illiterate Consumers and Some Implications for Marketing Management," Journal of Marketing 69 (January 2005): 19.

FIGURE 14.8

larger box, even if the label on the smaller sized package indicated a higher weight or greater volume. And through what might be referred to as "sight reading," they recognize brand logos the same way they might recognize people in a photograph. In fact, functionally illiterate consumers treat all words and numbers as pictorial elements. They also become anxious when shopping in a new store (they prefer to shop in the same store, especially if they have established a rapport with a friendly and helpful employee), and often give all their money to the cashier expecting him/her to return the proper change.[19] Table 14.11 presents the coping strategies used by functionally illiterate consumers. Note how such consumers avoid purchasing unknown brands and try to carry limited amounts of cash to the store.

TABLE 14.11	Coping Strategies of Functionally Illiterate Consumers
COPING STRATEGIES	**CLASSIFICATIONS**
AVOIDANCE	
Shop at the same store: avoids stress of unfamiliar environment	Problem focused: shops effectively Predecision: habitual choice about store helps with choices about products
Shop at smaller stores: avoids cognitive demands from product variety	Emotion focused: reduces stress Predecision: requires advance planning
Single-attribute decisions: avoids stressful and complex product comparisons	Problem focused: makes decisions manageable Emotion focused: preserves image of competence Predecision: requires advance planning
Avoid percentage- and fraction-off discounted items: avoids difficult numerical tasks	Emotion focused: reduces stress Problem focused: less chance of mistakes Predecision: implements habitually
Buy only known brands (loyalty): avoids risks from unknown brands	Problem focused: facilitates shopping Predecision: implements habitually
Rationalize outcomes to shift responsibility: avoids responsibility for outcomes	Emotion focused: protects self esteem Postdecision: implements after outcome is clear
Carry limited amounts of cash: avoids risks of overspending and being cheated	Problem focused: controls transactions Predecision: requires advance planning
Buy small amounts more often: avoids risk of large scale cheating	Problem focused: controls transactions Predecision: requires advance planning
Pretend disability: avoids revealing deficiencies and embarrassment	Problem focused: obtains assistance Emotion focused: preserves public image Predecision: requires advance planning
Pretend to evaluate products and prices: avoids revealing deficiencies indirectly	Emotion focused: preserves public image Predecision: requires advance planning
CONFRONTATIVE	
Shop with family members and friends: enables others to know deficiencies	Problem focused: helps shop on a budget Predecision: involves advance planning
Establish relationships with store personnel: enables others to know deficiencies	Emotion focused: avoids embarrassment and stress Predecision: Involves advance planning

(Continued)

TABLE 14.11	Continued	
Seek help in the store: enables others to know deficiencies	Problem focused: facilitates final decision Predecision: leads to a purchase decision
Give all money in pockets to cashier: admits deficiencies, plays on honesty standards	Problem focused: avoids not being able to count Predecision: implements habitually
Buy one item at a time: addresses the problem of loss of control when turning over cash	Problem focused: controls pace of transactions and flow of funds Predecision: requires advance planning
Confront store personnel and demand different treatment: focuses on responses and behaviors of others	Emotion focused: seeks to minimize or eliminate embarrassment and to preserve or restore public image Postdecision: implements in response to others
Plan expenditures with assistance from others: enables others to know deficiencies	Problem focused: facilitates a budget Predecision: involves advance planning

Source: Madhubalan Viswanathan, José Antonio Rosa, and James Edwin Harris, "Decision Making and Coping of Functionally Illiterate Consumers and Some Implications for Marketing Management," *Journal of Marketing* 69 (January 2005): 25.

Going Online to Secure Assistance in Decision Making For the past several years researchers have been examining how the Internet has impacted the way consumers make decisions. It is often hypothesized that because consumers have limited information-processing capacity, they must develop a choice strategy based on both individual factors (e.g., knowledge, personality traits, demographics) and contextual factors (characteristics of the decision tasks). The three major contextual factors that have been researched are *task complexity* (number of alternatives and amount of information available for each alternative), *information organization* (presentation, format, and content), and *time constraint* (more or less time to decide).[20] Table 14.12 compares these contextual factors for both the electronic and traditional environments.

A reason to go online is that a number of Web sites allow a consumer to build his or her own anything. For example, you can order M&Ms imprinted with your own message at **www.shop.mms.com/custom**, or order personalized shower gels and hand soaps at **www.samsoap.com**. About 75 percent of Mini Cooper purchasers pour through 70 options to design their vehicles online.[21]

Lifestyles as a Consumer Decision Strategy An individual's or family's decisions to be committed to a particular lifestyle (e.g., devoted followers of a particular religion) impacts on a wide range of specific everyday consumer behavior. For instance, the Trends Research Institute has identified "voluntary simplicity" as one of the top 10 lifestyle trends.[22] Researchers there estimate that 15 percent of all "boomers" seek a simpler lifestyle with reduced emphasis on ownership and possessions. Voluntary simplifiers are making do with less clothing and fewer credit cards (with no outstanding balances) and moving to smaller, yet still adequate, homes or apartments in less populated communities. Most importantly, it is not that these consumers can no longer afford their affluence or "lifestyle of abundance"; rather, they are seeking new, "reduced," less extravagant lifestyles. As part of this new lifestyle commitment, some individuals are seeking less stressful and lower-salary careers or jobs. In a telephone survey, for example, 33 percent of those contacted claimed that they would be willing to take a 20 percent pay cut in return for working fewer hours.[23] Time pressure may also play a role in the consumer's decision process, as research has positively associated this factor with both sale proneness (i.e., respond positively to cents-off coupons

TABLE 14.12	Comparison of Electronic and Traditional Information Environment		
		ELECTRONIC ENVIRONMENT **CONSUMERS USE BOTH "HEADS" AND COMPUTERS TO MAKE DECISIONS. THE TOTAL CAPACITY IS EXTENDED.**	**TRADITIONAL ENVIRONMENT** **CONSUMERS USE "HEADS" TO MAKE DECISIONS. THEIR COGNITIVE CAPACITY IS FIXED.**
ASSUMPTION			
Contextual Factors	Task Complexity	More alternatives and more information for each alternative are available.	Information is scattered and information search is costly.
	Information Organization	Information is more accessible. Information presentation format is flexible. It can be reorganized and controlled by consumers. Product utilities can be calculated by computers without consumers' direct examination of the attributes.	Information presentation format and organization are fixed. They can only be "edited" by consumers manually (e.g., using pencil and paper).
	Time Constraint	Time is saved by using computers to execute the decision rules; extra time is needed to learn how to use the application.	Complex choice strategies require more time to formulate and execute.

Source: Lan Xia, "Consumer Choice Strategies and Choice Confidence in the Electronic Environment," *American Marketing Association Conference Proceedings,* American Marketing Association, 10, 1999, 272.

or special offers) and display proneness (e.g., respond positively to in-store displays offering a special price).[24]

As another lifestyle issue, consider the humongous success of the Apple iPod. Especially among teenagers and young adults, the iPod is overwhelmingly the portable music player of choice. While some might argue that the introduction of the iPod Shuffle (starting at $99) cheapens the product's image, it could also be a way for Apple to offer a product that allows more modest income parents to placate their teenagers. One industry analyst has commented that "The cachet is not in the price, it's in the brand. iPod is an affordable luxury item, and they're simply bringing it to another level of buyers. People who want an iPod will forgo buying an MP3 player at all saying 'If I buy, I will buy an iPod.' "[25]

Incomplete Information and Noncomparable Alternatives   In many choice situations, consumers face incomplete information on which to base decisions and must use alternative strategies to cope with the missing elements. Missing information may result from advertisements or packaging that mentions only certain attributes, the consumer's own imperfect memory of attributes for nonpresent alternatives, or because some attributes are experiential and can only be evaluated after product use. There are at least four alternative strategies that consumers can adopt for coping with missing information:[26]

1. *Consumers may delay the decision until missing information is obtained.*
2. *Consumers may ignore missing information and decide to continue with the current decision rule (e.g., compensatory or noncompensatory), using the available attribute information.*
3. *Consumers may change the customarily used decision strategy to one that better accommodates missing information.*
4. *Consumers may infer ("construct") the missing information.*

In discussing consumer decision rules, we have assumed that a choice is made from among the brands (or models) evaluated. Of course, a consumer also may conclude that none of the alternatives offers sufficient benefits to warrant purchase. If this were to occur with a necessity, such as a home water heater, the consumer would probably either lower his or her expectations and settle for the best of the available alternatives or seek information about additional brands, hoping to find one that more closely meets predetermined criteria. On the other hand, if the purchase is more discretionary (a second or third NFL team jersey), the consumer probably would postpone the purchase. In this case, information gained from the search up to that point would be transferred to long-term storage (in the psychological field) and retrieved and reintroduced as input if and when the consumer regains interest in making such a purchase.

In Apply Decision Rules   It should be noted that, in applying decision rules, consumers may at times attempt to compare dissimilar (noncomparable) alternatives. For example, a consumer may be undecided about whether to buy a new computer system or a new set of golf clubs, because the individual can afford one or the other but not both. Another example: A consumer may try to decide between buying a new overcoat or a new raincoat. When there is great dissimilarity in the alternative ways of allocating available funds, consumers abstract the products to a level in which comparisons are possible. In the foregoing examples, a consumer might weigh the alternatives (golf clubs versus PC or overcoat versus raincoat) in terms of which alternative would offer more pleasure or which, if either, is more of a "necessity."

A Series of Decisions   Although we have discussed the purchase decision as if it were a single decision, in reality, a purchase can involve a number of decisions. For example, when purchasing an automobile, consumers are involved in multiple decisions such as choosing the make or country of origin of the car (foreign versus domestic), the dealer, the financing, and particular options. In the case of a replacement automobile, these decisions must be preceded by a decision as to whether or not to trade in one's current car.

Decision Rules and Marketing Strategy   An understanding of which decision rules consumers apply in selecting a particular product or service is useful to marketers concerned with formulating a promotional program. A marketer familiar with the prevailing decision rule can prepare a promotional message in a format that would facilitate consumer information processing. The promotional message might even suggest how potential consumers should make a decision. For instance, a direct-mail piece for a desktop computer might tell potential consumers "what to look for in a new PC." This mail piece might specifically ask consumers to consider the attributes of hard disk size, amount of memory, processor speed, monitor size and maximum resolution, video card memory, and CD burner speed.

Output

The output portion of the consumer decision-making model concerns two closely associated kinds of postdecision activity: **purchase behavior** and **postpurchase evaluation**. The objective of both activities is to increase the consumer's satisfaction with his or her purchase.

Purchase behavior

Consumers make three types of purchases: *trial purchases, repeat purchases*, and *long-term commitment purchases*. When a consumer purchases a product (or brand) for the first time and buys a smaller quantity than usual, this purchase would be considered a trial. Thus, a trial is the exploratory phase of purchase behavior in which consumers attempt to evaluate a product through direct use. For instance, when consumers purchase a new brand of laundry detergent about which they may be uncertain, they are likely to purchase smaller trial quantities than if it were a familiar brand. Consumers can also be encouraged to try a new product through such promotional tactics as free samples, coupons, and/or sale prices.

When a new brand in an established product category (toothpaste, chewing gum, or cola) is found by trial to be more satisfactory or better than other brands, consumers are likely to repeat the purchase. Repeat purchase behavior is closely related to the concept of *brand loyalty*, which most firms try to encourage because it contributes to greater stability in the marketplace. Unlike trial, in which the consumer uses the product on a small scale and without any commitment, a repeat purchase usually signifies that the product meets with the consumer's approval and that he or she is willing to use it again and in larger quantities.

Trial, of course, is not always feasible. For example, with most durable goods (refrigerators, washing machines, or electric ranges), a consumer usually moves directly from evaluation to a long-term commitment (through purchase) without the opportunity for an actual trial. While purchasers of the new Volkswagen Beetle were awaiting delivery of their just-purchased cars, they were kept "warm" by being sent a mailing that included a psychographic tool called "Total Visual Imagery" that was personalized to the point that it showed them the precise model and color they had ordered.[27]

Consider Eric and his decision concerning the selection of a digital camera. Since he lives and works in Manhattan, it was easy for him to visit several of the large camera stores. His first stop was Adorama, where all three of the cameras he was considering were on display. He was able to hold each one, play with all of the camera controls, and, since the store keeps batteries in its demo models, Eric was able to take pictures with each one. The salesperson was neutral in his opinion, feeling that all three cameras were essentially equivalent, and all took excellent pictures. A few days later, Eric stopped at B&H on his way home from the office. Again, he was able to handle all three cameras and take pictures with them. It seemed to him that the Canon felt better in his hands than the other two, and the controls seemed to fall right where he placed his fingers when holding the camera (a positive). Also, the Canon had an optical finder, which was the way Eric was used to taking pictures.

Next, Eric again went to the Internet. He had been told by a coworker that there were many digital camera discussion groups on the Internet, and that many of them were camera-model specific. So he spent one evening in his apartment reading owner/user comments on the forums of Digital Photography Review and Digital Camera Resource. He learned what some owners liked and disliked about each of the three cameras that he was considering. He also learned that the capacity of the memory cards packaged with each camera were too small to be of any use, and that along with purchasing a memory card with greater capacity he should also purchase a spare battery for whichever camera he bought. He also posted a message on the dpreview.com forum, asking which of the three cameras might be best for him, and within a day he had received five responses. The general sense was that all three cameras were excellent, but that the Canon, with its new, improved Digic II image processor, might be the best of the three because it would have the least amount of shutter lag (the hesitation of the camera between the time the shutter release is pressed and the camera actually takes the picture).

Eric is now convinced that the Canon is the digital camera he should purchase. It has a viewfinder, which is a feature that he likes and is used to, it is small and light in weight, and he considers its appearance to be very stylish. Also, he feels that he will have no difficulty carrying the camera by slipping it into his pants or jacket pocket. So he checks the prices for this camera both at the New York City retailers that he visited, and at several e-tailers. He finds that the lowest price for the camera is at Amazon.com, which includes free shipping, and he orders it. He had been told by friends that he can use any brand of SD memory card in the camera, and that rather than pay a lot of money for the genuine Canon battery (in order to have a spare), he should go online where he should be able to find a spare battery at less than half the cost of the genuine one. Eric goes to several e-tailer Web sites, and is able to find a 512MB SD card for $25 (after rebate), and a spare battery for $13—he orders both. Within the next week, UPS delivers his new Canon digital camera, as well as his SD memory card and spare battery.

Postpurchase evaluation

As consumers use a product, particularly during a trial purchase, they evaluate its performance in light of their own expectations. There are three possible outcomes of these evaluations: (1) actual performance matches expectations, leading to a neutral feeling; (2) performance exceeds expectations, causing what is known as *positive disconfirmation of expectations* (which leads to satisfaction); and (3) performance is below expectations, causing *negative disconfirmation of expectations* and dissatisfaction. For each of these three outcomes, consumers' expectations and satisfaction are closely linked; that is, consumers tend to judge their experience against their expectations when performing a postpurchase evaluation.

An important component of postpurchase evaluation is the reduction of any uncertainty or doubt that the consumer might have had about the selection. As part of their postpurchase analyses, consumers try to reassure themselves that their choice was a wise one; that is, they attempt to reduce *postpurchase cognitive dissonance*. They do this by adopting one of the following strategies: They may rationalize the decision as being wise; they may seek advertisements that support their choice and avoid those of competitive brands; they may attempt to persuade friends or neighbors to buy the same brand (and, thus, confirm their own choice); or they may turn to other satisfied owners for reassurance.

The degree of postpurchase analysis that consumers undertake depends on the importance of the product decision and the experience acquired in using the product. When the product lives up to expectations, they probably will buy it again. When the product's performance is disappointing or does not meet expectations, however, they will search for more suitable alternatives. Thus, the consumer's postpurchase evaluation "feeds back" as *experience* to the consumer's psychological field and serves to influence future related decisions. Although it would be logical to assume that customer satisfaction is related to customer retention (i.e., if a consumer is satisfied with his Nautica jacket, he will buy other Nautica products), a recent study found no direct relationship between satisfaction and retention. The findings show that customer retention may be more a matter of the brand's reputation—especially for products consumers find difficult to evaluate.[28]

What was Eric's postpurchase evaluation of his new digital camera? He absolutely loves it! First of all, because it is so small in size, he can carry it in his pants pocket anywhere he goes, and therefore is always ready to take pictures, which is something he very much enjoys doing. His 512MB secure digital card allows him to take about 200 photos before filling up, even using the camera's "best picture" setting. After coming back from a friend's party, where he took about 25 pictures, he quickly transferred the photos from his camera to his laptop (using the software and cord supplied with the camera), easily cropped a few of the photos and eliminated "red eye" in others, and then uploaded the 15 photos he really liked to the CVS Drugstore Web site. The next day, after work, he stopped by his local CVS store (located less than a block from his apartment) and picked up 4 × 6-inch reprints of his digital photos. He was absolutely thrilled with how sharp and colorful his pictures were, and couldn't wait to share these photos with his friends.

Beyond the decision: Consuming and possessing

Historically, the emphasis in consumer behavior studies has been on product, service, and brand choice decisions. As shown throughout this book, however, there are many more facets to consumer behavior. The experience of using products and services, as well as the sense of pleasure derived from *possessing, collecting,* or *consuming* "things" and "experiences" (mechanical watches, old fountain pens, or a baseball card collection) contributes to consumer satisfaction and overall quality of life. These consumption outcomes or experiences, in turn, affect consumers' future decision processes.

Thus, given the importance of possessions and experiences, a broader perspective of consumer behavior might view consumer choices as the beginning of a **consumption process**, not merely the end of a consumer decision-making effort. In this context, the choice or purchase decision is an *input* into a process of consumption. The input stage includes the establishment of a *consumption set* (an assortment or portfolio of products and their attributes) and a *consuming style* (the "rules" by which the individual or household fulfills consumption requirements). The *process* stage of a simple model of consumption might include (from the consumer's perspective) the *using, possessing* (or having), *collecting,* and *disposing* of things and experiences. The output stage of this process would include changes in a wide range of feelings, moods, attitudes, and behavior, as well as reinforcement (positive or negative) of a particular lifestyle (e.g., a devotion to physical fitness), enhancement of a sense of self, and the level of consumer satisfaction and quality of life.[37] Figure 14.9 presents a simple *model of consumption* that reflects the ideas discussed here and throughout the book.

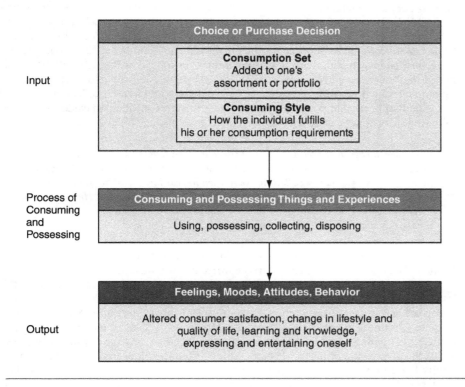

Input

Choice or Purchase Decision

Consumption Set
Added to one's
assortment or portfolio

Consuming Style
How the individual fulfills
his or her consumption requirements

Process of
Consuming
and
Possessing

Consuming and Possessing Things and Experiences

Using, possessing, collecting, disposing

Output

Feelings, Moods, Attitudes, Behavior

Altered consumer satisfaction, change in lifestyle and
quality of life, learning and knowledge,
expressing and entertaining oneself

**A Simple Model of
Consumption**

FIGURE 14.9

Products have special meanings and memories

Consuming is a diverse and complex concept. It includes the simple utility derived from the continued use of a superior toothpaste, the stress reduction of an island holiday, the stored memories of a DVD reflecting one's childhood, the "sacred" meaning or "magic" of a grandparent's wristwatch, the symbol of membership gained from wearing a school tie, the pleasure and sense of accomplishment that comes from building a model airplane, and the fun and even financial rewards that come from collecting almost anything (even jokers from decks of cards). In fact, one man's hobby of collecting old earthenware drain tiles has become the Mike Weaver Drain Tile Museum.[38] There are special possessions that consumers resist replacing, even with an exact replica, because the replica cannot possibly hold the same meaning as the original. Such possessions are often tied, in the consumer's mind, to a specific physical time or person.

Consider the male love affair with cars, which can manifest itself in many ways. Clearly, some men identify themselves with the automobiles that they own—it becomes an extension of the self, and some men personalize their vehicles in order to bond more fully with them (e.g., special paint color, custom wheels). Some individuals even take on the characteristics of their vehicles, with a powerful engine giving the owner a sense of greater power, and high performance handling providing the man with the notion that he is similarly capable of high performance. Some even feel that the "right" car will make them irresistible to women. Cars can also sometimes serve as children, lovers, and friends (e.g., "It's kind of like my baby—I wouldn't sell the car to just anyone—they must take care of the car or it would be like child abuse"), and some men attribute certain personality characteristics to their vehicles, call it a "she."[39] In a similar vein, a recent study of male motorcycle owners found that the type of "love" these bikers expressed toward their motorcycles was similar to interpersonal love—it is passionate, possessive, and selfless in nature.

Some possessions serve to assist consumers in their effort to create "personal meaning" and to maintain a sense of the past. To this end, it has been suggested that nostalgia permits people to maintain their identity after some major change in their life. This nostalgia can be based on family and friends; on objects such as toys, books, jewelry, and cars; or on special events, such as graduations, weddings, and holidays.[40] Providing the triple benefits of a sense of nostalgia, the fun of collecting, and the attraction of a potential return on investment, there is a strong interest in collecting Barbie® dolls. It is estimated that there are currently more than 100,000 Barbie doll collectors, who are dedicated to hunting down rare and valuable Barbie dolls to add to their collections.

And it appears that you're never too young to start collecting, as evidenced by the following story about a child who started collecting at the age of 2:

> Cars have always interested Kevin LaLuzerne, a fifth-grader at Oakhurst Elementary in Largo. He has boxes and boxes of Hot Wheels, Micro Machines and other cars— more than 600! He started collecting them when he was just 2, and he still enjoys seeing all of the different cars and trucks he has collected over the years. He even has a "Weinermobile," the Oscar Meyer hot dog car. Kevin's newest addition to his collection is a limited-edition Chevron car that has a cartoon mouth, eyes and ears.[41]

There is even a Web site devoted to kids who collect, which includes "An A to Z Guide to What Kids Can Collect" (**www.countrycollector.com/kids.html**).

At the other end of the age continuum, older consumers are often faced with the issue of how they should dispose of such special possessions. Indeed, in the past several years, a number of researchers have examined this subject area. Sometimes it is some precipitating event, such as the death of a spouse, illness, or moving out of one's home (to a nursing home or retirement community), that gets the consumer thinking about the disposition of his or her possessions. Often the older person wants to pass a family legacy on to a child, ensure a good home for a cherished collection, and/or influence the lives of others. The aim is not to "sell" the items, because they could do that themselves.

Relationship marketing

Many firms have established **relationship marketing** programs (sometimes called *loyalty programs*) to foster usage loyalty and a commitment to their company's products and services. Relationship marketing is exceedingly logical when we realize credit card research has shown that "75 percent of college students keep their first card for 15 years, and 60 percent keep that card for life."[42] This kind of loyalty is enhanced by relationship marketing, which at its heart is all about building *trust* (between the firm and its customers) and keeping *promises* ("making promises," "enabling promises," and "keeping promises" on the part of the firm and, possibly, on the part of the customer).[43]

Indeed, it is the aim of relationship marketing to create strong, lasting relationships with a core group of customers. The emphasis is on developing long-term bonds with customers by making them feel good about how the company interacts (or does business) with them and by giving them some kind of personal connection to the business. A review of the composition of 66 consumer relationship marketing programs revealed three elements shared by more than 50 percent of the programs. They are (1) fostering ongoing communication with customers (73 percent of the programs); (2) furnishing loyalty by building in extras like upgrades and other perks (68 percent of the programs); and (3) stimulating a sense of belonging by providing a "club membership" format (50 percent of the programs).[44] A real relationship marketing program is more than the use of database marketing tactics to better target customers—the consumer must feel that he or she has received something for being a participant in the relationship. In a positive vein, businesses have been finding that the Internet is an inexpensive, efficient, and more productive way to extend customer services. This has resulted in "permission marketing." It is the "art of asking consumers if they would like to receive a targeted e-mail ad, promotion, or message *before* it appears in their in-box." The opposite tact, sending a consumer spam and offering the option to "Click here to opt out," annoys consumers and is not permission marketing.[45]

Although direct marketing, sales promotion, and general advertising may be used as part of a relationship marketing strategy, relationship marketing stresses long-term commitment to the individual customer. Advances in technology (such as UPC scanning equipment, and relational databases) have provided techniques that make tracking customers simpler, thus influencing the trend toward relationship marketing. Indeed, Wal-Mart's database is second in size only to the database of the U.S. government.[46] Still further, a recent study suggests that relationship marketing programs are more likely to succeed if the product or service is one that buyers consider to be high involvement due to its association with financial, social, or physical risk.[47]

Relationship marketing programs have been used in a wide variety of product and service categories. Many companies call their relationship programs a club, and some even charge a fee to join. Membership in a club may serve as a means to convey to customers the notions of permanence and exclusivity inherent in a committed relationship. Additionally, those firms that charge a fee (such as the American Express Platinum card) increase customers' investment in the relationship that may, in turn, lead to greater commitment to the relationship and increased usage loyalty.

Airlines and major hotel chains, in particular, use relationship marketing techniques by awarding points to frequent customers that can be used to obtain additional goods or services from the company. This kind of point system may act as an exit barrier because starting a new relationship would mean giving up the potential future value of the points and starting from ground zero with a new service provider. That is why, for example, Hilton considers the 6.5 million members of the Hilton Honors loyalty program the most important customers the company has.[48]

Moreover, companies have recently been broadening the scope of such relationship programs. Still further, research has found that airline frequent flyer programs contribute in a positive way to the frequent business traveler's lifestyle and to his/her quality of life, perhaps by compensating for some of the negative aspects of frequent business

FIGURE 14.10

A Portrayal of the Characteristics of Relationship Marketing

Source: In part, this portrayal was inspired by: Mary Long, Leon Schiffman, and Elaine Sherman, "Understanding the Relationships in Consumer Marketing Relationship Programs: A Content Analysis," in *Proceedings of the World Marketing Congress VII-II*, eds. K. Grant and Walker (Melbourne, Australia: Academy of Marketing Science, 1995), 10/27–10/26.

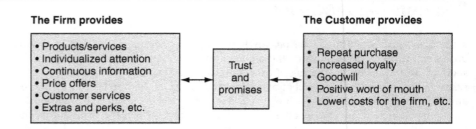

travel. In addition, happy frequent business travelers perceived themselves to be more loyal to a particular airline than their less happy counterparts.[49]

Ultimately, it is to a firm's advantage to develop long-term relationships with existing customers because it is easier and less expensive to make an additional sale to an existing customer than to make a new sale to a new consumer.[50] Figure 14.10 portrays some of the characteristics of the relationship between the firm and the customer within the spirit of relationship marketing.

Why is relationship marketing so important? Research indicates that consumers today are less loyal than in the past, due to six major forces: (1) the abundance of choice, (2) availability of information, (3) entitlement (consumers repeatedly ask "What have you done for me lately?"), (4) commoditization (most products/services appear to be similar—nothing stands out), (5) insecurity (consumer financial problems reduce loyalty), and (6) time scarcity (not enough time to be loyal). These six forces result in consumer defections, complaints, cynicism, reduced affiliation, greater price sensitivity, and litigiousness.[51]

chapter **15**

Perception

Elements of perception

Perception is defined as *the process by which an individual selects, organizes, and interprets stimuli into a meaningful and coherent picture of the world.* It can be described as "how we see the world around us." Two individuals may be exposed to the same stimuli under the same apparent conditions, but how each person recognizes, selects, organizes, and interprets these stimuli is a highly individual process based on each person's own needs, values, and expectations. The influence that each of these variables has on the perceptual process and its relevance to marketing will be explored later in the chapter. First, however, we will examine some of the basic concepts that underlie the perceptual process. These will be discussed within the framework of consumer behavior.

Sensation

Sensation is the immediate and direct response of the sensory organs to stimuli. A **stimulus** is any unit of input to any of the senses. Examples of stimuli (i.e., sensory input) include products, packages, brand names, advertisements, and commercials. **Sensory receptors** are the human organs (the eyes, ears, nose, mouth, and skin) that receive sensory inputs. Their sensory functions are to see, hear, smell, taste, and feel. All of these functions are called into play, either singly or in combination, in the evaluation and use of most consumer products. Human sensitivity refers to the experience of sensation. Sensitivity to stimuli varies with the quality of an individual's sensory receptors (e.g., eyesight or hearing) and the amount (or *intensity*) of the stimuli to which he or she is exposed. For example, a blind person may have a more highly developed sense of hearing than the average sighted person and may be able to hear sounds that the average person cannot.

Sensation itself depends on energy change within the environment where the perception occurs (i.e., on differentiation of input). A perfectly bland or unchanging environment, regardless of the strength of the sensory input, provides little or no sensation at all. Thus, a person who lives on a busy street in midtown Manhattan would probably receive little or no sensation from the inputs of such noisy stimuli as horns honking, tires screeching, and fire engines clanging, because such sounds are so commonplace in New York City. In situations in which there is a great deal of sensory input, the senses do not detect small changes or differences in input. Thus, one honking horn more or less would never be noticed on a street with heavy traffic.

As sensory input *decreases*, however, our ability to detect changes in input or intensity *increases*, to the point that we attain maximum sensitivity under conditions of minimal stimulation. This accounts for the statement, "It was so quiet I could hear a pin drop." The ability of the human organism to accommodate itself to varying levels of sensitivity as external conditions vary not only provides more sensitivity when it is needed but also serves to protect us from damaging, disruptive, or irrelevant bombardment when the input level is high.

One researcher pointed out that 83 percent of all communications today appeal to sight; also that smell, not sound, is the second most important sensory input. This study also reported that consumers preferred shoes and belts presented in a scented room rather than a non-scented room, and were also willing to pay higher prices for these products.[2] The importance of smell in communication was strongly supported by two Americans who developed a scientific explanation as to how people associate memories with smells (and won the 2004 Nobel Prize in Physiology for this work) and other studies demonstrating the impact of fragrance on product and store choices.[3]

The absolute threshold

The lowest level at which an individual can experience a sensation is called the **absolute threshold**. The point at which a person can detect a difference between "something" and "nothing" is that person's absolute threshold for that stimulus. To illustrate, the distance at which a driver can note a specific billboard on a highway is that individual's absolute threshold. Two people riding together may first spot the billboard at different times (i.e., at different distances); thus, they appear to have different absolute thresholds. Under conditions of constant stimulation, such as driving through a "corridor" of billboards, the absolute threshold increases (i.e., the senses tend to become increasingly dulled). After an hour of driving through billboards, it is doubtful that any one billboard will make an impression. Hence, we often speak of "getting used to" a hot bath, a cold shower, or the bright sun. As our exposure to the stimulus increases, we notice it less. In the field of perception, the term *adaptation* refers specifically to "getting used to" certain sensations; that is, becoming accommodated to a certain level of stimulation.

Sensory adaptation is a problem that concerns many national advertisers, which is why they try to change their advertising campaigns regularly. They are concerned that consumers will get so used to their current print ads and TV commercials that they will no longer "see" them; that is, the ads will no longer provide sufficient sensory input to be noted.

In an effort to cut through the advertising clutter and ensure that consumers note their ads, some marketers try to *increase* sensory input. For example, Apple Computer once bought all the advertising space in an issue of *Newsweek* magazine to ensure that readers would note its ads. From time to time, various advertisers have taken all of the bus cards on certain bus routes to advertise their products, ensuring that wherever a rider sits, he or she will be exposed to the ad. Other advertisers try to attract attention by *decreasing* sensory input. For example, some print ads include a lot of empty space in order to accentuate the brand name or product illustration, and some TV ads use silence, the absence of audio sound, to generate attention.

Some marketers seek unusual or technological media in which to place their advertisements in an effort to gain attention. Examples of such media include disks placed in bathroom sinks that play commercials when activated by running water, ads embedded in the floors of supermarkets, and small monitors that display weather and news, as well as advertising, placed in elevators. Researchers have reported that the use of an ambient scent in a retail environment enhances the shopping experience for many consumers and makes the time they spend examining merchandise, waiting in line, and waiting for help seem shorter than it actually is.[4] Some marketers have invested in the development of specially engineered scents to enhance their products and entice consumers to buy. Marketers try to form stronger bonds between young, design-oriented consumers and brands, using the store image itself to give "dimension" to their brands, and present them as "cool." For example, in one store selling sports footwear, the shoes are integrated into a huge sound system in the shape of a wall; in another store selling advertised high-definition TVs, the screens show works of art inside the store.[5]

The differential threshold

The minimal difference that can be detected between two similar stimuli is called the **differential threshold**, or the **just noticeable difference** (the **j.n.d.**). A nineteenth-century German scientist named Ernst Weber discovered that the j.n.d. between two stimuli was not an absolute amount, but an amount relative to the intensity of the first stimulus. **Weber's law**, as it has come to be known, states that the stronger the initial stimulus, the greater the additional intensity needed for the second stimulus to be perceived as different. For example, if the price of a half gallon container of premium, freshly squeezed orange juice is $5.50, most consumers will probably not notice an increase of 25 cents (i.e., the increment would fall below the j.n.d.), and it may take an increase of 50 cents or more before a differential in price would be noticed. However, a 50-cent increase in the price of gasoline would be noticed very quickly by consumers because it is a significant percentage of the initial (base) cost of the gasoline.

According to Weber's law, an additional level of stimulus equivalent to the j.n.d. must be added for the majority of people to perceive a difference between the resulting stimulus and the initial stimulus. Let us say that Goddard's, a 130-year-old manufacturer of fine polishes, wants to improve its silver polish sufficiently to claim that it retards tarnish longer than the leading competitive brand. In a series of experiments, the company determines that the j.n.d. for its present polish (which now gives a shine that lasts about 20 days) is 5 days, or one-fourth longer. That means that the shine given by the improved silver polish must last at least 25 days (or one-fourth) longer if the new polish is to be perceived by the majority of users as, in fact, improved. By finding this j.n.d. of 5 days, the company has isolated the minimum amount of time necessary to make its claim of "lasts longer" believable to the majority of consumers. If it had decided to make the polish effective for 23 days (just 3 extra days of product life), its claim of "lasts longer" would not be perceived as true by most consumers and, from the marketer's point of view, would be "wasted." On the other hand, if the company had decided to make the silver polish effective for 40 days, it would have sacrificed a good deal of repeat purchase frequency. Making the product improvement just equal to the j.n.d. thus becomes the most efficient decision that management can make.

An interesting application of the j.n.d. is the development of new food products. With the public alarm regarding the rapidly rising obesity rates, food marketers are looking for substances that can mimic the creamy and palate-coating food of fatty products such as pudding, cheese, and chocolate.[6] The challenge is to create fat substitutes with taste that is below, or at least not significantly above, consumers' j.n.d. for the original, fatty foods.

Marketing applications of the j.n.d.

Weber's law has important applications in marketing. Manufacturers and marketers endeavor to determine the relevant j.n.d. for their products for two very different reasons: (1) so that negative changes (e.g., reductions in product size or quality, or increases in product price) are not readily discernible to the public (i.e., remain below the j.n.d.), and (2) so that product improvements (e.g., improved or updated packaging, larger size, or lower price) are very apparent to consumers without being wastefully extravagant (i.e., they are at or just above the j.n.d.). For example, some years ago, in an apparent misunderstanding of the j.n.d., a silver polish manufacturer introduced an extension of its silver polish brand that prolonged the shine of the silver by months but raised its product price by merely pennies. By doing so, the company decreased its sales revenue because the new version cannibalized the sales of the old product and, at the same time, was purchased much less frequently than the old version. One marketing expert advised the company to double the price of the new product rather than make it just slightly more expensive than the old one.[7] However, for a nondurable consumer good, a product that has been improved dramatically but is doubled in price is inconsistent with the concept of the j.n.d. A better strategy would have been to introduce several successive versions of the polish; each version with a shine that lasts longer than the previous version (and at or slightly above the j.n.d.) and offered at a higher price (but a price that is lower than the j.n.d.).

When it comes to product improvements, marketers very much want to meet or exceed the consumer's differential threshold; that is, they want consumers to readily perceive any improvements made in the original product. Marketers use the j.n.d. to determine the amount of improvement they should make in their products. Less than the j.n.d. is wasted effort because the improvement will not be perceived; more than the j.n.d. is wasteful because it reduces the level of repeat sales. On the other hand, when it comes to price increases, less than the j.n.d. is desirable because consumers are unlikely to notice it.

Since many routinely purchased consumer goods are relatively inexpensive, companies are reluctant to raise prices when their profit margins on these items are declining. Instead, many marketers decrease the product *quantity* included in the packages, while leaving the prices unchanged—thus, in effect, increasing the per unit price. The manufacturer of Huggies reduced the number of diapers in a package from 240 to 228 (and continued pricing it at $31.99); PepsiCo reduced the weight of one snack food bag from 14.5 ounces to 13.5 ounces (and maintained the price at $3.29), and Poland Spring reduced its water-cooler-sized bottle from 6 to 5 gallons (and maintained the old price at $9.25).[8] The packages for these products remained virtually unchanged. Presumably, the decreases in the number of items or weight of these products reflect j.n.d.-focused research; the reductions in quantity were below most consumers' j.n.d. for these products.

Marketers often want to update their existing package designs without losing the ready recognition of consumers who have been exposed to years of cumulative advertising impact. In such cases, they usually make a number of small changes, each carefully designed to fall below the j.n.d., so that consumers will perceive minimal difference between succeeding versions. For example, Betty Crocker, the General Mills symbol, has been updated seven times from 1936 to 1996.

When Lexmark International Inc. bought the office supplies and equipment line from IBM in March 1991, it agreed to relinquish the IBM name by 1996. Recognizing the need to build a brand image for Lexmark while moving away from the well-known IBM name, Lexmark officials conducted a four-stage campaign for phasing in the Lexmark name on products. Stage 1 carried only the IBM name, Stage 2 featured the IBM name and downplayed Lexmark, Stage 3 featured the Lexmark name and downplayed IBM, and Stage 4 features only the Lexmark name.

Subliminal perception

Earlier we spoke of people being *motivated* below their level of conscious awareness. People are also *stimulated* below their level of conscious awareness; that is, they can perceive stimuli without being consciously aware that they are doing so. Stimuli that are too weak or too brief to be consciously seen or heard may nevertheless be strong enough to be perceived by one or more receptor cells. This process is called **subliminal perception** because the stimulus is beneath the threshold, or "limen," of conscious awareness, though obviously not beneath the absolute threshold of the receptors involved. (Perception of stimuli that are above the level of conscious awareness technically is called *supraliminal perception*, though it is usually referred to simply as perception.)

The effectiveness of so-called subliminal advertising was reportedly first tested at a drive-in movie in New Jersey in 1957, where the words "Eat popcorn" and "Drink Coca-Cola" were flashed on the screen during the movie. Exposure times were so short that viewers were unaware of seeing a message. It was reported that during the six-week test period, popcorn sales increased 58 percent and Coca-Cola sales increased 18 percent, but these findings were later reported to be false. Years later, a scientific study found that although the simple subliminal stimulus COKE served to arouse thirst in subjects, the subliminal command DRINK COKE did not have a greater effect, nor did it have any behavioral consequences.[9]

Since the 1950s, there have been sporadic reports of marketers using subliminal messages in their efforts to influence consumption behavior. For example, Disney was accused of using subliminal messages in the movies *Aladdin* (where the hero allegedly whispers "good teenagers, take off your clothes" in a subaudible voice), *The Little Mermaid* (where a minister officiating at a wedding ceremony allegedly displays an erection), and *The Lion King* (where the letters "S-E-X" are allegedly formed in a cloud of dust).[10] At times, it has been difficult to separate truth from fiction regarding such alleged manipulations. When some of the subliminal methods were tested methodically using scientific research procedures, the research results did not support the notion that subliminal messages can persuade consumers to act in a given manner.

Evaluating the effectiveness of subliminal persuasion

Despite the many studies undertaken by academicians and researchers since the 1950s, there is no evidence that subliminal advertising persuades people to buy goods or services. A review of the literature indicates that subliminal perception research has been based on two theoretical approaches. According to the first theory, constant repetition of very weak (i.e., subthreshold) stimuli has an incremental effect that enables such stimuli to build response strength over many presentations. This would be the operative theory when weak stimuli are flashed repeatedly on a movie screen or played on a soundtrack or audiocassette. The second approach is based on the theory that subliminal sexual stimuli arouse unconscious sexual motivations. This is the theory behind the use of sexual embeds in print advertising. But no studies have yet indicated that either of these theoretical approaches has been effectively used by advertisers to increase sales. However, there is some indication that subliminal advertising may provide new opportunities for modifying antisocial behavior through public awareness campaigns that call for individuals to make generalized responses to suggestions that enhance their personal performance or improve their attitudes.[11] There is also some (though not definitive) evidence that subliminal methods can indirectly influence attitudes and feelings toward brands.[12]

In summary, although there is some evidence that subliminal stimuli may influence affective reactions, there is no evidence that subliminal stimulation can influence consumption behavior. There continues to be a big gap between perception and persuasion. A recent review of the evidence on subliminal persuasion indicates that the only way for subliminal techniques to have a significant persuasive effect would be through long-term repeated exposure under a limited set of circumstances, which would not be economically feasible or practical within an advertising context.[13]

As to sexual embeds, most researchers are of the opinion that "what you see is what you get"; that is, a vivid imagination can see whatever it wants to see in just about any situation. And that pretty much sums up the whole notion of perception: Individuals see what they want to see (e.g., what they are motivated to see) and what they expect to see. Several studies concerned with public beliefs about subliminal advertising found that a large percentage of Americans know what subliminal advertising is, they believe it is used by advertisers, and that it is effective in persuading consumers to buy.[14] To correct any misperceptions among the public that subliminal advertising does, in fact, exist, the advertising community occasionally sponsors ads which ridicule the notion that subliminal techniques are effective or that they are used in advertising applications. The ethical issues related to subliminal advertising are discussed later in this chapter.

Dynamics of perception

The preceding section explained how the individual receives sensations from stimuli in the outside environment and how the human organism adapts to the level and intensity of sensory input. We now come to one of the major principles of perception: Raw sensory input by itself does not produce or explain the coherent picture of the world that most adults possess. Indeed, the study of perception is largely the study of what we subconsciously add to or subtract from raw sensory inputs to produce our own private picture of the world.

Human beings are constantly bombarded with stimuli during every minute and every hour of every day. The sensory world is made up of an almost infinite number of discrete sensations that are constantly and subtly changing. According to the principles of sensation, intensive stimulation "bounces off" most individuals, who subconsciously block (i.e., adapt to) a heavy bombardment of stimuli. Otherwise, the billions of different stimuli to which we are constantly exposed might serve to confuse us and keep us perpetually disoriented in a constantly changing environment. However, neither of these consequences tends to occur, because perception is not a function of sensory input alone. Rather, perception is the result of two different kinds of inputs that interact to form the personal pictures—the perceptions—that each individual experiences.

One type of input is *physical stimuli* from the outside environment; the other type of input is provided by individuals themselves in the form of certain predispositions (expectations, motives, and learning) based on *previous experience*. The combination of these two very different kinds of inputs produces for each of us a very private, very personal picture of the world. Because each person is a unique individual, with unique experiences, needs, wants, desires, and expectations, it follows that each individual's perceptions are also unique. This explains why no two people see the world in precisely the same way.

Individuals are very selective as to which stimuli they "recognize"; they subconsciously organize the stimuli they do recognize according to widely held psychological principles, and they interpret such stimuli (they give meaning to them) subjectively in accordance with their personal needs, expectations, and experiences. The following sections examine each of these three aspects of perception: the **selection**, **organization**, and **interpretation of stimuli**.

Perceptual selection

Consumers subconsciously exercise a great deal of selectivity as to which aspects of the environment (which stimuli) they perceive. An individual may look at some things, ignore others, and turn away from still others. In actuality, people receive (i.e., perceive) only a small fraction of the stimuli to which they are exposed. Consider, for example, a woman in a supermarket. She may be exposed to over 20,000 products of different colors, sizes, and shapes; to perhaps 100 people (looking, walking, searching, talking); to smells (from fruit, meat, disinfectant, people); to sounds within the store (cash registers ringing, shopping carts rolling, air conditioners humming, and clerks sweeping, mopping aisles, stocking shelves); and to sounds from outside the store (planes passing, cars honking, tires screeching, children shouting, car doors slamming). Yet she manages on a regular basis to visit her local supermarket, select the items she needs, pay for them, and leave, all within a relatively brief period of time, without losing her sanity or her personal orientation to the world around her. This is because she exercises *selectivity* in perception.

Which stimuli get selected depends on two major factors in addition to the nature of the stimulus itself: (1) consumers' *previous experience* as it affects their *expectations* (what they are prepared, or "set," to see) and (2) their *motives* at the time (their needs, desires, interests, and so on). Each of these factors can serve to increase or decrease the probability that a stimulus will be perceived.

Nature of the stimulus

Marketing stimuli include an enormous number of variables that affect the consumer's perception, such as the *nature* of the product, its *physical attributes*, the *package* design, the *brand* name, the *advertisements* and commercials (including copy claims, choice and sex of model, positioning of model, size of ad, typography), the *position* of a print ad or a commercial, and the *editorial* environment.

In general, *contrast* is one of the most attention-compelling attributes of a stimulus. Advertisers often use extreme attention-getting devices to achieve maximum contrast and, thus, penetrate the consumer's perceptual "screen." For example, a number of magazines and newspapers carry ads that readers can unfold to reveal oversized, poster-like advertisements for products ranging from cosmetics to automobiles, because of the "stopping power" of giant ads among more traditional sizes. However, advertising does not have to be unique to achieve a high degree of differentiation; it simply has to contrast with the environment in which it is run. The use of a dramatic image of the product against a white background with little copy in a print advertisement, the absence of sound in a commercial's opening scene, a 60-second commercial within a string of 20-second spots—all offer sufficient contrast from their environments to achieve differentiation and merit the consumer's attention. In an effort to achieve contrast, some advertisers use splashes of color in black-and-white print ads to highlight the advertised product.

With respect to packaging, astute marketers usually try to differentiate their packages to ensure rapid consumer perception. Since the average package on the supermarket shelf has about 1/10th of a second to make an impression on the consumer, it is important that every aspect of the package—the name, shape, color, label, and copy—provide sufficient sensory stimulation to be noted and remembered.

Expectations

People usually see what they expect to see, and what they expect to see is usually based on familiarity, previous experience, or preconditioned set (**expectations**). In a marketing context, people tend to perceive products and product attributes according to their own expectations. A student who has been told by his friends that a particular professor is interesting and dynamic will probably perceive the professor in that manner when the class begins; a teenager who attends a horror movie that has been billed as terrifying will probably find it so. On the other hand, stimuli that conflict sharply with expectations often receive more attention than those that conform to expectations.

For years, some advertisers have used blatant sexuality in advertisements for products to which sex is not relevant, in the belief that such advertisements would attract a high degree of attention. However, ads with irrelevant sexuality often defeat the marketer's objectives because readers tend to remember the sexual aspects of the ad (e.g., the innuendo or the model), not the product or brand advertised. Nevertheless, some advertisers continue to use erotic appeals in promoting a wide variety of products, from office furniture to jeans.

Motives

People tend to perceive the things they need or want; the stronger the need, the greater the tendency to ignore unrelated stimuli in the environment. A student who is looking for a new cell phone provider is more likely to notice and read carefully ads for deals and special offers regarding such services than his roommate, who may be satisfied with his present cellular service. In general, there is a heightened awareness of stimuli that are relevant to one's needs and interests and a decreased awareness of stimuli that are irrelevant to those needs. An individual's perceptual process simply attunes itself more closely to those elements in the environment that are important to him or her. Someone who is overweight is more likely to notice ads for diet foods; a sexually repressed person may perceive sexual symbolism where none exists.

Marketing managers recognize the efficiency of targeting their products to the perceived needs of consumers. For example, a marketer can determine through marketing research what different segments of consumers consider to be the ideal attributes of the product category or what they perceive their needs to be in relation to the product category. The marketer can then segment the market on the basis of those needs and vary the product advertising so that consumers in each segment will perceive the product as meeting their own special needs, wants, or interests.

Selective perception

As the preceding discussion illustrates, the consumer's "selection" of stimuli from the environment is based on the interaction of expectations and motives with the stimulus itself. These factors give rise to four important concepts concerning perception.

Selective Exposure   Consumers actively seek out messages that they find pleasant or with which they are sympathetic, and they actively avoid painful or threatening ones. They also selectively expose themselves to advertisements that reassure them of the wisdom of their purchase decisions.

Selective Attention   Consumers exercise a great deal of selectivity in terms of the attention they give to commercial stimuli. They have a heightened awareness of stimuli that meet their needs or interests and minimal awareness of stimuli irrelevant to their needs. Thus, consumers are likely to note ads for products that would satisfy their needs and disregard those in which they have no interest. People also vary in terms of the kinds of information in which they are interested and the form of message and type of medium they prefer. Some people are more interested in price, some in appearance, and some in social acceptability. Some people like complex, sophisticated messages; others like simple graphics.

Perceptual Defense   Consumers subconsciously screen out stimuli that they find psychologically threatening, even though exposure has already taken place. Thus, threatening or otherwise damaging stimuli are less likely to be consciously perceived than are neutral stimuli at the same level of exposure. Furthermore, individuals sometimes unconsciously distort information that is not consistent with their needs, values, and beliefs. One way to combat *perceptual defense* is to vary and increase the amount of sensory input. For example, since research showed that most Canadian smokers no longer pay attention to the written warning labels on cigarette packs, Canada now requires tobacco firms to feature graphic health warnings on cigarette packs; one such warning shows a damaged brain and warns about strokes; another shows a limp cigarette and states that tobacco can cause impotence.[15]

Perceptual Blocking Consumers protect themselves from being bombarded with stimuli by simply "tuning out"—blocking such stimuli from conscious awareness. They do so out of self-protection because of the visually overwhelming nature of the world in which we live. The popularity of such devices as *TiVo* and *ReplayTV*, which enable viewers to skip over TV commercials with great ease, is, in part, a result of *perceptual blocking*.

Perceptual organization

People do not experience the numerous stimuli they select from the environment as separate and discrete sensations; rather, they tend to organize them into groups and perceive them as unified wholes. Thus, the perceived characteristics of even the simplest stimulus are viewed as a function of the whole to which the stimulus appears to belong. This method of perceptual organization simplifies life considerably for the individual.

The specific principles underlying perceptual organization are often referred to by the name given the school of psychology that first developed it: **Gestalt psychology**. (*Gestalt*, in German, means pattern or configuration.) Three of the most basic principles of perceptual organization are *figure and ground, grouping*, and *closure*.

Figure and ground

As was noted earlier, stimuli that contrast with their environment are more likely to be noticed. A sound must be louder or softer, a color brighter or paler. The simplest visual illustration consists of a figure on a ground (i.e., background). The figure is perceived more clearly because, in contrast to its ground, it appears to be well defined, solid, and in the forefront. The ground is usually perceived as indefinite, hazy, and continuous. The common line that separates the figure and the ground is generally attributed to the figure rather than to the ground, which helps give the figure greater definition. Consider the stimulus of music. People can either "bathe" in music or listen to music. In the first case, music is simply background to other activities; in the second, it is figure. Figure is more clearly perceived because it appears to be dominant; in contrast, ground appears to be subordinate and, therefore, less important.

People have a tendency to organize their perceptions into **figure-and-ground** relationships. How a figure–ground pattern is perceived can be influenced by prior pleasant or painful associations with one or the other element in isolation. For example, a short time following the destruction of the World Trade Center on September 11, 2001 by airplanes hijacked by terrorists, a professor in New Jersey came across an ad for Lufthansa (Germany's national airline) that featured a flying jet, photographed from the ground up, between two glass high-rise buildings. Rather than focusing on the brand and the jet (i.e., the "figure"), all the viewer could think about was the two tall glass towers in the background (i.e., the "ground"), and the possibility of the jet crashing into them. When the professor presented the ad to his students, many expressed the same thoughts. Clearly, this figure–ground reversal was the outcome of the painful events that occurred in September 2001.

Advertisers have to plan their advertisements carefully to make sure that the stimulus they want noted is seen as figure and not as ground. The musical background must not overwhelm the jingle; the background of an advertisement must not detract from the product. Print advertisers often silhouette their products against a nondistinct background to make sure that the features they want noted are clearly perceived.

Marketers sometimes run advertisements that confuse the consumer because there is no clear indication of which is figure and which is ground. Of course, in some cases, the blurring of figure and ground is deliberate. The well-known Absolut Vodka campaign, started over 25 years ago, often runs print ads in which the figure (the shape of the Absolut bottle) is poorly delineated against its ground, challenging readers to search for the bottle; the resulting audience "participation" produces more intense ad scrutiny.

Grouping

Individuals tend to group stimuli so that they form a unified picture or impression. The perception of stimuli as groups or chunks of information, rather than as discrete bits of information, facilitates their memory and recall. **Grouping** can be used advantageously by marketers to imply certain desired meanings in connection with their products. For example, an advertisement for tea may show a young man and woman sipping tea in a beautifully appointed room before a blazing hearth. The overall mood implied by the grouping of stimuli leads the consumer to associate the drinking of tea with romance, fine living, and winter warmth.

Most of us can remember and repeat our Social Security numbers because we automatically group them into three "*chunks*," rather than try to remember nine separate numbers. Similarly, we recall and repeat our phone number in three segments—the area code, first three digits, and the last four digits. Also, for decades, Americans had five-digit zip codes grouped as a single chunk; as four digits are being added to our zip codes, the U.S. Postal Service faces a challenge in getting Americans to recall the extra digits and add a chunk to their recollection of zip codes.

Closure

Individuals have a need for **closure**. They express this need by organizing their perceptions so that they form a complete picture. If the pattern of stimuli to which they are exposed is incomplete, they tend to perceive it, nevertheless, as complete; that is, they consciously or subconsciously fill in the missing pieces. Thus, a circle with a section of its periphery missing is invariably perceived as a circle, not an arc.

Incomplete messages or tasks are better remembered than completed ones. One explanation for this phenomenon is that a person who hears the beginning of a message or who begins a task develops a need to complete it. If he or she is prevented from doing so, a state of tension is created that manifests itself in improved memory for the incomplete task. For example, hearing the beginning of a message leads to the need to hear the rest of it—like waiting for the second shoe to drop.

The need for closure has interesting implications for marketers. Promotional messages in which viewers are required to "fill in" information beg for completion by consumers, and the very act of completion serves to involve them more deeply in the message. In a related vein, advertisers have discovered that they can achieve excellent results by using the soundtrack of a frequently viewed television commercial on radio. Consumers who are familiar with the TV commercial perceive the audio track alone as incomplete; in their need for completion, they mentally play back the visual content from memory.

In summary, it is clear that perceptions are not equivalent to the raw sensory input of discrete stimuli, nor to the sum total of discrete stimuli. Rather, people tend to add to or subtract from stimuli to which they are exposed on the basis of their expectations and motives, using generalized principles of organization based on Gestalt theory.

Perceptual interpretation

The preceding discussion has emphasized that perception is a personal phenomenon. People exercise selectivity as to which stimuli they perceive, and they organize these stimuli on the basis of certain psychological principles. The interpretation of stimuli is also uniquely individual, because it is based on what individuals expect to see in light of their previous experiences on the number of plausible explanations they can envision, and on their motives and interests at the time of perception.

Stimuli are often highly ambiguous. Some stimuli are weak because of such factors as poor visibility, brief exposure, high noise level, or constant fluctuation. Even stimuli that are strong tend to fluctuate dramatically because of such factors as different angles of viewing, varying distances, and changing levels of illumination. Consumers usually attribute the sensory input they receive to factors they consider most likely to have caused the specific pattern of stimuli. Past experiences and social interactions help to form certain expectations that provide categories (or alternative explanations) that individuals use in interpreting stimuli.

When stimuli are highly ambiguous, an individual will usually interpret them in such a way that they serve to fulfill personal needs, wishes, interests, and so on. It is this principle that provides the rationale for projective tests. Such tests provide ambiguous stimuli (such as incomplete sentences, unclear pictures, untitled cartoons, or ink blots) to respondents who are asked to interpret them. How a person describes a vague illustration, or what meaning the individual ascribes to an ink blot, is a reflection not of the stimulus itself, but of the subject's own needs, wants, and desires. Through the interpretation of ambiguous stimuli, respondents reveal a great deal about themselves.

How close a person's interpretations are to reality, then, depends on the clarity of the stimulus, the past experiences of the perceiver, and his or her motives and interests at the time of perception.

Perceptual distortion

Individuals are subject to a number of influences that tend to distort their perceptions, such as physical appearances, stereotypes, first impressions, jumping to conclusions, and the halo effect.

Physical Appearances People tend to attribute the qualities they associate with certain people to others who may resemble them, whether or not they consciously recognize the similarity. For this reason, the selection of models for print advertisements and for television commercials can be a key element in their ultimate persuasiveness. Studies have found that attractive models are more persuasive and have a more positive influence on consumer attitudes and behavior than average-looking models; attractive men are perceived as more successful businessmen than average-looking men. Some research suggests that models influence consumers' perceptions of physical attractiveness, and through comparisons, their own self-perceptions.[16] Recent research indicates that using a highly attractive model may not necessarily increase message effectiveness. One study revealed that highly attractive models are perceived as having more expertise regarding enhancement products (e.g., jewelry, lipstick, perfume) but not problem-solving products (e.g., products that correct beauty flaws such as acne or dandruff).[17] Therefore, advertisers must ensure that there is a rational match between the product advertised and the physical attributes of the model used to promote it.

Stereotypes Individuals tend to carry pictures in their minds of the meanings of various kinds of stimuli. These stereotypes serve as expectations of what specific situations, people, or events will be like, and they are important determinants of how such stimuli are subsequently perceived. Several years ago, an ad for Benetton featuring two men—one black and one white—handcuffed together, which was part of the "united colors of Benetton" campaign promoting racial harmony, produced a public outcry because people perceived it as depicting a white man arresting a black man. Clearly, this perception was the result of stereotypes, since there was nothing in the ad to indicate that the white person was arresting the black person rather than the other way around. One study discovered the stereotypes regarding a product's country-of-origin influenced consumers' purchases, and also that such stereotypes had more impact on an impulse purchase than on a deliberate and planned purchase.[18]

First Impressions   First impressions tend to be lasting; yet, in forming such impressions, the perceiver does not yet know which stimuli are relevant, important, or predictive of later behavior. A shampoo commercial effectively used the line, "You'll never have a second chance to make a first impression." Since first impressions are often lasting, introducing a new product before it has been perfected may prove fatal to its ultimate success; subsequent information about its advantages, even if true, will often be negated by the memory of its early performance.

Jumping to Conclusions   Many people tend to jump to conclusions before examining all the relevant evidence. For example, the consumer may hear just the beginning of a commercial message and draw conclusions regarding the product or service being advertised. For this reason, many copywriters are careful to give their most persuasive arguments first. A recent study showed that consumers who ate foods with elaborate names such as "succulent Italian seafood filet" rated those foods as more tasty and appealing than those who ate the same foods with such regular names as "seafood filet."[19] Many consumers do not read the volume information on food labels. One study found that consumers purchase packages that they believe contain greater volume, whether or not this is actually so, and that they perceive elongated packaging to contain more volume than round packaging.[20] Clearly, these findings have important implications for package design, advertising, and pricing, and also represent some ethical dilemmas that are discussed later on in this chapter.

Halo Effect   Historically, the halo effect has been used to describe situations in which the evaluation of a single object or person on a multitude of dimensions is based on the evaluation of just one or a few dimensions (e.g., a man is trustworthy, fine, and noble because he looks you in the eye when he speaks). Consumer behaviorists broaden the notion of the halo effect to include the evaluation of multiple objects (e.g., a product line) on the basis of the evaluation of just one dimension (a brand name or a spokesperson). Using this broader definition, marketers take advantage of the halo effect when they extend a brand name associated with one line of products to another. The lucrative field of *licensing* is based on the halo effect. Manufacturers and retailers hope to acquire instant recognition and status for their products by associating them with a well-known name. A recent study discovered that brands are judged more positively than warranted when evaluated alone than when evaluated within a group of other brands.[21] These findings have implications for the placement of brands in stores and the position of a given brand's advertisements in relation to competing ads within a magazine or a commercial break.

Tampering with the perceived halo effect of a product or brand can have disastrous consequences. For example, in an attempt to enhance the image of JW Marriott, the Marriott hotel chain's upscale brand, Marriott took over the Righa Royal Hotel, an upscale hotel in New York City, and renamed it the JW Marriott New York. When the new name signs went up, the company discovered that scores of regular, upscale customers who always stayed at the Righa when visiting New York City canceled their reservations because they did not want to tell colleagues to contact them at the Marriott. The company restored the Righa Hotel name, with the JW Marriott name included in smaller print.[22]

Despite the many subjective influences on perceptual interpretation, individuals usually resolve stimulus ambiguity somewhat "realistically" on the basis of their previous experiences. Only in situations of unusual or changing stimulus conditions do expectations lead to wrong interpretations.

Consumer imagery

Consumers have a number of enduring perceptions, or images, that are particularly relevant to the study of consumer behavior. Products and brands have symbolic value for individuals, who evaluate them on the basis of their consistency (congruence) with their personal pictures of themselves. Earlier we discussed consumer self-images and how consumers attempt to preserve or enhance their self-images by buying products and using services that they believe are congruent with their self-images and by avoiding those that are not. The following section examines consumers' perceived images of products, brands, services, prices, product quality, retail stores, and manufacturers.

Product positioning

The essence of successful marketing is the image that a product has in the mind of the consumer—that is, its **positioning**. Positioning is more important to the ultimate success of a product than are its actual characteristics, although products that are poorly made will not succeed in the long run on the basis of image alone. The core of effective positioning is a unique position that the product occupies in the mind of the consumer. Most new products fail because they are perceived as "me too" offerings that do not offer potential consumers any advantages or unique benefits over competitive products.

Marketers of different brands in the same category can effectively differentiate their offerings only if they stress the *benefits* that their brands provide rather than their products' physical features. The benefits featured in a product's positioning must reflect attributes that are important to and congruent with the perceptions of the targeted consumer segment. For example, the two energy bars Nutrigrain and Balance are probably quite similar in terms of their nutritional composition and their physical characteristics; however, each one of the two brands is clearly positioned to offer a distinct benefit. Nutrigrain is positioned as an alternative to unhealthy snack foods in the morning, and Balance is positioned as an energy pickup for the late afternoon.

Positioning strategy is the essence of the marketing mix; it complements the company's definition of the competition, its segmentation strategy, and its selection of target markets. For example, in its positioning as a breakfast food, Nutrigrain competes with other breakfast foods. Through research, the manufacturer has determined the characteristics of people who are concerned about their health and appearance (and yet, eat unhealthy breakfast foods) and the media they read, listen to and watch. The marketers of Balance have determined the characteristics of those who need a pick-me-up in the late afternoon and their media habits, and developed a marketing plan that reflects all these elements.

Positioning conveys the concept, or meaning, of the product or service in terms of how it fulfills a consumer need. A good positioning strategy should have a two-pronged meaning: one that is congruent with the consumer's needs while, at the same time, featuring the brand against its competition. For example, the classic 7-Up slogan "The Un-Cola" was designed to appeal to consumers' desire for an alternative to the most popular soft drink (by using the prefix *un*), while also elevating the product by placing it in the same league with its giant competitor (by using the word *cola*). Also, as demonstrated by 7-Up's change in positioning strategy to "Caffeine—never had it, never will" to depict its core benefit, the same product (or service) can be positioned differently to different market segments or can be repositioned to the same audience, without being physically changed. Procter and Gamble has positioned its SURE deodorant as an essential travel necessity to take on safari—a positioning strategy designed to reach a strong, masculine, adventurous target audience.

The result of successful positioning strategy is a distinctive brand image on which consumers rely in making product choices. A positive brand image also leads to consumer loyalty, positive beliefs about brand value, and a willingness to search for the brand. A positive brand image also promotes consumer interest in future brand promotions and *inoculates* consumers against competitors' marketing activities. An advertiser's positioning strategy affects consumer beliefs about its brand's attributes and the prices consumers are willing to pay.

In today's highly competitive marketplace, a distinctive product image is most important, but also very difficult to create and maintain. As products become more complex and the marketplace more crowded, consumers rely more on the product's image and claimed benefits than on its actual attributes in making purchase decisions. The major positioning strategies are discussed in the following five sections.

Umbrella positioning

This strategy entails creating an overall image of the company around which a lot of products can be featured individually. This strategy is appropriate for very large corporations with diversified product lines. For example, McDonald's positioning approaches over the years include "You deserve a break today at McDonald's," "Nobody can do it like McDonald's can," and "Good times, great taste."

Positioning against the competition

A classic example of positioning against the competition is Wendy's "Where's the beef?" which was used to differentiate the smaller fast-food chain from much larger competitors. Visa's past slogan "We make American Express green with envy" is another good example of this strategy. A Sunkist ad featured a lemon, in the form of a salt shaker, with the caption "Salternative." The Hertz car rental company has run TV ads depicting other car rental companies as lacking in features that Hertz outlets generally possess, such as proximity to passenger terminals at airports (e.g., "Hertz? Not exactly.").

Positioning based on a specific benefit

FedEx created its highly reliable service image with the slogan "When it absolutely, positively has to be there overnight." Maxwell House Coffee is "good to the last drop." Bounty is "the quicker picker upper." These are examples of slogans that smartly and precisely depict key benefits of the brands they promote and have effectively positioned these brands in the minds of consumers. There are also many examples of products that failed because they were positioned to deliver a benefit that consumers either did not want or did not believe. For example, Gillette's "For Oily Hair Only" shampoo failed because most consumers do not acknowledge that they have oily hair. Effective depictions of a core benefit often include memorable imagery (e.g., the old lady featured in Wendy's "Where's the beef?" ad).

Finding an "unowned" position

In highly competitive markets, finding a niche not targeted by other companies is challenging but not impossible. For example, Long Island's *Newsday*, in a reference to two competitive daily newspapers published in New York City (*The Daily News* and the *New York Times*), is positioned as "On top of the news and ahead of the times." A clever approach to finding (or even creating) an "unowned" position was Palmolive's claim to ". . . soften your hands as you do the dishes"; today, even though many people no longer wash dishes by hand, Palmolive positions its dishwashing liquid as "tough on grease, soft on hands."

Filling several positions

Because unfilled gaps or "unowned" perceptual positions present opportunities for competitors, sophisticated marketers create several distinct offerings, often in the form of different brands, to fill several identified niches. For example, Visine's line of eye care offerings include versions for redness relief, eye lubrication, advanced redness relief and lubrication, lubrication and rewetting, and "tears" packaged in a single drop dispenser.[23] Crest Toothpaste's line includes offerings for whitening, tartar protection, multicare, cavity protection, sensitive teeth protection, and refreshing mouth and breath with baking soda. Many of these versions are offered as pastes, gels, liquid gels or striped pastes, in many flavors. There is also a separate line of toothpastes and gels for kids.[24] It would be difficult for a manufacturer to penetrate either the eye care or the toothpaste market with a product that offers a benefit that is not already provided by Visine or Crest, in their respective markets.

Product repositioning

Regardless of how well positioned a product appears to be, the marketer may be forced to reposition it in response to market events, such as a competitor cutting into the brand's market share or too many competitors stressing the same attribute. For example, rather than trying to meet the lower prices of high-quality private-label competition, some premium brand marketers have repositioned their brands to justify their higher prices, playing up brand attributes that had previously been ignored.

Another reason to reposition a product or service is to satisfy changing consumer preferences. For example, for years, GM tried to convince consumers that Oldsmobile is not an "old folks'" car by trying to reposition the car as "not your father's Oldsmobile." However, this effort failed because the "old folks'" image of the brand was very strongly set in the minds of car buyers, and GM discontinued this brand. Following consumers' frantic efforts to cut down on consuming carbohydrates, some brands of orange juice, vegetable juice, and beer were repositioned as products that provide "less carbs." One of the most successful product repositionings is the promotion of Arm & Hammer as America's standard for cleanliness and purity by showing it used as a product for the home, the family, and personal care. The brand's Web site lists about one dozen personal care uses, including using the product as a facial scrub, deodorant, bath soak, and mouth refreshent. The site also lists scores of possible uses of the product in every possible room of a typical house and its outside areas.

Perceptual mapping

The technique of **perceptual mapping** helps marketers to determine just how their products or services appear to consumers in relation to competitive brands on one or more relevant characteristics. It enables them to see gaps in the positioning of all brands in the product or service class and to identify areas in which consumer needs are not being adequately met. For example, if a magazine publisher wants to introduce a new magazine to Generation Y, he may use perceptual mapping to uncover a niche of consumers with a special set of interests that are not being adequately or equally addressed by other magazines targeted to the same demographic segment. This insight allows him to position the new magazine as specifically focused on these interests. Or, a publisher may discover through perceptual mapping that consumers perceive its magazine (let's call it *Splash*) to be very similar in editorial content and format to its closest competitors, *Bash* and *Crash*. By changing the focus of its editorial features to appeal to a new market niche, the publisher can reposition the magazine (e.g., from *Splash* to *Fashion Splash*). Figure 15.1 presents this example in a perceptual map.

Positioning of services

Compared with manufacturing firms, service marketers face several unique problems in positioning and promoting their offerings. Because services are intangible, image becomes a key factor in differentiating a service from its competition. Thus, the marketing objective is to enable the consumer to link a specific image with a specific brand name. Many service marketers have developed strategies to provide customers with visual images and tangible reminders of their service offerings. These include delivery vehicles painted in distinct colors, restaurant matchbooks, packaged hotel soaps and shampoos, and a variety of other specialty items. Many service companies feature real service employees in their ads (as tangible cues) and some use people-focused themes to differentiate themselves. For example, the Ritz-Carlton promotes

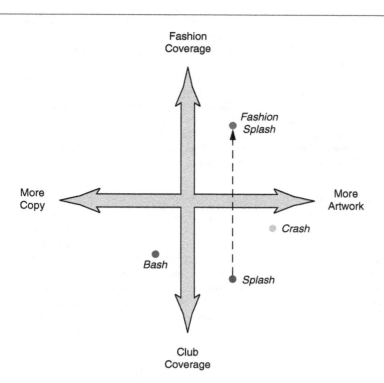

its "guest experience" with the corporate motto "We are ladies and gentlemen serving ladies and gentlemen."

Many service companies market several versions of their service to different market segments by using a differentiated positioning strategy. However, they must be careful to avoid perceptual confusion among their customers. For example, Marriott's Hotels and Resorts brand claims to provide customers with "superior service and genuine care"; the Renaissance Hotels and Resorts brand provides "distinctive décor, imaginative experiences and delights its customers' senses"; the Courtyard brand provides "essential services and amenities to business travelers"; the Residence Inn is designed for extended stays; and the Fairfield Inn provides rooms and suites at "prices that will make customers smile."[25] Although distinct brand names are important to all products or services, they are particularly crucial in marketing services due to the abstract and intangible nature of many services. For example, names such as Federal Express (later abbreviated to FedEx) and Humana (a provider of health services) are excellent names because they are distinctive, memorable, and relevant to the services they feature. On the other hand, Allegis—a short-lived brand name aimed at creating a business travel concept by combining United Airlines, Hertz, and Hilton and Westin Hotels under one umbrella—failed because it told consumers nothing about the type of services it offered.[26]

The design of the service environment is an important aspect of service positioning strategy and sharply influences consumer impressions and consumer and employee behavior. The physical environment is particularly important in creating a favorable impression for such services as banks, retail stores, and professional offices, because there are so few objective criteria by which consumers can judge the quality of the services they receive. The service environment conveys the image of the service provider with whom the service is so closely linked. Thus, the Polo Ralph Lauren store in its renovated 1895 mansion on New York's Upper East Side is the embodiment of the image Lauren wants to create for his clothes: traditionalism and Old World values. All the trappings of what one imagines to be the high-class and well-heeled ways of the very, very rich are here, from the baronial, hand-carved staircase lined with "family" portraits to the plush sitting rooms with working fireplaces. The Polo store image artfully extends the image of the clothing it sells and projects an Old World quality of living and shopping that its upscale target market finds appealing.

One study of service environments identified five environmental variables most important to bank customers: (1) privacy (both visually and verbally, with enclosed offices, transaction privacy, etc.); (2) efficiency/convenience (e.g., transaction areas that are easy to find, directional signs); (3) ambient background conditions (temperature, lighting, noise, music); (4) social conditions (the physical appearance of other people in the bank environment, such as bank customers and bank personnel); and (5) aesthetics (e.g., color, style, use of materials, and artwork).[27]

Perceived price

How a consumer perceives a price—as high, as low, as fair—has a strong influence on both purchase intentions and purchase satisfaction. Consider the perception of price fairness, for example. There is some evidence that customers do pay attention to the prices paid by other customers (such as senior citizens, frequent flyers, affinity club members), and that the differential pricing strategies used by some marketers are perceived as unfair by customers not eligible for the special prices. No one is happy knowing he or she paid twice as much for an airline ticket or a theater ticket as the person in the next seat. Perceptions of price unfairness affect consumers' perceptions of product value and, ultimately, their willingness to patronize a store or a service. One study, focused on the special challenges of service industries in pricing intangible products, proposed three types of pricing strategies based on the customer's perception of the value provided by the purchase: *satisfaction-based* pricing, *relationship* pricing, and *efficiency* pricing (see Table 15.1).

Reference prices

Products advertised as "on sale" tend to create enhanced customer perceptions of savings and value. Different formats used in sales advertisements have differing impacts, based on consumer **reference prices**. A reference price is *any price that a consumer uses*

TABLE 15.1	Three Pricing Strategies Focused on Perceived Value	
PRICING STRATEGY	**PROVIDES VALUE BY . . .**	**IMPLEMENTED AS . . .**
Satisfaction-based pricing	Recognizing and reducing customers' perceptions of uncertainty, which the intangible nature of services magnifies.	Service guarantees. Benefit-driven pricing. Flat-rate pricing.
Relationship pricing	Encouraging long-term relationships with the company that customers view as beneficial.	Long-term contracts. Price bundling.
Efficiency pricing	Sharing with customers the cost savings that the company has achieved by understanding, managing, and reducing the costs of providing the service.	Cost-leader pricing.

Source: Leonard L. Berry and Yadav S. Manjit, "Capture and Communicate Value in the Pricing of Services," *Sloan Management Review,* Summer 1996, 41–51.

as a basis for comparison in judging another price. Reference prices can be external or internal. An advertiser generally uses a higher *external reference price* ("sold elsewhere at . . .") in an ad offering a lower sales price, to persuade the consumer that the product advertised is a really good buy. *Internal reference prices* are those prices (or price ranges) retrieved by the consumer from memory. Internal reference prices play a major role in consumers' evaluations and perceptions of value of an advertised (external) price deal, as well as in the believability of any advertised reference price. However, consumers' internal reference prices change. For example, as the prices of flat-screen TVs declined sharply due to competition and manufacturers' abilities to produce them more cheaply, consumers' reference prices for this product have declined as well, and many no longer perceive flat-screen TVs as a luxury product that only few can afford. One study showed that consumers' price reference points include past prices, competitors' prices, and the cost of goods sold. The study also showed that these reference points do not adequately reflect the effects of inflation on costs, and that customers attribute price differentials to profit and fail to consider vendor costs.[28]

Some researchers proposed that two types of utility are associated with consumer purchases. **Acquisition utility** represents the consumer's perceived economic gain or loss associated with a purchase and is a function of product utility and purchase price. **Transaction utility** concerns the perceived pleasure or displeasure associated with the financial aspect of the purchase and is determined by the difference between the internal reference price and the purchase price.[29] For example, if a consumer wants to purchase a television set for which her internal reference price is approximately $500, and she buys a set that is sale-priced at $500, she receives no transaction utility. However, if either her internal reference price is increased or the sales price of the set is decreased, she will receive positive transaction utility, which increases the total utility she experiences with the purchase.

Consumers' perceptions of the credibility and fairness of stated prices is an important factor in overall satisfaction. Although many marketers assume that the traditional phrases "regular price" versus "sale price" have the same meaning for all consumers, this is unlikely given the evidence that perceptions of marketing stimuli vary widely among consumers.[30]

Several studies showed that consumers believe that the selling prices of a product or service are considerably higher than their perceived fair prices.[31] Several studies have investigated the effects on consumer price perceptions of three types of advertised reference prices: plausible low, plausible high, and implausible high. *Plausible low* prices are well within the range of acceptable market prices; *plausible high* are near the outer limits of the range but not beyond the realm of believability, and *implausible high* are well above the consumer's perceived range of acceptable market prices. As long as an advertised reference price is within a given consumer's acceptable price range, it is considered plausible and is assimilated. If the advertised reference point is outside the range of acceptable prices (i.e., implausible), it will be *contrasted* and thus will not be perceived as a valid reference point. This will adversely affect both consumer evaluations and the advertiser's image of credibility.[32]

Another study showed that when consumers encounter prices that are significantly different from their expectations, they engage in *dissonance reduction*. That is, they seek additional information to justify the high price or they trivialize their own expectations by, for example, saying that their expectations were unrealistic because it has been a while since they last were in the market to buy the product in question.[33] Table 15.2 depicts the possible changes in the perceptions of consumers who encounter unexpected prices.

Perceived quality

Consumers often judge the quality of a product or service on the basis of a variety of informational cues that they associate with the product. Some of these cues are **intrinsic** to the product or service; others are **extrinsic**. Either singly or together, such cues provide the basis for perceptions of product and service quality.

TABLE 15.2

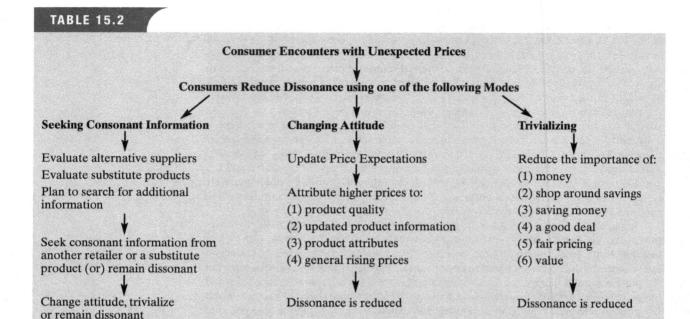

Consumer Encounters with Unexpected Prices

↓

Consumers Reduce Dissonance using one of the following Modes

Seeking Consonant Information	Changing Attitude	Trivializing
Evaluate alternative suppliers	Update Price Expectations	Reduce the importance of:
Evaluate substitute products		(1) money
Plan to search for additional information	Attribute higher prices to:	(2) shop around savings
	(1) product quality	(3) saving money
Seek consonant information from another retailer or a substitute product (or) remain dissonant	(2) updated product information	(4) a good deal
	(3) product attributes	(5) fair pricing
	(4) general rising prices	(6) value
Change attitude, trivialize or remain dissonant	Dissonance is reduced	Dissonance is reduced

Source: Joan Lindsey Mulliken, "Beyond Reference Price: Understanding Consumers' Encounters with Unexpected Prices," *Journal of Product and Brand Management,* 12, no. 3, 141.

Perceived quality of products

Cues that are *intrinsic* concern physical characteristics of the product itself, such as size, color, flavor, or aroma. In some cases, consumers use physical characteristics (e.g., the flavor of ice cream or cake) to judge product quality. Consumers like to believe that they base their evaluations of product quality on intrinsic cues, because that enables them to justify their product decisions (either positive or negative) as being "rational" or "objective" product choices. More often than not, however, they use extrinsic characteristics to judge quality. For example, though many consumers claim they buy a brand because of its superior taste, they are often unable to identify that brand in blind taste tests. One study discovered that the color of a powdered fruit drink product is a more important determinant than its label and actual taste in determining the consumer's ability to identify the flavor correctly. The study's subjects perceived the purple or grape-colored versions of the powdered product "tart" in flavor and the orange-colored version as "flavorful, sweet, and refreshing."[34] *Consumer Reports* found that consumers often cannot differentiate among various cola beverages and that they base their preferences on such *extrinsic cues* as packaging, pricing, advertising, and even peer pressure.[35] A study reported that both consumers who rated a popcorn's taste as unfavorable and those who rated the same taste as favorable consumed more of the product when the container size was increased.[36] In the absence of actual experience with a product, consumers often evaluate quality on the basis of cues that are external to the product itself, such as price, brand image, manufacturer's image, retail store image, or even the country of origin.

Many consumers use *country-of-origin* stereotypes to evaluate products (e.g., "German engineering is excellent" or "Japanese cars are reliable"). Many consumers believe that a "Made in the U.S.A." label means a product is "superior" or "very good." Yet for food products, a foreign image is often more enticing. For example, Haagen-Dazs, an American-made ice cream, has been incredibly successful with its made-up (and meaningless) Scandinavian-sounding name. The success of Smirnoff vodka, made in Connecticut, can be related to its so-called Russian derivation. Sorbet has become a very popular and chic dessert, now that it is no longer called sherbet. A recent study pointed out that consumers' perceptions of value, risk, trust, attitude towards the brand, satisfaction, familiarity, attachment, and involvement moderate the impact of country-of-origin on perceived quality.[37] Several researchers developed a scale that measures perceptions of brand luxury—a construct that is often related to perceived quality.

Perceived quality of services

It is more difficult for consumers to evaluate the quality of services than the quality of products. This is true because of certain distinctive characteristics of services: They are intangible, they are variable, they are perishable, and they are simultaneously produced and consumed. To overcome the fact that consumers are unable to compare competing services side-by-side as they do with competing products, consumers rely on surrogate cues (i.e., extrinsic cues) to evaluate service quality. In evaluating a doctor's services, for example, they note the quality of the office and examining room furnishings, the number (and source) of framed degrees on the wall, the pleasantness of the receptionist, and the professionalism of the nurse; all contribute to the consumer's overall evaluation of the quality of a doctor's services.

Because the actual quality of services can vary from day to day, from service employee to service employee, and from customer to customer (e.g., in food, in waitperson service, in haircuts, even in classes taught by the same professor), marketers try to standardize their services in order to provide consistency of quality. The downside of service standardization is the loss of customized services, which many consumers value.

Unlike products, which are first produced, then sold, and then consumed, most services are first sold and then produced and consumed simultaneously. Whereas a defective product is likely to be detected by factory quality control inspectors before it ever reaches the consumer, an inferior service is consumed as it is being produced; thus, there is little opportunity to correct it. For example, a defective haircut is difficult to correct, just as the negative impression caused by an abrupt or careless waiter is difficult to correct.

During peak demand hours, the interactive quality of services often declines, because both the customer and the service provider are hurried and under stress. Without special effort by the service provider to ensure consistency of services during peak hours, service image is likely to decline. Some marketers try to change demand patterns in order to distribute the service more equally over time. Long-distance telephone services, for instance, traditionally have offered a discount on telephone calls placed during off-peak hours (e.g., after 11:00 P.M. or on weekends); some restaurants offer a significantly less expensive "early bird" dinner for consumers who come in before 7:00 P.M. Service providers often try to reduce the perceived waiting time and the likely consequent negative service evaluation by filling the consumer's time. For example, diners may be invited to study the menu while waiting for a table; visitors who wait their turn at an attraction at Disney World are almost always distracted by video presentations or live entertainment.

The most widely accepted framework for researching service quality stems from the premise that a consumer's evaluation of service quality is a function of the magnitude and direction of the gap between the customer's *expectations of service* and the customer's *assessment (perception) of the service actually delivered*.[38] For example, a brand-new graduate student enrolled in an introductory marketing course at a highly reputable university has certain expectations about the intellectual abilities of her classmates, the richness of classroom discussions, and the professor's knowledge and communication skills. At the end of the term, her assessment of the course's quality is based on the differences between her expectations at the start of the term and her perceptions of the course at the end of the semester. If the course falls below her expectations, she will view it as a service of poor quality. If her expectations are exceeded, she will view the course as a high-quality educational experience. Of course, the expectations of a given service vary widely among different consumers of the same service. These expectations stem from word-of-mouth consumers have heard about the service, their past experiences, the promises made about the service in its ads and by its salespersons, the purchase alternatives available, and other situational factors.[39] Based on these factors, the sum total of a consumer's expectations of a service *before* receiving it is termed *predicted service*, services evaluated by the customer at the *end* of the service that significantly exceed the predicted service are perceived as offerings of high quality and generate more customer satisfaction, increased probability of repeat patronage, and favorable word-of-mouth.[40]

The SERVQUAL scale was designed to measure the gap between customers' expectations of services and their perceptions of the actual service delivered, based on the following five dimensions: reliability, responsiveness, assurance, empathy, and tangibility.[41] These dimensions are divided into two groups: the *outcome* dimension (which focuses on the reliable delivery of the core service) and the *process* dimension, which focuses on how the core service is delivered (i.e., the employees' responsiveness, assurance, and empathy in handling customers) and the service's tangible aspects.[42] The process dimension offers the service provider a significant opportunity to exceed customer expectations. For example, although Federal Express provides the same core service as other couriers (the *outcome* dimension), it provides a superior *process* dimension through its advanced tracking system, which can provide customers with instant information about the status of their packages at any time between pickup and delivery; it also provides call centers with knowledgeable, well-trained, and polite employees who can readily answer customers' questions and handle problems. Thus, FedEx uses the process dimension as a method to exceed customers' expectations and has acquired the image of a company that has an important, customer-focused competitive advantage among the many companies providing the same core service. Table 15.3 depicts the application of the five SERVQUAL dimensions in a study of tourists' perceptions of tour operators.

Perceptions of high service quality and high customer satisfaction lead to higher levels of purchase intentions and repeat buying. Service quality is a determinant of whether the consumer ultimately remains with the company or defects to a competitor. When service quality evaluations are high, customers' behavioral intentions tend to be favorable to the company, and they are likely to remain customers. When service evaluations are low, customer relationships are more likely to weaken, resulting in defection to a competitor. Another issue in the perception of service quality is time. A longitudinal research study using the SERVQUAL scale discovered that consumers' perceptions of service quality declined over time, that favorable perceptions of the service's tangible features declined the least, and that changes in perceptions impacted the intentions to purchase the service again.[43]

Today many services are delivered over the phone or the Internet, without direct visual contact between the customer and the service employee. Under these conditions, it is more difficult to research the factors that determine the customer's perception of service quality. Because more and more companies, including the manufacturers of many tangible products, use service-focused selling points to promote and differentiate their offerings, such consumer studies are crucial. Call centers are a key point for customer access to the company and also an important source of customer information. One study analyzed voice-to-voice encounters among customers and call-center employees, and developed a scale that measures customers' perceptions of such service experiences and their future intentions regarding the company represented by the call center contacted (see Table 15.4).

Price/quality relationship

Perceived product value has been described as a trade-off between the product's perceived benefits (or quality) and the perceived sacrifice—both monetary and non-monetary—necessary to acquire it. A number of research studies have found that consumers rely on price as an indicator of product quality, that consumers attribute different qualities to identical products that carry different price tags, and that such consumer characteristics as age and income affect the perception of value.[44] One study suggested that consumers using a **price/quality relationship** are actually relying on a well-known (and, hence, more

TABLE 15.3	Tour Operators Evaluated Under the Five SERVQUAL Dimensions

(1) ASSURANCE DIMENSION:

- being served by the appropriate personnel;
- reinforcement of tourists' confidence;
- experienced and competent tour and hotel escorts; and
- fluent and understandable communication with tourists.

(2) RESPONSIVENESS DIMENSION:

- sincere interest in problem solving;
- provision of adequate information about the service delivered;
- prompt response to tourists' requests;
- provision of information on local entertainment;
- willingness to help tourists; and
- advice on how to use free time.

(3) RELIABILITY DIMENSION:

- easy contact on arrival at airport;
- easy location of and contact with tour and hotel escorts;
- services delivered on time;
- right first time;
- keeping promises;
- insisting on error-free service;
- meeting the tour schedule; and
- no sudden increase in tour cost.

(4) EMPATHY DIMENSION:

- pleasant, friendly personnel;
- understanding of specific needs; and
- cultivation of friendly relationship.

(5) TANGIBLES DIMENSION:

- modern and technologically relevant vehicles;
- appealing accommodation facilities;
- availability of information documents and notes;
- physical appearance of tour and hotel escorts (tidiness etc.); and
- high-quality meals.

Source: Eda Atilgn, Serkan Akinaci, and Safak Aksoy, "Mapping Service Quality in the Tourism Industry," *Managing Service Quality*, 13, no. 5 (2003), 416

expensive) brand name as an indicator of quality without actually relying directly on price per se.[45] A later study found out that consumers use price and brand to evaluate the prestige of the product but do not generally use these cues when they evaluate the product's performance.[46] Because price is so often considered an indicator of quality, some product advertisements deliberately emphasize a high price to underscore the marketers' claims of quality. Marketers understand that, at times, products with lower prices may be interpreted as reduced quality. At the same time, when consumers evaluate more concrete attributes of a product, such as performance and durability, they rely less on the price and brand name

---

TABLE 15.4   **A Scale Measuring Customers' Perceptions of Call-Center Employees**

ATTENTIVENESS
1. The agent did not make an attentive impression.*
2. The agent used short, affirmative words and sounds to indicate that (s)he was really listening.

PERCEPTIVENESS
1. The agent asked for more details and extra information during the conversation.
2. The agent continually attempted to understand what I was saying.
3. The agent paraphrased what had been said adequately.

RESPONSIVENESS
1. The agent offered relevant information to the questions I asked.
2. The agent used full sentences in his or her answers instead of just saying yes or no.
3. The agent did not recognize what information I needed.*

TRUST
1. I believe that this company takes customer calls seriously.
2. I feel that this company does not respond to customer problems with understanding.*
3. This company is ready and willing to offer support to customers.
4. I can count on this company to be sincere.

SATISFACTION
1. I am satisfied with the level of service the agent provided.
2. I am satisfied with the way I was spoken to by the agent.
3. I am satisfied with the information I got from the agent.
4. The telephone call with this agent was a satisfying experience.

CALL INTENTION
1. I will very likely contact this company again.
2. Next time I have any questions I will not hesitate to call again.
3. I would not be willing to discuss problems I have with this company over the phone.*

---

*Negatively phrased item.

Source: Ko de Ruyter and Martin G. M. Wetzels, *Journal of Service Research*, "The Impact of Perceived Listening Behavior in Voice-to-Voice Service Encounters," February 2000, pp. 276–284, copyright © 2000 by Sage Publications Ltd. Reprinted by permission of Sage Publications.

as indicators of quality than when they evaluate the product's prestige and symbolic value.[47] For these reasons, marketers must understand all the attributes that customers use to evaluate a given product and include all applicable information in order to counter any perceptions of negative quality associated with a lower price.

In most consumption situations, in addition to price, consumers also use such cues as the brand and the store in which the product is bought to evaluate its quality. Consumers use price as a surrogate indicator of quality if they have little information to go on, or if they have little confidence in their own ability to make the product or service choice on other grounds. When the consumer is familiar with a brand name or has experience with a product (or service) or the store where it is purchased, price declines as a determining factor in product evaluation and purchase.

Retail store image

Retail stores have images of their own that serve to influence the perceived quality of products they carry and the decisions of consumers as to where to shop. These images stem from their design and physical environment, their pricing strategies, and product assortments. A study that examined the effects of specific store environmental factors on quality inferences found that consumer perceptions were more heavily influenced by ambient factors (such as the number, type, and behavior of other customers within the store and the sales personnel) than by store design features.[48] Another study discovered that consumers' preferences of apparel stores were determined by the availability of the desired clothing in stock, the outside store appearance, shopping hours, and advertising.[49]

A study of retail store image based on comparative *pricing strategies* found that consumers tend to perceive stores that offer a small discount on a large number of items (i.e., *frequency of price advantage*) as having lower prices overall than competing stores that offer larger discounts on a smaller number of products (i.e., *magnitude of price advantage*). Thus, frequent advertising that presents large numbers of price specials reinforces consumer beliefs about the competitiveness of a store's prices.[50] This finding has important implications for retailers' *positioning strategies.* In times of heavy competition, when it is tempting to hold frequent large sales covering many items, such strategies may result in an unwanted change in store image. For example, Lord & Taylor's in New York City, formerly positioned as an upscale, high-class department store, advertises sales so frequently and fills its aisles with sales racks proclaiming bargain prices, so that its upscale image has been tarnished, and its customer mix has changed. Marketers must also consider how price reductions of *specific* products impact consumers' perceptions. One study pointed out that some poorly chosen price promotions bring about discrepancies between the actual prices in the store and consumers' perceptions of the retailer's *overall store price image.*[51]

The *width of product assortment* also affects retail store image. Grocery retailers, for example, are often reluctant to reduce the number of products they carry out of concern that perceptions of a smaller assortment will reduce the likelihood that consumers will shop in their stores.[52] On the other hand, Whole Foods Markets—a relatively small supermarket chain—has carved itself a profitable niche by carrying a much smaller but highly selective range of products in comparison to conventional supermarkets. Whole Foods stores carry organic (perceived as healthier) products, many of which are bought from mom-and-pop producers; all food products carried are screened for artificial ingredients; and the chain is phasing out all products with hydrogenated fats. The chain has been much more profitable than conventional supermarkets in spite of its limited product assortment.[53] Clearly, the unique benefit that a store provides is more important than the number of items it carries in forming a favorable store image in consumers' minds.

The type of product the consumer wishes to buy influences his or her selection of a retail outlet; conversely, the consumer's evaluation of a product often is influenced by the knowledge of where it was bought. A consumer wishing to buy an elegant dress for a special occasion may go to a store with an elegant, high-fashion image, such as Saks Fifth Avenue. Regardless of what she actually pays for the dress she selects (regular price or marked-down price), she will probably perceive its quality to be high. However, she may perceive the quality of the identical dress to be much lower if she buys it in an off-price store with a low-price image.

Most studies of the effects of extrinsic cues on perceived product quality have focused on just one variable—either price *or* store image. However, when a second extrinsic cue is available (such as price *and* store image), perceived quality is sometimes a function of the interaction of both cues on the consumer. For example, when brand and retailer images become associated, the less favorable image becomes enhanced at the expense of the more favorable image. Thus, when a low-priced store carries a brand with a high-priced image, the image of the store will improve, whereas the image of the brand will be adversely affected. For that reason, marketers of prestigious designer goods often attempt to control the outlets where their products are sold. Also, when upscale stores sell leftover expensive items to discount stores, they remove the designer labels from these goods as part of the agreements they have with the manufacturers of these products.

Fads can have some unforeseen consequences on consumers' store choices. Recently, 99-cent and one-dollar stores, originally the terrain of lower-income consumers, became fashionable among affluent consumers, who bought there such items as beach balls with the logo "99-cents Only" imprinted on them (in giant letters), wines for under $5, and faux-bamboo picture frames. A study of one chain of dollar-stores found that 32 percent of the cars in the chains' parking lots were less than two years old and in excellent condition; in Los Angeles, Mercedes-Benzes, BMWs, and Rolls-Royces were routinely seen in the parking areas of low-status outlets.[54]

Manufacturers' image

Consumer imagery extends beyond perceived price and store image to the producers themselves. Manufacturers who enjoy a favorable image generally find that their new products are accepted more readily than those of manufacturers who have a less favorable or even a "neutral" image. Researchers have found that consumers generally have favorable perceptions of pioneer brands (the first in a product category), even after follower brands become available. They also found a positive correlation between *pioneer brand image* and an individual's *ideal self-image*, which suggests that positive perceptions toward pioneer brands lead to positive purchase intentions.[55] Studies show that consumers choose brands perceived as similar to their own *actual, ideal, social, ideal-social*, and *situational-ideal-social* images. Thus, if a consumer believes that using the brand is fun, she will buy it and use it when she is having fun with her friends and, to her, the brand will be worth what it costs, so long as she perceives it as fun.[56] These findings have important implications regarding the possible perils of repositioning brands.

Some major marketers introduce new products under the guise of supposedly smaller, pioneering (and presumably more forward-thinking) companies. The goal of this so-called *stealth* (or faux) *parentage* is to persuade consumers that the new brands are produced by independent, nonconformist free spirits, rather than by giant corporate entities. Companies sometimes use stealth parentage when they enter a product category totally unrelated to the one with which their corporate name has become synonymous. For example, when Disney Studios—a company with a wholesome, family-focused image—produces films that include violence and sex, it does so under the name Touchstone Pictures.

Today companies are using advertising, exhibits, and sponsorship of community events to enhance their images. Although some marketers argue that product and service advertising do more to boost the corporate image than *institutional* (image) advertising does, others see both types of advertising—product and institutional—as integral and complementary components of a total corporate communications program. When the reputation of Wal-Mart was tarnished by allegations of unfair labor practices, sexual discrimination and the publication of data indicating that the company caused most of America's trade imbalance with China, the company published ads stating that "Wal-Mart Is Working for Everyone." In addition, the company's executives appeared on TV talk shows and met with community groups and government officials to dispel the negative associations. In a further effort to improve its image, Wal-Mart sponsored a new TV reality show, *The Scholar*, on which high school seniors from across the country competed for college scholarships financed by Wal-Mart.[57]

Perceived risk

Consumers must constantly make decisions regarding what products or services to buy and where to buy them. Because the outcomes (or consequences) of such decisions are often uncertain, the consumer perceives some degree of "risk" in making a purchase decision. **Perceived risk** is defined as *the uncertainty that consumers face when they cannot foresee the consequences of their purchase decisions*. This definition highlights two relevant dimensions of perceived risk: uncertainty and consequences.

TABLE 15.5	Types of Perceived Risk

Functional risk is the risk that the product will not perform as expected. ("Can the new PDA operate a full week without needing to be recharged?")

Physical risk is the risk to self and others that the product may pose. ("Is a cellular phone really safe, or does it emit harmful radiation?")

Financial risk is the risk that the product will not be worth its cost. ("Will a new and cheaper model of a Plasma TV monitor become available six months from now?")

Social risk is the risk that a poor product choice may result in social embarrassment. ("Will my classmates laugh at my purple mohawk haircut?")

Psychological risk is the risk that a poor product choice will bruise the consumer's ego. ("Will I be embarrassed when I invite friends to listen to music on my five-year-old stereo?")

Time risk is the risk that the time spent in product search may be wasted if the product does not perform as expected. ("Will I have to go through the shopping effort all over again?")

The degree of risk that consumers perceive and their own tolerance for risk taking are factors that influence their purchase strategies. It should be stressed that consumers are influenced by risks that they perceive, whether or not such risks actually exist. Risk that is not perceived—no matter how real or how dangerous—will not influence consumer behavior. The major types of risks that consumers perceive when making product decisions include *functional risk, physical risk, financial risk, social risk, psychological risk*, and *time risk* (see Table 15.5).

Perception of risk varies

Consumer perception of risk varies, depending on the person, the product, the situation, and the culture. The amount of risk perceived depends on the specific consumer. Some consumers tend to perceive high degrees of risk in various consumption situations; others tend to perceive little risk. For example, adolescents who engage in high-risk consumption activities, such as smoking or drug use, obviously have lower perceived risk than those who do not engage in high-risk activities. *High-risk perceivers* are often described as **narrow categorizers** because they limit their choices (e.g., product choices) to a few safe alternatives. They would rather exclude some perfectly good alternatives than chance a poor selection. *Low-risk perceivers* have been described as **broad categorizers** because they tend to make their choices from a much wider range of alternatives. They would rather risk a poor selection than limit the number of alternatives from which they can choose.

An individual's perception of risk varies with product categories. For example, consumers are likely to perceive a higher degree of risk (e.g., functional risk, financial risk, time risk) in the purchase of a plasma television set than in the purchase of an automobile; this type of risk is termed *product-category* perceived risk. Researchers have also identified *product*-specific perceived risk. One study found that consumers perceive service decisions to be riskier than product decisions, particularly in terms of social risk, physical risk, and psychological risk.

The degree of risk perceived by a consumer is also affected by the shopping situation (e.g., a traditional bricks-and-mortar retail store, online, catalog, direct-mail solicitations, or door-to-door sales). The sharp increase in mail-order catalog sales in recent years suggests that on the basis of positive experiences and word-of-mouth, consumers now tend to perceive less risk in mail-order shopping than they once did, despite their inability to physically inspect the merchandise before ordering. The findings regarding the impact of perceived risk in shopping online are mixed. While some studies showed that the frequency of shopping online reduced consumers' perceived risk regarding such purchases, other studies showed no correlation between the two factors. Researchers also discovered that consumers' levels of involvement, brand familiarity, and the perceived benefits of shopping online impacted the perceived risk of electronic buying.[58]

How consumers handle risk

Consumers characteristically develop their own strategies for reducing perceived risk. These risk-reduction strategies enable them to act with increased confidence when making product decisions, even though the consequences of such decisions remain somewhat uncertain. Some of the more common risk-reduction strategies are discussed in the following sections.

Consumers seek information

Consumers seek information about the product and product category through word-of-mouth communication (from friends and family and from other people whose opinions they value), from salespeople, and from the general media. They spend more time thinking about their choice and search for more information about the product alternatives when they associate a high degree of risk with the purchase. This strategy is straightforward and logical because the more information the consumer has about the product and the product category, the more predictable the probable consequences and thus, the lower the perceived risk.

Consumers are brand loyal

Consumers avoid risk by remaining loyal to a brand with which they have been satisfied instead of purchasing new or untried brands. High-risk perceivers, for example, are more likely to be loyal to their old brands and less likely to purchase newly introduced products.

Consumers select by brand image

When consumers have had no experience with a product, they tend to "trust" a favored or well-known brand name. Consumers often think well-known brands are better and are worth buying for the implied assurance of quality, dependability, performance, and service. Marketers' promotional efforts supplement the perceived quality of their products by helping to build and sustain a favorable brand image.

Consumers rely on store image

If consumers have no other information about a product, they often trust the judgment of the merchandise buyers of a reputable store and depend on them to have made careful decisions in selecting products for sale. Store image also imparts the implication of product testing and the assurance of service, return privileges, and adjustment in case of dissatisfaction.

Consumers buy the most expensive model

When in doubt, consumers often feel that the most expensive model is probably the best in terms of quality; that is, they equate price with quality. (The price/quality relationship was discussed earlier in this chapter.)

Consumers seek reassurance

Consumers who are uncertain about the wisdom of a product choice seek reassurance through money-back guarantees, government and private laboratory test results, warranties, and prepurchase trial. For example, it is unlikely that anyone would buy a new car without a test drive. Products that do not easily lend themselves to free or limited trial, such as a refrigerator, present a selling challenge to marketers.

The concept of perceived risk has major implications for the introduction of new products. Because high-risk perceivers are less likely than low-risk perceivers to purchase new or innovative products, it is important for marketers to provide such consumers with persuasive risk-reduction strategies, such as a well-known brand name (sometimes achieved through licensing), distribution through reputable retail outlets, informative advertising, publicity stories in the media, impartial test results, free samples, and money-back guarantees. Also, most stores that carry a number of different brands and models of the same product, as well as manufacturers of such diverse model lines, now offer online consumers quick and easy ways to generate side-by-side comparisons with detailed charts of the features of all the available models.

Ethics and consumer perception

The ethical issues related to consumer perception focus on how marketers use the knowledge of perception to manipulate consumers. One technique marketers use is to blur the distinctions between *figure* and *ground*. For example, to combat fast-forwarding by consumers who wish to avoid TV commercials, marketers are increasingly turning to **product placements**, where the line between television shows and ads is virtually non-existent. In ABC's *Extreme Makeover: Home Edition*, Sears' Kenmore appliances and Craftsman tools are the "stars" of the show. Research indicates that many viewers were more likely to shop at Sears after seeing the show. Bags of Doritos and six-packs of Mountain Dew were given to the winners of personal challenge contests on *Survivor*, and the judges of "American Idol" always have a Coca-Cola within easy reach. A new product developed by Burger King went on sale the day after it was featured on *The Apprentice*, and another show of this series focused on developing an ad for Dove Cool Moisture Body Wash. Predictions have indicated that marketers are likely to increase expenditures substantially on such *branded entertainment.* In addition, online editions of newspapers often embed advertisements within the content of news. A newly formed consumer advocacy group, Commercial Alert, is lobbying for legislation that will require advertisers to disclose upfront those ads that are designed as product placements.[59]

Marketers also blend promotion and program content by positioning a TV commercial so close to the storyline of a program that viewers are unaware they are watching an advertisement until they are well into it. Because this was an important factor in advertising to children, the Federal Trade Commission has strictly limited the use of this technique. TV stars or cartoon characters are now prohibited from promoting products during the children's shows in which they appear. Other potential misuses of figure-and-ground are print ads (called *advertorials*) that closely resemble editorial matter, making it increasingly difficult for readers to tell them apart. Thirty-minute commercials (called *infomercials*) appear to the average viewer as documentaries, and thus command more attentive viewing than obvious commercials would receive.

As discussed earlier, marketers use their knowledge of the *just noticeable difference* to ensure that reductions in product quantity or quality and increases in prices go unnoticed by consumers. Marketers can also increase the quantity of the product consumed by the way it is physically packaged or presented. For example, studies showed that: (1) both children and adults consume more juice when the product is presented in short, wide glasses than in tall slender glasses; (2) candies placed in clear jars were eaten much quicker than those presented in opaque jars; (3) sandwiches in transparent wrap generated more consumption than those in opaque wraps; and (4) the visibility and aroma of tempting foods generated greater consumption.[60] Another study demonstrated that the organization of the merchandise, the size of the package, the symmetry of the display and its perceived variety served to impact consumption quantities. The consumer implications of these findings are listed in Table 15.6.[61]

Marketers can also manipulate consumers' perception and behavior by using the physical setting where consumption occurs. It is widely known that supermarkets routinely move products around to encourage consumers to wander around the store, and keep the stores relatively cold because colder temperatures make people hungrier and so they increase their food purchases. (Some nutritionists advise consumers to go food shopping directly after a filling meal.) At DisneyWorld, guests leaving rides, and presumably still under the spell of the thrill and enjoyment experienced, must exit through a corridor of stores featuring merchandise congruent with the themes of the rides.

TABLE 15.6	Implications for How Assortment Structure Influences Consumption Quantities				
	ORGANIZATION INFLUENCES CONSUMPTION	**SIZE INFLUENCES CONSUMPTION**	**SYMMETRY INFLUENCES CONSUMPTION**	**PERCEIVED VARIETY PARTIALLY MEDIATES CONSUMPTION**	**CONSUMPTION RULES INFLUENCE CONSUMPTION**
Consumer implications	Organization is relevant for mixed assortments in bowls (or "grab bags"), buffets, potlucks, or dinner table settings. It may also be relevant in retail contexts. Consumers may be able to control consumption by organizing less-structured offerings.	Assortment size or duplication is commonly found in the form of multiple product tastings, multiple offerings of party snacks, duplicate buffet lines, family dinners with multiple dishes, and perhaps even in retail displays. Duplicated offerings can stimulate consumption.	The symmetry of an assortment is an issue wherever multiple units (and perhaps sizes) of options are involved, such as at holiday dinners, toys in play areas, and collectables and collecting. Minimal variation in the size of serving bowls may overstimulate consumption.	People are often surprised at how much they consume, showing that they may have been influenced at a basic or perceptual level.	Large inventory levels in one's home pantry could increase the quantity of food one believes is appropriate for a meal. Health-care professionals and dieticians can stimulate consumption among nutritionally deficient individuals by offering smaller helpings of more items.

Source: Barbara E. Kahn and Brian Wansink, "The Influence of Assortment Structure on Perceived Variety and Consumption Quantities," *Journal of Consumer Research*, 30 (March 2004), 530. Reproduced with permission of the copyright owner. Further reproduction prohibited without permission.

Marketers can also manipulate consumers' interpretations of marketing stimuli through the context in which they are featured. For example, in QVC's "Extreme Shopping," during which rare and expensive products are offered, consumers perceived $200 art prints as reasonably priced when the prints were shown immediately after much more expensive items.[62] Inadvertently, marketers can also impact the content of news to which consumers are exposed. For example, many marketers carefully screen the context in which their messages are shown, because they recognize that advertisements are perceived more positively when placed within more positive programs. Thus, they may choose not to place ads in news broadcasts or programs that cover serious issues, such as wars and world hunger, where some of the content is bound to be unpleasant.

In 1973, a book entitled *Subliminal Seduction* charged that advertisers were using subliminal embeds in their print ads to persuade consumers to buy their advertised brands. It was alleged, for example, that liquor advertisers were trying to increase the subconscious appeal of their products by embedding sexually suggestive symbols in ice cubes floating in a pictured drink.[63] Subsequently, the Federal Communications Commission (FCC) studied the subject and concluded that subliminal messages, whether effective or not, are intended to deceive consumers and, therefore, contradict the public interest. However, because of the absence of any evidence that subliminal persuasion really works, no state or federal laws have been enacted to restrict the use of subliminal advertising.

Conveying socially undesirable stereotypes in products and advertisements is another ethical dilemma marketers may face. Some years ago, the makers of an American icon—G.I. Joe—introduced a substantially more muscular version of the doll and were subsequently accused of sanctioning the use of muscle-building drugs by teenagers. Similarly, the makers of Barbie—a doll that has gradually become thinner and bustier—were accused of conveying an unrealistic body image to young girls.[64] A recent example of perceived stereotypes in TV ads are ads that portray husbands and fathers as objects of ridicule and scorn (images that the creators of the messages believed to be a clever reversal of traditional sex roles).

chapter **16**

> **Attitude**

What are attitudes?

Consumer researchers assess attitudes by asking questions or making inferences from behavior. For example, if a researcher determines from questioning a consumer that she consistently buys Secret deodorant (**www.secret-deodorant.com**) and even recommends the product to friends, the researcher is likely to infer that the consumer possesses a positive attitude toward this brand of deodorant. This example illustrates that attitudes are not directly observable but must be inferred from what people say or what they do.

Moreover, the illustration suggests that a whole universe of consumer behaviors—consistency of purchases, recommendations to others, top rankings, beliefs, evaluations, and intentions are related to attitudes. What, then, are attitudes? In a consumer behavior context, an *attitude is a learned predisposition to behave in a consistently favorable or unfavorable way with respect to a given object.* Each part of this definition describes an important property of an attitude and is critical to understanding the role of attitudes in consumer behavior.

The attitude "object"

The word *object* in our consumer-oriented definition of attitude should be interpreted broadly to include specific consumption- or marketing-related concepts, such as product, product category, brand, service, possessions, product use, causes or issues, people, advertisement, Internet site, price, medium, or retailer. There is general agreement that an attitude "can be conceptualized as a summary evaluation of an object."[1]

In conducting attitude research, we tend to be *object specific.* For example, if we were interested in learning consumers' attitudes toward three major brands of popularly priced watches, our "object" might include Seiko, Fossil, and Casio; if we were examining consumer attitudes toward major brands of computer printers, our "object" might include HP, Dell, Brother, Canon, OKI, Lexmark, and Epson.

Attitudes are a learned predisposition

There is general agreement that attitudes are *learned.* This means that attitudes relevant to purchase behavior are formed as a result of direct experience with the product, word-of-mouth information acquired from others, or exposure to mass-media advertising, the Internet, and various forms of direct marketing (e.g., a retailer's catalog). It is important to remember that although attitudes may result from behavior, they are not synonymous with behavior. Instead, they reflect either a favorable or an unfavorable evaluation of the attitude object. As *learned predispositions,* attitudes have a motivational quality; that is, they might propel a consumer *toward* a particular behavior or repel the consumer *away* from a particular behavior.

Attitudes have consistency

Another characteristic of attitudes is that they are relatively consistent with the behavior they reflect. However, despite their *consistency,* attitudes are not necessarily permanent; they do change. (Attitude change is explored later in this chapter.)

It is important to illustrate what we mean by consistency. Normally, we expect consumers' behavior to correspond with their attitudes. For example, if a Canadian consumer reported preferring German over Japanese automobiles, we would expect that the individual would be more likely to buy a German brand when his current vehicle needed to be replaced. In other words, when consumers are free to act as they wish, we anticipate that their actions will be consistent with their attitudes. However, circumstances often preclude consistency between attitudes and behavior. For example, in the case of our Canadian consumer, the matter of affordability may intervene, and the consumer would find a particular Japanese car to be a more cost-effective choice than a German car. Therefore, we must consider possible *situational* influences on consumer attitudes and behavior.

Attitudes occur within a situation

It is not immediately evident from our definition that attitudes occur within and are affected by the *situation*.[2] By "situation," we mean events or circumstances that, at a particular point in time, influence the relationship between an attitude and behavior. A specific situation can cause consumers to behave in ways seemingly inconsistent with their attitudes. For instance, let us assume that Brad purchases a different brand of toothpaste each time he runs low. Although his brand-switching behavior may seem to reflect a negative attitude or dissatisfaction with the brands he tries, it actually may be influenced by a specific situation, for example, his wish to economize. Thus, he will buy whatever is the least expensive brand, and it is not a matter of a negative attitude.[3]

The opposite can also be true. If Sheryl stays at a Holiday Inn each time she goes out of town for business, we may erroneously infer that she has a particularly favorable attitude toward Holiday Inn. On the contrary, Sheryl may find Holiday Inn to be "just okay." However, because she owns her own business and travels at her own expense, she may feel that Holiday Inn is "good enough," given that she may be paying less than she would be paying if she stayed at a Marriott, Sheraton, or Hilton hotel.

Indeed, consumers can have a variety of attitudes toward a particular object, each corresponding to a particular situation or application. For instance, Saul may feel its alright to have a station wagon to drive the kids to their afterschool and weekend activities; or even to take his college-age daughter back and forth each year, with all her stuff, to State College, some two hundred and fifty miles away. However, when it comes to his growing interest in off-road driving, Saul feels strongly that only a high-quality sports utility vehicle (SUV) would provide the appropriate features to enable him to safely pursue his growing interest. So recently when it came time to replace the family's old station wagon, he opted for a new SUV, one that provided the "right" feature set to ensure his off-road interests.

It is important to understand how consumer attitudes vary from situation to situation. For instance, it is useful to know whether consumer preferences for various brands of SUVs (e.g., Honda Pilot, Jeep Liberty, and Ford Explorer) might depend on the anticipated driving task or most common driving situation (i.e., storage capacity, car pooling, and off-road driving). In Saul's case, his attitude and decision-making process lead him to select a Jeep 4x4. He feels it provides a win-win situation—in that the Jeep 4x4 would satisfy his need to car pool and transport his daughter to college, as well as his interest in off-road driving.

Clearly, when measuring attitudes, it is important to consider the situation in which the behavior takes place, or we can misinterpret the relationship between attitude and behavior. Table 16.1 presents additional examples of specific situations that might influence consumer attitudes toward specific brands of products or services.

Structural models of attitudes

Motivated by a desire to understand the relationship between attitudes and behavior, psychologists have sought to construct models that capture the underlying dimensions of an attitude.[4] To this end, the focus has been on specifying the composition of an attitude to better explain or predict behavior. The following section examines several important attitude models: the *tricomponent attitude model,* the *multiattribute attitude models,* the *trying-to-consume model,* and the *attitude-toward-the-ad models.* Each of these models provides a somewhat different perspective on the number of component parts of an attitude and how those parts are arranged or interrelated.

Tricomponent attitude model

According to the **tricomponent attitude model**, attitudes consist of three major components: a *cognitive* component, an *affective* component, and a *conative* component (see Figure 16.1).[5]

TABLE 16.1	Examples of How Situations Might Influence Attitudes	
PRODUCT/SERVICE	**SITUATION**	**ATTITUDE**
Claritan	Runny nose due to allergies	"I've got to stop my nose from running because I've got a date in two hours."
Hyundai Automobile	Buying a new car	"With my son starting college in the fall, I don't want to spend a lot of money on a car."
Northwestern Mutual	Life insurance	"Now that I've just become a father, I want to make sure that my family is provided for."
The New York Times	Need a job	"I graduated college last month, spent three weeks in Europe, and now it's time to find a job."
American Airlines	Family wedding	"My cousin is getting married and I want to be there."
Starbucks	Need to stay awake	"I have to pull an 'all-nighter' to finish this paper that has to be submitted by 9:00 A.M."
Softsoap Pump Soap	Messy bathroom counter	"I'm tired of cleaning soap off of the bathroom counter."

The cognitive component

The first part of the tricomponent attitude model consists of a person's *cognitions,* that is, the knowledge and perceptions that are acquired by a combination of direct experience with the *attitude object* and related information from various sources. This knowledge and resulting perceptions commonly take the form of *beliefs;* that is, the consumer believes that the attitude object possesses various attributes and that specific behavior will lead to specific outcomes.

There are two types of broadband Internet connections (e.g., cable and DSL). Steve's belief system for both types of connections consists of the same basic four attributes: speed, availability, reliability, and "other" features. However, Steve has somewhat different beliefs about the two broadband alternatives with respect to these attributes. For instance, he knows from friends that the local cable company's broadband

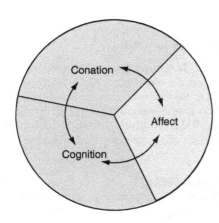

A Simple Representation of the Tricomponent Attitude Model

FIGURE 16.1

connection is much faster than DSL, but he does not like the fact that he will also have to begin subscribing to cable TV if he does not want to pay an extra $20 a month for the broadband Internet connection. Steve is thinking of asking a few of his friends about the differences between cable and DSL broadband Internet service and will also go online to a number of Web sites that discuss this topic (e.g., **www.cnet.com**).

The affective component

A consumer's *emotions* or *feelings* about a particular product or brand constitute the *affective component* of an attitude.[6] These emotions and feelings are frequently treated by consumer researchers as primarily *evaluative* in nature; that is, they capture an individual's direct or global assessment of the attitude object (i.e., the extent to which the individual rates the attitude object as "favorable" or "unfavorable," "good" or "bad").

Affect-laden experiences also manifest themselves as *emotionally charged states* (e.g., happiness, sadness, shame, disgust, anger, distress, guilt, or surprise). Research indicates that such emotional states may enhance or amplify positive or negative experiences and that later recollections of such experiences may impact what comes to mind and how the individual acts.[7] For instance, a person visiting a shopping center is likely to be influenced by his or her emotional state at the time. If the shopper is feeling particularly joyous at the moment, a positive response to the shopping center may be amplified. The emotionally enhanced response to the shopping center may lead the shopper to recall with great pleasure the time spent at the shopping center. It also may influence the individual shopper to persuade friends and acquaintances to visit the same shopping center and to make the personal decision to revisit the center.

In addition to using direct or global evaluative measures of an attitude object, consumer researchers can also use a battery of affective response scales (e.g., that measure feelings and emotions) to construct a picture of consumers' overall feelings about a product, service, or ad.

The conative component

Conation, the final component of the tricomponent attitude model, is concerned with the *likelihood* or *tendency* that an individual will undertake a specific action or behave in a particular way with regard to the attitude object. According to some interpretations, the conative component may include the actual behavior itself.

In marketing and consumer research, the conative component is frequently treated as an expression of the consumer's *intention to buy.* Buyer intention scales are used to assess the likelihood of a consumer purchasing a product or behaving in a certain way. Interestingly, consumers who are asked to respond to an intention-to-buy question appear to be more likely to actually make a brand purchase for positively evaluated brands (e.g., "I will buy it"), as contrasted to consumers who are not asked to respond to an intention question.[8] This suggests that a positive brand commitment in the form of a positive answer to an attitude intention question impacts in a positive way on the actual brand purchase.

Multiattribute attitude models

Multiattribute attitude models portray consumers' attitudes with regard to an attitude object (e.g., a product, a service, a direct-mail catalog, or a cause or an issue) as a function of consumers' perception and assessment of the key attributes or beliefs held with regard to the particular attitude object. Although there are many variations of this type of attitude model, we have selected the following three models to briefly consider here: the *attitude-toward-object model,* the *attitude-toward-behavior model,* and the *theory-of-reasoned-action model.*

The attitude-toward-object model

The **attitude-toward-object model** is especially suitable for measuring attitudes toward a *product* (or *service*) category or specific *brands.*[9] According to this model, the consumer's attitude toward a product or specific brands of a product is a function of the presence (or absence) and evaluation of certain product-specific beliefs and/or attributes. In other words, consumers generally have favorable attitudes toward those brands that they believe have an adequate level of attributes that they evaluate as positive, and they have unfavorable attitudes toward those brands they feel do not have an adequate level of desired attributes or have too many negative or undesired attributes. As an illustration, we return to the broadband Internet connection example. Each alternative has a different "mix" of features (a "feature set"). The defining features might include speed, reliability, cost, availability of 24/7 technical assistance, maximum file size that can be e-mailed, and so on. For instance, one of the two types of connections might be found to excel on core features, whereas the other may be really good on a few of the core features but offer more additional features. It is also possible that neither the cable nor the DSL carriers may be more than "second rate." However, what consumers will purchase is likely to be a function "how much they know," "what they feel are important features for them," and in the current example, their "awareness as to which type of broadband service possesses (or lacks) the valued attributes."

Conducting consumer attitude research with children, especially gauging their attitudes toward products and brands, is an ongoing challenge. What is needed are new and effective measurement approaches that allow children to express their attitudes toward brands. To this end, researchers have labored to develop an especially simple and short attitude measurement instrument for questioning children between 8 and 12 years of age.

The attitude-toward-behavior model

The **attitude-toward-behavior model** is designed to capture the individual's *attitude toward behaving* or *acting* with respect to an object rather than the attitude toward the object itself.[11] The appeal of the attitude-toward-behavior model is that it seems to correspond somewhat more closely to actual behavior than does the attitude-toward-object model. For instance, knowing Sam's attitude about the act of purchasing a Rolex wristwatch (i.e., his attitude toward the *behavior*) reveals more about the potential act of purchasing than does simply knowing his attitude toward expensive watches or specifically Rolex watches (i.e., the attitude toward the *object*). This seems logical, for a consumer might have a positive attitude toward an expensive Rolex wristwatch but a negative attitude as to his prospects for purchasing such an expensive wristwatch.

A recent study conducted in Taiwan examined the relationship between consumer characteristics and attitude toward the behavior of online shopping. The researcher found that attitudes toward online shopping are significantly different based on various consumer behavior factors. For example, the research identified the following nine benefits of online shopping: (1) effectiveness and modern, (2) purchase convenience, (3) information abundance, (4) multiform and safety, (5) service quality, (6) delivery speed, (7) homepage design, (8) selection freedom, and (9) company name familiarity. These nine attributes were selected because they tend to reflect consumers' attitude toward online shopping.[12] The researcher goes on to explore a model (see Figure 16.2) that suggests that *consumer characteristics* (on the left-side of the model) impact *attitudes toward online shopping* (in the middle of the model—the nine attitudinal attributes listed above) and the *rating of the online shopping experience* (on the right-side of the model).

Theory-of-reasoned-action model

The **theory-of-reasoned-action model** represents a comprehensive integration of attitude components into a structure that is designed to lead to both better explanation and better predictions of behavior. Like the basic tricomponent attitude model, the theory-of-reasoned-action model incorporates a *cognitive* component, an *affective* component, and a *conative* component; however, these are arranged in a pattern different from that of the tricomponent model (see Figure 16.3).

FIGURE 16.2

**Consumer
Characteristics,
Attitude, and Online
Shopping**

Source: Shwu-Ing Wu, "The
Relationship Between Consumer
Characteristics and Attitude
Toward Online Shopping,"
*Marketing Intelligence and
Planning* 21, no. 7 (2003): 40.

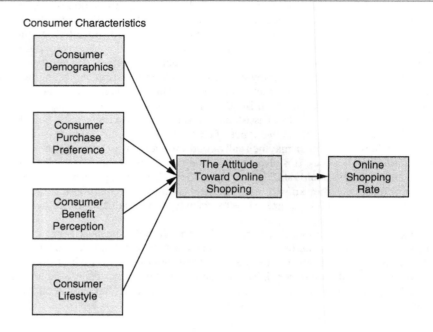

In accordance with this expanded model, to understand *intention* we also need to measure the *subjective norms* that influence an individual's intention to act. A subjective norm can be measured directly by assessing a consumer's feelings as to what relevant others (family, friends, roommates, coworkers) would think of the action being contemplated; that is, would they look favorably or unfavorably on the anticipated action? For example, if an undergraduate student was considering cutting her hair shorter and dying it red and stopped to ask herself what her parents or boyfriend would think of such behavior (i.e., approve or disapprove), such a reflection would constitute her subjective norm.

Consumer researchers can get behind the *subjective norm* to the underlying factors that are likely to produce it. They accomplish this by assessing the *normative beliefs* that the individual attributes to relevant others, as well as the individual's *motivation to comply* with each of the relevant others. For instance, consider the undergraduate student contemplating cutting her hair shorter and dying it red. To understand her subjective norm about the desired purchase, we would have to identify her relevant others (parents and boyfriend); her beliefs about how each would respond to her short red hair (e.g., "Mom would consider the shorter hair as too 'boyish,' but my boyfriend would love it"); and, finally, her motivation to comply with her parents and/or her boyfriend.[13] A recent study also indicates that incorporating the consumer's emotional experience into the multiattribute model has the potential of enhancing the predictability of motives and preferences.[14]

Theory of trying-to-consume model

There has been an effort underway to extend attitude models so that they might better accommodate consumers' goals as expressed by their "trying" to consume.[15] The **theory of trying to consume** is designed to account for the many cases in which the action or outcome is not certain but instead reflects the consumer's attempts to consume (i.e., purchase). In trying to consume, there are often *personal impediments* (a consumer is trying to find just the right shoes to go with a newly purchased dress for under $100 or trying to lose weight but loves chocolate bars) and/or *environmental impediments* (only the first 50 in line will be able to purchase this $200 MP3 player for the special Saturday 8:00 A.M. to 9:00 A.M. price of $99) that might prevent the desired action or outcome from occurring. Again, the key point is that in these cases of trying, the outcome (e.g., purchase, pos-

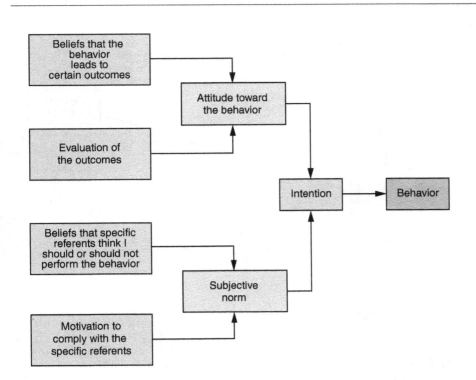

FIGURE 16.3

A Simplified Version of the Theory of Reasoned Action

Source: Adapted from Icek Ajzen and Martin Fishbein, *Understanding Attitudes and Predicting Social Behavior* (Upper Saddle River, NJ: Prentice Hall, 1980), 84. © 1980. Adapted by permission of Prentice Hall, Inc.

session, use, or action) is not and cannot be assumed to be certain. Researchers have recently extended this inquiry by examining those situations in which consumers do *not* try to consume—that is, *fail to try to consume*. In this case, consumers appear to (1) fail to see or are ignorant of their options and (2) make a conscious effort not to consume; that is, they might seek to self-sacrifice or defer gratification to some future time.[16]

Attitude-toward-the-ad models

In an effort to understand the impact of advertising or some other promotional vehicle (e.g., a catalog) on consumer attitudes toward particular products or brands, considerable attention has been paid to developing what has been referred to as **attitude-toward-the-ad models**.

Figure 16.4 presents a schematic of some of the basic relationships described by an attitude-toward-the-ad model. As the model depicts, the consumer forms various feelings (affects) and judgments (cognitions) as the result of exposure to an ad. These feelings and judgments in turn affect the consumer's *attitude toward the ad* and *beliefs about the brand* secured from exposure to the ad. Finally, the consumer's attitude toward the ad and beliefs about the brand influence his or her *attitude toward the brand*.[17]

Research among Asian Indian U.S. immigrants have explored attitudes toward 12 advertisements and purchase intention of six different products that the ads feature. The study found a positive relationship between attitude toward the advertisement and purchase intention for each of the advertised products; that is, if consumers "like" the ad, they are more likely to purchase the product.[18]

Finally, consumer socialization has also shown itself to be an important determinant of a consumer's attitudes toward advertising. One study, for example, found that parental communication, peer communication, social utility of advertising, amount of television watched, gender, and race were all associated with attitude toward advertising. African Americans and women were found to have more positive attitudes toward advertising.[19]

FIGURE 16.4

A Conception of the Relationship Among Elements in an Attitude-Toward-the-Ad Model

Source: Inspired by and based on Julie A. Edell and Marian Chapman Burke, "The Power of Feelings in Understanding Advertising Effects," *Journal of Consumer Research* 14 (December 1987): 431. Reprinted by permission of University of Chicago Press as publisher.

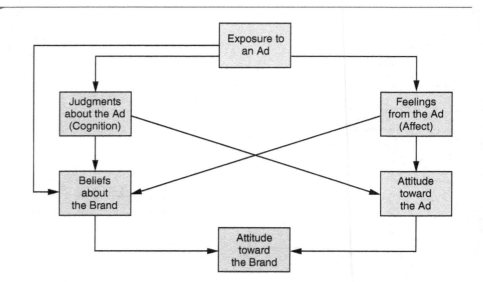

Attitude formation

How do people, especially young people, form their initial *general* attitudes toward "things"? Consider their attitudes toward clothing they wear, for example, underwear, casual wear, and business attire. On a more specific level, how do they form attitudes toward Fruit of the Loom or Calvin Klein underwear, or Levi's or Gap casual wear, or Anne Klein or Emporium Armani business clothing? Also, what about where such clothing is purchased? Would they buy their underwear, casual wear, and business clothing at Wal-Mart, Sears, JC Penney, or Macy's? How do family members and friends, admired celebrities, mass-media advertisements, even cultural memberships, influence the formation of their attitudes concerning consuming or not consuming each of these types of apparel items? Why do some attitudes seem to persist indefinitely while others change fairly often? The answers to such questions are of vital importance to marketers, for without knowing how attitudes are formed, they are unable to understand or to influence consumer attitudes or behavior.

Our examination of attitude formation is divided into three areas: *how attitudes are learned,* the *sources of influence* on attitude formation, and the impact of *personality* on attitude formation.

How attitudes are learned

When we speak of the formation of an attitude, we refer to the shift from having no attitude toward a given object (e.g., an MP3 player) to having *some* attitude toward it (e.g., having an MP3 player is great when you want to listen to music while on a treadmill at the gym). The shift from no attitude to an attitude (i.e., the *attitude formation*) is a result of learning.

Consumers often purchase new products that are associated with a favorably viewed brand name. Their favorable attitude toward the brand name is frequently the result of repeated satisfaction with other products produced by the same company. In terms of *classical conditioning,* an established brand name is an *unconditioned* stimulus that through past positive reinforcement resulted in a favorable brand attitude. A new product, yet to be linked to the established brand, would be the *conditioned* stimulus. To illustrate, by giving its Secret Platinum and Olay conditioners the benefit of two well-known and respected family names (i.e., Secret and Olay), P&G is expecting on a transfer of the favorable attitude already associated with these two brand names to the new product. They are counting on stimulus generalization from the two brand names to the new product. Research suggests that the "fit" between a parent brand (e.g., in this case both Secret and Olay) and a brand extension (e.g., in this case Secret Platinum and Olay conditioners) is a function of two factors: (1) the similarity between the preexisting product categories already associated with the parent brands (i.e., mostly products related to skin care) and the new extension and (2) the fit or match between the images of the parent brands and the new extension.[20]

Sometimes attitudes *follow* the purchase and consumption of a product. For example, a consumer may purchase a brand-name product *without* having a prior attitude toward it because it is the only product of its kind available (e.g., the last bottle of aspirin in a gas station mini-mart). Consumers also make trial purchases of new brands from product categories in which they have little personal involvement. If they find the purchased brand to be satisfactory, then they are likely to develop a favorable attitude toward it.

In situations in which consumers seek to solve a problem or satisfy a need, they are likely to form attitudes (either positive or negative) about products on the basis of information exposure and their own cognition (knowledge and beliefs). In general, the more information consumers have about a product or service, the more likely they are to form attitudes about it, either positive or negative. However, regardless of available information, consumers are not always ready or willing to process product-related information. Furthermore, consumers often use only a limited amount of the information available to them. Specifically, only two or three important beliefs about a product are likely to dominate in the formation of attitudes and that less important beliefs provide little additional input.[21] This suggests that marketers should fight off the impulse to include *all* the features of their products and services in their ads; rather, they should focus on the few key points that are at the heart of what distinguishes their product from the competition.

Sources of influence on attitude formation

The formation of consumer attitudes is strongly influenced by *personal experience,* the *influence* of family and friends, *direct marketing, mass media,* and the *Internet.*

A primary means by which attitudes toward goods and services are formed is through the consumer's direct experience in trying and evaluating them.[22] Recognizing the importance of direct experience, marketers frequently attempt to stimulate trial of new products by offering cents-off coupons or even free samples. In such cases, the marketer's objective is to get consumers to try and evaluate the product. If a product proves to be to their liking, then it is likely that consumers will form a positive attitude and be more likely to repurchase the product. In addition, from the information on the coupon the marketer is able to create a database of interested consumers.

As we come in contact with others, especially family, close friends, and admired individuals (e.g., a respected teacher), we form attitudes that influence our lives.[23] The family is an extremely important source of influence on the formation of attitudes, for it is the family that provides us with many of our basic values and a wide range of less central beliefs. For instance, young children who are rewarded for good behavior with sweet foods and candy often retain a taste for (and positive attitude toward) sweets as adults.

Marketers are increasingly using highly focused direct-marketing programs to target small consumer niches with products and services that fit their interests and lifestyles. (Niche marketing is sometimes called *micromarketing.*) Marketers very carefully target customers on the basis of their demographic, psychographic, or geodemographic profiles with highly personalized product offerings (e.g., watches for left-handed people) and messages that show they understand their special needs and desires. Direct-marketing efforts have an excellent chance of favorably influencing target consumers' attitudes, because the products and services offered and the promotional messages conveyed are very carefully designed to address the individual segment's needs and concerns and, thus, are able to achieve a higher "hit rate" than mass marketing.

In countries where people have easy access to newspapers and a variety of general and special-interest magazines and television channels, consumers are constantly exposed to new ideas, products, opinions, and advertisements. These mass-media communications provide an important source of information that influences the formation of consumer attitudes. Other research indicates that for consumers who lack direct experience with a product, exposure to an emotionally appealing advertising message is more likely to create an attitude toward the product than for consumers who have beforehand secured direct experience with the product category.[24] The net implications of these findings appear to be that emotional appeals are most effective with consumers who lack product experience.

Still another issue with regard to evaluating the impact of advertising messages on attitude formation is the level of realism that is provided. Research has shown that attitudes that develop through *direct experience* (e.g., product usage) tend to be more confidently held, more enduring, and more resistant to attack than those developed via *indirect experience* (e.g., reading a print ad). And just as television provided the advertiser with more realism than is possible in a radio or print ad, the Internet has an even greater ability to provide telepresence, which is the simulated perception of direct experience. The Internet also has the ability to provide the "flow experience," which is a cognitive state occurring when the individual is so involved in an activity that nothing else matters. Research on telepresence suggests that "perceptions of telepresence grew stronger as levels of interactivity and levels of vividness (i.e., the way an environment presents information to the senses) of web sites increased."[25]

Strategies of attitude change

The knowledge function

Individuals generally have a strong need to know and understand the people and things they encounter. The consumer's "need to know," a cognitive need, is important to marketers concerned with product positioning. Indeed, many product and brand positionings are attempts to satisfy the *need to know* and to improve the consumer's attitudes toward the brand by emphasizing its advantages over competitive brands. For instance, a message for a new OTC allergy medication might point out how it is superior to other OTC allergy medications in alleviating the symptoms of allergies. The message might even use a bar graph to contrast its allergy symptom relief abilities to other leading allergy medications. An ad for General Mills' Milk'n Cereal bars focuses on the product information panel for the two products. In addition, the ad goes on to state that they are "50% larger, twice the calcium, and three times the iron of Kellogg's bars." An important characteristic of the advertising is its appeal and usefulness to consumers' *need to know*.

Combining several functions

Because different consumers may like or dislike the same product or service for different reasons, a functional framework for examining attitudes can be very useful. For instance, three consumers may all have positive attitudes toward Suave hair care products. However, one may be responding solely to the fact that the products work well (the utilitarian function); the second may have the inner confidence to agree with the point "When you know beautiful hair doesn't have to cost a fortune" (an ego-defensive function). The third consumer's favorable attitudes might reflect the realization that Suave has for many years stressed value (equal or better products for less)—the knowledge function.

Resolving two conflicting attitudes

Attitude-change strategies can sometimes resolve actual or potential conflict between two attitudes. Specifically, if consumers can be made to see that their negative attitude toward a product, a specific brand, or its attributes is really not in conflict with another attitude, they may be induced to change their evaluation of the brand (i.e., moving from negative to positive).

For example, Stanley is a serious amateur photographer who has been thinking of moving from 35 mm photography into the realm of medium-format photography in order to take advantage of the larger negative size. However, with the growth of digital photography, Stanley is unsure of whether his move to the medium format will be worthwhile. Stanley loves the idea of having a bigger negative to work with in his darkroom (attitude 1), but he may feel that purchasing a medium-format camera is an unwise investment because these cameras may be supplanted in the near future by digital photography (attitude 2). However, if Stanley learns that Mamiya offers a medium-format camera that offers both a film capability and a digital capability, and even has recently introduced an entirely digital medium-format camera, he might change his mind and thereby resolve his conflicting attitudes.

Altering components of the multiattribute model

Earlier in this chapter we discussed a number of multiattribute attitude models. These models have implications for attitude-change strategies; specifically, they provide us with additional insights as to how to bring about attitude change: (1) changing the relative evaluation of attributes, (2) changing brand beliefs, (3) adding an attribute, and (4) changing the overall brand rating.

Changing the relative evaluation of attributes

The overall market for many product categories is often set out so that different consumer segments are offered different brands with different features or benefits. For instance, within a product category such as dishwashing liquids, there are brands such as Dawn that stress potency and brands such as Dove that stress gentleness. These two brands of dishwashing liquids have historically appealed to different segments of the overall dishwashing liquid market. Similarly, when it comes to coffee, the market can be divided into regular coffee and decaffeinated coffee, or when it comes to headache remedies, there is the division between aspirin (e.g., Bayer) and acetaminophen (e.g., Tylenol).

In general, when a product category is naturally divided according to distinct product features or benefits that appeal to a particular segment of consumers, marketers usually have an opportunity to persuade consumers to "cross over," that is, to persuade consumers who prefer one version of the product (e.g., standard bifocal eyeglass lenses) to shift their favorable attitudes toward another version of the product (e.g., progressive bifocal lenses).

Changing brand beliefs

A second cognitive-oriented strategy for changing attitudes concentrates on changing beliefs or perceptions about the brand itself. This is by far the most common form of advertising appeal. Advertisers constantly are reminding us that their product has "more" or is "better" or "best" in terms of some important product attribute. As a variation on this theme of "more," ads for Palmolive dishwashing liquid are designed to *extend* consumers' brand attitudes with regard to the product's gentleness by suggesting that it be used for hand washing of fine clothing items. In a similar fashion, Paul Mitchell hair care products have challenged the notion that hair damaged by chemicals, the environment, or heat cannot be helped. Paul Mitchell claims that the use of their Super Strong™ hair care products can strengthen damaged hair over 50 percent.

Within the context of brand beliefs, there are forces working to stop or slow down attitude change. For instance, consumers frequently resist evidence that challenges a strongly held attitude or belief and tend to interpret any ambiguous information in ways that reinforce their preexisting attitudes.[31] Therefore, information suggesting a change in attitude needs to be compelling and repeated enough to overcome the natural resistance to letting go of established attitudes.

Adding an attribute

Another cognitive strategy consists of *adding an attribute.* This can be accomplished either by adding an attribute that previously has been ignored or one that represents an improvement or technological innovation.

The first route, adding a previously ignored attribute, is illustrated by the point that yogurt has more potassium than a banana (a fruit associated with a high quantity of potassium). For consumers interested in increasing their intake of potassium, the comparison of yogurt and bananas has the power of enhancing their attitudes toward yogurt.

The second route of adding an attribute that reflects an actual product change or technological innovation is easier to accomplish than stressing a previously ignored attribute. To illustrate, Kenmore has introduced a refrigerator with PūR, an advanced and unique water filtration system. This is a powerful and attractive feature for a refrigerator, a feature that reflects Kenmore's continued efforts to create innovative products.

Sometimes eliminating a characteristic or feature has the same enhancing outcome as adding a characteristic or attribute. For instance, a number of skin care or deodorant manufacturers offer versions of their products that are unscented (i.e., *deleting an ingredient*). Indeed, Dove also markets an unscented version of its original Dove product.

Changing the overall brand rating

Still another cognitive-oriented strategy consists of attempting to alter consumers' *overall assessment of the brand* directly, without attempting to improve or change their evaluation of any single brand attribute. Such a strategy frequently relies on some form of global statement that "this is the largest-selling brand" or "the one all others try to imitate," or a similar claim that sets the brand apart from all its competitors. For instance, an advertisement announcing that the Chrysler 300C is "the most awarded new car ever" is the type of information that can increase consumers' positive attitudes, and also stimulate positive word-of-mouth, and even the purchase of a Chrysler 300C.

Changing beliefs about competitors' brands

Another approach to attitude-change strategy involves changing consumer beliefs about the *attributes of competitive* brands or product categories. For instance, a Motrin advertisement makes a dramatic assertion of product superiority over Advil and Aleve by claiming that "no other works faster or stronger on muscle pain." Similarly, Clorox Clean-Up that claims that Mr. Clean cannot remove certain types of tough stains that Clorox Clean-Up can. The main message is to proffer the insight that Clorox Clean-Up is a superior product to Mr. Clean's product (a principal competitor). While potentially very effective, such comparative advertising can boomerang by giving visibility to a competing brand and their claims.

The elaboration likelihood model (ELM)

Compared to the various specific strategies of attitude change that we have reviewed, the **elaboration likelihood model (ELM)** proposes the more global view that consumer attitudes are changed by two distinctly different "routes to persuasion": a central route or a peripheral route.[32] The *central route* is particularly relevant to attitude change when a consumer's motivation or ability to assess the attitude object is *high;* that is, attitude change occurs because the consumer actively seeks out information relevant to the attitude object itself. When consumers are willing to exert the effort to comprehend, learn, or evaluate the available information about the attitude object, learning and attitude change occur via the central route.

In contrast, when a consumer's motivation or assessment skills are low (e.g., low involvement), learning and attitude change tend to occur via the *peripheral route* without the consumer focusing on information relevant to the attitude object itself. In such cases, attitude change often is an outcome of secondary inducements (e.g., cents-off coupons, free samples, beautiful background scenery, great packaging, or the encouragement of a celebrity endorsement). Research indicates that even in low-involvement conditions (e.g., such as exposure to most advertising), in which both central and secondary inducements are initially equal in their ability to evoke similar attitudes, it is the central inducement that has the greatest "staying power"—that is, over time it is more persistent. Additionally, for subjects low in product knowledge, advertisements with terminology result in the consumer having a better attitude toward the brand and the ad.[33]

An offshoot of the elaboration likehood model is the *dual mediation model* (DMM). The DMM model adds a link between attitude towards the ad and brand cognitions.[34] It acknowledges the possibility that the central route to persuasion could be influenced by a peripheral cue (i.e., attitude towards the ad). Thus, this model demonstrated the interrelationship between the central and peripheral processes.

Behavior can precede or follow attitude formation

Our discussion of attitude formation and attitude change has stressed the traditional "rational" view that consumers develop their attitudes before taking action (e.g., "Know what you are doing before you do it"). There are alternatives to this "attitude precedes behavior" perspective, alternatives that, on careful analysis, are likely to be just as logical and rational. For example, *cognitive dissonance theory* and *attribution theory* each provide a different explanation as to why behavior might precede attitude formation.

Cognitive dissonance theory

According to **cognitive dissonance theory**, discomfort or dissonance occurs when a consumer holds conflicting thoughts about a belief or an attitude object. For instance, when consumers have made a commitment—made a down payment or placed an order for a product, particularly an expensive one such as an automobile or a personal computer—they often begin to feel cognitive dissonance *when they think of the unique, positive qualities of the brands not selected ("left behind")*. When cognitive dissonance occurs after a purchase, it is called *postpurchase dissonance*. Because purchase decisions often require some amount of compromise, postpurchase dissonance is quite normal. Nevertheless, it is likely to leave consumers with an uneasy feeling about their prior beliefs or actions—a feeling that they would seek to resolve by changing their attitudes to conform with their behavior.[35]

Thus, in the case of postpurchase dissonance, attitude change is frequently an *outcome* of an action or behavior. The conflicting thoughts and dissonant information following a purchase are prime factors that induce consumers to change their attitudes so that they will be consonant with their actual purchase behavior.

What makes postpurchase dissonance relevant to marketing strategists is the premise that *dissonance* propels consumers to reduce the unpleasant feelings created by the rival thoughts. A variety of tactics are open to consumers to reduce postpurchase dissonance. The consumer can rationalize the decision as being wise, seek out advertisements that support the choice (while avoiding dissonance-creating competitive ads), try to "sell" friends on the positive features of the brand (i.e., *"the consumer as a sales agent"*), or look to known satisfied owners for reassurance. For example, consider the response of a young man who just purchased an engagement ring for his girlfriend to the following ad headline he spots in a magazine: "How can you make two months' salary last forever?" This thought is likely to catch his attention. It says to him that although an engagement ring costs a great deal of money, it lasts forever because the future bride will cherish it for the rest of her life. Such an ad exposure is bound to help him reduce any lingering dissonance that he might have about how much he just spent on the ring.

While it has traditionally been viewed that with respect to a particular purchase, cognitive dissonance was something that a consumer either had or did not have, a recent study found that there can exist different types and levels of dissonance. The research studied consumer durable purchases, and found three distinct segments of consumers: a high dissonance segment, a low dissonance segment, and a "concerned about needing the purchase" segment.[36]

In addition to such consumer-initiated tactics for reducing postpurchase uncertainty, marketers can help consumers relieve their dissonance by including messages in their advertising specifically aimed at reinforcing consumers' decisions by complimenting their wisdom, offering stronger guarantees or warranties, increasing the number and effectiveness of its services, or providing detailed brochures on how to use its products correctly. However, with respect to product and service advertisements, there is evidence that as many as 75 percent of Americans feel that advertisers, on purpose, stretch the truth about their products in their advertising.[37]

Attribution theory

As a group of loosely interrelated social psychological principles, **attribution theory** attempts to explain how people assign causality (e.g., blame or credit) to events on the basis of either their own behavior or the behavior of others.[38] In other words, a person might say, "I contributed to UNICEF because it really helps people in need," or "She tried to persuade me to buy that unknown brand of DVD player because she'd make a bigger commission." In attribution theory, the underlying question is why: "Why did I do this?" "Why did she try to get me to switch brands?" This process of making inferences about one's own or another's behavior is a major component of attitude formation and change.

Attribution theory is certainly part of our everyday life, as companies continue to have their names on football stadiums and sponsor all types of charitable events. Research results indicate that the better the "match" between a sponsor and an event, the more positive the outcome is likely to be. Still further, there is evidence to suggest that consumers are willing to reward high-effort firms (i.e., they will pay more and/or evaluate the product higher) if they feel that the company has made an extra effort to make a better product or provide better consumer services.[39]

Self-perception theory

Of the various perspectives on attribution theory that have been proposed, **self-perception theory**—individuals' inferences or judgments as to the causes of their own behavior—is a good beginning point for a discussion of attribution.

In terms of consumer behavior, self-perception theory suggests that attitudes develop as consumers *look at and make judgments about their own behavior.* Simply stated, if a young Wall Street banker observes that he routinely purchases *The Wall Street Journal* on his way to the office, he is apt to conclude that he likes *The Wall Street Journal* (i.e., he has a positive attitude toward this newspaper).[40] Drawing inferences from one's own behavior is not always as simple or as clear-cut as the newspaper example might suggest. To appreciate the complexity of self-perception theory, it is useful to distinguish between **internal and external attributions**. Let us assume that Dana has just finished using a popular computer photoediting software (e.g., Adobe's Photoshop) for the first time and that her digital photographs were well received when they were shown to the members of the photography club that she belongs to. After receiving the compliments, she says to herself, "I'm really a natural at editing my digital photos," this statement would be an example of an *internal attribution.* It is an internal attribution because she is giving herself credit for the outcome (e.g., her ability, her skill, or her effort). That is, she is saying, "These photos are good because of me." On the other hand, if Dana concluded that the successful digital photoediting was due to factors beyond her control (e.g., a user-friendly photoediting program, the assistance of another club member, or just "luck"), this would be an example of an *external attribution*. In such a case, she might be saying, "My great photos are beginner's luck."

This distinction between internal and external attributions can be of strategic marketing importance. For instance, it would generally be in the best interests of the firm that produces the photoediting software if users, especially inexperienced users, *internalized* their successful use of the software package. If they internalized such a positive experience, it is more likely that they will repeat the behavior and become a satisfied regular user. Alternatively, however, if they were to *externalize* their success, it would be preferable that they attribute it to the particular software rather than to an incidental environmental factor such as "beginner's luck" or another's "foolproof" instructions. Additionally, recent studies suggest that when advertisers accurately target their message to consumers, with the proper cognitive generalizations about the self ("self-schema"), the consumer perceives the argument quality of the ad as being higher, and therefore has a more favorable attitude towards the message.[41]

According to the principle of **defensive attribution**, consumers are likely to accept credit personally for success (internal attribution) and to credit failure to others or to outside events (external attribution). For this reason, it is crucial that marketers offer uniformly high-quality products that allow consumers to perceive themselves as the reason for the success; that is, "I'm competent." Moreover, a company's advertising should serve to reassure consumers, particularly inexperienced ones, that its products will not let them down but will make them heroes instead.

Foot-in-the-door Technique   Self-perception theorists have explored situations in which consumer compliance with a minor request affects subsequent compliance with a more substantial request. This strategy, which is commonly referred to as the **foot-in-the-door technique**, is based on the premise that individuals look at their prior behavior (e.g., compliance with a minor request) and conclude that they are the kind of person who says "yes" to such requests (i.e., an internal attribution). Such self-attribution serves to increase the likelihood that they will agree to a similar more substantial request. Someone who donates twenty-five dollars to the American Heart Association might be persuaded to donate a much larger amount when properly approached. The initial donation is, in effect, the *foot in the door.*

Research into the foot-in-the-door technique has concentrated on understanding how specific incentives (e.g., cents-off coupons of varying amounts) ultimately influence consumer attitudes and subsequent purchase behavior. It appears that different-size incentives create different degrees of internal attribution, which, in turn, lead to different amounts of attitude change. For instance, individuals who try a brand without any inducements or individuals who buy a brand repeatedly are more likely to infer increasingly positive attitudes toward the brand from their respective behaviors (e.g., "I buy this brand because I like it"). In contrast, individuals who try a free sample are less committed to changing their attitudes toward the brand ("I tried this brand because it was free").

Thus, contrary to what might be expected, it is not the biggest incentive that is most likely to lead to positive attitude change. If an incentive is too big, marketers run the risk that consumers might externalize the cause of their behavior to the incentive and be *less* likely to change their attitudes and *less* likely to make future purchases of the brand. Instead, what seems most effective is a *moderate* incentive, one that is just big enough to stimulate initial purchase of the brand but still small enough to encourage consumers to internalize their positive usage experience and allow a positive attitude change to occur.[42]

In contrast with the foot-in-the-door technique is the **door-in-the-face technique**, in which a large, costly first request that is probably refused is followed by a second, more realistic, less costly request. Under certain situations, this technique may prove more effective than the foot-in-the-door technique.[43]

Attributions toward others

In addition to understanding self-perception theory, it is important to understand **attributions toward others** because of the variety of potential applications to consumer behavior and marketing. As already suggested, every time a person asks "why?" about a statement or action of another or "others"—a family member, a friend, a salesperson, a direct marketer, a shipping company—attribution theory is relevant. To illustrate, in evaluating the words or deeds of others, say, a salesperson, a consumer tries to determine if the salesperson's motives are in the consumer's best interests. If the salesperson's motives are viewed as favorable to the consumer, the consumer is likely to respond favorably. Otherwise, the consumer is likely to reject the salesperson's words and go elsewhere to make a purchase. In another case, a consumer orders a new digital camera from a major direct marketer such as **Buy.com** or **Newegg.com**. Because the consumer wants it immediately, she agrees to pay an extra $8 to $15 for next-day delivery by FedEx or UPS. If on the next day the package with the digital camera fails to show up as expected, the consumer has two possible "others" to which she might attribute the failure—that is, the direct marketer (failing to get the product out on time) or the delivery service (failing to get the package to the consumer on time). In addition, she might blame them both (a dual failure); or if the weather was really bad, she might conclude that it was the bad weather (an attribution that neither of them was at fault).[44]

Attributions toward things

Consumer researchers also are interested in consumers' **attributions toward things** because products (or services) can readily be thought of as "things." It is in the area of judging product performance that consumers are most likely to form product attributions. Specifically, they want to find out why a product meets or fails to meet their expectations. In this regard, they could attribute the product's successful performance (or failure) to the product itself, to themselves, to other people or situations, or to some combination of these factors.[45] To recap an earlier example, when Dana edited a set of challenging digital photos, she could attribute her success to the Photoshop software (product attribution), to her own skill (self or internal attribution), or to a fellow photo club member who helped her (external attribution).

How we test our attributions

After making initial attributions about a product's performance or a person's words or actions, we often attempt to determine whether the inference we made is correct. According to a leading attribution theorist, individuals acquire conviction about particular observations by acting like "naive scientists," that is, by collecting additional information in an attempt to confirm (or disconfirm) prior inferences. In collecting such information, consumers often use the following criteria:[46]

1. Distinctiveness—The consumer attributes an action to a particular product or person if the action occurs when the product (or person) is present and does not occur in its absence.
2. Consistency over time—Whenever the person or product is present, the consumer's inference or reaction must be the same, or nearly so.
3. Consistency over modality—The inference or reaction must be the same, even when the situation in which it occurs varies.
4. Consensus—The action is perceived in the same way by other consumers.

FIGURE 16.5

Testing Attributions of a Corporate Grant to Support an After-School Program

Source: Andrea M. Sjovall and Andrew C. Talk, "From Actions to Impressions: Cognitive Attribution Theory and the Formation of Corporate Reputation," *Corporate Reputation Review* 7 (Fall 2004): 277.

Consensus	Distinctiveness	Consistency	Resulting attribution
High *Many groups support the after-school program*	**High** *The corporation supports only the school*	**High** *The corporation supports the school regularly*	→ **External influence** *Support of the school is related to the quality of the school*
Low *Only the corporation supports the after-school program*	**Low** *The corporation supports several schools and other programs*	**High** *The corporation supports the school regularly*	→ **Internal disposition** *Support of the school is related to the benevolence of the corporation*
Either **High or Low**	**Either** **High or Low**	**Low** *The corporation gave a grant to the school only once*	→ **External influence** *Support of the school is related to an undefined aspect of the particular situation that occurred at the time of the grant*

To illustrate how the process of testing our attributions work, Figure 16.5 provides three scenarios that depict (for three of the four "attributions testing criteria"), how people might use information to determine why a corporation has given a grant for an after-school program to benefit public school children, and whether the giving is either internally or externally driven or caused.

The following example illustrates how each of these criteria might be used to make inferences about product performance and people's actions.

If Mike, a city bus driver who loves do-it-yourself projects, observes that the edges on wooden tables that he builds seem to be smoother when using his new DeWalt router (**www.dewalt.com**), he is likely to credit the new DeWalt power tool with the improved appearance of his tables (i.e., distinctiveness). Furthermore, if Mike finds that his new DeWalt router produces the same high-quality results each time he uses it, he will tend to be more confident about his initial observation (i.e., the inference has consistency over time). Similarly, he will also be more confident if he finds that his satisfaction with the DeWalt power tool extends across a wide range of other related tasks, from making dovetail joints for drawers to cutting patterns in wood (i.e., consistency over modality). Finally, Mike will have still more confidence in his inferences to the extent that his friends who own DeWalt routers also have similar experiences (i.e., consensus).

Much like Mike, we go about gathering additional information from our experiences with people and things, and we use this information to test our initial inferences.

chapter **17**

› **Learning**

The elements of consumer learning

Because not all learning theorists agree on how learning takes place, it is difficult to come up with a generally accepted definition of learning. From a marketing perspective, however, consumer learning can be thought of as *the process by which individuals acquire the purchase and consumption knowledge and experience that they apply to future related behavior.* Several points in this definition are worth noting.

First, consumer learning is a *process;* that is, it continually evolves and changes as a result of newly acquired *knowledge* (which may be gained from reading, from discussions, from observation, from thinking) or from actual *experience.* Both newly acquired knowledge and personal experience serve as *feedback* to the individual and provide the basis for *future behavior* in similar situations.

The role of *experience* in learning does not mean that all learning is deliberately sought. Though much learning is *intentional* (i.e., it is acquired as the result of a careful search for information), a great deal of learning is also *incidental,* acquired by accident or without much effort. For example, some ads may induce learning (e.g., of new products under familiar brand names such as the ones discussed earlier), even though the consumer's attention is elsewhere (on a magazine article rather than the advertisement on the facing page). Other ads are sought out and carefully read by consumers contemplating a major purchase decision.

The term **learning** encompasses the total range of learning, from simple, almost reflexive responses, to the learning of abstract concepts and complex problem solving. Most learning theorists recognize the existence of different types of learning and explain the differences through the use of distinctive models of learning.

Despite their different viewpoints, learning theorists in general agree that in order for learning to occur, certain basic elements must be present. The elements included in most learning theories are *motivation, cues, response,* and *reinforcement.* These concepts are discussed first because they tend to recur in the theories discussed later in this chapter.

Motivation

The concept of **motivation** is important to learning theory. Remember, motivation is based on needs and goals. Motivation acts as a spur to learning. For example, men and women who want to take up bicycle riding for fitness and recreation are motivated to learn all they can about bike riding and also to practice often. They may seek information concerning the prices, quality, and characteristics of bicycles and "learn" which bicycles are the best for the kind of riding that they do. They will also read any articles in their local newspapers about bicycle trails and may seek online information about "active vacations" that involve biking or hiking. Conversely, individuals who are not interested in bike riding are likely to ignore all information related to the activity. The goal object (bicycle riding in order to relax and stay fit) simply has no relevance for them. The degree of relevance, or *involvement,* determines the consumer's level of motivation to search for knowledge or information about a product or service. (*Involvement theory,* as it has come to be known, is discussed later in the chapter.) Uncovering consumer motives is one of the prime tasks of marketers, who then try to teach motivated consumer segments why and how their products will fulfill the consumers' needs.

Cues

If motives serve to stimulate learning, **cues** are the stimuli that give direction to these motives. An advertisement for an exotic trip that includes bike riding may serve as a cue for bike riders, who may suddenly "recognize" that they "need" a vacation. The ad is the cue, or *stimulus,* that suggests a specific way to satisfy a salient motive. In the marketplace, price, styling, packaging, advertising, and store displays all serve as cues to help consumers fulfill their needs in product-specific ways.

Cues serve to direct consumer drives when they are consistent with consumer expectations. Marketers must be careful to provide cues that do not upset those expectations. For example, consumers expect designer clothes to be expensive and to be sold in upscale retail stores. Thus, a high-fashion designer should sell his or her clothes only through exclusive stores and advertise only in upscale fashion magazines. Each aspect of the marketing mix must reinforce the others if cues are to serve as the stimuli that guide consumer actions in the direction desired by the marketer.

Response

How individuals react to a drive or cue—how they behave—constitute their **response**. Learning can occur even when responses are not overt. The automobile manufacturer that provides consistent cues to a consumer may not always succeed in stimulating a purchase. However, if the manufacturer succeeds in forming a favorable image of a particular automobile model in the consumer's mind, it is likely that the consumer will consider that make or model when he or she is ready to buy.

A response is not tied to a need in a one-to-one fashion. Indeed, a need or motive may evoke a whole variety of responses. For example, there are many ways to respond to the need for physical exercise besides riding bicycles. Cues provide some direction, but there are many cues competing for the consumer's attention. Which response the consumer makes depends heavily on previous learning; that, in turn, depends on how related responses have been reinforced.

Reinforcement

Reinforcement increases the likelihood that a specific response will occur in the future as the result of particular cues or stimuli. For example, a certain ad presents a three-step process for facial skin care based on three products (i.e., cues). This ad is instructional and designed to generate consumer learning. If a college student finds that the cleansing routine based on the three products featured in this ad relieves his acne problem, he is likely to continue buying and using these products. Through positive reinforcement, learning has taken place, since the facial cleansing system lived up to expectations. On the other hand, if the products had not provided relief from the problem when first used, the student would have no reason to associate the brand with acne relief in the future. Because of the absence of reinforcement, it is unlikely that he would buy that brand again.

With these basic principles established, we can now discuss some well-known theories or models of how learning occurs.

Behavioral learning theories

Behavioral learning theories are sometimes referred to as **stimulus-response theories** because they are based on the premise that observable responses to specific external stimuli signal that learning has taken place. When a person acts (responds) in a predictable way to a known stimulus, he or she is said to have "learned." Behavioral theories are not so much concerned with the *process* of learning as they are with the *inputs* and *outcomes* of learning; that is, in the stimuli that consumers select from the environment and the observable behaviors that result. Two behavioral theories with great relevance to marketing are **classical conditioning** and **instrumental** (or **operant) conditioning**.

Classical conditioning

Early classical conditioning theorists regarded all organisms (both animal and human) as relatively passive entities that could be taught certain behaviors through repetition (i.e., *conditioning*). In everyday speech, the word *conditioning* has come to mean a kind of "knee-jerk" (or automatic) response to a situation built up through repeated exposure. If you get a headache every time you think of visiting your Aunt Gertrude, your reaction may be conditioned from years of boring visits with her.

Ivan Pavlov, a Russian physiologist, was the first to describe conditioning and to propose it as a general model of how learning occurs. According to Pavlovian theory, conditioned learning results when a stimulus that is paired with another stimulus that elicits a known response serves to produce the same response when used alone.

Pavlov demonstrated what he meant by **conditioned learning** in his studies with dogs. The dogs were hungry and highly motivated to eat. In his experiments, Pavlov sounded a bell and then immediately applied a meat paste to the dogs' tongues, which caused them to salivate. Learning (conditioning) occurred when, after a sufficient number of repetitions of the bell sound followed almost immediately by the food, the bell sound alone caused the dogs to salivate. The dogs associated the bell sound (the *conditioned* stimulus) with the meat paste (the *unconditioned* stimulus) and, after a number of pairings, gave the same unconditioned response (salivation) to the bell alone as they did to the meat paste. The unconditioned response to the meat paste became the conditioned response to the bell. Figure 17.1A models this relationship. An analogous situation would be one in which the smells of dinner cooking would cause your mouth to water. If you usually listen to the 6 o'clock news while waiting for dinner to be served, you would tend to associate the 6 o'clock news with dinner, so that eventually the sounds of the 6 o'clock news alone might cause your mouth to water, even if dinner was not being prepared and even if you were not hungry. Figure 17.1B diagrams this basic relationship.

In a consumer behavior context, an **unconditioned stimulus** might consist of a well-known brand symbol (such as the Neutrogena name) that implies dermatologists' endorsement and pure (chemically free) products (i.e., containing few potentially irritating ingredients, such as perfume scents commonly added to personal cleansing products). This previously acquired consumer perception of Neutrogena is the *unconditioned response*. **Conditioned stimuli** might consist of new products bearing the well-known symbol, and the *conditioned response* would be trying these products because of the belief that they embody the same attributes with which the Neutrogena name is associated.

Cognitive associative learning

Contemporary behavioral scientists view classical conditioning as the learning of associations among events that allows the organism to anticipate and "represent" its environment. According to this view, the relationship (or contiguity) between the conditioned stimulus and the unconditioned stimulus (the bell and the meat paste) influenced the dogs' expectations, which in turn influenced their behavior (salivation). Classical conditioning, then, rather than being a reflexive action, is seen as **cognitive associative learning**—not the acquisition of new reflexes, but the acquisition of new knowledge about the world.[2] According to some researchers, optimal conditioning—that is, the creation of a strong association between the conditioned stimulus (CS) and the unconditioned stimulus (US)—requires (1) forward conditioning (i.e., the CS should precede the US); (2) repeated pairings of the CS and the US; (3) a CS and US that logically belong together; (4) a CS that is novel and unfamiliar; and (5) a US that is biologically or symbolically salient. This model is known as **neo-Pavlovian conditioning**.

Under neo-Pavlovian theory, the consumer can be viewed as an information seeker who uses logical and perceptual relations among events, along with his or her own preconceptions, to form a sophisticated representation of the world. Conditioning is the learning that results from exposure to relationships among events in the environment; such exposure creates expectations as to the structure of the environment.

Strategic applications of classical conditioning

Three basic concepts derive from classical conditioning: *repetition, stimulus generalization,* and *stimulus discrimination.* Each of these concepts is important to the strategic applications of consumer behavior.

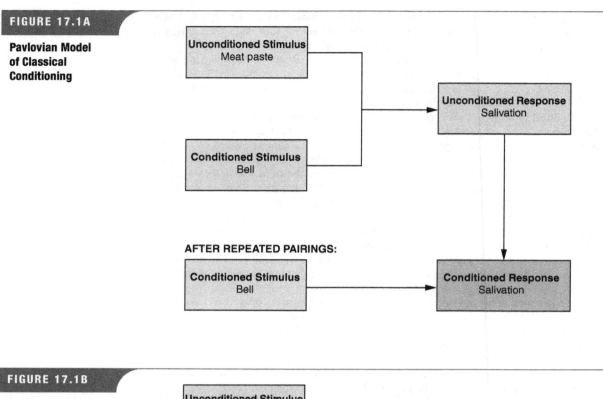

FIGURE 17.1A

Pavlovian Model of Classical Conditioning

FIGURE 17.1B

Analogous Model of Classical Conditioning

Repetition   **Repetition** increases the strength of the association between a conditioned stimulus and an unconditioned stimulus and slows the process of forgetting. However, research suggests that there is a limit to the amount of repetition that will aid retention. Although some overlearning (i.e., repetition beyond what is necessary for learning) aids retention, at some point an individual can become satiated with numerous exposures, and both attention and retention will decline. This effect, known as **advertising wearout**, can be moderated by varying the advertising message. Some marketers avoid wearout by using *cosmetic variations* in their ads (using different backgrounds, different print types, different advertising spokespersons) while repeating the same advertising theme. For example, the classic, decades-old Absolut Vodka campaign has used the same theme with highly creative and varied backgrounds, relating the product to holidays, trends, and cultural symbols in the United States and across the world. One study showed that brand familiarity impacted the effectiveness of repeating ads. The effectiveness of repeated ads for an unfamiliar brand declined over time, but when the same advertising was used for a well-known and familiar brand, repetition wearout was postponed.[3]

Substantive variations are changes in advertising content across different versions of an advertisement. Varied ads provide marketers with several strategic advantages. Consumers exposed to substantively varied ads process more information about product attributes and have more positive thoughts about the product than those exposed to cosmetic variations. Attitudes formed as a result of exposure to substantively varied ads are more resistant to change in the face of competitive attack.

Although the principle of repetition is well established among advertisers, not everyone agrees on how much repetition is enough. Some marketing scholars believe that just three exposures to an advertisement are needed: one to make consumers aware of the product, a second to show consumers the relevance of the product, and a third to remind them of its benefits. This is known as the *three-hit theory.* Others think it may take 11 to 12 repetitions to increase the likelihood that consumers will actually receive the three exposures basic to the so-called three-hit theory.

The effectiveness of repetition is somewhat dependent upon the amount of competitive advertising to which the consumer is exposed. The higher the level of competitive ads, the greater the likelihood that *interference* will occur, causing consumers to forget previous learning that resulted from repetition.

Stimulus Generalization   According to classical conditioning theorists, learning depends not only on repetition but also on the ability of individuals to generalize. Pavlov found, for example, that a dog could learn to salivate not only to the sound of a bell but also to the somewhat similar sound of jangling keys. If we were not capable of **stimulus generalization**—that is, of making the same response to slightly different stimuli—not much learning would take place.

Stimulus generalization explains why some imitative "me-too" products succeed in the marketplace: Consumers confuse them with the original product they have seen advertised. It also explains why manufacturers of private-label brands try to make their packaging closely resemble the national brand leaders. They are hoping that consumers will confuse their packages with the leading brand and buy their product rather than the leading brand. Similarly packaged competitive products result in millions of lost sales for well-positioned and extensively advertised brands.

Product Line, Form, and Category Extensions   The principle of stimulus generalization is applied by marketers to *product line, form,* and *category extensions.* In **product line extensions**, the marketer adds related products to an already established brand, knowing that the new products are more likely to be adopted when they are associated with a known and trusted brand name.

Marketers also offer **product form extensions**, such as Crest Toothpaste to Crest Whitestrips, Listerine mouthwash to ListerinePaks, and Ivory bath soap to Ivory liquid soap to Ivory shower gel. Marketers also offer **product category extensions** that generally target new market segments.

The success of product extensions depends on a number of factors. If the image of the parent brand is one of quality and the new item is logically linked to the brand, consumers are more likely to bring positive associations to the new offerings introduced as product line, form, or category extensions. For example, Tylenol, a highly trusted brand, initially introduced line extensions by making its products available in a number of different forms (tablets, capsules, gelcaps), strengths (regular, extra strength, and children's), and package sizes. It then extended its brand name to a wide range of related remedies for colds, flu, sinus congestion, and allergies, further segmenting the line for adults, children, and infants. The number of different products affiliated with a brand strengthens the brand name, as long as the company maintains a quality image across all brand extensions. Failure to do so, in the long run, is likely to negatively affect consumer confidence and evaluations of all the brand's offerings. One study showed that brands that include diverse products are likely to offer more successful brand extensions than brands that include similar products. The study also confirmed that the likely associations between the benefits offered by the brand and its new extension are the key to consumers' reactions to the brand extension.[4]

Family Branding **Family branding**—the practice of marketing a whole line of company products under the same brand name—is another strategy that capitalizes on the consumer's ability to generalize favorable brand associations from one product to others. Campbell's, originally a marketer of soups, continues to add new food products to its product line under the Campbell's brand name (such as canned soups, frozen meals, soup to be eaten on-the-go, and tomato juice), thus achieving ready acceptance for the new products from satisfied consumers of other Campbell's food products. The Ralph Lauren designer label on men's and women's clothing helps to achieve ready acceptance for these products in the upscale sportswear market. Clearly, managing a family brand is more complex than managing a brand that includes only closely related items. One study demonstrated that consumers are likely to expect variability in the performances of the products under the family brand if the company does not address this issue in the information provided with new products introduced; the study singles out the importance of consistent positioning even as the number of offerings under a given name increases.[5]

On the other hand, Procter & Gamble (P&G) was built on the strength of its many individual brands in the same product category. For example, the company offers multiple brands of laundry products, of antiperspirants, and of hair care products, including shampoo. Although offering many brands of the same product is expensive, the combined weight of its brands has always provided Procter & Gamble (the **umbrella brand**) with great power in negotiating with advertising media and securing desirable shelf space for its products in the United States and around the world. It also enables the company to effectively combat any competitors who may try to introduce products in markets dominated by P&G.

Donald Trump, the real estate tycoon, made his own surname into a brand name, *Trump*, a name attached to multiple buildings, hotels, and casinos to give consumers feelings of confidence in their quality. He extended this brand into television with his highly successful reality show *The Apprentice*, which has itself developed brand extensions. Real estate developers offer Mr. Trump a percentage in their new developments in return for the use of his name. However, he has to be vigilant that the Trump name is not attached to inferior buildings or hotels or TV shows because the brand would lose its carefully built up quality image.

Retail private branding often achieves the same effect as family branding. For example, Wal-Mart used to advertise that its stores carried only "brands you trust." Now, the name Wal-Mart itself has become a "brand" that consumers have confidence in, and the name confers brand value on Wal-Mart's store brands.

Licensing **Licensing**—allowing a well-known brand name to be affixed to products of another manufacturer—is a marketing strategy that operates on the principle of *stimulus generalization.* The names of designers, manufacturers, celebrities, corporations, and even cartoon characters are attached for a fee (i.e., "rented") to a variety of products, enabling the licensees to achieve instant recognition and implied quality for the licensed products. Some successful licensors include Liz Claiborne, Tommy Hilfiger, Calvin Klein, and Christian Dior, whose names appear on an exceptionally wide variety of products, from sheets to shoes and luggage to perfume. Figure 17.2 shows an ad for eyeglasses bearing the name of the well-known shoe manufacturer Kenneth Cole.

Corporations also license their names and trademarks, usually for some form of brand extension, where the name of the corporation is licensed to the maker of a related product and thereby enters a new product category (e.g., Godiva chocolates licensed its name for Godiva liqueur). Corporations also license their names for

FIGURE 17.2

Source: Courtesy of Kenneth
Cole Productions, Inc.

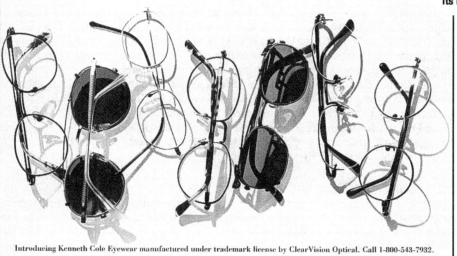

No matter what your point of view, we hope you see things our way.

—Kenneth Cole

**Shoe Manufacturer Licenses
Its Name**

Introducing Kenneth Cole Eyewear manufactured under trademark license by ClearVision Optical. Call 1-800-543-7932.

purely promotional licensing, in which popular company logos (such as "Always Coca-Cola") are stamped on clothing, toys, coffee mugs, and the like. The Vatican Library licenses its name for a variety of products from luggage to bed linens, and the Mormon Church has expanded its licensing activities to apparel and home decorating items.

The increase in licensing has made *counterfeiting* a booming business, as counterfeiters add well-known licensor names to a variety of products without benefit of contract or quality control. Aside from the loss of sales revenue because of counterfeiting, the authentic brands also suffer the consequences associated with zero quality control over counterfeit products that bear their names. It is also increasingly difficult to identify fakes of such expensive and upscale goods as Christian Dior bags, Gucci shoes, and Chanel No. 5 perfume. Many firms are now legally pursuing retailers that sell counterfeit branded goods; many also are employing specialized technology to make their products more counterfeit-proof.[6]

Stimulus Discrimination   **Stimulus discrimination** is the opposite of stimulus generalization and results in the selection of a specific stimulus from among similar stimuli. The consumer's ability to discriminate among similar stimuli is the basis of positioning strategy, which seeks to establish a unique image for a brand in the consumer's mind.

Positioning   In our over-communicated society, the key to stimulus discrimination is effective **positioning**, a major competitive advantage. The image—or position—that a product or service holds in the mind of the consumer is critical to its success. When a marketer targets consumers with a strong communications program that stresses the unique ways in which its product will satisfy the consumer's needs, it wants the consumer to differentiate its product from among competitive products on the shelf. Unlike the imitator who hopes consumers will *generalize* their perceptions and attribute special characteristics of the market leader's products to its own products, market leaders want the consumer to *discriminate* among similar stimuli. Major marketers are constantly vigilant concerning store brand look-alikes, and they quickly file suit against retailers that they believe are cannibalizing their sales. They want their products to be recognized as uniquely fulfilling consumers' needs. Studies have shown that the favorable attitudes resulting from effective positioning and stimulus discrimination are usually retained long enough to influence future purchase behavior.[7]

Product Differentiation   Most product differentiation strategies are designed to distinguish a product or brand from that of competitors on the basis of an attribute that is relevant, meaningful, and valuable to consumers. However, many marketers also successfully differentiate their brands on an attribute that may actually be irrelevant to creating the implied benefit, such as a noncontributing ingredient or a color.

It often is quite difficult to unseat a brand leader once stimulus discrimination has occurred. One explanation is that the leader is usually first in the market and has had a longer period to "teach" consumers (through advertising and selling) to associate the brand name with the product. In general, the longer the period of learning—of associating a brand name with a specific product—the more likely the consumer is to discriminate and the less likely to generalize the stimulus.

Classical conditioning and consumer behavior

The principles of classical conditioning provide the theoretical underpinnings for many marketing applications. Repetition, stimulus generalization, and stimulus discrimination are all major applied concepts that help to explain consumer behavior in the marketplace. However, they do not explain all behavioral consumer learning. Although a great deal of consumer behavior (e.g., the purchase of branded convenience goods) is shaped to some extent by repeated advertising messages stressing a unique competitive advantage, a significant amount of purchase behavior results from careful evaluation of product alternatives. Our assessments of products are often based on the degree of satisfaction—the rewards—we experience as a result of making specific purchases; in other words, from instrumental conditioning.

Instrumental conditioning

Like classical conditioning, **instrumental conditioning** requires a link between a stimulus and a response. However, in instrumental conditioning, the stimulus that results in the most satisfactory response is the one that is learned.

Instrumental learning theorists believe that learning occurs through a trial-and-error process, with habits formed as a result of rewards received for certain responses or behaviors. This model of learning applies to many situations in which consumers learn about products, services, and retail stores. For example, consumers learn which stores carry the type of clothing they prefer at prices they can afford to pay by shopping in a number of stores. Once they find a store that carries clothing that meets their needs, they are likely to patronize that store to the exclusion of others. Every time they purchase a shirt or a sweater there that they really like, their store loyalty is rewarded (*reinforced*), and their patronage of that store is more likely to be repeated. Whereas classical conditioning is useful in explaining how consumers learn very simple kinds of behaviors, instrumental conditioning is more helpful in explaining complex, goal-directed activities.

The name most closely associated with instrumental (*operant*) conditioning is that of the American psychologist B. F. Skinner. According to Skinner, most individual learning occurs in a controlled environment in which individuals are "rewarded" for choosing an appropriate behavior. In consumer behavior terms, instrumental conditioning suggests that consumers learn by means of a trial-and-error process in which some purchase behaviors result in more favorable outcomes (i.e., rewards) than other purchase behaviors. A favorable experience is "instrumental" in teaching the individual to repeat a specific behavior.

Like Pavlov, Skinner developed his model of learning by working with animals. Small animals, such as rats and pigeons, were placed in his "Skinner box"; if they made appropriate movements (e.g., if they depressed levers or pecked keys), they received food (a positive reinforcement). Skinner and his many adherents have done amazing things with this simple learning model, including teaching pigeons to play Ping-Pong and even to dance. In a marketing context, the consumer who tries several brands and styles of jeans before finding a style that fits her figure (positive reinforcement) has engaged in instrumental learning. Presumably, the brand that fits best is the one she will continue to buy. This model of instrumental conditioning is presented in Figure 17.3.

Reinforcement of behavior

Skinner distinguished two types of reinforcement (or reward) that influence the likelihood that a response will be repeated. The first type, **positive reinforcement**, consists of

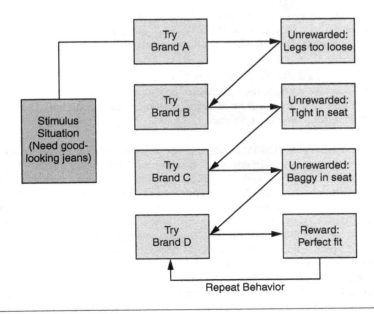

A Model of Instrumental Conditioning

FIGURE 17.3

events that strengthen the likelihood of a specific response. Using a shampoo that leaves your hair feeling silky and clean is likely to result in a repeat purchase of the shampoo. **Negative reinforcement** is an unpleasant or negative outcome that also serves to encourage a specific behavior. An advertisement that shows a model with wrinkled skin is designed to encourage consumers to buy and use the advertised skin cream.

Fear appeals in ad messages are examples of negative reinforcement. Many life insurance advertisements rely on negative reinforcement to encourage the purchase of life insurance. The ads warn husbands of the dire consequences to their wives and children in the event of their sudden death. Marketers of headache remedies use negative reinforcement when they illustrate the unpleasant symptoms of an unrelieved headache, as do marketers of mouthwash when they show the loneliness suffered by someone with bad breath. In each of these cases, the consumer is encouraged to avoid the negative consequences by buying the advertised product.

Either positive or negative reinforcement can be used to elicit a desired response. However, negative reinforcement should not be confused with punishment, which is designed to *discourage* behavior. For example, parking tickets are not negative reinforcement; they are a form of "punishment" designed to discourage drivers from parking illegally.

Extinction and Forgetting   When a learned response is no longer reinforced, it diminishes to the point of *extinction,* that is, to the point at which the link between the stimulus and the expected reward is eliminated. If a consumer is no longer satisfied with the service a retail store provides, the link between the stimulus (the store) and the response (expected satisfaction) is no longer reinforced, and there is little likelihood that the consumer will return. When behavior is no longer reinforced, it is "unlearned." There is a difference, however, between extinction and *forgetting.* A couple who have not visited a once-favorite restaurant for a very long time may simply forget how much they used to enjoy eating there and not think to return. Thus, their behavior is unlearned because of lack of use rather than lack of reinforcement. Forgetting is often related to the passage of time; this is known as the process of *decay.* Marketers can overcome forgetting through repetition, and can combat extinction through the deliberate enhancement of consumer satisfaction. Sometimes, marketers may cause extinction deliberately and "undo" a previously learned association. For example, a large car service in New York City known for many years as Tel Aviv Car Service is now advertising itself as the "Dial 7s" car service in reference to its phone number (consisting of seven consecutive sevens) and, quite possibly, to undo its association in the consumer's mind with Israeli ownership.

Strategic applications of instrumental conditioning
Marketers effectively utilize the concepts of consumer instrumental learning when they provide positive reinforcement by assuring customer satisfaction with the product, the service, and the total buying experience.

Customer Satisfaction (Reinforcement)   The objective of all marketing efforts should be to maximize customer satisfaction. Marketers must be certain to provide the best possible product for the money and to avoid raising consumer expectations for product (or service) performance beyond what the product can deliver. Aside from the experience of using the product itself, consumers can receive reinforcement from other elements in the purchase situation, such as the environment in which the transaction or service takes place, the attention and service provided by employees, and the amenities provided. For example, an upscale beauty salon, in addition to a beautiful environment, may offer coffee and soft drinks to waiting clients and provide free local telephone service at each hairdressing station. Even if the styling outcome is not so great, the client may feel so pampered with the atmosphere and service that she looks forward to her next visit. On the other hand, even with the other positive reinforcements in place, if the salon's employees are so busy talking with each other while the service is being rendered that the client feels ignored, she is not likely to return.

Recent data from the American Customer Satisfaction Index—the benchmark source regarding customer satisfaction with businesses—illustrate that many companies wrongly assume that lower prices and more diverse product lines make customers more satisfied. Instead, it appears that companies that create personal connections with customers, and also offer diverse product lines and competitive prices, are the ones providing the best reinforcement, resulting in satisfaction and repeat patronage.[8] Some hotels offer reinforcements in the form of small amenities, such as chocolates on the pillow or bottled water on the dresser; others send platters of fruit or even bottles of wine to returning guests to show their appreciation for continued patronage. Most frequent shopper programs are based on enhancing positive reinforcement and encouraging continued patronage. The more a consumer uses the service, the greater the rewards. Kellogg's provides a frequent user program by including coupons on the top of its cereal boxes that can be accumulated and exchanged for various premiums, such as a coffee mug or denim shirt emblazoned with the company's logo.

Relationship marketing—developing a close personalized relationship with customers—is another form of nonproduct reinforcement. Knowing that she will be advised of a forthcoming sale or that selected merchandise will be set aside for her next visit cements the loyalty that a consumer may have for a retail store. The ability to telephone his "personal" banker to transfer funds between accounts or to make other banking transactions without coming into the bank reinforces the satisfaction a consumer may have with his bank. Service companies are particularly vulnerable to interruptions in customer reinforcement because of service failures that cannot be controlled in advance. As a result, astute service providers have implemented *service recovery* measures that provide extra rewards to customers who have experienced service failures. Studies indicate that customers who emotionally bonded with the service provider were less forgiving than other customers because they felt truly "betrayed," and that the effectiveness of service recovery measures had the strongest impact on loyal customers.[9]

Reinforcement Schedules Marketers have found that product quality must be consistently high and provide satisfaction to the customer with each use for desired consumer behavior to continue. However, they have also discovered that some nonproduct rewards do not have to be offered each time the transaction takes place; even an occasional reward provides reinforcement and encourages consumer patronage. For example, airlines may occasionally upgrade a passenger at the gate, or a clothing discounter may from time to time announce a one-hour sale over the store sound system. The promise of possibly receiving a reward provides positive reinforcement and encourages consumer patronage.

Marketers have identified three types of reinforcement schedules: *total* (or continuous) reinforcement, *systematic* (fixed ratio) reinforcement, and *random* (variable ratio) reinforcement. An example of a total (or continuous) reinforcement schedule is the free after-dinner drink or fruit plate always served to patrons at certain restaurants. Needless to say, the basic product or service rendered is expected to provide total satisfaction (reinforcement) each time it is used.

A *fixed ratio* reinforcement schedule provides reinforcement every "*n*th" time the product or service is purchased (say, every third time). For example, a retailer may send a credit voucher to account holders every three months based on a percentage of the previous quarter's purchases. A *variable ratio* reinforcement schedule rewards consumers on a random basis or on an average frequency basis (such as every third or tenth transaction). Gambling casinos operate on the basis of variable ratios. People pour money into slot machines (which are programmed to pay off on a variable ratio), hoping for the big win. Variable ratios tend to engender high rates of desired behavior and are somewhat resistant to extinction—perhaps because, for many consumers, hope springs eternal. Other examples of variable ratio schedules include lotteries, sweepstakes, door prizes, and contests that require certain consumer behaviors for eligibility.

Shaping   Reinforcement performed *before* the desired consumer behavior actually takes place is called **shaping**. Shaping increases the probabilities that certain desired consumer behavior will occur. For example, retailers recognize that they must first attract customers to their stores before they can expect them to do the bulk of their shopping there. Many retailers provide some form of preliminary reinforcement (shaping) to encourage consumers to visit only their store. For example, some retailers offer loss leaders—popular products at severely discounted prices—to the first hundred or so customers to arrive, since those customers are likely to stay to do much of their shopping. By reinforcing the behavior that's needed to enable the desired consumer behavior to take place, marketers increase the probability that the desired behavior will occur. Car dealers recognize that in order to sell new model cars, they must first encourage people to visit their showrooms and to test-drive their cars. Hopefully, the test-drive will result in a sale. Using shaping principles, many car dealers encourage showroom visits by providing small gifts (such as key chains and DVDs), larger gifts (e.g., a $10 check) to test-drive the car, and a rebate check upon placement of an order. They use a multi-step shaping process to achieve desired consumer learning.

Massed versus distributed learning

As illustrated previously, *timing* has an important influence on consumer learning. Should a learning schedule be spread out over a period of time (*distributed learning,*) or should it be "bunched up" all at once (*massed learning*)? The question is an important one for advertisers planning a media schedule, because massed advertising produces more initial learning, whereas a distributed schedule usually results in learning that persists longer. When advertisers want an immediate impact (e.g., to introduce a new product or to counter a competitor's blitz campaign), they generally use a massed schedule to hasten consumer learning. However, when the goal is long-term repeat buying on a regular basis, a distributed schedule is preferable. A distributed schedule, with ads repeated on a regular basis, usually results in more long-term learning and is relatively immune to extinction.

Modeling or observational learning

Learning theorists have noted that a considerable amount of learning takes place in the absence of direct reinforcement, either positive or negative, through a process psychologists call **modeling** or **observational learning** (also called *vicarious learning*). Consumers often observe how others behave in response to certain situations (stimuli) and the ensuing results (reinforcement) that occur, and they imitate (model) the positively reinforced behavior when faced with similar situations. Modeling is *the process through which individuals learn behavior by observing the behavior of others and the consequences of such behavior.* Their role models are usually people they admire because of such traits as appearance, accomplishment, skill, and even social class.

Advertisers recognize the importance of observational learning in their selection of models—whether celebrities or unknowns. If a teenager sees an ad that depicts social success as the outcome of using a certain brand of shampoo, she will want to buy it. If her brother sees a commercial that shows a muscular young athlete eating Wheaties—"the breakfast of champions"—he will want to eat it, too. Indeed, vicarious (or observational) learning is the basis of much of today's advertising. Consumer models with whom the target audience can identify are shown achieving positive outcomes to common problem situations through the use of the advertised product. Children learn much of their social behavior and consumer behavior by observing their older siblings or their parents. They imitate the behavior of those they see rewarded, expecting to be rewarded similarly if they adopt the same behavior.

Sometimes ads depict negative consequences for certain types of behavior. This is particularly true of public policy ads, which may show the negative consequences of smoking, of driving too fast, or of taking drugs. By observing the actions of others and the resulting consequences, consumers learn vicariously to recognize appropriate and inappropriate behavior.

Cognitive learning theory

Not all learning takes place as the result of repeated trials. A considerable amount of learning takes place as the result of consumer thinking and problem solving. Sudden learning is also a reality. When confronted with a problem, we sometimes see the solution instantly. More often, however, we are likely to search for information on which to base a decision, and we carefully evaluate what we learn in order to make the best decision possible for our purposes.

Learning based on mental activity is called **cognitive learning**. Cognitive learning theory holds that the kind of learning most characteristic of human beings is *problem solving,* which enables individuals to gain some control over their environment. Unlike behavioral learning theory, cognitive theory holds that learning involves complex *mental processing of information.* Instead of stressing the importance of repetition or the association of a reward with a specific response, cognitive theorists emphasize the role of motivation and mental processes in producing a desired response.

Information processing

Just as a computer processes information received as input, so too does the human mind process the information it receives as input. **Information processing** is related to both the consumer's cognitive ability and the complexity of the information to be processed. Consumers process product information by attributes, brands, comparisons between brands, or a combination of these factors. Although the attributes included in the brand's message and the number of available alternatives influence the intensity or degree of information processing, consumers with higher cognitive ability apparently acquire more product information and are more capable of integrating information on several product attributes than consumers with lesser ability.

Individuals also differ in terms of **imagery**—that is, in their ability to form mental images—and these differences influence their ability to recall information. Individual differences in imagery processing can be measured with tests of *imagery vividness* (the ability to evoke clear images), *processing style* (preference for and frequency of visual versus verbal processing), and *daydream (fantasy) content* and *frequency.*[10]

The more experience a consumer has with a product category, the greater his or her ability to make use of product information. Greater familiarity with the product category also increases cognitive ability and learning during a new purchase decision, particularly with regard to technical information. Some consumers learn by analogy; that is, they transfer knowledge about products they are familiar with to new or unfamiliar products in order to enhance their understanding. One study found that when people exerted more cognitive effort in processing information about a product, they experienced a process-induced negative effect toward that alternative and were more likely to choose a product that required less effort to evaluate. However, the negative effect did not influence product choice for a clearly superior product.[11]

How consumers store, retain, and retrieve information

Of central importance to the processing of information is the human memory. A basic research concern of most cognitive scientists is discovering how information gets stored in memory, how it is retained, and how it is retrieved.

Because information processing occurs in stages, it is generally believed that there are separate and sequential "storehouses" in memory where information is kept temporarily before further processing: a *sensory store,* a *short-term store,* and a *long-term store.*

Sensory Store   All data come to us through our senses; however, the senses do not transmit whole images as a camera does. Instead, each sense receives a fragmented piece of information (such as the smell, color, shape, and feel of a flower) and transmits it to the brain in parallel, where the perceptions of a single instant are synchronized and perceived as a single image, in a single moment of time. The image of a sensory input lasts for just a second or two in the mind's **sensory store**. If it is not processed, it is lost immediately. We are constantly bombarded with stimuli from the environment and subconsciously block out a great deal of information that we do not "need" or cannot use. For marketers, this means that although it is relatively easy to get information into the consumer's sensory store, it is difficult to make a lasting impression. Furthermore, the brain automatically and subconsciously "tags" all perceptions with a value, either positive or negative; this evaluation, added to the initial perception in the first microsecond of cognition, tends to remain unless further information is processed. This would explain why first impressions tend to last and why it is hazardous for a marketer to introduce a product prematurely into the marketplace.

Short-term Store   The **short-term store** (known as "working memory") is the stage of real memory in which information is processed and held for just a brief period. Anyone who has ever looked up a number in a telephone book, only to forget it just before dialing, knows how briefly information lasts in short-term storage. If information in the short-term store undergoes the process known as *rehearsal* (i.e., the silent, mental repetition of information), it is then transferred to the long-term store. The transfer process takes from 2 to 10 seconds. If information is not rehearsed and transferred, it is lost in about 30 seconds or less. The amount of information that can be held in short-term storage is limited to about four or five items.

Long-term Store   In contrast to the short-term store, where information lasts only a few seconds, the **long-term store** retains information for relatively extended periods of time. Although it is possible to forget something within a few minutes after the information has reached long-term storage, it is more common for data in long-term storage to last for days, weeks, or even years. Almost all of us, for example, can remember the name of our first-grade teacher. Figure 17.4 depicts the transfer of information received by the sensory store, through the short-term store, to long-term storage.

Rehearsal and Encoding   The amount of information available for delivery from short-term storage to long-term storage depends on the amount of **rehearsal** it is given. Failure to rehearse an input, either by repeating it or by relating it to other data, can result in fading and eventual loss of the information. Information can also be lost because of competition for attention. For example, if the short-term store receives a great number of inputs simultaneously from the sensory store, its capacity may be reduced to only two or three pieces of information.

The purpose of rehearsal is to hold information in short-term storage long enough for encoding to take place. **Encoding** is the process by which we select a word or visual image to represent a perceived object. Marketers, for example, help consumers encode brands by using brand symbols. Kellogg's uses Tony the Tiger on its Frosted Flakes; the Green Giant Company has its Jolly Green Giant. Dell Computer turns the *e* in its logo on its side for quick name recognition; Microsoft uses a stylized window, presumably on the world.

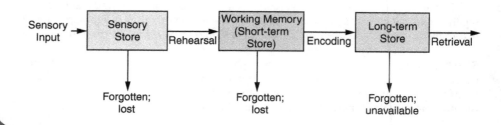

Information Processing and Memory Stores

FIGURE 17.4

"Learning" a picture takes less time than learning verbal information, but both types of information are important in forming an overall mental image. A print ad with both an illustration and body copy is more likely to be encoded and stored than an illustration without verbal information. A study that compared the effects of visual and verbal advertising found that, when advertising copy and illustrations focus on different product attributes, the illustrations disproportionately influence consumer inferences.[12] Another study found that high-imagery copy had greater recall than low-imagery copy, whether or not it was accompanied by an illustration; for low-imagery copy, however, illustrations were an important factor in audience recall.[13]

Researchers have found that the encoding of a commercial is related to the context of the TV program during (or adjacent to) which it is shown. Some parts of a program may require viewers to commit a larger portion of their cognitive resources to processing (e.g., when a dramatic event takes place versus a casual conversation). When viewers commit more cognitive resources to the program itself, they encode and store less of the information conveyed by a commercial. This suggests that commercials requiring relatively little cognitive processing may be more effective within or adjacent to a dramatic program setting than commercials requiring more elaborate processing.[14] Viewers who are very involved with a television show respond more positively to commercials adjacent to that show and have more positive purchase intentions. Men and women exhibit different encoding patterns. For example, although women are more likely than men to recall TV commercials depicting a social relationship theme, there is no difference in recall among men and women for commercials that focus on the product itself.[15]

When consumers are presented with too much information (called **information overload**), they may encounter difficulty in encoding and storing it all. Often, it is difficult for consumers to remember product information from ads for new brands in heavily advertised categories. Consumers can become cognitively overloaded when they are given a lot of information in a limited time. The result of this overload is confusion, resulting in poor purchase decisions.

Retention Information does not just sit in long-term storage waiting to be retrieved. Instead, information is constantly organized and reorganized as new links between chunks of information are forged. In fact, many information-processing theorists view the long-term store as a network consisting of nodes (i.e., concepts), with links between and among them. As individuals gain more knowledge about a subject, they expand their network of relationships and sometimes their search for additional information. This process is known as *activation,* which involves relating new data to old to make the material more meaningful. Consumer memory for the name of a product may also be activated by relating it to the spokesperson used in its advertising. For many people, Michael Jordan means Nike sneakers. The total package of associations brought to mind when a cue is activated is called a *schema.*

Product information stored in memory tends to be brand based, and consumers interpret new information in a manner consistent with the way in which it is already organized. Consumers are confronted with thousands of new products each year, and their information search is often dependent upon how similar or dissimilar (discrepant) these products are to product categories already stored in memory. Therefore, consumers are more likely to recall the information they receive on new products bearing a familiar brand name, and their memory is less affected by exposure to competitive ads.

One study demonstrated that *brand imprinting*—messages that merely establish the brand's identity—conducted before the presentation of the brand's benefits facilitates consumer learning and retention of information about the brand.[16] Studies also showed that a brand's *sound symbolism* (a theory suggesting that the *sounds* of words convey meanings) and the brand's *linguistic characteristics* (e.g., unusual spelling) impacted the encoding and retention of the brand name.[17]

Consumers recode what they have already encoded to include larger amounts of information (called **chunking**). Marketers should research the kinds and numbers of groupings (chunks) of information that consumers can handle. When the chunks offered in an advertisement do not match those in the consumer's frame of reference, information recall may be hampered. The extent of prior knowledge is also an important consideration. Knowledgeable consumers can take in more complex chunks of information than those who are less knowledgeable about the product category. Thus, the amount and type of technological information contained in a computer ad can be much more detailed in a magazine such as *PC Magazine* or *Wired* than in a general-interest magazine such as *Time*.

Information is stored in long-term memory in two ways: *episodically* (by the order in which it is acquired) and *semantically* (according to significant concepts). We may remember having gone to a movie last Saturday because of our ability to store data episodically, and we may remember the plot, the stars, and the director because of our ability to store data semantically. Learning theorists believe that memories stored semantically are organized into frameworks by which we integrate new data with previous experience. For information about a new brand or model of printer to enter our memory, for example, we would have to relate it to our previous experience with printers in terms of such qualities as speed, print quality, resolution, and memory.

Retrieval **Retrieval** is the *process by which we recover information from long-term storage*. For example, when we are unable to remember something with which we are very familiar, we are experiencing a failure of the retrieval system. Marketers maintain that consumers tend to remember the product's benefits rather than its attributes, suggesting that advertising messages are most effective when they link the product's attributes with the benefits that consumers seek from the product; this view is consistent with the previous discussion of product positioning strategies. Consumers are likely to spend time interpreting and elaborating on information they find relevant to their needs and to activate such relevant knowledge from long-term memory.

Incongruent (or unexpected) message elements pierce consumers' perceptual screens and improve the memorability of an ad when these elements are relevant to the advertising message. For example, an ad for a brand of stain-resistant, easy-to-clean carpet shows an elegantly dressed couple in a beautiful dining room setting where the man inadvertently knocks the food, the flowers, and the china crashing to the floor. The elegance of the actors and the upscale setting make the accident totally incongruous and unexpected, whereas the message remains highly relevant: The mess can be cleaned up easily without leaving a stain on the carpet.

Incongruent elements that are not relevant to an ad also pierce the consumer's perceptual screen but provide no memorability for the product. An ad showing a nude woman sitting on a piece of office furniture would very likely attract readers' attention, but would provide no memorability for the product or the advertiser because of the irrelevance of the nudity to the advertising message. One study discovered that false cues in post-experience advertising influence recollection. Also, when the false verbal cues and picture appeared together they were more likely to be integrated into memory than false verbal cues without pictures.[18]

Interference The greater the number of competitive ads in a product category, the lower the recall of brand claims in a specific ad. These **interference effects** are caused by confusion with competing ads, and make information retrieval difficult. Ads can also act as retrieval cues for a competitive brand. An example of such consumer confusion occurred when consumers attributed the long-running and attention-getting television campaign featuring the Eveready Energizer Bunny to the leader in the field, Duracell. Advertisements for competing brands or for other products made by the same manufacturer can lower the consumer's ability to remember advertised brand information. Such effects occur in response to even a small amount of advertising for similar products.

The level of interference experienced can depend on the consumer's previous experiences, prior knowledge of brand attribute information, and the amount of brand

TABLE 17.1	Models of Cognitive Learning				
	PROMOTIONAL MODEL	TRICOMPONENT MODEL	DECISION-MAKING MODEL	INNOVATION ADOPTION MODEL	INNOVATION DECISION PROCESS
Sequential Stages of Processing	Attention	Cognitive	Awareness Knowledge	Awareness	Knowledge
	Interest Desire	Affective	Evaluation	Interest Evaluation	Persuasion
	Action	Conative	Purchase Postpurchase Evaluation	Trial Adoption	Decision Confirmation

information available at the time of choice. There are actually two kinds of interference: *New learning* can interfere with the retrieval of previously stored material, and *old learning* can interfere with the recall of recently learned material. With both kinds of interference, the problem is the similarity of old and new information. Advertising that creates a distinctive brand image can assist in the retention and retrieval of message contents.

Limited and extensive information processing

For a long time, consumer researchers believed that all consumers passed through a complex series of mental and behavioral stages in arriving at a purchase decision. These stages ranged from awareness (exposure to information) to evaluation (preference, attitude formation), to behavior (purchase), to final evaluation (adoption or rejection). This same series of stages is often presented as the *consumer adoption process*.

A number of models have been developed over the years to express the same notion of sequential processing of information by consumers (see Table 17.1). Initially, marketing scholars believed that extensive and complex processing of information by consumers was applicable to all purchase decisions. However, on the basis of their own subjective experiences as consumers, some theorists began to realize that there were some purchase situations that simply did not call for extensive information processing and evaluation; that sometimes consumers simply went from awareness of a need to a routine purchase, without a great deal of information search and mental evaluation. Such purchases were considered of minimal personal relevance, as opposed to highly relevant, search-oriented purchases. Purchases of minimal personal importance were called *low-involvement purchases*, and complex, search-oriented purchases were considered *high-involvement purchases*. The following section describes the development of **involvement theory** and discusses its applications to marketing strategy.

Involvement theory

Involvement theory developed from a stream of research called **hemispheral lateralization**, or split-brain theory. The basic premise of *split-brain theory* is that the right and left hemispheres of the brain "specialize" in the kinds of information they process. The left hemisphere is primarily responsible for cognitive activities such as reading, speaking, and attributional information processing. Individuals who are exposed to verbal information cognitively analyze the information through left-brain processing and form mental images. Unlike the left hemisphere, the right hemisphere of the brain is concerned with nonverbal, timeless, pictorial, and holistic information. Put another way, the left side of the brain is rational, active, and realistic; the right side is emotional, metaphoric, impulsive, and intuitive.[19]

Involvement theory and media strategy

Building on the notion of hemispheral lateralization, a pioneer consumer researcher theorized that individuals *passively* process and store right-brain (nonverbal, pictorial) information—that is, without active involvement.[20] Because TV is primarily a pictorial medium, TV viewing was considered a right-brain activity (passive and holistic processing of images viewed on the screen), and TV itself was therefore considered a low-involvement medium. This research concluded that **passive learning** occurs through repeated exposures to a TV commercial (i.e., low-involvement information processing) and produces changes in consumer behavior (e.g., product purchases) *prior* to changes in the consumer's attitude toward the product. This view contradicts the models presented in Table 17.1, all of which maintain that cognitive evaluation and favorable attitude toward a product take place before the actual purchase behavior.

To extend this line of reasoning, cognitive (verbal) information is processed by the left side of the brain; thus, print media (e.g., newspapers and magazines) and interactive media (the Internet) are considered high-involvement media. According to this theory, print advertising is processed in the complex sequence of cognitive stages depicted in classic models of information processing (i.e., high-involvement information processing).

The right-brain theory of passive processing of information is consistent with classical conditioning. Through repetition, the product is paired with a visual image (e.g., a distinctive package) to produce the desired response: purchase of the advertised brand. According to this theory, in situations of passive learning (generated by low-involvement media), repetition is the key factor in producing purchase behavior. In marketing terms, the theory suggests that television commercials are most effective when they are of short duration and repeated frequently, thus ensuring brand familiarity without provoking detailed evaluation of the message content.

The right-brain processing theory stresses the importance of the *visual component* of advertising, including the creative use of symbols. Under this theory, highly visual TV commercials, packaging, and in-store displays generate familiarity with the brand and induce purchase behavior. Pictorial cues are more effective at generating recall and familiarity with the product, whereas verbal cues (which trigger left-brain processing) generate cognitive activity that encourages consumers to evaluate the advantages and disadvantages of the product.

There are limitations to the application of split-brain theory to media strategy. Although the right and left hemispheres of the brain process different types of cues, they do not operate independently of each other but work together to process information. Some individuals are *integrated processors* (they readily engage both hemispheres during information processing). Integrated processors have better overall recall of both the verbal and the visual portions of print ads than individuals who exhibit right or left hemispheral processing.

Involvement theory and consumer relevance

From the conceptualization of high- and low-involvement media, involvement theory next focused on the consumer's involvement with products and purchases. It was briefly hypothesized that there are high- and low-involvement consumers; then, that there are high- and low-involvement purchases. These two approaches led to the notion that a consumer's level of involvement depends on the degree of personal relevance that the product holds for that consumer. Under this definition, high-involvement purchases are those that are very important to the consumer (e.g., in terms of perceived risk) and thus provoke extensive problem solving (information processing). An automobile and a dandruff shampoo both may represent high-involvement purchases under this scenario—the automobile because of high perceived financial risk, the shampoo because of high perceived social risk. Low-involvement purchases are purchases that are not very important to the consumer, hold little relevance, and have little perceived risk, and, thus, provoke very limited information processing. Highly involved consumers find fewer brands acceptable (they are called **narrow categorizers**); uninvolved consumers are likely to be receptive to a greater number of advertising messages regarding the purchase and will consider more brands (they are **broad categorizers**).

Central and peripheral routes to persuasion

The theory of **central** and **peripheral routes to persuasion** illustrates the concepts of extensive and limited problem solving for high- and low-involvement purchase situations. The major premise of this theory is that consumers are more likely to carefully evaluate the merits and weaknesses of a product when the purchase is of high relevance to them. Conversely, the likelihood is great that consumers will engage in very limited information search and evaluation when the purchase holds little relevance or importance for them. Thus, for high-involvement purchases, the *central route to persuasion*—which requires considered thought and cognitive processing—is likely to be the most effective marketing strategy. For low-involvement purchases, the *peripheral route to persuasion* is likely to be more effective. In this instance, because the consumer is less motivated to exert cognitive effort, learning is more likely to occur through repetition, the passive processing of visual cues, and holistic perception.

Various researchers have addressed the relationship between the theory of central and peripheral routes to persuasion and consumer information processing. Numerous studies have found that high involvement with a product produces more extensive processing of information, including extensive information search on the Internet.[21] It is apparent that highly involved consumers use more attributes to evaluate brands, whereas less involved consumers apply very simple decision rules. In marketing to highly involved consumers, the quality of the argument presented in the persuasive message, rather than merely the imagery of the promotional message, has the greater impact on the consumption decision.

Many studies investigated the relationship between the level of information processing and the product and promotional elements of the marketing mix. For example, one study found that comparative ads are more likely to be processed centrally (purposeful processing of message arguments), whereas noncomparative ads are commonly processed peripherally (with little message elaboration and a response derived from other executional elements in the ad).[22] Another study found that the use of metaphors and figures of speech that deviate from the expected in print ads places added processing demands on the readers and increases the ad's persuasiveness and memorability. The metaphors examined in this study were such slogans as "It forced other car makers into the copier business" (Mercury Sable) and "In the Caribbean, there's no such thing as a party of one" (Malibu Caribbean Rum).[23] Another study demonstrated that the correlation between a consumer's product involvement and objective product knowledge is higher for utilitarian products than in products designed to bring about pleasure (termed *hedonic products*); in the case of hedonic products, the correlation between subjective knowledge and product involvement is higher than for utilitarian products.[24] Assuming that *subjective knowledge* is the result of interpreting the imagery presented in the ad while *objective knowledge* is the outcome of the factual information that the ad provides, marketers should consider the degree of the product's utilitarianism in selecting either the central or peripheral route in promoting that product.

The Elaboration Likelihood Model   The **elaboration likelihood model (ELM)** suggests that a person's level of involvement during message processing is a critical factor in determining which route to persuasion is likely to be effective. For example, as the message becomes more personally relevant (i.e., as involvement increases), people are more willing to expend the cognitive effort required to process the message arguments. Thus, when involvement is high, consumers follow the central route and base their attitudes or choices on the message arguments. When involvement is low, they follow the peripheral route and rely more heavily on other message elements (such as spokespersons or background music) to form attitudes or make product choices.

Measures of involvement

Given that involvement theory evolved from the notion of high- and low-involvement media, to high- and low-involvement consumers, to high- and low-involvement products and purchases, to appropriate methods of persuasion in situations of high and low product relevance, it is not surprising to find there is great variation in the conceptualization and measurement of involvement itself. Researchers have defined and conceptualized involvement in a variety of ways, including ego involvement, commitment, communications involvement, purchase importance, extent of information search, persons, products, situations, and purchase decisions.[25] Some studies have tried to differentiate between *brand* involvement and *product* involvement.[26]

The lack of a clear definition about the essential components of involvement poses some measurement problems. Researchers who regard involvement as a cognitive state are concerned with the measurement of ego involvement, risk perception, and purchase importance. Researchers who focus on the behavioral aspects of involvement measure such factors as the search for and evaluation of product information. Others argue that involvement should be measured by the degree of importance the product has to the buyer.

Because of the many different dimensions and conceptualizations of involvement, it makes the most sense to develop self-administered measures that assess the consumer's cognitions or behaviors regarding a particular product or product category, and where involvement is measured on a continuum rather than as a dichotomy consisting of two mutually exclusive categories of "high" and "low" involvement.

Marketing applications of involvement

Involvement theory has a number of strategic applications for the marketer. For example, the left-brain (cognitive processing)/right-brain (passive processing) paradigm seems to have strong implications for the content, length, and presentation of both print, television, and interactive advertisements. There is evidence that people process information extensively when the purchase is of high personal relevance and engage in limited information processing when the purchase is of low personal relevance. Uninvolved consumers appear to be susceptible to different kinds of persuasion than highly involved consumers. Therefore, for high-involvement purchases, marketers should use arguments stressing the strong, solid, high-quality attributes of their products, thus using the central (or highly cognitive) route. For low-involvement purchases, marketers should use the peripheral route to persuasion, focusing on the method of presentation rather than on the content of the message (e.g., through the use of celebrity spokespersons or highly visual and symbolic advertisements).

Marketers can take steps to increase customer involvement with their ads. For example, advertisers can use sensory appeals, unusual stimuli, and celebrity endorsers to generate more attention for their messages. Since highly involved consumers are more likely to engage in long-term relationships with products and brands, marketers should simultaneously increase customer involvement levels and create bonds with their customers.[27] Of course, the best strategy for increasing the personal relevance of products to consumers is the same as the core of modern marketing itself: Provide benefits that are important and relevant to customers, improve the product and add benefits as competition intensifies, and focus on forging *bonds* and *relationships* with customers rather than just engaging in *transactions*.

Measures of consumer learning

For many marketers, the dual goals of consumer learning are increased market share and brand-loyal consumers. These goals are interdependent: Brand-loyal customers provide the basis for a stable and growing market share, and brands with larger market shares have proportionately larger groups of loyal buyers. Marketers focus their promotional budgets on trying to teach consumers that their brands are best and that their products will best solve the consumers' problems and satisfy their needs. Thus, it is important for the marketer to measure how effectively consumers have "learned" its message. The following sections will examine various measures of consumer learning: *recognition* and *recall measures, cognitive measures,* and the *attitudinal and behavioral measures of brand loyalty.*

Recognition and recall measures

Recognition and **recall tests** are conducted to determine whether consumers remember seeing an ad, the extent to which they have read it or seen it and can recall its content, their resulting attitudes toward the product and the brand, and their purchase intentions. Recognition tests are based on *aided recall*, whereas recall tests use *unaided recall*. In recognition tests, the consumer is shown an ad and asked whether he or she remembers seeing it and can remember any of its salient points. In recall tests, the consumer is asked whether he or she has read a specific magazine or watched a specific television show, and if so, can recall any ads or commercials seen, the product advertised, the brand, and any salient points about the product.

A number of syndicated research services conduct recognition and recall tests, such as the Starch Readership Service, which evaluates the effectiveness of magazine advertisements. After qualifying as having read a given issue of a magazine, respondents are presented with the magazine and asked to point out which ads they *noted,* which they *associated with the advertiser,* and which they *read most.* They are also asked which parts of the ads they *noted* and *read most.* An advertiser can gauge the effectiveness of a given ad by comparing its readership recognition scores to similar-sized ads, to competitive ads, and to the company's own prior ads. A recent study using Starch readership scores demonstrated that consumers received more information from advertisements for *shopping products* (e.g., high-priced clothing and accessories) than from ads for *convenience goods* (e.g., low-priced items purchased routinely) and, surprisingly, from ads for *search products* (e.g., very expensive, durable items purchased infrequently following an extensive information search). These findings show that marketers may be under-informing consumers when advertising search products.[28]

Cognitive responses to advertising

Another measure of consumer learning is the degree to which consumers accurately comprehend the intended advertising message. **Comprehension** is a function of the message characteristics, the consumer's opportunity and ability to process the information, and the consumer's motivation (or level of involvement). To ensure a high level of comprehension, many marketers conduct **copy testing** either *before* the advertising is actually run (called **pretesting**) or *after* it appears (**posttesting**). Pretests are used to determine which, if any, elements of an advertising message should be revised before major media expenses are incurred. Posttests are used to evaluate the effectiveness of an ad that has already run and to identify which elements, if any, should be changed to improve the impact and memorability of future ads.

Attitudinal and behavioral measures of brand loyalty

Brand loyalty is the ultimate desired outcome of consumer learning. However, there is no single definition of this concept. The varied definitions of brand loyalty reflect the models presented earlier in Table 17.1. They are summarized in Table 17.2, together with their shortcomings and weaknesses in the context of potential competitive responses.

Marketers agree that brand loyalty consists of both attitudes and actual behaviors toward a brand and that both must be measured. **Attitudinal measures** are concerned with consumers' overall feelings about the product and the brand (i.e., evaluation), and their purchase intentions. **Behavioral measures** are based on observable responses to promotional stimuli—repeat purchase behavior rather than attitude toward the product or brand. A recent study pointed out that marketers must distinguish between two attitudinal measures of brand loyalty; the study demonstrated that the degree of commitment toward buying the brand and the propensity to be brand loyal are two *separate* dimensions but did not conclusively determine which construct is more useful for explaining buying behavior.[29]

TABLE 17.2	Definitions of Brand Loyalty and Their Shortcomings	
STAGE	**IDENTIFYING MARKER**	**VULNERABILITIES**
Cognitive	Loyalty to information such as price, features, and so forth.	Actual or imagined better competitive features or price through communications (e.g., advertising) and vicarious or personal experience. Deterioration in brand features or price. Variety seeking and voluntary trial.
Affective	Loyalty to a liking: "I buy it because I like it."	Cognitively induced dissatisfaction. Enhanced liking for competitive brands, perhaps conveyed through imagery and association. Variety seeking and voluntary trial. Deteriorating performance.
Conative	Loyalty to an intention: "I'm committed to buying it."	Persuasive counterargumentative competitive messages. Induced trial (e.g., coupons, sampling, point-of-purchase promotions). Deteriorating performance.
Action	Loyalty to action, coupled with the overcoming of obstacles.	Induced unavailability (e.g., stocklifts—purchasing the entire inventory of a competitor's product from a merchant). Increased obstacles generally. Deteriorating performance.

Source: Reprinted with permission from 1999 Special Issue of Journal of Marketing, published by the American Marketing Association, Richard L. Oliver, 1999, vol. 63, 33–34.

Behavioral scientists who favor the theory of instrumental conditioning believe that brand loyalty results from an initial product trial that is reinforced through satisfaction, leading to repeat purchase. *Cognitive* researchers, on the other hand, emphasize the role of mental processes in building brand loyalty. They believe that consumers engage in extensive problem-solving behavior involving brand and attribute comparisons, leading to a strong brand preference and repeat purchase behavior. Therefore, brand loyalty is the synergy among such attitudinal components as perceived product superiority, customer satisfaction and the purchase behavior itself.

Recently, brain imaging technologies, commonly used in medicine, were used to study brand loyalty and yielded some fascinating results. Brain scans of some Japanese women taken while they were answering questions about everyday events showed similar patterns, but these patterns became distinctive when women who were brand loyal to a given store responded to the statement "this is the perfect store for me."

The brain scans of consumers who were split as to whether they prefer Coke or Pepsi and were given blind taste tests indicated that two different brain regions were at play. When the subjects tasted either of the soft drinks, their brain's reward system was activated. But when these persons were told which brand they were drinking, their brains' memory region (where information regarding brand loyalty is stored) was activated and overrode the preferences the participants indicated after tasting the soft drink, but before knowing which brand they had tasted.[30]

Behavioral definitions (such as frequency of purchase or proportion of total purchases) lack precision, because they do not distinguish between the "real" brand-loyal buyer who is intentionally faithful and the spurious brand-loyal buyer who repeats a brand purchase out of mere habit or because it is the only one available at the store. Often consumers buy from a mix of brands within their acceptable range. The greater the number of acceptable brands in a specific product category, the less likely the consumer is to be brand loyal to one specific brand. Conversely, products having few competitors, as well as those purchased with great frequency, are likely to have greater brand loyalty. Thus, a more favorable attitude toward a brand, service, or store, compared to potential alternatives, together with repeat patronage, are seen as the requisite components of customer loyalty. A recent study related the attitudinal and purchase aspects of brand loyalty to market share and the relative prices of brands. The study showed that brand trust and brand affect, combined, determine purchase loyalty and attitudinal loyalty. Purchase loyalty leads to a higher market share, and attitudinal loyalty often enables the marketer to charge a higher price for the brand relative to competition.[31]

An integrated conceptual framework views consumer loyalty as the function of three groups of influences: (1) consumer drivers (i.e., personal degree of risk aversion or variety seeking); (2) brand drivers (i.e., the brand's reputation and availability of substitute brands); and (3) social drivers (i.e., social group influences and peers' recommendations). These influences produce four types of loyalty: (1) *no loyalty*—no purchase at all and no cognitive attachment to the brand; (2) *covetous loyalty*—no purchase but strong attachment and predisposition towards the brand that was developed from the person's social environment; (3) *inertia loyalty*—purchasing the brand because of habit and convenience but without any emotional attachment to the brand; and (4) *premium loyalty*—high attachment to the brand and high repeat purchase.[32] This framework also reflects a correlation among consumer involvement and the cognitive and behavioral dimensions of brand loyalty. Due to social perceptions regarding the importance of a car, and the symbolism of a particular car brand (e.g., Mercedes) as representing prestige and achievement, consumers may become involved with and attached to the brand without purchasing it (covetous loyalty), but may purchase the brand when they have the money to do so. Low involvement leads to exposure and brand awareness and then to brand habit (inertia loyalty). Consumers operating in this condition perceive little differentiation among brands and buy the brand repeatedly due to familiarity and convenience. On the other hand, premium loyalty represents truly brand-loyal consumers who have a strong commitment to the brand, are less likely to switch to other brands in spite of the persuasive promotional efforts of competitors, and may even go out of their way to obtain the strongly preferred brand.

Loyalty programs are generally designed with the intention of forming and maintaining brand loyalty. One study showed that brand managers believe that all reward programs impact incremental purchases and that low and moderate reward programs are the most cost-effective. The study proposed three types of brand-loyalty reward programs.[33] This research illustrates the options of tailoring loyalty programs to the purchase patterns of different market segments and the importance of doing so.

Unlike tangible products, where switching to another brand is relatively easy, it is often difficult to switch to another "brand" of service. For example, it is costly and time consuming to transfer one's business to a new attorney or accountant or even to get used to a new hair stylist. One study showed that the reasons that cause customers to switch service providers play a role in their loyalty behaviors toward subsequent providers. Thus, service marketers should research past customer behavior and use these data to increase the loyalty of new customers.[34]

Brand equity

The term **brand equity** refers to the value inherent in a well-known brand name. This value stems from the consumer's perception of the brand's superiority, the social esteem that using it provides, and the customer's trust and identification with the brand. For many companies, their most valuable assets are their brand names. Well-known brand names are referred to as **megabrands**. Among the best-known brands are Coca-Cola, Campbell's Soup, Hallmark Cards, and United Parcel Service. Their names have become "cultural icons" and enjoy powerful advantages over the competition.

Because of the escalation of new-product costs and the high rate of new-product failures, many companies prefer to leverage their brand equity through brand extensions rather than risk launching a new brand. Brand equity facilitates the acceptance of new products and the allocation of preferred shelf space, and enhances perceived value, perceived quality, and premium pricing options. Brand equity is most important for low-involvement purchases, such as inexpensive consumer goods that are bought routinely and with little processing of cognitive information. A study found that very strong brand cues, such as the ones conveyed by brands with high equity, may actually "block" the learning of quality-related cues for specific product attributes.[35] Thus, competitors of a strong brand will find it difficult to "teach" brand-loyal customers about the benefits of their brands.

Because a brand that has been promoted heavily in the past retains a cumulative level of name recognition, companies buy, sell, and rent (i.e., license) their brand names, knowing that it is easier for a new company to buy, rather than to create, a brand name that has enduring strength. Brand equity enables companies to charge a price premium—an additional amount over and above the price of an identical store brand. A relatively new strategy among some marketers is **co-branding** (also called double branding). The basis of co-branding, in which two brand names are featured on a single product, is to use another product's brand equity to enhance the primary brand's equity. For example, Cranberry Newtons is a product of Nabisco and Ocean Spray, bearing both brand names. Some experts believe that using a second brand's equity may imply that the host brand can no longer stand on its own. Others question whether a co-branded product causes consumer confusion as to who actually makes the product, and whether the host brand can survive if the second brand endorsement is taken away.

Brand equity reflects brand loyalty, which, as presented here, is a *learned* construct and one of the most important applications of learning theory to consumption behavior. Brand loyalty and brand equity lead to increased market share and greater profits. To marketers, the major function of learning theory is to teach consumers that their product is best, to encourage repeat purchase, and, ultimately, to develop loyalty to the brand name and brand equity for the company.

chapter **18**

› **Business Buying**
Behavior

Business markets and business buyer behavior

In one way or another, most large companies sell to other organizations. Companies such as DuPont, Boeing, IBM, Caterpillar, and countless other firms sell *most* of their products to other businesses. Even large consumer-products companies, which make products used by final consumers, must first sell their products to other businesses. For example, General Mills makes many familiar consumer brands—Big G cereals (Cheerios, Wheaties, Total, Golden Grahams); baking products (Pillsbury, Betty Crocker, Gold Medal flour); snacks (Nature Valley, Chex Mix, Pop Secret); Yoplait Yogurt; Haagen-Das ice cream; and others. But to sell these products to consumers, General Mills must first sell them to its wholesaler and retailer customers, who in turn serve the consumer market.

Business buyer behavior refers to the buying behavior of the organizations that buy goods and services for use in the production of other products and services that are sold, rented, or supplied to others. It also includes the behavior of retailing and wholesaling firms that acquire goods to resell or rent to others at a profit. In the *business buying process,* business buyers determine which products and services their organizations need to purchase and then find, evaluate, and choose among alternative suppliers and brands. *Business-to-business (B-to-B) marketers* must do their best to understand business markets and business buyer behavior. Then, like businesses that sell to final buyers, they must build profitable relationships with business customers by creating superior customer value.

Business buyer behavior
The buying behavior of the organizations that buy goods and services for use in the production of other products and services or for the purpose of reselling or renting them to others at a profit.

Business markets

The business market is *huge*. In fact, business markets involve far more dollars and items than do consumer markets. For example, think about the large number of business transactions involved in the production and sale of a single set of Goodyear tires. Various suppliers sell Goodyear the rubber, steel, equipment, and other goods that it needs to produce the tires. Goodyear then sells the finished tires to retailers, who in turn sell them to consumers. Thus, many sets of *business* purchases were made for only one set of *consumer* purchases. In addition, Goodyear sells tires as original equipment to manufacturers who install them on new vehicles, and as replacement tires to companies that maintain their own fleets of company cars, trucks, buses, or other vehicles.

In some ways, business markets are similar to consumer markets. Both involve people who assume buying roles and make purchase decisions to satisfy needs. However, business markets differ in many ways from consumer markets. The main differences are in *market structure and demand,* the *nature of the buying unit,* and the *types of decisions and the decision process* involved.

Market structure and demand

The business marketer normally deals with *far fewer but far larger buyers* than the consumer marketer does. Even in large business markets, a few buyers often account for most of the purchasing. For example, when Goodyear sells replacement tires to final consumers, its potential market includes the owners of the millions of cars currently in use in the United States and around the world. But Goodyear's fate in the business market depends on getting orders from one of only a handful of large automakers. Similarly, Black & Decker sells its power tools and outdoor equipment to tens of millions of consumers worldwide. However, it must sell these products through three huge retail customers—Home Depot, Lowe's, and Wal-Mart—which, combined, account for more than half its sales.

Further, business demand is **derived demand**—it ultimately derives from the demand for consumer goods. Hewlett-Packard and Dell buy Intel microprocessor chips because consumers buy personal computers. If consumer demand for PCs drops, so will the demand for computer chips. Therefore, B-to-B marketers sometimes promote their products directly to final consumers to increase business demand. For example, Intel

Derived demand
Business demand that ultimately comes from (derives from) the demand for consumer goods.

advertises heavily to personal computer buyers through selling them on the virtues of Intel microprocessors. In ads, it tells consumers that "great computing starts with Intel inside." The increased demand for Intel chips boosts demand for the PCs containing them, and both Intel and its business partners win.

Many business markets have *inelastic demand;* that is, total demand for many business products is not affected much by price changes, especially in the short run. A drop in the price of leather will not cause shoe manufacturers to buy much more leather unless it results in lower shoe prices that, in turn, will increase consumer demand for shoes.

Finally, business markets have more *fluctuating demand.* The demand for many business goods and services tends to change more—and more quickly—than the demand for consumer goods and services does. A small percentage increase in consumer demand can cause large increases in business demand. Sometimes a rise of only 10 percent in consumer demand can cause as much as a 200 percent rise in business demand during the next period.

Nature of the buying unit

Compared with consumer purchases, a business purchase usually involves *more decision participants* and a *more professional purchasing effort.* Often, business buying is done by trained purchasing agents who spend their working lives learning how to buy better. The more complex the purchase, the more likely it is that several people will participate in the decision-making process. Buying committees made up of technical experts and top management are common in the buying of major goods. Beyond this, B-to-B marketers now face a new breed of higher-level, better-trained supply managers. Therefore, companies must have well-trained marketers and salespeople to deal with these well-trained buyers.

Types of decisions and the decision process

Business buyers usually face *more complex* buying decisions than do consumer buyers. Purchases often involve large sums of money, complex technical and economic considerations, and interactions among many people at many levels of the buyer's organization. Because the purchases are more complex, business buyers may take longer to make their decisions. The business buying process also tends to be *more formalized* than the consumer buying process. Large business purchases usually call for detailed product specifications, written purchase orders, careful supplier searches, and formal approval.

Finally, in the business buying process, the buyer and seller are often much *more dependent* on each other. B-to-B marketers may roll up their sleeves and work closely with their customers during all stages of the buying process—from helping customers define problems, to finding solutions, to supporting after-sale operation. They often customize their offerings to individual customer needs. In the short run, sales go to suppliers who meet buyers' immediate product and service needs. In the long run, however, business-to-business marketers keep a customer's sales and create customer value by meeting current needs *and* by partnering with customers to help them solve their problems.

In recent years, relationships between customers and suppliers have been changing from downright adversarial to close and chummy. In fact, many customer companies are now practicing *supplier development,* systematically developing networks of supplier-partners to ensure an appropriate and dependable supply of products and materials that they will use in making their own products or resell to others. For example, Caterpillar no longer calls its buyers "purchasing agents"—they are managers of "purchasing and supplier development." Wal-Mart doesn't have a "Purchasing Department," it has a "Supplier Development Department." And giant Swedish furniture retailer IKEA doesn't just buy from its suppliers, it involves them deeply in the process of delivering a stylish and affordable lifestyle to IKEA's customers.

Business buyer behavior

At the most basic level, marketers want to know how business buyers will respond to various marketing stimuli. Figure 18.1 shows a model of business buyer behavior. In this

FIGURE 18.1

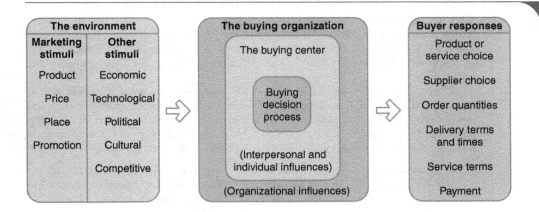

model, marketing and other stimuli affect the buying organization and produce certain buyer responses. These stimuli enter the organization and are turned into buyer responses. In order to design good marketing strategies, the marketer must understand what happens within the organization to turn stimuli into purchase responses.

Within the organization, buying activity consists of two major parts: the buying center, made up of all the people involved in the buying decision, and the buying decision process. The model shows that the buying center and the buying decision process are influenced by internal organizational, interpersonal, and individual factors as well as by external environmental factors.

The model in Figure 18.1 suggests four questions about business buyer behavior: What buying decisions do business buyers make? Who participates in the buying process? What are the major influences on buyers? How do business buyers make their buying decisions?

Major types of buying situations

There are three major types of buying situations.[39] At one extreme is the *straight rebuy*, which is a fairly routine decision. At the other extreme is the *new task*, which may call for thorough research. In the middle is the *modified rebuy,* which requires some research.

In a **straight rebuy**, the buyer reorders something without any modifications. It is usually handled on a routine basis by the purchasing department. Based on past buying satisfaction, the buyer simply chooses from the various suppliers on its list. "In" suppliers try to maintain product and service quality. They often propose automatic reordering systems so that the purchasing agent will save reordering time. "Out" suppliers try to find new ways to add value or exploit dissatisfaction so that the buyer will consider them.

In a **modified rebuy**, the buyer wants to modify product specifications, prices, terms, or suppliers. The modified rebuy usually involves more decision participants than does the straight rebuy. The in suppliers may become nervous and feel pressured to put their best foot forward to protect an account. Out suppliers may see the modified rebuy situation as an opportunity to make a better offer and gain new business.

A company buying a product or service for the first time faces a **new-task** situation. In such cases, the greater the cost or risk, the larger the number of decision participants and the greater their efforts to collect information will be. The new-task situation is the marketer's greatest opportunity and challenge. The marketer not only tries to reach as many key buying influences as possible but also provides help and information.

The buyer makes the fewest decisions in the straight rebuy and the most in the new-task decision. In the new-task situation, the buyer must decide on product specifications, suppliers, price limits, payment terms, order quantities, delivery times, and service terms. The order of these decisions varies with each situation, and different decision participants influence each choice.

Straight rebuy
A business buying situation in which the buyer routinely reorders something without any modifications.

Modified rebuy
A business buying situation in which the buyer wants to modify product specifications, prices, terms, or suppliers.

New task
A business buying situation in which the buyer purchases a product or service for the first time.

**Systems selling
(or solutions selling)**
Selling a complete solution to a problem, helping buyers to avoid all the separate decisions involved in a complex buying situation.

Many business buyers prefer to buy a complete solution to a problem from a single seller instead of buying separate products and services from several suppliers and putting them together. The sale often goes to the firm that provides the most complete *system* for meeting the customer's needs and solving its problems. Such **systems selling** (or **solutions selling**) is often a key business marketing strategy for winning and holding accounts.

Thus, transportation and logistics giant UPS does more than just ship packages for its business customers. It develops entire solutions to customers' transportation and logistics problems. For example, UPS bundles a complete spectrum of services that support Nikon's consumer products supply chain—including logistics, transportation, freight, and customs brokerage services—into one smooth-running system.[40]

> When Nikon entered the digital camera market, it decided that it needed an entirely new distribution strategy as well. But rather than handling distribution in-house, it asked transportation and logistics giant UPS to design a complete system for moving its entire electronics product line from its Asian factories to retail stores throughout the United States, Latin America, and the Caribbean. Now, products leave Nikon's Asian manufacturing centers and arrive on American retailers' shelve in as few as two days, with UPS handling everything in between. UPS first manages air and ocean freight and related customs brokerage to bring Nikon products from Korea, Japan, and Indonesia to its Louisville, Kentucky operations center. There, UPS can either "kit" the Nikon merchandise with accessories such as batteries and chargers or repackage it for in-store display. Finally, UPS distributes the products to thousands of retailers across the United States or exports them to Latin American or Caribbean retail outlets and distributors. Along the way, UPS tracks the goods and provides Nikon with a "snap shot" of the entire supply chain, letting Nikon keep retailers informed of delivery times and adjust them as needed.

Participants in the business buying process

Who does the buying of the trillions of dollars' worth of goods and services needed by business organizations? The decision-making unit of a buying organization is called its **buying center**: all the individuals and units that play a role in the business purchase decision-making process. This group includes the actual users of the product or service, those who make the buying decision, those who influence the buying decision, those who do the actual buying, and those who control buying information.

The buying center is not a fixed and formally identified unit within the buying organization. It is a set of buying roles assumed by different people for different purchases. Within the organization, the size and makeup of the buying center will vary for different products and for different buying situations. For some routine purchases, one person—say a purchasing agent—may assume all the buying center roles and serve as the only person involved in the buying decision. For more complex purchases, the buying center may include 20 or 30 people from different levels and departments in the organization.

The buying center concept presents a major marketing challenge. The business marketer must learn who participates in the decision, each participant's relative influence, and what evaluation criteria each decision participant uses. This can be difficult. "In the good old days, the decision maker was easy to find," notes one sales manager. "Now it's tougher. There are consensus decisions, committee decisions, decision teams, subcommittees, influencers . . . it's a regular jungle out there."[41]

For example, the medical products and services group of Cardinal Health sells disposable surgical gowns to hospitals. It identifies the hospital personnel involved in this buying decision as the vice president of purchasing, the operating room administrator, and the surgeons. Each participant plays a different role. The vice president of purchasing analyzes whether the hospital should buy disposable gowns or reusable gowns. If analysis favors disposable gowns, then the operating room administrator compares competing products and prices and makes a choice. This administrator considers the gown's absorbency, antiseptic quality, design, and cost and normally buys the brand that meets requirements at the lowest cost. Finally, surgeons affect the decision later by reporting their satisfaction or dissatisfaction with the brand.

The buying center usually includes some obvious participants who are involved formally in the buying decision. For example, the decision to buy a corporate jet will probably involve the company's CEO, chief pilot, a purchasing agent, some legal staff, a member of top management, and others formally charged with the buying decision. It may also involve less obvious, informal participants, some of whom may actually make or strongly affect the buying decision. Sometimes, even the people in the buying center are not aware of all the buying participants. For example, the decision about which corporate jet to buy may actually be made by a corporate board member who has an interest in flying and who knows a lot about airplanes. This board member may work behind the scenes to sway the decision. Many business buying decisions result from the complex interactions of ever-changing buying center participants.

Major influences on business buyers

Business buyers are subject to many influences when they make their buying decisions. Some marketers assume that the major influences are economic. They think buyers will favor the supplier who offers the lowest price or the best product or the most service. They concentrate on offering strong economic benefits to buyers. However, business buyers actually respond to both economic and personal factors. Far from being cold, calculating, and impersonal, business buyers are human and social as well. They react to both reason and emotion.

Today, most B-to-B marketers recognize that emotion plays an important role in business buying decisions. For example, you might expect that an advertisement promoting large trucks to corporate fleet buyers would stress objective technical, performance, and economic factors. However, one ad for Volvo heavy-duty trucks shows two drivers arm-wrestling and claims, "It solves all your fleet problems. Except who gets to drive." It turns out that, in the face of an industry-wide driver shortage, the type of truck a fleet provides can help it to attract qualified drivers. The Volvo ad stresses the raw beauty of the truck and its comfort and roominess, features that make it more appealing to drivers. The ad concludes that Volvo trucks are "built to make fleets more profitable and drivers a lot more possessive."[42]

When suppliers' offers are very similar, business buyers have little basis for strictly rational choice. Because they can meet organizational goals with any supplier, buyers can allow personal factors to play a larger role in their decisions. However, when competing products differ greatly, business buyers are more accountable for their choice and tend to pay more attention to economic factors. Figure 18.2 lists various groups of influences on business buyers—environmental, organizational, interpersonal, and individual.

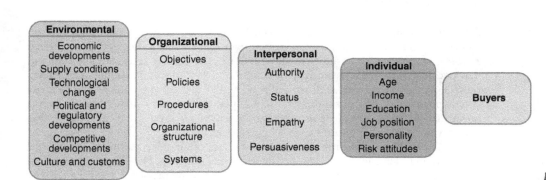

Major influences on Business Buyer Behavior

FIGURE 18.2

Environmental Factors   Business buyers are heavily influenced by factors in the current and expected economic environment, such as the level of primary demand, the economic outlook, and the cost of money. Another environmental factor is shortages in key materials. Many companies now are more willing to buy and hold larger inventories of scarce materials to ensure adequate supply. Business buyers also are affected by technological, political, and competitive developments in the environment. Finally, culture and customs can strongly influence business buyer reactions to the marketer's behavior and strategies, especially in the international marketing environment. The business buyer must watch these factors, determine how they will affect the buyer, and try to turn these challenges into opportunities.

Organizational Factors   Each buying organization has its own objectives, policies, procedures, structure, and systems, and the business marketer must understand these factors well. Questions such as these arise: How many people are involved in the buying decision? Who are they? What are their evaluative criteria? What are the company's policies and limits on its buyers?

Interpersonal Factors   The buying center usually includes many participants who influence each other, so *interpersonal factors* also influence the business buying process. However, it is often difficult to assess such interpersonal factors and group dynamics. Buying center participants do not wear tags that label them as "key decision maker" or "not influential." Nor do buying center participants with the highest rank always have the most influence. Participants may influence the buying decision because they control rewards and punishments, are well liked, have special expertise, or have a special relationship with other important participants. Interpersonal factors are often very subtle. Whenever possible, business marketers must try to understand these factors and design strategies that take them into account.

Individual Factors   Each participant in the business buying decision process brings in personal motives, perceptions, and preferences. These individual factors are affected by personal characteristics such as age, income, education, professional identification, personality, and attitudes toward risk. Also, buyers have different buying styles. Some may be technical types who make in-depth analyses of competitive proposals before choosing a supplier. Other buyers may be intuitive negotiators who are adept at pitting the sellers against one another for the best deal.

The business buying process

Figure 18.3 lists the eight stages of the business buying process.[43] Buyers who face a new-task buying situation usually go through all stages of the buying process. Buyers making modified or straight rebuys may skip some of the stages. We will examine these steps for the typical new-task buying situation.

Problem Recognition   The buying process begins when someone in the company recognizes a problem or need that can be met by acquiring a specific product or service. *Problem recognition* can result from internal or external stimuli. Internally, the company may decide to launch a new product that requires new production equipment and materials. Or a machine may break down and need new parts. Perhaps a purchasing manager is unhappy with a current supplier's product quality, service, or prices. Externally, the buyer may get some new ideas at a trade show, see an ad, or receive a call from a salesperson who offers a better product or a lower price.

   In fact, in their advertising, business marketers often alert customers to potential problems and then show how their products provide solutions. For example, a Sharp ad notes that a multifunction printer can present data security problems and asks "Is your MFP a portal for identity theft?" The solution? Sharp's data security kits "help prevent sensitive information from falling into the wrong hands."

Stages of the Business Buying Process FIGURE 18.3

```
┌──────────────┐      ┌──────────────┐      ┌──────────────┐      ┌──────────────┐
│   Problem    │ ═▷   │ General need │ ═▷   │   Product    │ ═▷   │   Supplier   │
│ recognition  │      │ description  │      │specification │      │    search    │
└──────────────┘      └──────────────┘      └──────────────┘      └──────────────┘

┌──────────────┐      ┌──────────────┐      ┌──────────────┐      ┌──────────────┐
│   Proposal   │ ═▷   │   Supplier   │ ═▷   │ Order-routine│ ═▷   │ Performance  │
│ solicitation │      │  selection   │      │specification │      │    review    │
└──────────────┘      └──────────────┘      └──────────────┘      └──────────────┘
```

General Need Description   Having recognized a need, the buyer next prepares a *general need description* that describes the characteristics and quantity of the needed item. For standard items, this process presents few problems. For complex items, however, the buyer may need to work with others—engineers, users, consultants—to define the item. The team may want to rank the importance of reliability, durability, price, and other attributes desired in the item. In this phase, the alert business marketer can help the buyers define their needs and provide information about the value of different product characteristics.

Product Specification   The buying organization next develops the item's technical *product specifications,* often with the help of a value analysis engineering team. **Value analysis** is an approach to cost reduction in which components are studied carefully to determine if they can be redesigned, standardized, or made by less costly methods of production. The team decides on the best product characteristics and specifies them accordingly. Sellers, too, can use value analysis as a tool to help secure a new account. By showing buyers a better way to make an object, outside sellers can turn straight rebuy situations into new-task situations that give them a chance to obtain new business.

Supplier Search   The buyer now conducts a *supplier search* to find the best vendors. The buyer can compile a small list of qualified suppliers by reviewing trade directories, doing computer searches, or phoning other companies for recommendations. Today, more and more companies are turning to the Internet to find suppliers. For marketers, this has leveled the playing field—the Internet gives smaller suppliers many of the same advantages as larger competitors.

The newer the buying task, and the more complex and costly the item, the greater the amount of time the buyer will spend searching for suppliers. The supplier's task is to get listed in major directories and build a good reputation in the marketplace. Salespeople should watch for companies in the process of searching for suppliers and make certain that their firm is considered.

Proposal Solicitation   In the *proposal solicitation* stage of the business buying process, the buyer invites qualified suppliers to submit proposals. In response, some suppliers will send only a catalog or a salesperson. However, when the item is complex or expensive, the buyer will usually require detailed written proposals or formal presentations from each potential supplier.

Business marketers must be skilled in researching, writing, and presenting proposals in response to buyer proposal solicitations. Proposals should be marketing documents, not just technical documents. Presentations should inspire confidence and should make the marketer's company stand out from the competition.

Supplier Selection   The members of the buying center now review the proposals and select a supplier or suppliers. During *supplier selection,* the buying center often will draw up a list of the desired supplier attributes and their relative importance. Such attributes include product and service quality, reputation, on-time delivery, ethical corporate behavior, honest communication, and competitive prices. The members of the buying center will rate suppliers against these attributes and identify the best suppliers.

Buyers may attempt to negotiate with preferred suppliers for better prices and terms before making the final selections. In the end, they may select a single supplier or a few suppliers. Many buyers prefer multiple sources of supplies to avoid being totally dependent on one supplier and to allow comparisons of prices and performance of several suppliers over time. Today's supplier development managers want to develop a full network of supplier-partners that can help the company bring more value to its customers.

Order-Routine Specification   The buyer now prepares an *order-routine specification*. It includes the final order with the chosen supplier or suppliers and lists items such as technical specifications, quantity needed, expected time of delivery, return policies, and warranties. In the case of maintenance, repair, and operating items, buyers may use blanket contracts rather than periodic purchase orders. A blanket contract creates a long-term relationship in which the supplier promises to resupply the buyer as needed at agreed prices for a set time period.

Many large buyers now practice *vendor-managed inventory,* in which they turn over ordering and inventory responsibilities to their suppliers. Under such systems, buyers share sales and inventory information directly with key suppliers. The suppliers then monitor inventories and replenish stock automatically as needed.

Performance Review   In this stage, the buyer reviews supplier performance. The buyer may contact users and ask them to rate their satisfaction. The *performance review* may lead the buyer to continue, modify, or drop the arrangement. The seller's job is to monitor the same factors used by the buyer to make sure that the seller is giving the expected satisfaction.

The eight-stage buying-process model provides a simple view of the business buying as it might occur in a new-task buying situation. The actual process is usually much more complex. In the modified rebuy or straight rebuy situation, some of these stages would be compressed or bypassed. Each organization buys in its own way, and each buying situation has unique requirements.

Different buying center participants may be involved at different stages of the process. Although certain buying-process steps usually do occur, buyers do not always follow them in the same order, and they may add other steps. Often, buyers will repeat certain stages of the process. Finally, a customer relationship might involve many different types of purchases ongoing at a given time, all in different stages of the buying process. The seller must manage the total customer relationship, not just individual purchases.

E-procurement: Buying on the Internet

Advances in information technology have changed the face of the B-to-B marketing process. Online purchasing, often called *e-procurement,* has grown rapidly in recent years.

Companies can do e-procurement in any of several ways. They can conduct *reverse auctions,* in which they put their purchasing requests online and invite suppliers to bid for the business. Or they can use online *trading exchanges,* through which companies work collectively to facilitate the trading process. For example, Exostar is an online trading exchange that connects buyers and sellers in the aerospace and defense industry. Its goal is to improve trading efficiency and reduce costs among industry trading partners. Initially a collaboration between five leading aerospace and defense companies—Boeing, Lockheed Martin, Raytheon, BAE Systems, and Rolls-Royce—Exostar has now connected more than 300 procurement systems and 34,000 trading partners in 20 countries around the world.

Companies can conduct e-procurement by setting up their own *company buying sites.* For example, General Electric operates a company trading site on which it posts its buying needs and invites bids, negotiates terms, and places orders. Or the company can create *extranet links* with key suppliers. For instance, they can create direct procurement accounts with suppliers such as Dell or Office Depot, through which company buyers can purchase equipment, materials, and supplies.

E-procurement gives buyers access to new suppliers, lowers purchasing costs, and hastens order processing and delivery. In turn, business marketers can connect with customers online to share marketing information, sell products and services, provide customer support services, and maintain ongoing customer relationships.

So far, most of the products bought online are MRO materials—maintenance, repair, and operations. For instance, Hewlett-Packard spends 95 percent of its $13 billion MRO budget via e-procurement. And last year Delta Air Lines purchased $6.2 billion worth of fuel online. National Semiconductor has automated almost all of the company's 3,500 monthly requisitions to buy materials ranging from the sterile booties worn in its fabrication plants to state-of-the-art software. Even the Baltimore Aquarium uses e-procurement to buy everything from exotic fish to feeding supplies. It recently spent $6 billion online for architectural services and supplies to help construct the new exhibit "Animal Planet Australia: Wild Extremes."[45]

The actual dollar amount spent on these types of MRO materials pales in comparison to the amount spent for items such as airplane parts, computer systems, and steel tubing. Yet, MRO materials make up 80 percent of all business orders, and the transaction costs for order processing are high. Thus, companies have much to gain by streamlining the MRO buying process on the Web.

Business-to-business e-procurement yields many benefits. First, it shaves transaction costs and results in more efficient purchasing for both buyers and suppliers. A Web-powered purchasing program eliminates the paperwork associated with traditional requisition and ordering procedures. One study found that e-procurement cuts down requisition-to-order costs by an average of 58 percent.[46]

E-procurement reduces the time between order and delivery. Time savings are particularly dramatic for companies with many overseas suppliers. Adaptec, a leading supplier of computer storage, used an extranet to tie all of its Taiwanese chip suppliers together in a kind of virtual family. Now messages from Adaptec flow in seconds from its headquarters to its Asian partners, and Adaptec has reduced the time between the order and delivery of its chips from as long as 16 weeks to just 55 days—the same turnaround time for companies that build their own chips.

Finally, beyond the cost and time savings, e-procurement frees purchasing people to focus on more strategic issues. For many purchasing professionals, going online means reducing drudgery and paperwork and spending more time managing inventory and working creatively with suppliers. "That is the key," says the HP executive. "You can now focus people on value-added activities. Procurement professionals can now find different sources and work with suppliers to reduce costs and to develop new products."[47]

The rapidly expanding use of e-purchasing, however, also presents some problems. For example, at the same time that the Web makes it possible for suppliers and customers to share business data and even collaborate on product design, it can also erode decades-old customer-supplier relationships. Many firms are using the Web to search for better suppliers.

E-purchasing can also create potential security disasters. Although e-mail and home banking transactions can be protected through basic encryption, the secure environment that businesses need to carry out confidential interactions is often still lacking. Companies are spending millions for research on defensive strategies to keep hackers at bay. Cisco Systems, for example, specifies the types of routers, firewalls, and security procedures that its partners must use to safeguard extranet connections. In fact, the company goes even further—it sends its own security engineers to examine a partner's defenses and holds the partner liable for any security breach that originates from its computer.

chapter 19

Price

What is a price?

In the narrowest sense, **price** is the amount of money charged for a product or service. More broadly, price is the sum of all the values that customers give up in order to gain the benefits of having or using a product or service. Historically, price has been the major factor affecting buyer choice. In recent decades, nonprice factors have gained increasing importance. However, price still remains one of the most important elements determining a firm's market share and profitability.

Price is the only element in the marketing mix that produces revenue; all other elements represent costs. Price is also one of the most flexible marketing mix elements. Unlike product features and channel commitments, prices can be changed quickly. At the same time, pricing is the number-one problem facing many marketing executives, and many companies do not handle pricing well. One frequent problem is that companies are too quick to reduce prices in order to get a sale rather than convincing buyers that their product's greater value is worth a higher price. Other common mistakes include pricing that is too cost oriented rather than customer-value oriented, and pricing that does not take the rest of the marketing mix into account.

Some managers view pricing as a big headache, preferring instead to focus on the other marketing mix elements. However, smart managers treat pricing as a key strategic tool for creating and capturing customer value. Prices have a direct impact on a firm's bottom line. According to one expert, "a 1 percent price improvement generates a 12.5 percent profit improvement for most organizations."[5] More importantly, as a part of a company's overall value proposition, price plays a key role in creating customer value and building customer relationships. "Instead of running away from pricing," says the expert, "savvy marketers are embracing it."

Price
The amount of money charged for a product or service, or the sum of all the values that customers give up in order to gain the benefits of having or using a product or service.

Factors to consider when setting prices

The price the company charges will fall somewhere between one that is too high to produce any demand and one that is too low to produce a profit. Figure 19.1 summarizes the major considerations in setting price. Customer perceptions of the product's value set the ceiling for prices. If customers perceive that the price is greater than the product's value, they will not buy the product. Product costs set the floor for prices. If the company prices the product below its costs, company profits will suffer. In setting its price between these two extremes, the company must consider a number of other internal and external factors, including its overall marketing strategy and mix, the nature of the market and demand, and competitors' strategies and prices.

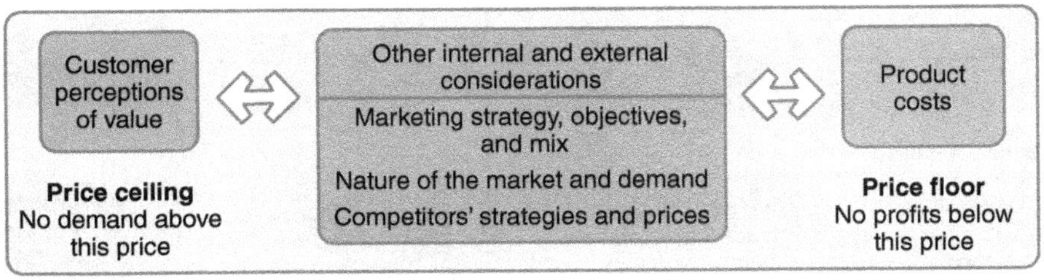

Considerations in Setting Price

FIGURE 19.1

Value-based pricing

In the end, the customer will decide whether a product's price is right. Pricing decisions, like other marketing mix decisions, must start with customer value. When customers buy a product, they exchange something of value (the price) in order to get something of value (the benefits of having or using the product). Effective, customer-oriented pricing involves understanding how much value consumers place on the benefits they receive from the product and setting a price that captures this value.

Value-based pricing

Setting price based on buyers' perceptions of value rather than on the seller's cost.

Good pricing begins with a complete understanding of the value that a product or service creates for customers. **Value-based pricing** uses buyers' perceptions of value, not the seller's cost, as the key to pricing. Value-based pricing means that the marketer cannot design a product and marketing program and then set the price. Price is considered along with the other marketing mix variables *before* the marketing program is set.

Figure 19.2 compares value-based pricing with cost-based pricing. Cost-based pricing is product driven. The company designs what it considers to be a good product, adds up the costs of making the product, and sets a price that covers costs plus a target profit. Marketing must then convince buyers that the product's value at that price justifies its purchase. If the price turns out to be too high, the company must settle for lower markups or lower sales, both resulting in disappointing profits.

Value-based pricing reverses this process. The company first assesses customer needs and value perceptions. It then sets its target price based on customer perceptions of value. The targeted value and price then drive decisions about what costs can be incurred and the resulting product design. As a result, pricing begins with analyzing consumer needs and value perceptions, and price is set to match consumers' perceived value.

It's important to remember that "good value" is not the same as "low price." For example, prices for a Hermes Birkin Bag start at about $7,000 and can top $25,000—a less-expensive handbag might carry as much, but some consumers place great value on the intangibles they receive from a one-of-a-kind handmade bag that has a year-long waiting list. Similarly, some car buyers consider the luxurious Bentley Continental GT automobile a real value, even at an eye-popping price of $150,000:

> Stay with me here, because I'm about to [tell you why] a certain automobile costing $150,000 is not actually expensive, but is in fact a tremendous value. Every Bentley GT is built by hand, an Old World bit of automaking requiring 160 hours per vehicle. Craftsmen spend 18 hours simply stitching the perfectly joined leather of the GT's steering wheel, almost as long as it takes to assemble an entire VW Golf. The results are impressive: Dash and doors are mirrored with walnut veneer, floor pedals are carved from aluminum, window and seat toggles are cut from actual metal rather than plastic, and every air vent is perfectly chromed.... The sum of all this is a fitted cabin that approximates that of a $300,000 vehicle, matched to an engine the equal of a $200,000 automobile, within a car that has brilliantly incorporated ... technological sophistication. As I said, the GT is a bargain. [Just ask anyone on the lengthy waiting list.] The waiting time to bring home your very own GT is currently half a year.[6]

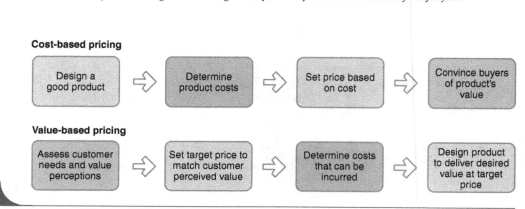

Value-Based Pricing Versus Cost-Based Pricing

FIGURE 19.2

A company using value-based pricing must find out what value buyers assign to different competitive offers. However, companies often find it hard to measure the value customers will attach to its product. For example, calculating the cost of ingredients in a meal at a fancy restaurant is relatively easy. But assigning a value to other satisfactions such as taste, environment, relaxation, conversation, and status is very hard. And these values will vary both for different consumers and different situations.

Still, consumers will use these perceived values to evaluate a product's price, so the company must work to measure them. Sometimes, companies ask consumers how much they would pay for a basic product and for each benefit added to the offer. Or a company might conduct experiments to test the perceived value of different product offers. According to an old Russian proverb, there are two fools in every market—one who asks too much and one who asks too little. If the seller charges more than the buyers' perceived value, the company's sales will suffer. If the seller charges less, its products sell very well. But they produce less revenue than they would if they were priced at the level of perceived value.

We now examine two types of value-based pricing: *good-value pricing* and *value-added pricing*.

Good-value pricing

During the past decade, marketers have noted a fundamental shift in consumer attitudes toward price and quality. Many companies have changed their pricing approaches to bring them into line with changing economic conditions and consumer price perceptions. More and more, marketers have adopted **good-value pricing** strategies—offering just the right combination of quality and good service at a fair price.

> **Good-value pricing**
> Offering just the right combination of quality and good service at a fair price.

In many cases, this has involved introducing less-expensive versions of established, brand name products. Fast-food restaurants such as Taco Bell and McDonald's offer "value menus." Armani offers the less-expensive, more-casual Armani Exchange fashion line. Volkswagen recently reintroduced the Rabbit, an economical car with a base price under $15,000, to help "get VW on the shopping list of more buyers."[7] In other cases, good-value pricing has involved redesigning existing brands to offer more quality for a given price or the same quality for less.

An important type of good-value pricing at the retail level is *everyday low pricing (EDLP)*. EDLP involves charging a constant, everyday low price with few or no temporary price discounts. In contrast, *high-low pricing* involves charging higher prices on an everyday basis but running frequent promotions to lower prices temporarily on selected items. In recent years, high-low pricing has given way to EDLP in retail settings ranging from Saturn car dealerships to Costco warehouse clubs to furniture stores such as Room & Board. The king of EDLP is Wal-Mart, which practically defined the concept. Except for a few sale items every month, Wal-Mart promises everyday low prices on everything it sells.

Value-added pricing

In many marketing situations, the challenge is to build the company's *pricing power*—its power to escape price competition and to justify higher prices and margins without losing market share. To retain pricing power, a firm must retain or build the value of its market offering. This is especially true for suppliers of commodity products, which are characterized by little differentiation and intense price competition. If companies "rely on price to capture and retain business, they reduce whatever they're selling to a commodity," says an analyst. "Once that happens, there is no customer loyalty."[8]

> **Value-added pricing**
> Attaching value-added features and services to differentiate a market offering and support higher prices, rather than cutting prices to match competitors.

To increase their pricing power, many companies adopt **value-added pricing** strategies. Rather than cutting prices to match competitors, they attach value-added features and services to differentiate their offers and thus support higher prices. Consider this example:

The monsoon season in Mumbai, India, is three months of near-nonstop rain. For 147 years, most Mumbaikars protected themselves with a Stag umbrella from venerable Ebrahim Currim & Sons. Like Ford's Model T, the basic Stag was sturdy, affordable, and of any color, as long as it was black. By the end of the 20th century, however, the Stag was threatened by cheaper imports from China. Stag responded by dropping prices and scrimping on quality. It was a bad move: For the first time since the 1940s, the brand began losing money.

Finally, however, the company came to its senses. It abandoned the price war and vowed to improve quality. Surprisingly, even at higher prices, sales of the improved Stag umbrellas actually increased. Then the company started innovating. Noting the new fashion consciousness of Indian men, it launched designer umbrellas in funky designs and cool colors. Teenagers and young adults lapped them up. Stag then launched umbrellas with a built-in high-power flashlight for those who walk unlit roads at night, and models with prerecorded tunes for music lovers. For women who walk secluded streets after dark, there's Stag's Bodyguard model, armed with glare lights, emergency blinkers, and an alarm. Customers willingly pay up to a 100 percent premium for the new products. Under the new value-added strategy, the Stag brand has now returned to profitability. Come the monsoon in June, the grand old black Stags still reappear on the streets of Mumbai—but now priced 15 percent higher than the imports.[9]

"Even in today's economic environment, it's not about price," says a pricing expert. "It's about keeping customers loyal by providing [features and] service they can't find anywhere else."[10]

Company and product costs

Whereas customer-value perceptions set the price ceiling, costs set the floor for the price that the company can charge. **Cost-based pricing** involved setting prices based on the costs for producing, distributing, and selling the product plus a fair rate of return for its effort and risk. A company's costs may be an important element in its pricing strategy. Many companies, such as Southwest Airlines, Wal-Mart, and Dell, work to become the "low-cost producers" in their industries. Companies with lower costs can set lower prices that result in greater sales and profits.

Cost-based pricing
Setting prices based on the costs for producing, distributing, and selling the product plus a fair rate of return for its effort and risk.

Types of costs

A company's costs take two forms, fixed and variable. **Fixed costs** (also known as overhead) are costs that do not vary with production or sales level. For example, a company must pay each month's bills for rent, heat, interest, and executive salaries, whatever the company's output. **Variable costs** vary directly with the level of production. Each PC produced by Hewlett-Packard involves a cost of computer chips, wires, plastic, packaging, and other inputs. These costs tend to be the same for each unit produced. They are called variable because their total varies with the number of units produced. **Total costs** are the sum of the fixed and variable costs for any given level of production. Management wants to charge a price that will at least cover the total production costs at a given level of production.

Fixed costs
Costs that do not vary with production or sales level.

Variable costs
Costs that vary directly with the level of production.

Total costs
The sum of the fixed and variable costs for any given level of production.

The company must watch its costs carefully. If it costs the company more than competitors to produce and sell its product, the company will need to charge a higher price or make less profit, putting it at a competitive disadvantage.

Cost-based pricing

The simplest pricing method is **cost-plus pricing**—adding a standard markup to the cost of the product. For example, an appliance retailer might pay a manufacturer $20 for a toaster and mark it up to sell at $30, a 50 percent markup on cost. The retailer's gross margin is $10. If the store's operating costs amount to $8 per toaster sold, the retailer's profit margin will be $2.

Cost-plus pricing
Adding a standard markup to the cost of the product.

The manufacturer that made the toaster probably used cost-plus pricing. If the manufacturer's standard cost of producing the toaster was $16, it might have added a 25 percent markup, setting the price to the retailers at $20. Similarly, construction companies submit job bids by estimating the total project cost and adding a standard markup for profit. Lawyers, accountants, architects, and other professionals typically price by adding a standard markup to their costs. Some sellers tell their customers they will charge cost plus a specified markup; for example, aerospace companies price this way to the government.

Does using standard markups to set prices make sense? Generally, no. Any pricing method that ignores demand and competitor prices is not likely to lead to the best price. Still, markup pricing remains popular for many reasons. First, sellers are more certain about costs than about demand. By tying the price to cost, sellers simplify pricing—they do not need to make frequent adjustments as demand changes. Second, when all firms in the industry use this pricing method, prices tend to be similar and price competition is thus minimized. Third, many people feel that cost-plus pricing is fairer to both buyers and sellers. Sellers earn a fair return on their investment but do not take advantage of buyers when buyers' demand becomes great.

Another cost-oriented pricing approach is **break-even pricing**, or a variation called **target profit pricing**. The firm tries to determine the price at which it will break even or make the target profit it is seeking. Target pricing uses the concept of a *break-even chart*, which shows the total cost and total revenue expected at different sales volume levels. Figure 19.3 shows a break-even chart for the toaster manufacturer discussed here. Fixed costs are $6 million regardless of sales volume, and variable costs are $5 per unit. Variable costs are added to fixed costs to form total costs, which rise with volume. The slope of the total revenue curve reflects the price. Here, the price is $15 (for example, the company's revenue is $12 million on 800,000 units, or $15 per unit).

At the $15 price, the company must sell at least 600,000 units to *break even* [break-even volume = fixed costs ÷ (price – variable costs) = $6,000,000 ÷ ($15 − $5) = 600,000]. That is, at this level, total revenues will equal total costs of $9 million. If the company wants a target profit of $2 million, it must sell at least 800,000 units to obtain the $12 million of total revenue needed to cover the costs of $10 million plus the $2 million of target profits. In contrast, if the company charges a higher price, say $20, it will not need to sell as many units to break even or to achieve its target profit. In fact, the higher the price, the lower the company's break-even point will be.

The major problem with this analysis, however, is that it fails to consider customer value and the relationship between price and demand. As the *price* increases, *demand* decreases, and the market may not buy even the lower volume needed to break even at

Break-even pricing (target profit pricing)
Setting price to break even on the costs of making and marketing a product; or setting price to make a target profit.

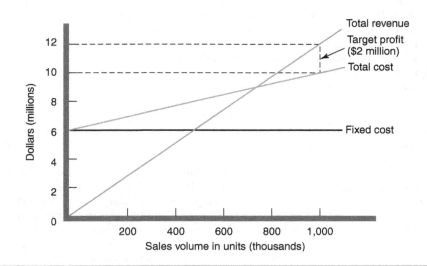

Break-Even Chart for Determining Price

FIGURE 19.3

the higher price. For example, suppose the company calculates that given its current fixed and variable costs, it must charge a price of $30 for the product in order to earn its desired target profit. But marketing research shows that few consumers will pay more than $25. In this case, the company must trim its costs in order to lower the break-even point so that it can charge the lower price consumers expect.

Thus, although break-even analysis and target profit pricing can help the company to determine minimum prices needed to cover expected costs and profits, they do not take the price-demand relationship into account. When using this method, the company must also consider the impact of price on sales volume needed to realize target profits and the likelihood that the needed volume will be achieved at each possible price.

Other internal and external considerations affecting price decisions

Customer perceptions of value set the upper limit for prices and costs set the lower limit. However, in setting prices within these limits, the company must consider a number of other internal and external factors. Internal factors affecting pricing include the company's overall marketing strategy, objectives, and marketing mix, as well as other organizational considerations. External factors include the nature of the market and demand, competitors' strategies and prices, and other environmental factors.

Overall marketing strategy, objectives, and mix

Price is only one element of the company's broader marketing strategy. Thus, before setting price, the company must decide on its overall marketing strategy for the product or service. If the company has selected its target market and positioning carefully, then its marketing mix strategy, including price, will be fairly straightforward. For example, when Toyota developed its Lexus brand to compete with European luxury-performance cars in the higher-income segment, this required charging a high price. In contrast, when it introduced its Yaris model—"the car that you can afford to drive is finally the car you actually want to drive"—this positioning required charging a low price. Thus, pricing strategy is largely determined by decisions on market positioning.

General pricing objectives might include survival, current profit maximization, market share leadership, or customer retention and relationship building. At a more specific level, a company can set prices to attract new customers or to profitably retain existing ones. It can set prices low to prevent competition from entering the market or set prices at competitors' levels to stabilize the market. It can price to keep the loyalty and support of resellers or to avoid government intervention. Prices can be reduced temporarily to create excitement for a brand. Or one product may be priced to help the sales of other products in the company's line. Thus, pricing may play an important role in helping to accomplish the company's objectives at many levels.

Price is only one of the marketing mix tools that a company uses to achieve its marketing objectives. Price decisions must be coordinated with product design, distribution, and promotion decisions to form a consistent and effective integrated marketing program. Decisions made for other marketing mix variables may affect pricing decisions. For example, a decision to position the product on high-performance quality will mean that the seller must charge a higher price to cover higher costs. And producers whose resellers are expected to support and promote their products may need to build larger reseller margins into their prices.

Companies often position their products on price and then tailor other marketing mix decisions to the prices they want to charge. Here, price is a crucial product-positioning factor that defines the product's market, competition, and design. Many firms support such price-positioning strategies with a technique called **target costing**, a potent strategic weapon. Target costing reverses the usual process of first designing a new product, determining its cost, and then asking, "Can we sell it for that?" Instead, it starts with an ideal selling price based on customer-value considerations and then targets costs that will ensure that the price is met. For example, when Toyota set out to design the Yaris, it began with the "car you can afford to drive" positioning and price point firmly in mind.

Target costing
Pricing that starts with an ideal selling price, then targets costs that will ensure that the price is met.

It then designed a car with costs that allowed it to give target consumers "a car you actually want to drive" at that targeted price.

Other companies deemphasize price and use other marketing mix tools to create *nonprice* positions. Often, the best strategy is not to charge the lowest price but rather to differentiate the marketing offer to make it worth a higher price. For example, Viking builds more value into its kitchen appliance products and charges a higher price than many competitors. Customers recognize Viking's higher quality and are willing to pay more to get it.

Some marketers even position their products on *high* prices, featuring high prices as part of their product's allure. For example, Grand Marnier offers a $225 bottle of Cuvée du Cent Cinquantenaire that's marketed with the tagline "Hard to find, impossible to pronounce, and prohibitively expensive." Porsche proudly advertises its curvaceous Cayman as "Starting at $49,400," actually a reasonable price given the brand's high-end prestige, quality, and innovation in performance and design.

Thus, marketers must consider the total marketing strategy and mix when setting prices. If the product is positioned on nonprice factors, then decisions about quality, promotion, and distribution will strongly affect price. If price is a crucial positioning factor, then price will strongly affect decisions made about the other marketing mix elements. But even when featuring price, marketers need to remember that customers rarely buy on price alone. Instead, they seek products that give them the best value in terms of benefits received for the prices paid.

Organizational considerations

Management must decide who within the organization should set prices. Companies handle pricing in a variety of ways. In small companies, prices are often set by top management rather than by the marketing or sales departments. In large companies, pricing is typically handled by divisional or product line managers. In industrial markets, salespeople may be allowed to negotiate with customers within certain price ranges. Even so, top management sets the pricing objectives and policies, and it often approves the prices proposed by lower-level management or salespeople.

In industries in which pricing is a key factor (airlines, aerospace, steel, railroads, oil companies), companies often have pricing departments to set the best prices or to help others in setting them. These departments report to the marketing department or top management. Others who have an influence on pricing include sales managers, production managers, finance managers, and accountants.

The market and demand

As noted earlier, good pricing starts with understanding how customers' perceptions of value affect the prices they are willing to pay. Both consumer and industrial buyers balance the price of a product or service against the benefits of owning it. Thus, before setting prices, the marketer must understand the relationship between price and demand for the company's product. In this section, we take a deeper look at the price-demand relationship and how it varies for different types of markets. We then discuss methods for analyzing the price-demand relationship.

Pricing in Different Types of Markets The seller's pricing freedom varies with different types of markets. Economists recognize four types of markets, each presenting a different pricing challenge.

Under *pure competition,* the market consists of many buyers and sellers trading in a uniform commodity such as wheat, copper, or financial securities. No single buyer or seller has much effect on the going market price. A seller cannot charge more than the going price, because buyers can obtain as much as they need at the going price. Nor would sellers charge less than the market price, because they can sell all they want at this price. If price and profits rise, new sellers can easily enter the market. In a purely competitive market, marketing research, product development, pricing, advertising, and sales promotion play little or no role. Thus, sellers in these markets do not spend much time on marketing strategy.

Under *monopolistic competition,* the market consists of many buyers and sellers who trade over a range of prices rather than a single market price. A range of prices occurs because sellers can differentiate their offers to buyers. Either the physical product can be varied in quality, features, or style, or the accompanying services can be varied. Buyers see differences in sellers' products and will pay different prices for them. Sellers try to develop differentiated offers for different customer segments and, in addition to price, freely use branding, advertising, and personal selling to set their offers apart. Thus, Moen differentiates its faucets and other fixtures through strong branding and advertising, reducing the impact of price. Because there are many competitors in such markets, each firm is less affected by competitors' pricing strategies than in oligopolistic markets.

Under *oligopolistic competition,* the market consists of a few sellers who are highly sensitive to each other's pricing and marketing strategies. The product can be uniform (steel, aluminum) or nonuniform (cars, computers). There are few sellers because it is difficult for new sellers to enter the market. Each seller is alert to competitors' strategies and moves. If a steel company slashes its price by 10 percent, buyers will quickly switch to this supplier. The other steelmakers must respond by lowering their prices or increasing their services.

In a *pure monopoly,* the market consists of one seller. The seller may be a government monopoly (the U.S. Postal Service), a private regulated monopoly (a power company), or a private nonregulated monopoly (DuPont when it introduced nylon). Pricing is handled differently in each case. In a regulated monopoly, the government permits the company to set rates that will yield a "fair return." Nonregulated monopolies are free to price at what the market will bear. However, they do not always charge the full price for a number of reasons: a desire not to attract competition, a desire to penetrate the market faster with a low price, or a fear of government regulation.

Analyzing the Price-Demand Relationship   Each price the company might charge will lead to a different level of demand. The relationship between the price charged and the resulting demand level is shown in the **demand curve** in Figure 19.4. The demand curve shows the number of units the market will buy in a given time period at different prices that might be charged. In the normal case, demand and price are inversely related; that is, the higher the price, the lower the demand. Thus, the company would sell less if it raised its price from P_1 to P_2. In short, consumers with limited budgets probably will buy less of something if its price is too high.

In the case of prestige goods, the demand curve sometimes slopes upward. Consumers think that higher prices mean more quality. For example, Gibson Guitar Corporation once toyed with the idea of lowering its prices to compete more effectively with Japanese rivals such as Yamaha and Ibanez. To its surprise, Gibson found that its instruments didn't sell as well at lower prices. "We had an inverse [price-demand relationship]," noted Gibson's chief executive. "The more we charged, the more product we sold." At a time when other guitar manufacturers have chosen to build their instruments

Demand curve

A curve that shows the number of units the market will buy in a given time period, at different prices that might be charged.

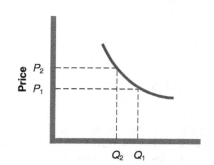

Demand Curve

FIGURE 19.4

more quickly, cheaply, and in greater numbers, Gibson still promises guitars that "are made one-at-a-time, by hand. No shortcuts. No substitutions." It turns out that low prices simply aren't consistent with "Gibson's century-old tradition of creating investment-quality instruments that represent the highest standards of imaginative design and masterful craftsmanship."[11] Still, if the company charges too high a price, the level of demand will be lower.

Most companies try to measure their demand curves by estimating demand at different prices. The type of market makes a difference. In a monopoly, the demand curve shows the total market demand resulting from different prices. If the company faces competition, its demand at different prices will depend on whether competitors' prices stay constant or change with the company's own prices.

Price Elasticity of Demand   Marketers also need to know **price elasticity**—how responsive demand will be to a change in price. If demand hardly changes with a small change in price, we say demand is *inelastic*. If demand changes greatly, we say the demand is *elastic*.

Price elasticity
A measure of the sensitivity of demand to changes in price.

If demand is elastic rather than inelastic, sellers will consider lowering their prices. A lower price will produce more total revenue. This practice makes sense as long as the extra costs of producing and selling more do not exceed the extra revenue. At the same time, most firms want to avoid pricing that turns their products into commodities. In recent years, forces such as deregulation and the instant price comparisons afforded by the Internet and other technologies have increased consumer price sensitivity, turning products ranging from telephones and computers to new automobiles into commodities in some consumers' eyes.

Marketers need to work harder than ever to differentiate their offerings when a dozen competitors are selling virtually the same product at a comparable or lower price. More than ever, companies need to understand the price sensitivity of their customers and prospects and the trade-offs people are willing to make between price and product characteristics. In the words of marketing consultant Kevin Clancy, those who target only the price sensitive are "leaving money on the table."

Competitors' strategies and prices

In setting its prices, the company must also consider competitors' costs, prices, and market offerings. Consumers will base their judgments of a product's value on the prices that competitors charge for similar products. A consumer who is thinking about buying a Canon digital camera will evaluate Canon's customer value and price against the value and prices of comparable products made by Kodak, Nikon, Sony, and others.

In addition, the company's pricing strategy may affect the nature of the competition it faces. If Canon follows a high-price, high-margin strategy, it may attract competition. A low-price, low-margin strategy, however, may stop competitors or drive them out of the market. Canon needs to benchmark its costs and value against competitors' costs and value. It can then use these benchmarks as a starting point for its own pricing.

In assessing competitors' pricing strategies, the company should ask several questions. First, how does the company's market offering compare with competitors' offerings in terms of customer value? If consumers perceive that the company's product or service provides greater value, the company can charge a higher price. If consumers perceive less value relative to competing products, the company must either charge a lower price or change customer perceptions to justify a higher price.

Next, how strong are current competitors and what are their current pricing strategies? If the company faces a host of smaller competitors charging high prices relative to the value they deliver, it might charge lower prices to drive weaker competitors out of the market. If the market is dominated by larger, low-price competitors, the company may decide to target unserved market niches with value-added products at higher prices. For example, your local independent bookstore isn't likely to win a price war against Amazon.com or Barnes & Noble. It would be wiser to add special customer services and personal touches that justify higher prices and margins.

Finally, the company should ask, How does the competitive landscape influence customer price sensitivity?[12] For example, customers will be more price sensitive if they see few differences between competing products. They will buy whichever product costs the least. The more information customers have about competing products and prices before buying, the more price sensitive they will be. Easy product comparisons help customers to assess the value of different options and to decide what prices they are willing to pay. Finally, customers will be more price sensitive if they can switch easily from one product alternative to another.

What principle should guide decisions about what price to charge relative to those of competitors? The answer is simple in concept but often difficult in practice: No matter what price you charge—high, low, or in between—be certain to give customers superior value for that price.

Other external factors

When setting prices, the company also must consider a number of other factors in its external environment. *Economic conditions* can have a strong impact on the firm's pricing strategies. Economic factors such as boom or recession, inflation, and interest rates affect pricing decisions because they affect both consumer perceptions of the product's price and value and the costs of producing a product.

The company must also consider what impact its prices will have on other parties in its environment. How will *resellers* react to various prices? The company should set prices that give resellers a fair profit, encourage their support, and help them to sell the product effectively. The *government* is another important external influence on pricing decisions. Finally, *social concerns* may need to be taken into account. In setting prices, a company's short-term sales, market share, and profit goals may need to be tempered by broader societal considerations. We will examine public policy issues in pricing later in the chapter.

We've now seen that pricing decisions are subject to a complex array of customer, company, competitive, and environmental forces. To make things even more complex, a company sets not a single price but rather a *pricing structure* that covers different items in its line. This pricing structure changes over time as products move through their life cycles. The company adjusts prices to reflect changes in demand and costs and to account for variations in buyers and situations. As the competitive environment changes, the company considers when to initiate price changes and when to respond to them.

We now examine the major dynamic pricing strategies available to marketers. In turn, we look at *new-product pricing strategies* for products in the introductory stage of the product life cycle, *product mix pricing strategies* for related products in the product mix, *price-adjustment strategies* that account for customer differences and changing situations, and strategies for initiating and responding to *price changes*.

New-product pricing strategies

Pricing strategies usually change as the product passes through its life cycle. The introductory stage is especially challenging. Companies bringing out a new product face the challenge of setting prices for the first time. They can choose between two broad strategies: *market-skimming pricing* and *market-penetration pricing*.

Market-skimming pricing (price skimming)
Setting a high price for a new product to skim maximum revenues layer by layer from the segments willing to pay the high price; the company makes fewer but more profitable sales.

Market-skimming pricing

Many companies that invent new products set high initial prices to "skim" revenues layer by layer from the market. Sony frequently uses this strategy, called **market-skimming pricing** (or **price skimming**). When Sony introduced the world's first high-definition television (HDTV) to the Japanese market in 1990, the high-tech sets cost $43,000. These televisions were purchased only by customers who could afford to pay a high price for the new technology. Sony rapidly reduced the price over the next several years to attract new buyers. By 1993, a 28-inch HDTV cost a Japanese buyer just over $6,000. In 2001, a Japanese consumer could buy a 40-inch HDTV for about $2,000, a price that many more customers could afford. An entry-level HDTV set now sells for less than $500 in the United States, and prices continue to fall. In this way, Sony skimmed the maximum amount of revenue from the various segments of the market.[13]

Market skimming makes sense only under certain conditions. First, the product's quality and image must support its higher price and enough buyers must want the product at that price. Second, the costs of producing a smaller volume cannot be so high that they cancel the advantage of charging more. Finally, competitors should not be able to enter the market easily and undercut the high price.

Market-penetration pricing

Rather than setting a high initial price to skim off small but profitable market segments, some companies use **market-penetration pricing**. They set a low initial price in order to *penetrate* the market quickly and deeply—to attract a large number of buyers quickly and win a large market share. The high sales volume results in falling costs, allowing the company to cut its price even further. For example, Wal-Mart and other discount retailers use penetration pricing. And Dell used penetration pricing to enter the personal computer market, selling high-quality computer products through lower-cost direct channels. Its sales soared when HP, Apple, and other competitors selling through retail stores could not match its prices.

Market-penetration pricing
Setting a low price for a new product in order to attract a large number of buyers and a large market share.

Several conditions must be met for this low-price strategy to work. First, the market must be highly price sensitive so that a low price produces more market growth. Second, production and distribution costs must fall as sales volume increases. Finally, the low price must help keep out the competition, and the penetration pricer must maintain its low-price position—otherwise, the price advantage may be only temporary. For example, Wal-Mart has faced challenges from other low-cost retailers, such as Costco and Kohl's. However, through its dedication to low operating and purchasing costs, Wal-Mart has retained its price advantage and established itself as the world's number-one retailer.

Product mix pricing strategies

The strategy for setting a product's price often must be changed when the product is part of a product mix. In this case, the firm looks for a set of prices that maximizes the profits on the total product mix. Pricing is difficult because the various products have related demand and costs and face different degrees of competition. We now take a closer look at the five product mix pricing situations summarized in Table 19.1: *product line pricing, optional-product pricing, captive-product pricing, by-product pricing,* and *product bundle pricing.*

TABLE 19.1	Product Mix Pricing Strategies
STRATEGY	**DESCRIPTION**
Product line pricing	Setting prices across an entire product line
Optional-product pricing	Pricing optional or accessory products sold with the main product
Captive-product pricing	Pricing products that must be used with the main product
By-product pricing	Pricing low-value by-products to get rid of them
Product bundle pricing	Pricing bundles of products sold together

Product line pricing

Product line pricing
Setting the price steps between products in a product line based on cost differences and customer perceptions of the value.

Companies usually develop product lines rather than single products. For example, Samsonite offers some 20 different collections of bags of all shapes and sizes at prices that range from under $50 for a Sammie's child's backpack to more than $1,250 for a bag from its Black Label Vintage Collection.[14] In **product line pricing**, management must decide on the price steps to set between the various products in a line.

The price steps should take into account cost differences between the products in the line. More importantly, they should account for differences in customer perceptions of the value of different features. For example, Quicken offers an entire line of financial management software, including Basic, Deluxe, Premier, and Home & Business versions priced at $29.99, $59.99, $79.99, and $89.99. Although it costs Quicken no more to produce the CD containing the Premier version than the CD containing the Basic version, many buyers happily pay more to obtain additional Premier features, such as financial-planning and investment-monitoring tools. Quicken's task is to establish perceived value differences that support the price differences.

Optional-product pricing

Optional-product pricing
The pricing of optional or accessory products along with a main product.

Many companies use **optional-product pricing**—offering to sell optional or accessory products along with their main product. For example, a car buyer may choose to order an in-car entertainment system and Bluetooth wireless communication. Refrigerators come with optional ice makers. And when you order a new PC, you can select from a bewildering array of processors, hard drives, docking systems, software options, and carrying cases.

Pricing these options is a sticky problem. Automobile companies must decide which items to include in the base price and which to offer as options. Until recent years, General Motors' normal pricing strategy was to advertise a stripped-down model at a base price to pull people into showrooms and then to devote most of the showroom space to showing option-loaded cars at higher prices. The economy model was stripped of so many comforts and conveniences that most buyers rejected it. Then, GM and other U.S. automakers followed the examples of the Japanese and German companies and included in the sticker price many useful items previously sold only as options. Thus, most advertised prices today represent well-equipped cars.

Captive-product pricing

Captive-product pricing
Setting a price for products that must be used along with a main product.

Companies that make products that must be used along with a main product are using **captive-product pricing**. Examples of captive products are razor blade cartridges, video games, and printer cartridges. Producers of the main products (razors, video game consoles, and printers) often price them low and set high markups on the supplies. Thus, Gillette sells low-priced razors but makes money on the replacement cartridges. HP makes very low margins on its printers but very high margins on printer cartridges and other supplies.

Companies using captive-product pricing must be careful—consumers trapped into buying expensive supplies may come to resent the brand that ensnared them. Kodak hopes to reverse the process with its new EasyShare inkjet printers:

> *Until recently, printers have been sold at a loss, with profits being made up by the later sales of high-margin ink cartridges. Kodak plans to turn that model upside-down by selling premium-priced printers with no discounts, then selling much cheaper ink cartridges. The printers will be priced from $149 to $299. The company will then sell ink cartridges at $9.99 for black and $14.99 for color. "Our strategy . . . is to crystallize for consumers that they're not only buying a printer today but also buying into three to four years of ink purchases," says a Kodak marketing executive. The strategy is risky—Kodak will need to educate consumers on the benefits of paying more up front in order to reduce long-run printing costs. Initial ads will be built around the idea and visual image "think," with the first two letters in black and the*

last three in white, creating a "think ink" message. Also, Kodak initially sold the print-ers only in Best Buy stores to take advantage of the retailer's on-the-floor sales staff and ability to educate buyers.[15]

In the case of services, this captive-product pricing is called *two-part pricing*. The price of the service is broken into a *fixed fee* plus a *variable usage rate*. Thus, at Six Flags and other amusement parks, you pay a daily ticket or season pass charge plus additional fees for food and other in-park features. Theaters charge admission and then generate additional revenues from concessions. And cell phone companies charge a flat rate for a basic calling plan, then charge for minutes over what the plan allows. The service firm must decide how much to charge for the basic service and how much for the variable usage. The fixed amount should be low enough to induce usage of the service; profit can be made on the variable fees.

By-product pricing

Producing products and services often generates by-products. If the by-products have no value and if getting rid of them is costly, this will affect the pricing of the main product. Using **by-product pricing**, the company seeks a market for these by-products to help off-set the costs of disposing of them and to help make the price of the main product more competitive. The by-products themselves can even turn out to be profitable. For example, papermaker MeadWestvaco has turned what was once considered chemical waste into profit-making products.

By-product pricing
Setting a price for by-products in order to make the main product's price more competitive.

> *MeadWestvaco created a separate company, Asphalt Innovations, which creates useful chemicals entirely from the by-products of MeadWestvaco's wood-processing activi-ties. In fact, Asphalt Innovations has grown to become the world's biggest supplier of specialty chemicals for the paving industry. Using the salvaged chemicals, paving companies can pave roads at a lower temperature, create longer-lasting roads, and more easily recycle road materials when roads need to be replaced. What's more, sal-vaging the by-product chemicals eliminates the costs and environmental hazards once associated with disposing of them.[16]*

Product bundle pricing

Using **product bundle pricing**, sellers often combine several of their products and offer the bundle at a reduced price. For example, fast-food restaurants bundle a burger, fries, and a soft drink at a "meal" price. Resorts sell specially priced vacation packages that include airfare, accommodations, meals, and entertainment. And Comcast, Time Warner, and other cable companies bundle cable service, phone service, and high-speed Internet connections at a low combined price. Price bundling can promote the sales of products consumers might not otherwise buy, but the combined price must be low enough to get them to buy the bundle.[17]

Product bundle pricing
Combining several products and offering the bundle at a reduced price.

Price-adjustment strategies

Companies usually adjust their basic prices to account for various customer differences and changing situations. Here we examine the seven price adjustment strategies summa-rized in Table 19.2: *discount and allowance pricing, segmented pricing, psychological pricing, promotional pricing, geographical pricing, dynamic pricing,* and *international pricing.*

Discount and allowance pricing

Most companies adjust their basic price to reward customers for certain responses, such as early payment of bills, volume purchases, and off-season buying. These price adjust-ments—called *discounts* and *allowances*—can take many forms.

TABLE 19.2	Price Adjustment Strategies
STRATEGY	**DESCRIPTION**
Discount and allowance pricing	Reducing prices to reward customer responses such as paying early or promoting the product
Segmented pricing	Adjusting prices to allow for differences in customers, products, or locations
Psychological pricing	Adjusting prices for psychological effect
Promotional pricing	Temporarily reducing prices to increase short-run sales
Geographical pricing	Adjusting prices to account for the geographic location of customers
Dynamic pricing	Adjusting prices continually to meet the characteristics and needs of individual customers and situations
International pricing	Adjusting prices for international markets

Discount
A straight reduction in price on purchases under stated conditions or during a stated period of time.

The many forms of **discounts** include a *cash discount,* a price reduction to buyers who pay their bills promptly. A typical example is "2/10, net 30," which means that although payment is due within 30 days, the buyer can deduct 2 percent if the bill is paid within 10 days. A *quantity discount* is a price reduction to buyers who buy large volumes. Such discounts provide an incentive to the customer to buy more from one given seller, rather than from many different sources.

A *functional discount* (also called a *trade discount*) is offered by the seller to trade-channel members who perform certain functions, such as selling, storing, and record keeping. A *seasonal discount* is a price reduction to buyers who buy merchandise or services out of season. For example, lawn and garden equipment manufacturers offer seasonal discounts to retailers during the fall and winter months to encourage early ordering in anticipation of the heavy spring and summer selling seasons. Seasonal discounts allow the seller to keep production steady during an entire year.

Allowance
Promotional money paid by manufacturers to retailers in return for an agreement to feature the manufacturer's products in some way.

Allowances are another type of reduction from the list price. For example, *trade-in allowances* are price reductions given for turning in an old item when buying a new one. Trade-in allowances are most common in the automobile industry but are also given for other durable goods. *Promotional allowances* are payments or price reductions to reward dealers for participating in advertising and sales support programs.

Segmented pricing

Segmented pricing
Selling a product or service at two or more prices, where the difference in prices is not based on differences in costs.

Companies will often adjust their basic prices to allow for differences in customers, products, and locations. In **segmented pricing**, the company sells a product or service at two or more prices, even though the difference in prices is not based on differences in costs.

Segmented pricing takes several forms. Under *customer-segment* pricing, different customers pay different prices for the same product or service. Museums, for example, may charge a lower admission for students and senior citizens. Under *product-form pricing,* different versions of the product are priced differently but not according to differences in their costs. For instance, a 1-liter bottle (about 34 ounces) of Evian mineral water may cost $1.59 at your local supermarket. But a 5-ounce aerosol can of Evian Brumisateur Mineral Water Spray sells for a suggested retail price of $11.39 at beauty boutiques and spas. The water is all from the same source in the French Alps and the aerosol packaging costs little more than the plastic bottles. Yet you pay about 5 cents an ounce for one form and $2.28 an ounce for the other.

Using *location pricing,* a company charges different prices for different locations, even though the cost of offering each location is the same. For instance, theaters vary their seat prices because of audience preferences for certain locations, and state universities charge higher tuition for out-of-state students. Finally, using *time pricing,* a firm varies its price by the season, the month, the day, and even the hour. Some public utilities vary their prices to commercial users by time of day and weekend versus weekday. Resorts give weekend and seasonal discounts.

Segmented pricing goes by many names. Robert Cross, a longtime consultant to the airlines, calls it *revenue management.* According to Cross, the practice ensures that "companies will sell the right product to the right consumer at the right time for the right price." Airlines, hotels, and restaurants call it *yield management* and practice it religiously. The airlines, for example, routinely set prices hour-by-hour—even minute-by-minute—depending on seat availability, demand, and competitor price changes.

For segmented pricing to be an effective strategy, certain conditions must exist. The market must be segmentable, and the segments must show different degrees of demand. The costs of segmenting and watching the market cannot exceed the extra revenue obtained from the price difference. Of course, the segmented pricing must also be legal. Most importantly, segmented prices should reflect real differences in customers' perceived value. Otherwise, in the long run, the practice will lead to customer resentment and ill will.

Psychological pricing

Price says something about the product. For example, many consumers use price to judge quality. A $100 bottle of perfume may contain only $3 worth of scent, but some people are willing to pay the $100 because this price indicates something special.

In using **psychological pricing**, sellers consider the psychology of prices and not simply the economics. For example, consumers usually perceive higher-priced products as having higher quality. When they can judge the quality of a product by examining it or by calling on past experience with it, they use price less to judge quality. But when they cannot judge quality because they lack the information or skill, price becomes an important quality signal:

> Some years ago, Heublein produced Smirnoff, then America's leading vodka brand. Smirnoff was attacked by another brand, Wolfschmidt, which claimed to have the same quality as Smirnoff but was priced at one dollar less per bottle. To hold on to market share, Heublein considered either lowering Smirnoff's price by one dollar or holding Smirnoff's price but increasing advertising and promotion expenditures. Either strategy would lead to lower profits and it seemed that Heublein faced a no-win situation. At this point, however, Heublein's marketers thought of a third strategy. They raised the price of Smirnoff by one dollar! Heublein then introduced a new brand, Relska, to compete with Wolfschmidt. Moreover, it introduced yet another brand, Popov, priced even lower than Wolfschmidt. This clever strategy positioned Smirnoff as the elite brand and Wolfschmidt as an ordinary brand, producing a large increase in Heublein's overall profits. The irony is that Heublein's three brands were pretty much the same in taste and manufacturing costs. Heublein knew that a product's price signals its quality. Using price as a signal, Heublein sold roughly the same product at three different quality positions.

Another aspect of psychological pricing is **reference prices**—prices that buyers carry in their minds and refer to when looking at a given product. The reference price might be formed by noting current prices, remembering past prices, or assessing the buying situation. Sellers can influence or use these consumers' reference prices when setting price. For example, a company could display its product next to more expensive ones in order to imply that it belongs in the same class. Department stores often sell women's clothing in separate departments differentiated by price: Clothing found in the more expensive department is assumed to be of better quality.

For most purchases, consumers don't have all the skill or information they need to figure out whether they are paying a good price. They don't have the time, ability, or inclination to research different brands or stores, compare prices, and get the best deals.

Psychological pricing
A pricing approach that considers the psychology of prices and not simply the economics; the price is used to say something about the product.

Reference prices
Prices that buyers carry in their minds and refer to when they look at a given product.

Instead, they may rely on certain cues that signal whether a price is high or low. For example, the fact that a product is sold in a prestigious department store might signal that it's worth a higher price.

Interestingly, such pricing cues are often provided by sellers. A retailer might show a high manufacturer's suggested price next to the marked price, indicating that the product was originally priced much higher. Or the retailer might sell a selection of familiar products for which consumers have accurate price knowledge at very low prices, suggesting that the store's prices on other, less familiar products are low as well. The use of such pricing cues has become a common marketing practice.

Even small differences in price can signal product differences. Consider a stereo receiver priced at $300 compared to one priced at $299.99. The actual price difference is only 1 cent, but the psychological difference can be much greater. For example, some consumers will see the $299.99 as a price in the $200 range rather than the $300 range. The $299.99 will more likely be seen as a bargain price, whereas the $300 price suggests more quality. Some psychologists argue that each digit has symbolic and visual qualities that should be considered in pricing. Thus, 8 is round and even and creates a soothing effect, whereas 7 is angular and creates a jarring effect.[19]

Promotional pricing

Promotional pricing
Temporarily pricing products below the list price, and sometimes even below cost, to increase short-run sales.

With **promotional pricing**, companies will temporarily price their products below list price and sometimes even below cost to create buying excitement and urgency. Promotional pricing takes several forms. Supermarkets and department stores will price a few products as *loss leaders* to attract customers to the store in the hope that they will buy other items at normal markups. For example, supermarkets often sell disposable diapers at less than cost in order to attract family buyers who make larger average purchases per trip. Sellers will also use *special-event pricing* in certain seasons to draw more customers. Thus, linens are promotionally priced every January to attract weary Christmas shoppers back into stores.

Manufacturers sometimes offer *cash rebates* to consumers who buy the product from dealers within a specified time; the manufacturer sends the rebate directly to the customer. Rebates have been popular with automakers and producers of durable goods and small appliances, but they are also used with consumer packaged goods. Some manufacturers offer *low-interest financing, longer warranties,* or *free maintenance* to reduce the consumer's "price." This practice has become another favorite of the auto industry. Or, the seller may simply offer *discounts* from normal prices to increase sales and reduce inventories.

Promotional pricing, however, can have adverse effects. Used too frequently and copied by competitors, price promotions can create "deal-prone" customers who wait until brands go on sale before buying them. Or, constantly reduced prices can erode a brand's value in the eyes of customers. Marketers sometimes become addicted to promotional pricing, using price promotions as a quick fix instead of sweating through the difficult process of developing effective longer-term strategies for building their brands. The use of promotional pricing can also lead to industry price wars. Such price wars usually play into the hands of only one or a few competitors—those with the most efficient operations. For example, in the face of intense competition with Intel, computer chip maker Advanced Micro Devices (AMD) began to aggressively reduce its prices. Intel retaliated with even lower prices. In the resulting price war, AMD has seen its margins and profits skid against those of its larger rival.[20]

The point is that promotional pricing can be an effective means of generating sales for some companies in certain circumstances. But it can be damaging for other companies or if taken as a steady diet.

Geographical pricing

A company also must decide how to price its products for customers located in different parts of the country or world. Should the company risk losing the business of more distant customers by charging them higher prices to cover the higher shipping costs? Or should the company charge all customers the same prices regardless of location? We will look at five **geographical pricing** strategies for the following hypothetical situation:

> *The Peerless Paper Company is located in Atlanta, Georgia, and sells paper products to customers all over the United States. The cost of freight is high and affects the companies from whom customers buy their paper. Peerless wants to establish a geographical pricing policy. It is trying to determine how to price a $100 order to three specific customers: Customer A (Atlanta), Customer B (Bloomington, Indiana), and Customer C (Compton, California).*

One option is for Peerless to ask each customer to pay the shipping cost from the Atlanta factory to the customer's location. All three customers would pay the same factory price of $100, with Customer A paying, say, $100 for shipping; Customer B, $150; and Customer C, $250. Called *FOB-origin pricing*, this practice means that the goods are placed *free on board* (hence, *FOB*) a carrier. At that point the title and responsibility pass to the customer, who pays the freight from the factory to the destination. Because each customer picks up its own cost, supporters of FOB pricing feel that this is the fairest way to assess freight charges. The disadvantage, however, is that Peerless will be a high-cost firm to distant customers.

Uniform-delivered pricing is the opposite of FOB pricing. Here, the company charges the same price plus freight to all customers, regardless of their location. The freight charge is set at the average freight cost. Suppose this is $150. Uniform-delivered pricing therefore results in a higher charge to the Atlanta customer (who pays $150 freight instead of $100) and a lower charge to the Compton customer (who pays $150 instead of $250). Although the Atlanta customer would prefer to buy paper from another local paper company that uses FOB-origin pricing, Peerless has a better chance of winning over the California customer. Other advantages of uniform-delivered pricing are that it is fairly easy to administer and it lets the firm advertise its price nationally.

Zone pricing falls between FOB-origin pricing and uniform-delivered pricing. The company sets up two or more zones. All customers within a given zone pay a single total price; the more distant the zone, the higher the price. For example, Peerless might set up an East Zone and charge $100 freight to all customers in this zone, a Midwest Zone in which it charges $150, and a West Zone in which it charges $250. In this way, the customers within a given price zone receive no price advantage from the company. For example, customers in Atlanta and Boston pay the same total price to Peerless. The complaint, however, is that the Atlanta customer is paying part of the Boston customer's freight cost.

Using *basing-point pricing*, the seller selects a given city as a "basing point" and charges all customers the freight cost from that city to the customer location, regardless of the city from which the goods are actually shipped. For example, Peerless might set Chicago as the basing point and charge all customers $100 plus the freight from Chicago to their locations. This means that an Atlanta customer pays the freight cost from Chicago to Atlanta, even though the goods may be shipped from Atlanta. If all sellers used the same basing-point city, delivered prices would be the same for all customers and price competition would be eliminated. Industries such as sugar, cement, steel, and automobiles used basing-point pricing for years, but this method has become less popular today. Some companies set up multiple basing points to create more flexibility: They quote freight charges from the basing-point city nearest to the customer.

Finally, the seller who is anxious to do business with a certain customer or geographical area might use *freight-absorption pricing*. Using this strategy, the seller absorbs all or part of the actual freight charges in order to get the desired business. The seller might reason that if it can get more business, its average costs will fall and more than compensate for its extra freight cost. Freight-absorption pricing is used for market penetration and to hold on to increasingly competitive markets.

Dynamic pricing

Throughout most of history, prices were set by negotiation between buyers and sellers. *Fixed price* policies—setting one price for all buyers—is a relatively modern idea that

Geographical pricing
Setting price based on the buyer's geographic location.

Dynamic pricing
Adjusting prices continually to meet the characteristics and needs of individual customers and situations.

arose with the development of large-scale retailing at the end of the nineteenth century. Today, most prices are set this way. However, some companies are now reversing the fixed pricing trend. They are using **dynamic pricing**—adjusting prices continually to meet the characteristics and needs of individual customers and situations.

For example, think about how the Internet has affected pricing. From the mostly fixed pricing practices of the past century, the Web seems now to be taking us back—into a new age of fluid pricing. The flexibility of the Internet allows Web sellers to instantly and constantly adjust prices on a wide range of goods based on demand dynamics. In many cases, this involves regular changes in the prices that Web sellers set for their goods. In others, such as eBay or Priceline, consumers negotiate the final prices they pay.

Dynamic pricing offers many advantages for marketers. For example, Internet sellers such as Amazon.com can mine their databases to gauge a specific shopper's desires, measure his or her means, instantaneously tailor products to fit that shopper's behavior, and price products accordingly. Catalog retailers such as L. L. Bean or Spiegel can change prices on the fly according to changes in demand or costs, changing prices for specific items on a day-by-day or even hour-by-hour basis.

Buyers also benefit from the Web and dynamic pricing. A wealth of *shopping bots*—such as Yahoo! Shopping, Bizrate.com, NexTag.com, epinions.com, PriceGrabber.com, mysimon.com, and PriceScan.com—offer instant product and price comparisons from thousands of vendors. Epinions.com, for instance, lets shoppers browse by category or search for specific products and brands. It then searches the Web and reports back links to sellers offering the best prices along with customer reviews. In addition to simply finding the best product and the vendor with the best price for that product, customers armed with price information can often negotiate lower prices.

Buyers can also negotiate prices at online auction sites and exchanges. Suddenly the centuries-old art of haggling is back in vogue. Want to sell that antique pickle jar that's been collecting dust for generations? Post it on eBay, the world's biggest online flea market. Want to name your own price for a hotel room or rental car? Visit Priceline.com or another reverse auction site. Want to bid on a ticket to a Coldplay show? Check out Ticketmaster.com, which now offers an online auction service for concert tickets.

Dynamic pricing can also be controversial. Most customers would find it galling to learn that the person in the next seat on that flight from Gainesville to Galveston paid 10 percent less just because he or she happened to call at the right time or buy through the right sales channel. Amazon.com learned this some years ago when it experimented with lowering prices to new customers in order to woo their business. When regular customers learned through Internet chatter that they were paying generally higher prices than first-timers, they protested loudly. An embarrassed Amazon.com halted the experiments.

Dynamic pricing makes sense in many contexts—it adjusts prices according to market forces, and it often works to the benefit of the customer. But marketers need to be careful not to use dynamic pricing to take advantage of certain customer groups, damaging important customer relationships.[22]

International pricing

Companies that market their products internationally must decide what prices to charge in the different countries in which they operate. In some cases, a company can set a uniform worldwide price. For example, Boeing sells its jetliners at about the same price everywhere, whether in the United States, Europe, or a third-world country. However, most companies adjust their prices to reflect local market conditions and cost considerations.

The price that a company should charge in a specific country depends on many factors, including economic conditions, competitive situations, laws and regulations, and development of the wholesaling and retailing system. Consumer perceptions and preferences also may vary from country to country, calling for different prices. Or the company may have different marketing objectives in various world markets, which require changes in pricing strategy. For example, Samsung might introduce a new product into mature markets in highly developed countries with the goal of quickly gaining mass-market share—

this would call for a penetration-pricing strategy. In contrast, it might enter a less-developed market by targeting smaller, less price-sensitive segments; in this case, market-skimming pricing makes sense.

Costs play an important role in setting international prices. Travelers abroad are often surprised to find that goods that are relatively inexpensive at home may carry outrageously higher price tags in other countries. A pair of Levi's selling for $30 in the United States might go for $63 in Tokyo and $88 in Paris. A McDonald's Big Mac selling for a modest $2.90 here might cost $6.00 in Reykjavik, Iceland, and an Oral-B toothbrush selling for $2.49 at home may cost $10 in China. Conversely, a Gucci handbag going for only $140 in Milan, Italy, might fetch $240 in the United States. In some cases, such *price escalation* may result from differences in selling strategies or market conditions. In most instances, however, it is simply a result of the higher costs of selling in another country—the additional costs of product modifications, shipping and insurance, import tariffs and taxes, exchange-rate fluctuations, and physical distribution.

Price has become a key element in the international marketing strategies of companies attempting to enter emerging markets, such as China, India, and Brazil. Thus, international pricing presents some special problems and complexities.

Price changes

After developing their pricing structures and strategies, companies often face situations in which they must initiate price changes or respond to price changes by competitors.

Initiating price changes

In some cases, the company may find it desirable to initiate either a price cut or a price increase. In both cases, it must anticipate possible buyer and competitor reactions.

Initiating price cuts

Several situations may lead a firm to consider cutting its price. One such circumstance is excess capacity. Another is falling demand in the face of strong price competition. In such cases, the firm may aggressively cut prices to boost sales and share. But as the airline, fast-food, automobile, and other industries have learned in recent years, cutting prices in an industry loaded with excess capacity may lead to price wars as competitors try to hold on to market share.

A company may also cut prices in a drive to dominate the market through lower costs. Either the company starts with lower costs than its competitors, or it cuts prices in the hope of gaining market share that will further cut costs through larger volume. Bausch & Lomb used an aggressive low-cost, low-price strategy to become an early leader in the competitive soft contact lens market. Costco used this strategy to become the world's largest warehouse retailer.

Initiating price increases

A successful price increase can greatly improve profits. For example, if the company's profit margin is 3 percent of sales, a 1 percent price increase will boost profits by 33 percent if sales volume is unaffected. A major factor in price increases is cost inflation. Rising costs squeeze profit margins and lead companies to pass cost increases along to customers. Another factor leading to price increases is overdemand: When a company cannot supply all that its customers need, it may raise its prices, ration products to customers, or both. Consider the worldwide oil and gas industry.

When raising prices, the company must avoid being perceived as a price gouger. Customers have long memories, and they will eventually turn away from companies or even whole industries that they perceive as charging excessive prices. There are some techniques for avoiding this problem. One is to maintain a sense of fairness surrounding any price increase. Price increases should be supported by company communications telling customers why prices are being raised. Making low-visibility price moves first is also a good technique: Some examples include dropping discounts, increasing minimum order sizes, and curtailing production of low-margin products. The company sales force should help business customers find ways to economize.

Wherever possible, the company should consider ways to meet higher costs or demand without raising prices. For example, it can consider more cost-effective ways to produce or distribute its products. It can shrink the product or substitute less-expensive ingredients instead of raising the price, as candy bar manufacturers often do. Or it can "unbundle" its market offering, removing features, packaging, or services and separately pricing elements that were formerly part of the offer. IBM, for example, now offers training and consulting as separately priced services.

Buyer reactions to price changes

Customers do not always interpret price changes in a straightforward way. They may view a price *cut* in several ways. For example, the Manolo brand name has become synonymous with expensive shoes. But what would you think if designer Manolo Blahnik were to suddenly cut his shoe prices from $400 to $65? You might think that you are getting a better deal on a good pair of designer shoes. More likely, however, you'd think that quality had been reduced or that Manolo had licensed his name to a mass-market shoemaker.

Similarly, a price *increase,* which would normally lower sales, may have some positive meanings for buyers. What would you think if Manolo Blahnik *raised* the price of his latest shoe? On the one hand, you might think that the item is even more exclusive or better made. On the other hand, you might think that Manolo Blahnik is simply being greedy by charging what the traffic will bear.

Competitor reactions to price changes

A firm considering a price change must worry about the reactions of its competitors as well as those of its customers. Competitors are most likely to react when the number of firms involved is small, when the product is uniform, and when the buyers are well informed about products and prices.

How can the firm anticipate the likely reactions of its competitors? The problem is complex because, like the customer, the competitor can interpret a company price cut in many ways. It might think the company is trying to grab a larger market share, or that it's doing poorly and trying to boost its sales. Or it might think that the company wants the whole industry to cut prices to increase total demand.

The company must guess each competitor's likely reaction. If all competitors behave alike, this amounts to analyzing only a typical competitor. In contrast, if the competitors do not behave alike—perhaps because of differences in size, market shares, or policies—then separate analyses are necessary. However, if some competitors will match the price change, there is good reason to expect that the rest will also match it.

Responding to price changes

Here we reverse the question and ask how a firm should respond to a price change by a competitor. The firm needs to consider several issues: Why did the competitor change the price? Is the price change temporary or permanent? What will happen to the company's market share and profits if it does not respond? Are other competitors going to respond? Besides these issues, the company must also consider its own situation and strategy and possible customer reactions to price changes.

Figure 19.5 shows the ways a company might assess and respond to a competitor's price cut. Suppose the company learns that a competitor has cut its price and decides that this price cut is likely to harm company sales and profits. It might simply decide to hold its current price and profit margin. The company might believe that it will not lose too much market share, or that it would lose too much profit if it reduced its own price. Or it might decide that it should wait and respond when it has more information on the effects of the competitor's price change. However, waiting too long to act might let the competitor get stronger and more confident as its sales increase.

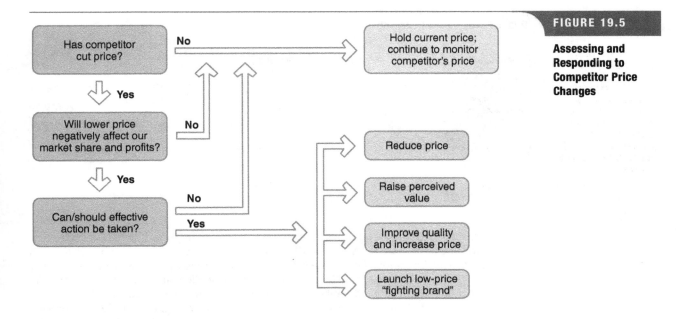

FIGURE 19.5

**Assessing and
Responding to
Competitor Price
Changes**

If the company decides that effective action can and should be taken, it might make any of four responses. First, it could *reduce its price* to match the competitor's price. It may decide that the market is price sensitive and that it would lose too much market share to the lower-priced competitor. Cutting the price will reduce the company's profits in the short run. Some companies might also reduce their product quality, services, and marketing communications to retain profit margins, but this will ultimately hurt long-run market share. The company should try to maintain its quality as it cuts prices.

Alternatively, the company might maintain its price but *raise the perceived value* of its offer. It could improve its communications, stressing the relative value of its product over that of the lower-price competitor. The firm may find it cheaper to maintain price and spend money to improve its perceived value than to cut price and operate at a lower margin. Or, the company might *improve quality and increase price,* moving its brand into a higher price-value position. The higher quality creates greater customer value, which justifies the higher price. In turn, the higher price preserves the company's higher margins.

Finally, the company might *launch a low-price "fighting brand"* —adding a lower-price item to the line or creating a separate lower-price brand. This is necessary if the particular market segment being lost is price sensitive and will not respond to arguments of higher quality. Thus, to counter store brands and other low-price entrants, Procter & Gamble turned a number of its brands into fighting brands. Luvs disposable diapers give parents "premium leakage protection for less than pricier brands." And P&G offers popular budget-priced Basic versions of several of its major brands. For example, Charmin Basic is "the quality toilet tissue at a price you'll love." And Bounty Basic is "Practical. Not Pricey." It offers "great strength at a great price—the paper towel that can take care of business without costing a bundle." In all, the Bounty brand claims an astounding 42.5 percent share of the paper towel market, and Bounty Basic has accounted for much of the brand's recent growth.[24]

Public policy and pricing

Price competition is a core element of our free-market economy. In setting prices, companies usually are not free to charge whatever prices they wish. Many federal, state, and even local laws govern the rules of fair play in pricing. In addition, companies must

FIGURE 19.6   **Public Policy Issues in Pricing**

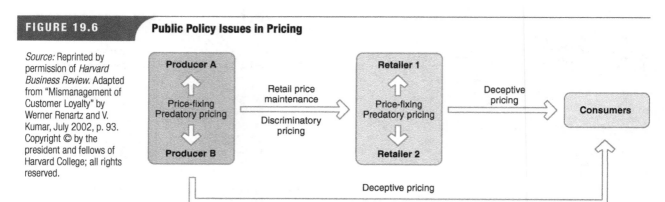

consider broader societal pricing concerns. The most important pieces of legislation affecting pricing are the Sherman, Clayton, and Robinson-Patman acts, initially adopted to curb the formation of monopolies and to regulate business practices that might unfairly restrain trade. Because these federal statutes can be applied only to interstate commerce, some states have adopted similar provisions for companies that operate locally.

Figure 19.6 shows the major public policy issues in pricing. These include potentially damaging pricing practices within a given level of the channel (price-fixing and predatory pricing) and across levels of the channel (retail price maintenance, discriminatory pricing, and deceptive pricing).[25]

Pricing within channel levels

Federal legislation on *price-fixing* states that sellers must set prices without talking to competitors. Otherwise, price collusion is suspected. Price-fixing is illegal per se—that is, the government does not accept any excuses for price-fixing. Companies found guilty of such practices can receive heavy fines.

Recently, governments at the state and national levels have been aggressively enforcing price-fixing regulations in industries ranging from gasoline, insurance, and concrete to credit cards, CDs, and computer chips. For example, Samsung and two other computer memory-chip makers agreed to pay $160 million to settle a suit alleging a four-year price-fixing conspiracy to artificially constrict the supply of D-Ram (dynamic random access memory) chips to computer makers such as Dell and Apple. This control of the supply helped keep prices artificially high, producing higher profits for the conspiring companies. Since that settlement, U.S. state and federal governments and the European Union have filed additional price-fixing lawsuits against various computer memory-chip makers.[26]

Sellers are also prohibited from using *predatory pricing*—selling below cost with the intention of punishing a competitor or gaining higher long-run profits by putting competitors out of business. This protects small sellers from larger ones who might sell items below cost temporarily or in a specific locale to drive them out of business. The biggest problem is determining just what constitutes predatory pricing behavior. Selling below cost to unload excess inventory is not considered predatory; selling below cost to drive out competitors is. Thus, the same action may or may not be predatory depending on intent, and intent can be very difficult to determine or prove.

In recent years, several large and powerful companies have been accused of predatory pricing. For example, Wal-Mart has been sued by dozens of small competitors charging that it lowered prices in their specific geographic areas or on specific products—such as gasoline and generic drugs—to drive them out of business. In fact, the State of New York passed a bill requiring companies to price gas at or above 98 percent of cost to "address the more extreme cases of predatory pricing by big-box stores" such as Wal-Mart. Yet, in North Dakota, the same gas pricing proposal was rejected because state representatives did not view the practice as predatory pricing. And in Colorado, a bill was passed that allowed below-cost fuel.[27]

Pricing across channel levels

The Robinson-Patman Act seeks to prevent unfair *price discrimination* by ensuring that sellers offer the same price terms to customers at a given level of trade. For example, every retailer is entitled to the same price terms from a given manufacturer, whether the retailer is Sears or your local bicycle shop. However, price discrimination is allowed if the seller can prove that its costs are different when selling to different retailers—for example, that it costs less per unit to sell a large volume of bicycles to Sears than to sell a few bicycles to the local dealer.

The seller can also discriminate in its pricing if the seller manufactures different qualities of the same product for different retailers. The seller must prove that these differences are proportional. Price differentials may also be used to "match competition" in "good faith," provided the price discrimination is temporary, localized, and defensive rather than offensive.

Laws also prohibit *retail (or resale) price maintenance*—a manufacturer cannot require dealers to charge a specified retail price for its product. Although the seller can propose a manufacturer's *suggested* retail price to dealers, it cannot refuse to sell to a dealer who takes independent pricing action, nor can it punish the dealer by shipping late or denying advertising allowances. For example, the Florida attorney general's office investigated Nike for allegedly fixing the retail price of its shoes and clothing. It was concerned that Nike might be withholding items from retailers who were not selling its most expensive shoes at prices the company considered suitable.

Deceptive pricing occurs when a seller states prices or price savings that mislead consumers or are not actually available to consumers. This might involve bogus reference or comparison prices, as when a retailer sets artificially high "regular" prices then announces "sale" prices close to its previous everyday prices. For example, Overstock.com recently came under scrutiny for inaccurately listing manufacturer's suggested retail prices, often quoting them higher than the actual price. Such comparison pricing is widespread.

Comparison pricing claims are legal if they are truthful. However, the FTC's *Guides Against Deceptive Pricing* warns sellers not to advertise a price reduction unless it is a saving from the usual retail price, not to advertise "factory" or "wholesale" prices unless such prices are what they are claimed to be, and not to advertise comparable value prices on imperfect goods.[28]

Other deceptive pricing issues include *scanner fraud* and price confusion. The widespread use of scanner-based computer checkouts has led to increasing complaints of retailers overcharging their customers. Most of these overcharges result from poor management—from a failure to enter current or sale prices into the system. Other cases, however, involve intentional overcharges. *Price confusion* results when firms employ pricing methods that make it difficult for consumers to understand just what price they are really paying. For example, consumers are sometimes misled regarding the real price of a home mortgage or car leasing agreement. In other cases, important pricing details may be buried in the "fine print."

Many federal and state statutes regulate against deceptive pricing practices. For example, the Automobile Information Disclosure Act requires automakers to attach a statement to new-car windows stating the manufacturer's suggested retail price, the prices of optional equipment, and the dealer's transportation charges. However, reputable sellers go beyond what is required by law. Treating customers fairly and making certain that they fully understand prices and pricing terms is an important part of building strong and lasting customer relationships.